CTS®-D
Certified Technology Specialist-Design
Exam Guide

Brad Grimes

Mc
Graw
Hill
Education

New York • Chicago • San Francisco
Athens • London • Madrid • Mexico City
Milan • New Delhi • Singapore • Sydney • Toronto

Cataloging-in-Publication Data is on file with the Library of Congress

McGraw-Hill Education books are available at special quantity discounts to use as premiums and sales promotions, or for use in corporate training programs. To contact a representative, please visit the Contact Us pages at www.mhprofessional.com.

CTS®-D Certified Technology Specialist-Design Exam Guide

1234567890 DOC DOC 109876

ISBN: Book p/n 978-0-07-183566-4 and CD p/n 978-0-07-183567-1
of set 978-0-07-183568-8

MHID: Book p/n 0-07-183566-0 and CD p/n 0-07-183567-9
of set 0-07-183568-7

Sponsoring Editor Timothy Green	**Technical Editor** Michelle Streffon	**Production Supervisor** Pamela Pelton
Editorial Supervisor Jody McKenzie	**Copy Editor** Kim Wimpsett	**Composition** Cenveo Publisher Services
Project Manager Vasundhara Sawhney, Cenveo® Publisher Services	**Proofreader** Mike McGee	**Illustration** Cenveo Publisher Services
Acquisitions Coordinators Amy Stonebraker Claire Yee	**Indexer** Jack Lewis	**Art Director, Cover** Jeff Weeks

CONTENTS

Part V   Appendixes

InfoComm International has been serving the professional audiovisual industry for more than 75 years. Throughout those years, AV technology—like all technology—has changed dramatically. As a result, the jobs of people who make AV technology come to life have changed.

AV designers have had a front-row seat to the change happening all around them. That is because on an AV project, it's the designer—the professional who conceptualizes the solution from beginning to end—who often must know the most about the various specialties and technologies that impact a finished AV system. How will a client's network infrastructure impact the desired AV solution? The designer needs to know. How might the AV system communicate with the client's building systems, including lighting, HVAC, and security? The designer understands how it's possible. At the end of the day, the more an AV designer knows about how an AV system fits in with a client's overall mission, the greater the chance of designing and overseeing completion of a technology solution that meets that client's needs and exceeds expectations.

One of InfoComm's core purposes is to support the AV industry through professional development and certification. This means collecting and making available technical knowledge and best practices pertinent to your job from a network of expert volunteers who work in the AV industry. That knowledge, in turn, helps inform InfoComm certification.

AV industry certification demonstrates to your employer, to industry partners, to the business world at large, and to yourself, that you are committed to a higher level of professionalism and expertise in all aspects of AV integration and design. InfoComm's general Certified Technology Specialist (CTS) designation demonstrates knowledge of the widest breadth of AV solutions, tasks, and operations. After you attain your CTS credential and want to take your skills to the next level, you may pursue a more focused certification, such as Certified Technology Specialist-Design (CTS-D).

As you will learn in this book, a CTS-D works with clients to understand their needs, designs AV systems that meet those needs, prepares the necessary design documents, coordinates with other professionals to create AV systems, and ultimately ensures that the final product meets the clients' requirements. People who hold the CTS-D credential, like its counterpart for the AV installation community, the Certified Technology Specialist-Installation (CTS-I), are members of a special group of AV pros who have gone beyond foundational experience and dedicated themselves to quality work, focused expertise, and the confidence of the people they work with. And because a CTS-D has already spent years in the AV industry, he or she forms the basis of a growing, global marketplace expected to be worth $114 billion in 2016.

The CTS-D credential is accredited by the American National Standards Institute (ANSI) under the International Organization of Standardization (ISO) and the International Electrotechnical Commission (IEC) ISO/IEC 17024 General Requirements for Bodies Operating Certification Schemes of Persons program. For many, an ANSI/ISO/IEC certification is an additional mark of distinction because ANSI/ISO/IEC is recognized across many different industries. For example, the Building Performance Institute offers ANSI/ISO/IEC-accredited certifications. So do Cisco Systems, the Computing Technology Industry Association, the Green Building Certification Institute, the Project Management Institute, the Society of Industrial Security Professionals, and many other, non-technical trades. Holding a professional certification that meets the same high standards as that of another trade certification can help raise your profile in a company of large project teams that include many diverse individuals.

The fact that all InfoComm certifications meet ANSI/ISO/IEC requirements has other implications. In accordance with globally recognized principles, no single publication or class can necessarily prepare you for the CTS-D exam, nor are you obligated to enroll in InfoComm courses to take the exam. As you will learn, on-the-job experience is a critical prerequisite for taking the CTS-D exam. Because of the way InfoComm certifications are developed—in accordance with ANSI/ISO/IEC standards and separate from InfoComm's own professional training, including this book—relying on a single source of exam preparation may not prove successful for every AV professional. Put another way—specifically with regard to this exam guide—no prep tool is permitted to "teach to the test" and still maintain ANSI/ISO/IEC accreditation. InfoComm, through its AV design classes and publications, attempts to offer prospective designers the latest knowledge; prospective designers must then apply that knowledge to the CTS-D exam—and to their design careers. For other ways that InfoComm can help establish your professional qualifications, visit us at www.infocomm.org/ctsd.

CTS-D Certified Technology Specialist-Design Exam Guide includes the latest information that AV designers need to create solutions in a converged AV/IT world. Yes, all the bread-and-butter skills are here, too, such as how to perform a thorough needs assessment and document an AV design. But so are tips and background information for configuring and troubleshooting modern protocols, such as Extended Display Identification Data (EDID) and High-bandwidth Digital Content Protection (HDCP)—two important attributes of today's high-definition video systems. Plus, you'll find important information about current multimedia transmission technologies, such as High-Definition Multimedia Interface (HDMI), DisplayPort, Mobile-High Definition Link, and more. And with all the talk about ultra high-definition "4K" video, AV designers need to understand when it's really needed, how it's achieved, and how it impacts an overall system design. This book has you covered.

Finally, CTS-D holders—and AV designers in general—must know how to integrate and control AV gear on a network. They must understand Internet protocol, network security, and other IT-related issues to help ensure that networked AV systems operate as promised without impacting other IT services. This book includes several chapters that encapsulate important AV/IT skills.

CTS-D Certified Technology Specialist-Design Exam Guide represents InfoComm's knowledge base for aspiring CTS-D holders. Even if you never take the CTS-D exam, this guide is a handy reference. It reflects what professionals like you—InfoComm volunteers—say goes into being a modern AV designer. It also reflects the CTS-D exam as it has changed over time and will help prepare you for the test but won't automatically turn you into a CTS-D. For more on the CTS-D exam itself, see Chapter 2.

Again, this guide is not required reading, but it's an excellent place to start. You may decide to burnish your design skills in other ways. InfoComm University offers three levels of AV design training—though they're also not required—which are available in classrooms or online. It also offers a four-week CTS-D Prep Virtual Classroom. You can find information at www.infocomm.org/education.

If you have decided to pursue your CTS-D certification, congratulations. If you have been looking for a valuable resource to use on the job, you've found one. We hope this guide helps you reach your goals. As I've told many people in many different settings, now is an exciting time to be part of the AV industry. By certifying your skills, you show that you're committed to your own success and to the success of AV professionals everywhere. You're ready to be a leader in this industry, and we thank you for your commitment. Good luck.

David Labuskes, CTS, RCDD
Executive Director and CEO
InfoComm International

ABOUT THE AUTHOR

Brad Grimes is Director of Communications for InfoComm International and the former editor of *Pro AV* magazine. He has been writing about technology for 25 years, including covering information technology for Ziff Davis, International Data Group, PostNewsweek Tech Media (now 1105 Media), and Hanley Wood. His work has been recognized by the American Business Media, the American Society of Business Publication Editors, and the American Society of Magazine Editors.

Grimes edited the McGraw-Hill Education books *CTS Certified Technology Specialist Exam Guide, Second Edition* (2013) and *Networked AV Systems* (2014). He's been an adjunct faculty member of InfoComm University and received his master's degree from Northwestern University's Medill School of Journalism.

About the Technical Editor

Michelle Streffon, CTS, is Standards Manager for InfoComm International. She has developed training materials for the audiovisual industry since 2011 and served as a technical editor for McGraw-Hill Education's 2013 publication *CTS Certified Technology Specialist Exam Guide, Second Edition,* and 2015 publication *CTS-I Certified Technology Specialist-Installation Exam Guide*. Streffon graduated from Hillsdale College in 2012 with a bachelor's degree in English.

ACKNOWLEDGMENTS

It's not written on any subsequent page, but here's what I know about today's AV designers: They're wicked smart. AV designers often have the broadest expertise on a project because they need to anticipate the requirements of the entire team, including those of the client, installer, electrical engineer, architect, network administrator, and others. I've met many AV designers over the years, and many more have volunteered their time and expertise not only to the book you're holding, which reflects their collective knowledge and valuable contributions to InfoComm International, but also to the Certified Technology Specialist-Design (CTS-D) certification.

People don't always realize that the volunteers who develop InfoComm's AV design education and the volunteers who administer the CTS-D certification represent—by necessity—two different camps. That is to say, there are twice as many people to acknowledge on this page than you might think. I want to thank all the professionals who've ever taught a design-related class, taken a class, added to InfoComm's curriculum, written a CTS-D exam question, and much more. The AV industry is better and stronger for your efforts. I want to thank members of the InfoComm Certification Steering Committee—past and present—for their volunteer role in developing and maintaining the most respected professional credentials in the audiovisual industry.

More specifically, thanks to InfoComm's Michelle Streffon, Amanda Beckner, Michael Hewitt, Mel Girardin, Alla Orlova, Joseph Valerio, Marcus Yarborough, and former InfoComm editor Nermina Miller for corralling all this knowledge and working with subject-matter experts to present the most complete picture of a certified AV designer. InfoComm's staff instructors hone this information every day and take it directly to industry professionals, and for that we're all grateful. Thanks to everyone at McGraw-Hill Education, including Tim Green, Amy Stonebraker, Jody McKenzie, and Kim Wimpsett, as well as their behind-the-scenes team, for turning this all into a useful resource.

And thanks very, very much to my wonderful family.

To all you wicked smart AV designers, good luck on your CTS-D exam. You've got a lot to work with in this guide. I hope it will serve as the springboard for a rewarding career. Thank *you* for making this an amazing time to be an AV professional.

—Brad Grimes, 2016

2016 InfoComm Board of Directors

Matt Emerson, CTS, CEAVCO Audio Visual Co. Inc., Leadership Search Committee Chair

Craig Janssen, LEED AP, Idibri, President

Gary Hall, CVE, CTS-D, CTS-I, Cisco, President-Elect

Julian Phillips, Whitlock, Secretary-Treasurer

Zane Au, CTS-D, LEED AP, BD+C, Shen Milsom & Wilke

Deb Britton, CTS, K2 Audio

Frank Culotta, CTS, Symco Inc.

Jeff Day, Bluewater Technologies

Maru Gaitán, GrupoNiza

Ratnesh Javeri, CTS-D, Innovative Systems and Solutions Pvt. Ltd.

Kevin Kelly, Stampede

Joe Pham, Ph.D., QSC Audio Products, LLC

InfoComm Staff

David Labuskes, CTS, RCDD, Executive Director and CEO

Alex Damico, Chief Operating Officer

Amanda Beckner, CTS, Vice President of Learning

Brad Grimes, Director of Communications

Alla Orlova, Director of Curriculum Development

Rachel Bradshaw, M. Ed., Director of Exposition Content

Mel Girardin, CTS, Director of Training

Nicole Verardi, Director of Marketing, Membership & Education

Michelle Streffon, CTS, Standards Manager

Tom Kehr, CTS-D, CTS-I, Senior Staff Instructor

Rod Brown, CTS-D, CTS-I, Staff Instructor

Chuck Espinoza, CTS-D, CTS-I, Staff Instructor

Andre LeJeune, CTS, Staff Instructor

Marcus Yarborough, CTS-I, Staff Instructor

Joseph Valerio, Training Developer

Michael Hewitt, Learning Systems Content Manager

Scott Wills, CTS-D, CTS-I, Senior Director of International Member Services

Bill Thomas, CTS-I, Director of International Education

PART I

The Certified Technology Specialist-Design

CHAPTER 1

What Is a Certified Technology Specialist-Design?

In this chapter, you will learn about
- InfoComm certifications and audiovisual (AV) industry standards
- The benefits of earning a Certified Technology Specialist-Design (CTS-D) credential
- What types of work an AV designer does
- Eligibility criteria for taking the CTS-D exam

You might be holding this book for many reasons. You could be a professional audiovisual systems designer in search of a handy reference. You could be a user or operator of AV systems at a company, school, house of worship, or other organization and need in-depth information to make sure those systems work properly and deliver the best possible experience. Or you're a Certified Technology Specialist (CTS). You've already proven yourself to be an expert AV professional, committed to a higher standard of workmanship and to keeping abreast of the fast-moving technology and best practices that characterize this highly dynamic industry. But now you're ready for more.

As a current CTS holder, you've decided to take your skills to the next level and become a Certified Technology Specialist-Design. CTS-D is a specialized industry accreditation, recognized by employers, customers, and international standards bodies. A CTS-D demonstrates the broad expertise of a CTS but also the skills and knowledge required to design AV systems. You demonstrate the skills and knowledge by excelling on the CTS-D exam. Throughout this book, you will learn what you need to know to be a CTS-D holder, but first let's align your ambition with what's expected of a CTS-D.

Introducing InfoComm International

InfoComm International created and administers the Certified Technology Specialist program. Founded in 1939, InfoComm is the leading nonprofit association serving the professional audiovisual communications industry worldwide. Through activities that include tradeshows, education, certification, standards, government relations, outreach, and information services, InfoComm promotes the industry and enhances members' ability to conduct business successfully and competently.

InfoComm has offered certification programs for nearly 35 years, as well as industry-specific and general business training and education for people seeking careers in professional AV. Every year, InfoComm certifies more qualified AV professionals than anyone else in the industry.

InfoComm is also an American National Standards Institute (ANSI)–accredited standards developer, creating voluntary performance standards for the AV industry. InfoComm develops both independent and ANSI-approved standards, as well as joint standards with other professional associations. It is important for certified professionals to recognize, understand, and (if appropriate) apply relevant standards when designing AV systems. Although implementing InfoComm standards is not a requirement for being a CTS-D, the standards themselves are available to CTS-D exam item writers and could be referenced on the exam. The following are the current approved standards:

- Audio Coverage Uniformity in Enclosed Listener Areas
- Audio, Video and Control Architectural Drawing Symbols
- Audiovisual Systems Energy Management
- Audiovisual System Performance Verification
- Standard Guide for Audiovisual Systems Design and Coordination Processes
- Projected Image System Contrast Ratio

Many standards are in development. Visit the standards website at www.infocomm .org/standards to learn more.

Why Earn Your CTS-D Credential?

Certification shows your commitment to being among the best in a professional field. This benefits you, your company, and your clients.

In the field of AV and information communications, the CTS credential is recognized worldwide as the leading credential. Being a CTS holder shows your professionalism and technical proficiency. It increases your credibility and boosts customers' confidence in your work.

There are currently three available CTS certifications:

- Certified Technology Specialist (CTS)
- Certified Technology Specialist-Design (CTS-D)
- Certified Technology Specialist-Installation (CTS-I)

All three of InfoComm's certifications have achieved accreditation through the International Organization of Standardization (ISO) and the International Electrotechnical Commission (IEC) as administered by ANSI in the United States. They have been accredited by ANSI to the ISO/IEC 17024:2012 personnel standard—the AV industry's only third-party accredited personnel certification program. These are the only certifications in the AV industry to achieve ANSI accreditation.

The certification programs are administered independently by InfoComm's certification committee. You can learn more about how the exams are developed and administered, as well as how to maintain your certification, by visiting the certification website at www.infocomm.org/certification.

Although certification is not a guarantee of performance by certified individuals, CTS holders at all levels of certification have demonstrated AV knowledge and skills. They adhere to the CTS Code of Ethics and Conduct and maintain their status through continued education. Certification demonstrates commitment to professional growth in the audiovisual industry and is strongly supported by InfoComm.

Why take the next step toward specialized certification? Simply put, you're ready for more. You have a deep understanding of the many aspects of a successful AV system, from the AV components themselves to the other building systems and networks with which they integrate. You know how to translate what clients say they need into a technology solution that helps them achieve their goals. And you know how to build a team of professionals from inside and outside the AV industry that can execute on time and on budget. We've just described a CTS-D.

A career in AV design is a commitment. You're dedicating your professional life to a higher level of excellence that can be achieved only through education and expertise in the AV field. The continuing education that accompanies CTS-D certification will help keep you up to date on advancing technologies and position you as a major player on project teams. In short, pursuing advanced certification is an excellent decision for your career and your company.

What Does a CTS-D Do?

A CTS-D is a leader in the AV industry. As a designer of AV systems, from conference spaces to performance venues, a CTS-D often takes the reins early in a project and performs specific tasks to assess a client's needs, design appropriate AV systems, prepare supporting documents, and coordinate and collaborate with other professionals to create systems that satisfy the client's requirements. A CTS-D is more than a technologist and recognizes that the goal of an AV system is to create an experience for the client that combines content, space, and technology so that the client and the client's clients can communicate better, work more efficiently, or be entertained.

To identify specifically what a CTS-D does, InfoComm developed a job task analysis (JTA). The JTA is a comprehensive list of the key responsibilities (referred to as *domains*) and tasks in which an AV designer should demonstrate proficiency. You will learn more about the JTA in Chapter 2, but in general, the many tasks that a CTS-D must perform fall into four general categories.

- Conducting a needs assessment and identifying a scope of work
- Collaborating with other professionals, including architects, engineers, electricians, interior designers, and more
- Developing AV designs, drawings, and documentation to describe the required audio, video, and network systems
- Conducting project implementation activities, from verifying system performance to troubleshooting

Based on the JTA, InfoComm's independent certification committee created a CTS-D exam content outline. Both the JTA and outline are available at the organization's website and are included in the free *CTS-D Candidate Handbook* (available in print and online at www.infocomm.org/ctsd).

It is important to note that the content and practice exercises in this book do not follow the CTS-D exam content outline perfectly. Nor do they follow the order in which actual CTS-D exam questions may be presented. Instead, the book follows the real-world course of an AV design, from conducting the needs analysis to commissioning and supporting AV systems. It is organized into three parts:

- Environment, which covers information for laying the groundwork of an AV design
- Infrastructure, which covers acoustic, lighting, mechanical, and other considerations that affect an AV design
- Applied design, which details specific aspects of an AV design, including audio, video, network, security, and other specifications

Upon completing this book, you will have been exposed to the knowledge and skills identified by the JTA and included in the exam outline.

 NOTE A JTA is a study conducted to identify the knowledge, skills, and abilities necessary for professional competence in a particular field. Such an analysis is often conducted to determine the content and competencies that should be included in a certification or exam. InfoComm's independent certification committee conducts periodic JTAs to make sure the various CTS exams and certification processes align with the real-world skills required of AV professionals.

Are You Eligible for the CTS-D Exam?

To be considered eligible to take the CTS-D exam, you must meet the following pre-requisites:

- Hold a current CTS certification
- Be in good standing with the certification committee (in other words, have no ethics cases or sanctions)
- Have two years of audiovisual industry experience in design

There are several other prerequisites, such as an application form, proof of identity, and application fee. You can find information about all requirements and more in the *CTS-D Candidate Handbook*.

 Throughout this book, you will see references to online videos that reinforce what you read and offer additional insight into the CTS-D exam. You can find links to all the videos in Appendix C. To get you started, watch a video on demystifying InfoComm certification and beginning preparation for the CTS-D exam at www.infocomm.org/CertVideo.

Chapter Review

A CTS-D is a jack-of-all-trades and master of pretty much everything about an AV project. Proficient in audiovisual and other technology principles, a CTS-D also understands how to coordinate the efforts of many different trades and translate the stated needs of users into a solution that meets their goals.

Achieving CTS-D certification demonstrates an AV designer's mastery of everything from conducting a needs analysis to coordinating audiovisual and network technologies to training users on a system once it's been installed. The CTS-D exam measures an aspiring professional's skills and knowledge in a series of tasks identified by experienced industry peers. Good luck in your pursuit of CTS-D accreditation and in your professional AV career.

The CTS-D Exam

In this chapter, you will learn about
- The scope of the CTS-D exam
- The skills and knowledge that the exam covers
- Exam preparation and math strategies
- The process required to apply for, schedule, and complete the CTS-D exam
- The types of questions you might encounter on the exam

Now you're ready. You understand the role of an AV designer and appreciate the professional commitment it takes to earn your CTS-D. It's time to start preparing.

This chapter takes you inside the CTS-D exam, from what it covers in general terms to specific examples of questions you might see on the test. Along the way, we'll describe helpful preparation strategies, point you to additional resources, and detail exactly how to apply for the exam (and plan for the big day). We will even take you through a quick-and-dirty review of some basic math concepts you'll absolutely need to know to succeed on the exam and in your chosen field—AV design.

The Scope of the CTS-D Exam

As noted earlier, the CTS-D exam tests the knowledge and skills required by an AV professional to earn CTS-D certification. To create the CTS-D exam, a group of volunteer audiovisual subject-matter experts (SMEs), guided by professional test development experts, participated in a job task analysis focused on AV design. The results of this study form the basis of a valid, reliable, fair, and realistic assessment of the skills, knowledge, and abilities required for certified AV design professionals.

In creating the JTA, the group of volunteer SMEs identified major categories, or *domains*, of knowledge, as well as topics within each domain, based on the tasks that a certified individual might perform on an AV design job. The exam development team examined the importance, criticality, and frequency of AV design tasks and used the data to determine the number of CTS-D exam questions related to each domain and task.

Based on the JTA, the CTS-D exam content outline divides design tasks into four domains of knowledge, each of which will be addressed on the exam. The *CTS-D Certified Technology Specialist-Design Exam Guide* was written to cover the exam content in a manner that spends the most time on areas that make up the largest portion of the exam. At the same time, topics are covered in a logical manner, meaning the book doesn't go in exactly the same order as the content outline. As you proceed through the book, you will see information at the beginning of each chapter, called "Domain Checks," that describe how the material in the chapter relates to domains and tasks in the CTS-D exam content outline.

The complete CTS-D exam content outline is shown in Table 2-1.

CTS-D Domains/Tasks	% of Exam	# of Items
Domain A: Conducting a Needs Assessment	**15.2%**	**19**
Task 1: Identify stakeholders/decision-makers	1.6%	2
Task 2: Identify skill level of end users	1.6%	2
Task 3: Educate the AV client	0.8%	1
Task 4: Review client technology master plan	1.6%	2
Task 5: Identify clients' procurement process	0.8%	1
Task 6: Research clients' business process	0.8%	1
Task 7: Research clients' business environment	0.8%	1
Task 8: Define AV needs (absolutes)	2.4%	3
Task 9: Identify scope of work	2.4%	3
Task 10: Identify regulatory requirements and project certification goals	2.4%	3
Domain B: Collaborating with Other Professionals	**25.6%**	**32**
Task 1: Review architectural and engineering (A/E) drawings	4%	5
Task 2: Coordinate architectural/interior design criteria	3.2%	4
Task 3: Coordinate structural/mechanical criteria	3.2%	4
Task 4: Coordinate electrical criteria	3.2%	4
Task 5: Coordinate lighting criteria	3.2%	4
Task 6: Coordinate IT and network security criteria	4%	5
Task 7: Recommend acoustical criteria	2.4%	3
Task 8: Coordinate life safety and security criteria	2.4%	3
Domain C: Developing AV Designs	**49.6%**	**62**
Task 1: Create draft AV design	10.4%	13
Task 2: Confirm site conditions	8%	10
Task 3: Produce infrastructure drawings	10.4%	13
Task 4: Produce AV system documents	11.2%	14
Task 5: Produce AV build documentation	9.6%	12
Domain D: Conducting Project Implementation Activities	**9.6%**	**12**
Task 1: Participate in project implementation communication	2.4%	3
Task 2: Perform system verifications	4%	5
Task 3: Conduct system close out activities	3.2%	4

Table 2-1   CTS-D Exam Domains and Tasks

Exam Preparation Strategies

You can prepare for the CTS-D exam in many ways, including studying this book. In fact, studying this book alone may not be enough to help you pass the exam. You are required to have two years of design experience and a valid CTS, so real-world training is key to your success. That said, another way to start your CTS-D studies is by performing a self-assessment of your existing AV design knowledge to identify your strengths and weaknesses. You will find a free practice test composed of questions that are similar to the questions presented on the CTS-D exam on the accompanying CD. You will also find helpful questions in the "Chapter Review" sections throughout this book, though such questions are not actual practice exam questions.

Keep in mind that because the CTS-D exam is designed to comply with ANSI standards, the CTS-D practice exam cannot include actual exam questions. In fact, the practice exam questions may not be informed by the exam itself. Any practice question you find here or elsewhere is written to be *similar* to an actual CTS-D exam question.

InfoComm provides other resources to help you prepare for the CTS-D exam. The glossary toward the end of this book covers most of the acronyms, technical terms, and other language you will need to be versed in to navigate the CTS-D exam and life as a certified designer. Also, refer to Appendix A, "AV Math for Design," for a handy reference to important math formulas used in AV design. InfoComm also offers online courses, such as *AV Math Online, AV Math for Design Online,* and *AV Design Levels 1 – 3 Online* for a fee. Courses are discounted for InfoComm members. (Read more about math strategies later in this chapter.)

As you prepare for the CTS-D exam, keep the exam content outline and JTA handy. Figure out not only where you're strongest but also where the JTA has placed the most emphasis.

Not surprisingly, the part of the exam that covers developing AV designs (Domain C) counts the most (50 percent). So, spend extra time on sections that inform the five tasks in Domain C, which have a lot to do with drawings and documentation—critical components of a good AV design. You will find information about drawings and documentation, for example, in Part II, "Environment," where we discuss the needs analysis, program reports, AV documentation, and more. You will find more information about drawings and documentation near the end of the book, in Part IV, "Applied Design," where we discuss closing out a project and handing over documentation to the client. Documenting an AV design is an important part of a CTS-D's job and occurs throughout a project.

In addition, as you prepare to take the CTS-D exam, refer frequently to the *CTS-D Candidate Handbook,* which you can download from www.infocomm.org/ctsd. In addition to information about the exam, the JTA, and the exam content outline, the *CTS-D Candidate Handbook* lays out the important knowledge and professional attributes required of CTS-D candidates. From there, download and refer to the entire JTA, also available at www.infocomm.org/ctsd, for a complete breakdown of knowledge, attributes, and skills required across all domains and tasks.

NOTE Make sure to download the most up-to-date free edition of the *CTS-D Candidate Handbook* for important policy and procedure updates by going to the InfoComm website at www.infocomm.org/ctsd.

For example, under Domain A: Conducting a Needs Assessment, Task 4: Review client technology master plan, the detailed JTA indicates CTS-D candidates should have good written and verbal skills, plus knowledge of the following:

- Basic fiscal planning terminology (return on investment, and so on)
- Client's structured cabling system
- Equipment life cycles
- Restriction of hazardous substances (RoHS) and other green issues

As another example, under Domain B: Collaborating With Other Professionals, Task 2: Coordinate architectural/interior design criteria, the JTA indicates CTS-D candidates should demonstrate the following attributes:

- The ability to calculate area
- The ability to identify three-dimensional interference issues from two-dimensional plans
- The ability to visualize spatial relationships from plans
- An understanding of AV maintenance requirements
- An understanding of AV systems operational requirements
- An understanding of equipment space and access requirements
- An understanding of ergonomic best practices
- An understanding of Inverse Square Law
- The ability to utilize reference materials

This type of information is detailed in the JTA and can help guide your thinking as you work through the *CTS-D Certified Technology Specialist-Design Exam Guide*. The content and practice questions in this book are based on the same JTA and exam content outline as the CTS-D exam. However, because the exam questions are confidential, there can be no guarantee that this book will cover every question on the exam or that the exam will address every topic in this book. This exam guide prepares you for a career as a certified AV designer—not just for the credentialing exam.

And as you might expect, technology and best practices change over time. Therefore, the CTS-D exam must change. When InfoComm revises the CTS-D exam, it will publish such revisions on its website, www.infocomm.org/ctsd.

NOTE   No book, course, or other study material is required to take the CTS-D exam. By the same token, no book, course, or other study material can guarantee you will pass the exam.

Math Strategies

Some of the questions on the CTS-D exam can be answered only by solving math equations. When you earned your CTS certification, chances are you had to brush up on a pair of important mathematical concepts, which we will review briefly: the order of operations and Ohm's law. Both are important math principles for AV professionals and will serve you long after you've taken the CTS-D exam.

There are a lot of mathematical formulas associated with AV design, but you don't have to memorize them all. On test day, CTS-D candidates have access to relevant math formulas on the computer screen while they test. The formula sheet does not cover every possible formula that you may encounter on the exam, but it does contain many common (and complicated) formulas. You can download the list ahead of time and use it to practice AV math functions before test day. Find it at www.infocomm .org/CTSDmath.

You are not allowed to bring a calculator into the CTS-D exam room. You will, however, have access to a virtual, computer-based calculator that simulates a Texas Instruments TI-30XS MultiView calculator (see Figure 2-1). The TI-30XS is a scientific calculator, designed to perform complex operations that are not common in everyday

Figure 2-1
The TI-30XS
MultiView
calculator

math (for example, exponent and square root). Many AV design tasks call for complex calculations, so you should learn how to use a scientific calculator.

As you work your way through this exam guide, keep an actual TI-30XS MultiView calculator handy. Even though you won't be able to use it on exam day, you should become familiar with its functions so you can easily navigate the onscreen calculator.

Order of Operations

Many AV math formulas use addition, subtraction, multiplication, division, exponents, and logarithms. These formulas require a solid foundation in the order of operations. The order of operations helps you correctly calculate the desired result by prioritizing which part of the formula to use first. It is a way to rank the order in which you work your way through a formula.

This is the order of operations:

1. Any numbers within parentheses or brackets
2. Any exponents, indices, or orders
3. Any multiplication or division
4. Any addition or subtraction

If there are multiple operations with the same priority, then proceed from left to right: parentheses, exponents, multiplication, division, addition, and subtraction. You can remember the order of operations by using the acronym PEMDAS.

Practice Exercise 1: Order of Operations

Solve the following equation using the order of operations:

$$2 + (5 / 8^2 * 9)$$

Step 1 Anything inside parentheses is processed first. Inside the parentheses, calculate the exponent first.

$$2 + (5 / 8^2 * 9)$$
$$2 + (5 / 64 * 9)$$

Step 2 Inside the parentheses are now two operations that have the same priority: multiply and divide.

Because they are the same priority, begin solving them from left to right.

$$2 + (5 / 64 * 9)$$
$$2 + (0.078125 * 9)$$
$$2 + (0.703125)$$

This step is typically where a mistake might be made. If the formula is at a stage where the operations are of the same priority, continue solving from *left to right*. If this step is not completed, you will arrive at the wrong answer.

Examine the following *incorrect* processing shown here:

2 + (5 / 64 * 9)
2 + (5 / 576)
2 + (0.009) .

In this example of incorrect processing, multiplication was performed first. The incorrect processing of right to left within the parentheses means that the final answer will be wrong.

Step 3 Now the only remaining operation is addition.

2 + (0.703125) = 2.703125

Answer Rounded to the nearest tenth, the result is 2.7.

Practice Exercise 2: Order of Operations

Solve the following equation using the order of operations:

$6^2 + 4 / (3 * 8) - 8$

Step 1 Anything inside parentheses is processed first. Inside the parentheses, multiply first.

$6^2 + 4 / (24) - 8$

Step 2 There are no more operations in parentheses. Calculate the exponent next.

36 + 4 / 24 - 8

Step 3 The next operation is divide. Calculate the division.

36 + 0.16667 - 8

Step 4 The only two operations remaining are addition and subtraction. Both addition and subtraction are the same priority. Solve the formula from left to right. Remember to process from *left to right*.

36.16667 - 8 = 28.16667

Answer Rounded to the nearest tenth, the result is 28.2.

Ohm's Law and Electrical Circuits

Now that you've practiced basic mathematical principles, you can apply them to a fundamental concept in AV design: Ohm's law. Ohm's law can be hard to understand without a basic understanding of electricity, so let's first review the essentials of circuit theory. Then you'll practice Ohm's law calculations.

Figure 2-2
Simple
illustration of a
circuit path

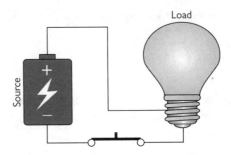

An electrical circuit is a closed-loop path that goes from a power source, through a load, and back to the power source. As shown in Figure 2-2, all circuits must have these three physical items connected together:

- Conductive material, such as wires
- Voltage source, such as a battery
- Load, such as a light source

When the switch is set to the "on" position, the circuit is closed, and four factors (current, voltage, resistance, and power) work together to make a light bulb glow, for example.

It is important to know what the words *current, voltage, resistance,* and *power* represent and to understand the relationship between them.

- *Current* is the rate of electrons flowing through a circuit per second. It is typically represented in math by I for "intensity" or A for "amperes." Current is measured in amps.

- *Voltage* is the electrical potential to create current flow in a circuit. It is represented in math by the letter V for "volts" or E for "electromotive force." Voltage is measured in volts.

- *Resistance* is the property opposition of the flow of electrical current. It is typically represented in math by the letter R for "resistance." Resistance is measured in ohms.

- *Power* is equivalent to an amount of energy consumed per unit time. Energy expended in one form manifests itself into another form—motion, heat, or light. Power is the rate at which energy is utilized. Power is represented by the letter P and is measured in watts (W).

TIP   The term *resistance* is used when you are working with direct current (DC) circuits, such as those that are powered by a battery. In alternating current (AC) circuits, such as loudspeaker circuits, the term *impedance* is used in place of resistance. Impedance is measured in ohms and typically represented in math by the letter Z. The calculations in this chapter help you approximate impedance measurements for AC circuits.

In the AV industry, Ohm's law and the power equation are used to calculate and predict voltage, current, resistance, and power. These elements help AV professionals calculate the total electrical impedance of a group of loudspeakers that are connected by cabling, and they help calculate the amount of current required to power the AV equipment in a rack. They can also be used to determine signal level at the end of a long cable run.

Ohm's law defines the electrical relationships in DC circuits. It will also help approximate for AC circuits. However, AC circuit calculations are frequency dependent, and Ohm's law does not account for the influence of frequency in a circuit. The results of Ohm's law or power equation calculations are given to a professional electrician or an AV systems designer to incorporate into a design.

The Simple Ohm's Law Formula Wheel

The simple Ohm's law formula wheel can help you remember how to calculate voltage, current, and resistance (see Figure 2-3). If you know the value of two of these variables, you can easily calculate the third.

To use the wheel, locate the value you want to calculate.

- V = Voltage (volts)
- I = Current (amps)
- R = Resistance (ohms)

Calculate the value by performing the operation between the two remaining variables (see Figure 2-4).

- If variables are on top of each other, divide the top variable by the bottom.
- If variables are next to each other, multiply them.

Ohm's law defines the relationship between current, voltage, and resistance in an electrical circuit as proportional to applied voltage and inversely proportional to resistance.

Current and Voltage

Current, voltage, resistance, and power interact with each other in a predictable way.

Figure 2-3
Simple Ohm's law
formula wheel

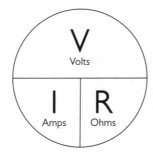

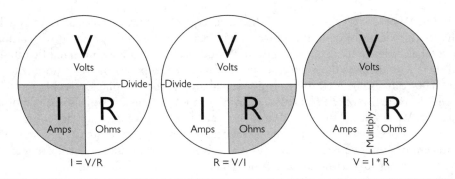

Figure 2-4 Three Ohm's law formula wheels

Current Formula (Ohm's Law)

The formula for calculating current using Ohm's law is

$$I = V / R$$

where:

- I = Current
- V = Voltage
- R = Resistance

The current in an electrical circuit is proportional to the applied voltage, meaning that an increase in voltage produces an increase in current if resistance stays the same.

Current and Resistance

The relationship between current and resistance is inversely proportional, meaning that an increase in resistance produces a decrease in current if voltage stays the same.

As an analogy of the relationship between current and resistance, think of a sink with a stopper. The water pressure in the sink basin is like voltage. It has the potential to go down the drain, but it hasn't yet. If you remove the stopper, the volume of water flowing through the drain pipe is like current. The pipe diameter presents a resistance to the current. A wider pipe will drain more quickly than a narrower pipe. Thus, the total volume of flowing water will increase because the pipe is wider (less resistance allows for an increase in the flow of current) than the narrower pipe (there is higher resistance in a narrower pipe).

Current and Power

Just as Ohm's law describes the relationship between current, voltage, and resistance, the power equation describes the relationship between power, current, and voltage.

Power is created when current, voltage, and resistance are present. However, unlike current, power is consumed as it travels along the circuit, and it never makes it back to the source. Typically, it is used up performing some work, such as moving a speaker cone, or in the form of heat.

Power Equation

The formula to calculate power is

$$P = I * V$$

where:

- P = Power
- I = Current
- V = Voltage

If current increases, so does power. If the voltage increases, so does power.

The Simple Power Formula Wheel

The simple power formula wheel can help you remember how to calculate power, current, and voltage (see Figure 2-5). If you know two of these variables, you can easily calculate the third.

To use the wheel, locate the value you want to calculate.

- P = Power, measured in watts
- I = Current, measured in amps
- V = Voltage, measured in volts

Figure 2-5
Simple power
equation formula
wheel

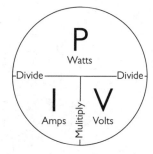

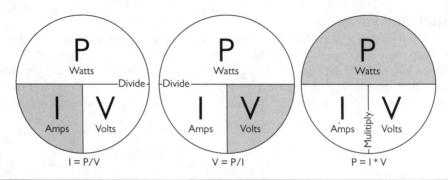

Figure 2-6 Simple power formula wheels

Calculate the value by performing the operation between the two remaining variables (see Figure 2-6).

- If variables are on top of each other, divide the top variable by the one below.

- If variables are next to each other, multiply them.

Memorize the simple power formula wheel; one simple wheel will help you remember three formulas. As soon as you sit down for the exam, draw this wheel on the erasable whiteboard that is provided in your test cubicle.

Combined Formula Wheel

These simple Ohm's law and power formula wheels appear as a combined formula wheel on the CTS-D Master List of Formulas and Symbology Descriptions sheet (see Figure 2-7). The simple wheels, however, are easy to memorize and utilize on the exam.

To use the combined wheel, first locate the measurement you want to determine in the "hub" of the wheel. Then locate the two measurements you know in the same quadrant of the outer wheel. You can then perform the mathematical operation shown in the outer wheel, and the result will be the value or the measurement you are seeking. For example, if you want to determine the number of watts or power (P) resulting when there are 3 amps of current (I) at 12 volts (V), simply find the *P* in the center of the wheel

Figure 2-7
Combined
formula wheel

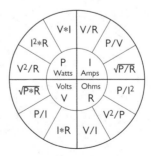

and then find the *V* and *I* in the same quadrant. Apply the math operation shown (*, or multiply) to the values for *V* and *I* (12 * 3), and the result (36) is the number of watts.

Apply the math operation shown here:

$$P = V * I$$
$$P = 12 * 3$$
$$P = 36$$

There are 36 watts of power.

Practice Exercise 1: Ohm's Law Calculation

Perform the following calculation using Ohm's law:

Calculate the current in a circuit where the voltage is 2V and the resistance is 8 ohms.

Step 1   Ohm's law formulas all have three variables. If any two of the three are known, you can solve the formula.

In this example, volts and resistance are known, and you are solving for current. Because you already have values for voltage and resistance, the correct formula to use is $I = V / R$.

Step 2   Divide voltage by resistance.

$$I = 2 / 8$$
$$I = 0.25 \text{ A}$$

Answer

$$I = 0.25 \text{ A}$$

Practice Exercise 2: Ohm's Law Calculation

Perform the following calculation using Ohm's law:

Calculate the voltage in a circuit where the current is 4 amps and the resistance is 25 ohms.

Step 1   In this example, current and resistance are known, and you are solving for voltage. Because you already have values for current and resistance, the correct formula to use is $V = I * R$.

Multiply current times resistance.

$$V = 4 * 25$$

Step 2   Calculate.

$$V = 100 \text{ V}$$

Answer

V = 100 V

Practice Exercise 3: Ohm's Law Calculation

Perform the following calculation using Ohm's law:

Calculate the resistance in a circuit where the voltage is 4 V and power is 2 watts.

Step 1 In this case, you have only one known Ohm's law variable: voltage. However, you have two known power equation variables: voltage and power. You can use the power formula to derive another Ohm's law variable, current, and then solve for resistance.

First, use the power equation to solve for current.

I = P / V
I = 2 / 4
I = 0.5

The current is 0.5 A.
Now that you know the current, use Ohm's law to solve for resistance.

R = V / I
R = 4 / 0.5
R = 8

Answer The resistance is 8 ohms.

Practice Exercise 4: Ohm's Law Calculation

Perform the following calculation using Ohm's law:

Calculate the voltage in a circuit where the resistance is 16 ohms and power is 4 watts.

Step 1 In this example, resistance and power are known, and you are solving for voltage. Because you already have values for power and resistance, the correct formula to use is the following:

$V = \sqrt{(P * R)}$

Enter the values from the question.

$V = \sqrt{(16 * 4)}$

Step 2 Calculate the value in parentheses first.

$V = \sqrt{(64)}$

Step 3   Calculate the square root.

V = 8

Answer   The voltage is 8 V.

 Watch *Ohm's Law and the Power Formula,* a short video tutorial that explains how to use the Ohm's law formula wheel. Appendix C provides a link to the video, or you can find it at www.infocomm.org/OhmsVideo.

The CTS-D Exam Process

When you're ready to take the CTS-D exam, review the application process. All the information you need is posted on InfoComm's website at www.infocomm.org/ctsd and in the *CTS-D Candidate Handbook.* Bear in mind the following:

- You must meet all eligibility requirements as of the date of the application.

- You may apply for the exam using the application in the *CTS-D Candidate Handbook* or by downloading the most recent application. Mail, fax, or e-mail the application to the InfoComm certification office for review and subsequent approval.

- Applications will not be processed unless all required information on the application is completed and the application fee is received.

- You must provide phone and e-mail contact information to facilitate e-mail confirmation of receipt of the application and any necessary phone contact prior to or following the exam.

- InfoComm will review and respond to your application within approximately 10 business days. For applications that are incomplete or lack documentation and/or payment, InfoComm will contact the applicant regarding the missing requirements. Once you have been approved for eligibility, InfoComm will notify you within one day of notifying Pearson VUE of your eligibility. You may then contact Pearson VUE after a 24-hour period to make your testing appointment. You can find the list of available testing locations at www.pearsonvue.com/infocomm.

- Your application is approved for a period of 120 days from the date of the eligibility approval notice, and you must arrange for and be tested during that 120-day period. The exam application fee must be paid by using a major credit card or by check at the time the application is submitted.

Getting to the Testing Center

On the scheduled day of the CTS-D exam, you should report to the exam center as instructed in your appointment confirmation letter. Plan to arrive at least 30 minutes prior to your scheduled start time. Allow extra travel time for unforeseen events, such as traffic delays. If you arrive after your assigned exam time, you will be considered a "no-show" and will not be admitted. To take the exam, you will need to reapply by contacting InfoComm and paying a reinstatement fee.

It is not necessary (although it is preferred) to bring your e-mail or letter of confirmation with you. However, you must have proper identification (as described shortly). The name on the ID must match the information on file with InfoComm and the vendor responsible for presenting the exam.

 TIP   If you live more than an hour from the exam center, consider staying at a nearby hotel the night before so you can get a good night's rest and make sure you arrive on time. It may also be a good idea to visit the testing center prior to the exam to ensure you know exactly where to go and how to get there.

Identification Requirements

Candidates must check in at the testing center with two forms of valid ID, one of which must be a government-issued photo ID with signature (driver's license, government ID, or passport). (See the "On the Day of the Exam" section in the *CTS-D Candidate Handbook*.) For testing center identification purposes, you must bring both a valid government-issued ID and a secondary ID that has a matching signature to the name on the government ID. *The first and last names on the ID must match exactly the name submitted on the application or you will be denied admission.*

Candidates can make changes to their names by contacting InfoComm (certification@ infocomm.org) prior to scheduling their exam appointment. Candidates will also be required to provide a digital signature and have a digital photo taken when checking in. This information is retained in a secure database for no more than five years from the last exam date. The candidate's electronic signature is not linked to the candidate's personal identification information, such as address or credit card information.

For certain Asian countries, specifically, China, Hong Kong, and Taiwan, identification requirements may differ. Please see the *CTS-D Candidate Handbook* for more details.

Items Restricted from the Exam Room

You are not allowed to bring anything into the exam room. Secure lockers are provided to store personal items while taking the exam. The following are examples of items that are *not* permitted in the exam room or testing center:

- Slide rules, papers, dictionaries, or other reference materials
- Phones and signaling devices such as pagers
- Alarms
- Recording/playback devices of any kind
- Calculators (a calculator will be displayed on the test computer screen)

- Photographic or image-copying devices
- Electronic devices of any kind
- Jewelry or watches (time will be displayed on the computer screen and wall clocks in each testing center)
- Caps or hats (except for religious reasons)

This list is not exhaustive. To be safe, you shouldn't expect to be allowed to bring *any* item into the testing room.

About the Exam

You will take the exam on a computer. The exam includes multiple-choice questions. For each question, the computer will display four possible answers (A, B, C, and D). One of the answers represents the single correct response, and credit is granted only if you select that response.

Candidates get 180 minutes to answer 135 questions, 10 of which don't count because they're pilot questions used to study future additions to the CTS-D exam. They won't be scored, but you will not know which are the pilot questions.

There is a brief onscreen computer-based tutorial just prior to starting the exam and a brief online survey at the end of the exam. The time necessary to complete the tutorial and survey do not count against the 180 minutes you're given to finish the exam.

To get familiar with the testing interface, use the online tutorial practice exam from Pearson VUE's InfoComm International Testing page at www.pearsonvue.com /infocomm. The questions you find there are not AV-related; the tutorial is simply intended to familiarize you with the testing interface. You can use this free resource any time before you take the CTS-D exam.

During the Exam

What is it like inside the exam room? Knowing ahead of time should help you plan for any eventuality. Bear in mind the following:

- Candidates should listen carefully to the instructions given by the exam supervisor and read all directions thoroughly.
- Questions concerning the content of the exam will not be answered during the exam.
- The exam center supervisor will keep the official time and ensure that the proper amount of time is provided for the exam.
- Restroom breaks are permitted, but the clock will not stop during the 180 minutes allotted for the actual exam.
- During the exam, candidates will be reminded when logging in to the testing center computer screen and prior to being allowed to take the exam that they have agreed to follow the CTS Code of Ethics and Conduct and nondisclosure agreements presented earlier in the application process.

- Candidates will have access to a computer-based calculator and a wipe-off note board provided by the testing center.
- Candidates will have the ability to provide comments for any question, as well as mark questions and return to them for review.
- There will be an onscreen reminder when only five minutes remain to complete the exam.
- No exam materials, notes, documents, or memoranda of any kind can be taken from the exam room.

For best results, pace yourself and periodically check your progress. This will allow you to adjust the speed at which you answer questions, if necessary. Remember that the more questions you answer, the better your chance of achieving a passing score. In other words, don't leave any question unanswered. If you are unsure of a response, eliminate as many options as possible and choose from the answers that remain. You will also be allowed to mark questions for review prior to the end of the exam.

 TIP Be sure to record an answer for every question, even if you're not sure which answer is correct. You can note which questions you want to review and return to them later. There is no penalty for wrong answers, and each correct answer is worth one point. So, marking an answer to all questions will maximize your chances of passing.

Dismissal or Removal from the Exam

During the exam, the exam supervisor may dismiss a candidate from the exam for any of the following reasons:

- The candidate's admission to the exam is unauthorized
- A candidate creates a disturbance or gives or receives help
- A candidate attempts to remove exam materials or notes from the testing room
- A candidate possesses items that are not permitted in the exam room
- A candidate exhibits behavior consistent with attempting to memorize or copy exam items

Any individual who removes or attempts to remove exam materials, or is observed cheating in any manner while taking the exam, will be subject to disciplinary or legal action. Sanctions could result in removing the credential or denying the candidate's application for any InfoComm credential.

Any unauthorized individual found in possession of exam materials will be subject to disciplinary procedures in addition to possible legal action. Candidates in violation of InfoComm testing policies are subject to forfeiture of the exam fee.

Hazardous Weather or Local Emergencies

Hey, you never know. In the event of hazardous weather conditions or any other unforeseen local emergencies occurring on the day of the exam, the exam presentation vendor will determine whether circumstances require cancellation. Every attempt will be made to administer all exams as scheduled.

When an exam center must be closed, the vendor will contact all affected candidates to reschedule the exam date and time. Under those circumstances, candidates will be contacted through every means available: e-mail and all phone numbers on record. This is an important reason for candidates to provide and maintain up-to-date contact information with InfoComm and the exam vendor.

Special Accommodations for Exams

InfoComm complies with the Americans with Disabilities Act (or country equivalent) and is interested in ensuring that no individual is deprived of the opportunity to take the exam solely by reason of a disability as defined under the Americans with Disabilities Act (or equivalent). Two forms must be submitted to receive special accommodations:

- Request for InfoComm (CTS, CTS-D, CTS-I) Exam Special Accommodations
- InfoComm (CTS, CTS-D, CTS-I) Exam, Healthcare Documentation of Disability Related Needs

Applicants must complete both forms and submit them with their application information to the InfoComm certification office no later than 45 days prior to the desired exam date.

Requests for special testing accommodations require documentation of a formally diagnosed or qualified disability by a qualified professional who has provided evaluation or treatment for the candidate.

You can find these forms, along with more information about the process, at the InfoComm CTS-D website and in the *CTS-D Candidate Handbook*.

Exam Scoring

Candidates receive their results immediately upon test completion. The final passing score for each examination is established by a panel of SMEs using a criterion-referenced process. This process defines the minimally acceptable level of competence and takes into consideration the difficulty of the questions used on each examination.

Candidates who do not pass the exam receive their score and the percentages of questions they answered correctly in each domain. InfoComm provides these percentages to help candidates identify their strengths and weaknesses, which may assist them in studying for a retest. It is not possible to arrive at your total exam score by averaging these percentages because there are different numbers of exam items in each domain on the exam.

Retesting

If you do not pass the CTS-D exam, you may take it again two more times following your original exam date. There is a minimum 30-day waiting period between each retest.

After your retest application has been approved, you have 120 days from the date of the reissued eligibility notice to retake the exam.

If, after two retests, you still have not passed the exam, you must wait 90 days before restarting the application process. This period gives you time to adequately prepare and prevents overexposure to the exam. Candidates must meet all eligibility requirements in effect at the time of any subsequent application. You can find the CTS-D Exam Retest Application form and current retest fees at the InfoComm website.

Currently certified CTS-D individuals may not retake the CTS-D exam, except as specified by InfoComm's CTS-D renewal policy.

CTS-D Exam Practice Questions

To reiterate, the CTS-D exam consists of 135 multiple-choice questions that address each of the domains and tasks listed in Table 2-1. The questions focus primarily on issues that an AV professional may encounter when working on a specific job or task, rather than on general AV technology knowledge.

Let's take a look at examples of CTS-D exam questions. For each question, the domain and task from which the question is drawn are identified first. Not to sound like a broken record, but remember that these are sample questions, not actual CTS-D exam questions. They may be similar to exam questions, but because of the way the CTS-D exam is designed to meet ANSI standards, there can be no guarantee that these practice questions reflect the actual exam. That said, both the practice questions and the exam questions are guided by the same JTA.

1. [Conducting a Needs Assessment/Review client technology master plan]

   How do you determine the client's long-term plans and needs in terms of equipment and support maintenance?

   A. Ask advice from other AV industry experts and vendors

   B. Contract with a consulting company to determine client needs

   C. Consult the owner, examine standards and design manuals, and create the project report

   D. Design a generic system that fits any organization of that size

2. [Conducting a Needs Assessment/Identify regulatory requirements and project certification goals]

   In a proposed presentation room with a flat floor and theater-style seating, which has the greatest influence on the visibility of a projection screen?

   A. Ceiling height

   B. Projection room location

   C. Location of windows

   D. Width of the room

3. [Collaborating With Other Professionals/Coordinate architectural/interior design criteria]

For a flat-floor auditorium with rows of staggered seats, evenly spaced for proper horizontal viewing, which row or rows will determine the preferred minimum height of the bottom of the image on a display at the front of the room?

   A. First three front rows of the room

   B. Ends of the back row of the room

   C. Rear three rows of the room

   D. Second row from the back of the room

4. [Developing AV Designs/Create draft AV design]

Which of the following signals can coexist in one conduit without interference?

   A. Serial control and video

   B. Speaker level audio and serial control

   C. Video and microphone-level audio

   D. Data network and line-level audio

5. [Conducting Project Implementation Activities/Participate in project implementation communication]

In an AV project involving a courtroom, sightlines from the jury box are obscured by an architectural feature. How should the issue be addressed?

   A. Communicate with the project manager

   B. Contact the architect with recommended changes

   C. Let the judge manage the situation

   D. No consult necessary; move forward with your recommendations

NOTE   If you encounter a question or topic in this book that is unfamiliar to you, write it down for further study. That way, you know to focus on these topics when you develop your personal study plan.

Answers to CTS-D Practice Questions

Did you peek or read ahead? Here are the answers to the preceding practice questions:

   1. C. When determining a client's long-term plans and needs in terms of equipment and support maintenance, you should consult the owner, examine standards and design manuals, and create the project report.

   2. A. Ceiling height has the greatest influence on the visibility of a projection screen in a presentation room with a flat floor and theater-style seating.

3. **C.** For a flat-floor auditorium with rows of staggered seats, evenly spaced for proper horizontal viewing, the rear three rows of the room will determine the preferred minimum height of the bottom of the image on a display at the front of the room.

4. **A.** Serial control and video signals can coexist in one conduit without interference.

5. **A.** If you have sightline issues from the jury box of a courtroom, communicate with the project manager.

Chapter Review

Upon completion of this chapter, you should have a clear understanding of the following:

- How the CTS-D exam is designed
- The skills, knowledge, and AV design-related tasks that the exam covers and why
- How and why this guide covers the exam material differently than the exam content outline
- How to study and prepare for the CTS-D exam
- How to solve AV-related mathematical equations using the order of operations
- How to solve calculations using Ohm's law
- How to apply for the exam
- What to expect on the day of the exam
- What the CTS-D exam questions might look like (but not exactly)

Now you're ready to delve into the specific knowledge, skills, and responsibilities you will need to succeed in your career as a CTS-D–certified AV designer.

PART II

Environment

Communicating Design Intent

In this chapter, you will learn about

- The phases of an AV design project
- The documentation necessary for communicating a design to the necessary stakeholders
- Creating accurate AV design drawings
- Reading architectural drawings and identifying the elements that impact your AV design
- Identifying end users' requirements through a needs analysis process
- Creating a program report for an AV system installation

AV systems are complex. They're integrated with other building systems, such as network; electrical; heating, ventilation, and air conditioning (HVAC); and building automation/ energy conservation systems. In many cases, AV systems provide operational functionality to an owner, requiring a thoughtful and well-organized approach to commonly accepted planning, design, and integration procedures. As you proceed through a design, you must constantly review and adjust assumptions to ensure the needs of the customer are met given the available environment.

Any seasoned AV designer will tell you that a design project is not linear. That is, you don't complete tasks 1, 2, and 3 in order. Rather, the process is more like, "Do task 1 first, then task 2, then go back to task 1, before jumping to task 3 and then task 2 again. Oh, and simultaneously finish task 4." What's more, the AV design and systems integration processes may span and parallel a lengthy construction cycle, resulting in input and review from key personnel in many different trades and disciplines.

Throughout everything, it is critical that an AV designer be able to communicate—in words and drawings—the intent of a design. Such design intent comprises everything from a client's expectations to the details of a system that meets those expectations, from how a design works within the architecture of a space to how it fits within a client's budget. Successfully communicating design intent requires a phased approach.

Domain Check

This chapter relates directly to the following tasks on the CTS-D Exam Content Outline:

- Domain A Task 1: Identify stakeholders/decision makers
- Domain A Task 2: Identify skill level of end users
- Domain A Task 5: Identify clients' procurement processes
- Domain A Task 6: Research clients' business process
- Domain A Task 8: Define AV needs (absolutes)
- Domain B Task 1: Review A/E (architectural and engineer) drawings
- Domain B Task 2: Coordinate architectural/interior design criteria
- Domain B Task 3: Coordinate structural/mechanical criteria
- Domain C Task 3: Produce infrastructure drawings

These tasks comprise 28 percent of the exam (about 35 questions). This chapter may also relate to other tasks.

The Phases of an AV Design Project

Even though design is iterative and there is no precise step-by-step process, there are still logical phases to the project. ANSI/INFOCOMM 2M-2010, *Standard Guide for Audiovisual Systems Design and Coordination Processes,* lays out the steps of an AV design. If you follow them, you will find yourself laying the five important building blocks of a successful design, as shown in Figure 3-1.

The ANSI/INFOCOMM 2M-2010 standard was created to describe the methods, procedures, tasks, and deliverables typically recommended by AV systems designers and systems integrators. By using the standard, clients, designers, and construction team members can be confident that everyone on the project team delivers on expectations.

 Watch a video about planning an AV design at www.infocomm.org/ PlanningVideo. Appendix C provides links to all the helpful videos in this guide.

As a designer, your job is to analyze and define performance needs, functional requirements, and system budgets prior to ordering and installing equipment. You need to record clearly the client's needs and expectations through written documents and formal architectural drawings. To help you accomplish this goal, use the phases described in the ANSI/INFOCOMM 2M-2010 standard as your guide. Let's take a quick look at design phases before going into more detail later in the chapter.

Figure 3-1
The building blocks of an AV design

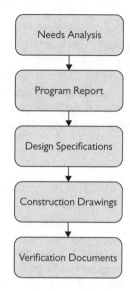

A Word About Meetings

All parties involved in an AV project want the finished product to meet the design intent—on time and within budget. But before you can design anything, you need to hold planning and coordination meetings, sometimes called *pre-construction meetings*, each with a potentially different focus. These will be the first of many meetings throughout the project.

You should adjust the type, timing, and quantity of meetings to reflect project requirements, and there should be a contract that specifies the number and location of meetings to be held throughout the design effort. It is important to come out of every meeting with some form of written documentation. Meeting minutes, notes, and contracts help reinforce discussions and record any decisions that are made.

Meetings will serve a variety of purposes during a project and should include the following:

- Technology programming meetings, to understand the client's goals and level of technical sophistication
- Design coordination and review meetings, held at major milestones to review with the client the progress of the design and to coordinate with the rest of the team
- Pre-bid and pre-construction meetings, held with the client and potential contractors to review the scope of the project
- Construction meetings, to observe the progress of the work and address issues onsite
- Post-construction meeting, held with the client to review the project.

NOTE Here's an example of the nonlinear nature of a design project: Let's say, early in a project, you determine that a large direct-view monitor would be best for your customer's needs. However, later in the project, you discover that the large screen does not fit in the building's elevators and can't be delivered to the room. In such a case, you would need to review the design selection to ensure it's still the best choice given the limitation. Moreover, changing screen specifications may impact other parts of your design.

Program Phase

Once you have met with your customers and determined the shape and structure of your project, you can begin the *program phase* of your design. The purpose of the program phase (alternatively called the *briefing* or *concept design phase*) is to discuss, clarify, and document the client's needs, concerns, expectations, and constraints. These will guide the design team in its approach to the functionality and cost of the AV systems.

There are two key components of the program phase: the needs analysis and program report. Keep in mind, this phase of the project is not for discussing particular equipment; it's to define the needs, contexts, methods, and wants of the client.

For architects, *programming* is the process by which the overall requirements of building are defined. Architects document the needs of owners and occupants as a preliminary step to putting lines on paper in what will become a set of blueprints or other engineering design.

The architectural program document describes the facility in terms of square footage, space configuration, and overall building quality. For AV professionals, *programming* may also refer to the separate process of software coding of programmable AV devices, such as control systems and digital signal processing (DSP) equipment.

Design Phase

Designers use the results of the program phase, including the program report, to create two more sets of documents in what's known as the *design phase*. These documents provide the backbone for communication and coordination among the design team, the contractors, and the clients. The design phase and its associated documents are meant to identify the functional, physical, and system design requirements that meet the clients'—or building owners'—needs.

The first set of documents includes specification and AV system documents. They describe functional, operational, and technical performance specifications (e.g., frequency response, speech intelligibility goals, and image contrast ratio). The specifications may also provide information about equipment manufacturers, models, and quantities required to implement the design, as well as installation and testing procedures, warranty information, and other details.

The second set of documents is a collection of drawings. These drawings comprise a graphical representation of the facility (architecture and infrastructure) and indicate how the AV equipment will integrate with the built environment—for instance, the locations of such visible items as loudspeakers, projectors, cameras, equipment racks, and so on. The drawings also include system diagrams that show what equipment will be provided and how it will connect.

It's worth noting that architects and some other trades break down design into subphases, described next.

 Watch a video about the design phase of an AV project at www.infocomm.org/ DesignPhaseVideo. Appendix C provides links to all the helpful videos in this guide.

Conceptual Design Phase

Following architectural programming, the architect sometimes creates a conceptual design—a diagram that graphically portrays the program information for space shapes, adjacencies, and sizes.

Schematic Design Phase

The conceptual design is developed to a more detailed level, beginning to show more detail such as double lines for walls, door locations, and room orientations. In addition, the architect defines the overall "massing" or general shape and size of the buildings, and a schematic narrative generally describes the major systems to be included in the building.

Design Development Phase

The goal of design development is to move beyond major coordination issues to the basic floor plans. During this phase, all major design decisions are made and finalized with the owner so the building floor plan is set, engineering systems are selected, and detailing can commence. This is an intense period of design consulting and decision making for the design team and the owner. The end result is the final architectural and engineering design.

Within the architectural design process, the design development phase is a go/no-go decision point. Usually, enough design information has been gathered by the end of this phase to know with a fair degree of accuracy how much the facility construction will cost. For some projects, this is the stage at which the owner may decide that a project should be abandoned because of budget or other issues before proceeding into the construction phase.

Construction Phase

Let's get back to the AV design phases. In the *construction phase*, you will turn your design documents into construction drawings. These drawings, provided in Portable Document Format (PDF) or other unalterable document format, should include sufficient detail to convey to the AV installation team the physical configuration of the AV systems. These drawings are also known as *submittal drawings, workshop drawings,* or *shop drawings.* As the AV designer, you must make sure these documents are handed off to the team responsible for implementing your design.

Throughout the construction phase, accurate drawings that correctly depict the system and its components are critical. Inaccurate documentation leads to change orders, which can delay a project and frustrate everyone involved. Changes *will* occur, but minimizing them is a major goal of accurate construction documentation.

The construction phase involves three efforts that are interconnected and repeatedly feed one another. Think of them as three parts of a braid: coordination, procurement, and installation. These efforts feed off documents created during the design phase, namely, drawings, specifications, and equipment schedules. These contract documents will be used to create more detailed drawings, called *shop* or *installation drawings*, which will be used for onsite fabrication at the contractor's shop and onsite installation. They will also be used to procure equipment and materials, and they will lay the groundwork for system testing, adjustment, and training when the project nears completion.

Verification Phase

After you've handed off the design documents to the installation team, your job is not over. You are still responsible for ensuring that the client's new AV system is installed according to your specifications. This means having a process in place to check that every component was installed properly and performs up to expectations.

When the project installation is coming to a close, using standards for the verification and optimization of AV systems demonstrates that the installation meets the design intent. Years after the project is completed, the next AV provider can refer to your design and verification documentation and know the initial delivery was professionally installed.

ANSI/INFOCOMM 10:2013, *AV Systems Performance Verification*, offers a framework and set of processes for determining which elements of an AV system need to be verified. It also details the timing of systems verification within the project delivery cycle, a process for determining verification metrics, and reporting procedures.

The Design Process—A Mnemonic Device

As mentioned earlier, AV design is an iterative process, which means you often find yourself repeating steps to get the interrelated parts of a design working properly together. That said, if it helps you remember what you're trying to accomplish during an AV design, think in terms of these four actions:

1. **Think it**   Take time to speak with clients. Find out what they need so you can address their problems with your design.

2. **Draw it**   Draw or write down what clients tell you and then show them what you're thinking. This way, everyone can verify that they're on the same page.

3. Math it Once a client has agreed with your idea, make sure your design works. Don't waste time designing systems for ideas that won't work in a space or with other equipment. Make calculations, determine specifications, and take measurements. After you've determined that your plans will or will not work, communicate the results to the client.

4. Detail it Document all your ideas in a formal design that AV installers will use to build the systems. This step includes determining specific equipment, creating detail drawings, and coordinating your AV system with allied trades.

This process is not part of the ANSI/INFOCOMM 2M-2010 standard, and it is not meant to limit you to an inflexible structure. But by thinking in these terms, you may find yourself moving fluidly between the different phases and seeing the "big picture" of your design. How will the system address your client's needs? How will the gear work together to create a seamless, pleasant AV experience?

Reading Construction Drawings

Throughout the phases of an AV project, designers need to be comfortable reading construction drawings. This means being familiar with the following:

- Drawing scales
- Drawing types
- Drawing symbols
- Drawing abbreviations

As you develop a plan and communicate with everyone involved in the project, you will inevitably have to review construction drawings. To understand these drawings, however, you need to be familiar with drawing scales. Accurate conversions between scaled drawings and the real object are necessary for implementing a design according to the documentation.

Scaled Drawings

Construction drawings are drawn to a reduced size. Scales, like those on a map, are used to show large objects accurately but at a manageable size. A scaled drawing has a relationship, or proportion, between a length on a drawing and the actual length of an object. As an example, for a drawing produced at 1:100 scale, every 1 millimeter (mm) on the drawing represents an actual length of 100 mm.

TIP When reading an architect's or engineer's drawings, make sure to note the scale of the drawing. In addition, check that the physical size of the printed drawing is accurate. Besides checking the scale noted on the drawing, it is always a good idea to confirm the scale using common building elements such as doors or ceiling grid tiles. Drawings may have been unintentionally rescaled during printing, photocopying, faxing, or PDF conversion.

A scale ruler provides a quick method for measuring an object drawing to scale on paper and interpreting its true size in the actual space.

Most metric scale rulers look similar to normal rulers, except that the marking has different numbers, with a different scale, along each edge. A ratio at the left end indicates the scale measured using that side. The numbers along the scale indicate the length of an actual object when measured against its scaled representation on the drawing.

Traditional U.S. customary scale rulers are prism-shaped tools. A whole or fractional number to the left or right edge of the measurement tool indicates the scale those numbers represent.

The selected scale of a drawing is usually written in the title block in the lower-right corner of the drawing but may be located anywhere on the sheet. Converting the scale length to actual length is required to determine height, length, and width, as well as cable run estimates.

Watch a video about how to use a scale ruler at www.infocomm.org/ScaleVideo. Appendix C provides links to all the helpful videos in this guide.

Converting Dimensions on Scaled Drawings

Being able to accurately measure using a scale ruler is an important skill when working with scaled drawings. Scale drawings are used to communicate the dimensions of a full-size project on a paper or electronic document. The selected scale is usually in the title block in the lower-right corner of the drawing but may be located anywhere on the plans. A set of drawings may include more than one scale, so you must check each drawing page for its scale. Some drawings may even have multiple scales on the same sheet. Occasionally, several details may need to be called out, but they may not be large enough to require their own sheet. Check the identifying information adjacent to the item to confirm its scale. Converting the scale length to actual length is required to determine actual height, length, width, and cable run estimates.

Two different scale systems can be found on drawings: U.S. customary and metric. Drawings using U.S. customary measurements usually state a scale using a particular fraction of an inch (in) to represent a foot (ft). For example, you might find a scale on a drawing that shows 1/4 inch equaling 1 foot.

This means that a 1/4-inch length on the drawing is equal to a 1-foot length in reality. The "1/4 in = 1 ft" scale is the most common in the United States and is also referred to as 1/48 size because there are 48 units of 1/4 in in 12 in.

Figure 3-2
Customary U.S.
scales

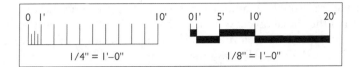

Figure 3-2 shows two different U.S. customary scales. The 1/4-in scale on the left indicates that for every 1/4 in measured there is 1 ft of real distance.

Most regions outside of the United States use the metric International System of Units (SI). Millimeters are the standard unit used in architectural drawings and construction language for commercial projects, and 1:50 and 1:100 are the most common scales. This means that for a drawing using 1:100, 1 unit of length on a drawing equals 100 units of the same length in reality.

1:20, 1:10, and other larger scales are generally used only for details. 1:200, 1:500, and 1:1000 are only used for small-scale drawings with little detail, such as the whole floor of a large building or a site plan.

Figure 3-3 shows a metric scale ruler. The 1:50 scale on the left indicates that for every 1 mm measured, there are 50 mm of real distance. The adjacent markings show that the ruler is reading 1950 mm for the room dimension, which is the same as the dimension printed on the drawing. Note that below these markings is the 1:500 scale.

TIP If the scale of a metric drawing is 1:50, every unit that you measure on the drawing translates into 50 units in the actual room. You could measure with a normal ruler (metric or inches) and multiply the measurement by the scale.

1:50 and 1:100 are the practical equivalents of the U.S. customary 1/4-in and 1/8-in scales, respectively.

Figure 3-3
A metric scale
ruler

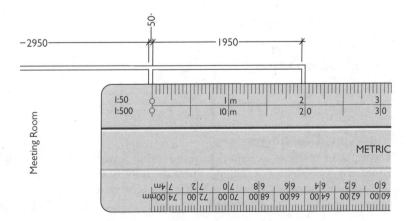

If you measured 51 millimeters on a 1:50 drawing using a normal metric ruler, the length of the actual object would be 51 × 50 = 2550 mm. If you then measured the same item using a normal-inch ruler, you would get a reading of just over 2 in, which converts to 2 × 50 = 100 in. Allowing for reading accuracy, the two measurements are almost identical: 2500 mm = 98.4 in.

Always note the scale on the drawing. Also, check that the printed physical scale of the drawing is correct.

Consider what would happen if you took a drawing that is the correct scale on a piece of U.S. Letter-sized paper that is 8.5 in × 11 in (216 mm × 279 mm) and tried to print it on metric A4 paper that is 210 mm × 297 mm (8.27 in × 11.7 in). The printer may rescale the image to fit the different sized paper, which will result in an inaccurate printout.

All your measurements taken from these printed copies would be incorrect.

You should always check that the document was printed accurately before making measurements and conversions. Make sure all construction drawings are printed so that 1 unit of the printed document equals 1 unit of the original drawing. This can be done by checking the measurement of a dimensioned object or an object of known size.

Drawings can be inaccurate because of any form of copying or processing. While most original plots from a computer-aided drawing (CAD) file should be accurate (though human mistakes can and do happen), anything that has been plotted to "fit" the sheet of paper, rather than to a specific scale, is likely to be scaled incorrectly.

In addition to providing detailed information that is essential to ensuring the AV system design is accurately depicted, construction drawings also tell you where in a space to install an AV system.

Drawing Types

Designers create drawings to show where each component will be located and how each component should be physically installed. The package typically contains functional diagrams, connection details, plate and panel details, patch panel details, equipment diagrams, rack elevation diagrams, and the control panel layout.

The following are a few of the different types and subsets of drawings you will typically encounter:

- Plan view drawings
- Reflected ceiling plans
- Elevation drawings
- Section drawings
- Detail drawings

Plan View Drawings

Floor plans provide an orientation to the space. You should slice through the building or room at 4 feet (about 1.2 meters) above the floor to illustrate a floor plan.

A plan drawing, as shown in Figure 3-4, is a view of the room taken from directly above, showing the floor plan or site plan. The floor plan identifies the room locations

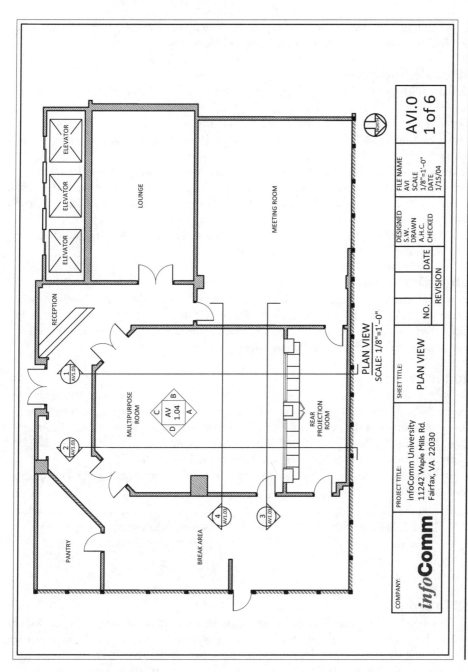

Figure 3-4 A plan drawing

and layout dimensions, such as locations of walls, doors, and windows. A floor plan view may also include indicators to other more detailed view drawings.

Reflected Ceiling Plans

A reflected ceiling plan, shown in Figure 3-5, illustrates elements in the ceiling with respect to the floor. It is called reflected because it is intended to be interpreted as though the floor was a mirrored surface, reflecting the ceiling plan. The reflected ceiling plan shows the locations of such elements as ventilation diffusers and returns, sprinkler heads, and lights.

The drawings are of interest to the AV designer and installer because locations of AV equipment such as loudspeakers and projectors will require coordination with allied trades. For example, placement of lights and HVAC diffusers may conflict with required locations of projection screens or loudspeakers to meet performance standards.

The reflected ceiling plan is an especially important plan for an AV designer because it depicts the features included within the ceiling.

Elevation Drawings

An elevation drawing (see Figure 3-6) is a drawing that looks at the environment from a front, side, or back view. Elevations provide a true picture of what the interior wall will look like. Elevations show anything that might be on the walls, such as electrical outlets, windows, doors, AV faceplates, and chair rails.

Section Drawings

A view of the interior of a building in the vertical plane is called a *section drawing* (see Figure 3-7). A section drawing shows the space as if it was cut apart, and the direction you are looking is indicated by an arrow in the plan drawing. Section drawings show walls bisected, which allows you to view what is behind the wall and the internal height of the infrastructure. A section drawing can be rendered at an angle.

AV professionals use section drawings to plan for installation needs, such as mounting locations and cable runs.

 TIP To help understand the difference between elevation drawings and section drawings, think of elevations as pictures and sections as cutouts.

Detail Drawings

Detail drawings (see Figure 3-8) indicate small items that need magnified views to show how they must be installed. Detail drawings depict items too small to see at the project's typical drawing scale. Details may show how small items are put together or illustrate mounting requirements for a specific hardware item, such as a ceiling projector mount.

PART II

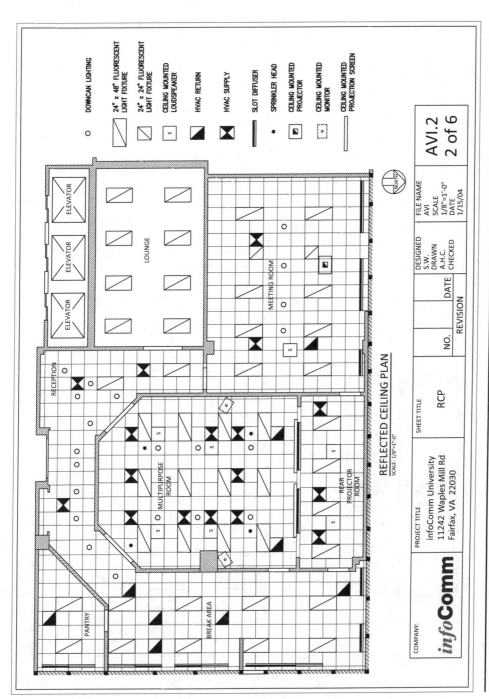

Figure 3-5   A reflected ceiling plan

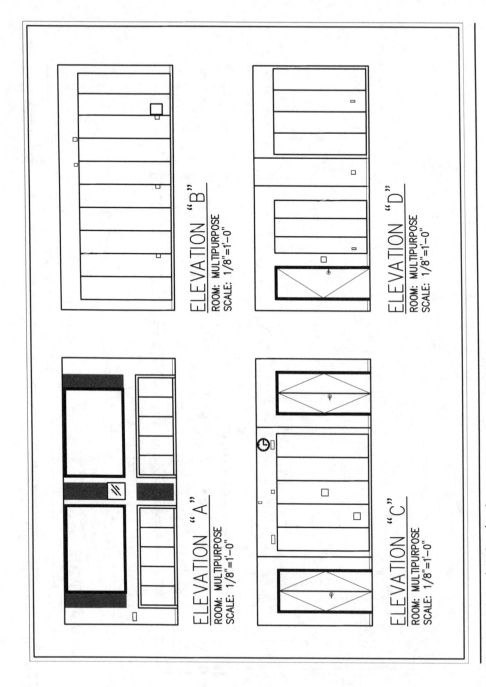

Figure 3-6 An elevation drawing

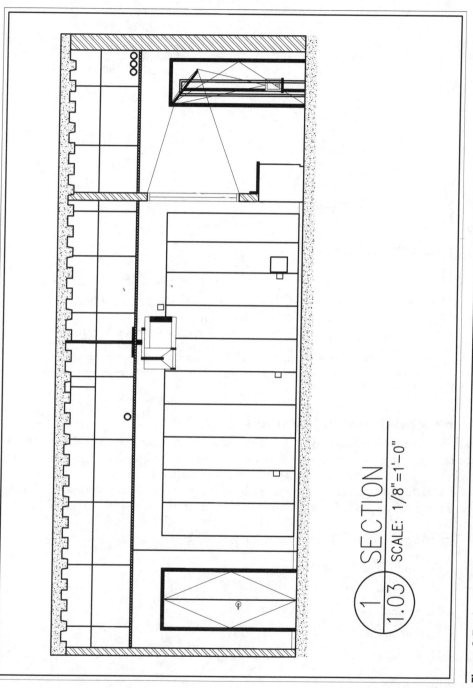

Figure 3-7 A section drawing

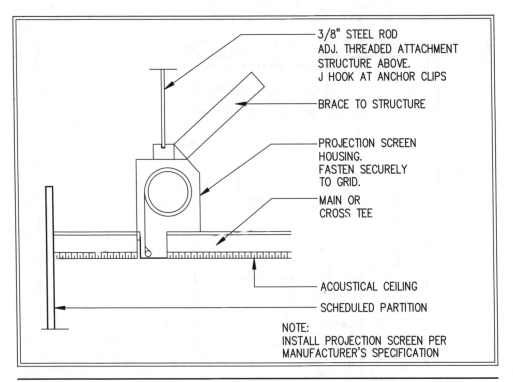

Figure 3-8 Detail drawings

Architectural Drawing Symbols

Each project drawing has different symbols and icons that are used to depict specific elements of the project design or the relationship between multiple drawings, such as where a room depiction in one drawing is continued on another drawing.

Architectural symbols are standardized by country or region, and normally a drawing set will include a legend. As long as they are defined in the legend, the actual object does not matter.

Typical symbols you will see include the following:

- Column lines
- Match lines
- Elevation flags
- Section cut flags
- Detail flags

Column Lines

A grid system, also known as a *column line,* is used to indicate the locations of columns, load-bearing walls, and other structural elements within the building layout, prior to

Figure 3-9
Column lines

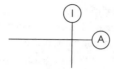

the room locations being defined. Grid lines are used to reference the schedule and for dimensioning. Vertical grid lines should have designators at the top and be numbered from left to right. Horizontal grid lines should have designators at the right and be alphabetized from bottom to top.

The grid system can be used to find your way around a work site in the early construction phase. Contractors will refer to a point in the space with respect to where it exists on the drawing, as in "4 meters west of B6." Since the space may not yet be divided into rooms, identifying a point by the grid system ensures that everyone at the site understands the location.

Figure 3-9 illustrates a column line. You should orient the point of the circles to the column line with the letters in one direction and the numbers in the other direction.

Match Lines

Technicians use match lines (Figure 3-10) to show how each subdrawing matches to another page of the drawing. For example, it may take multiple pages to depict one area of a building. To assemble the separate drawings so you can see the big picture, the individual pieces are aligned using the match lines as a guide. The shaded portion of the line is the side that is considered.

TIP Remember to include page numbers to identify the adjacent drawing element.

Elevation Flags

Elevation flags (Figure 3-11) are used on plan drawings to indicate related elevation drawings. The picture displayed is an example of an elevation flag. The center number

Figure 3-10
Match lines

Figure 3-11
Elevation flags

D4
D3 A4.0 D1
D2

indicates the page number where the elevation drawings can be found. The letters in the triangle portions of the figure identify the elevation drawing on that page.

Each elevation view for a room may be drawn in order and presented in a clockwise manner. This way, you can "look around the room" as if you were standing on the elevation flag and viewing the walls.

Section Cut Flags

Section cut flags indicate which section drawing depicts a section of a master drawing in more detail, as shown in Figure 3-12.

The bottom number indicates the page number where the section drawing can be found. The top number is the section drawing identification, because multiple section drawings may be on the same page. A line extends from the center of the symbol indicating the path of the section cut. The right angle of the triangle is an arrow indicating the view direction of the section drawing.

Section views are similar to elevation views. They depict specific wall sections, based on the section cut line indicators on the master floor plan drawing.

Detail Flags

Detail flags indicate the small items that need to be blown up to show how they need to be installed. These items are too small to draw or see at the project's typical drawing scale.

In a large system, there may be hundreds of areas requiring more detail to read accurately. Each instance is numbered. The bottom number indicates the page number where the detail drawing can be found. The top number is the detail drawing identification, because multiple detail drawings may be on the same page. In Figure 3-13, the symbol refers to detail number 1, where you can find more information about drawing AV1.06.

 CAUTION   Abbreviations are not the same in all countries.

Figure 3-12
Section cut flags

Figure 3-13
Detail flags

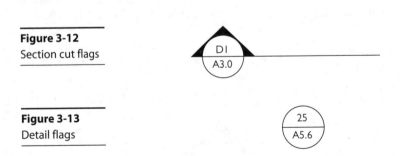

Abbreviation	Definition
AFF	Above finished floor
AS	Above slab
CL	Center line
CM	Construction manager
DIA	Diameter
E.	East
E.C.	Empty conduit
EC	Electrical contractor
(E) or #XG	Existing
EL	Elevation
ELEC	Electrical
FUT	Future
GC	General contractor
MISC	Miscellaneous
NIC	Not in contract
NTS	Not to scale
OC	On center
OD	Outer diameter
OFCI	Owner furnished, contractor installed
OFE	Owner furnished equipment
OFOI	Owner furnished, owner installed
PM	Project manager
RCP	Reflected ceiling plan
SECT	Section
VIF	Verify in field

Table 3-1 Common Architectural Drawing Abbreviations

Common Architectural Drawing Abbreviations

See Table 3-1 for common architectural drawing abbreviations.

The AV Design Package

You can't design or install AV systems without considering other system designs. Because in the course of your work you will be communicating with members of the architecture, engineering, and consultant teams, refer to the standards of all applicable organizations for guidelines on effective communication.

The *AV design package* represents a written method of communicating design intent to allied trades. It also conveys architectural details that may impact the AV-enabled environment.

Design documents must include enough information to convey the intent of the AV design. In addition to system design information, certain administrative contract language will form the basis of the actual installation contract. The design package is the basis of most—if not all—of the contract that an AV integrator signs when the project is awarded.

Major components of the design package include the following:

- Administrative front-end specifications
- Architectural and infrastructure drawings
- AV system drawings
- AV system specifications

 Watch a video about the components of an AV design package at www.infocomm .org/Package Video. Appendix C provides links to all the helpful videos in this guide.

Front-End Documentation

A construction contract typically has an administrative front-end section. This section explains how the contractor and owner will interact by specifying what documentation, meetings, reports, and record drawings are required.

Front-end documentation usually includes the following:

- **Invitation to bid**   This is a cover letter that formally invites potential bidders to respond to the bid package. It includes contract information, dates, times, and schedules associated with the bid process.

- **Request for quote (RFQ)**   This is a statement that invites potential bidders to submit a "resume" of their qualifications for the job.

- **Bid response form**   This organizes responses from potential bidders and indicates what information is required.

- **General conditions**   The architect for the base building contract provides the general conditions. Typical sections of the general conditions include the following:
  - Project work conditions and terms
  - Definitions of terminology
  - Safety and accident prevention
  - Permits, regulations, and taxes
  - Insurance
  - Overall quality control
  - Submittals
  - Substitutions schedule
  - Changes in the scope of work

- Initiating and processing change orders
- Warranty
- Non-discrimination and affirmative action
- Contract termination options
- Arbitration
- Invoicing and payments
- **Money matters in the contract**   Within the general conditions—and sometimes within a consultant's specifications section—are the terms related to invoicing and payment.

Architectural and Infrastructure Drawings

Architectural drawings indicate where the systems will be installed, what infrastructure exists, and what may be required for AV systems. These indicate available power, signal conduit, data outlets, and structural accommodations for AV equipment.

Architectural drawings provide a technical illustration of all construction details, including the following:

- Site work
- Foundation
- Structure
- Power and lighting systems
- Plumbing
- Sprinklers
- Audiovisual equipment
- Electrical
- Mechanical
- Finishes
- Details

3D Modeling and CAD Drawings

When working on an AV design, you will need to express your needs to various allied trades. For ease of communication, you should present your design in a format that will be compatible with documentation from those allied trades.

Many design firms and allied trades use 3D or solid modeling. Also known as computer-aided design, CAD programs allow multiple trades to communicate their needs and flag possible conflicts. For example, if a light fixture was placed in the lighting plan in the same spot where a loudspeaker was placed in an AV plan, a quick comparison of each trade's CAD drawings would be the easiest way to spot the conflict.

3D modeling helps establish efficient communication. Changes to 3D-modeled documents are reflected quickly and accurately. In addition, 3D modeling allows engineers to explore a greater number of design iterations during product development. When utilized with building information modeling (BIM), 3D modeling allows for concurrent engineering, whereby engineering and manufacturing processes are enabled simultaneously through shared data.

3D modeling also leads to lower unit costs because of reduced development and prototype expenses. All of these advantages lead to a quality project.

Building Information Modeling

BIM describes a data repository for building design, construction, and maintenance information used by multiple trades on a single project. It includes CAD drawings, as well as information such as bid and contract documents, bills of materials (BOMs), timelines, specifications, price lists, installation and maintenance guides, cable lists, and cable label guidelines.

According to the National BIM Standard, "A BIM is a digital representation of physical and functional characteristics of a facility. As such it serves as a shared knowledge resource for information about a facility forming a reliable basis for decisions during its lifecycle from inception onward."

As an AV designer, BIM may impact your design in several ways. Most importantly, many of the allied trades you will be working with—especially architects—will probably use BIM. You need to ensure that your documentation is compliant with theirs. Early in the design, get in touch with your project architects and other allied trades. This will keep your design compatible and compliant from the beginning.

Detail Drawings: Custom or Integrated Millwork and Casework

When designing a room that contains audiovisual equipment, be aware of the architectural elements that are commonly used to house such equipment. Two items that fit that classification would be *millwork* and *casework*.

Millwork refers to items that are custom-cut for the project, such as moldings or trim. AV designers often design the millwork detail for structures that hold a projection screen in place, for example, as shown in Figure 3-14. As you determine the locations of a projection screen or loudspeaker, you need to ensure that the architectural elements will allow them to be placed in exactly the right spot.

Casework is similar to furniture, with the distinction that casework is built into the room. Casework includes such items as cabinets, credenzas, benches, and lecterns. There is a range of integration questions associated with the casework that an AV designer will need to help answer, including the following:

- What equipment is expected to be installed in the casework?
- How large should the casework components be?
- What connections are required to interface with the AV system?
- Is the casework adequately sized for the equipment including mounting, cable management, and serviceability?
- What are the electrical and signal connection requirements for the equipment to be installed in the casework?
- What are the cooling requirements, and how will they be implemented?
- Does the casework meet any disabled person codes or requirements?

Figure 3-14
Detail drawing
showing
millwork detail
for a projection
screen

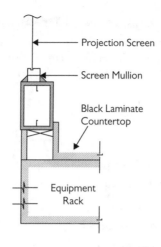

Projection Screen

Screen Mullion

Black Laminate
Countertop

Equipment
Rack

AV designers often partner with interior designers to create detailed drawings for the custom millwork or casework required to accommodate AV equipment. These drawings communicate to allied trade the exact dimensions, style, shape, color, finishes, ventilation, and so on, that the AV systems require. Therefore, you should understand how to communicate the installation and millwork requirements to the architect. The level of detail required will vary, depending on the project.

Color Schemes

AV designers should work with the interior designer and architect to help ensure that a room's visual design is compatible with the AV presentation needs. The interior designer will be responsible for the color and texture of the finishes. Your job is to remind them that contrast around an image is important. For example, visual design is important when considered from a videoconferencing camera's point of view. This means verifying that a room is designed with complementary colors, minimal patterns, and no strong lines.

Interior design coordination includes the following:

- Locations for key AV components
- Connection plate finishes
- Connection plate mounting heights
- The level of exposure or hidden integration of AV equipment
- Shapes, finishes, and placement of furniture

Coordinate color, materials, and patterns with the architect and interior designer to ensure compatibility with the overall interior design.

AV System Drawings: Facility Drawings

AV system drawings depict the AV system itself. These should reflect equipment configurations, interconnections, details, plate layouts, and other graphic depictions of the system installation. Typical components of the design drawings package include the following:

- Title and index
- Power, grounding, and signal wiring details
- Floor and reflected ceiling plans showing device locations
- System functional diagrams
- Rack elevations
- Custom plate and panel details
- Speaker aiming information
- Large-scale plans, such as equipment or control room plans
- Architectural elevations showing AV devices, their locations, and their relationships to other items on the walls
- Custom-enclosure or mounting details for projectors, microphones, loudspeakers, media players, and others
- Furniture integration details
- Any special circumstances or details that may be required for the installers to understand the design intent

Architectural and facilities drawings are used to perform sightline studies and determine viewing areas, audience listening areas, camera angles of view, and so on.

AV designers use these drawings to coordinate and locate AV elements such as displays, screens, projectors, equipment racks, loudspeakers, specialized lighting, microphones, lecterns, equipment storage, conduit for AV cabling, wall boxes, connection plates, electrical and data receptacles needed for AV equipment, and so on.

AV System Drawings: System Diagrams

Architectural and facilities drawings are used to perform sightline studies and determine viewing areas, audience listening areas, camera angles of view, and so on.

AV designers use these drawings to coordinate and locate AV elements such as displays, screens, projectors, equipment racks, loudspeakers, specialized lighting, microphones, lecterns, equipment storage, conduit for AV cabling, wall boxes, connection plates, electrical and data receptacles needed for AV equipment, and so on.

For the AV system itself, AV designers create system diagrams. These system diagrams could be as simple as a one-line conceptual drawing that shows the system's intent but not the specific connections. More detailed system drawings show all specific connection points and other important system details. These drawings include the following:

- Video system flows
- Audio system flows
- Control system flows
- Rack elevations
- Connection plate details
- Digital signal processor settings

AV System Specifications

Specifications are sort of like the project's manual, in that they explain how AV systems should be installed and tested. They describe the system, components, codes, references, and other requirements. They also contain information concerning submittal requirements, shop drawing requirements, components, and system testing requirements.

 Now that you have studied all the components of design documentation, take a video tour of the AV design package at www.infocomm.org/DesignTourVideo. Appendix C provides links to all the helpful videos in this guide.

The Basics of AV-Enabled Rooms

AV designers must take a big-picture view of a room to ensure that they understand exactly how it will be used. They also must be able to read blueprints to identify architectural details that may impact AV and communicate those issues to other professionals. For example, room size and how people move in a room will affect design. Keep the following in mind:

- The form of the room should follow the function of the room.
- The number of people in the room will help define the size.
- Circulation and work patterns within the room will help define the form.

All AV-enabled rooms have as their primary function the communication of ideas and information. This concept of a room's function should be at the center of all design decisions, and all other design characteristics, such as HVAC, lighting, and windows, should be integrated so as to augment the function of the room.

Most AV-enabled rooms include audience, presenter, control, and projection areas. You should also look at other rooms and areas (such as break areas, reception, etc.) to determine whether those spaces might impact the overall performance of the room you're designing for. In short, work with the architect to ensure that the layout of a room and associated spaces is appropriate for the tasks that will take place in the room.

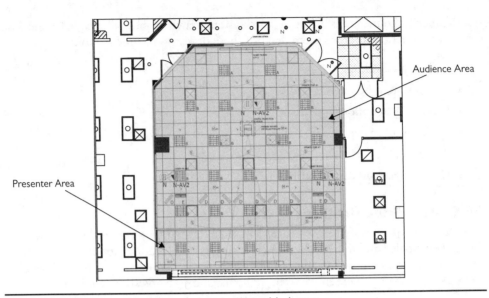

Figure 3-15   Audience a presenter areas in an AV-enabled room

Audience and Presenter Areas

When planning your room layout, you need to consider both the audience and presenter areas, as shown in Figure 3-15. While there are some considerations unique to each area, many are common to both. The following are some of the commonalities:

- **Equipment and materials**   Is there enough room for presentation equipment, people's personal devices, books, and writing materials?

- **Connection points**   Where are AC power, network connections (wired or wireless), and display connections required?

- **Comfort**   What furniture will the room need? Consider ease of movement for both access and egress.

- **Sightlines**   Will everyone be able to see the presenter and their presentation materials?

- **Audio coverage**   Will everyone be able to hear what they are supposed to hear?

When it comes specifically to the presenter area, there are several design considerations you need to address. The presenter area refers to the designated location in a room where presenters (teachers, speakers, etc.) will operate. The area typically includes a lectern, microphones, and a control system interface. The following are some of the design issues to consider in the presentation area:

- **Presenter workstation**   Is the lectern/console well laid out for the range of presentation needs identified by the client?

- **Presenter equipment**   Is there enough room for the presenter and the presenter's equipment, such as notebook computers or presentation notes? Also keep in mind that a presenter may want to move around during a presentation and not be anchored to the lectern.

- **Power, voice, and data**   Are the power, data, and computer connections in front of the room adequate to meet the needs of presenters?

- **Sightlines**   Specific to the presenter area, can the audience see both the presenter and projected images? For example, if a presenter is too close to the screen, it may be necessary to limit the amount of the lighting on the presenter because ambient light may interfere with a projected image. And if that's the case, cutting back on light may make it difficult to see the presenter.

- **Versatility**   Have you met *all* the needs of the client? For example, the client may not want a lectern permanently attached to a specific location. They may intend to move the presenter area to different locations when changing the room orientation to accommodate different audiences. Can they?

Looking out from the presenter area is the audience area—where people sit to take in a presentation. The following are some of the design issues to consider in the audience area:

- **Visuals.**   Can everyone in the audience see the presenter and the presentation? Consider screen size, image resolution, task requirements, sightlines, and more.

- **Sound**   Can everyone in the audience hear the presentation? Consider the acoustics of the room and determine the appropriate configuration of microphones and loudspeakers.

- **Ease of movement**   Can everyone in the audience enter and exit with ease? A properly designed seating layout is essential.

- **Audience comfort**   Will people be comfortable in their seats? Ensure that there is sufficient room between the seats and in the aisles for the required number of persons, given the desired audience seating layout. And be sure to consider the needs of people with disabilities, in compliance with the Americans with Disabilities Act.

Control and Projection Areas

Depending on the size and scope of a room, the AV system may require a dedicated control or projection room. Think of the control/projection room at the back of an auditorium, for example. The design issues associated with a control or projection area are usually technical in nature and include the following:

- **Equipment space**   In some cases, AV operators may be required to support a presentation. Is there enough room for both AV operators and the projection equipment? If an operator is required to remain within the control area for long periods, then the room should be designed to provide an adequate level of comfort.

- **Heating and cooling**   Can the heat generated by AV equipment be removed from the room? Coordinate the design requirements with the architect and HVAC designer to ensure adequate ventilation.

- **Power requirements**   Is there sufficient power for the required equipment?

- **Voice and data**   Does the area include appropriate telephone and data communication? For example, a network cable may be required to ensure computer-based presentations can access required data. Phone communication with the presenter area may also be desirable.

- **Task lighting**   There needs to be enough lighting for operators to see system controls without adversely affecting the quality of a projected image.

- **Sound isolation**   Noise from the area, such as cooling fans, must be controlled and minimized so that it does not distract the audience.

- **Monitoring**   Operators must be able to hear what's going on in the main room to support the presentation or other activity. They shouldn't be "tucked away in a closet," as sometimes happens.

NOTE   There are other spaces that support a room, its occupants, and the activities in a building, such as lounges, breakout rooms, reception areas, and restrooms. Often, the design of these associated spaces can impact the success of the rooms an AV designer creates. For example, a reception desk adjacent to the presenter area of a room can be a source of noise that might interfere with the presentations taking place within the room.

Programming

In AV and information technology (IT) fields, the term *programming* often refers to software coding of programmable devices, such as control systems and digital signal processing equipment. But for other allied trades, such as architects, programming is the process by which the overall requirements for the building are defined. Architects document the needs of the owner and end user as a preliminary step to putting lines on paper that represent the space plan. The architectural program document discusses the facility in terms of square footage, space configuration, and overall quality of the building.

Applying an AV design begins with careful planning and time spent identifying and discussing the end-user's needs. Therefore, let's take an in-depth look at this crucial step of the AV design process.

The Needs Analysis

A needs analysis requires identifying the activities that end users need to perform using AV and developing the functional descriptions of the systems that support those needs. Conducting a needs analysis is the most crucial stage of the design process. It determines the nature of the systems, their infrastructure, and the project's budget.

Figure 3-16
The needs
analysis pyramid

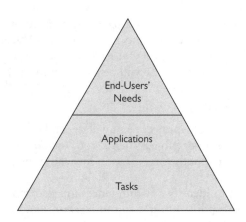

When you ask a client and the client's end users why they need an AV system, they may not always know. However, they do know what tasks they need to accomplish to do their jobs. This is where an AV design educates clients and helps fill in the missing information, making connections between jobs tasks and the capabilities of an AV system.

Figure 3-16 shows the needs analysis pyramid, a visual representation of how needs relate to an AV system's functionality, first through the applications they enable and the tasks they help accomplish.

But first, it's important to understand who we're talking about when we talk about your client's end users and why you need their input on a project.

Who Are the End Users?

The client is the person paying for the AV system. It might be a business owner, a chief technical officer, or a facilities manager.

End users are people who operate a system day to day. They can be technical end users who know a lot about the system, such as a technology manager or production engineer. Or they can be nontechnical people who need the system to work at the push of a button, such as a teacher or an executive using a conference system. You need to understand the needs of both the person holding the purse strings (the client) and the person using the system (the end user).

End-user input is essential when designing an AV system. The fact is, other client representatives may not really understand how a room and its AV system will be used. Ignore end users at your peril—you'll hear from them if they're dissatisfied with the final product.

Asking end users probing questions helps fill in the blanks when determining what they really need. Ask not only what they plan on doing in a space but also how they plan to do it. And depending on who you're talking to during the needs analysis, figure out who can get you what you need. For example, ask for scale drawings of the space and its surrounding infrastructure. Get a feel for estimated or fixed budgets. And figure out whether there will be any constraints placed on the AV team by the client, such as work hours during the project (i.e., do you have to install systems on weekends?), acceptable ambient noise levels, or what else will be going on in the building at the same time.

Clients on a Project

The actual who's who of a project team will depend on the size and nature of the project. An AV designer has other project clients, too, including the project manager (if not the architect or a member of the organization for whom the project is being built) and other design specialists.

It is important to identify any differences in approach and opinion among end users, decision makers, funding groups, support groups, and even external contractors, such as project and design team members. The difference between a good and unsatisfactory project outcome can be in the AV designer's ability to recognize and manage varying expectations.

Some end users may be low in an organization's hierarchy but have the best knowledge of what an AV system should achieve. Others, with more authority but less understanding, may have different expectations or place constraints on the project, in terms of timing and budget. The AV designer must find ways to communicate with, educate, and understand the perspectives of each stakeholder.

For example, at times, end users will have unrealistically high expectations and ask for functionality (equipment and features) that is not justified by their needs or that are unaffordable based on the available budget. The AV designer has to know when to support end users and argue for better funding and when to recognize that a budget is realistic and help end users appreciate that some of the things they're asking for are "wish list" items.

The following sections discuss some of the key players you may encounter as you work on your AV design.

The Owner Team

Depending on the type and size of the owner organization, participants may consist of a small number of people or a large group. An owner can be a corporation, a government agency, or an individual. In some cases, the owner of a building is fitting out a space to be leased to another company that is the actual purchaser of the AV systems. Some owner configurations are more complicated, such as in some state university systems, and some are simple, as in the case of a small private company, such as a law firm or a small manufacturer.

The owner typically has its own representatives in the building design process. Representatives range from nontechnical administrative employees to chief executive officers (CEOs) and from facilities managers to in-house architects, if the client owns or leases a lot of property. Sometimes a team or committee represents the owner. The owner team can include one or many of the following types of people.

End Users

As noted earlier, end users are the people who will ultimately use the AV systems and the spaces where they will be installed. It is important to note that end users may not be employed by the owner's organization, although in most cases they are. In addition, later mentions of the owner may or may not represent the end users, depending on the structure of the project.

In terms of AV systems, there are generally two types of end user.

- **Technical end users**   In the AV industry, technical end users, also known as *technology managers*, are responsible for operating, setting up, maintaining, scheduling, and managing an AV system. Most are familiar with the IT network and how the AV systems relate to it; some are also responsible for the IT systems.

- **Nontechnical end users**   They are sometimes referred to as the "real" end users. These are the presenters and meeting participants who use AV systems for their intended purpose: information communication. These may be teachers, trainers, students, salesmen, CEOs, or anyone who participates in an event that utilizes an AV system.

Facility Managers

Larger organizations have a facility manager heading up a department that covers everything from janitorial services to renovation work and from planning to operations. Facility managers are concerned with physical facility standards (standard finishes, cabling schemes, and electrical/mechanical services) and construction schedules from the owner's operational perspective. Their areas of AV concern may include space allocation, cabling standards, and installation schedules because large AV installations often overlap with occupancy periods, after a general contractor has finished its own work.

AV Department Manager

Many organizations have someone on staff who manages the current AV systems, schedules usage, and maintains the AV spaces. The AV manager usually coordinates training for end users once the system has been installed. The AV manager may also act as the owner's representative or point of contact throughout the AV project.

Smaller organizations may not have a dedicated AV position. In that case, responsibility often rests with someone who has similar experience or expertise, often in the IT department.

Buyer, Purchasing Agent, or Contract Representative

Medium to large organizations often have a department or individual whose role is to manage contracts, select vendors, and establish or negotiate contract pricing and terms. These personnel may be involved in the construction document preparation (particularly the administrative portions), the bidding and contract negotiation processes for designers and installers, and the administration of billing, paying, and contract close-out tasks.

Building by Committee

Sometimes, a project involves several divisions or departments of an organization, including a large number of administrative and technical stakeholders. In this case, the owner may create an internal committee to steer the process of building a new facility. This type of committee should have representation from the technical staff, which can provide valuable input to the design process.

Conducting the Needs Analysis

Now you know who is involved in the needs analysis. Next you'll talk to stakeholders, review existing documentation, evaluate the site environment, conduct program meetings, and write the program report. That's a lot, but each step is important. We'll break them down.

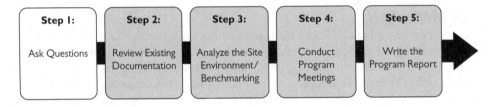

Step 1: Ask Questions

First, you'll talk to as many stakeholders as feasible. Knowing that there are many ways clients can use AV, how can you find out what they need so you recommend just the right solution? Just ask. But ask in the right way.

When you create a good dialogue with a client and a client's end users, everyone will better understand the project's goals. Good dialogue is also friendlier and less threatening.

Questions foster dialogue. Questions also help gather important information, get the client involved, and persuade more effectively (and softly) than statements. Use them often and intelligently. When asking questions, employ the following:

- Open-ended questions
- Closed-ended questions
- Directive questions

When you want the client to give a full, informative response—or just start talking—ask open-ended questions that are hard to answer in a word or two. Here are a few examples:

- How do people in your organization like to present content in meetings?
- What kinds of meetings are held in this facility?

- How would you describe the current effectiveness of your training?
- What would you like to see be done differently or better?

Answers to questions like these tell you how your client thinks, how much they know, and what they consider important. If you need factual or specific information, ask closed-ended questions, such as the following:

- How many people will the room need to seat?
- Are there any windows or columns in that room?
- When do you expect construction to start?

When it's time to bring a client to your point of view or persuade them that one of your ideas will work well, ask directive questions. These are questions that suggest their own answer—sometimes the one you want to hear—such as the following:

- Can you see the added value of a maintenance agreement to protect your equipment investment?
- Wouldn't it be great if everyone knew how to take full advantage of this room?
- Would you get more use out of the liquid crystal display (LCD) display or the projector and screen?

Step 2: Review Existing Documentation

Once you've talked to key stakeholders, your next step is to gather and review the available documentation. This documentation is usually available with information about the existing physical, organizational, and technical aspects of the project.

Ask the client for the existing documentation. It may include items such as scale and engineering drawings (blueprints, CAD drawings), architectural program documents, organizational project directories, design manuals, standards, best practices, and other owner and end-user information. Ensure that you have a full set of drawings for the rooms your AV design will address. Be sure to examine all elements that might potentially affect the layout, mounting, installation, and operation of AV system components. If no documentation is available, you may need to create new material based on existing conditions.

At this point, it's also important to ask the client about budget. Providing a fixed budget and setting expectations will go a long way toward addressing concerns the client may have. Be sure to ask which part of the budget is for AV and which part is for other contractors' work. The customer may not be aware that other trades share in the project.

Step 3: Evaluate the Site Environment/Benchmarking

If the AV systems are to be installed in an existing facility, it is important to tour those areas during the needs analysis process to gather information about physical characteristics and how the spaces are currently being used. It is important to learn about any issues that may impact your ability to work at the client site once the design and installation tasks begin, such as building security and access. In many cases, the design and installation teams can identify a method to work around constraints, such as working during certain hours or in areas where they are less likely to disrupt operations.

When touring and evaluating an existing facility's environment for the first time, make note of room elements such as the acoustics, lighting, and electrical infrastructure. Use handheld light meters and audio analyzers for quick, useful measurements. Getting an idea of the ambient light levels could inform future contrast ratio decisions, and ambient noise readings can give you a ballpark idea of audio reinforcement needs. You're not trying to make a detailed analysis; you're just getting to know the space.

You should also consider visiting other similar facilities for review and comparison. This is known as *benchmarking* and gives the owner and the design team a common (and sometimes expanded) vision of what the user wants and needs. Seeing a number of locations of similar size, type, and usage establishes a benchmark or guide on which to base the new facility design.

Benchmarking offers the following benefits:

- It provides an opportunity to see varying approaches to design versus budget.
- It may inspire new design ideas.
- The team can identify successful (and unsuccessful) designs and installations similar to the project at hand.
- It can help determine which functions and designs are most applicable to the current project.
- It allows stakeholders to establish a communication path with other building managers and end users about what they learned in the design and construction process and to discuss what they would do the same or differently if they needed to do it over again.

Benchmarking can't occur on all projects. Sometimes you can save the time and money required to visit similar sites by letting the client look through a portfolio of your firm's work on similar projects or by asking them to provide you with pictures of projects they've seen and liked.

Step 4: Conduct Program Meetings

Once you've collected feedback from stakeholders, reviewed existing documentation, and evaluated the environment, you can schedule program meetings.

Program meetings should include representatives of both the design team and the owner. During these meetings, the architect, AV professionals, and other design team members discover more about the end-users' needs by examining required applications and the tasks and functions that support those applications. In other words, you've learned what they want; now you're discussing in-depth how they'll get it. If you don't know who you should be meeting with, go back to the section "Clients on a Project."

As you already understand, one or more people will use the AV system you design. Others may manage or maintain it. And still others may pay for it. So, it follows that some will care about functionality, others about upkeep, and others about cost. A safe way to find out how decisions will be made during program meetings is to ask your contact, "Who, in addition to you, will be involved in this decision?" Words are important: You don't want to suggest that your contact has no authority.

A good follow-up question might be, "What is their primary interest or concern?" This will help you target your message to each stakeholder based on what they care about most. Yes, they all care about the whole project, but they also have their own areas of focus: operations, security, maintenance, financing, and so on.

Here's another good question for a program meeting: "How far along are you in your budgeting process?" This asks in a nonthreatening way whether the client has a realistic budget in place or they're able to make the investment a certain design decision may require. It'll also help you learn more about the client's planning and decision-making processes.

AV solutions are often—although not always—scalable to a client's needs and budget. But it's unsafe to guess about expectations because you will usually guess wrong. Not only does this waste your time and theirs, it can create hard feelings and damage relationships. The basic rule is never guess about what you can find out for sure by careful questioning.

 TIP In each meeting with your client, make it a point to learn who else has an interest in AV and look for opportunities to meet them. Never go around your contacts or over their heads. Offer to arrange meetings and introductions between your colleagues and theirs. Naturally, each meeting needs a purpose; it can't only be something nice to do.

Step 5: Write the Program Report

At the conclusion of the program meetings, information is captured in a written report of the findings, including an interpretation of the users' needs with respect to the AV systems. The report should include a conceptual system description, along with necessary information about its impact on spaces that have already been programmed, designed, or built.

The program report is a functional description of the system that your design team intends to deliver. It functions as your project's scope of work, in that it contains the milestones, reports, deliverables, and end products that you agree to deliver to the project customer. It should also lay out change order, escalation, sign-off, and payment procedures. Many designers will also include a list of equipment in the program report because it helps with the cost estimation, though a program report should contain much more information than a simple bill of materials.

The objectives of the program report are as follows:

- Communicate to decision makers about the overall systems and budget
- Communicate to users the system configurations that would serve their needs as identified during the program meetings

- Communicate to the design team a general description of the AV systems and what impact they may have on other trades
- Communicate the scope and functionality of the AV systems to be designed and installed

NOTE A scope of work can describe many elements of an AV project, including aspects of the design, such as the program report. The scope of work is often the most comprehensive description of the project and may include any or all of the following: information about all contractors, a description of the solution (with drawings and products), key assumptions, pricing, project milestones, responsibilities, project-management procedures, warranty information, and terms and conditions.

A Closer Look at the Program Report

At the conclusion of the program meetings and needs analysis process, you need to document what you learned in what is called a *program report*. This nontechnical document describes the client's needs, the AV system's purpose and functionality, and your best estimate of probable cost, and it ultimately documents the client's approval.

NOTE Other names for the program report include AV narrative, discovery phase report, return brief, or the concept design report.

What follows are the common contents of a program report. Exact contents will vary because every project is unique.

- **Executive summary** This section provides an overview of the project, the programming process, systems, special issues, and overall budget.
- **Space planning** This section provides advice to the design team, where necessary, about the space requirements of AV systems. This may include equipment closets, projection rooms, observation rooms, internal room layouts, room adjacencies, and so on.
- **System descriptions** This section is a nontechnical description of the client's desired functionality for each system. It may include AV sketches, drawings, diagrams, photos, product data, and other graphics, such as touch-panel interfaces, to illustrate the capabilities of the proposed systems.
- **Infrastructure considerations** This section describes the electrical, voice, IT, mechanical, lighting, acoustic, structural, and architectural infrastructure needed to support the AV systems.

- **Budget recommendations**   This section outlines the probable costs to procure, install, and commission the proposed AV systems, as well as any additional costs, such as tax, "builders work in connection" (BWIC), markups, service, support, and contingencies.

Once the document is distributed to stakeholders, reviewed, and approved, it becomes the basis for the upcoming design phase. The review and approval process may go through several rounds before obtaining client or end-user sign-off.

NOTE   Your program report will vary from project to project. There is no single correct way to order the information, but using the list of items outlined in the ANSI/INFOCOMM 2010-2M Standard as a table of contents is a reasonable starting point.

AV Budget Terms

As noted earlier, the program report should include an opinion—or estimate—of how much the AV system will cost. As you form your opinion, pay attention to the following budget terms. Using them incorrectly may lead to confusion and financial consequences later in the project.

Opinion of Probable Cost

This term describes an early attempt to determine the cost of a system before there is enough detailed design to produce a line-item estimate. The opinion of probable cost is an "educated guess" based on experience and some line-item costs for large equipment, such as projectors or large-matrix switchers. Final costs cannot be applied until the system is designed and the actual equipment selected.

Estimate

An estimate implies that there is a more objective basis for the cost provided. It is an "approximate calculation" that includes a line-item analysis of equipment and labor (perhaps including taxes and other ancillary costs); it would be more accurate than an opinion of probable cost.

Quote

A quote is a detailed and enforceable estimate. It should be provided and identified as such only if it's based on a program report and an AV system design. If it isn't, the client, the end users, and the AV provider are at risk of a painful mismatch of needs, capabilities, and cost.

Budget

Although the term *budget* is often used in the context of terms described earlier, by strict definition it applies only to what the owner or project team has allocated for a particular system, trade, or facility. In the correct relationship of these terms, the budget should be established based on an opinion of probable cost or an estimate. A quote is then submitted by a provider based on a Request for Proposal (RFP). The quote is subsequently compared to the budget before acceptance by the owner.

Distribution and Approval

A program report may contain sensitive information. It should be distributed on a need-to-know basis and never to anyone outside the project team without permission from its writer and the client (or authorized representative). Distribution to unauthorized parties could reveal confidential information about the client, project, or other details. In particular, it should not be distributed to individuals and organizations with connections to the AV industry. Doing so could undermine the competitive bid process or a project where an integrator is not already engaged. Apart from leaked cost information, which could potentially affect the owner, unauthorized distribution of the program report opens a door to suppliers and others inappropriately lobbying project team members and/or manipulating prices.

Watch a video about writing a program report at www.infocomm.org/ ProgramReportVideo. Appendix C provides links to all the helpful videos in this guide.

Assuming you distribute the program report to the appropriate parties, you need to establish a set period of time for comments and responses. At its conclusion, any necessary revisions should be made and the report either redistributed or submitted for approval if only minor changes were required. Depending on the nature of the feedback, more program meetings may be required to address any major issues or deficiencies.

Once the program report is signed and approved, it can be used as the basis for the design of the AV systems and their supporting infrastructure. In this formalized, approved state, it protects the owner, consultant, and designer by ensuring everyone defines the project in the same, unambiguous way.

Chapter Review

In this chapter, you learned about the phases of an AV design project, including the program, design, construction, and verification phases. You also learned about what goes into an AV design package, including drawings and diagrams. AV designers must be able to read and interpret such drawings and diagrams to collaborate with other professionals on an AV project.

Perhaps the most important part of the AV design is the needs analysis, which occupies a significant chunk of the program phases. Being able to discern the various stakeholders on a project and illicit information about their needs and wants is critical to designing the best possible AV system to meet those needs and ensuring it delivers as promised. All the documentation that comes out of the program phase will serve to guide the project to its successful completion.

Review Questions

The following questions are based on the content covered in this chapter and are intended to help reinforce the knowledge you have assimilated. These questions are not extracted from the CTS-D exam, and they are not necessarily CTS-D practice exam questions. For an official CTS-D practice exam, see the accompanying CD.

1. What is the primary goal of a needs assessment?

   A. Identifying the intended use of a space

   B. Selecting the right equipment

   C. Establishing the "first use" date

   D. Meeting the budget requirements

2. The total length of a measurement from a metric (SI) scaled drawing of 1:50 is 100 mm. What is the actual length?

   A. 5 meters

   B. 50 meters

   C. 0.5 meters

   D. 150 meters

3. Which of the following architectural drawing symbols is a detail flag?

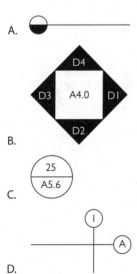

   A.

   B.

   C.

   D.

4. The total length of a measurement from a U.S. customary scaled drawing of 1/8 inch is 3.5 inches. What is the length of the real object?

   A. 18 feet

   B. 25 feet

   C. 28 feet

   D. 35 feet

5. What type of drawing would you use to find out exactly how the projector should be mounted to the ceiling?

   A. Reflected ceiling plan

   B. Mechanical drawing

   C. Detail drawing

   D. Section drawing

6. Which abbreviation on a drawing tells you that you will not need to install a specific display screen?

   A. OFOI

   B. OC

   C. OD

   D. NTS

7. Technical end users are sometimes referred to as:

   A. Teachers

   B. Technology managers

   C. Clients

   D. Architects

8. Which is the following is not a step in conducting a needs analysis?

   A. Review existing documentation

   B. Evaluate the site environment

   C. Conduct program meetings

   D. Educate allied trades

9. Benchmarking is a process by which AV designers and clients:

   A. Evaluate the performance of AV systems

   B. List specifications required on AV equipment

   C. Examine the AV designs of other facilities

   D. Compare expected results to actual results

10. Which of the following would not be considered part of the system drawings for an AV design?

    A. DSP settings

    B. Rack elevations

    C. Control system flows

    D. Color schemes

Answers

1. **A.** The primary goal of a needs assessment is to identify the intended use of a space.

2. **A.** When the total length of a measurement from a metric (SI) scaled drawing of 1:50 is 100 mm, the actual length is 5 meters.

3. **C.** Figure C shows a detail flag.

4. **C.** When the total length of a measurement from a U.S. customary scaled drawing of 1/8 inch is 3.5 inches, the length of the real object is 28 feet.

5. **C.** You would use a detail drawing to find out exactly how a projector should be mounted to the ceiling.

6. **A.** OFOI (which means "owner furnish, owner installed") on a drawing would tell you that you will not need to install a specific display screen (or other OFOI equipment).

7. **B.** Technical end users are sometimes referred to as technology managers.

8. **D.** Educating allied trades is not part of the needs analysis.

9. **C.** Benchmarking is a process by which AV designers and clients examine the AV designs of other facilities.

10. **D.** Color schemes would not be considered part of the system drawings for an AV design.

Ergonomics in AV Design

In this chapter, you will learn about
- What ergonomics means in the context of AV design
- Identifying the limitations of a viewer's visual field
- Creating optimal sightlines based on the seating layout of a room
- Selecting the furniture for an AV design project

AV systems are tools for improving human communication; therefore, the human element—and specifically, human comfort—is an important consideration in AV system design.

Ergonomics, also known as *human-factors engineering,* is the scientific study of the way people interact with a system. The purpose of ergonomics is to limit injury, fatigue, and discomfort in a work environment. Factored properly into an AV design, ergonomics can help the users of AV systems enjoy greater effectiveness, efficiency, productivity, comfort, and safety, while at the same time reducing the errors, fatigue, frustration, and stress that could otherwise come from interacting with technology.

Domain Check

This chapter relates directly to the following tasks on the CTS-D Exam Content Outline:

- Domain B Task 2: Coordinate architectural/interior design criteria
- Domain B Task 3: Coordinate structural/mechanical criteria
- Domain C Task 1: Create draft AV design

These tasks comprise 14.4 percent of the exam (about 21 questions). This chapter may also relate to other tasks.

AV designers should strive to ensure that a system follows ergonomic principles. For example, consider eye and head levels when conducting sightline studies, and factor in reach distances when deciding where to place a control or input panel. The goal is to create an optimal experience that takes into account users, technology, content, and the room environment. Achieving that end requires the proper design and layout of physical equipment, displays, and system interfaces.

Human Dimensions and Visual Field

Because so much of the audiovisual experience today is about what people see, it's important that the video portion of an AV design create the proper experience. (You will learn about the human perception of sound and subjects such as loudspeaker coverage in Chapter 6, "Audio Principles of Design.")

When you design a visual system, the screens or monitors need to be placed in locations that are comfortable for viewers. This means accounting for visual ergonomics and ensuring projected and displayed images sit within what is called the *visual field*.

The visual field is the point in space that can be seen when a person's head and eyes are absolutely still. It's measured in terms of angular magnitude, or degrees. The visual field of a single eye is called *monocular vision,* and the visual field where the perceived image from both eyes overlaps is called *binocular vision*.

Each human eye, when looking straight ahead, can see comfortably about 15 degrees side to side, as shown in Figure 4-1. This range is the optimum field of vision, meaning that when you design your visual system, the image should fall comfortably within this range so that audience members can experience it with no extra effort.

Of course, many variables go into designing a visual system for optimal viewing. Chief among them is the content that the system will display. Let's drill down further into visual field so you understand more about how viewers experience your systems.

To give you a better understanding of ergonomics for AV design, watch a pair of videos at www.infocomm.org/Ergo1Video and www.infocomm.org/Ergo2Video. Appendix C provides links to all the helpful videos in this guide.

Figure 4-1
The basic visual field of a human eye

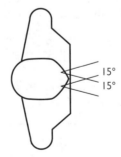

The Horizontal Visual Field

As you know from your everyday life, a human's visual field spans side to side and up and down. Let's first explore the visual field along the horizontal plane (side to side).

Remember, the visual field is measured in degrees. The horizontal zero-degree line is the standard line of sight—what's right in front of a person. This is the area of sharpest focus and where depth perception occurs. A person's total field of vision—without rotating his or her head—typically extends 60 degrees from the line of sight in either direction. That doesn't mean you have 60 degrees of visual field to work with. Depending on the content that the visual system will display, there are limits to what viewers can recognize or comprehend within the field of vision (see Figure 4-2). The following list is a simple set of guidelines:

- People can recognize words, fine details, and color information up to about 10 to 20 degrees from the standard line of sight. This is the limit of word recognition. If the main content will include words, the visual system should be placed within this range.

- Depending on size, shape, and detail, people can identify symbols between 5 and 30 degrees from the standard line of sight. This is the limit of symbol, or picture (image), recognition. For graphical displays of information, you have a slightly wider visual field to work with.

- The limits of color discrimination are between 30 and 60 degrees in each direction, depending on the color. In other words, if someone is meant to discern words or images, this is beyond the viable horizontal field of vision. However, depending on the visual application, there may be a useful visual field up to 60 degrees from straight ahead. A digital signage display, for example, may have a two-step goal: first to draw attention and second to convey information. Because viewers can discern colors up to 60 degrees, that would be considered the range in which people could perceive some colorful or dynamic content before turning to the visual system and into a field more suitable for conveying words or imagery.

Figure 4-2

The visual field along a horizontal plane

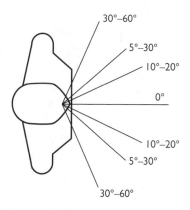

The Vertical Visual Field

To complete the picture, it is important to understand the visual field from a vertical perspective (up and down). Once again, the zero-degree line represents the standard line of sight.

It's important to note that in the real world the natural line of sight is not perfectly perpendicular to the human body but actually angles downward. In fact, the natural line of sight is about 10 degrees below straight ahead when standing and about 15 degrees when sitting. When a viewer is relaxed or lounging, the natural line of sight may drift even farther downward. It's just more comfortable for people to rotate their eyes downward than upward. (Try it at home!)

The following tips are for your reference:

- Optimal eye rotation along a vertical plane is 30 degrees below the standard line of sight. The maximum eye rotation above the standard line of sight is 25 degrees. Note the difference: It's more comfortable to cast a gaze downward.

- The limit of color discrimination is between 40 degrees below the standard line of sight and 30 degrees above the standard line of sight.

- The limit of the total visual field along the vertical plane is 70 degrees below the standard line of sight and 50 degrees above the standard line of sight.

The important thing to remember is that people view objects most comfortably in the lower visual field. Therefore, placing a screen more than 25 degrees above the standard line of sight would be exhausting and uncomfortable for viewers (see Figure 4-3).

Figure 4-3
The visual field along a vertical plane

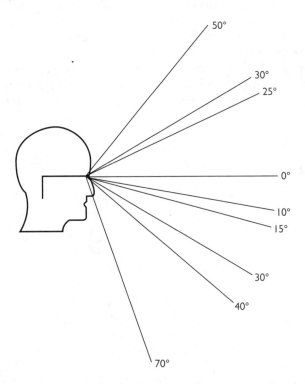

Figure 4-4
Head rotation
along the
horizontal plane

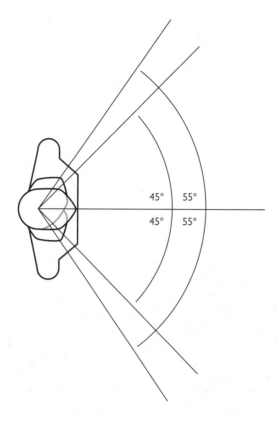

Head Rotation

As you've no doubt noticed, the earlier descriptions of visual field assumed that a viewer kept his or her head perfectly level and still. When does that happen? Human necks have a range of motion, and the real-world viewable area is often affected by the range of eye *and* head movement. Still, for the most comfortable and ergonomically designed visual system, you should not assume a wider visual field based on neck movement. Think of the front rows of a traditional movie theater. Yes, people could turn their heads upward for the length of the feature, but is it comfortable?

That said, it's important to know how much rotation may be reasonable. Along the horizontal plane, the human head can move 55 degrees in each direction. Comfortable head movement falls between the 45-degree lines (see Figure 4-4).

Along the vertical plane, the average human head can move within the 50- to 40-degree area in Figure 4-5. Comfortable head movement, however, falls between the 30-degree lines (remember the movie theater).

Sightlines

Your understanding of the visual field informs one of the most important ergonomic considerations of an AV design: the sightline. A *sightline* is the unobstructed view between a person and the object or content that he or she needs to see. A *sightline study* helps

Figure 4-5
Head rotation
along the vertical
plane

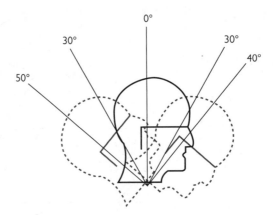

determine the most appropriate seating layout, for example, to ensure a clear field of view. Such a study identifies such AV design criteria as the lowest visible point on a display wall, the nearest viewers' line of sight, the farthest viewers' line of sight, the possible distortion of an image from off-axis viewing locations, and other ergonomic factors that affect preferred field of vision and viewing comfort tolerances.

In a conference room, classroom, or other AV space, the designer is responsible for designing a seating layout that creates the best viewing environment for the audience. Sightline studies are used to verify that everyone in the audience will have a clear view of the presenter area (see Chapter 3). These studies determine the lowest visible point on the front wall of the presenter area, for example. This information helps the designer determine how low a screen can be mounted.

Sightline studies are based on three factors.

- Seating types
- Floor types
- The limits of comfortable viewing (ergonomics)

Sightlines should not be confused with viewing angles, which are used to verify that a given display in the presenter area can be viewed on an axis as much as possible from the audience. In other words, it is possible to have great sightlines for viewing a presenter at a lectern but poor sightlines for a screen on the wall (screen too small, too high, too low, off-center).

Human Sightlines

When doing a sightline study, you can determine the minimum distance between the nearest viewer and a display. This can be determined by drawing a sightline from the top of the projected image to the eye of the closest viewer at a 30-degree angle (see Figure 4-6).

Figure 4-6
Determining a
sightline from
the top of a
projected image
to the eye of the
closest viewer

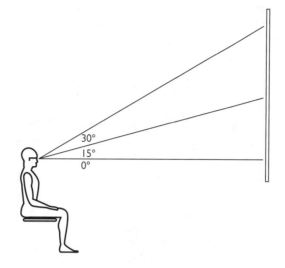

Conversely, if you have already placed your audience members, you can use sightlines to determine the maximum image height. Simply draw a sightline from the eye of the closest viewer at a 30-degree angle. The point at which that line intersects the wall will be your maximum image height.

As you'll recall, the standard line of sight for humans is at zero degrees. The more perpendicular a sightline is to the display plane, the greater the viewing comfort will be. The center of the screen should therefore fall at a 15-degree angle above the standard line of sight.

Eye Height

The eye height of viewers is a critical variable in a sightline study. In Figure 4-7, the person on the left represents the stature of a short viewer, while the person on the right represents the stature of a tall viewer. If the large viewer were to sit in front of the short viewer, the short viewer would not be able to see over the large viewer's head and shoulders.

When seated, assume the tall viewer's eye height is about 33.9 in (861 mm), plus the distance between the floor and the chair seat. For the short viewer, that height is 28.1 in (714 mm), plus the distance between the floor and chair seat.

You can mitigate height differences in several ways. Adjustable chairs will permit the eye height of the seated viewer to be raised or lowered. An adjustment range between 15 and 18 in, or 381 and 457 mm, will accommodate the eye height requirements of about 90 percent of viewers.

Often, adjustable seats won't fit the bill. In those cases, you can stagger your seating layouts or even adjust the floor of a space into a tiered or sloped layout, as discussed in the next section.

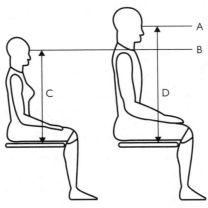

A. Sightline: Tall Viewer
B. Sightline: Short Viewer
C. Seated Eye Height: Small Viewer
D. Seated Eye Height: Tall Viewer

Figure 4-7 Seated sightlines of typical tall and short viewers. The seated eye height "C" is 28.1 in (714 mm) for a North American woman in the 95th percentile, and the seated eye height "D" is 33.9 in (861 mm) for a North American man in the 95th percentile.

Seating Layouts

When designing a visual system for a larger room or space, you have two primary options for arranging viewers: aligned or staggered.

In an *aligned seating arrangement,* viewers are placed directly behind the viewer in front of them (see Figure 4-8). On a flat floor, the view of people in the back rows will obviously be obstructed. As you move farther back through an aligned seating arrangement,

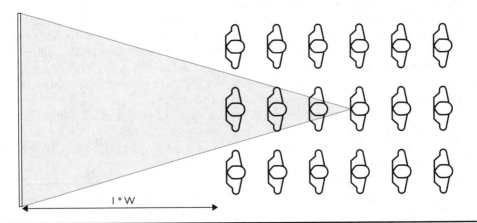

Figure 4-8 Aligned seating

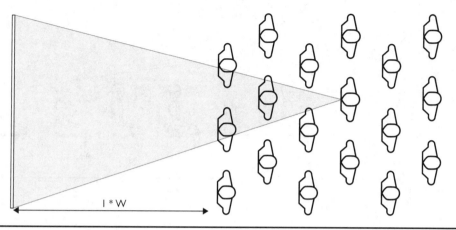

Figure 4-9 Staggered seating

you will need to raise sightlines higher to clear the bodies of viewers seated closer to the screen or presenter.

Compare this with a *staggered seating arrangement* (see Figure 4-9). In this layout, people are placed so they can view the image between the shoulders of the viewers in front of them. This lowers the sightlines significantly in comparison to an aligned seating layout.

NOTE If your needs analysis determines that the people using the AV room will be seated at least part of the time, you must consider seating ergonomics. You need to ensure that your end users will be able to see any displays or talkers comfortably from their seated positions.

Floor Layouts

Ultimately, the type of seating you choose for your AV design will depend on the room's infrastructure. A key element of that infrastructure is the floor.

Flat floors are the most common. However, as you can see in Figure 4-10, flat floors make it hard for viewers in the back to see what is being displayed or communicated. Sightlines for the farthest viewers need to clear obstructions, such as nearer viewers' heads, to see displayed images. Poor seating alignment, such as aligned seating on a flat floor, will force those sightlines higher and higher.

Sloped and tiered floors, which are typically found in amphitheaters, training facilities, and other large-capacity meeting spaces, represent an ideal design solution to challenging sightlines. Figure 4-11 shows how tiered seating can dramatically lower sightlines for the farthest viewers, even in cases of aligned seating. If you combine a tiered or sloped floor with a staggered-seating alignment, you could lower sightlines even more because viewers can look between the shoulders of the people in front of them.

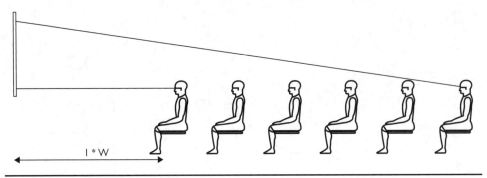

Figure 4-10 A flat floor

Figure 4-11 A tiered floor

Furniture

It certainly doesn't seem high tech, but furniture is part of an AV design. And you need to apply ergonomic principles when selecting furniture. For example, the layout of furniture within a space will depend on the room's function and design considerations, such as your sightline study.

But you also need to take the furniture into account. When communicating furniture needs to an architect or interior designer, be sure to include dimensions and coordinate color schemes and finishes. If furniture is custom designed, make sure to include detailed drawings as part of the audiovisual drawing package, as shown in Figure 4-12. That way, other contractors can build exactly what you need to complement the rest of your AV design.

Let's discuss briefly some of the furniture that factors into an AV design.

Tables and Chairs

Tables and chairs are some of the most basic elements of an AV design project. For example, certain types of tables may be required by the architect or interior designer to

Figure 4-12
Furniture
drawing for the
design package

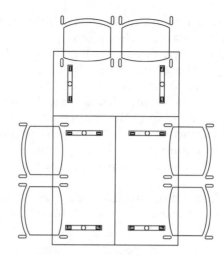

support specific presentation needs. The AV designer may be required to provide tables with AV system input/output connections. And in a room that will host videoconferencing or any other on-camera applications, tables should be light in color. The size and location of tables will depend on activities that users intend to conduct in the room. These are the types of considerations an AV designer is trusted to understand.

Chairs for both presenters and audience come in a wide range of styles and sizes. The architect or interior designer will likely pick out the chairs for a room, but they should be comfortable, plain, medium in color, and with no specular features that might be distracting in video applications.

Stackable, multipurpose chairs are common, as are ergonomic chairs. Keep in mind that a room layout may need to accommodate the use of storage dollies to deliver and remove chairs. Depending on the AV in the room, this could affect equipment placement or other aspects.

In addition, when collaborating with the architect or interior designer, consider the amount of time people will be sitting in the room. Hour-long meetings and multiday training sessions may have different seating requirements. During your needs analysis, you will have determined how much of each the client intends to use the room for. Communicate this to other project team members.

Many types of furniture have standard dimensions, designed to match the average size of the human body. Here are some of them:

- Tables are typically 29 in high (736 mm) but can range from 25 to 32 in (635 to 812 mm).

- Chair widths are typically 18 to 22 in (457 mm to 558 mm) for most fixed-seating situations and 22 to 26 in (558 mm to 660 mm) for most movable chairs.

- Counters are typically 36 in (914 mm) high but can range from 32 to 42 in (812 mm to 1066 mm).

When creating a layout for a space, the AV designer can usually assume that furniture will comply with these standard dimensions.

As you determine where furniture will go in a room, consider the total amount of space each person will occupy. Specifically, table and chair configurations should be designed so each occupant feels comfortable in the space provided.

Seated people need to be able to sit down and stand up easily. Experts recommend a minimum distance of 48 in (1219 mm) between the edge of a table and the nearest physical obstruction, such as a wall. This amount of space accounts for chair clearance and circulation (moving around). If the design plans for less space than that, you run the risk of seated users having to sidestep or interfere with each other when moving around the room.

Standing people also need circulation space. For passageway clearance, such as in an aisle or walkway, specify about 30 to 36 in (762 to 914 mm) of circulation space.

NOTE Circulation space is the amount of area a person needs to turn around without disturbing other people. According to best practices, this area is 10 to 13 square feet, or 0.93 to 1.21 square meters per person.

In addition to circulation space, seated people should also have enough room for materials, such as meeting notes, reference books, or electronic devices. The width of a seated person's area (a desk or shared table) should also accommodate for human dimensions and body position (to account for elbows, for example).

The optimal range of table space width is 24 to 30 in (610 to 762 mm) per seated person. The optimal range of table space depth is 16 to 18 in (406 to 457 mm).

Lecterns

Despite the growing popularity of presentation formats such as TED Talks or so-called town hall meetings, in which presenters roam a stage rather than stand in one place, lecterns remain important to AV spaces. Boardrooms, classrooms, and hotel conference spaces still commonly feature lecterns.

The location and design of a lectern are important. AV designers should ensure that they follow ergonomic principles when integrating a system with a lectern. The goal is to create an optimal environment for users, not only in the way they present their material but also in the way they interact with the audiovisual equipment.

Users will vary widely. AV designers should strive to meet the needs of *all* users by taking several things into account.

The architect or interior designer may want to craft the lectern or at least select it for use within the room. Lecterns can be premanufactured or custom-designed to meet specific design requirements. No matter how nice the lectern looks in the room, AV designers need to coordinate with architects and interior designers on where to put it within a space. Nothing will ruin a new room faster than a beautiful, custom-built lectern that blocks the audience's view of part of the presenter area or can't accommodate the AV controls the user wants.

Remember that some presenters have limited mobility. Taking mobility issues into account may change lectern design specifications. Some countries have accessibility requirements that also need to be addressed.

When presenters are at a lectern, they may want access to system controls either built into or adjacent to the lectern. This requirement should have surfaced during the needs analysis. Keep in mind that presenters shouldn't have to search for common controls or when trying to use technology.

In addition, consider the placement of microphones, ventilation for heat dissipation if equipment will be housed in a lectern, and all required power and space presentation media. Lecterns offer a good location for presentation source equipment, such as overhead projections and document cameras, just make sure your design includes provisions for wiring and equipment integration when using a lectern as an AV source.

Other Furniture

Other types of AV-related furniture may factor into your design.

- *Carts* can be used to hold projectors and monitors. A monitor should be secured to a cart with straps to minimize the potential for damage or personal injury should the monitor slip from the cart.

- *Whiteboards* are required in many installations. They can take up an entire wall or just part of a presenter area.

- *Electronic whiteboards* provide a method for electronically sharing or transferring information from the writing surface to a computer, display, or other end point. Electronic whiteboards can be wall-mounted or portable; just remember that they need an AC power source.

- *Flip charts* are simple tools still used by a wide range of clients and found in many meeting rooms. The AV designer may have nothing to do with a flip chart, but if there is going to be one, its location and the space required to utilize it could affect other parts of the design.

 NOTE Whiteboards make poor projection screens. They should not be used as a substitute for a traditional front-projection screen.

Chapter Review

In this chapter, you learned about ergonomics, human dimensions, sightlines, and the role of furniture decisions in an AV design. You learned that the foundation of an AV design begins with planning for human comfort. Having completed this chapter, you should be able to begin preparing a sightline study, which is critical to planning a visual system. You will build on this knowledge in Chapter 5, "Visual Principles of Design."

Review Questions

The following questions are based on the content covered in this chapter and are intended to help reinforce the knowledge you have assimilated. These questions are not extracted from the CTS-D exam nor are they necessarily CTS-D practice exam questions. For an official CTS-D practice exam, see the accompanying CD.

1. When considering viewers' visual field along a horizontal plane, people can recognize words, fine details, and color at what angle from the standard line of sight?

   A. 0 to 10 degrees

   B. 10 to 20 degrees

   C. 25 to 30 degrees

   D. 40 to 50 degrees

2. Which of the following methods can be used to improve sightlines in an auditorium?

   A. Lowering the height of the display

   B. Using an aligned seating layout

   C. Providing a sloped or tiered-seating layout

   D. Installing seats with taller dimensions

3. In a sightline study, you can determine the minimum distance between the nearest viewer and a display by drawing a sightline from the top of the projected image to the eye of the closest viewer at what angle?

   A. 10 degrees

   B. 20 degrees

   C. 30 degrees

   D. 40 degrees

4. People view objects more comfortably when the objects are located _____.

   A. To the left of their standard line of sight

   B. To the right of their standard line of sight

   C. Higher than their standard line of sight

   D. Lower than their standard line of sight

5. Circulation space is _____.

   A. The area a person needs to turn around without disturbing other people

   B. The area around AV equipment that allows it to ventilate

   C. The area below a lectern where AV sources are housed

   D. The space behind a rear-projection screen

Answers

1. **B.** When considering viewers' visual field along a horizontal plane, people can recognize words, fine details, and color 10 to 20 degrees from the standard line of sight.

2. **C.** Providing a sloped or tiered-seating layout can improve sightlines in an auditorium.

3. **C.** You can determine the minimum distance between the nearest viewer and a display by drawing a sightline from the top of the projected image to the eye of the closest viewer at a 30-degree angle.

4. **D.** People view objects more comfortably when the objects are located lower than their standard line of sight.

5. **A.** Circulation space is the area a person needs to turn around in without disturbing other people.

Visual Principles of Design

In this chapter, you will learn about
- Determining image specifications for a video system, including character height, farthest and nearest viewing locations, and good and acceptable viewing areas
- Calculating the aspect ratio of a display, given its height, width, or diagonal
- The advantages and disadvantages of front-screen and rear-screen projection
- The basics of videowalls
- Measuring reflected light bouncing off a screen and into a viewer's eyes
- Calculating lumens, projector brightness, and task-light levels for a given projection system
- Using industry standards to calculate contrast ratio correctly

The visual display components of an AV system drive room design. Designers must configure the space to ensure that an audience has a high-quality viewing experience. They must then design the other elements of the room to fit that layout.

The display system (also referred to as the *video system*) consists of the display devices themselves (flat-panel display, projector and screen, etc.) and the components that support those devices (sources, switchers, etc.). Every aspect of the video system affects what the audience sees; therefore, it all requires careful consideration by the AV designer.

Domain Check
This chapter relates directly to the following tasks on the CTS-D Exam Content Outline:

- Domain A Task 2: Identify skill level of end users
- Domain A Task 8: Define AV needs (absolutes)
- Domain A Task 9: Identify scope of work

(Continued)

- Domain B Task 1: Review A/E (architectural and engineering) drawings
- Domain B Task 2: Coordinate architectural/interior design criteria
- Domain B Task 3: Coordinate structural/mechanical criteria
- Domain C Task 1: Create draft AV design
- Domain C Task 2: Confirm site conditions

These tasks comprise 35.2 percent of the exam (about 44 questions). This chapter may also relate to other tasks.

Determining Image Specifications

When designing a video system, your first task is to determine image specifications. After all, you can't select effective video equipment if you don't know what needs to be displayed and who's going to be displaying/looking at it. For example, where will the viewers be located? Will they be sitting? Where should the screen go so the most people can see it? How tall should any displayed text be so viewers can read it?

If you determine this information first, you can use it later when you select the display gear needed to produce the right image to communicate the intended message.

An AV designer must consider four parameters before selecting an actual display: text size, farthest viewing distance, nearest viewing distance, and good or acceptable viewing areas.

Determining Text Size

When designing a video system, you should first consider the size of any text the user wants to display. After all, people should be able to read information on the display from a given distance. And if customers can't read digital signs, what good are they? Once you determine the required text size, you can explore the presentation medium.

Displays are characterized by resolution; the human eye is characterized by acuity. Resolution describes a video system's ability to reproduce highly detailed information. Visual acuity is an eye's ability to discern fine details. Put another way, visual acuity is what an individual set of eyes can see, but screen resolution is what an electronic display can output.

There are several different kinds of acuity, including *resolution acuity,* which is the ability to detect that there are two stimuli, rather than one, in a visual field. Resolution acuity is measured in terms of the smallest angular separation between two stimuli that can still be seen as separate.

Recognition acuity is the ability to identify correctly a visual target. In terms of text onscreen, it's the ability to differentiate between a *G* and a *C*, for example. Usually—but not always—recognition acuity is measured in terms of the angular dimension of the smallest target that can be discriminated. A clinical eye chart, where visual-acuity testing is performed using letters, is a form of recognition-acuity testing.

 Watch a video about determining image specifications at www.infocomm.org/ ImageSpecVideo. Appendix C provides a link to the video.

Visual Acuity and the Snellen Eye Chart

You're probably familiar with standard eye charts. Figure 5-1 shows a Snellen chart. It's a great reference for understanding acuity. The Snellen chart displays several characters, called *optotypes,* which look like letters. An optotype is a character used to assess a person's visual acuity. It looks like a block letter and is drawn with specific and rigid geometric rules. Only ten optotypes are used on the traditional Snellen eye chart: C, D, E, F, L, N, O, P, T, and Z. The perception of five out of six letters (or a similar ratio) is called the

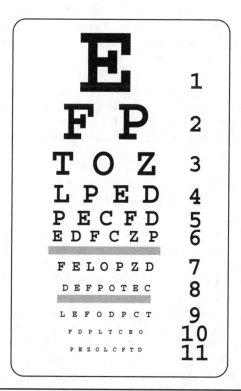

Figure 5-1 A Snellen eye chart

Snellen fraction. In this chart, the thickness of the lines equals the thickness of the white spaces between lines and the thickness of the gap in the letter *C*. In addition, the height and width of the letter are five times the thickness of the line.

Character Height

When determining text size, your design goal is to create a text height that is easy to read and won't cause eye strain or fatigue. Imagine an audience looking at PowerPoint presentations for three days.

Eye charts are designed to have a high contrast and a clear font. AV presentations likely won't have this kind of contrast, especially in situations of front-screen projection. You also cannot control the creation of the presenter's material, backgrounds, text color, or font style.

There is a rule for determining whether onscreen text is legible.

Text height × 150 = maximum distance from the screen

For example, if a line of text is 3 in (75 mm) high, the maximum viewing distance for this font is about 37.5 feet (about 11.5 meters). You can determine this by multiplying 3 in by 150, which gives you 450 in (450/12 = 37.5 feet). In metric, that would be 75 mm multiplied by 150, which gives you 11,250 mm, or 11.25 meters.

License plates are an excellent example of visual acuity in the real world. After all, they're designed to be legible from a distance. In Nevada, the laws governing license plates read, "The Director may determine and vary the size, shape and form and the material of which license plates are made, but each license plate must be of sufficient size to be plainly readable from a distance of 100 feet (about 30.5 meters) during daylight. All license plates must be treated to reflect light and to be at least 100 times brighter than conventional painted number plates. When properly mounted on an unlighted vehicle, the license plates, when viewed from a vehicle equipped with standard headlights, must be visible for a distance of not less than 1,500 feet (about 457 meters) and readable for a distance of not less than 110 feet (about 33.5 meters). (This is an angle of 7.16 or 1.43 times larger than 20/20 vision)."

The United States isn't the only country with such laws. The Department for Transport in the United Kingdom specifies that each character in a registration mark must be 79 mm high and 57 mm wide.

Technically, both the Nevada and United Kingdom laws exceed the 150 rule. This is because they include provisions for people who don't have 20/20 vision.

The AV designer plans for where viewers will (and won't) be positioned to see a quality image. This means considering the height of the font in light of the viewing task or purpose of the space. Let's consider an airport display wall.

Figure 5-2 shows an airport departure display at Washington Dulles airport. An AV designer, when developing this installation, considered questions like, "Who will be viewing this sign, and why? Where is the viewing area? Should viewers be able to walk and read at the same time, or will they have to stand still?"

This videowall consists of eight individual screens: two high by four wide (2 by 4). Each 32 by 24 in (813 × 610 mm) screen is 800 by 600 pixels and displays 21 rows of information. Because the videowall comprises eight screens, it can display 168 lines of text.

Figure 5-2
An airport
display wall

The font height is 12 mm, and the pixel count is 12. Because you know the height of the font used for the board, you can calculate the farthest viewing distance using the 150 rule: 12mm × 150 = 1.8 meters (5.9 feet). This puts the farthest viewing distance right at the edge of the carpeted area and just on the tiled walkway. Perfect. The smaller font forces people to move out of the walkway and closer to the sign. It also makes people slow down or stop to get the required information.

Conversely, if you know where the people need to stand, you can figure out how big text needs to be—or more specifically, what size font you should use for your display. Characters are measured in both inches/millimeters and pixels. The screen size and font size in inches/millimeters are directly proportional to the screen size and font size in pixels. A fairly standard 10-point font (Arial or Times Roman, for example) will be 10 pixels tall when viewed at 100 percent. Some flashier fonts may not adhere to this concept, but because of readability and other factors, users are less likely to use such fonts for presentations, digital signage, and so on.

Earlier, you learned to use the 150 rule for the farthest viewer to determine the font size in inches/meters. When you know how tall a font must be in inches/meters, you can convert that to pixels to recommend the right font size. If you know the screen height in inches or millimeters, you can calculate the font size in points. With that information in hand, you'll know the screen height and font height in inches/meters.

Determining the Farthest Viewing Distance

When people view content on a screen or display, they're performing a viewing task. The viewer expects to see the displayed content comfortably. If you know the maximum distance of the farthest viewer, you can determine the required image height that best suits the task. Conversely, if you know the height of the image, you determine how far the farthest viewer should be.

For the purposes of determining the farthest viewing distance for a display system, AV designers group viewing tasks into three general areas.

- **Observing content** This could be for any type of motion picture viewing where details are not critical. This task is also known as *general viewing*.

- **Inspecting content, or observing content with clues**   This could be reviewing web pages, spreadsheets, or simple presentations. In addition, words sometimes offer clues to the meaning of images for easier interpretation. This viewing task—a combination of words and images—is known as *reading with clues*.

- **Inspecting content without clues**   This could be analyzing engineering drawings or medical images. For this task, there are no words displayed to help interpret an image's meaning. This task is also known as *inspection*.

One way to determine a comfortable viewing experience is to base the height of the image on two criteria.

- What the viewers are going to see
- Where the farthest viewer will be seated

These two factors are important because viewers may need a larger screen to see more detail without having to strain their eyes. They may also need to move closer to a display to view material comfortably.

The formula for determining image height based on a viewing task is as follows:

$$I_H/I_D = D_T/V_T$$

where:

- I_H = Image height.
- I_D = Distance from the farthest viewer to the image.
- D_T = Viewing task ratio (height). This will always be 1.
- V_T = Viewing task ratio (distance).

The image height formula reveals that tasks requiring more detail require bigger images. For the viewing task ratio, which is based on levels of detail, use a factor of 8 when viewers will observe content (general viewing), use 6 when viewers will inspect content with clues (reading with clues), and use 4 when the viewers will inspect content without clues (inspection). Figure 5-3 shows a seated display area with a screen to the left and three curves showing maximum viewing distances based on factors of 4, 6, and 8.

Figure 5-3
Viewing
distances based
on tasks

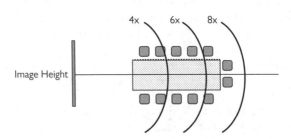

Figure 5-4

The simple image height formula wheel

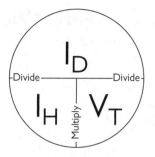

The Simple Image Height Formula Wheel

The relationship between image height, viewing task, and farthest viewer distance can also be represented as a wheel, as shown in Figure 5-4. Just as with the Ohm's law wheel, if you know two of the variables, you can easily calculate the third.

To use the wheel, locate the value you want to calculate. Here's a reminder:

- I_D = Farthest viewer distance
- I_H = Image height
- V_T = Viewing task

Calculate the value by performing the operation between the two remaining variables. If variables are on top of each other, divide the top variable by the bottom. If variables are next to each other, multiply them, as shown in Figure 5-5.

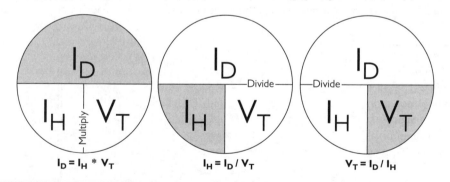

$$I_D = I_H * V_T \qquad I_H = I_D / V_T \qquad V_T = I_D / I_H$$

Figure 5-5   Derivative formulas from the simple image height formula wheel

Determining the Nearest Viewing Distance

Designers need to lay out a viewing area to ensure the audience gets the best visual quality from the display screens. To do this, you need to know the position of the audience, and the first question you need to ask is, "How close is too close?" The answer to this question will determine the location of your nearest viewer.

Not surprisingly, viewers can be too close to a screen. How close is too close? Info-Comm states no less than 1× the screen width, which closely matches your eyes' viewing angle (approximately 60 degrees for color discrimination), is too close. Therefore, a useful rule of thumb is to make sure that the distance to the first row in a viewing area is no less than the image width (see Figure 5-6). This allows viewers to see the entire screen within a natural field of vision.

When determining the closest viewing position, designers should also consider the height of the image. You don't want viewers in the front row to have to turn their heads up through an entire presentation. When specifying image dimensions, the top of a screen should be no higher than 30 degrees above the standard line of sight for a seated viewer in the nearest viewing position. The middle of the screen should fall about 15 degrees above the standard line of sight (see Figure 5-7).

Figure 5-6 The first row of a viewing area should be no closer than the image width.

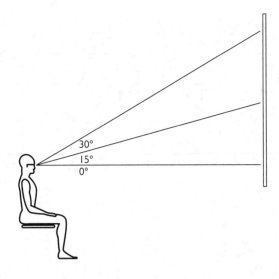

Figure 5-7
A screen size based on comfortable viewing angles for the nearest viewer

30°
15°
0°

Determining the Viewing Range

Earlier, you learned how to calculate the farthest viewer using the 4, 6, and 8 rule. Then you learned how to find the location of the nearest viewer based on an image's width. The space between these two positions is your viewing range.

Next, you need to determine how far to the left and right viewers can sit and still see the image, as shown in Figure 5-8. Once you have these dimensions, you will have a complete picture of the viewing area.

Screens have limitations that can reduce the viewing range. Off-axis viewing angles limit a viewer's ability to make out characters. The maximum acceptable viewing angle is 45 degrees from the far edge of the screen. Beyond that, characters or image elements may become indecipherable.

What we'll call the *good viewing area* is the best place to view a screen. It is typically defined as any point within 45 degrees to the left or right from the straight-on axis (see Figure 5-9). Therefore, the total good viewing area is 90 degrees.

Figure 5-8
Optimal viewing areas

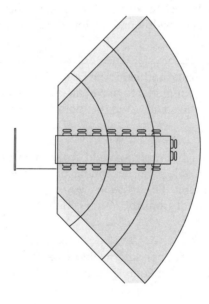

Figure 5-9
A good viewing area is 45 degrees off-axis in either direction.

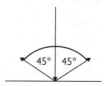

Figure 5-10
A good viewing area, taking into account the distance to the first row, farthest viewers, and viewing angles

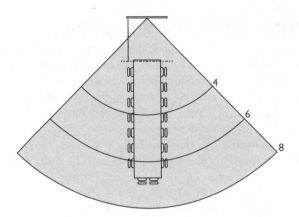

A major part of designing an AV-enabled room is ensuring that an audience can see what's presented while seated in the good viewing area. In Figure 5-10, the good viewing area is within 45 degrees of the display axis. The short line coming off the screen represents 1× the screen width, and the long lines coming out of the screen represent the farthest viewer length.

NOTE Take another look at Figure 5-10. If the room had a larger screen, you might be required to move the table farther back. Such a design decision might impact access to the room and pathways for getting in and out.

Of course, although a design should strive to ensure a good viewing area, you may need only an acceptable area, depending on your needs analysis, examination of the space, and other criteria. The *acceptable viewing area* for a screen falls within a 45-degree line extending outward from the left and right edges of a displayed image, rather than the center.

Watch a video about determining a viewing area at www.infocomm.org/ViewingVideo. Appendix C provides a link to the video.

Display Device Selection

Once you've done the math and determined the specifications needed for your images, you are ready to determine which equipment you need for your system, starting with display sources. In digital video systems, the term *format* refers to the source of the image. Digital sources can include Blu-ray players, DVD players, streaming media players, personal computers, cloud-based services, and personal devices, such as tablets and smartphones.

Knowing your customer's source media, resolution, refresh rate, color space, audio format, and more will help you identify the proper player for that media. Remember, as you specify display devices, it is important to employ the highest-quality signal available while still maintaining system functionality.

To that end, let's start breaking down some of the important characteristics of display equipment.

Video Resolution

Graphic chips, regardless of the type of source they come in, produce many different display resolutions. It's up to the AV professional to select a resolution output that looks good on the display used in a video system.

A display device has a "native" resolution, which is the resolution that is optimized for the display. For example, if a display has 1024 pixels horizontally and 768 pixels vertically, it has a native resolution of 1024×768.

If an image is larger or smaller than the display's native resolution, it might not look good. If a source image is a different height or width than the display, the display's scaler may stretch the image or create unsightly borders. Whenever possible, you should match the resolution of the source to the native resolution of the display.

A higher-resolution display means more pixels, greater detail, and better image quality. It also means the system requires more information to build an image. Figure 5-11 shows a variety of display resolutions.

Aspect Ratio

Human vision is oriented horizontally. Your eyes' angle of view is wider than it is high— landscape rather than portrait. Therefore, people naturally frame a scene horizontally. This perceptual quality is translated into a mathematical equivalent known as *aspect ratio,* which is the ratio of image width to image height.

Aspect ratio is expressed as two whole numbers, separated by a colon (for example, 16:9), or by the decimal equivalent of the implied division (for example, 1.77). Common video aspect ratios include the following:

- 4:3 (1.33) for standard-definition (SD) video
- 16:9 (1.77) for high-definition (HD) video

Figure 5-11
Common video display resolutions

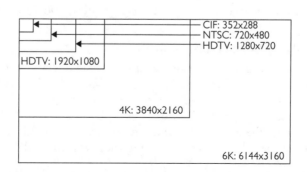

CIF: 352x288
NTSC: 720x480
HDTV: 1280x720
HDTV: 1920x1080
4K: 3840x2160
6K: 6144x3160

Some computer and video production displays operate at a 16:10 (1.6) aspect ratio. Your ability to determine the correct aspect ratio for any image, screen, or display will help you specify the right product for your design, match a projector's image to the correct screen size, or select the correct image size for a given environment. Without a solid understanding of aspect ratio, you could make a costly error.

The worst-case scenario is a mismatch between a screen and projector *and* a mismatch from image to projector. In such a scenario, the size of the image will be reduced. When an image gets smaller, the audience will have to move closer to get a good view. Moving closer will, in turn, change viewing angles and the closest/farthest viewer calculations.

Calculating Aspect Ratio

An HDTV display with a 1920×1080 resolution has an aspect ratio of 1920:1080 or 16:9 or 1.77. Using this aspect ratio, if you know one of the image dimensions, you can easily find the other.

Let's say you need a projected HD image to fill a custom space above the chair rail in a room. You measure and find the height to be 63 in (1600 mm). By multiplying 63 in (1600 mm) by 1.77, you will get the width for a 16:9 HD image, which is 111.5 in (2832 mm). Conversely, if you know the width and are looking for the height, you simply divide the width by 1.77 to find the height required to show a 16:9 image. If you have a width of 102 in (2600 mm) and divide that by 1.77, you will get a height of 57.6 in (1469 mm).

So, let's try it. Find the width of an image 60 in high with a 16:9 aspect ratio. Width/height = 16/9:

X/60 = 16/9

Cross multiply:

9 * X = 60 * 16
9 * X = 960

Divide both sides by 9:

(9 * X) / 9 = 960 / 9
X = 106.666666…

Rounded to the nearest tenth, the image width is 106.7 inches.

Calculating Screen Diagonal

The width and height of an image can also be used to determine a screen's diagonal measurement using the Pythagorean theorem: $A^2 + B^2 = C^2$, where A is the height of a screen, B is the width of a screen, and C is the diagonal length of a screen. Doing the math, a 16:9 image has a diagonal of 18.36.

If you know the aspect ratio and any dimension—width, height, or diagonal—you can calculate the other dimensions using the "cross multiply and divide" method. Let's give it a shot. A screen has an aspect ratio of 16:9:18.36. The diagonal of the screen is 2.5 meters. What is the width?

Cross multiply.

$2.5 * 16 = X * 18.36$
$40 = X * 18.36$

Divide both sides by 18.36.

$40/18.36 = (X/18.36)/18.36$
$X = 2.178649$

Rounded to the nearest tenth, the width is 2.2 meters.

Display Types

There are many display options on the market. The type an AV designer chooses will depend on different factors. In general, display options include projected, direct, and interactive.

Projection systems can be inexpensive and create large images. Increasingly, creative AV designers can "map" projected images onto buildings, cars, or other objects that aren't shaped like traditional screens. With projection, however, image quality can suffer in some situations because of ambient light.

Direct-display systems, such as popular LCD or LED flat-panel TVs, can provide bright, excellent images, but they are usually limited in size. Large direct displays come at a price premium. Still, direct-display systems offer excellent contrast ratios, and there is no projected light path for viewers or presenters to block.

Interactive displays allow users to make electronic notes directly on an image. An interactive display can use a projection system or a special overlay on a direct-view display. Some interactive displays are large, purpose-built touch screens.

In this section, we will focus on three popular display designs: front-projection systems, rear-projection systems, and videowalls.

Front Projection

Although flat-panel, direct displays are getting bigger, cheaper, and more ubiquitous as the primary screens used for video systems, projection systems are still popular for certain types of installations. As such, AV designers need to know how to integrate these two-piece display systems into spaces.

For starters, a designer needs to understand the properties of projection screens to enhance the projection environment. Projectors produce light, but they do not direct the light toward viewers. Projection screens, however, give substance and quality to projected images. They help direct and focus light to the audience and define image limits by separating them from the wall.

Projection screens are passive devices. This means they cannot amplify or create light energy. They can reflect light rays back at wide or narrow angles. *Screen gain* is the ability of a screen to reflect or redirect light energy in a narrower viewing area, making projected images appear brighter to viewers sitting on-axis. The higher the gain number of a screen, the narrower the viewing angle over which it provides optimal brightness.

A *matte white screen* diffuses light uniformly along both horizontal and vertical planes. In this way, a matte white screen creates a wide viewing area, which can be up to 180 degrees along both axes. Such screens provide good color rendition and may be the best choice for projection applications that incorporate sufficiently bright projectors.

Ambient light rejection—the ability of a screen surface to negate the effects of distracting, ambient light in a space—generally increases as screen gain increases. This is because as the screen gain increases, the angle at which light hits the screen becomes more important. Ambient light that is not on-axis between the projector and viewer (light from exit signs, hallways, windows, etc.) is reflected away from the viewer. This makes the screen appear darker, increasing the contrast ratio. The *contrast ratio* of a display system is the ratio of the luminance of the brightest color (white) to that of the darkest color (black). A better contrast ratio means viewers can see or read images onscreen more easily. We will discuss contrast ratio in more detail later in this chapter.

Where ambient light is too great and can't be adequately controlled using curtains or other solutions, a high-gain screen is often used. A screen with high gain directs most of the light energy from the projector away from the audience. The screen is therefore more tolerant of high-ambient light conditions because any ambient light that hits the screen can be directed away from viewers. The angle of incidence (light striking the surface) equals the angle of reflectance (light bouncing off the surface).

In general, front projection requires less floor space than rear projection because the projector is often placed in the audience area. Front projection is also less costly and easier to install than rear projection. For these main reasons, front-projection screens are the most common screens.

However, putting a projector in the same space as viewers poses some issues that must be addressed. For example, most projectors have cooling fans that create noise. Moreover, when a projector is in the same space as its users, people such as presenters or instructors, especially, can interfere with the image by walking in front of the projected light (which, frankly, can also be annoying for the presenter).

Front-Projection Screens

With front projection, the image is viewed from the same side of the screen as the projector's location. As mentioned, front-projection screens are passive reflectors of light. This means they allow light to bounce off of them toward the viewing area. The contrast ratio of a front-projection system is largely dependent on the AV designer's ability to control ambient light in a space, but the brightness of the projector and the screen material are also important.

Matte white screens evenly disperse light 180 degrees horizontally and vertically, creating a wide viewing area. Such screens have a smooth, nonglossy surface, similar to a white sheet. They provide accurate color rendition and completely uniform reflection, which makes them the best choice for data and graphics applications. However, because reflected light will diffuse equally in all directions, room lights can be a problem when using matte white screens.

 NOTE A matte white screen is a projection screen made of magnesium carbonate or a similar substance that provides a perfect diffuser for the redistribution of light. In other words, the light energy striking the screen surface is scattered identically in all directions. Matte white is a reference surface, with a screen gain of 1.0 (also known as *unity gain*).

There are also angularly reflective screen surfaces, which reflect light at various angles, rather than a uniform 180-degree reflection. Such surfaces perform like a mirror and have a gain greater than five. The light is reflected at the same angle, it strikes the screen but on the other side of the screen's axis. If a projector is mounted at a height equal to the top center of the screen, the light would be directed back at the audience in a downward direction. This screen type works well for motion video.

Specifying Front-Screen Projection

A designer must consider several factors when specifying front-projection screens.

- Will the screen be fixed, manual, or electric? Electric screens have motors that are offset or inserted into the roll. Offset motors require a larger cutout than the screen to accommodate the motor.

- How will the screen be mounted? For example, will it be mounted to the wall or ceiling? Will it be recessed in the ceiling? Will it be foldable? Roller screens are the most common mounted screens. Tension screens are made of a thinner material and have "arms" that gently stretch the material flat. Fixed-mount screens are stretched and mounted to the wall.

- Where in a room will the screen be mounted? If it's mounted near air diffusers, will the screen vibrate as air blows on the screen? The image can also be shaken by structural vibrations. You need to pay attention to the location of other wall-mounted devices, such as exit signs, fire alarms, and whiteboards.

- How far does the screen need to lower to get into the proper position? Will it require extra fabric, called *extra drop,* at the top or bottom? Designers should specify whether extra drop is required to compensate for ceiling or projection height. This drop should be communicated to the screen manufacturer and written into the specs.

- Do you need to specify reverse wrap? Usually, screens wrap (roll up) toward the back and around. This allows the screen to be placed close to the wall. With a reverse wrap, the screen wraps toward the front and around, which puts it a few inches out from the wall. Such placement, with reverse wrap, allows the screen to be located where it avoids other mounted items, such as chalk trays or whiteboards.

- What size screen do you need, and can it be easily delivered to the required location through doors or up elevators? Will multiple people be required to deliver it?

- Do you need to specify a masking system? A masking system (active or passive) allows you to change the aspect ratio of the visible area of a screen.

NOTE When specifying a front-projection screen in the United States, you may need to specify a plenum-rated box in which to roll it up and store it when not in use. Plenum is the breathable air space above the ceiling that serves as an environmental air-return pathway. Cables, loudspeakers, projector screen cases, and other AV gear mounted in this area must be plenum rated, meaning if it caught fire, it would not release toxic fumes into the air space. Wooden boxes for screens are not plenum rated.

Rear Projection

Rear-screen projection describes a presentation system in which the image is projected from behind and through a translucent screen, toward the audience on the opposite side. It is a transmissive system, in which light passes through the screen toward the viewer.

Rear projection requires more space for installation because it needs a projection room or cabinet behind the screen to accommodate the projector. Mirrors are commonly used to save space in rear-projection applications. Generally, in spaces that suffer from high ambient light, a rear-projection system can deliver better contrast and color saturation than a front-projection system.

Rear-projection systems have a number of characteristics that make them especially suited to specific AV installations, including the following:

- **High tolerance of ambient light**   The images on a rear-projection screen can usually be seen clearly without requiring the room to be as dark as it might be for a front-projection screen.

- **Unobtrusive equipment placement**   Because the projector is out of sight in a rear-projection area, it will not interfere with the room layout or sightlines.

- **System black level**   Rear-projection screens can create a system black level (the level of brightness at the darkest—blackest—part of an image) that is superior to front-projection screens. This can translate into brighter images and greater contrast.

- **Contrast**   Images produced by a rear-projection system usually benefit from a better contrast ratio than those produced by a front-projection system. Sometimes, rear-projection systems can also focus projected light on viewers, further reducing ambient light and improving contrast.

- **Low noise**   Because the projector and associated equipment go into a rear-projection room, the noise they produce is isolated.

- **User mobility**   Presenters can walk in front of a rear-projection screen without disturbing the projected image, making such screens more appropriate for certain types of rooms, such as command-and-control centers or visualization spaces.

All that said, rear-projection systems have their downsides, too, including the following:

- **High cost**   On average, the mirrors, mounts, and screen material required for a rear-projection system add up to cost more than a front-projection system would cost. This is why the needs analysis is so important when deciding between a rear-projection system and a front-projection system.

- **Required floor space**   Because rear-projection systems need space to house the projector behind the screen, they require more floor space than front-projection systems do. Moreover, the projector room needs to be kept clear of objects that could block the light path or push the projector out of alignment. Users can't think of their rear-projector room as extra storage space!

Rear-Projection Screens

Diffusion screen material for rear projection is usually rigid acrylic, glass, or vinyl fabric. These materials provide a diffused, coated, or frosted surface on which to focus an image. The ambient light rejection of these materials is considered moderate, based on the viewer-side material's reflectivity or sheen. Assuming the projection room is painted flat black, any ambient light behind the screen will be absorbed while still in the room.

Rear-projection screen materials offer a wide viewing angle—horizontally and vertically—but with little or no gain. The light from the projector is transmitted through the screen with relatively little bending. You may see some hot spotting with rear projection, where an image is unevenly illuminated, because of the transparency of the screen fabric and the vertical placement of the projector in relation to the audience.

Optical-pattern rear-projection screens capture and concentrate light to maximize the amount passing through to the audience. An image can appear less bright if viewers or the projector are moved off-axis. Therefore, the projector must be at the focal point indicated by the manufacturer.

For permanent rear-projection applications, you'll want to use optical screen material. This type of screen system comprises a series of lenses formed into the screen material. The most common is a two-lens system, in which the lens that faces the projector is a *Fresnel lens*. It is a flat glass or acrylic lens in which the curvature of a normal lens surface has been collapsed, creating concentric circles on the lens surface. This lens gathers the light from the projector. The second lens, molded to the other side of the acetate or to another sheet, is a *vertical lenticular lens*. It must be flat to avoid hot spots. The lenticular lens faces the viewing audience and spreads the light horizontally, providing a relatively large viewing area. See Figure 5-12.

When creating specifications for a rear-projection screen, AV designers should consider the following:

- **The required size of the screen**   The raw screen should be of sufficient size to account for mounting and framing. This means the screen will need to be larger than the desired viewing area. Other size issues to consider include the type of framing to specify and whether the screen will fit through the doors of the building (because a rigid screen cannot be folded or broken down into separate pieces). The size will also factor into the size of the wall opening required for installation.

Figure 5-12

Types of rear-screen projection material

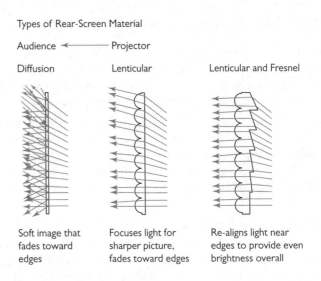

Types of Rear-Screen Material

Audience ←——————— Projector

Diffusion	Lenticular	Lenticular and Fresnel
Soft image that fades toward edges	Focuses light for sharper picture, fades toward edges	Re-aligns light near edges to provide even brightness overall

NOTE When specifying the size of a rear-projection screen, anticipate mounting requirements. Most screen manufacturers offer mounting and framing options. Remember, the frame will reduce the actual viewing area slightly. You will need to provide the general contractor (GC) with the "rough opening" size for your screen and frame assembly. Given the room dimensions and the preferred projector and lens, most screen manufacturers can help with screen recommendations, mirror assembly drawings, framing options, and more to make the design and installation go smoothly.

- **Delivery**   Some screens will be larger than the doors to the space they're intended for and should be delivered prior to wall completion. Rear-projection screens are delicate and must be protected if stored onsite while a space is being completed. If the screen is installed early in the construction process, it must be protected from accidental damage by other trades, using plywood, for example.

- **The side that will face the audience**   There are two sides of a projection screen—the projector side and the audience side. Typically, the projector side is smooth and clear, while the audience side is rougher. Always refer to the manufacturer of the screen to identify which side is designed to face the audience. Failure to do so will reduce the quality of the image.

- **Other attributes**   Rear-screen material can be lighter or darker in color. The darker the screen, the darker the blacks in an image will be. Whites will be less so, but overall contrast should improve. In addition, optical screens need to be matched to the lens of the projector because both have optical specifications. There are screens designed for short-throw projectors and other special applications.

Rear-Projection Design Considerations

A designer must consider a number of factors when designing a rear-projection system, including the following:

- **Screen materials** Diffusion rear-projection screens need to be specified with the required density, tinting, and protective coatings.

- **Screen frames** Frames of the appropriate type, finish, and size create borders around a rear-projection screen.

- **Space requirements** Because of the need for a rear-projection room, designers must determine whether the advantages are worth the amount of floor space required.

- **Mirrors** Mirror systems can help reduce the size of a rear-projection room, but they require more time and skill to design and install.

- **Lens local length** Short focal-length lenses can also help reduce the size of a rear-projection room. But they can also create distortion and reduce screen brightness compared to longer focal-length lenses, which create a straighter light throw that is more closely aligned with the viewers.

- **Sources of light reflections** Shiny objects in a rear-projection room can reflect light onto the screen and reduce viewability for the audience. All surfaces in the projection room need to be specified matte black, including doors and hardware.

Videowalls

A videowall features several monitors, video screens, display cubes, video projectors, or flat-screen TVs that are configured on top of each other or side by side to form a single, large, contiguous display.

Depending on the component technology used, a videowall can give clients a large display surface with uniform brightness and clarity that can be harder to accomplish with traditional, single-projector systems.

Because videowalls often comprise multiple smaller displays, they can be designed in many sizes and shapes, depending on the display environment. Not only will the size of the room dictate the size and shape of a videowall (a high or low ceiling, for example, is often a determining factor), but so will the available wall space. Available space will also determine the display technology used. One of the advantages of a videowall designed to incorporate flat-panel monitors, for example, is that it requires less physical space than a videowall that incorporates projection technology or video cubes, which are often deeper than flat panels.

When designing a videowall, it is important to specify displays that can be color matched in applications where one or few images will span multiple screens. Remember that the sum of the parts will need to appear as one display when all is said and done, so the reds on one screen need to match the reds on another.

In a simple videowall system, a videowall processor will take a single image and divide it among many screens. Alternately, the processor can route several different sources to different parts of the videowall. The processor maps the appropriate image (or portion of an image) to each display and synchronizes them. More advanced videowall processors can adjust the output image size for display on videowall screens that aren't necessarily identical in shape or size.

Common Videowall Applications

The choice to design a videowall is driven by the application. Videowalls can be more expensive and intricate than more traditional video systems, so there should be a compelling reason to include one. That said, as video technology becomes better and less costly, more and more clients see videowalls as a way not only to accomplish their business goals but also to create visually engaging experiences—the "wow" factor. Here are some typical videowall applications:

- Digital signage
- Corporate lobbies
- Boardrooms
- Command-and-control centers
- Emergency operations centers
- Scientific visualization
- Simulation and training
- Sports bars

In general, videowalls are fertile ground for AV designers to be creative and tailor video solutions to their clients' needs. Designers can mix and match technologies, screen orientations, source content, and more in unique solutions.

Videowall Design

Because videowalls can vary widely in their composition, it is especially important to understand what the client intends to use a videowall for. A videowall can be a significant investment, so a thorough needs analysis is needed to determine whether it's the best solution for the video application. Many of the questions you will ask are similar to those for other video systems.

- How much room is there for a videowall?
- Is there an equipment closet or other space for processors, switchers, and so on, as necessary?
- What type of information will be displayed? Is any of it protected content?
- How many people will view it, and what will the room layout be?
- What and how many video sources will feed images to the videowall?

Most of the principles that dictate other video systems design also apply to videowall design. You will need to determine image specifications, viewing distances, and viewing angles. You will also need to take into account ergonomics and human factors (see Chapter 4). But videowalls also require some unique considerations, including but not limited to the following:

- **Bezels** Because they consist of individual screens, videowalls can include gaps or borders (mullions) where the screens come together. This is most prominent when flat-panel displays are used; projection displays and cubes don't typically show noticeable gaps. It is important to determine from the client how much of a gap or border around screens will be tolerated. The more the client is trying to create a single, uninterrupted image, the more necessary it may be to specify displays with thin to no bezels—the frames that hold the screen in place. Videowall processors or technology built into many videowall screens can help compensate for gaps, which can make moving or still imagery look poor or unnatural when it spans multiple screens across bezels.

- **Hours of operation** Some videowalls are intended to be on 24/7—whether for digital signage or a command-and-control room. Knowing this will help guide your design. A more mission-critical videowall will require sturdier, reliable components. In addition, should there be a technical problem with one or more screens in a videowall, the client's reliability requirements may guide you to a solution that is easier to maintain. For example, some videowall displays can be serviced from the front of the wall.

- **Source inputs and processing** Depending on the application, videowall sources—and their location—can vary greatly. In a more centralized design, the sources are local to the videowall and feed directly either into the processor (or, in the case of a simple videowall, directly into the displays) or into a switcher, or both. But videowall sources can also be remote, as in the case of an emergency operations center that needs to be able to patch in remote camera feeds to view situations in the field. In this case, the format of video sources can vary significantly, and they likely will be delivered over a network. Such a scenario may require a more distributed processing model.

- **Blending**   Videowalls can include video from multiple projectors, combined to create one, seamless image. When this is the case, the projected images overlap at the edges. A video design that includes processing to blend those edges is necessary.

Videowalls are a rapidly emerging specialty of AV design. If, during the needs analysis, you and the client determine a videowall is a proper solution, you will determine other factors beyond the scope of this guide, such as screen orientation, wall composition, source resolutions and formats, pixel density, user control, and more.

Display Environment

Once you've performed image specification and display selection, the next step is to consider how the display environment will impact a video system. Mostly, this comes down to making calculated predictions and measurements about how light will affect your design. For example, you need to know how much reflected light might bounce off a screen and into viewers' eyes. And you should be able to calculate precisely projector brightness given ambient light, screen area and gain, contrast ratio, and other factors. Much of how an AV design accounts for the display environment comes down to the designer's understanding of light.

Measuring Light

When people first set out to quantify visible light, they chose a source that was familiar to be their standard—a candle. It was a specifically sized candle, made of a specific material, and molded in a specific way, but it was an ordinary candle nonetheless. The amount of light emitted from such a candle became the first and most fundamental unit of brightness. That unit is one *candlepower*.

Looking at a lit candle in the center of an otherwise darkened room, early scientists observed that light energy radiates equally in all directions, creating a sphere of light around the flame. They also observed that the farther you get from the flame at the center of the light sphere, the more the light energy is spread out, and the less the light appears to be shedding.

You may think of light in terms of AV systems, but light affects every aspect of a user's experience in the environment. It is used for everything from reading and writing to walking through a building. You must therefore be able to measure and quantify the types of light in your environment.

Light is measured using two types of meters. An *incident meter* (also referred to as an *illuminance meter*) measures light coming directly from a source, such as a lightbulb, projector, or monitor. A *spot meter* (sometimes called a *luminance meter*) measures the light that is reflected off an object back to the meter and can vary based upon the attributes of the subject being measured.

Incident Light Measurements

Using an incident light meter, you can measure the brightness of an emitting light source. There are three units of measure that are commonly used in the audiovisual industry. See Figure 5-13.

- Lumens
- Footcandles
- Lux

Lumens is the most common measurement term used for describing light output from a projector or lightbulb. A lumen is a measure of the light quantity emitted from a constant light source across 1 square meter. Manufacturers state brightness measurements in lumens on their product literature. A higher lumen rating means a brighter displayed image.

 NOTE Different organizations measure lumens by different methods. The most common standard for the lumen measurement worldwide is from the American National Standards Institute (ANSI). Officially, the two ANSI lumen standards, ANSI/NAPM IT7.228-1997 and ANSI/PIMA IT7.227-1998, were retired in July 2003. However, most manufacturers still use them today. The International Electrotechnical Commission has a similar standard, IEC 61947-1.

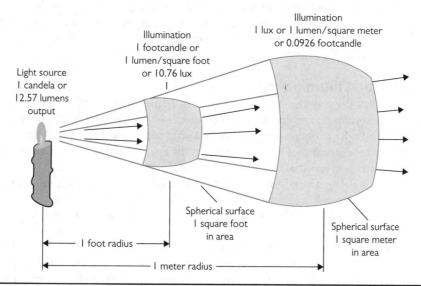

Figure 5-13 Units of light measurement

Footcandle (fc) is also a unit of measurement for direct light. It is an English unit of measurement expressing the intensity of light illuminating an object and describes the illumination from one candle falling on a surface of 1 square foot at a distance of 1 foot. Footcandles are customary U.S. measurements; one footcandle equals 10.78 lux.

Lux is a contraction of the words *luminance* and *flux*. One lux is equal to 1 lumen per square meter, or 0.093 footcandles. Again, 10.78 lux is equal to 1 footcandle. Lux is usually associated with metric measurements. Generally, the lux measurement is taken at a task area, which could be a video screen, note-taking location, or reading area.

TIP   Lux and footcandle are units for the same measurement, just different metrics (like millimeters and inches).

Reflected Light Measurements

Originally, light measurements were based on a candle's light output. Today, the candela, which is an SI unit, has replaced the candlepower standard.

The measurement of light reflected off a screen, the value of which depends on the intensity of the light and screen gain, is measured in candelas per meter squared (cd/m²). In fact, you can use the candela to measure the amount of light that is reflected off any surface. Candelas measure luminance. It differs from footcandles and lux because they measure reflected, not direct, light.

NOTE   Technically, a *candela* is defined as the luminous intensity, in a given direction, of a source that emits monochromatic radiation of frequency 540×1012 hertz and that has a radiant intensity in that direction of 1/683 watt per steradian. (A *steradian* is a unit of solid angular measure—a conical shape in a sphere.)

Luminance and Illuminance

As you've learned, the way an AV system performs should be all about people. The human eye (and a video camera, for that matter) can react only to luminance. Luminance is the photometric quantity most closely associated with a person's perception of brightness. It usually refers to the amount of light that reaches the eye of the observer measured in units of luminous intensity (candelas) per unit area (m²).

Luminance is the quantitative measure of the brightness of a light source or illuminated surface, measured in candelas per meter squared (cd/m2). It can be direct from a light source or from a reflective surface, and AV professionals measure it with a *luminance meter*.

Keep in mind that the luminance for a camera is not the same as for lighting. In video, luminance (Y) is the monochromatic, or black and white, picture information. The imager of a camera passes red, green, and blue color signals into the camera's circuitry. The circuitry takes the three signals and combines them into a single luminance signal while also producing color difference signals.

Illuminance is light that falls on a surface, measured in footcandles (fc) or lux (lx). It is not visible to the human eye except in the form of reflected luminance. For designers, illuminance is expressed as *IL-luminance* or *Incident Light-Luminance*.

System Black

Projectors can't project black light. Instead, a bright projected image tricks the brain into perceiving a black area by making whites brighter.

System black is the lowest level of luminance a system is capable of producing for a task under defined operating conditions. System black is defined by three parameters.

- The material of the display screen
- The ambient light level
- The light from the display with a solid black image input

Contrast Ratio

In the AV industry, the level of contrast between black and white in a displayed image is critical. A person who views a display needs to be able to distinguish clearly the edges of objects and the subtle changes of color that result from proper contrast. If the difference between black and white is not great enough, the resulting images are difficult to see and text is difficult to read.

Contrast ratio describes the dynamic video range of a display device as a numeric relationship between the brightest color (typically white) and the darkest color (typically black) that a system is capable of producing.

Ensuring a high-contrast ratio will make projected images appear crisper and seem to have more depth. High-contrast ratios will make reading text easier because viewers' eyes will be able to find the edges of the characters.

A checkerboard pattern projected onto a screen shows eight areas of white and eight areas of black (see Figure 5-14). Using a light meter, AV professionals take measurements of the whites and blacks. When both sets of measurements are averaged and expressed as a ratio (white:black), you arrive at the contrast ratio.

Figure 5-14   Checkerboard pattern for measuring contrast ratio in accordance with ANSI/ INFOCOMM 3M-2011 *Projected Image System Contrast Ratio (PISCR)* standard

According to the ANSI/INFOCOMM 3M-2011 standard (often referred to as PISCR), the formula for calculating contrast ratio is as follows:

$$Contrast\ Ratio = Luminance_{average\ max} / Luminance_{average\ min}$$

where:

- Luminance $_{average\ max}$ = the average level of luminance of all eight white squares
- Luminance $_{average\ min}$ = the average level of luminance of all eight black squares

ANSI/INFOCOMM 3M-2011

Because projected images are often the centerpiece of AV systems, the image contrast ratio is one of the most important criteria. The ANSI/INFOCOMM 3M-2011, *Projected Image System Contrast Ratio (PISCR),* standard was developed to ensure high-quality images.

This standard applies to front- and rear-projection systems. It defines four acceptable contrast ratios for various use cases, based on certain criteria within a space, including ambient room light. The following are the four contrast ratios:

- 7:1 for passive viewing
- 15:1 for basic decision making
- 50:1 for analytical decision making
- 80:1 for full-motion video (home theater)

The standard includes a set of simple measurements to verify that a system conforms to the desired contrast ratio of the viewing task. We will explore the PISCR standard in more detail in the following sections.

Five Viewing Positions

The ANSI/INFOCOMM 3M-2011 PISCR standard calls for taking measurements in five viewing locations: closest left and right, farthest left and right, and center. If there is an obstruction in the center, such as a table, designers should use the first available position behind the obstruction.

Designers—or during actual installation, AV technicians—should measure contrast ratio using a 16-position checkerboard test pattern and calculate the contrast ratio at each viewing location using a spot meter. See Figure 5-15.

Four Viewing Tasks

As mentioned earlier, the ANSI/INFOCOMM 3M-2011, *Projected Image System Contrast Ratio (PISCR),* standard defines four viewing categories. It's important to understand what they are and how they relate to the needs analysis conducted for the AV space where the display systems will be located.

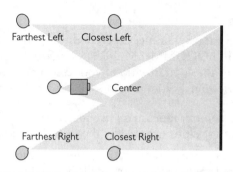

Figure 5-15 Five viewing positions for measuring contrast ratio, according to the *Projected Image System Contrast Ratio (PISCR)* standard

Passive Viewing

The viewer is able to recognize the images on a screen and can separate text or the main image from the background under typical lighting conditions for the viewing environment. The content does not require assimilation and retention of detail, but the general intent should be understood. There may be passive engagement with the content, such as noncritical or informal viewing of video or data. Passive viewing requires a minimum contrast ratio of 7:1.

Basic Decision Making

The viewer can make basic decisions based on the displayed image. The decisions are not dependent on critical details within the image, but it allows for the assimilation and retention of information. The viewer is actively engaged with the content, such as with information displays, presentations containing detailed images, classrooms, boardrooms, multipurpose rooms, and product illustrations. Basic decision making requires a minimum contrast ratio of 15:1.

Analytical Decision Making

The viewer can make critical decisions by analyzing details within the displayed image. The viewer is fully engaged with the details of the content, as in medical imaging, architectural/engineering drawings, forensic evidence, or photographic image inspection. Analytical decision making requires a minimum contrast ratio of 50:1.

Full-Motion Video

The viewer is able to discern key elements present in a video, including details included by the cinematographer or videographer necessary to support the story line and intent. This could be in a home theater, business screening room, or broadcast postproduction suite.

For more examples of where these viewing requirements are relevant, see the chart on page 19 of the standard (which has been copied into the instructor version of the ANSI/INFOCOMM contrast ratio activity). Full-motion video requires a minimum contrast ratio of 80:1.

3M Conformance

Standards conformance means you meet the conditions laid out in a standard. Conforming to the ANSI/INFOCOMM 3M-2011, *Projected Image System Contrast Ratio (PISCR)*, standard means the contrast ratio of your display design matches the standard specifications from all viewing locations. Here's a breakdown of conformance:

- **Conforms**   The contrast ratios at all five measurement (viewing) locations meet or exceed the contrast ratios required by the identified viewing category.
- **Partially conforms**   The contrast ratio of one location—but no more than four measurement (viewing) locations—falls below the required ratio for the identified viewing category by no more than 10 percent.
- **Fails to conform**   The contrast ratio at any one of the measured locations falls below the identified viewing category by more than 10 percent.

Projector Positioning

Calculating the correct projector position can be complex. The formula for projector position depends on the specific equipment. Manufacturer specifications include instructions for positioning the gear.

Projection positioning calculations are usually made in three dimensions, as shown in Figure 5-16.

- x, the horizontal offset of the projector to the screen
- y, the vertical offset of the projector to the screen
- z, the throw distance

If you don't have access to a manufacturer-specific formula, estimating the third variable, throw distance, can be useful all on its own. Estimating throw distance reveals how far away the projector needs to be from the screen. Your goal is to have an image fill the entire screen surface.

Figure 5-16
Projector position in relation to horizontal offset (*x*), vertical offset (*y*), and throw distance (*z*)

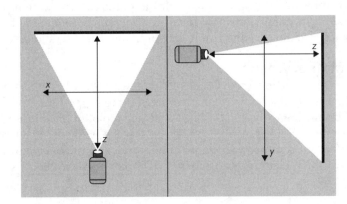

Projector Light Path

When designing a front-projection system, you need to make sure that the projector sightlines are unobstructed. Obstructions can be found in the ceiling, such as lighting fixtures, fire sprinklers, soffits, uneven ceiling, or loudspeakers. They're also on the floor, in the form of standing or sitting people, lecterns, tables, and microphone stands.

If you know that a room will be used for presentations, place presenters and their lecterns out of the light path. Viewers may become frustrated if the image is frequently obscured by presenters. From the presenter's point of view, staring at a bright projector bulb for an extended period of time will be uncomfortable.

Projection Throw

Throw distance refers to the distance that a specific combination of projector and lens needs to be from the projection screen to project a specific image size. Throw distance ratios can vary widely depending on the model, manufacturer, and lens type of a projector.

Manufacturers tend to have specific formulas that provide the best results for their projector and lens combination. Refer to the owner's manual of your specific projector and lens combination to find the most accurate throw distance and projector position relative to the screen. The projector manual will contain the correct lens information and reference point of measurement (e.g., screen to front of lens). Remember that all lenses are not the same. Also, the distance from the projection screen may vary because screen size and lens zoom ratio will impact projector location. In addition, image processors within each projector can create images of different sizes.

The formula for estimating throw distance is as follows:

*Distance = Screen width * Throw ratio*

where:

- *Distance* is the distance from the front of the lens to the closest point on the screen.
- *Screen width* is the width of the projected image.
- *Throw ratio* is the ratio of throw distance to image width.

You may need to refer to the owner's manual of your chosen projector and lens combination to find an accurate formula for your specific projector.

Let's try the throw distance formula. Say a projector has an installed lens with a throw ratio of 2:1 (you'll get that information from the manufacturer documentation). The width of the screen in the room is 72 inches. What's the throw distance?

*Distance = Screen width * throw ratio*
*Distance = 72 inches * 2*
Distance = 144 inches

In metric, if the screen were 1830 mm with a throw ratio of 2:1, the calculation would be as follows:

> *Distance = Screen width * throw ratio*
> *Distance = 1830 mm * 2*
> *Distance = 3660 mm*

And let's try it again. A projector has an installed lens with a throw ratio of 2.5:1. The width of the screen in the room is 72 inches. What's the throw distance?

> *Distance = Screen width * throw ratio*
> *Distance = 72 inches * 2.5*
> *Distance = 180 inches*

In metric, let's assume the same screen of 1830 mm, and a throw ratio of 2.5:1. What's the throw distance?

> *Distance = Screen width * throw ratio*
> *Distance = 1830 mm * 2.5*
> *Distance = 4575 mm*

Compare those two calculations. Notice that the screen width stays the same, but the throw ratio determines how far away the projector is from the screen.

 TIP When using a lens that has a zoom feature, use two throw ratio calculations that provide the range from closest distance (minimum) to farthest distance (maximum) for a given combination of projector and zoom lens.

Predicting Projector Brightness

Image brightness is impacted by several factors.

- Brightness of screen
- Screen gain
- Lumen rating of the projector
- Age of projector lamp
- The lens aperture and f-stop settings

Designers will need to employ more math calculations to determine a suitable brightness level for a viewing environment. Let's go over several of the factors that will go into brightness calculations.

Screen Gain

A projection screen is a passive device and does not have the capacity to amplify or create brightness. But the surface of a screen can focus reflected light to help increase projector brightness.

Screen gain is the ability of a screen to redirect projected light to make the image appear brighter within the viewer area. As a result of this ability, off-axis viewing is actually diminished. Screen gain refers to the amount of light reflected by the screen materials, not the amplification of light.

The higher the gain number of a screen, the brighter the picture viewed on-axis. When someone is seated within the good viewing area, a screen should provide uniform brightness over the entire image area, with no dim areas or hot spots.

Ambient light rejection generally increases as screen gain increases. This is because the light becomes more directional as screen gain increases and reflected ambient light appears outside the viewing cone.

 NOTE Ambient light will have its own viewing cone, which should be outside the projected image's viewing cone. If this is not the case, you'll need to adjust the lights.

A gain of 1.0 refers to a matte white screen surface that does not absorb or channel light, is uniformly reflective, and can be seen from all directions. A glass-beaded screen that has a gain reading of 1.3 or 1.5 is highly reflective, less uniformly reflective, and has more hot spotting.

Hot Spotting

As gain increases, so does hot spotting. A hot spot is the part of a displayed image that is unevenly illuminated, usually appearing as a bright area in the center.

Hot spotting is caused by the properties of the screen surface. It manifests itself as a brighter area on the screen. For example, when shining a flashlight on a wall, the reflected spot is not of uniform brightness. The brightest area in that spot is the hot spot.

Screen manufacturers develop surfaces to yield high gain with minimal hot spotting. Hot spotting is one of the trade-offs for screen gain in front-projection screens and some rear-projection screens and is most noticeable when viewing a projected image off-axis.

Lamp Life

A projector's brightness will be greatest on the first day of installation and decline over the life of the projector's lamp (see Figure 5-17). Projector lamps become dimmer over time. When calculating light levels, you will need to account for derating the lumen specification of the projector. This will allow you to factor in the average amount of decay over the life of a projector lamp.

Figure 5-17
Lamp life derating over time. Operating hour figures are not displayed because each lamp is specified differently.

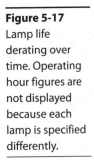
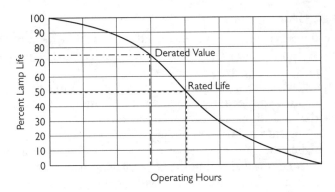

Lamp life is defined as the time it takes for a lamp to reach 50 percent of its initial light output. After or near the 50 percent point, not only will the lamp get dimmer, but its color temperature will change.

For the purposes of derating a projector's specified lamp output, we select the halfway point between 100 percent and 50 percent brightness, or 75 percent. This means the projector should be derated by 25 percent of its specified brightness. The derating factor will be important to calculating a projector's required brightness, which we will discuss in the section "Calculating Required Projector Brightness."

Projector Lens

When a projector manufacturer writes its specifications, it usually describes the lens and electronics as a complete package. The projector's lens has a specific f-stop, or *focal ratio*. This indicates the amount of light that is lost as it travels through the lens.

In case you select a lens that's not the lens supplied with the projector, it is important to compare the new lens f-stop with that of the old lens. The difference in f-stops can mean the projector's light output goes up or down. A full f-stop—going from f2 to f4, for instance—will cut the specified light output in half. Similarly, going from f8 to f4 will double your light output. Either way, if you don't plan around the f-stop of a projector lens, it can lead to major issues with the system's performance.

Ambient Light Levels

Figure 5-18 represents a simple display environment. The screen is a front-projection screen with a gain of 1. A projector is hung from the ceiling to project some amount of light on the screen. A lightbulb represents the task light required for the audience to see around the room and take notes. The other lightbulb represents all the ambient light that strikes the screen (lighting fixtures, sun, and light from the projected image that's reflected around the room). When designing a display environment, there is natural competition between ambient light levels and the projector light levels as they impact the viewing area (the screen).

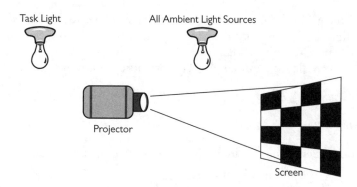

Figure 5-18
Sources of light in a projection environment

Reducing ambient light at the screen location is the most important element of creating a good contrast ratio for the projected image. It can also be the most difficult thing to do.

In new construction, communicate often with lighting designers and electrical contractors. These allied trades have more flexibility to control ambient lighting. The lighting designer will be able to give you the planned light levels so you can factor them into your projector brightness specifications. This is also an opportunity for you, as the AV designer, to discuss issues that are important to the AV design, such as screen placement, lighting zones, and dimming systems.

As a designer, it's important that you develop an awareness of lighting levels by using a light meter on all projects. Taking accurate measurements and making specific recommendations will help you communicate your needs to allied trades.

Calculating Required Projector Brightness

When you select a projector, you need to make sure the one you choose is bright enough for your viewing environment. That means taking a number of variables into account.

Because most front screens are matte white finish, it is fairly easy to assume that the ambient light reading near the screen location will be nearly the same as a measurement of black at the screen. This is because a white screen can only get brighter when light is applied, but the screen can never become darker. So, with no light from the projector, what you have is a screen that is as black as it will ever be. To calculate what the white level would be with a contrast ratio of 15:1, for example, you simply multiply the black level by 15.

Once the white level and screen dimensions are known, you can find the rated projected output level. Just remember that you need to account for the projector lamp's derating factor because of its loss of light output over its useful life.

When calculating projector brightness, your black level is a measurement of the ambient light at the screen. To achieve a 15:1 contrast ratio—or to know the white level—multiply the ambient light at the screen by 15 (note that this works only for a front matte white screen). Multiply the result by the area of the screen. Because the light is spread across the screen, you need to consolidate the light to the projector lamp. Divide the previous answer by the gain of the screen. You divide because the light will need to be less if the gain is higher; conversely, if the gain is low, you will need a brighter projector. Dividing the final result by (1 to 0.25) will increase the projector brightness to account for the lamp loss over its life.

The formula for required projector brightness is as follows:

$$Lumens = L * C * A \, S_G / D_R$$

where:

- *Lumens* = The required brightness of the projector in lumens.
- L = The ambient light level.
- A = The screen area.
- C = The required contrast ratio.
- S_G = The gain of the screen. Assume a screen gain of 1 unless otherwise noted.
- D_R = The projector derating value. Assume a derating value of 0.75 unless otherwise noted.

TIP   Projectors are typically derated by 25 percent (1 − 0.25 = 0.75). DR is therefore typically equal to 0.75.

Measuring OFE Projector Brightness

As you see, it's possible to calculate brightness requirements for a given application to specify a projector. However, how can you be sure that a projector you already have on hand (owner-furnished equipment, or OFE) is actually producing the amount of light needed? When using a client's existing equipment in a design, you should test it to ensure it still meets its original specifications. Even the performance of new equipment should be verified.

Calculating the brightness of a fixed-resolution projector requires a light meter, which takes a reading of the received light and provides a value in lux or footcandles, and requires an ANSI lumens nine-zone graphic, projected on the screen. The amount of light energy delivered to the screen is measured in lumens. This is one of the primary issues when considering the amount of light that should be produced by the lamp for the viewing environment.

The ANSI method for determining lumens was developed to provide a standardized method of measuring the light output of projector lamps. This is the measurement detailed in most projector specifications. The ANSI standard was retired in 2003 and is now maintained by the International Electrotechnical Commission in standards 61947-1 and 61947-2.

Here is the formula for calculating the ANSI brightness of a screen:

$$Lumens = [(Z_1 + Z_2 ... Z_9)/9] * (S_H * S_W)$$

where:

- Z_n = One of the nine zones on a screen (lux)
- S_H = Height of the image (in feet or meters)
- S_W = Width of the image (in feet or meters)

 TIP When calculating projector brightness, your incident light and area measurements must match. If your light measurement is in lux, a metric unit, but your screen area measurement is in feet, a U.S. customary unit, you must convert square feet to square meters before calculating the required projector brightness. To do this, multiply square feet by 0.0929.

Task-Light Levels

The difference between the white levels of an image and a viewer's work surface, or task area, should be within a range of three times greater and three times less than the white image. The purpose of keeping this level within three times is to keep eye strain at a minimum. Greater differences in the two light levels (projected and task) can cause a viewer's iris to contract and dilate too often, causing eye strain and some discomfort.

In many cases, task lighting can raise the ambient light in the room. This is especially true if the task lighting is broadly directed and the room treatments (wall coverings, table surfaces, ceiling, and floor) reflect light to a large degree. In a properly designed room, the task-light measurements should be independent of the ambient-light measurements at the screen. Consider moving or directing light fixtures closer to the task area and away from the screen. Ideally, the lighting system would combine directed fixtures and a dimming controller.

Luminance differences are normally necessary for vision. Print, for instance, can be seen and interpreted because of the difference in luminance between the white page and the black print. In a display space, luminance variations are a function of both the reflectance of the surfaces and the distribution of light on those surfaces.

Large variations in luminance can be problematic. Office interiors should be lit to provide for good visibility with distracting glare. Direct and reflected glare should be avoided. However, it is important to provide enough variation in luminance (or color) to contribute to a stimulating, attractive environment. Where there are no prolonged visual tasks, as in lobbies, corridors, reception areas, and lounges, greater variations in luminance are a good idea, using attractive colors and appropriate focal points of high contrast to catch the eye.

In a working office environment, luminance near each task area and other parts of the office within the field of view should be balanced with task luminance. Two separate phenomena are influenced by luminance ratios within the field of view: *transient adaptation* and *disability glare*. To limit the effects of these phenomena, the luminance ratios generally should not exceed the following:

- **Between paper task and adjacent screen**   3:1 or 1:3
- **Between task and adjacent dark surroundings**   3:1 or 1:3
- **Between task and remote (nonadjacent) surfaces**   10:1 or 1:10

It is not, however, practical or aesthetically desirable to maintain these ratios throughout the entire environment. For visual interest and distant focus (for periodic eye muscle relaxation throughout the day), small visual areas that exceed the luminance-ratio recommendations are desirable. This would include artwork, accent finishes on walls, ceilings or floors, small window areas, accent finishes on chairs and accessories, and accent focal lighting.

Calculating Task-Light Levels

Once you know the projector brightness, you can solve for task lighting. The objective is to have a task-light level that is in a range of plus or minus three times the white level, in lux. Once you have selected a projector, you can find its lumen output within the projector's specifications. From this, you can calculate how bright the white level should be on the screen.

The following are the formulas for task-light levels:

$$Task\ Light_{upper} = [(Lumens\ /\ A) * S_G * D_R] * 3$$

and

$$Task\ Light_{lower} = [(Lumens\ /\ A) * S_G * D_R] / 3$$

where:

- *Task Light$_{upper}$/Light$_{lower}$* = The task-light levels at the top and bottom of the acceptable range
- *Lumens* = Specified projector brightness
- *A* = Area of the screen
- *S$_G$* = Screen gain
- *D$_R$* = 1 minus projector derating percentage

NOTE   Remember to keep like measurements throughout your calculations. If the screen is in feet and you measure in footcandles, you will get the same answer as if you used a lux meter and a metric screen size.

Chapter Review

In this chapter, you studied the fundamental principles needed to determine image specifications, including text size, farthest and nearest viewers, and viewing area. All are critical components to consider early in your design.

With an understanding of image specifications, you're ready for display selection. Available options include front-projection, rear-projection, and videowall systems. It is always important to remember how aspect ratios play a role in ensuring a quality image in your design.

Finally, you learned how environmental factors affect image quality and how to apply measurements to perfect your design. With the information you gained from this chapter, you can appropriately position and select equipment for your display design.

Review Questions

The following questions are based on the content covered in this chapter and are intended to help reinforce the knowledge you have assimilated. These questions are not extracted from the CTS-D exam nor are they necessarily CTS-D practice exam questions. For an official CTS-D practice exam, see the accompanying CD.

1. A conference room requires videoconferencing and AV presentation capabilities. Which of the following design elements are defined by the architectural dimensions and orientation of the room?

   A. Display size

   B. Display type

   C. Display aspect ratio

   D. Display brightness

2. What is the recommended (highest) ambient lighting level illuminating a front-projection screen within a videoconferencing space?

   A. 5 footcandles (50 lux)

   B. 30 footcandles (108 lux)

   C. 45 footcandles (161 lux)

   D. 25 footcandles (215 lux)

3. If a font height is 2 in (50 mm), the screen height is 60 in (1,525 mm), and screen resolution is 1080 pixels high, what is the font size in pixels?

   A. 28 point

   B. 32 point

   C. 36 point

   D. 40 point

4. A matte white screen surface has a gain of _____.

   A. 0.5

   B. 0.75

   C. 1.0

   D. 1.25

5. A 16:9 screen will be installed in a lecture hall. The screen's diagonal is 72 in (1,829 mm). What is its width?

   A. 50 in (1270 mm)

   B. 63 in (1594 mm)

   C. 70 in (1778 mm)

   D. 72 in (1829 mm)

6. If you have a projector that is 2500 ANSI lumens on a 5.5 m² standard matte white screen, what should be the limits of the task lighting? Note that the projector specification is derated by 25 percent.

   A. 113.6 to 1022.7 lux

   B. 120 to 175 lux

   C. 515 to 1001 lux

   D. 527 to 632 lux

7. Lamp life is defined as the time it takes for a lamp to reach _____ percent of initial output.

   A. 10

   B. 25

   C. 50

   D. 75

8. You need to project an image that has a 4:3 aspect ratio. You measure the screen height and determine that it is 2,286 mm high and 3,048 mm wide. Can you use this screen for the 4:3 image?

   A. Yes

   B. No

   C. Not enough information to determine

   D. All of the above

9. You require a 16:9 screen with a height of 60 in (1,524 mm). What will the screen's diagonal be?

   A. 90 in

   B. 1,524 mm

   C. 3,109 mm

   D. 100 in

10. In videowall design, _____ is the process of adjusting for the edges of multiple projected images.

   A. Blending

   B. Pixel mapping

   C. Processing

   D. Orienting

Answers

1. **A.** For visual systems, the architectural dimensions and orientation of the room will determine display size.

2. **A.** The highest recommended ambient lighting level for a front-projection screen in a videoconferencing space is 5 footcandles, or 50 lux.

3. **C.** In this case, 2/60 = X/1080. Cross multiply and divide to arrive at 36 pixels, or a 36-point font.

4. **C.** A matte white screen surface has a gain of 1.0.

5. **B.** Width/diagonal = Width ratio/diagonal ratio, and width/72 = 16/18.36. Therefore, width = 63, rounded to the nearest inch.

6. **A.** Task light = [(2500/5.5) * 1 * (1 − 0.25)]. For the upper limit, multiply by 3; for the lower limit, divide by 3. Your task-light range is 113.6 to 1022.7 lux.

7. **C.** Lamp life is defined as the time it takes for a lamp to reach 50 percent of initial output.

8. **A.** Yes, because 3,048:2,286 is the same as 4:3, or 3,048/2,286 = 4/3.

9. **C.** At 16:9, length = 106.7 inches; $60^2 + 106.7^2 = C^2$; C = 122.4 inches, or 3,109 mm.

10. **A.** In videowall design, blending is the process of adjusting for the edges of multiple projected images.

Audio Principles of Design

In this chapter, you will learn about

- Calculating the change in a sound and signal level using decibel equations, as well as power and distance using 10-log and 20-log functions
- Plotting loudspeaker coverage in a room and wiring loudspeakers
- Transformers and amplifiers
- Different types of microphones and polar-response patterns
- The benefits of using an automatic microphone mixer
- The qualities of an effective sound-reinforcement system
- Determining whether an audio system will be stable by comparing potential acoustic gain (PAG) and needed acoustic gain (NAG) calculations

Much of what you need to know as an audiovisual professional revolves around sound: how sounds are generated, how sound moves through a medium (such as air), how you might control its propagation, how sound interacts with the environment, and how you receive and process sound. As an AV designer, you need to apply math concepts and accurate measurements to support the human perception of sound as intended by your design. With an understanding of sound and sound systems, you will be better positioned to meet the needs of your clients.

For example, if you determine a loudspeaker system is necessary, your design will need to specify where the loudspeakers will be located. Your goal is to provide adequate audio coverage for listeners. To accomplish this, you will need to evaluate coverage patterns, loudspeaker locations, and power requirements.

Microphones play a vital role in ensuring your audio design supports your client's message, giving the audience an exceptional listening environment. Special calculations, such as PAG and NAG, reduce the possibility of audio feedback within a system. PAG and NAG determinations are among the many that AV designers make when creating a stable, effective audio system design.

Introduction to the Decibel

When discussing audio, you need a way to talk about how people experience the sound that a system produces. The most common unit of measurement for sound is the decibel.

But a decibel doesn't really measure sound. It measures change. In technical terms, a decibel is a base-10 logarithmic ratio between two values. Remember, the logarithmic scale is used to describe a large range of values, which can vary over several orders of magnitude. A ratio is just simply a comparison of two numbers. In other words, a decibel is a measurement of how much change a person will actually perceive as a linear value changes.

Before we delve further into decibels, let's pause to discuss logarithms. The logarithm of a number is how many times the number 10 must be multiplied by itself to get a certain value. For example, the log of 10,000 is 4, and the log of 0.0001 is –4.

Logarithmic scales make ratio values easier to express. For example, the ratio between the threshold of hearing (when sounds become audible) and the threshold of pain is 1 to 1,000,000. No one wants to count that many zeros.

Think of a standard ruler. Each unit on the ruler represents a unit of 1 wherever it is located on the ruler, whether it's an inch, millimeter, or whatever. It's a one-to-one relationship between the units shown and the units represented. This is a *linear* scale.

What if the value of each unit on that ruler represented something other than a single unit? What if each time you moved to the right, each unit represented ten times as much as before? Or, each time you moved a unit to the left it represented one-tenth as much as before? In this case, comparing adjacent units on a scale would represent a ratio of 1:10 or 10:1. This is a *logarithmic* scale.

In Figure 6-1, the top row represents a linear scale, and the bottom row represents a logarithmic scale.

Figure 6-1

Linear and logarithmic scales

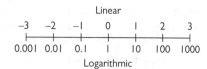

You can write 10 * 10 * 10 = 1,000 or 10^3 = 1,000 (10 multiplied by itself three times). You have just used a logarithm with a base of 10 and an exponent of 3 as a shortcut for an equation that uses multiplication. Therefore, you could substitute 10^1, 10^2, and 10^3 at the bottom of Figure 6-1 for the numbers 10, 100, and 1,000.

Humans perceive differences in sound levels logarithmically, not linearly. Because of this, a base-10 logarithmic scale is used to measure, record, and discuss sound level differences.

If you used a linear scale to describe the perceived difference in sound pressure level from the threshold of hearing to the threshold of pain, you would need to use numbers from 1 to well over 1 million.

When it comes to sounds and decibels, there are some accepted generalities related to human hearing.

- A 1 decibel (dB) change is the smallest perceptible change noticeable. Unless they're listening carefully, most people will not discern a 1 dB change.

- A "just noticeable" change—either louder or softer—requires a 3 dB change (e.g., 85 dB sound pressure level [SPL] to 88 dB SPL).

- A 10 dB change is required for listeners to perceive subjectively a sound that is twice or one-half as loud as it was before. For example, a change from 85 dB SPL to 95 dB SPL is perceived to be twice as loud.

Why Use Decibels?

Even before you got into the audiovisual industry, you probably heard sound described in decibels. Did you know that you can also use decibels to measure distance, power, and voltage? Because a decibel measures perceived change—not actual pressure or sound—you can use it to quantify many kinds of changes. For this reason, the decibel is dimensionless and cannot be properly called a unit.

A decibel change in distance, voltage, or power will result in the same decibel change in sound pressure. If you want to increase the loudness of a sound system by 5 dB, you just need to increase the power or voltage by 5 dB.

Calculating Decibel Changes

As you've learned, a decibel doesn't really measure anything. It's a ratio—a comparison of two values. To compare, you need a start point and an end point. Those values will be real measurements, in linear units such as pascals, volts, watts, or meters. They must be like units; you can compare only volts to volts, watts to watts, meters to meters, and so on. Once you've converted the values to decibels, you can compare them to each other.

Calculating the decibel change from one distance, voltage, or power measurement to another will tell you how much louder or softer the output of a sound system will seem after the change. To convert linear measurements, such as meters, volts, or watts, to the logarithmic decibel, you use a logarithmic equation.

To calculate the change in decibels between two power measurements, use the *10-log equation*. The formula for calculating a decibel change for power is as follows:

$$dB = 10 * log (P_1/P_r)$$

where:

- dB = The change in decibels
- P_1 = The new or measured power measurement
- P_r = The original or reference power measurement

The result of this formula will be either positive or negative. If it is positive, the result is an increase, or gain. If it is negative, the result is a decrease, or loss.

NOTE *Gain* refers to the electronic amplification of a signal.

To calculate the change in decibels between two voltage or distance measurements, use the *20-log equation*. The formula for calculating decibel changes in sound pressure level over distance is as follows:

$$dB = 20 * log (D_1/D_2)$$

where:

- dB = The change in decibels
- D_1 = The original or reference distance
- D_2 = The new or measured distance

As before, the result of this calculation will be either positive or negative. If it is positive, the result is an increase, or gain. If it is negative, the result is a decrease, or loss.

The formula for calculating decibel changes in voltage is as follows:

$$dB = 20 * log (V_1/V_r)$$

where:

- dB = The change in decibels

- V_1 = The new or measured voltage
- V_r = The original or reference voltage

Once again, the result of this calculation will be either positive or negative. If it is positive, the result is an increase, or gain. If it is negative, the result is a decrease, or loss.

TIP In AV, the 10-log formula is for power calculations only. The 20-log formula is for voltage, pressure, and distance calculations. Just remember: 10 for power, 20 for everything else.

Reference Level

A decibel can be a comparison of two values, or it can be a comparison of a value to a predetermined starting point, known as a *reference level*. This is also sometimes referred to as a *zero reference*. For example, you could compare two voltages and use a 20-log formula to discover the decibel change between them.

In the context of decibel measurements, the reference level is the established starting point, represented as 0 dB. The reference level varies according to linear unit and application. It is typically indicated by the decibel abbreviations. Table 6-1 shows decibel abbreviations and reference levels for various common measurements.

To use a reference level as a starting point, you have to know what the reference is. For sound pressure, the reference level is the threshold of human hearing at 1 kHz, 0.00002 Pa. Humans perceive that sound pressure level as silence. Any unit you might quantify in decibels has its own reference level.

NOTE This guide doesn't teach you how to convert pascals to dB SPL. That's because you never have to perform such math on the job. When you take a measurement using an SPL meter, the meter senses pressure in pascals and automatically compares its reading to the dB SPL zero reference, 0.00002 Pa.

Decibels will be abbreviated differently to indicate the reference level used. For example, dB SPL indicates that the reference level is a sound pressure level of 0.00002 Pa at 1 kHz. Meanwhile, dBV indicates that the reference level is a voltage of 1 V.

Table 6-1	Measurement	Decibel Abbreviation	Reference Level
Decibel Abbreviations and Reference Levels	Sound pressure	dB SPL	0.00002 pascal (Pa) at 1 kHz
	Voltage	dBV	1 V
	Voltage	dBu	0.775 V
	Power	dBW	1 W
	Power	dBm	0.001 W, or 1 mW

Some units, such as volts and watts, have more than one zero reference. Use the one that makes sense for the application. If you're taking power measurements at a radio station, use dBW. If you're measuring the power of wireless microphones, use dBm.

TIP You will encounter specifications expressed as negative decibel values. For instance, you might see a microphone sensitivity specification of −54 dBu. That doesn't mean the microphone has negative voltage. Remember, a negative decibel measurement means "less than before" or, in this case, "less than the reference level." The specification of −54 dBu just means that the mic signal voltage is 54 dB less than 0.775 V, the reference voltage level for 0 dBu.

Decibels are often qualified with a suffix. These suffixes indicate the reference quantity. Two suffixes often found in the AV industry are dBu and dBV. Both reference voltage ratios.

0 dBu is equivalent to 0.775 volts.

Pro-audio line level is often expressed as +4 dBu, which expresses a voltage above the 0.775 reference point, or 1.23 volts. If you have a microphone level of −50 dBu, that does not mean the device has "negative voltage." Instead, it is expressing a voltage level less than the 0.775 volt reference point, or 2 millivolts.

0 dBV is equivalent to 1 volt.

The consumer line level is often expressed as −10 dBV, or 316 millivolts. A good clue that a device's level might be −10 dBV is the use of the phono or RCA connector.

As an AV professional, you should commit certain decibel values to memory.

- Sound pressure level should always fall between 0 and 140 dB SPL.
- Microphone level, which is typically measured in dBu, should be −60 to −50 dBu, well below the zero reference of 0.775 volts for the dBu.
- Line level on the other hand, should be between 0 and +4 dBu for pro audio.
- The consumer audio level is −10 dBV (0.316 V).

NOTE The dBu uses a lowercase *u*, while the dBV uses an uppercase *V*. This is to avoid confusion between the two.

Let's try a 10-log decibel calculation. An audio amplifier is delivering 15 watts, and its output is decreased to 5 watts. What is the change in decibels?

- **Step 1** Ask yourself, "What do I expect to happen?" If the amplifier will be delivering less power, then there will be less sound coming out of the system. In the AV industry, this is called a *loss*.

- **Step 2** Which number do you put first? If you expect a gain, place the higher number first. If you expect a loss, place the smaller number first. In this example, you are expecting a loss, so the smaller number (5) goes first (5/15 = 0.33).

- **Step 3** Calculate the log. In this example, the problem concerns power. Therefore, you need to use the 10-log formula. In step 2, you completed the division. Now enter 0.33 in your calculator and press the "log" button.

  *10 * log (P_1/P_2)*

  *10 * log (0.33)*

  *10 * (−0.48)*

- **Step 4** Multiply −0.48 by 10.

  *10 * (−0.48)*

  Answer: −4.8 dB

Sound Pressure Level

Figure 6-2 shows a graph of the equal loudness curves. These contours were formed using short-duration, pure tones. Levels shown are referenced to a 1kHz tone, which takes into account the ear's relative insensitivity to low-frequency energy at low overall listening levels.

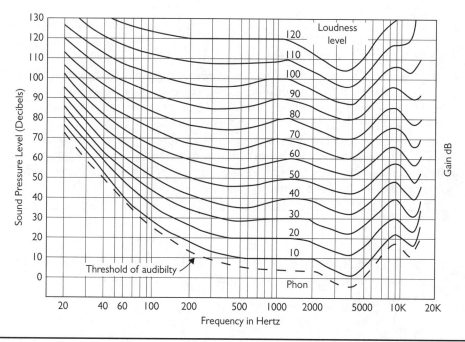

Figure 6-2 Fletcher-Munson equal loudness contour

The threshold of human hearing is 0 dB SPL at 1 kHz. The graph in Figure 6-2 shows how loud different frequencies must be for the human ear to perceive them as equally loud as another.

What sound pressure level would a 40 Hz tone require to be perceived equally as loud as a 1 kHz tone? The dotted curve represents the threshold of human hearing, which is what the human ear perceives. The x-axis of the graph shows actual frequency, and the y-axis shows actual dB SPL.

A 40 Hz tone must be about 50 dB SPL louder before the human ear can perceive it equally as loud as 1 kHz. A 200 Hz tone, however, would only have to be 15 dB SPL louder to be perceived equally as loud as the 1 Hz tone.

TIP   As part of your needs assessment, you should document your customer's SPL needs. Speech and program audio may have different sound-level requirements. Your rationale for determining the level above ambient noise, for example, should take into account your customer's input. Designers must document such agreed-upon levels so installers can set them.

Notice that at overall louder listening levels the hearing response curve begins to flatten. Human perception of the energy across the audible spectrum is more even at overall louder listening levels. Also note that your ears' sensitivity is where normal speech frequencies are located, 500 to 4,000 Hz. And your ears are most sensitive to higher-pitched sounds, such as a crying baby.

Notes from the Field: Home Stereos

For an example of how equal loudness curves work, think of a home stereo. Typical home stereos have a loudness button that emphasizes or provides a "boost" for low frequencies. At low listening levels, you could engage the loudness button to hear the kick drum or bass guitar.

As the listening level increases, however, you should find that the low frequencies are now over-emphasized, and you would then disengage the loudness button for a more appropriate spectrum balance. At low listening levels, the human ear is simply less sensitive to low-frequency information.

Watch a video about human perception of loudness across sound frequencies at www.infocomm.org/LoudnessVideo. Appendix C provides a link to this and other videos.

SPL Meters

Sound pressure level is a measurement of all the acoustic energy in an environment. It is typically expressed in decibels (dB SPL). Sound pressure refers to the pressure deviation from the ambient atmospheric pressure caused by the vibration of air particles. SPL is expressed in decibels to correlate with the human perception of changes in loudness.

An SPL meter reports a single-number measurement of the sound pressure at the meter's microphone location. The meter has a calibrated microphone and the necessary circuitry to detect and display the sound level. Its function is simple: An SPL meter converts the sound pressure levels in the air into corresponding electrical signals. These signals are measured and processed through internal filters, and the results are displayed in decibels.

NOTE Although a single SPL number has its usefulness, you can't use it to optimize a system or fully analyze noise in an environment. Additional data points are required. This is true of any "one-number" reading or measurement; it has limitations, and more information may be required for proper application or analysis.

SPL Meter Settings

Always reference the project specifications to obtain the necessary SPL meter settings for properly verifying the audio performance of a system. If the verification requirements do not specify settings for the SPL meter, you can apply a weighting to the SPL meter measurements to correlate the meter's readings with how people perceive loudness. A meter will typically have three settings.

- **A-weighting**   A setting commonly used for environmental, hearing conservation, and noise ordinance enforcement. It closely reflects the response of the human ear to noise and its insensitivity to lower frequencies at lower listening levels.

- **C-weighting**   More uniform response over the entire frequency range.

- **Z-weighting**   A flat frequency response, with no filtering.

Historically, there used to be B-weighting (where filtering fell between the A and C weightings) and D-weighting (like for jet engines), but they are not included in the latest standards.

In addition to applying a weighting to SPL readings when verifying performance, you can select a specific response.

- *Fast,* to capture transient (momentary) levels.

- *Slow,* which is more like how your ears react to sound. Use this response for more consistent noise levels or for averaging rapidly changing fluctuations in sound levels.

Keep in mind, an audio system may need to comply with a standard. SPL meter performance falls under two different standards. Internationally, the standard is governed by the International Electrotechnical Commission (IEC); in the United States, it's the American National Standards Institute (ANSI).

The IEC standard relates to frontal-incidence correction, while the ANSI standard relates to random-incidence correction. In other words, does the microphone have to be oriented directly on-axis with the noise source to be compliant (IEC), or can it be off-axis up to a certain point (ANSI)? These two different standards have more to do with the response than weighting.

Measuring Background Noise

Although there are better metrics for quantifying background noise levels and their effect on listeners, a simple method is to measure the SPL of the background noise. To gauge background noise levels, the SPL should be measured using an A-weighted scale.

One standard, ANSI/ASA S12.60, specifies that maximum, one-hour background SPL levels, including that from building services (HVAC, etc.), should not exceed 35 dB SPL A-weighted. This is for spaces 20,000 square feet (566 square meters) or less, such as classrooms and other learning spaces.

Given the maximum background noise level of 35 dB SPL A-weighted specified in the standard, and the fact that a space should acoustically have a minimum 25 dB acoustic signal-to-noise ratio (the level of a desired signal compared to the level of background noise), you arrive at a targeted speech level of 60 dB SPL A-weighted. However, a sound reinforcement system for speech may more typically operate in the range of 70 to 75 dB SPL.

SPL Meter Classes

When selecting an SPL meter, you want to use one that can take extremely accurate readings. SPL meters are classified based on allowable tolerances. Devices that are not classified do not conform to a standard and are not reliable for measurement and testing purposes. How do you know which class of meter to use for the task?

- **Class 0**   A lab-reference standard. It supports the strictest tolerances and should be used when extreme precision is needed.

- **Class 1**   Precision measurement. It is useful for taking flat, engineering-grade measurements, rather than wide-range or field measurements.

- **Class 2**   For general purpose. It has the widest tolerances with respect to level linearity and frequency response. Class 2 meters are required only to support A-weighting. Other weightings are optional. For many audio purposes, a Class 2 meter is acceptable.

- **Class 3**   Intended for noise surveys. Class 2 meters are simple SPL meters meant to determine whether a noise problem exists. If a problem does exist, diagnosing it will require a higher-class meter.

SPL Meter Weighting Curves

You can see the differences in SPL weighting by examining the weighting curve chart, pictured in Figure 6-3.

The line marked "A" on this chart represents the A-weighted filter setting on an SPL meter. You can see that A-weighting discriminates against low-frequency energy. The A-weighting curve is almost the inverse of the equal loudness curve at a low listening level. The human ear perceives low-frequency energy as a lower dB SPL than it actually is. The energy is still there; it's just that listeners are not as sensitive to it at these levels.

The A-weighting, therefore, is useful in low-listening-level situations, roughly 20 to 55 dB SPL. It lowers the dB SPL reading of low-frequency sounds to reflect how a human being perceives those sounds.

As the listening level increases to the 85 to 140 dB SPL range, the human ear response "flattens out." You may then choose a C-weighted filter (indicated by the line marked "C" in Figure 6-3), whose curve is far less steep.

Loudness vs. Weighting

Figure 6-4 shows a side-by-side comparison of an equal loudness curve on the left and a weighting curve on the right. The equal loudness curve is a measure of sound pressure over the frequency spectrum of human hearing. It is an absolute value, using 0 dB SPL as a reference. The weighting curve represents standard filter contours used to make test instruments approximate the human ear. Therefore, the different weighting curves are

Figure 6-3
SPL weighting curves

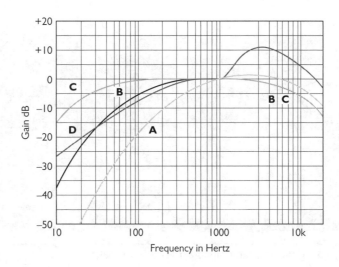

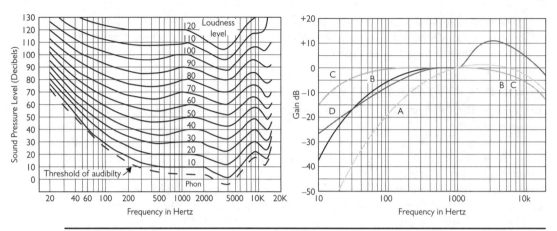

Figure 6-4 Equal loudness curves (left) and SPL weighting curves (right)

meant to represent what the ear hears at various intensity levels. These measurements are a relative value and depend on where or what you are referencing for your measurement.

SPL Meter Weighting: Spectrum Analysis

Let's take a look at two spectrum-analyzer readings taken from the same room. The first reading, shown in Figure 6-5 and fairly flat, was taken with no weighting applied. Notice that the overall dB SPL reading is 70.

The second reading, shown in Figure 6-6, was taken using an A-weighted filter. The overall level, especially the low-frequency energy, is shown as reduced; now the meter

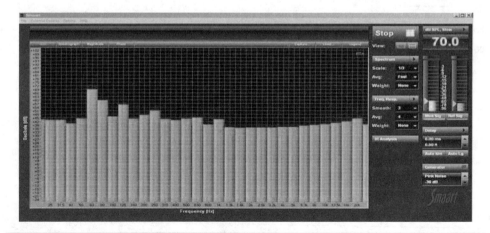

Figure 6-5 Unfiltered audio signal on a spectrum analyzer

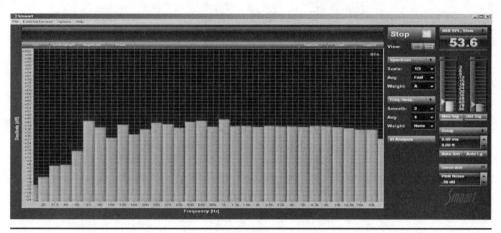

Figure 6-6   Audio signal on a spectrum analyzer with an A-weighted filter

reads 53.6 dB SPL. This reading reflects how a listener would actually perceive the noise in the room.

TIP   If you use a filter when taking an SPL reading, you must note which filter you applied. When recording the readings in Figures 6-5 and 6-6, you would write the first reading down as "70 dB SPL" because no filter was used. The second reading should be written "53.6 dB SPL A-wtd" to indicate that you used an A-weighting filter when you took the reading.

Loudspeaker Directivity

A distributed loudspeaker system employs multiple loudspeakers that are separated from each other by some distance. This is most usually accomplished by installing the speakers in the ceiling above an audience area.

To design a distributed layout, you first must know how much area the sound from each of your selected loudspeakers will cover. For starters, use the polar-pattern directivity information provided by the loudspeaker manufacturer to create an elevation section view of a loudspeaker and the pattern. This will allow you to create a circular area that each unit will cover.

Loudspeaker coverage patterns are frequency dependent. This means that the exact pattern of coverage will depend on frequency. In other words, a loudspeaker rated a 90-by-40-degree loudspeaker covers only 90 by 40 degrees at a certain frequency. Remember that each frequency has a physical wavelength associated with it. A loudspeaker does not have the same coverage pattern across the entire audible frequency range.

Balloon plots are typically part of a loudspeaker's specifications and are often available in computer files for use in various modeling programs, such as EASE. Computer modeling is commonplace (and necessary) in all but the simplest installations.

PART II

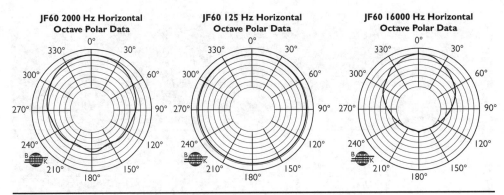

Figure 6-7   Polar plots of different frequency bands for a loudspeaker

Figure 6-7 shows some of the plots from an EAW JF60 loudspeaker. Each concentric circle on these charts represents a change of 5 dB SPL. A polar pattern shows how far off-axis a loudspeaker's coverage pattern extends at a given frequency. You can see that at high frequencies this loudspeaker's energy drops off steeply as you move off-axis. As you move off-axis, look for the point at which the range of frequencies you're using drops off by 6 dB SPL. The "6 dB down" point is typical for defining a loudspeaker's coverage pattern.

The specification sheet for this loudspeaker says its "nominal beam width" (coverage pattern) is 100 degrees horizontal by 100 degrees vertical. The axial grids are 5 dB divisions. Notice that the coverage pattern (dispersion) at 2 kHz is about 100 degrees wide. In other words, when comparing the level on-axis with the level 50 degrees off-axis, you should find a reduction in level of about 6 dB at 2 kHz.

The pattern shown at 125 Hz disperses in an omnidirectional pattern. Does this mean that low frequencies are omnidirectional? Not at all. It has to do with wavelength. It takes a larger device to control the dispersion pattern associated with the longer wavelengths of lower frequencies.

Realistically, the pattern shown for 2,000 Hz is the only one of these three that comes close to being 100 degrees by 100 degrees.

TIP   Coverage is typically stated at the 6 dB down points. This means the level at the edge of the stated coverage pattern would be found to be 6 dB less than the energy measured on-axis.

Calculating Loudspeaker Coverage

To create a loudspeaker layout, you must first determine two things: loudspeaker coverage angle and listener ear level.

By referencing the polar pattern information, you find the angle at which your highest target frequency is 6 dB below the on-axis level. For example, this might be at 40 degrees off-axis, which would provide a full 80 degrees of coverage for that target frequency.

Next, you must determine the listening ear height—the highest level being of most interest. For example, if you are designing a multipurpose room where the audience may be standing for some presentations and seated for others, design for the standing audience. The size of a loudspeaker coverage circle can be dramatically different when you factor in a low ceiling and a standing audience versus a higher ceiling and a seated audience, even with the same loudspeaker. See Figure 6-8 to help visualize your loudspeaker coverage calculation.

The formula for calculating the diameter (twice the radius) of the circle that represents the coverage area of a loudspeaker is as follows:

$$D = 2 * (H - h) * tan (C\angle / 2)$$

where:

- *D* is the diameter of the coverage area.
- *H* is the ceiling height.
- *h* is the height of the listeners' ears.
- *C∠* is the loudspeaker's angle of coverage in degrees.

For example, if your loudspeaker provides 80-degree coverage, your ceiling height is 12 feet, and the audience is seated with an ear level of 4 feet, the following would give you your coverage area:

$$D = 2 * (H - h) * tan (C\angle / 2)$$
$$D = 2 * (12 - 4) * tan (80/2)$$
$$D = 2 * (8) * tan\ 40$$

Figure 6-8
Calculating
loudspeaker
coverage

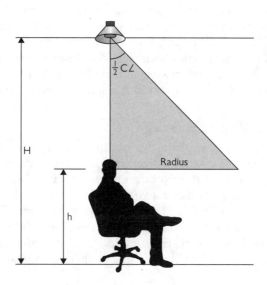

$D = 16 * 0.839$
$D = 13.4\ feet,\ or\ a\ radius\ of\ 6.7\ feet$

In metric, if your ceiling height is 3.7 meters and your seated audience has an ear level of 1.2 meters, the following would give you your coverage area:

$D = 2 * (H - h) * tan\ (C\angle\ /\ 2)$
$D = 2 * (3.7 - 1.2) * tan\ (80/2)$
$D = 2 * (2.5) * tan\ 40$
$D = 5 * 0.839$
$D = 4.2\ meters,\ or\ a\ radius\ of\ 2.1\ meters$

Distributed Layout Options

When distributing loudspeakers, the goal is to place them in a strategic pattern to create a uniform sound source. You might design a distributed loudspeaker system when it's not possible to implement a point-source system. For example, a certain ceiling height may be inadequate for a centralized, point-source speaker system because all listeners don't have a good line of hearing to a central speaker or cluster.

You can use a number of patterns for a distributed loudspeaker system. As the amount of background noise in a space increases or the reverberation becomes high, loudspeaker pattern control becomes very important. Ultimately, the pattern you choose may be a compromise between the ideal and the attainable. Often, the available space for loudspeakers—or the budget—is less than desirable.

Uniformity of coverage is the greatest difference between distributed loudspeaker patterns. Generally, the more dense the pattern, the more uniform the coverage will be, but density will increase interaction among loudspeakers.

Designers should strive to minimize coverage where it's not needed or where it can create problems. For example, you shouldn't place loudspeakers where the audio will strike a wall before reaching listeners' ears. This can cause uneven frequency response and phase cancellation at the listener position. Too much sound at the head of a conference table can cause feedback, so designers should make sure to implement a way to reduce levels or turn off offending loudspeakers in that area—or don't put them there in the first place.

Figure 6-9 shows six common arrangements for distributed ceiling systems.

Edge-to-Edge Coverage

Edge-to-edge coverage places the loudspeakers in such a way that the furthest extent of their acoustic energy comes together at listeners' ear level. There is no overlap with edge-to-edge patterns and therefore significant gaps. One loudspeaker's coverage area is simply adjacent to the next; therefore, the distance between loudspeakers in this layout is two times the radius of the loudspeaker's coverage pattern: $(D = 2 * r)$.

This approach is inexpensive and results in minimum interaction between loudspeakers within a room. But an edge-to-edge configuration may result in an uneven SPL with low spots in the corners of the coverage area. This is least favorable in a

Figure 6-9
Six common
coverage
configurations
for distributed
loudspeakers

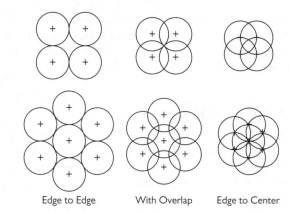

Edge to Edge   With Overlap   Edge to Center

business communication setting but may be appropriate for general paging or simple background music.

Maximum to minimum coverage variations for this configuration are around 4.35 dB. When deployed in a hexagon edge-to-edge pattern, coverage variations are around 5.4 dB.

Partial Overlap Coverage

Coverage patterns with minimal or *partial overlap* are among the most common methods of laying out distributed loudspeakers. In partial overlap systems, each loudspeaker's coverage pattern overlaps about 20 percent of the adjoining speaker's coverage pattern. Specifically, the minimum overlap in a square layout should be the radius of the loudspeaker polar pattern, multiplied by the square root of 2: ($D = r * 1.4$). In a hexagonal layout, that distance is the radius of the loudspeaker polar pattern, multiplied by the square root of 3: ($D = r * 1.7$).

Partial overlap provides good coverage at most frequencies, with 3 dB of variation, and ensures few or no "low" spots. However, this approach may not produce a perfectly even frequency response because dispersion patterns vary according to the frequency of the sound. In addition, partial overlap may also create some negative interaction between nearby loudspeakers.

Edge-to-Center Coverage

An *edge-to-center* layout, or 50 percent overlap, will provide excellent coverage at most frequencies (with 1.4 dB variation). However, this is a costly approach because it requires many loudspeakers and will likely provide more coverage than required. Additional power amplification may also be required, plus additional installation labor.

Such a large amount of pattern overlap may also result in some negative interaction with the sound from nearby loudspeakers, such as uneven frequency response. This is because a dense overlap pattern may create too much pattern overlap within the space. Adding additional acoustic energy into a space can also reduce intelligibility, which will make it difficult for listeners to understand presenters.

In 50 percent overlap systems, each loudspeaker's coverage pattern overlaps half of the adjoining coverage pattern, which can provide even SPL coverage. Whether using a square or hexagonal layout, the spacing distance between loudspeakers in a 50 percent overlap system equals the radius of the coverage circle: ($D = r$).

Ohm's Law Revisited

In the audiovisual industry, Ohm's law and the power equation are used to calculate and predict four properties of an electrical circuit: voltage, current, resistance, and power. They can help calculate the amount of current required to power the AV equipment within a rack or determine signal level at the end of a long cable run.

Ohm's law defines the electrical relationships in direct current (DC) circuits. It can also help approximate for alternating current (AC) circuits. AC circuit calculations are frequency dependent, and Ohm's law does not account for the influence of frequency in a circuit.

The results of Ohm's law or power equation calculations can be given to a professional electrician or an AV systems designer to incorporate into a design. Before we go further in our discussion of loudspeakers, you may want to review Ohm's law in Chapter 2.

 TIP The term *resistance* is used when you are working with DC circuits, such as those that are powered by a battery. In AC circuits, such as loudspeaker circuits, the term *impedance* is used in place of resistance. The calculations within this lesson will help you approximate impedance measurements for AC circuits.

Loudspeaker Impedance

Ohm's law helps AV professionals calculate the total electrical impedance of a group of loudspeakers that are connected by cabling. Impedance is the opposition to the flow of electrons in an AC circuit. Like a DC circuit, an AC circuit contains resistance, but it also includes forces that oppose changes in current (inductive reactance) and voltage (capacitive reactance). Impedance takes into account all three of these factors.

Impedance is frequency-dependent, measured in ohms, and symbolized by the letter Z. If you know how to calculate voltage, current, and resistance using Ohm's law, you can determine the impedance of loudspeakers as you're setting them up and wiring them together.

On the back of almost any loudspeaker, you will see a nominal impedance rating. It is an important specification for loudspeakers, power amplifiers, and the inputs and outputs of equipment. Most common loudspeakers have a nominal impedance rating of 4, 8, or even 16 ohms. You may even see some that have an impedance of 6 ohms.

Audio signals are AC waveforms; therefore, you express audio signals in terms of frequency (cycles per second). Because impedance in an AC circuit is frequency-dependent, as frequency changes, so does the impedance of the circuit.

You will need to determine the resulting impedance of the loudspeaker line as you're connecting and wiring together the loudspeakers.

Impedance and Amplifiers

How you wire loudspeakers together determines the circuit's impedance. You need to be certain that the power amplifier you choose to drive those speakers is rated for that load.

If you're wiring only a couple of loudspeakers, determining the circuit's impedance and checking the power amplifier's rating are simple processes. Amplifier makers specify a certain impedance for their products, which they expect to be connected to their amps' output terminals. Matching this impedance with the loudspeaker load maximizes the energy transfer from amplifier to loudspeaker to acoustic energy.

Wiring Loudspeakers

Before installing loudspeakers, one of your first tasks is to verify the expected impedance of the loudspeaker-system circuit. If you don't, you risk damaging equipment, personal injury, or simply poor system performance.

Ideally, you can complete this step before leaving for the jobsite. But sometimes, circumstances require you to make calculations in the field. If the expected impedance is not indicated on drawings or documentation, then you need to come up with it yourself. The formula you use depends on how the loudspeakers will be wired: in a series, in parallel, or a combination of the two. Let's examine each scenario.

TIP Parallel loudspeaker circuits are easier to install and troubleshoot than series circuits.

Loudspeakers Wired in a Series

When loudspeakers are wired in a series, each loudspeaker's coil is connected to the next loudspeaker in the series, in sequence. The power amplifier's positive output terminal connects to the positive terminal of the first loudspeaker. The first loudspeaker's negative terminal connects to the second loudspeaker's positive terminal. The second loudspeaker's negative terminal connects to the third loudspeaker's positive terminal, and so on. The last loudspeaker's negative terminal completes the circuit by connecting to the amplifier's negative terminal.

The formula for calculating the total impedance of a series loudspeaker circuit is as follows:

$$Z_T = Z_1 + Z_2 + Z_3 + \dots Z_N$$

Figure 6-10
Speakers wired in
a series

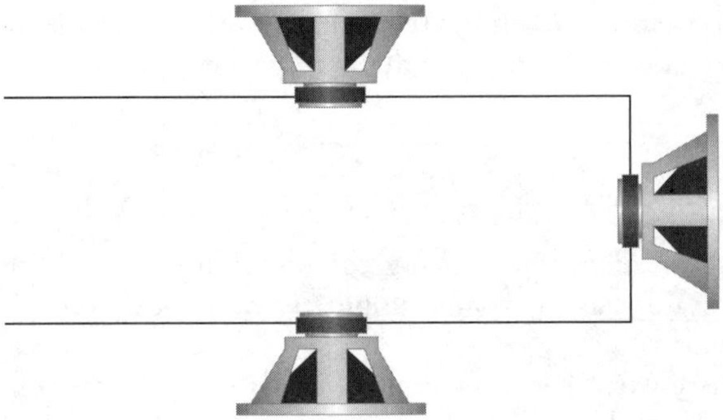

where:

- Z_T is the total impedance of the loudspeaker circuit.
- Z_N is the impedance of each loudspeaker.

Figure 6-10 shows three loudspeakers wired in series—plus to minus to plus to minus. If you want to calculate the total impedance of this loudspeaker circuit, you would simply add the impedances of the individual loudspeakers.

If each of these loudspeakers has a nominal impedance of 8 ohms, the total impedance is 24 ohms.

Loudspeakers Wired in Parallel, Same Impedance

Another method of connecting loudspeakers in a circuit is to wire them in parallel. This means that the positive output of the amplifier connects to every loudspeaker's positive terminal, and each loudspeaker's negative terminal connects to the amplifier's negative terminal.

Loudspeakers wired in parallel can have the same or different impedances. The formula for finding the circuit impedance for loudspeakers wired in parallel with the same impedance is as follows:

$$Z_T = Z_1 / N$$

where:

- Z_T is the total impedance of the loudspeaker system.
- Z_1 is the impedance of one loudspeaker.
- N is the quantity of loudspeakers in the circuit.

Figure 6-11 shows three loudspeakers wired in parallel. If all the loudspeakers have the same impedance, the impedance of the loudspeaker divided by the number of loudspeakers wired in parallel equals the impedance of the circuit. If you have three

Figure 6-11
Speakers wired in
parallel

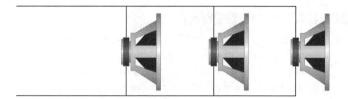

loudspeakers wired in parallel, each rated at 8 ohms, the circuit's impedance is 2.67 ohms (8 ohms/3).

Loudspeakers Wired in Parallel, Different Impedances

If loudspeakers wired in parallel have different impedances, you must use a different formula for finding the total impedance of the circuit. The formula for finding the circuit impedance for loudspeakers wired in parallel with differing impedance is as follows:

$$Z_T = \frac{1}{\frac{1}{Z_1} + \frac{1}{Z_2} + \frac{1}{Z_3} \cdots \frac{1}{Z_N}}$$

where:

- Z_T is the total impedance of the loudspeaker circuit.
- Z_{1-N} is the impedance of each individual loudspeaker.

If you have three loudspeakers wired in parallel, with the first rated at 4 ohms, the second rated at 8 ohms, and the third rated at 16 ohms, the circuit's impedance is 2.29 ohms, or $Z_T = 1/((1/4 \text{ ohms})+(1/8 \text{ ohms})+(1/16 \text{ ohms}))$.

Loudspeakers Wired in a Series and Parallel Combination

In a series/parallel loudspeaker circuit, groups of loudspeakers, called *branches,* are wired together in series. Typically, loudspeakers in the same branch have the same impedance. Each branch is connected to the positive and negative lines of the amplifier in parallel.

To calculate the total impedance of a series/parallel circuit, you must do the following:

- Calculate the total impedance of each branch using the series circuit impedance formula, as described earlier.
- Calculate the total circuit impedance of the circuit using the parallel circuit impedance formula, as described earlier.

NOTE It is rare to encounter loudspeakers wired in a series/parallel combination in the field. Although the idea of implementing a series/parallel combination would be to present a proper load to the output of the power amplifier, such systems are difficult to troubleshoot.

Measuring Impedance

Before electrically testing the loudspeaker circuit, refer to your impedance calculations and compare it to readings from an impedance meter. An impedance meter is a piece of test equipment used to measure the true impedance in an entire loudspeaker or loudspeaker circuit. Most are portable and battery operated, similar to a multimeter.

When working with large systems, check the line impedance often. Do not wait until all the loudspeakers are wired to find out that one is bad. As you install a group of loudspeakers, test it to make sure there are no problems before you install the next group. Be sure to write down the final measured impedance. This final measurement will be useful for future system service and maintenance.

Moreover, always check the system load prior to connecting the loudspeakers to an amplifier. Too little impedance on the output of the amplifier will cause the amplifier to drive too much current into the loudspeakers and may cause the amplifier to fail.

To measure impedance, take the following steps:

1. Disconnect the wires from the amplifier.
2. Calibrate the meter by doing the following (analog meters only):
   a. Connecting the test leads to the meter
   b. Using the three range buttons and selecting the scale that is appropriate for your expected value for greatest accuracy
   c. Holding the test leads together so the tips are touching, or pressing and holding the "zeroing" button
   d. Rotating the calibration knob until the reading indicates 0
3. Connect one lead to each of the wires on the first loudspeaker in the chain. Polarity is not important.
4. Observe the reading and compare it with the expected reading. It should be within a certain tolerance; otherwise, there may be problems.
5. Reconnect the loudspeaker wires and power on the amplifier.

Transformers

Voltage can be manipulated in an electrical circuit by using transformers. Transformers are common electrical devices that are used in power supplies, audio/video circuits, and loudspeaker systems.

Transformers work by placing two coils against each other, usually wound around a common piece of iron. A coil may also be known as a *winding*. Basic physics explains that alternating current, such as audio signals, flowing through a coil will create a magnetic field.

The input coil is often referred to as the *primary winding,* and the output coil is the *secondary winding.*

The current is transferred by electromagnetic induction, a process that transfers a current from an input to an output coil. This means that the current from the source, flowing through the first coil, creates a magnetic field.

Because the two coils in electromagnetic induction are not physically connected to each other, the input and output are "isolated" from each other. This is where the term *isolation transformer* comes from.

Transformers can increase or decrease the voltage in a circuit; they can also keep it the same. If the ratio of turns in the input and output coils are 1 to 1, the voltage output will be the same as the input, minus what is known as *insertion loss*.

You can use a 1:1 isolation transformer (Figure 6-12) to isolate one circuit (audio or video) from another to solve a ground loop problem, such as an audio hum or rolling lines in a video image.

If the ratio of turns in the input and output coils are 1 to 2, the voltage output will be doubled. This is known as a *step-up transformer*. A 1:2 step-up transformer (see Figure 6-13) has twice as many windings on the secondary side as it does on the primary side. With twice as many windings, twice as much voltage will be induced into the secondary side. In other words, the magnetic lines of force (flux) from the conductors on the primary side will cut across twice as many conductors on the secondary side. This means that the voltage will be induced across twice as many conductors as compared to the primary side.

If the ratio of turns in the input and output coils are 2 to 1, the voltage output will be lowered by 1/2. This is known as a *step-down transformer*.

A 2:1 step-down transformer (see Figure 6-14) has half as many windings on the secondary side as opposed to the number of windings on the primary side. Even though the voltage will be carried on half as many windings, the power will be equal on both sides, minus a small amount of insertion loss. Instead, either the voltage will increase or the current will decrease.

Figure 6-12
A 1:1 transformer

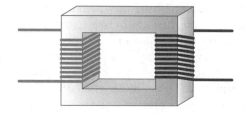

Figure 6-13
A 1:2 step-up
transformer

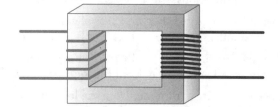

Figure 6-14
A 2:1 step-down
transformer

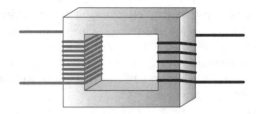

Loudspeaker Taps

Most transformers have multiple wires on the primary side that allow you to adjust the voltage level to each loudspeaker. These wires are commonly referred to as *taps*. Either the transformer manufacturer will code these wires in some way and provide a chart for their values or you can write the values on the wires themselves. They may also provide a selectable switch.

You can select taps based on the amount of power in watts or impedance steps they'll deliver to the loudspeaker. Just keep in mind, the taps should comply with the designer's intention for loudspeaker performance.

Many transformer manufacturers pre-strip the tap wires for termination. When terminating, be sure that the wires from the amplifier are connected to the proper tap points, as indicated on the designer's drawings. The consequences of connecting the wrong wire include exceeding the capability of the amplifier or decreasing the signal to a barely audible level.

Specifying a Power Amplifier

Once loudspeaker locations have been determined, the next step is to calculate how much power is needed at the loudspeaker to provide adequate SPL at the listener location. This calculation would also include the necessary headroom appropriate to the application. Headroom is the difference in dB SPL between the peak and average-level performance of an audio system. For a speech application, the recommended value is 10 dB; for program audio, it's as much as 20 dB.

To determine the power required at the loudspeaker, you need to know the following:

- The sound pressure level required from the sound system at the listener position. For speech applications, this is typically 70 dB SPL.

- The headroom required. For speech applications, 10 dB is considered adequate. For music applications, as much as 20 dB or more may be required.

- Loudspeaker sensitivity. Typically this will be stated as SPL in decibels expected at a distance of 1 meter away from the loudspeaker with 1 watt applied.

- Distance to the farthest listener from the loudspeaker.

Once you have this information, you can calculate the amount of power needed at the loudspeaker, also known as the electrical power required (EPR), or wattage at the loudspeaker. You calculate EPR using this formula:

$$EPR = 10^{\wedge\left(\dfrac{\left[L_p + H - L_s(20\,Log(D_2/D_r))\right]}{10}\right)} * W_{ref}$$

where:

- *EPR* is the amount of electrical power required at the loudspeaker.
- L_p is the SPL required at distance D_2.
- *H* is the headroom required.
- L_s is the loudspeaker sensitivity reference, usually 3.28 feet (1 m).
- D_2 is the distance from the loudspeaker to the farthest listener.
- D_r is the distance reference value.
- W_{ref} is the wattage reference value; assume a W_{ref} of 1, unless otherwise noted.

Headroom Requirements

A sound reinforcement system needs to be loud enough for the listeners to hear it. When choosing a loudspeaker, you must verify that the loudspeaker is sensitive enough to boost the sound signal with enough headroom.

System headroom is the difference between the audio system's typical operation level and the maximum level the system can attain. If a sound system usually operates at +1 dBV but could operate as high as +20 dBV, then it has 19 dB of headroom. It is important to have enough headroom to handle momentary performance boosts.

As noted earlier, for a speech-only sound reinforcement system, 10 dB of headroom is appropriate. For a music reinforcement system, as much as 20 dB of headroom is needed to avoid clipping musical peaks.

Loudspeaker Sensitivity

Like microphones, loudspeakers are rated based on their ability to convert one energy form into another. This rating is called a *sensitivity specification,* and it defines the loudspeaker's acoustic output signal level, given a reference input level. Put another way, sensitivity defines how efficiently a loudspeaker transduces—or converts—electrical energy into acoustic energy.

Given the same reference electrical input level into two different loudspeakers, a more sensitive loudspeaker would provide a higher acoustical energy output than a less sensitive loudspeaker.

Loudspeakers vary quite a bit when it comes to efficiency. Does this mean that lower-sensitivity loudspeakers are of lesser quality? Not at all. Like microphones, loudspeakers are designed and chosen to meet specific uses.

Power Amplifiers

Now that you know how many watts are needed at the listener position, you can specify the power amplifier. A power amplifier boosts the audio signal enough to move the loudspeakers.

Power amplifiers are designed to be connected to a specific load (impedance)—either a low-impedance load (typically 2 to 8 ohms) or a high-impedance load, such as with a distributed or constant-voltage loudspeaker system. The power amplifier's specifications should tell you what kind of impedance load it can be connected to. Some power amplifiers have a switch that allows them to connect to various impedance loads. Other power amplifiers may require an internal or external transformer to function with a 70 V or 100 V load.

 TIP The term *constant voltage* implies that an amplifier configured for a 70 V line, for example, will never output more than 70 V regardless of the number of loudspeakers connected to the output of the power amplifier. However, the actual number of loudspeakers you can connect will be limited by the power (watts) available from the power amplifier.

Specifying a Power Amplifier for Direct-Connection Audio

To specify a power amplifier for direct connection audio, follow these steps:

1. Determine the SPL at the listener position.
2. Add 10 dB for voice or 20 dB for music.
3. Find the loss over distance in dB by taking the 20log of the dB-SPL at the listener position (D_2) divided by the loudspeaker's sensitivity in dB-SPL (D_r). Written another way, this is $20\log(D_2/D_r)$.
4. Determine the power (watts) required at the loudspeaker using the EPR formula.
5. Round the result up to an amplifier value that can be readily purchased.

Specifying a Power Amplifier for Distributed Audio

This is a process for specifying a power amplifier for a distributed audio system. In this type of audio system, you need to specify your tap settings before you can determine your amplifier need.

1. Determine SPL at the listener position.
2. Add 10 dB for voice or 20 dB for music.
3. Find the loss over distance in dB by taking the 20log of the dB-SPL at the listener position (D_2) divided by the loudspeaker's sensitivity in dB-SPL (D_r). Written another way, this is $20\log(D_2/D_r)$.

4. Determine the power (watts) required at the loudspeaker using the EPR formula.

5. Select the appropriate tap value for the loudspeaker based on watts required.

6. Repeat steps 1–5 for each loudspeaker.

7. Sum the tap settings from all loudspeakers.

8. Increase the total tap settings by a factor of 1.5.

9. Round the result up to an amplifier value that can be readily purchased.

Microphones

If you're designing an audio system, chances are it will include microphones. Clients use microphones to be heard—in presentations, conferences, or performances. In this section, you will learn about the special qualities of microphones and how they factor into AV systems. We'll start by discussing the different types of microphones you might specify in a design.

Handheld Microphones

Handheld microphones are used mainly for speech or singing. Because they're constantly moving, handheld microphones include internal shock-mounting to reduce handling noise. Handheld microphones can be held in the hand or mounted on a lectern or stand for hands-free operation.

Instrument, Lavalier, and Head Microphones

Lavalier and head microphones are worn by users. A lavalier (also called a *lav* or *lapel* microphone) is attached directly to clothing, such as a necktie or lapel (pictured in the following illustration).

A head microphone (also called a *headmic*), is a microphone that is attached to a small, thin boom and fitted around the ear (on the right).

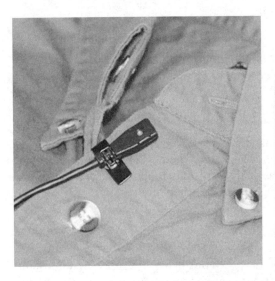

Because size, appearance, and color are key considerations for these types of microphones, lavaliers and headmics are often electret microphones, a type of condenser microphone that can be powered with small batteries. We will discuss electret microphones later in this chapter. Lavaliers and head mics are usually worn by presenters and commonly used in television and theater productions.

Boundary and Gooseneck Microphones

Boundary microphones (sometimes known as *pressure-zone microphones* [PZMs]) are mounted directly against a hard surface, such as a conference table, wall, or ceiling. They rely on reflected sound from the surrounding surface and are also called *surface-mount microphones*. Keep in mind that the acoustically reflective properties of the mounting surface affect the microphones' performance.

Although they can be much less obtrusive in a conference table than a gooseneck mic, boundary microphones may be subject to papers accidently being placed over them, laptop fans blowing on them, and more.

Mounting a microphone on a ceiling typically yields the poorest performance because the sound source is much farther away from the intended source and much closer to other noise sources, such as ceiling-mounted projectors, heating, ventilation, and air conditioning (HVAC) diffusers, and other devices.

Gooseneck microphones (as seen in the following illustration) are often used on lecterns and conference tables. Such microphones are attached to flexible or bendable stems, which come in varying lengths.

Shock mounts are available to isolate the microphone from table or lectern vibrations.

On a conference table, although goosenecks generally get the microphone closer to the source than a boundary microphone, they can create an undesirable appearance in the space or, in the case of videoconferencing, on camera. (Picture what's sometimes called a *gooseneck farm*.)

Shotgun Microphones

Shotgun microphones are named for their physical shape, as well as their long and narrow polar pattern. A shotgun microphone is a long, cylindrical, highly sensitive, unidirectional microphone used to pick up sound from a great distance.

Most often used in film, television, and field production work, a shotgun microphone can be attached to a long pole called a *fish pole* or *studio boom*. The boom is often used by a boom operator (as seen in the following illustration) or fitted to the top of a camera.

Microphone Construction

Microphones come in two main versions, based on construction: dynamic and condenser. A dynamic microphone is a pressure-sensitive microphone with a moving-coil design that transduces sound into electricity using electromagnetic principles.

Dynamic microphones are economical, durable, and capable of handling high sound pressure levels. Unlike condenser microphones, they don't require a source of power, often called *phantom power*.

 NOTE Phantom power is the remote power required to power a microphone. It typically ranges from 12 to 48 volts DC. It is often available from an audio mixer and may be switched on or off at each individual microphone input. If phantom power is not available from the audio mixer, separate phantom power supplies may be used.

Condenser microphones transduce sound into electricity using electrostatic principles. Condenser microphones are generally sensitive, which means you'll get more electrical signal and higher sound quality from a condenser microphone than from a dynamic microphone. They are excellent for boardrooms or classrooms where you need to pick up quieter signals, such as a person talking.

Condensers aren't as durable as dynamic microphones, however, and they *do* require phantom power.

NOTE An electret microphone is a type of condenser microphone. It gets its name from the prepolarized material—electret—applied to the microphone's diaphragm or backplate. This provides a permanent, fixed charge, which eliminates the need for the higher voltage required for powering the typical condenser microphone and allows the electret microphone to be powered using small batteries, as well as the normal phantom power. Electrets are small, lending themselves to a wide variety of uses and quality levels.

Microphone Polar Response

One of the characteristics to consider when selecting a microphone is its polar response or pickup pattern. The pickup pattern describes the microphone's directional capabilities—its ability to pick up the desired sound from a certain direction while rejecting unwanted sounds from other directions.

Pickup patterns are defined by the directions in which the microphone is most sensitive. These patterns help you determine which microphone type to use for a given purpose.

There will be occasions when you want a microphone to pick up sound from all directions (such as an interview), and there will be occasions when you do not want a microphone to pick up sounds from nearby sources surrounding it (such as people talking or papers rustling). The pickup pattern is also known as the *polar pattern*, or the microphone's directionality.

Different types of pickup patterns include the following:

- **Omnidirectional** Sound pickup is uniform in all directions.
- **Cardioid (unidirectional)** Pickup is from the front of the microphone only (one direction) in a cardioid pattern. It rejects sounds coming from the side but mostly rejects sound from the rear of the microphone. The term *cardioid* refers to the heart-shaped polar plot.
- **Hypercardioid** A variant of cardioid. It's more directional than a regular cardioid mic because it rejects more sound from the sides. The trade-off is that it will pick up some sound from directly behind the microphone.
- **Supercardioid** Provides better directionality than hypercardioid, with less rear pickup.
- **Bidirectional** Pickup is equal in opposite directions with little or no pickup from the sides. This is sometimes also referred to as a *figure-eight* pattern, referring to the shape of its polar plot.

Polar Plot

The polar plot is a graphical representation of a microphone's directionality and electrical response characteristics (see Figure 6-15).

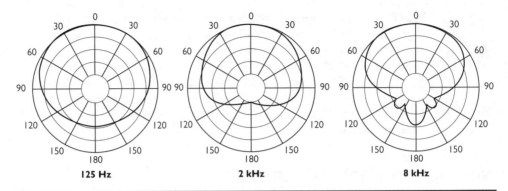

Figure 6-15 Polar plots of one microphone at 125 Hz, 2 kHz, and 8 kHz

Although a frequency-response graph shows the level of decibels at a given frequency, the polar plot shows the level of decibels by angle, or the pickup pattern of the microphone. Typically, microphone specifications will include several polar plots, each showing the pickup pattern at a different frequency.

Imagine a microphone in the center of the plot, pointing straight at 0 degrees. If you stood at the 0-degree point, you'd be standing right in front of the microphone. At the 180-degree point on the plot, you would be directly behind the microphone.

The polar plot shows the angles from which the microphone picks up and transduces sound at the highest voltage. It extends farthest toward the 0-degree point, which shows that the microphone is best at detecting sounds coming from directly in front of it. To the left and right of the 0-degree mark, the curve falls away. This means as you move farther to the left or right of this microphone, it "hears" you a little less well. In Figure 6-15, the microphone picks up no sound at all from directly behind at 2 kHz, though it picks up some sound from behind at 125 Hz and 8 kHz.

Polar plots help you select and position a microphone. For example, say you need a microphone to pick up audio in a conference room. You want people on all sides of the table to be heard, so you would choose a mic whose polar pattern displays even pickup in all directions in the frequency range of the human voice.

The Right Mic for the Job

Have you ever handed a presenter a lavalier microphone and watched him pin it to his lapel—pointing sideways? If the microphone had an omnidirectional pickup pattern, that's probably OK. However, if the pickup pattern is directional, he just pointed it 90 degrees away from its optimum position.

As one InfoComm University expert puts it, "I always ask, 'Who's going to be pinning the microphone to the presenter? Does that person know how to use a directional mic?' If a sound technician is going to pin the lav to the presenter, I'll give the customer a directional mic. If the presenter's going to pin it to him or herself, I'll probably use an omni."

Microphone Frequency Response

The frequency-response specification is an important measure of a microphone's performance. It defines the microphone's electrical output level over the audible frequency spectrum, which in turn helps to determine how a microphone "sounds."

Frequency response is a way of expressing a device's amplitude response versus frequency characteristic, as shown in Figure 6-16. A frequency response is usually presented as a graph or plot of a device's output on the vertical axis versus the frequency on the horizontal axis.

A microphone's frequency response gives the range of frequencies, from lowest to highest, that the microphone can transduce. It is often shown as a plot on a two-dimensional frequency response graph. A microphone's frequency response graph shows the voltage of its output signal relative to the frequency of the sounds it picks up.

With directional microphones, the overall frequency response will be best directly into the front of the microphone. As you move off-axis from the front of the microphone, not only will the sound be reduced, but the frequency response will change.

Microphone Signal Levels

A microphone, regardless of the type, produces a signal level called *mic level*. Mic level is a low-level signal—only a few millivolts (abbreviated as mV to express one-thousandth of a volt). Table 6-2 shows the relative voltages of different signal levels.

Because mic level operates at only a few millivolts, it is prone to interference. A microphone preamplifier amplifies the mic level signal to line level for routing and processing. Line level is the strength of a regular audio signal and is used for all routing and processing between components. In a professional audio system, line level is about 1.23 volts (+4 dBu); consumer line level is 0.316 V (–10 dBV). When you see an RCA or phono connector, it often indicates a consumer-level signal.

Once the audio system has routed and processed the signal, it is sent to the power amplifier for final amplification up to loudspeaker level. The loudspeaker takes that amplified electrical signal and transduces the electrical energy into acoustical energy (see Figure 6-17).

Figure 6-16
Microphone
frequency
response

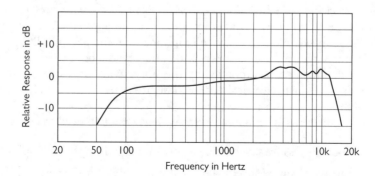

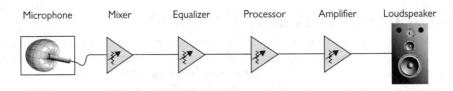

Figure 6-17   Mic level to line level to loudspeaker level

Table 6-2	Description	Voltage Level
Comparing Signal Levels	Mic level	0.001 to 0.003 volts (-60 to -50 dBu)
	Line level (professional)	1.23 volts (+4 dBV)
	Line level (consumer)	0.316 volts (-10 dBV)
	Loudspeaker level	4 to < ~100 volts

Microphone Sensitivity

Another important performance criterion that characterizes a microphone is its sensitivity specification. Sensitivity defines how efficiently a microphone converts acoustic energy into electrical energy. It is expressed as decibels of voltage per pascal of sound pressure (dBV/PA).

For example, a microphone may have a sensitivity specification that reads as follows: *–54.5 dBV/PA (1.85 mV) 1 Pa = 94 dB SPL.* This means that with a reference level of 94 dB SPL into the microphone, it will produce a voltage level of –54.5 dBV (0.00185 V) out.

One pascal is equal to 94 dB SPL. If a microphone with the previous specification receives less than 94 decibels of sound pressure, it will output less than –54.5 dBV. Less acoustical energy in will result in less electrical energy out.

If you expose two different microphones to an identical sound input level, a more sensitive microphone provides a higher electrical output than a less sensitive microphone. Condenser microphones are usually more sensitive than dynamic microphones.

Does this mean that lower-sensitivity microphones mean lesser quality? Not at all. Microphones are designed and chosen for specific uses. A professional singer using a microphone up close can produce a high SPL. In contrast, a presenter speaking behind a lectern and a foot or two away from the microphone produces much less sound pressure. The singer needs a less sensitive microphone than the person talking.

For the singer, a dynamic microphone may be the best choice because it will typically handle the higher SPL produced by the singer without distortion while still providing more than adequate electrical output. The presenter would benefit from a more sensitive microphone, such as a condenser mic.

When determining microphone sensitivity, you will need to consider three factors.

- **Sound pressure level**   The acoustic energy is at the microphone.
- **Electrical signal level**   The goal is to have a line-level signal after the preamplification.

- **Matching levels** Can the signal level from the microphone/preamp combination be amplified to the line-level signal that the audio system (mixer) requires?

Microphone Pre-Amp Gain

Let's say you need to choose a microphone for a new auditorium. Your sound source is a presenter located 2 feet (609.6 mm) away from the microphone, with a measured SPL of 72 dB. To route and process that signal, you need to amplify the microphone-level signal to line level (0 dBu). Most microphone preamplifiers will provide around 60 dB of amplification.

You have a choice between two microphones (remember, 1 Pascal = 94 dB SPL).

- Dynamic Microphone A, with an equivalent voltage specification of –54.5 dBV /Pa (1.85 mV)

- Condenser Microphone B, with an equivalent voltage specification of –35.0 dBV /Pa (17.8 mV)

In this scenario, your microphone specification sheets tell you that if you put 94 dB SPL into each microphone, −54.5 dBV and −35.0 dBV will be produced, respectively. You need to select a microphone that will provide an adequate signal level for the application. To do this, you need to know what the required microphone pre-amp gain is for each microphone. Refer to Figure 6-18 for the formula.

To calculate the pre-amp gain for your microphones, follow these steps:

1. Determine the level (in dB SPL) that is measured with an SPL meter at the microphone position. Record this at position 1.

2. Determine your microphone reference level (dB SPL). You will find this number on your microphone specification sheets. Record this at position 2.

3. Determine the microphone sensitivity value (dBV). This is the negative number indicated on the specification sheet. Record this at position 3.

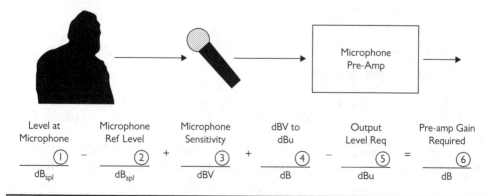

Figure 6-18 Microphone pre-amp gain formula

4. Convert the dBV value from step 3 to dBu. The formula for this is *20log(dBu/dBV)* = *20log(1/0.77) = 2.2 dB*. Record this value at position 4.

5. Record the output level required at position 5. This is generally 0 dBu or +4 dBu.

6. Now do the match: The pre-amp gain required is position 1 − 2 + 3 + 4 − 5.

In this example, the pre-amp gain required for Dynamic Microphone A is −74.29 dBu. The pre-amp gain required for Condenser Microphone B is −54.79 dBu.

Assuming you have a 60 dB gain in your microphone pre-amp, Dynamic Microphone A is not sensitive enough for this application. The closer you can get to 0 dBu, the better the microphone will be for the application. You need 83.5 dB, but you have only 74.29 dB gain, leaving you 9.21 dB short.

Does this make Dynamic Microphone A a bad mic? No. It is designed for a different application—speaking or singing at a much closer range than 2 feet (610 mm) and with much more acoustic input. In this case, the mixer's preamplifier would normally be more than adequate to amplify Dynamic Microphone A's signal to line level.

With a pre-amp gain of −54.79 dBu, Condenser Microphone B is sensitive enough for this application. The combination of the more sensitive microphone and the gain available from the microphone preamplifier in the mixer can take the mic level signal to the 60 dBu level needed for signal routing and processing.

Microphone Mixing and Routing

Aside from microphones amplified to line level, your audio system will include other sources, originating at line level. For professional audio line sources, little, if any, amplification will be required for routing and processing. Consumer line level may require some amplification.

An automatic microphone mixer is meant to control the number of open microphones (NOM) to the loudspeaker. The user can set NOM on the mixer, but generally it's limited to one. The following are some of the settings where using an auto mixer would be ideal:

- Conference rooms
- Courtrooms
- Meeting spaces
- Live events with handheld microphones

In these settings, you have multiple people speaking and need a way to control the different line sources. The big question is, "How many people need to talk at any one time?"

If there are multiple people who need to speak, you can assign a NOM that reflects that number. However, keep in mind that the number of open microphones affects the chances of feedback in the system. The fewer microphones open, the fewer chances of feedback or extraneous noise coming through the loudspeaker.

There are two ways an auto mixer can limit the NOM in a design: gated or gain sharing. With *gated sharing,* each channel is set to an adjustable sound threshold that a microphone needs to surpass to be turned on. If it falls below that threshold, it is muted. The threshold must be set high enough to keep the channel from being opened by background noise yet low enough to open when someone is speaking. This creates a binary effect—each microphone is either on or off. But there is a chance that the system can't pick up the first-spoken syllables of a low talker if not set correctly and varying levels from conference participants (soft to loud) can lead to choppy audio.

With *gain sharing,* the available gain is shared among all of the channels, and microphones with more signal get more gain. (Those with less receive less.) Because all the microphones are splitting gain depending on activity, pick up is gradual, resulting in smoother operation and greater sophistication than a gated design.

Microphone Placement: A Conference Table

Let's say you need to place microphones around a conference table. Here are two possible options:

- Six cardioid mics—one microphone per every two participants, with one each for the participants at the ends of the table (see Figure 6-19).

- Two omnidirectional mics (see Figure 6-20). Although two omnimicrophones would seem to cover the participants, you must also consider the environment. Omnidirectional mics are equally sensitive to sounds coming from all directions, so ask yourself, for example, "Will there be a projector above the table?" and "How loud will background noise from the HVAC system be?"

Figure 6-19

A conference table with a cardioid microphone coverage pattern

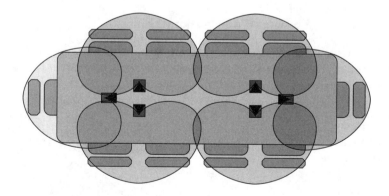

Figure 6-20
A conference table with an ominidirectional microphone coverage pattern

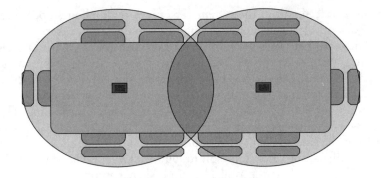

Microphone Placement: The 3:1 Rule

When using multiple microphones, consider how the sound from a presenter will reach the microphones.

In Figure 6-21, each person has been given their own microphone. When a presenter speaks, their voice is picked up by three microphones. The microphone directly in front picks up the sound louder than the off-axis microphones do. In addition, because they are farther away, the sound that these two microphones pick up may be out of phase.

Let's say the mics are separated by 1 foot and are 1 foot away from the person talking. The front mic picks up the talker at 65 dB SPL. What are the two mics picking up?

The outside mics are this far away:

$$C = \sqrt{(1^2 + 1^2)}$$
$$C = \sqrt{(1 + 1)}$$
$$C = \sqrt{2}$$
$$C = 1.41$$

The loss over distance is as follows:

$$dB = 20\log(1.41/1)$$
$$dB = 2.98 \text{ or about 3 dB less (not very much)}$$

In an analog mixer, the three microphones would be "mixed" together. The phase differences between the microphones create a comb-filter effect in the sound's frequency response, which gives it a thin, hollow tone quality.

Figure 6-21
Each mic is 1 foot away from one presenter and 1 foot away from all other mics.

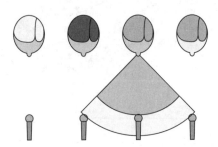

Figure 6-22
Each mic is 3 feet
away from each
other and 1 foot
away from one
presenter.

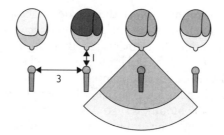

In Figure 6-22, the microphones are separated at a greater distance, this time at a ratio of 3:1. That is, the distance between each microphone is three times the distance between the microphone and a presenter.

By separating the microphones using the 3:1 rule, the outside microphones are this far away:

$$C = \sqrt{(12 + 32)}$$
$$C = \sqrt{(1 + 9)}$$
$$C = \sqrt{(10)}$$
$$C = 3.16$$

The loss over distance is as follows:

$$dB = 20\log(3.16/1)$$
$$dD = 9.48 \text{ or about 10 dB less, which sounds half as loud}$$

When the three microphones are mixed together in an analog mixer, the phase differences between the microphones will still affect the sound. However, the levels being mixed are greatly reduced because of the distance, which makes the comb filtering less noticeable.

NOTE   In signal processing, a comb filter adds a delayed version of a signal to itself, causing constructive and destructive interference. The frequency response of a comb filter consists of a series of regularly spaced spikes, giving the appearance of a comb.

Reinforcing a Presenter

If you need to mic only one specific person, you have a few options for reinforcing their voice.

Wireless lavalier microphones are effective for film or training presentations where the microphone needs to be "invisible." The best position for a wireless lavaliere will be in the center of the chest, just below the hollow of the throat. You want to get the microphone as close to the presenter's mouth as possible, but take care to avoid any positions that might cause unwanted contact.

An ear-worn microphone is another hidden microphone solution. Ear microphones should be placed about a quarter-inch (10 mm) away from the corner of the performer's mouth. Do not position the element directly in front of the mouth because it will pick up "plosives" (*P*s, *D*s, and *T*s) and breath sounds. Place the element so it does not directly contact or rub the cheek of the presenter.

If an ear microphone is not available, a lavalier placed along the center of the chest, as close as possible to the mouth, is best. Ask the presenter to tilt their chin down as low to the chest as they possibly can and place the microphone just below that point.

Handheld microphones will always give better gain before feedback when held as close to the mouth as possible. Advise presenters to hold the mic just below their chin.

 TIP   If you need to place microphones at a lectern, only one microphone should be active. Additional microphones won't give you more gain and should be used only for backup or redundancy. If you need more gain, try using a more sensitive microphone. This solution is cheaper and won't introduce comb filtering issues.

Microphones and Clothing

When reinforcing (micing) a presenter, you need to consider the presenter's clothing. Here are some examples:

- If the presenter is wearing a suit, you may be able to hide the microphone inside the knot of a tie.

- Avoid placing the microphone near silk. Silk blouses and ties can sound scratchy if they move against the microphone.

- There are protective mounts that can be taped to the performer's chest and prevent rustling noises from clothing.

- If your project involves a wardrobe manager, working closely with that person may make microphone placement easier.

Polar Plots for Reinforcing a Presenter

When reinforcing a presenter with a lavalier microphone, you need to consider microphone placement and polar patterns. A lavalier microphone with a cardioid polar pattern will capture the presenter's voice without capturing background noise from other directions (see Figure 6-23).

This directional microphone is an excellent choice, but only if you know that the end users are all trained in how to place the microphone. For example, what if the user places the cardioid microphone off-center, on their lapel? What if they place the microphone upside down?

Instead of specifying a microphone with a cardioid polar pattern, consider specifying one with an omnidirectional polar pattern. An omnidirectional microphone will pick up the presenter's voice, even if it is placed off-center or upside down (see Figure 6-24).

Figure 6-23
Proper
placement of a
cardioid lavalier
microphone

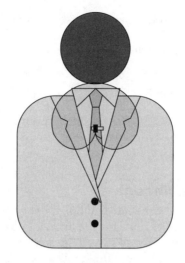

Figure 6-24
Proper
placement of an
omnidirectional
lavalier
microphone

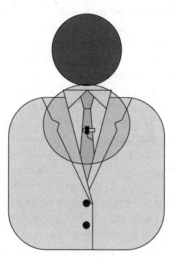

Audio System Quality

Now that you've learned how humans perceive sound and how sound is measured, you need to ensure the quality of the audio system and how it functions in the space. For one thing, you need to determine whether the audio system will be stable by comparing a couple of calculations, namely, potential acoustic gain and needed acoustic gain. You also need to check your sound-reinforcement design to make sure it will be effective based on the client's audio system needs.

Sound reinforcement is the combination of microphones, audio mixers, signal processors, power amplifiers, and loudspeakers that are used to electronically amplify and distribute sound.

To work properly, a sound system must accomplish three things.

- It must be loud enough.
- It must be intelligible.
- It must remain stable.

Before we delve into PAG-NAG equations and a fundamental goal of audio system design—eliminating nasty feedback—let's discuss further these three measures of audio system quality.

It Must Be Loud Enough

Can the listener hear the intended audio? If the answer is no, you have a problem. This may be a simple matter of changing the listener or loudspeaker location or increasing the volume. It may also be a sign of a much greater issue, such as unfriendly acoustics.

"Loud enough" depends on the application. Although sound systems encompass everything from conference rooms to rock 'n' roll concerts, for now, at least, we'll focus on the context of a typical boardroom, conference room, or lecture hall.

For each audio system, you need a target sound pressure level. For a typical speech reinforcement system, that level is around 60 to 65 dB SPL. That is the speech level of a human about 2 feet (0.6 meters) away. Through the audio system you're designing, your goal is to replicate that conversational level with the audience. One key consideration in achieving this is the signal-to-noise (S/N) ratio and its effect on audio loudness.

Signal-to-noise ratio is the ratio, measured in decibels, between the audio (or video) signal and the noise accompanying the signal. In your design, look for an acoustic signal-to-noise (S/N) ratio of 25 dB. This means you should have 25 dB between the level of the sound system, your signal, and the level of the room's background noise level.

Using a 25 dB S/N ratio, you can arrive at the required loudness of the audio system two different ways. First, imagine you've measured a background noise level of 55 dB SPL. Your system target level then needs to be 25 dB above that—80 dB SPL. But 80 dB SPL would be a loud level for conversation.

Coming at it from a different direction, start with your target. Say you want to achieve 65 dB SPL. Your background noise level should be 25 dB less than that—40 dB SPL. Think of this as the signal-to-noise level of the acoustic environment and design your acoustic space with that in mind.

NOTE You may have heard that an audio system should have a 60 dB S/N ratio. This is the *electronic* S/N ratio of the electronic components. The signal level in the system should be at least 60 dB above the combined noise inherent in all the electronics in the signal path. In today's systems, a properly adjusted system should have no problem meeting a minimum 60 dB S/N ratio. But don't get the electronic S/N ratio of 60 dB confused with the *acoustic* S/N ratio of 25 dB.

It Must Be Intelligible

Intelligibility describes an audio system's ability to produce a meaningful reproduction of sound. For example, an intelligible sound-reinforcement system can reproduce accurately the vowels and consonants of a source, which helps listeners identify words and sentence structure, giving the sound meaning.

In audio system design, intelligibility deals with the intensity and time arrival of the indirect sound. Reflected and reverberated sound energy arrives at the listener's ear after direct sound, which comes directly from the loudspeaker. Late reflections sound like distinct echoes, and excessive reverberation masks intelligible speech.

Whether in amplified or unamplified speech presentation, the requirements of speech intelligibility are very much the same.

- **Speech loudness level**   Average speech levels should be in the 60 to 65 dB range, if people with normal hearing are to understand it without effort. Under noisy conditions, the speech level should be raised accordingly.

- **Speech signal-to-noise ratio**   For ease in listening, average speech levels should be at least 25 dB higher than the prevailing noise level. However, at elevated speech levels, in noisy environments, a somewhat lesser speech-to-noise ratio is possible. Typically, a 15 dB S/N ratio may suffice in situations where considerable noise is expected, such as live sports where there are spectators.

Normal face-to-face speech communication is about 60 to 65 dB SPL, but most speech reinforcement systems operate between 70 and 75 dB SPL. If the level of amplified speech increases beyond that range, to about 85 to 90 dB SPL, overall intelligibility won't increase much, and most listeners will complain of excessive levels. Any louder, and intelligibility will diminish because listeners will feel oppressed by the high levels.

The direct-to-reflected sound ratio is a measure of the different energy in a space. It takes the level of direct sound—from source to listener—and compares it to the level of reflected sound, all of which arrives at the listener by an indirect pathway and determines the intelligibility.

Whether reflected sound is a problem or not comes down to two things.

- How late did it arrive at the listener in relation to the direct sound?
- At what energy level did that reflection arrive at the listener?

If the reflection arrives at the listener 50 to 80 milliseconds or later than the direct sound and at a sufficient energy level, it is considered an echo, and it adversely affects intelligibility.

TIP   Harmonic distortion can also diminish audio quality. Harmonics are multiples of a fundamental frequency, and harmonic distortion describes energy that wasn't there originally. Harmonic distortion can occur in both an audio system's electronic components and loudspeakers, which makes it one of the most common types of distortion. Analyzing all the harmonics together and comparing them to the fundamental frequency gives you a measure of total harmonic distortion (THD). The lower the THD percentage, the better the audio signal quality.

It Must Remain Stable

Stability applies to audio systems that employ microphones in the same space. Can the client turn up the volume loud enough to be heard without causing feedback? If someone must make constant adjustments to eliminate feedback, chances are the system wasn't designed properly.

To determine whether an audio system is stable, a designer calculates *gain before feedback*—how loud the loudspeakers get before the microphones pick them up. Gain before feedback is frequently referred to as *potential acoustic gain,* which you will learn about later in this chapter.

Gain before feedback is largely a design issue. It has to do with distance relationships between the source (such as a presenter) and the microphone, the microphone and the loudspeakers, and the loudspeakers and the listeners.

The designer must also determine the amount of gain—or amplification—required from the audio system to produce an adequate sound level. How loud do the loudspeakers need to be for listeners to hear the intended audio? This is known as *needed acoustic gain,* which you will also learn about later.

By comparing PAG to NAG, you can determine whether a system will be stable. If the system exhibits more potential acoustic gain than needed acoustic gain, it will be stable. But if its needs exceed its potential, either the client won't be able to turn the volume up loud enough or feedback may occur.

 TIP　You can perform calculations that help predict whether an audio system will create feedback, but as general rules, loudspeakers should be as close to listeners and as far from microphones as possible, and microphones should be as close to the presenter as possible.

PAG/NAG

As you learned earlier, the quality of an audio system can be summed up by three easily understood concepts: Is the audio loud enough? Can the audio be understood? Does the audio system operate in a stable manner?

To reiterate, audio system stability refers to the system's ability to amplify sound from a microphone without feedback or distortion. Proper equipment selection and placement are significant contributors to system stability (think acoustic treatment, equalization, feedback suppression, and mix-minus), but controlling acoustic gain is also an important method. A sufficient PAG/NAG ratio will minimize the potential for feedback.

NAG is the gain the audio system requires to achieve an equivalent acoustic level at the farthest listener equal to what the nearest listener would hear without sound reinforcement. It tells the designer how much you need to increase the amplitude of a sound wave on a microphone for it to be equivalent to some closer location, where no amplification would be required. Again, NAG is relevant only for systems incorporating microphones that are being reinforced in the same space.

Before you can solve for NAG, you need to understand *equivalent acoustic distance* (EAD). EAD is the farthest distance one can go from the source without needing sound amplification or reinforcement to maintain good speech intelligibility. It is a design parameter dependent on the level of the presenter and the noise level in the room. A simple illustration of this principle is two people talking as one person backs away until they can no longer communicate clearly. The farthest distance at which they can still communicate clearly is the EAD.

For your calculations, the farthest listener in a space is at a position D_0 and should be in the same ambient noise situation as the EAD listener—the listener who can hear without amplification. Using the NAG formula, the resultant dB level indicates how many additional decibels of sound pressure are required for the farthest listener to hear as well as the EAD listener.

 TIP Although EAD will be very different depending on whether you're working with music or voice, an EAD of 4 feet (1.2 meters) is often a safe bet for voice. This assumes a 25 dB acoustic S/N ratio.

The purpose of the NAG calculation is to determine how much gain is needed to deliver the same level of sound to all the listeners in the space. The reference for the necessary sound level is determined by the EAD. Logically, excessive background noise level will cause the EAD to decrease.

The formula for NAG is as follows:

$$NAG = 20log(D_0/EAD)$$

The answer is in dB and indicates the amount of acoustical loss from the EAD position to the farthest listener. Designers use this formula to decide whether any equipment is necessary to overcome the loss over distance. Because you calculate NAG before equipment is employed, no equipment is represented in the NAG formula.

Figure 6-25 shows an EAD chart, which allows you to calculate the maximum physical distance where a talker and a listener could stand apart and easily be heard and understood without a sound system. For example, let's say you are talking at a comfortable volume of 70 dBA at 2 feet (0.7 meters). If you look at the EAD chart where 2 feet (0.7 meters) on the x-axis meets 70 dBA on the y-axis, your plot would land within the "normal voice" range on the chart. Let's say that you change the amount of decibels to 53 dB. By following the normal voice line along the chart, the EAD would need to be 16 feet (4.8 meters) to stay within the normal voice range.

PAG describes the ability of a system to amplify live sound without creating feedback. You will usually compare PAG to NAG for a given space. The potential of the system needs to exceed the need of listeners.

Whereas NAG is theoretical, PAG deals with actual equipment and comprises four distance factors in its calculation, as shown in Figure 6-26. The distance factors are as follows:

- D_0 The distance between the talker and the farthest listener
- D_1 The distance between the closest loudspeaker to the microphone and the microphone

Figure 6-25
Equivalent
acoustical
distance by
distance (x-axis)
and ambient
noise level
(y-axis)

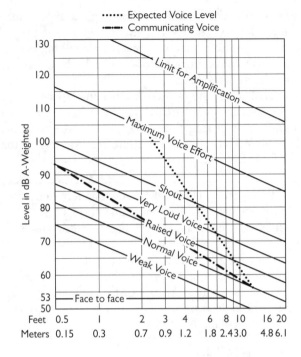

- **D_2** The distance between the loudspeaker closest to the farthest listener and the farthest listener
- **D_S** The distance between the sound source (talker) and the microphone

The formula for PAG is as follows:

$$PAG = 20log[(D_0 * D_1) / (D_2 * D_S)]$$

Figure 6-26
Distance
variables from
the NAG-PAG
equations

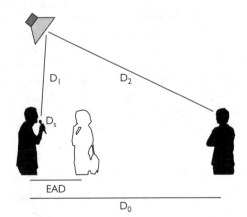

It is important to keep in mind that the PAG formula assumes you're using an omnidirectional microphone and loudspeaker. A directional microphone could increase PAG by picking up the presenter's voice and rejecting the loudspeaker's power easier than an omnidirectional microphone could. A directional loudspeaker could increase PAG by aiming more of the power to the listener and away from the microphone. A directional loudspeaker could also reduce feedback potential by producing less room reverberation and reducing the reverberant level at the microphone.

But directional equipment isn't always a good thing. As long as directional mics and speakers point away from each other, you're fine. But if they point toward each other, it could be a worst-case scenario.

More Variables: NOM and FSM

Now that you've learned about PAG and NAG, you need to consider two other factors when ensuring audio system stability: *number of open microphones* (NOM) and *feedback stability margin* (FSM).

In speech-reinforcement or conferencing applications, NOM becomes an issue for a variety reasons. For example, each time the number of open microphones increases, the system gain also increases. In other words, each decibel of gain is a decibel closer to feedback. Similarly, every time the number of open microphones doubles, acoustic power doubles, so when you double the number of open microphones (one to two, two to four, etc.), you lose 3 dB before feedback. In conferencing applications, the level increases with each open microphone, which could introduce signal distortion.

FSM refers to how close the system is to actual feedback. Any system on the edge of feedback will produce a ringing behavior prior to actual feedback. The FSM in a carefully equalized system is typically 6 dB.

Putting NOM and FSM on the PAG side of a formula makes sense, because microphones and equalizers are pieces of equipment and PAG is relevant to equipment. Ultimately, you will compare PAG and NAG to determine whether an audio system will be stable and whether it can be built as designed. PAG must be greater than or equal to NAG.

PAG/NAG in Action

Now that you have learned about the NAG formula, the PAG formula, and how NOM and FSM affect them, you can put them all together in one formula.

Remember, for a sound system to be stable, PAG must be greater than or equal to NAG. Conversely, NAG must be less than or equal to PAG. Although this chapter presents NOM and FSM on the PAG side of the formula, you could also factor them into the NAG side. For our purposes, here is the formula:

NAG < PAG

This is also represented by the following complete formula:

$20log\ (D_0/EAD) < 20log\ [(D_0 * D_1)/(D_2 * D_S)] - 10log\ (NOM) - FSM$

Here's how to solve the equation:

1. Document the EAD and the distances D_0, D_1, D_2, and D_S, for the presenter and farthest listener positions.
2. Document the number of active microphones (NOM).
3. Document the feedback stability margin (FSM).
4. Perform the NAG calculation using the formula given earlier.
5. Perform the PAG calculation using the formula given earlier.
6. Account for NOM and FSM, by subtracting *10log(NOM) – FSM* from the PAG side of the equation.
7. Compare NAG to PAG. To have a stable sound system, NAG must be less than or equal to PAG.

If it helps, keep track of the various PAG/NAG variables in a table such as this:

Variable	Measurement
EAD	
D_0	
D_1	
D_2	
D_S	
NOM	
FSM	
NAG	
PAG	

Chapter Review

In this chapter, you learned how people perceive sound. You learned how sound is generated, moves through space, and interacts with the environment. Most importantly, you learned how to receive and process sound, as well as control its propagation to meet a client's needs.

Upon completion of this chapter, you should be able to do the following:

- Calculate the change in a sound and signal level using decibel equations
- Calculate power and distance using the 10-log and 20-log functions
- Relate a given sound pressure level measurement to human perception
- Identify three qualities of an effective sound reinforcement system

- Plot loudspeaker coverage in a room so that the SPL level is consistent within a range of 3 dB throughout a defined listener area

- Specify a power amplifier for a sound reinforcement system by calculating the amount of wattage needed to achieve a target SPL at the listener position

- Explain the purpose of the microphone preamplifier and identify the signal level used for routing and processing

- Select the appropriate microphone for a given application by evaluating the environment

- Determine whether a given audio system will be stable by comparing NAG and PAG calculations

Review Questions

The following questions are based on the content covered in this chapter and are intended to help reinforce the knowledge you have assimilated. These questions are not extracted from the CTS-D exam nor are they necessarily CTS-D practice exam questions. For an official CTS-D practice exam, see the accompanying CD.

1. When creating a schematic diagram of audio signal flow for a project, what must be included in the diagram?

    A. Microphones, mixers, switchers, routers, and processors

    B. Inputs, outputs, equipment rack locations, ceiling venting

    C. Conduit runs, pull boxes, bends

    D. Construction materials, wall panels, acoustic tiles

2. Sound pressure level should always fall between _____.

    A. −10 and 100 dB SPL

    B. 0 and 140 dB SPL

    C. 0 and 200 dB SPL

    D. 10 and 140 dB SPL

3. Using a 20-log decibel calculation and assuming a loudspeaker is generating 80 dB SPL at a distance of 22 feet (7 m) from the source, what would the level be at 88 feet (27 m) away?

    A. 40 dB SPL

    B. 52 dB SPL

    C. 68 dB SPL

    D. 72 dB SPL

4. A presenter is speaking to a large audience. Listener #1 is 2 meters away from the presenter, and listener #2 is 15 meters away from the presenter. What is the expected gain in SPL at the listener #1 position? Hint: This is a 20-log problem.

   A. −1.7

   B. −7

   C. −17.5

   D. 17.5

5. The threshold of human hearing is 0 dB SPL at what kHz?

   A. 0 kHz

   B. 1 kHz

   C. 3 kHz

   D. 10 kHZ

6. Calculating for loudspeaker coverage takes into account which of the following?

   A. Ceiling height, listeners' ear height, and the speaker's angle of coverage

   B. Dispersal patterns, room dimensions, and number of speakers

   C. Number of speakers, type of speakers, acoustic treatments

   D. Number of listeners, type of audio, speaker power

7. Assuming a loudspeaker coverage angle of 90 degrees, a mounted loudspeaker height of 12 feet (3.7 meters), and listeners who are seated, what is the diameter of coverage?

   A. 9 feet (2.7 meters)

   B. 15.4 feet (4.7 meters)

   C. 16 feet (4.9 meters)

   D. 16.4 feet (5 meters)

8. How many watts are required at the loudspeaker with a sound pressure requirement of 70 dB SPL, a loudspeaker with a sensitivity of 88 dB SPL 1 w/1 m, 10 dB SPL of headroom, and a listener position of 14 feet (4267 mm) from the loudspeaker? Hint: You'll need the EPR formula.

   A. 2.89 watts

   B. 4 watts

   C. 4.33 watts

   D. 5.12 watts

9. A(n) _____ microphone picks up sound uniformly from all directions.

    A. Bidirectional

    B. Cardioid

    C. Hypercardioid

    D. Omnidirectional

10. PAG and NAG are important calculations for ensuring an audio system is:

    A. Loud enough

    B. Intelligible

    C. Stable

    D. All of the above

Answers

1. **A.** When creating a schematic diagram of audio signal flow, you should include microphones, mixers, switchers, routers, and processors.

2. **B.** Sound pressure level should always fall between 0 and 140 dB SPL.

3. **C.** 68 dB SPL. To calculate the loss, because you're calculating for a distance farther away, $dB = 20 * log (D_1/D_2) = dB = 20 * log (22/88) = (12)$ dB. Therefore, 80 dB – 12 dB = 68 dB SPL.

4. **D.** The gain is 17.5 SPL. $dB = 20 * log (D_1/D_2) = 20 * log (15/2) = 20 * log(7.5) = 17.5$.

5. **B.** The threshold of human hearing is 0 dB SPL at 1 kHz.

6. **A.** Calculating for loudspeaker coverage takes into account ceiling height, the listeners' ear height, and the speaker's angle of coverage.

7. **C.** 16 feet (4.9 meters)

$$D = 2 * (H - h) * tan(C\angle /2) = 2 * (12 - 4) * tan(90/2) = 2 * 8 * 1 = 16 \text{ feet}$$

$$EPR = 10^{\wedge \left(\frac{\left[L_p + H - L_r (20Log(D_2/D_r)) \right]}{10} \right)} * W_{ref}$$

8. **A.** 2.89 watts

First, calculate the exponent part of the equation.

$L_p + H - L_S + 20\log (D_2 / D_r)$
$70 + 10 - 88 + 20\log (14 / 3.28)$
$(80 - 88) + 12.6$
$(-8 + 12.26) = 4.6$

Second, divide by 10.

4.6/10 = 0.46

Third, complete the exponent calculation.

EPR = $10^{0.46}$
EPR = 2.89

Finally, multiply 2.89 by the reference value, which is 1 in this problem.

EPR = 2.89 * 1
EPR = 2.89

9. D. An omnidirectional microphone picks up sound uniformly from all directions.

10. C. PAG and NAG are important calculations for ensuring an audio system is stable.

PART III

Infrastructure

CHAPTER 7

Communicating with Allied Trades

In this chapter, you will learn about

- The related professionals you work with on an AV project
- Three common organizational tools used to track an AV project
- The purpose of industry standards and the role they play in working with allied trades
- The importance of detail in specifying your design

The infrastructure that supports an AV design is handled by electricians, lighting designers, mechanical engineers, and others. As you specify what will go into your design, you will need to communicate those elements to your allied trade partners.

Each trade requires certain information from you, which we will discuss in Chapters 8 through 11. But before you learn about working with individual allied trades, we will discuss briefly the general fabric of communicating with these professionals.

Domain Check

This chapter relates directly to the following tasks on the CTS-D Exam Content Outline:

- Domain A Task 1: Identify stakeholders/decision-makers
- Domain A Task 2: Identify skill level of end users
- Domain A Task 3: Educate the client
- Domain A Task 6: Research client's business process
- Domain D Task 1: Participate in project implementation communication

These tasks comprise 7.2 percent of the exam (about 9 questions). This chapter may also relate to other tasks.

Communicating with Stakeholders

All AV professionals must work with people from outside their organization to serve their customers' needs.

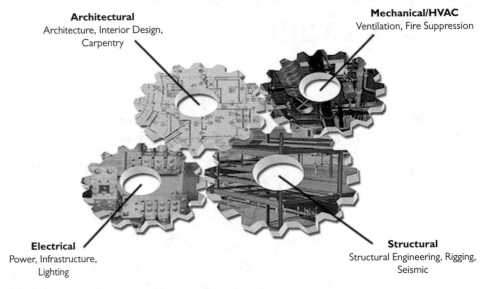

Architectural
Architecture, Interior Design, Carpentry

Mechanical/HVAC
Ventilation, Fire Suppression

Electrical
Power, Infrastructure, Lighting

Structural
Structural Engineering, Rigging, Seismic

Allied trades are the businesses that collaborate with AV professionals to complete integrated solutions for customers. Each trade has its own priorities and areas of expertise, but they must all work together to satisfy the customer. Typically, you will need to work with these other professionals in the design phase of the project to create proper spaces for AV systems. Cooperating and identifying issues early will produce the best results.

Table 7-1 shows some of the AV industry's allied trades and the areas where they might collaborate with AV professionals. This table is not exhaustive. A more complex or unusual AV project might involve even more allied trades.

Allied Trade	Collaborate with AV Professionals on...
Architects	Window placement in display environments; space requirements.
Interior designers	Furniture; equipment positioning; wall and window treatments.
Electrical professionals	Wiring installation; power requirements.
IT professionals	Network connectivity; media storage; equipment control.
Telecom professionals	Telephone systems; intercoms; Internet lines.
Heating, ventilation, and air conditioning (HVAC) professionals	Equipment mounting; HVAC noise.
Content developers	Digital signage content.
Subject-matter experts	Topics specific to a particular project or vertical market. For example, a teacher might advise an AV professional on the requirements for a classroom.

Table 7-1   Areas of Collaboration with Allied Trades

Tracking the Project

Engaging with allied trades and understanding each other's needs are crucial to figuring out how you're going to design an AV system. In the process, it is important to develop a feasible timeline with your client and team so that everyone is aware of the dates by which certain milestones should be accomplished. Although this is more of a project management function, it's important that AV designers understand how it works.

Project coordination covers many different aspects of a project, not just the AV portion. Sometimes, other parts of a project must be completed before you can begin or finish certain AV elements. It is common for the AV team to wait until construction is finished before scheduling the installation of sensitive equipment.

The AV project manager must also monitor other parts of the project to ensure that considerations for AV equipment or specifications are met, such as monitoring where, specifically, an HVAC or sprinkler system is installed in a space to keep it from being collocated with a projector or cable run.

The most common way to coordinate the completion of such tasks and to track the overall project is to create an organizational chart. There are three basic types:

- A *work breakdown structure* (WBS), which defines products or services
- A *Gantt chart,* which provides a timeline for all the activities
- A *logic network diagram,* which shows what tasks must be completed before you can begin your work

Work Breakdown Structure

One important tool or technique for project management is the work breakdown structure (WBS), as shown in Figure 7-1. It is a deliverables-oriented representation of project components, created in hierarchical form, which helps organize and define the scope of work. A WBS shows how deliverables and components are interconnected and dependent on one another. The visual elements of the WBS define products or services and are always expressed in nouns.

Figure 7-1
A work breakdown structure

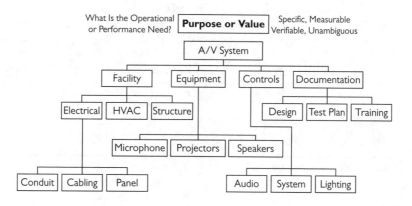

The WBS serves many critical purposes, the most important of which is defining the work to be performed and breaking it into manageable parts. A well-defined WBS helps ensure that all team members working on a project clearly understand what the client expects to receive.

NOTE A work breakdown structure tells you only "what." It does not address who, when, or how much.

Gantt Chart

The most common way to present a project schedule is through a Gantt chart (see Figure 7-2). A Gantt chart depicts the timeline for tasks and subtasks as horizontal bars, showing the sequence in which tasks should be performed. The chart also includes project milestones, such as the completion of major tasks.

Gantt charts are a great tool for actually showing your client a project as it progresses. It's important to be able to offer clients a graphical representation of their projects so they understand which activities impact others and which project activities are the responsibilities of allied trades.

Figure 7-2 is a simplified version of a Gantt chart, but it illustrates the concept well. The top of the chart shows project dates. On the left side, you see activities and milestones.

The shaded areas represent milestones, which are the tasks that have to happen before the subsequent task. If the milestones are not met, the project will not be able to move forward and continue. The milestones might shift one way or another. If you receive approval quickly, the milestone can move to the left (earlier in the project), but if the activity requires revision, the milestone might move to the right (later in the project).

Task	Duration	Start	Finish	4-Feb-16	11-Feb-16	18-Feb-16	25-Feb-16
Needs Analysis Phase	12 days	2/4/2016	2/15/2016				
Kick off-meeting	1 day	2/4/2016	2/4/2016				
Needs Analysis interviews	3 days	2/5/2016	2/7/2016				
Facility survey	3 days	2/6/2016	2/8/2016				
Inventory existing equipment	2 days	2/7/2016	2/8/2016				
Additional requirements review	3 days	2/11/2016	2/13/2016				
Program report preparation	3 days	2/12/2016	2/14/2016				
Report presentation and sign-off	1 day	2/15/2016	2/15/2016				
Design Phase	21 days	2/18/2016	3/10/2016				
Logical topology	5 days	2/18/2016	2/22/2016				
Architechural reqs	5 days	2/18/2016	2/22/2016				
QoS reqs	2 days	2/25/2016	2/26/2016				
Acoustical reqs	2 days	2/25/2016	2/26/2016				
Electrical and HVAC reqs	3 days	2/27/2016	3/1/2016				
Workmanship and techinique reqs	3 days	3/4/2016	3/6/2016				
Design drawings finalized	7 days	3/4/2016	3/10/2016				

Figure 7-2 A Gantt chart

Because some tasks must be completed before others can start, the Gantt chart identifies types of dependencies in a manner that clearly shows their sequence. For example, walls within a room must be finished and painted prior to mounting sensitive and fragile AV components, so the start dates of these AV tasks will be identified as dependent on the end dates of the room-preparation tasks.

TIP When creating project charts for AV systems, it's important to coordinate your charts with those for other parts of the project, which may track such elements as the installation of electrical conduit and ceiling tiles. Their milestones need to work with your milestones because if theirs slip, it could impact yours.

Logic Network Diagram

A logic network diagram represents the same information as a Gantt chart except the information is laid out in a different way, showing the relationship among project activities and the effort (amount of time) each will take (see Figure 7-3).

Logic network diagrams are useful when discussing with a client what other tasks need to be finished before you can begin yours. For example, say you allocate five weeks to install a certain AV system and the client asks if you can do it in two. A logic network diagram helps visualize what is or is not possible, based on other contingencies, such as whether a sprinkler system still needs to be installed in a space. You can't install your AV system first without risking damage; therefore, until the sprinkler-installation activity is completed (and the diagram should show how long it will take), the AV system must wait.

As with Gantt charts, coordinating AV activities and milestones with those of allied trades is critical to ensuring a logic network diagram reflects the project in a comprehensive way.

NOTE Gantt charts and logic network diagrams can be as simple or as complicated as you want to make them.

Figure 7-3
A logic network
diagram

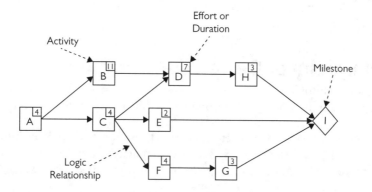

Industry Standards as Common Language

AV projects are complex. Out of necessity, they're guided by standards, both in the AV industry and in those of allied trades.

A standard is a document that provides requirements, specifications, guidelines, or characteristics that can be used consistently to ensure that materials, products, processes, and services are fit for their purpose. Standards serve as a common platform for understanding and teamwork; they're a language for conducting day-to-day business. Standards are often voluntary, but they can also become regulation or code.

There are many kinds of standards: technical, management, performance, measurement, methodology, and even de facto standards. De facto standards are not necessarily written down but become standard because they are overwhelmingly accepted by the public or a particular market. In the AV and technology-related industries, technical standards help ensure that diverse products from different companies work together, which creates efficiency, consistency, and interoperability. Performance standards help ensure that a system operates optimally or as intended so that it meets a client's expectations.

Standards are developed by specific organizations to establish agreed-upon rules, regulations, specifications, measurements, and protocols. These organizations often create standards that meet other standards, which gives them the added weight of authority and encourages implementations.

Standards groups that are important to the AV and IT industries include the International Organization for Standards (ISO), the International Electrotechnical Commission (IEC), and regional standard coordinators such as the American National Standards Institute (ANSI). In 2008, InfoComm International became an ANSI Accredited Standards Developer to bring performance standards to the AV industry. Because other industries also develop their own standards, the likelihood that related trades will acknowledge and accept the role of AV-related standards increases.

The first AV performance standard was ANSI/InfoComm 1M-2009, *Audio Coverage Uniformity in Enclosed Listener Areas*. For more information, visit www.infocomm.org/standards.

NOTE Standards differ throughout the world. If you are interested in discovering AV standards relevant to your region, start your search at www .nssn.org or www.iso.org.

Hierarchy of Design Consultation

Although InfoComm and allied trades offer standards that lend uniformity and professionalism to each project, there is a hierarchy of design consultation that goes beyond standards (see Figure 7-4).

As you consider which references you'll use for basic project information or as the basis for key decisions, always start with regulatory requirements. From there, you can work your way down the hierarchy to identify sources that will help you make and

Figure 7-4
The hierarchy
of design
consultation

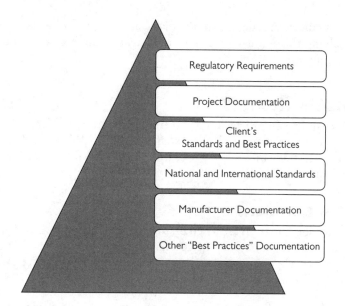

Regulatory Requirements

Project Documentation

Client's
Standards and Best Practices

National and International Standards

Manufacturer Documentation

Other "Best Practices" Documentation

defend your decisions. For example, you may be working with an allied trade partner to resolve a conflict between lighting positions in a room. Although the lighting designer might refer to a manufacturer's recommendation for fixture placement, you might refer to a national standard that recommends a different solution. Instead of going with a personal preference, you can use your knowledge of the standard to solve the problem with the lighting designer. When you consult a higher voice of authority, you can be more confident in the decision-making process.

Ultimately, your goal is to reference the proper source and use this knowledge to justify your design solutions.

Showing Workmanship

As you progress through the AV design and documentation process, your most important ally is the integrator. The specifications you create for electricians, lighting designers, and other trades comprise the same documentation that an integrator will use to verify that the design you developed is the one the client sees. Integrators will be the people who ultimately install, set up, and verify the AV design based on your specifications.

With that in mind, don't assume anything. Your specifications are the lens through which allied trades and integrators picture the project; therefore, you don't want that vision to be anything but clear. For example, if the designer fails to specify clearly important details, such as the display contrast ratio or loudspeaker placement, the AV design intent may or may not be achieved. Even small details, such as how items should be labeled on input wall plates or the color of user-accessible input cables, can affect the overall success of a system.

Specify the details, document the math, and use professional guidelines in your design. Maintaining this mind-set will safeguard against unnecessary confusion and limit misconceptions.

Chapter Review

In this chapter, you reviewed the basic tools, resources, and strategies that are the foundation for communicating with allied trades during an AV design. You should now be ready to study each trade individually to learn exactly what they'll need from you as you design the AV infrastructure.

Review Questions

The following questions are based on the content covered in this chapter and are intended to help reinforce the knowledge you have assimilated. These questions are not extracted from the CTS-D exam nor are they necessarily CTS-D practice exam questions. For an official CTS-D practice exam, see the accompanying CD.

1. What is the first design reference you need to consider in your design consultation?

   A. Project documentation

   B. Regulatory requirements

   C. Manufacturer documentation

   D. Client's standards and best practices

2. What is a common way to track a project?

   A. Spreadsheet

   B. Note taking

   C. Work breakdown structure

   D. Statement of work

3. Who must monitor other areas of the project to ensure that considerations for AV equipment or specifications are met, such as monitoring where an HVAC and sprinkler system are installed?

   A. HVAC installer

   B. AV project manager

   C. Facilities manager

   D. Building owner

4. In which phase does a project manager need to work with allied trades to create proper workspaces?

   A. Training phase

   B. Installation phase

   C. Maintenance phase

   D. Design phase

5. Which document provides a common language for communicating with teams from different industries?

   A. Standards

   B. Project documentation

   C. Manufacturer documentation

   D. Meeting notes

Answers

1. **B.** In the hierarchy of design consultation, regulatory requirements are your first point of reference when making key decisions.

2. **C.** A work breakdown structure is one common way to track an AV project.

3. **B.** An AV project manager should monitor all aspects of a project to ensure that considerations for AV equipment are met.

4. **D.** A project manager should work with allied trades during the design phase to create proper workspaces.

5. **A.** Standards provide a common language for communicating with teams from different industries.

Lighting Specifications

In this chapter, you will learn about

- The characteristics of light that impact human perception
- Selecting luminaires for an AV system based on a room's application
- Creating zoning plans for a room's lighting based on application
- Determining lighting-level presets for each zone in an AV space
- Addressing factors specific to maintaining lighting quality for videoconferencing
- Safety expectations in your design

An AV designer must specify lighting requirements for the space in which an AV system will be installed and operated. The goal of this chapter isn't to turn you into a lighting engineer. It's to make you aware of lighting specifications that can improve the quality of your AV design. Ultimately, you will likely coordinate with a lighting consultant to execute your design.

Light can come from many sources, such as natural light from windows or artificial light from lamps and AV equipment (in other words, projectors and displays). All light sources, whether natural or artificial, must be included in an AV design so they meet the client's needs and allow end users to operate an AV system effectively.

Keep in mind, users need enough ambient light to move safely around a space, view collateral materials (objects, printed pages), and see the presenter well enough to comprehend the intended message. Such ambient light, while necessary, can impact the effectiveness of display systems and will affect the design. Users also need enough light coming from the AV equipment to perceive displayed images as faithful reproductions. Moreover, in situations where video cameras are required, you need to specify lighting that illuminates participants and the space so that they can be seen clearly (and in a flattering light), whether the video will be transmitted across a distance, as in a videoconference, or recorded and watched later.

Domain Check

This chapter relates directly to the following tasks on the CTS-D Exam Content Outline:

- Domain A Task 9: Identify scope of work
- Domain B Task 2: Coordinate architectural/interior design criteria
- Domain B Task 5: Coordinate lighting criteria
- Domain C Task 1: Create draft AV design
- Domain C Task 2: Confirm site conditions

These tasks comprise 27.2 percent of the exam (about 34 questions). This chapter may also relate to other tasks.

Basics of Lighting

When considering lighting for an AV design, it is important to understand human perception. How humans perceive brightness, contrast, and color will help determine whether your design serves its intended purpose, as identified during the needs analysis, and will help users communicate effectively.

Visual perception in an AV space requires a light source (the luminaire), receptor (the human eye), and analyzer (the brain). It's up to the designer to control the light within a room so that users can accurately perceive, receive, and analyze information.

The human eye is stimulated by light that comes directly from a source, as well as light that reflects off surfaces before entering the eye. The brain interprets the various light waves it receives through the eye, causing people to see color, contrast, and shape. Everything humans see is the product of light absorbed by, transmitted through, and reflected back from the surfaces of objects. Two important characteristics of light, which designers must consider, are brightness and color temperature.

Brightness

For the eye to recognize color and contrast, there needs to be enough light directed toward and reflecting off surfaces in a room. The brightness, or *luminance,* perceived by humans depends on the amount of light coming from a source to a surface and on the amount of light reflected back to the eyes from that surface. Luminance is light emitted from or reflected by an object. It is measured in *candelas per square meter* (cd/m^2, also referred to as a *nit*) or footlamberts (fL). One nit (cd/m^2) = 0.292 fL.

NOTE Illuminance is light falling on a surface, measured in lux (lx) or footcandles (fc). One lux = 0.09 fc. It is not visible to the human eye except in the form of reflected luminance.

Both direct (luminance) and reflected (illuminance) light can be measured using special instruments.

- *Incident light meters* measure the direct light coming from a source, such as a lightbulb, projector, or monitor.
- *Reflected light meters,* also known as spot meters, measure the light that bounces off an object, such as a projection screen or work surface.

For more information about light measurement, see the section about display environments in Chapter 5.

Color Temperature

The lamps you choose for an AV space will be a determining factor in what wavelengths of light will reach users' eyes. An important element of those light sources is *color temperature*. Color temperature is the quantification of the color of "white" light, as rated on a numerical scale. Low color temperature light (about 2000 kelvin [K]) has a warm (reddish) appearance, while light with a high color temperature (about 6000 K) has a colder (blueish) appearance.

All white light consists of varying amounts of color wavelengths from the visible light spectrum. Depending on how much of each color is present, the human eye will perceive the warmth or coolness of that light.

The lamps you choose will have a perceived color. If you have outdoor light coming into your room, you need lamps that match the outdoor color temperature. If you have no windows, you can choose a warmer, yellow light that is more pleasing to the human eye indoors.

Characteristics of color temperature can be expressed in a couple ways, by correlated color temperature and by color rendering index.

Correlated Color Temperature

Correlated color temperature (CCT) measures the light color that a lamp emits as a single number and indicates the "warmth" or "coolness" of the light. The curved line in the middle of Figure 8-1, known as the Planckian locus, indicates the color of a theoretical *black body* as it's heated to the temperature indicated in kelvin. In physics, a black body is an ideal physical object that absorbs all incident radiation. Think of a piece of steel in a blacksmith's shop. As the metal heats, it starts to glow. It gets redder and redder until it is orange and then finally blue in color. The blue numbers indicate the monochrome wavelength values of the image.

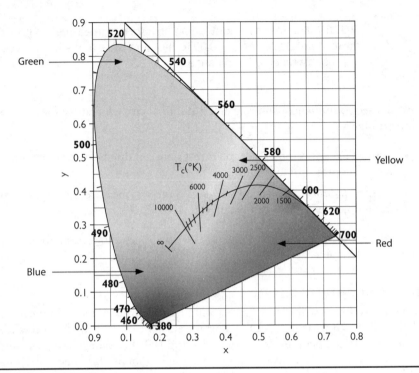

Figure 8-1   A chromaticity diagram

Typically, most commercial light sources range from 2700 to 6500 K, with lamp CCTs appearing "warm" below 3200 K and "cool" above 4000 K. For example, the CCT of LED lamps can span from warm white (2700 K) to cool white (greater than 4000 K) to daylight (5600 K). Which you choose may depend on the space, such as a ballroom in which you want the light to appear either harsh or soft depending on the event.

Table 8-1 shows CCTs for various light sources.

Correlated Color Temperature (K)	Light Source
1900	Candlelight
2200	High-pressure sodium lamp
3200 to 3400	Tungsten lamp
4200	Cool white fluorescent bulb
5400	Daylight
5500	Direct daylight, noon, cloudless sky
6500	Reference white, as defined by the Society of Motion Pictures and Television Engineers (SMPTE)

Table 8-1   Correlated Color Temperature

TIP The higher the CCT, the bluer the light. The lower the CCT, the redder the light.

Color Rendering Index

While CCT measures the color that a light source emits, the *color rendering index* (CRI) measures how accurately a light source replicates a desired set of parameters. It is the effect a light source has on the perceived color of objects relative to an incandescent source of the same CCT. In lighting, a lamp is tested for its ability to render faithfully several test colors, and then those measurements are averaged to produce one CRI number.

CRI values range from negative numbers to 100. The most accurate replication of colors is indicated by 100. Typically, incandescent lights are the best color replicators, followed by LEDs, which are somewhere in the 90s range. This information is important in the AV industry. If your AV system is displaying a company logo, critical information on a projection screen, or a live video feed of a chief executive officer (CEO) leading a meeting through a videoconference, it needs to produce the right colors.

CRI values are often expressed by their equivalent CIE R_a value, which is an international standard. When you see R_a listed for a commercial lighting product, think CRI. The R_a is the average test color value, or CRI, of each lamp (see Figure 8-2). Using an LED lamp with a higher CRI (R_a) would change the look of whatever object it's illuminating.

TIP It's important that you understand the link between the correlated color temperature and the color rendering index. If you're given a light-emitting diode (LED) blend with a perceived kelvin reading of 6500 K, you might think that it's perfect for your application. However, if it has a CRI in the 20s, it may be worthless.

	R_a	R1	R2	R3	R4	R5	R6	R7
D50 fluorescent lamp	91	94	91	86	90	93	89	90
Natural white fluorescent lamp	79	89	89	54	82	81	72	86
LED lamp	68	65	74	79	68	65	62	81

	R8	R9	R10	R11	R12	R13	R14	R15
D50 fluorescent lamp	90	77	78	93	81	93	92	91
Natural white fluorescent lamp	76	16	40	63	55	92	70	92
LED lamp	54	−39	36	61	31	66	88	59

Figure 8-2 Average test color values (R_a)

Energy Consumption

Another factor you'll have to consider is a lamp's energy consumption. Just as a car's performance can be measured in miles per gallon, a lamp's performance can be measured in lumens per watt. The number of lumens you get per watt is known as *efficacy*. You arrive at this number by dividing the initial lumens by the nominal lamp watts.

Sustainability efforts, along with local and national regulations, have sought to limit the waste of energy coming from lamps, so many manufacturers have been investing in light designs with better efficacy. Figure 8-3 shows the range of efficacies for various lamps.

Keep in mind, however, that the highest-efficacy lamp may not always be the right one for your AV design, regardless of sustainability efforts. Efficacy is only one measure among many that you need to consider when determining the proper lighting. You must also take into account intensity, color, lamp life, and control capabilities.

Lighting the Space

Planning for the various lamps, luminaires, and other lighting-related equipment in your AV design requires information gathered during the needs analysis. In that analysis, you and the client, along with your fellow allied trade representatives, should have discussed the different tasks that users will perform in a space. Given room applications, you can start thinking about task lighting, shades and blackout drapes, and lamps and luminaires.

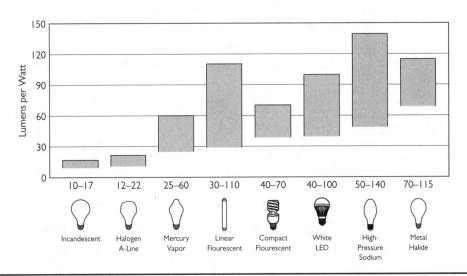

Figure 8-3   Lamp efficacy ranges

TIP It is important to know the difference between a lamp and a luminaire. A *lamp* describes the light source and light-producing components (bulb, filament, fuse, and so on). A *luminaire* is the light source plus the structures attached to it that control and distribute light (the lamp plus sockets, housing, and so on). Often you'll hear *lighting fixture* and *luminaire* used interchangeably in the AV industry, but *luminaire* is preferred when communicating with the lighting trade.

Task Lighting

The Illuminating Engineering Society (IES) *Lighting Handbook* recommends task light levels in AV areas to be from 200 to 500 lux or from 20 to 50 fc.

Task lighting concerns the amount of light you want to direct *toward* people for things such as note-taking, reading manuals, and operating equipment. It will need to be balanced against the amount of light you want to direct *away* from things such as a front-projection screen or videoconferencing camera.

Ultimately, in planning for luminaires, you want to specify the following in your design:

- Light you want
- Light you don't want
- Light you need to control

For more information about task lighting, see the section about task light levels in Chapter 5.

Shades and Blackout Drapes

Not all the light in a room comes from lamps. Nor is all light desirable at every location of the room. Because there is usually *ambient light*—or general light filling a space—you will need to consider how to control it so that it doesn't negatively impact your design. Ambient light may strike the screen or the walls in the room and reflect into the viewing area, competing with the displayed image by reducing contrast and washing out the picture.

Consider the ANSI/INFOCOMM 3M-2011 standard, *Projected Image System Contrast Ratio,* which sets a minimum contrast ratio of 15:1 for basic decision-making applications, including information displays, presentations containing detailed images, classrooms, boardrooms, multipurpose rooms, and product illustrations. Achieving compliance with the standard starts with limiting the amount of ambient light falling on a screen. AV designers should specify the ambient light limits for these locations. A great starting point is the Illuminating Engineering Society DG-17-05 standard, *Fundamentals of Lighting for Videoconferencing,* which recommends the following:

- Less than 50 lux (5 fc) at front-projection screens
- Less than 150 lux (15 fc) at rear-projection screens
- Less than 200 lux (20 fc) at direct displays

One way to control the ambient light at a display is to specify shades and blackout drapes for rooms with windows that allow excessive natural light. Yes, natural light can help set a mood or meet energy-savings requirements. But the amount and color of natural light isn't always consistent. Color temperatures can range from a warm 1000 to 1800 K at sunrise to a cool 5000 K at noon. And natural light can vary in spectra and distribution depending on whether the skies outside are blue or cloudy. That's why if an AV space includes windows, it is important to block out natural light, especially for videoconferencing or displaying critical images.

Choosing Lamps

Once you've specified your task light levels and your ambient light limits, you can consider the types of lamps and luminaires you'll want in the room. Lamps can be broken into three main groups.

- Incandescent
- Fluorescent
- LED

Incandescent lamps work by heating a filament with electricity, which causes the tungsten wire to glow. The advantages of incandescent lamps are low initial cost and high CRI, while the disadvantages are low efficacy and high heat output.

Fluorescent lights work by heating both an inert gas and mercury to the point of producing visible light by the phosphor coating on the bulb. The advantages of fluorescent lights are higher efficacy and cooler operation, while the disadvantages are higher initial cost and sensitivity to external temperatures.

LED lights work by converting electrical energy directly into photons through semiconductor materials. The advantages of LED lights are long lamp life, high efficacy, good performance in cold weather, and longer durability. The disadvantages are high initial cost and heat sensitivity.

 TIP Many LED lamps on the market offer extremely poor performance. The United States requires LED makers to include "Lighting Facts" on their cut sheets, which helps to make an informed purchase decision.

Because incandescent lights become hot when illuminated, designers must account for the heat they generate. Heat and AV equipment don't usually mix well, so make sure the heating, ventilation, and air conditioning (HVAC) engineer provides adequate air-conditioning capacity for the AV space. Of course, in a few years, it might not matter because incandescent lamps are being phased out completely in many parts of the world.

Choosing Luminaires

Luminaires include not only the light source but also the physical features that control and distribute light. A luminaire is a complete lighting unit consisting of a lamp (or lamps) and ballast (or ballasts), when applicable, together with the parts designed to distribute light, position and protect the lamps, and connect the lamps to the power supply.

Luminaires are intended to utilize absorption, reflection, transmission, and other physical properties of light to control it in a way that complements human perception in a room. From various plastic blends that cover the lamp to shaped reflectors that direct light, luminaires come in a range of designs for different lighting needs.

Luminaires can be grouped based on several characteristics, but the following are the most common:

- By the type of light source, determined by the type of lamp they employ, such as incandescent, fluorescent, LED, and so on

- By mounting style, such as surface-mounted, recessed, semi-recessed, track, or suspended

- By light distribution, classified by the IES as direct, indirect, semi-direct, semi-indirect, direct-indirect, and general diffuse. Such descriptions are based on the percentage of light output above and below a horizontal plane.

NOTE When you add a ballast and housing unit to a lamp, its efficacy can change. The term that describes the difference in percentage between the lumen output of a lamp alone and the lumen output of the lamp within a luminaire is *efficiency*.

Lighting Coverage

When choosing luminaires, it is important to assess available photometric data. This will help you design for lighting coverage. Photometric data is collected on luminaires to gauge the light intensity and includes many measurements to help you choose a luminaire suitable for your room application. Three important reports to consider are candlepower distribution curves, spacing criterion, and lamp and ballast data.

Candlepower distribution curves are usually graphed as polar plots that look similar to microphone and loudspeaker plots (see Figures 8-4 to 8-7). These graphs show the distribution of light from the vertical field and help give you a sense of the direction that light will be spread in an area of a room. This is helpful to an AV design because, for example, there are places in a space where you don't want light to be directed, such as at a front-projection screen. Although a luminaire that distributes generally diffuse light might be applicable in an audience setting, it would not be acceptable near the projection screen.

Spacing criterion data will provide you with the recommended ratio between each light's center and the distance above the task area. This is to ensure an even distribution of light and can help you properly coordinate with your loudspeaker layout in a reflected ceiling plan or keep an even wall wash for videoconferencing lighting.

Figure 8-4
A candlepower
distribution
curve

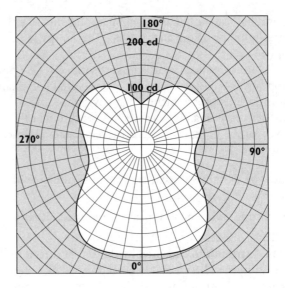

Lamp and ballast data includes lamp type, CCT information, and CRI information. It also includes ballast descriptions, such as electronic, dimmable, and energy efficient. These specifications will affect everything from the color temperature of the room to the way the ballast utilizes light energy.

Figure 8-5 The
center of the plot
shows where the
light source is
emanating from.

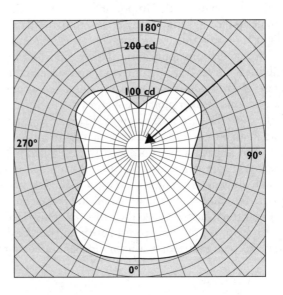

Figure 8-6
The intensity
of the light is
measured in
candelas.

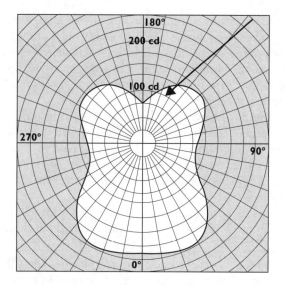

Documenting Luminaires

Having studied luminaires, you should now be able to specify their type and location. You want to sketch out lighting positions across the space and specify type in detail (for example, direct-reflected fluorescents for the front of the room with less than 50 lux falling on the front-projector screen, plus general diffuse fluorescents with task light of at least 200 to 500 lux).

Figure 8-7
The direction
of the intended
light path is
indicated by the
0° mark.

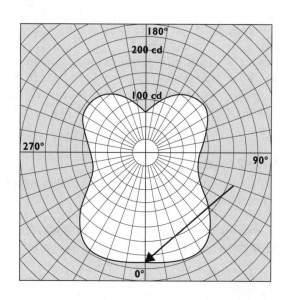

Although documenting luminaires for an AV design might seem straightforward, it's often a process that's better accomplished using computer-modeling software. Such software can produce artful and scientifically calculated models, based on your lighting design information. More importantly, by using software, the luminaires you specify for your design can be imported into the lighting designer's modeling software, putting the AV needs front and center.

Your lighting documentation also needs to take into other possible systems, such as HVAC and sprinklers, which compete for space in the ceiling. Furthermore, you will have to consider your own loudspeaker coverage pattern, if applicable, and your sightline study. This is where you will want to review reflected-ceiling plans (see Figure 8-8). You cannot put a luminaire where a loudspeaker is, and you cannot suspend luminaires that impede sightlines.

The bottom line is, be thoughtful and specific. Your fellow trades people cannot meet your AV design needs if you do not communicate them through documentation.

 NOTE While you document luminaires, know that some energy codes will impact the type and quantity of luminaires in the room. Some energy codes that may affect your design are the *International Energy Conservation Code* (IECC) from the International Code Council (ICC) and *Energy Standard for Buildings Except Low-Rise Residential Buildings 90.1* from the American Society of Heating, Refrigerating, and Air-Conditioning Engineers (ASHRAE).

Creating a Zoning Plan

Different tasks require different lighting, so your design specifications will need to include a way to alter luminaires throughout the space. During a video presentation, when note-taking is required, your system should utilize different groups of lights than it does during a videoconference to achieve proper contrast ratios.

Lights are often grouped together in *zones*. A zone is a grouping of luminaires (lighting fixtures) that are controlled together.

Lighting zones are usually grouped by the luminaire's intended function, which may or may not determine their position in a room. A zone can be as simple as a single row of lights near a display wall or as complex as individually addressable luminaires.

Figure 8-9 shows a room's lighting zones organized by luminaire function and labeled with letters.

Determining Zones

Determining which luminaires go in which zone depends on the needs analysis. Keeping in mind how the space should function will help you determine the complexity of the zoning plan.

If you have a room that will be used only for PowerPoint presentations and general meetings, you might create two separate zones: the lighting above the meeting space and

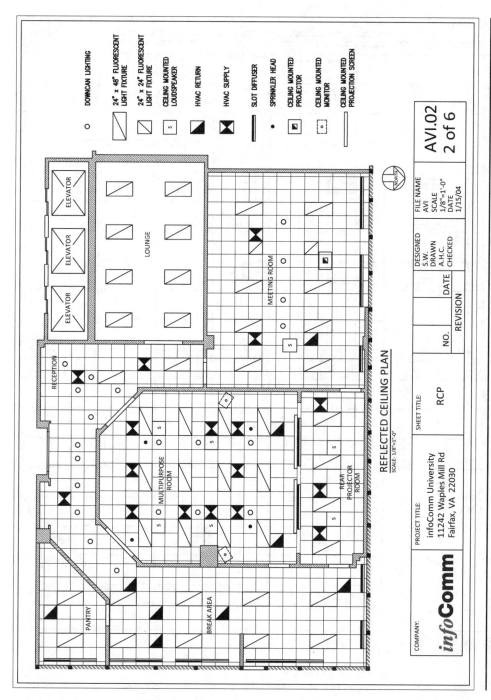

Figure 8-8 Reflected ceiling plan

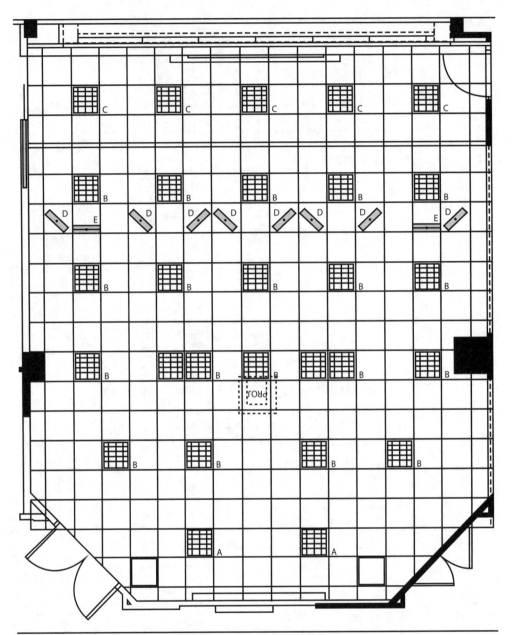

Figure 8-9 Lighting zones organized by letter

the lighting closest to the projection screen. Such a simple zoning plan would allow users to adjust the lights manually based on the room's function. Notice in Figure 8-10 that groups of lights are zoned together so they can be manipulated to meet the needs of various tasks in the room.

PART III

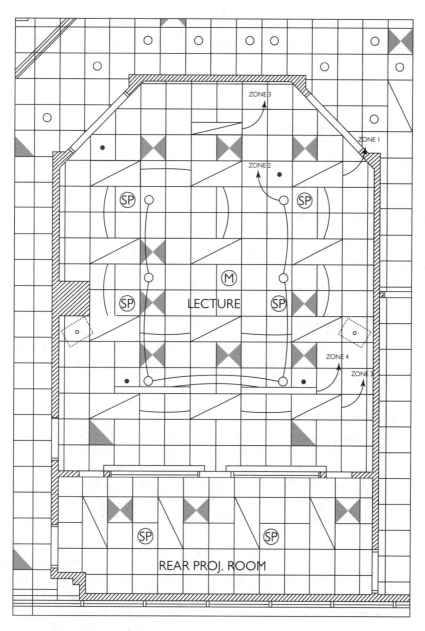

SCENE	ZONE			
	1	2	3	4
MEETING	100%	0%	0%	0%
PRESENT	75%	75%	100%	0%
AV PRESENT	75%	100%	25%	0%
VIDEO CONFERENCE	100%	100%	100%	100%
OFF	0%	0%	0%	0%

Figure 8-10   Lighting zones based on tasks

If you are designing for a space that will host videoconferences, the IES publication this should be a space *Fundamentals of Lighting for Videoconferencing* recommends the following zones:

- Ambient, or general illumination
- Videoconference task lighting
- Lighting of vertical and perimeter surfaces
- Image-display lighting or luminaires located in front of the projection screen or monitor
- Additional zones for task lighting on the table, accent, and display lighting

The more complex the AV space, the more complex the zoning required to meet various needs.

As with luminaires, you should document your lighting zones to show which lights will be working together. As you document the zoning plan, be logical. You can color code them, if that helps, or you can label them using symbols and a key.

Lighting Control

After zoning your lights, you will then need to consider how the end user will interact with them. This means determining how lights will be controlled, setting up preset levels, and incorporating control interfaces.

On/Off vs. Dimmable

The simplest way of adjusting lighting levels is a switch. Switches give you the option of two conditions: on and off. They can control a single light or an entire zone.

The most basic lighting design for an AV room would be two zones of switched lights. Typically, the lights in front of the projection screen can be turned off separately from the rest of the room. Switches are rated by the amount of current they can safely pass. When a number of luminaires are grouped onto one zone, it is common to control them using a higher current-capable controller.

Another, more complex way of controlling a lighting system is through dimmers, which give users greater flexibility to set light levels based on the task at hand. Dimmers are controls that can reduce the percent of lumens coming from a light source by varying the voltage (or current) to the luminaires. They can be simple, such as a switch/dimmer on the wall for manual control, or complex, such as a computer controller.

Dimmers are rated according to their power-handling capability and, therefore, are different for incandescent and fluorescent lamps.

It is common practice to use only 80 percent of a dimmer's capacity for incandescent loads. For example, if a dimmer is rated at 2400 W, the designed load should not exceed 1920 W (80 percent of 2400).

Fluorescent loads have an inherent surge, and dimmers that control them are commonly derated by 30 to 50 percent. Fluorescents can't be dimmed unless fitted with appropriate dimmable ballasts.

Lighting Scenes

A *scene* or *preset* is a recallable configuration of lighting levels for one or more zones. If your design specifies dimmable lighting, then it can be controlled through scenes or presets that dictate the lighting levels in every zone, regardless of method. These should be specified based on the task.

Thinking back to the needs analysis for the room, you should be able to specify the number of lux or footcandles you need from each zone and preset to create the proper scene. You can reference the IES *Lighting Handbook* to find the various categories necessary for your particular tasks. If you specify dimmable lighting, you can calculate these zones more precisely.

For any given scene, every zone is working together to produce the correct lighting for a particular task. In a scene/preset for "Presentations," Zone 1 is turned off to keep light away from the projection screen, Zone 2 is dimmed to 75 percent for task lighting, and Zone 3 is on to direct light at the person speaking. When a user presses the "Presentations" button, the lighting in all three zones is automatically adjusted to support that task.

Figure 8-11 shows a lighting control panel with seven scenes, an off switch, and dimming options. Each scene will recalibrate the lighting in the room for different tasks. As you consider the usability of this panel, would you be able to walk into the room and instantly set the scene for a videoconference? Probably not, because the numbers don't tell you much about what each preset is meant to do. As a designer, you should be thinking about how your users will interact with your AV system. In this case, specifying a panel that labels scenes by task would better meet the needs of the client.

Figure 8-11
A panel with
seven scenes

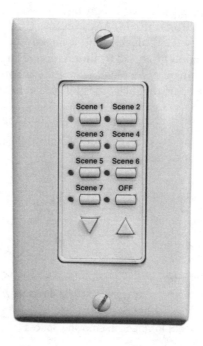

Keep in mind, not every wall panel works with every dimming control system. Specifying a scene panel with dimmers and other features is beneficial only if the dimming system interface can yield the intended results. You don't want a scene selection/dimming unit that doesn't interface with the dimming control system.

 TIP Be sure to specify control-override features and keep window treatments and lights independently addressable. Override features allow end users to operate the lights when daylight-saving timers alter a room, for example. Keeping shades separate from lighting presets allows people to adjust the window treatments without having to cycle through lighting scenes.

Lighting a Videoconference

Videoconferencing requires a particular set of design criteria to address both the viewers in a space and the camera that is capturing images. Although people in a room are capable of capturing and processing images using both their eyes and their brains, a video camera simply captures images. Humans have the ability to adjust to a far greater range of image contrasts, movement speeds, and luminance variations than a camera.

With this in mind, when designing a room to support videoconferencing, you must think of the people in the room and the camera. Your lighting requirements need to strike the right balance between the two, as described in Table 8-2.

Glare

Chances are, you've experienced bright light in your eyes or seen a TV screen partially washed out by light from the sun. Any excessive bright light that causes discomfort or a reduction in visibility is called *glare,* and it negatively impacts your AV design.

Glare is the sensation produced by luminance within the visual field that is sufficiently greater than the luminance to which the eyes are adapted and causes annoyance, discomfort, or loss in visual performance or visibility. There are two types of glare.

- *Direct glare,* or any excessive bright light coming directly into the eyes or camera
- *Indirect glare,* or any excessive bright light reflecting off a surface before coming into the eyes or camera

Participant Need	Camera Need
Visually comfortable room	Proper vertical illumination on faces
Views without glare on video displays and tasks	Appropriate contrasts between subjects and room surfaces
Proper contrast of displays	Correct subject to camera distance
Unobstructed view of other displays that might be used (whiteboards and so on)	No direct views of luminaires or of video display monitors; specific seating arrangement

Table 8-2 Lighting Needs in Videoconferencing Spaces

When it comes to videoconferencing, your goal is to avoid direct glare from light sources entering the camera, as well as indirect glare, called *veiling reflections,* from reflecting light off nonmatte surfaces and washing out critical text and details. Some ways of addressing glare include the following:

- Specifying the location of the camera
- Specifying the luminaire distribution
- Specifying the wall and furniture finishes

Light Balance

Videoconferencing systems require proper light balance to produce high-quality images. In general, three-point lighting of a presenter will create suitable lighting in many AV designs, but it's especially true of videoconferencing. A fourth light can be aimed at the rear wall to help with the camera's auto-iris setting (see Figure 8-12). Four layers of light are often considered in videoconference rooms.

- Key light
- Fill light
- Back light
- Wall wash

Here is what the letters mean in Figure 8-12:

- A is the key light, the brightest light on the subject.
- B is the fill light, filling in the dark spot created by the key light.
- C is the back light. It shines on the subject's shoulders and hair. This creates an outline around the subject and separates the subject from the wall behind.
- D is the wall wash that lights the background. It helps to produce a pleasing image when using an auto-iris camera.

Lighting for video can be a challenge because the contrast of the image must not exceed the contrast ratio of the camera's pickup device. If the contrast ratio of the device is exceeded, then clipping can occur. Clipping may cause the person's face to appear

Figure 8-12
Four layers of light

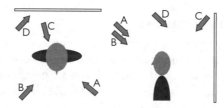

too white on camera. If the lighting is too dark, noise can enter the image because of automatic gain settings in the camera. When flat, low-contrast lighting is used, images can look washed out and dull. Proper lighting will create images that look good and are interesting to watch.

This is why specifying dimmable lighting is essential in videoconference scenes.

NOTE In many cases, back lighting and wall washing are optional. The key and fill lights may produce enough light on the wall to make them unnecessary. It is also important to note that fill light can come from a lamp that is providing key light on an adjacent area.

Color Temperature

Some video cameras have a manual setting for color temperature; it should be set to the color temperature of the lamps used. If the camera uses auto white balance, then it will adjust automatically. It is important that wall colors do not "fool" a camera into thinking the wall is white. This will make for incorrect white settings that affect skin tones, which, in turn, may create images that are tinted green or pink.

Correlated color temperature is important when lighting videoconferences. Here are two examples of how you will see CCT applied:

- Video cameras are not as forgiving of variations in CCT as the human eye. Therefore, electronic adjustments are often made for what "white" should be.

- A monitor or projector may have a CCT selection feature. This allows you to alter the "whiteness" of the image for the lighting conditions in the environment. You can make the "white" of the displayed images match the "white" of a piece of paper under the room's lighting conditions.

IES's *Fundamentals of Lighting for Videoconferencing* recommends that fluorescent sources have a CCT of 3000 to 3500 K, with a minimum CRI of 80; halogen sources should have a CCT of 2800 K or greater. Other types of light sources are not recommended.

NOTE Projected-image or direct-display devices often have a different CCT than the videoconference room lighting. The room lighting is often in the 3000 to 3500 K range, while the display might be 5000 K or greater. This is an issue only if the light from images are seen on the users' faces.

Wall and Table Finishes

When designing a space to support videoconferencing, remember that the materials, colors, and reflections within the camera's field of view can significantly impact the camera's ability to capture the intended images. There are many surfaces that affect a camera, from the materials on the walls, ceiling, floor, tables, chairs, and furniture to the colors and

Finishes/Furniture	Suggested Reflectance Values
Walls	40 to 60 percent reflectance; no small patterns/stripes; no specular finishes; avoid black, orange, yellow, green, and red; grays, blues, and mauves are good
Floor	Less than 60 percent reflectance
Ceiling	70 to 90 percent reflectance
Windows	Blackout shades are required for all windows; interior finish of shades as per wall finishes above
Whiteboards	40 to 60 percent reflectance gray, not white
Tables	20 to 60 percent reflectance; monolithic, neutral colors such as gray, buff, taupe, and lighter; modesty panels for multilevel rooms; no specular finishes; avoid rectangular shape
Chairs	As per wall finish requirements stated earlier in the table

Table 8-3 Reflectance Values of Various Surfaces

properties of surfaces. When light encounters such materials, the characteristics of light will change depending on their properties. Here are some examples:

- Polished material, such as marble or mirror, creates specular (mirrorlike) reflections, similar to the sky on the horizon of a body of water.

- Irregular material, such as etched metal, creates spread reflections similar to specular but with a more cone-shaped reflection.

- Matte materials, such as plaster and matte paint, create diffuse reflections that reflect light without direction and achieve a wide distribution of light.

As you coordinate with allied trades, you will want to specify the reflectance values of various surfaces throughout the space to achieve a good distribution of light. See Table 8-3 for guidance.

 NOTE During the design process, you need to make sure multiple stakeholders take the time to talk to each other. Getting the lighting designer and the interior designer or architect together on a conference call helps to ensure that everyone is taking room and furniture finishes into account with lighting. For example, a glass table will affect lighting levels. A conference call may draw attention to the issue.

Emergency Lighting

AV spaces may need to include emergency lights that are not attractive but are necessary for the building. As you're designing, remember to ask yourself where these signs will be located within your space. Will they cause problems? How can you design around them? Ultimately, these light sources cannot be turned off and cannot be covered up.

For example, you can't place a ceiling-mounted loudspeaker or luminaire near an exit sign. You probably don't want to design your projection screen near an emergency light that stays on in a darkened room either. If you do either of these without realizing the ramification, you may have to restart your design, which could cost time and money.

 TIP Check your local codes for other safety considerations that may affect your lighting design.

Chapter Review

In this chapter, you learned about important lighting specifications you will need to consider as you design the lights within your space. You will use this information when communicating with the lighting consultant and architect about your design, and ultimately you will hand these specifications over to your integrator as a way for them to verify the work.

Review Questions

The following questions are based on the content covered in this chapter and are intended to help reinforce the knowledge you have assimilated. These questions are not extracted from the CTS-D exam nor are they necessarily CTS-D practice exam questions. For an official CTS-D practice exam, see the accompanying CD.

1. For light coming directly from a source such as a lightbulb, what measure and instrument should be used?

    A. Foot lambert with an STL

    B. Candela with an incident meter

    C. Lux with an incident meter

    D. Footcandle with a light impedance meter

2. Considering a 2400 W lighting dimmer is available, the design load for the system should *not* exceed:

    A. 1300 watt

    B. 1750 watt

    C. 1920 watt

    D. 2400 watt

3. What is the highest recommended ambient lighting level illuminating a front-projection screen within a videoconferencing space?

   A. 5 footcandles (50 lux)

   B. 30 footcandles (108 lux)

   C. 45 footcandles (161 lux)

   D. 25 footcandles (215 lux)

4. What other type of light, besides light coming directly from a source, must be measured?

   A. Refracted

   B. Distorted

   C. Fluorescent

   D. Ambient

5. When lighting a room for videoconferencing, the Illuminating Engineering Society recommends that fluorescent light sources have a correlated color temperature of _____.

   A. 2000 to 2500 K

   B. 3000 to 3500 K

   C. 4000 to 4500 K

   D. 5000 to 5500 K

Answers

1. **B.** Use candelas and an incident meter to measure light coming directly from a source.

2. **C.** With a 2400 W lighting dimmer, the design load for the system should not exceed 1920 W (80 percent of capacity).

3. **A.** The highest recommended ambient lighting level illuminating a front-projection screen in a videoconferencing space is 5 footcandles (50 lux).

4. **D.** When considering lighting for an AV design, you should measure ambient light as well as light coming directly from a source.

5. **B.** When lighting a room for videoconferencing, the Illuminating Engineering Society recommends that fluorescent light sources have a correlated color temperature of 3000 to 3500 K.

Structural and Mechanical Considerations

In this chapter, you will learn about

- Building codes and issues that have an impact on AV design
- Equipment mounting requirements
- Mounting requirements in racks and how to calculate power consumption and heat loads
- Heating, ventilation, and air conditioning (HVAC) and fire safety issues that impact AV systems
- The *Audiovisual Systems Energy Management* standard and how you can use it to conserve energy in your AV systems

In a building, there is a limited amount of space for infrastructure, and AV systems aren't the only types of systems that need to be installed. There are HVAC, fire suppression, electrical, lighting, and other systems. And like AV systems, these others comprise not only the actual equipment but also power, cabling, cable pathways, and more. To ensure the systems integrate seamlessly, coordinating the AV design with the members of the architect, engineer, and construction (AEC) team is paramount. Moreover, the standards of all applicable trade groups must be carefully considered and effectively communicated.

This chapter—divided into mechanical and structural topic areas—will discuss various infrastructure elements that are important to your design so you can better communicate with others on the design team. We start by delving into rules and regulations governing the design of the structural and mechanical elements of an AV design.

Domain Check

This chapter relates directly to the following tasks on the CTS-D Exam Content Outline:

- Domain B Task 2: Coordinate architectural/interior design criteria
- Domain B Task 3: Coordinate structural/mechanical criteria
- Domain B Task 8: Coordinate life safety and security criteria
- Domain C Task 3: Produce infrastructure drawings

These tasks comprise 19.2 percent of the exam (about 24 questions). This chapter may also relate to other tasks.

Codes and Regulations

Building codes exist to protect life and safety. They define standards for the design and construction of electric systems, fire protection, and structural systems. The regulatory bodies tasked with overseeing the construction of public spaces want to know the answers to the following questions:

- How many people should we permit within a space?
- How much room is required for exiting?
- How should we protect the people during an emergency situation?
- How should people be protected from accidental electrical shock?
- What construction materials are appropriate (and inappropriate)?

There are many code considerations an AV professional should learn. Most codes are logical and serve a good purpose. Even if they are not enforced in your area, you may want to consider codes as best practices. The following are some examples:

- The Health and Safety Executive in the United Kingdom has a regulation that limits the exposure of employees to certain sound pressure levels. *Local Authority Circular 59/5: Advice on the Enforcement of the Noise at Work Regulations 1989 in Leisure Premises (Where Recorded or Amplified Music is Played)* states that employees should not be subjected to more than an average of 85 A-weighted decibels (dBA) over an eight-hour period without some protective action taken.

- The National Fire Protection Association (NFPA) publishes *NFPA 101B: Code for Means of Egress from Buildings and Structures*. This code provides guidance on the width of aisles for typical seating, the width of exit rows, and furniture arrangement, which are all critical to AV design.

- The *Americans with Disabilities Act* (ADA) offers guidelines to ensure all people, regardless of disability, have the same experience in a space. Australia's *Disabilities Act* and the United Kingdom's *Disabilities Discrimination Act* are similar to the U.S. guidelines.

First we'll go into more depth on specific design elements that consider the needs of people with disabilities. Then we'll discuss some of the electrical and construction codes that affect AV design.

Designing for Equal Access

Many regions, including the United States, have laws or codes that prohibit discrimination based on disability. These laws often impact structural considerations in new construction. In the United States, the Americans with Disabilities Act identifies a range of other construction standards that AV designers must be aware of when laying out a room. For example, everyone should have equal access to a space, and passageways must be kept clear of protruding elements that could interfere with a person's passage through the space.

When it comes to designing for equal access, you will need to refer to the different governing bodies in your location. Governing bodies provide building code provisions for equal access to people with disabilities. For example, the ADA states that the same experience must be provided to all people. However, it does not detail the specific solutions required to meet that requirement.

In the case of AV systems, guidelines dictate that every presenter or end user must have access to the same control functions. This typically means that operator controls should be between 15 and 54 in above the floor, depending on whether someone in a wheelchair is directly in front of the equipment or approaching from the side. This allows a person in a wheelchair to insert media or operate controls. If the equipment must be approached from the front because a wheelchair cannot come beside it, then the access points should be between 15 and 48 in (380 and 1220 mm) high (see Figure 9-1). See the "Ergonomics" section in this chapter for more information.

Figure 9-1
ADA guidelines for access to control functions

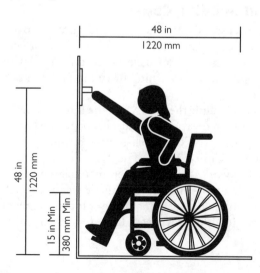

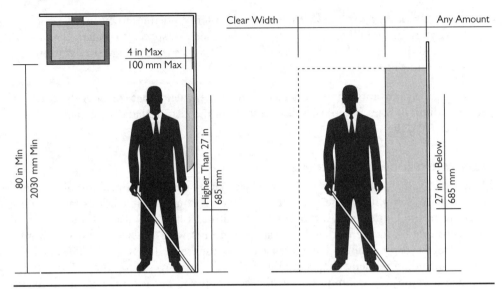

Figure 9-2 ADA guidelines for head and aisle clearance

The guidelines also dictate that every presenter must have access to all sources, including slides, video, and recordings. For example, if there is fixed seating and an audio system, an assistive listening system should be provided for the hearing impaired.

The ADA also recommends certain design guidelines related to head and aisle clearance (Figure 9-2). For example, equipment, such as a display, should protrude no farther than 4 in (101.6 mm) from a wall. And when hanging screens, projectors, or other devices from a ceiling, it's important to note that ADA guidance states that 80 in (2.03 m) is the minimum height for any passageway.

Electric and Building Codes

Codes are an extensive compilation of minimum standards for construction purposes. They protect the health and safety of people who use or occupy buildings and structures. Typically, the authors of codes have no enforcement power. They are merely experts offering their opinions. A governing or ruling body takes these suggestions and adopts them as their own.

Some examples include the NFPA and the International Code Council (ICC), authors of guidelines on the construction and occupancy of buildings. The NFPA authors the *National Electric Code* (NEC), a well-respected source of electrical installation and usage guidelines for the United States. The ICC develops the *International Building Code* (IBC), a reference work for construction materials and practices.

A country may adopt uniform rules that cover any or all of these items. For instance, the Australian Building Codes Board is a joint initiative of all levels of government in Australia. Its mission is to provide guidance for design, construction, and use of buildings through nationally consistent building codes, standards, regulatory requirements, and regulatory systems.

A country may also choose to let smaller governing bodies make the rules. This is the case in the United States. The individual states can develop their own codes, and regions and cities may add their own. They typically reference and adopt portions of the NEC or IBC material. You will revisit electric and building codes in Chapter 10.

 NOTE Make sure you are aware of the codes at work in your area, as prescribed by the *authority having jurisdiction* (AHJ), or regional regulatory authority. Ignorance is never an excuse. In some cases, several conflicting codes from jurisdictions may overlap. In a case like this, it is important that you follow the most restrictive code.

Mounting Considerations

The building structure is the part of a building that is capable of supporting other materials. This may be structural steel, concrete, or wood trusses. Keep in mind, there are portions of the building structure that you can see, but they may not be true structural components.

You can have the perfect design with all the right equipment to fulfill a client's needs, but if the building structure can't sustain the weight of mounted AV components, the installation will be unsafe. To create a plan for mounting AV devices as necessary, ask the following questions at the beginning of the project:

- Will the building structure hold each piece of equipment?
- Will the mounted support system hold each piece of equipment?

To answer these questions, you should determine what type of building material is behind finished walls and ceilings. What looks like a solid wall may, in fact, be old plaster with no structural integrity.

Mounting Options

You have a few options for mounting AV equipment in a space—on the floor, wall, or overhead. This allows you to offer alternatives depending on the structure of the room or building.

Floor Mounting

Floor mounting is the simplest form of mounting because gravity is working in your favor. The equipment is mounted to the floor (see Figure 9-3), simultaneously ensuring that the equipment is securely attached and protected from theft or misuse.

Alignment of a rear-projection mirror assembly takes many hours of labor. It needs to be performed in a way that prevents accidental movement and resulting damage. Once

Figure 9-3
Bolts hold rear-
projection mirror
mounts in place.

the alignment is complete, the assembly can be attached to the floor permanently. However, this task should not be performed without the building owner's permission.

Wall Mounting

When it comes to mounting equipment to a wall, an AV designer has to consider several structural elements, in addition to the equipment weight.

Suppose you intend to mount a remote-controlled video camera to the wall of a training room. The camera assembly weighs 30 lb (13.6 kg), and the mounting bracket offers a footprint of 6 by 6 in (152.4 by 152.4 mm) for support.

It may seem like attaching the mounting bracket to the wall is a simple solution, but there are other considerations.

- Can the wall withstand the load of this camera assembly? You should investigate the construction of the wall.
- Will the weight of the camera on the end of the mounting bracket pull the assembly out of the wall? The camera suspended from the wall on a bracket creates a lever.

One of the most important aspects of wall mounting is to include proper blocking. Blocking is the support system or construction material that is added to the wall, typically before the wall finish is applied (see Figure 9-4).

The general contractor may install heavy wood into the wall assembly across three or more studs prior to applying sheet rock or drywall. Once the finish is applied to the wall, the blocking is invisible to the eye. This cannot be accomplished without planning and coordination among the AV designer, architect, and builder.

Overhead Mounting

Any time you suspend or hang overhead equipment, you need to think about supporting the equipment's weight. And because you always want to attach mounting support

Figure 9-4
Blocking for
wall-mounted
equipment

to the building structure and not the ceiling itself, you're less concerned with the type of ceiling in a space than what's behind it. How is the building constructed? Is it poured, pan-style concrete? Is it post-tension construction, in which smooth concrete includes high-tension cables running through it for support?

Construction stability is vital. If someone on your project drills through a cable in post-tension flooring, the cable could snap with such great force that it tears off the outside of the building. Always verify the depth and location of these cables with the building owner before attempting to mount equipment to a ceiling or floor. If this information is not available for the building, then an X-ray of the proposed drilling or trenching site must be conducted and interpreted by specialists.

When you're planning for mounting to a wall or overhead, check the load limit in the mounting equipment specifications to find out the weight at which the item will structurally fail.

Load Limit

Load limit is an important part of AV equipment's specifications. One element of the load limit is the safe working load (SWL), or a similar rating called the working load limit (WLL), which is the weight that must not be exceeded. Note that the load factor specified for the mount refers only to the mount and not to the bolts or any other components used in mounting. Each individual component has its own load factor, and you should be able to identify the weakest link.

If you exceed the load limit, your device won't just fall; it could also cause damage to other equipment and the space itself, not to mention possibly injure people nearby. When considering load limits and possible mounting malfunctions, you need to guard against the following:

- Improper calculation of loads.
- Shear (see Figure 9-5), or the separation between the wall and the mounting. It's measured by how much weight is necessary to break the mounting from the wall.

Figure 9-5
Shearing of a bolt

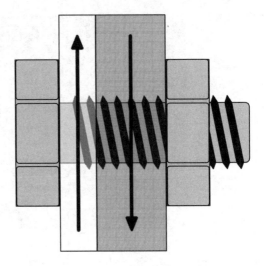

- Tensile strength (see Figure 9-6), or the maximum amount of tension—pulling apart—that the hardware can withstand before it fails.

- Pullout (see Figure 9-7), which takes into account the pounds of force needed to pull a fastener from the wall.

- The placement of bolts. In general, bolts placed at the top of a mounting carry more stress than bolts placed lower down. Placement should match manufacturers' instructions.

Figure 9-6
Tensile stress
of bolt

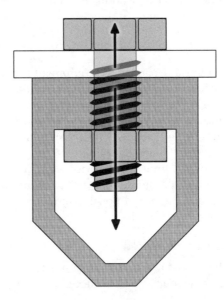

Figure 9-7
Pullout of a bolt

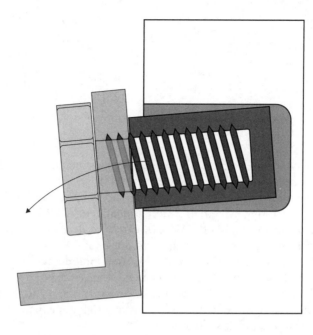

TIP   When your goal is to mount equipment safely (which is always), multiply published design weights by no less than five. Five is the safety factor, also known as the design factor, load factor, or safety ratio. If a loudspeaker with mounting hardware weighs 100 lb (45kg), you should use mounting hardware that can handle 500 lb (227 kg).

Mounting Hardware

When it comes time to mount AV equipment, installers will need the following:

- The product to be mounted
- The mount
- The appropriate hardware
- Cable dressing as needed

The choice of mounting hardware, or *fasteners,* depends on the type of mounting surface. For example, your options for mounting in concrete will not necessarily work for hollow block. Hardware specifications will be categorized by type and manufacturer and the method of sinking into the material.

To select the correct mounting hardware, consider the holes or slots in the mounting (and note that holes are stronger than slots), as well as their location. The number of bolts used in a mount determines the structural strength per attach point. Understand

Figure 9-8
Bolt grades

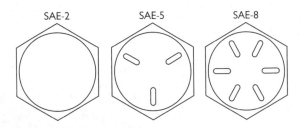

the size, type, and length of the bolts, as well as the number and size of threads. This will all help AV installers successfully execute your design.

Standards organizations, such as the Society of Automotive Engineers (SAE), American Society of Testing Materials International (ASTM International), and International Organization for Standardization (ISO), have developed ways to categorize mounting hardware by composition, quality, and durability.

The ASTM International and SAE use a unique marking technique for bolt heads. The raised bumps on the head of the bolt indicate the bolt's *grade,* as shown in Figure 9-8.

If there are none, then it is Grade 2 and very soft. One raised bump is Grade 3. The more bumps, the stronger the bolt. Selecting the proper hardware for mounting is critical for a sturdy and safe installation.

The ISO has a different numbering scheme. It uses a numerical marking system called a *property classification* (see Figure 9-9). The property class numbers relate to the hardware's material strength. The higher the number, the stronger the bolt.

TIP   When designing for mounted equipment, specify ASTM and SAE bolts that are at least Grade 5. When using an ISO-rated hardware, use 8.8 and above for AV installations. It is best to procure your fasteners from an AV hardware vendor. A local hardware store may not have Grade 5 or 8.8 hardware in stock.

Mounting considerations include size, couplings, length/depth, thread size, and the gauge of steel. Usually a pipe or threaded rod is used to suspend a device. Black iron provides substantial strength, but there are other material choices.

The term *schedule* associated with pipe utilization refers to the material thickness, similar to wire gauge. For long runs, specify a single piece of pipe without couplings. Each coupling gives the mounting two additional weak spots or points of failure. A threaded rod should be used only for vertical mounts.

Figure 9-9
Bolt property
classes

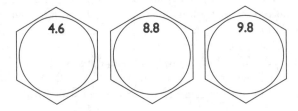

TIP When using black iron pipe, any threaded junction should have some form of locking function, such as a set screw or an alignment hole with a through bolt. This will prevent the assembly from unscrewing over time and use.

Designing the Rack

As an AV professional, you know that some equipment gets mounted, and some goes in a rack. What does a rack do? The most obvious purpose is to group together systems and subsystems. But racks also protect the elements of your AV design and provide security after installation. They can also prolong the life of the design by maintaining system integrity.

Racks come in many different styles, including the following:

- **Fixed racks**, which are used for most AV equipment. Fixed racks have rails that hold AV equipment and can be either stand-alone or"gangable." Gangable racks can be attached together to create larger racks.

- **Wall-mounted racks**, which can be attached to any type of wall with the proper hardware. These racks swing open so technicians can access equipment.

- **Slide-out (built-in) racks**, which come in handy where service area is limited. The whole rack can be pulled out for installation or service. Such racks may also rotate or spin in place for easier access.

- **Portable racks**, which comprise metal, wood, or plastic racks with casters and handles for moving around. There are portable racks for specific rack-mounted equipment, such as mixing consoles, as well as trunks, cases, and custom solutions for just about any kind of AV system that requires protection in storage or transit.

- **Portable shock-mounted racks**, where the rack shell is encased in foam or suspended by shock-absorbing mounts and designed to withstand transport by truck or air.

Racks of all types come in various sizes to match the width and height of specific components. Many of the sizes are industry standard to make designing a rack easier.

Rack Sizes

A standard AV equipment rack is 19 in (482.6 mm) wide. Height is specified in terms of *rack units* (RUs); 1 RU (basically, a single slot in a rack) is an Electronic Industries Alliance (EIA) standard of 1.75 in (44.5 mm) tall. Therefore, a device that takes up 3 RUs will be up to 5.25 in (133.4 mm) tall. (When talking about rack height, people often drop the *R* in RU and describe, for example, a rack enclosure with 44 units as a 44U rack.)

A rack's height is specified to accommodate the number of installed components and provide adequate space for ventilation. The specification is given in the number of rack units available for equipment mounting. Rack heights vary considerably depending on whether the rack is a standard or custom configuration. The total number of rack units available will usually range up to 44 RUs, or 77 in (1955.8 mm) tall.

Rack sizes may also be determined by the size of the space into which they will be installed. For example, a rack must be able to fit into an acceptable equipment closet or fit through the building passages. Rack depth typically varies from 12 to 32+ in (304.8 to 812.8+ mm).

In an AV design, you should provide enough rack space for all current equipment, as well as extra equipment to support the system's future growth.

NOTE   Although a lot of rack space is handy, some taller racks may not fit through standard doorways or in an elevator. Because integrators will likely build racks off-site to ensure they work properly, transporting racks to the client site must be carefully considered.

AV equipment is also measured in rack units. An audio mixer might be 1 RU high (1U), while an amplifier might be 2 RUs high (2U). Some bigger equipment, such as switchers, can be 10 RUs or larger.

The hole spacing on standard rack units is designed to match various RU dimensions. On each side of the mounting rail, there are typically three screw holes for one rack unit. The proper hole spacing provides stability for mounting equipment (see Figure 9-10).

The dark arrows in Figure 9-11 indicate the center of a rack unit and standard EIA spacing for mounting holes. Note that the holes are not evenly spaced. Equipment that is manufactured for a rack has *ears*—extensions on both sides of the faceplate that align with the holes in the mounting rail. Sometimes the ears are ordered separately and attached to the sides of equipment first. Rack screws through the ear holes secure the equipment in the rack.

Figure 9-10
Rack-mount hole
spacing

Figure 9-11
Standard
equipment
mount holes

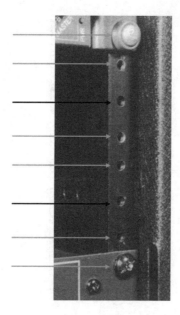

Ergonomics

When designing a rack, it's important to keep in mind the user-interface components, namely, buttons, dials, switches, and control panels that users will need to access to operate AV systems. Applying ergonomic principles ensures that such elements are within easy reach of everyone using the rack.

Equipment with user-interface components, such as Blu-ray players, should be placed within easy reach of standing and sitting users. For example, you want the player at a convenient height for the end user to insert a disc. In the United States, it is important to follow the Americans with Disabilities Act guidelines for equal experience, which dictate "reach ranges" for people in wheelchairs who need to insert media or operate controls from the front or side of a rack. Forward and side reaches are between 15 and 48 in (381 and 1219.2 mm) above the finished floor (AFF).

Media players and control panels usually go between eye height for a standing and sitting user, as shown in Figure 9-12. Devices that users won't necessarily interact with (such as wireless microphone receivers or patch panels, which often include connector jacks for AV and network equipment) can be located at the top or bottom of a rack.

Weight Distribution

Not only must the equipment in a rack be placed where it's accessible, its weight should be distributed strategically (as shown in the following illustration). For example, a typical 60 lb (27.22 kg) audio amplifier may be the heaviest device designed for an equipment

Figure 9-12
Important height references in a rack

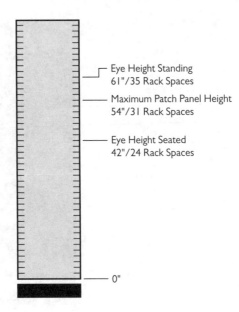

Eye Height Standing
61"/35 Rack Spaces

Maximum Patch Panel Height
54"/31 Rack Spaces

Eye Height Seated
42"/24 Rack Spaces

0"

rack. The rack in question may not provide additional stability, meaning it isn't designed to be bolted to the floor or mounted to a wall. If the amplifier gets installed near the top of the rack, the rack may tip over because of its weight. In such a situation, the best place for the amplifier is at the bottom of the rack.

Most equipment is supported entirely by the rack screws in the front mounting rail. Heavier equipment typically occupies two or more RUs, providing more support. Some equipment may need the additional support of a rear-mount rail.

Professional equipment has built-in or removable rack ears for mounting, which help support rack-mounted devices. Heavier equipment, such as power amplifiers, includes additional mounting provisions at the rear of the equipment, which are secured to additional rack mounting rails located in the rear of the rack. Always check the manufacturer's manual for mounting and spacing requirements.

Signal Separation

In rack layout design, it is common to group equipment according to function. For instance, you may want to specify that all video components be installed together in one area of the rack (as shown in the following illustration). This practice is called *signal separation*.

Signal separation protects against the effects of electromagnetic interference (EMI)—*noise* or *crosstalk*. For example, the cables coming out of rack-mounted equipment and carrying microphone-level signals (0.0001 V) should be kept separate from cables carrying power (120 V). This maintains signal integrity.

Signal separation allows your audio wiring to remain shorter because most of that cable will be between the audio components. Shorter cable means less opportunity for the cables to pick up induced noise.

Block Diagrams

Before installers can start wiring everything together in a rack, they have to be able to visualize the signal flow among the various components within a system. To help them do that, you should create block diagrams.

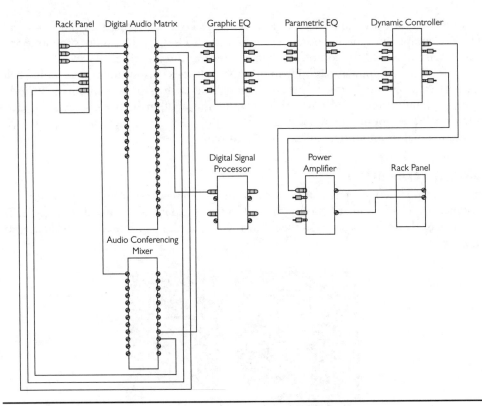

Figure 9-13 Block diagram

A *block diagram* illustrates the signal path through a system. It is drawn with simple icons (triangles, circles, or boxes) representing the system's devices, as shown in Figure 9-13.

Interconnecting lines (sometimes with arrows) indicate the signal path. They are drawn or read from left to right and from top to bottom.

A designer typically provides block diagrams to installers. A good diagram will have well-marked icon labels because several common symbol variations are used in block diagrams. For example, an amplifier is usually, but not always, symbolized as a triangle.

The goal of a diagram is to visualize the signal flow. Analyze two connected icons at a time and ask yourself, "Will this work?" Then work your way into greater detail. This process will reveal any potential problem areas.

In your AV design, you also have to calculate how much heat is produced during normal operation by all electronic equipment within an AV rack.

Heat Load

Any piece of electronic equipment that is powered on generates heat, whether it is idle or doing work. The resulting *heat load* is measured in British thermal units (BTU). The following are common BTU unit conversions:

- One BTU equals about 1,055 joules.
- One watt per hour equals 3.41 BTU.

An AV designer typically calculates the total BTU in a system and provides that information to the HVAC engineer. Designers can then design appropriate cooling to prevent equipment failure and balance HVAC systems so people can be comfortable in the space. Consult the owner's manual or device labels for the allowed wattage a piece of equipment can have in the AV rack.

The formula for calculating heat load is as follows:

$$Total\ BTU = W_E \times 3.41$$

where:

- W_E is the total watts of all equipment used in the room.
- 3.41 is the conversion factor, where 1 watt of power generates 3.41 BTU of heat per hour.

This formula does not account for the heat load generated by amplifiers.

NOTE As the number of digital signals that have to be processed continues to grow, AV equipment becomes more "computer like." Digital devices tend to draw more current and generate more heat than their analog counterparts because of analog-to-digital (A/D) and digital-to-analog (D/A) conversions and digital processing. Managing heat dissipation in racks, credenzas, lecterns, and any enclosures that house AV equipment becomes increasingly important.

Calculating Heat Load from Power Amplifiers

Power amplifiers are distinctly different from other components in the amount of heat they dissipate. By far, they will typically have the highest wattage rating of all the equipment you are handling, with the only exception perhaps being the projector.

A multichannel power amplifier that is rated at 200W per channel may also have a power consumption rating of 600W maximum. Designers are less interested in the wattage per channel rating than the consumption rating, but the maximum consumption of 600W does not tell the whole story. Here are some factors that need to be considered with power amplifiers:

- The efficiency of the amplifier. Of the power that is consumed, how much of it is used up within the mounted case compared with the amount transferred to the loudspeakers?

- Voice paging, music, rock music, and pink noise have drastically different demands on the amplifier. This is referred to as the *duty cycle*—how much of the time it is powered on and how much it is at rest. What kind of program material is being amplified?

- How much power will be demanded of the amplifier? Just because it is capable of producing 200W per channel, are you designing it to do so?

- How often is the power amplifier turned on? Is it always on and operational or only one hour per week?

It would be improper to simply take a 600W consumption and multiply that by 3.41 BTU to come up with 2,046 BTU. This ignores all the previously mentioned factors.

The amount of heat the equipment generates is directly related to its power consumption. For example, a 20W equalizer produces less heat than a 40W equalizer. If electronic equipment gets too hot, it may cease to operate. Therefore, manufacturers incorporate methods to circulate cooler air in and hot air out of electronic equipment.

Cooling a Rack

With all the heat-generating equipment contained close together in a rack, it is up to the AV designers and technicians to direct a flow of cool air into the rack and hot air out.

There are two main methods of cooling a rack, shown in Figure 9-14.

- Pressurization
- Evacuation

When you *pressurize* a rack with air, cooler air is blown into the rack with fans. The fans may have a filter to prevent dust and dirt from entering the rack. Vents on the sides and top of the rack provide an escape for the hot air.

The *evacuation* cooling method uses fans to draw air out of the rack, usually through the top vents. Cool air is drawn into the rack from the side and bottom vents. Since there is no filtering over every vent or slot, dirt can infiltrate the equipment rack. It is important to keep the equipment rack dust and dirt free with periodic maintenance.

Most electronics have vents where the hot air can escape, typically in the back of the unit, and slots or vents where cool air can enter. Pay attention to the heat flow between component vents. Avoid mounting equipment with opposite heat flows next to each other because such placement will cause circulation of only the hot air.

Figure 9-14
Rack-cooling
methods

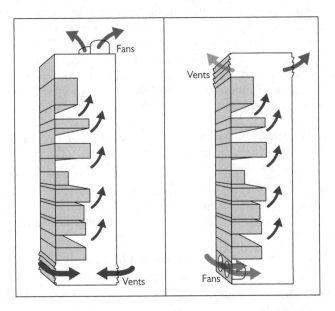

You should separate pieces of equipment that produce a lot of heat with blank or vented panels in between. Equipment producing a greater amount of heat should be placed near the top of the rack.

TIP Amplifiers create a dichotomy because they are heavy, so they can cause the rack to tip over. Amplifiers also create a lot of heat, which is best vented out if the gear is near the top of the rack. When the rack is securely mounted in place to the wall or floor, then it is OK to place the amp at a higher rack elevation.

You know all about removing the heat from the equipment rack, but you should now think in terms of where that heat should go. How do you remove it from the room? HVAC systems are the physical systems that control the environmental (temperature and humidity) conditions of a workspace. Let's talk about AV-related HVAC requirements.

HVAC Considerations

AV designers are primarily concerned with the relationship between HVAC systems and the maintenance of temperature and humidity in the AV equipment, as well as the associated noises created in presentation spaces.

AV designers are not responsible for, and in many cases are barred from, the design of HVAC systems. However, an AV designer should coordinate HVAC requirements with an HVAC designer and make the HVAC designer aware of the AV system's impact on an HVAC system.

Heat load is considered a load to the HVAC system. An AV designer will typically calculate the total BTU in a system and provide that information to the HVAC engineer. They will then design appropriate cooling to create a more comfortable environment for the equipment and the people.

All HVAC systems generally have the same basic components. A system consists of components that do the following:

- Extract heat to and from the environment
- Extract heat to and from the conditioned spaces
- Move air throughout the conditioned spaces

HVAC Issues that Impact Design

A designer should understand how HVAC systems affect AV systems. HVAC is usually the main source of noise that a designer will have to address. Being aware of the issues can help an AV designer collaborate with a mechanical engineer.

Background noise within a room can affect speech intelligibility, which creates additional challenges for AV designers. One common source of background noise is the building HVAC system. HVAC system components that can generate noise include the following:

- **Fans** Motor vibrations and air turbulence.
- **Diffusers** Passage of supply or return air through the diffuser vents. HVAC diffusion vents can generate a substantial amount of noise and unwanted airflow if they are not designed and balanced carefully for the space's function.

- **Ducts** Passage of air. The ductwork also can carry noise generated by other sources throughout the building. This is especially problematic in conferencing spaces. If you requisition oversized diffusers, they will cure many problems before they appear.

Sound systems typically need to perform 25 dB above the noise level. You should use an A-weighted sound pressure level (SPL) meter and measure the noise level of the HVAC system. For example, if the HVAC ambient noise measures 45 dB SPL, add 25 dB SPL. The loudspeaker system would need to produce at least 70 dB SPL at the listener's ear level.

Vibration is another source of noise. The AV designer, architect, and mechanical engineer should work together to ensure large mechanical units are not placed directly adjacent to the spaces that require a low-noise floor.

Mechanical vibration and noise created by vibration are often major complaints in buildings. The low rumble of a chiller or large fan can resonate throughout a building if it is not designed properly and given the proper vibration isolation. Low-frequency vibration should also be considered because it can affect the stability of display devices attached to the building structure.

Many components can be used to control vibration. Larger pieces of equipment are often provided with spring isolators, air mounts, or rubber padding. Piping systems can also be isolated with the use of flexible pipe connectors between sections of metal pipe to control vibrations traveling down the pipe walls.

The cooling diffusers should be located in a way that ensures cooler air is available to the presenter area. You should not count on diffusers from the audience area to make the presenter area cool, or the audience will continually complain about being too cold. The air flow from a diffuser can also cause a projection screen to sway.

Current construction techniques conserve space by using the open cavity above the visible ceiling as a pathway for breathable air. It gets recycled via this space to the ventilation system. In this instance, the space is called a *return air plenum*. Placing anything into this return air plenum will require special materials and methods.

If a fire breaks out in the return air plenum space, the smoke will recirculate throughout the building. Any toxic smoke from burning materials in this space could cause serious physical harm to people. All material should be rated for use within the return air plenum. In many locations, it is a violation of rules set forth by the authorities to use materials that are not rated for plenum space use. In the United States, the NEC spells out permissible materials and methods for these areas.

AV designers must be aware of the locations and installation requirements of HVAC system components to create a compatible overall system design. And AV drawings assist with the discovery process.

AV Drawings

A *reflected ceiling plan* (see Figure 9-15) is an especially important plan for AV designers since it depicts the features included within the ceiling. It includes AV components, such as loudspeakers, as well as other features that can interfere with the location and/or installation of AV components, such as the HVAC ducts or diffusers or indirect lighting hanging from the ceiling.

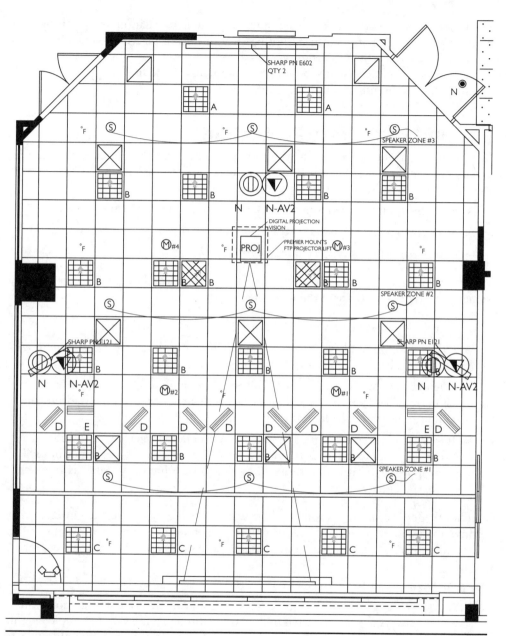

Figure 9-15   Reflected ceiling plan

The designer should check the air duct placement in relation to any projector-mounting locations or any screen-mounting locations. A misplaced air vent with a high air velocity may cause the projection screens to shake or wave.

In addition to HVAC systems, buildings incorporate fire and life safety systems, which also need to be accounted for in AV design.

Fire and Life Safety Protection

In case of fire, a fire alarm system will attempt to alert the occupants so they can be evacuated from the space. The AV professional may need to integrate the AV system with the fire alarm system to do any of the following:

- Mute the sound from an ongoing AV system to allow the alarm to be heard
- Send visual messages to a display
- Return lighting to the "on" state to allow egress

Fire suppression systems may also be installed and employed by the life safety professionals. You should be aware of the following:

- Wet systems are fire protection systems that use pressurized water.
- Dry systems do not have water constantly present in the system. Dry systems are pressurized by the fire department in the event of a fire.
- Chemical systems replace the room air with fire-inhibiting gas, such as halon, CO^2, or halocarbon agents (chemical agents that contain chlorine, fluorine, or iodine, either individually or in some combination).
- Inert gas systems are designed to reduce the ambient oxygen concentration in a protected space to between 10 and 14 percent, a level that is breathable but will not support flaming combustion. These systems use inert gases such as argon and nitrogen, either as mixtures or alone.

The AV designer must coordinate their work with the mechanical engineer so that sprinkler systems are not located over projectors, which would hinder the flow of water to a fire, and projection screens, which would hide alarm indicators when they are deployed.

Fire Safety

While drilling through a firewall is sometimes unavoidable, there are ways to do so safely. For instance, always use *firestop* when pulling cable through a firewall. Firestop comes in many forms, such as foam, blocks, or plugs, but it all has the same basic function. It acts as an impenetrable insulator against flames.

When mounting AV equipment in the ceiling, you may find firestop in the way of your installation. Scrape off as little firestop as necessary, and make sure you replace it immediately.

Energy Management

Before we close out this chapter, we need to discuss one more element of structural and mechanical systems—energy management. You will find ANSI/InfoComm 4, *Audiovisual Systems Energy Management Standard,* invaluable in your design. We use the term *power meter* to describe the individual AV devices that you've installed and configured, which allows you to measure what's in the actual space. You can think of this standard as adding a huge power meter to a room that already has AV in it.

Adhering to the *Energy Management Standard* is a long-term, ongoing commitment. There are seven conformance requirements in the standard.

- *An energy management plan* (EMP) identifies energy reduction goals.
- An *energy management manager* (EMM) is a role that provides leadership and management of the system.
- A *wiring diagram* illustrates how power to AV components is controlled and monitored and how the energy management system is connected to the AV system.
- A *visual display* shows end users and management the continuous power usage of the AV system.
- Use of *automated devices* and *power-state changes* ensure the AV system is energy-efficient.
- A *method for continuous power measurement* collects power consumption data.
- *End-user operation training* leads to understanding, participation, and behavior modification.

The standard centers on three big ideas.

- Data collection
- Automation
- Education and training

Each of these concepts warrants special treatment. We'll discuss them in detail next.

Data Collection

Data collection is all about the *power factor* of devices and how they're measured. If the point is to conserve energy, you have to quantify it first—how much energy is my AV system using? You add hardware to the room to gather all the data so you can analyze it.

When it comes to data collection, AV devices inside and outside of the rack collect the measurements. Measuring within the rack is easy, but devices such as projectors, displays, and digital signage add a layer of complexity.

Data collection is not just about powering the measuring devices in the rack; you have to think about remote monitoring and relay devices. Remote monitoring and relay devices are attached to an AV device in the room and allow users to monitor when the device is on, off, how much power it's using, and so on. That information is sent to a computer, which you can then use to run reports.

NOTE How do you know if someone is in the room? Occupancy sensors are a great way to collect data about access to the space. You've probably been in a room where you walk in and the lights come on automatically. This is what occupancy sensors do. In terms of your AV systems, you can set them up to react when someone walks into the room. The sensor has technology in it that's routable to the control system.

Automation

Suppose you install all your AV devices and you collect and analyze the data to find that too many devices are powered on at the same time. A critical design concept is not what should be on—it's what should be off. This is known as *off thinking*.

Device power status is a major design issue. Think of a projector: It has optional power states such as on, off, disconnected, or standby. What needs to be on all the time? What can go into standby? This information is kept in the system state matrix created by the AV designer, which keeps track of the power states for individual devices in an AV system.

You should think of system design in terms of functions. Functions can include presentations, videoconferencing, and so on. The matrix allows you to keep track of what's on, what's off, or what's in standby (see Figure 9-16). You can then organize all that information and integrate it into your control system so that when you switch functions, the right devices go on or off.

Figure 9-16
Sample automated setup

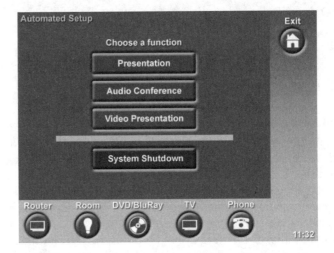

Well-designed automation systems are those that the end user doesn't need to think about. Unified systems, such as room lighting, screen deployment, and audio settings, should work in harmony, delivering an experience appropriate to the use of the room.

Programming and data collection lose value if people don't make improvements based on the information obtained about the AV system. Incorporating an energy management component into a system may lead to more responsible energy consumption. Educating end users about power consumption helps to achieve that goal.

Education and Training

End users may walk into a room, turn everything on, and use only a flip chart. Devices don't have to be on all the time, and if you know that your system is managing energy, then it's going to change how you think about an AV-enabled room.

Some end users don't want to turn off the AV system because they don't fully understand how it works. Other end users may be impatient and keep turning the system on and off because they're not sure if it's powered on.

The role of an energy management manager is to provide training to end users and work with the designer and integrator to understand how the system operates and how the system has been designed. Proper training ultimately enables end users to make energy-conserving decisions.

 NOTE Some companies take power conservation so seriously that they turn it into a competition. To assist with that, designers can set up a display outside the room to show how many kilowatt/hours of power are used by the room each day.

Chapter Review

Mechanical systems, including the HVAC and fire suppression systems, have a significant impact on the design and layout of an AV system. The AV designer must carefully consider these elements to make sure the end users are comfortable and the equipment functions as expected.

The designer must also consider how the AV system will be integrated into the building's structure. This includes making sure the equipment is mounted securely, accessible to the end user, and in accordance with relevant codes. Once again, the structural considerations include issues of both functionality and safety. Once you complete this chapter review, you'll be ready to tackle the electrical infrastructure requirements of your design.

Review Questions

The following questions are based on the content covered in this chapter and are intended to help reinforce the knowledge you have assimilated. These questions are not extracted from the CTS-D exam nor are they necessarily CTS-D practice exam questions. For an official CTS-D practice exam, see the accompanying CD.

1. If an amplifier draws 7 amperes (A) at 120 V of alternating current (VAC), without considering amplifier efficiency, what is the heat load it generates?

   A. 2856 BTU/hr

   B. 1212 BTU/hr

   C. 840 BTU/hr

   D. 1505 BTU/hr

2. What factors need to be considered when designing and drawing rack elevation diagrams?

   A. User mobility, competence of the technician, quality of the rack material

   B. Equipment manufacturer, model year of equipment, number of USB ports

   C. Ergonomics, weight distribution, RF and IR reception, heat loads, signal separation

   D. Amount of RJ-45 connectors used, amount of conduit used

3. According to best practices, what is the safe working load (SWL) requirement for overhead mounting of a 75 lb (34 kg) projector?

   A. 500 lb (227 kg)

   B. 375 lb (170 kg)

   C. 300 lb (136 kg)

   D. 275 lb (125 kg)

4. When installing conduit, it is important to remember that the conduit will require the following:

   A. Room to expand 45 percent because of latent heating

   B. Internal insulation, usually an injected polyurethane jell

   C. Adequate mounting support to withstand cable pulling

   D. A slip sleeve to ensure adequate air space for cable

5. What is the best place to install a 60 lb (27.22 kg) audio amplifier in a freestanding equipment rack?

   A. Top of the rack.

   B. Middle of the rack.

   C. Bottom of the rack.

   D. The location is irrelevant.

Answers

1. **A.** If an amplifier draws 7 amperes (A) at 120 V of alternating current (VAC), without considering amplifier efficiency, it generates 2856 BTU/hr.

2. **C.** When designing and drawing rack elevation diagrams, you need to consider ergonomics, weight distribution, RF and IR reception, heat loads, signal separation, and other things.

3. **B.** The safe working load (SWL) requirement for overhead mounting of a 75 lb (34 kg) projector is 5 * 75 = 375 lb (170 kg).

4. **C.** When installing conduit, it is important to remember that the conduit will require mounting support to withstand cable pulling.

5. **C.** The best place to install a 60 lb (27.22 kg) audio amplifier in a freestanding equipment rack is at the bottom of the rack.

CHAPTER 10

Specifying Electrical Infrastructure

In this chapter, you will learn about

- How current, voltage, resistance, impedance, and power interact so you can apply them to the power and grounding required for an AV system
- Specifying the circuits needed to support AV equipment
- Differentiating among system and equipment grounding schemes so that you can identify and specify them within a given AV system
- Specifying infrastructure that will protect AV equipment from magnetic and electric interference
- Specifying AV conduits, calculating jam ratio, and accounting for floor boxes
- Common power and grounding issues

As an AV professional, you are responsible for requesting the appropriate power for your system's needs. This will require you to calculate those needs and physically specify the location of outlets in the design space. You will have to integrate your AV system with existing power and grounding infrastructure and work with the electrical trade to verify that your power needs are met.

Power/grounding may seem simple, but it is one of the most misunderstood topics in the AV industry. There are many electrical terms that sound similar but often mean different things. When specifying electrical requirements, you need to apply safe principles. A lack of foundational knowledge can lead to improper recommendations and serious consequences.

Moreover, correctly applying power and grounding principles will prevent common audio problems. As you will learn, some symptoms in audio system performance can indicate problems with the electrical system. You will learn about the sources of these problems so you can avoid or troubleshoot them. A solid foundation in power and grounding theory will help you identify the source of an issue and then formulate and implement the necessary corrective measures.

Domain Check
This chapter relates directly to the following tasks on the CTS-D Exam Content Outline:

- Domain B Task 4: Coordinate electrical criteria

This task comprises 3.2 percent of the exam (about 4 questions). This chapter may also relate to other tasks.

Circuit Theory

Before learning about the power system, you need to be able to trace how current moves through a circuit. In his *Illustrated Guide to Basic Electrical Theory Textbook, 3rd Edition,* Mike Holt writes, "Electrical current is the unseen movement of electrons that flow from the power source through the electrical circuit of the appliance or equipment and then return to the power source. The complete path the electrons take is called the electrical circuit."

An electrical circuit is a closed-loop path that sends electrons from a power source, through a circuit to a load, and back to the power source. All circuits must have these three physical items that are connected.

- Conductive material, such as wires
- A voltage source, such as a battery
- A "load," such as a light source

When the circuit's switch is set to the "on" position, the circuit is closed, and four properties work together to make the light source glow. We covered these properties in Chapter 2, but to review, in the context of specifying electrical infrastructure, they are as follows:

- **Current**   The rate of electrons flowing through a circuit per second. Current is measured in amperes. It is typically represented in math by I for "intensity" or A for "amperes." Devices that require electrical power are said to "draw" current from a circuit. An increase in current is an increase in the quantity of electricity.

- **Voltage**   The electrical potential to create current flow in a circuit. It is represented in math by the letter V for "volts" or E for "electromotive force."

- **Resistance**   The property opposition of the flow of electrical current. Resistance is measured in ohms. It is typically represented in math by the letter R for resistance. The amount of resistance in a conductor is based on the size—or gauge—of the wire used. A thicker wire cable will have less resistance, and thus a better electrical transfer, than a thinner wire will. Plus, resistance increases with cable length; therefore, a longer run of the same gauge cable will result in a weaker signal at the far end of the wire.

- **Power** The energy dissipated or consumed when an electrical device is working. It is represented by the letter P and is measured in watts.

NOTE A *resistor* is a passive electrical component that produces equal impedance to current flow. Current passes through a resistor in direct proportion to voltage, independent of frequency, as outlined in Ohm's law.

There are two types of electrical current: direct current (DC) and alternating current (AC), as shown in Figure 10-1. Direct current travels in one direction only. Power supplies, computer signals, and batteries usually use direct current. A simple example of direct current is a battery-powered light source. As the battery discharges, the voltage will decrease, and the filament will glow less brightly. As the voltage drops, the current flow will drop as well.

Alternating current reverses its direction periodically. It is used in home and commercial power sources. The speed of the current change is its frequency, or cycles per second, measured in *hertz* (Hz). There are two common frequencies used worldwide: 50 Hz and 60 Hz.

The voltage of an AC wall outlet is typically 120 V in North America or 230 to 240 V in most other parts of the world. It is important that you know which voltage system you are using and the power requirements of each piece of AV equipment you specify.

AV equipment uses power from the outlet, but there are other voltages your AV design may employ, such as for loudspeaker and control systems, that are typically less than the voltage from the outlet. Sometimes these types of systems are classified as *low voltage*.

Each country has rules or codes that determine which types of workers are allowed to install or work with differing voltage levels. The definition of *low voltage* varies among jurisdictions, so check with your local authority having jurisdiction (AHJ) to figure out who can perform what kind of work on your project.

Ohm's Law and Power Formulas

As you learned in Chapter 2, Ohm's law and the power equation (Figure 10-2) are used to calculate and predict the four properties of an electrical circuit: voltage, current, resistance, and power. They are also used to approximate *impedance,* which is the total opposition to current flow in an AC circuit. Like a DC circuit, an AC circuit contains resistance, but it also includes forces that oppose changes in current (inductive reactance)

Figure 10-1
The difference in voltage over time in direct current (left) and alternating current (right)

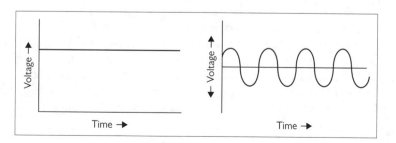

Figure 10-2

Ohm's law and
power formulas

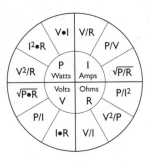

and voltage (capacitive reactance). Impedance takes into account all three of these factors. It is frequency-dependent, measured in ohms and symbolized by the letter Z.

The formulas are used in many AV calculations, such as when calculating the total electrical impedance of a group of loudspeakers that are connected by cabling or when calculating the amount of current required to power the AV equipment in a rack. You can also use the power formulas to determine signal level at the end of a long cable run.

Ohm's law defines the electrical relationships in DC circuits. It will also, however, help approximate for AC circuits. AC-circuit calculations are frequency-dependent, and Ohm's law does not account for frequency in a circuit. The results of Ohm's law or power-equation calculations can be given to professional electricians and AV integrators for incorporation into a system design.

More on Resistance and Impedance

Resistance restricts the flow of current and is frequency-independent, which means the resistance value does not change with the frequency of the current passing through it.

Impedance is like resistance in that it restricts the flow of current. However, impedance is frequency-dependent. There will be different values for low and high frequencies.

The term *resistance* is used when you are working with DC, such as currents that are powered by a battery or other DC source. In AC circuits, such as electrical power, loudspeaker circuits, and audio interfaces, the term *impedance* is used in place of *resistance*. For loudspeaker calculations, treat impedance as resistance to keep the calculations simple. While the calculations used in this guide do not account for the *reactive* components in the AC circuit, the calculations will help you approximate impedance for AC circuits.

AC circuits have both resistance and *reactance*. Reactance is the opposition to the changes in voltage and current associated with the AC waveform. Impedance, therefore, is the total of the resistive and reactive components in an AC circuit.

Audio signals are an AC waveform. Therefore, you will express audio signals in terms of frequency (cycles per second), or hertz. This is why you also see the term *impedance* rather than *resistance* in relation to audio circuits.

Figure 10-3
Current through
a series circuit

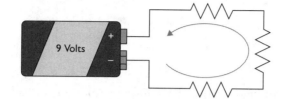

Series vs. Parallel Circuits

A key concept of circuit theory is that electrons flow from a power source, go through a circuit, and return to the power source. A common misconception is that all current seeks to go to ground (meaning the earth). This is not true. Current does not try to find a path to ground or earth; it seeks to return to the source—whatever that source may be. You can see how this works by studying a basic series and parallel circuit.

In a *series circuit* (Figure 10-3), all the electrons leave the source of power (such as a battery), travel through each part of the circuit, and return to the source. The current flows through the entire circuit, and voltage is divided across the loads. Wire has resistance; therefore, it's considered a load in the circuit.

In a *parallel circuit* (Figure 10-4), the voltage remains the same across the loads. Current divides and takes all available paths to return to the source, while the resistance of each path determines how much current flows through each path.

Although the majority of the current in a parallel circuit will flow through the path of least resistance, remember that current will take any and all available pathways, even if it's an unintentional path. The voltage will be constant in all parts of the circuit.

Capacitors

A *capacitor* is a circuit component that stores electrical energy. It is sort of like a battery, except it can't produce new electrons. Instead, it stores energy created by a battery or other source. Capacitors consist of two metal plates that are separated by a nonconducting substance, called a *dielectric*. When the plates are connected to a charging device, such as a battery, electrons are transferred from one plate to the other. The greater the voltage—and the larger or closer the plates are—the greater the charge that can be stored.

A charged capacitor discharges when a conducting path is present between the plates. For a given *capacitance* value, expressed in *farads,* a capacitor will have a greater opposition to AC current flow at lower frequencies than at higher frequencies. This property is known as *capacitive reactance.*

Figure 10-4
Current through
a parallel circuit

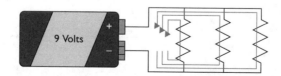

Figure 10-5
A capacitor
symbol

If you're reading electrical diagrams, the capacitor is what's shown in Figure 10-5. In electronic circuits, capacitors serve four primary purposes.

- Capacitors store charge for high-speed use, especially with lasers.
- Capacitors eliminate ripples in DC voltage. Capacitors can even out uneven voltage by absorbing peaks and filling in valleys.
- Capacitors can block DC current from flowing between two circuit elements while allowing AC current to pass.
- Capacitors are used to form "tuned" circuits, which are used in radios and speaker crossovers, to name a few applications.

Figure 10-6 shows a capacitor in series with a load, shown as a resistor. The capacitor impacts the flow of current through this circuit.

As frequency increases in this circuit, so does current flow. Capacitors pass high frequencies and block lower frequencies. Because cables themselves act as capacitors, this concept can be applied to *signal loss over distance*. More cable creates more capacitance, resulting in a greater loss of high frequencies.

NOTE The shield and center conductor in a coaxial cable act as a capacitor. They are separated by a dielectric.

Inductors

An inductor, also known as a *coil*, has the opposite effect of a capacitor. It *opposes* any change in current. Inductors pass low frequencies and block higher frequencies. For a given *inductance* value, expressed in *henries* (plural of *henry*), the inductor will have a greater opposition to AC current flow at higher frequencies than at lower frequencies. Inductance is the property of a circuit that opposes any change in current.

Figure 10-6
A capacitor (top)
in a series circuit

Figure 10-7
An inductor
(top), or coil, in a
series circuit

Figure 10-7 shows an inductor, or coil, in a series circuit. The load is shown as a resistor. As the frequency of the circuit increases, the current flow decreases.

Coils and Magnetic Induction

Coils carrying current create magnetic fields. These magnetic fields can spread across other components in a circuit and induce current flow. This is how a *transformer* works; it creates a field that gets picked up by a secondary coil.

A transformer is a passive electromagnetic device usually consisting of at least two coils of wire (inductors) with no electrical connection between them. Often, these coils share an iron-based core. This common core helps concentrate the magnetic force created by current flow in one coil (primary), thereby inducing a voltage in the other coil (secondary). Coils are used in every transformer.

Sometimes the induced voltage is unintended, which creates noise. Figure 10-8 shows magnetic fields crossing from one conductor to another. We will discuss transformers in more depth later in this chapter.

Coils, Capacitors, and Resistors in a Series Circuit

In a series circuit, AC current can flow only where the frequency coil and capacitor cross over. Figure 10-9 shows a series circuit in which the capacitor blocks lower-frequency current, while the coil blocks higher-frequency current.

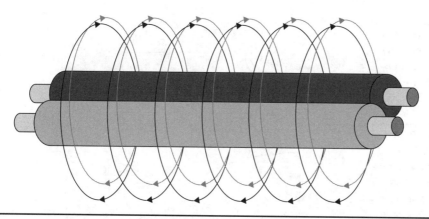

Figure 10-8   Conductors create magnetic fields.

Figure 10-9
A series circuit with a capacitor and a coil

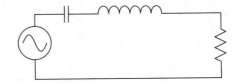

Figure 10-10
Where coil current flow and capacitor current flow intersect, you have a crossover.

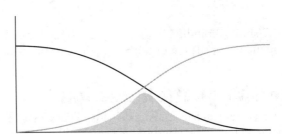

In Figure 10-10, the circuit's current is represented along the y-axis and its frequency along the x-axis. The darker curve represents the coil current flow; the lighter curve is the capacitor current flow. The shaded area beneath is the total circuit current flow.

The intersection of the two curves creates an x, which is known as the *crossover* or *x-over*. This is where the effects of the capacitor and coil cross. Current can flow in this circuit only in this frequency region. The result is that only a portion of the frequency range can pass current. This is a *band-pass filter*.

Coils, Capacitors, and Resistors in a Parallel Circuit

In a parallel circuit, AC current flows *except* at the frequency crossover point. In the parallel circuit shown in Figure 10-11, the capacitor passes higher-frequency current, while the coil passes lower-frequency current.

In Figure 10-12, the circuit's current is represented along the y-axis and its frequency along the x-axis. The darker curve represents the coil current flow; the lighter curve is the

Figure 10-11
A parallel circuit with a coil and capacitor

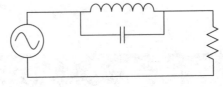

Figure 10-12
A notch filter, where the current flows intersect, marks a reduction in total circuit current flow.

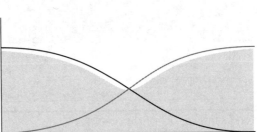

capacitor current flow. The shaded area is the total circuit current flow. The dip at the crossover represents a reduction in current flow. This is a *notch filter*. You can find these types of circuits in audio equalizers.

Specifying Electrical Power

When a building is built or a room remodeled, an electrical engineer plans for supplying electricity throughout the space. These general plans don't usually include requirements for AV systems, in part because each AV system is different—from a single projector and screen to a fully integrated and custom videoconferencing suite.

AV designers need to do everything from specify receptacles and power locations to calculate expected current loads for each piece of AV equipment. You may also find you have some specialized electrical power and grounding requirements based upon the size and signal-to-noise requirements of an AV system.

In addition to specifying power locations and requirements, AV designers do the following:

- Specify or design interface and connection plates
- Specify junction-box sizes and locations
- Perform conduit-fill calculations
- Size conduit and cable trays
- Create conduit riser diagrams
- Review electrical plans and schedules to confirm they meet AV requirements

To do all this properly, an AV designer must know local codes and regulations so that the infrastructure is safe, conforms to standards and best practices, and can be understood by electrical engineers and contractors.

Established Terms

You may come across slang terms while working with power and grounding. The IEEE Standard 1100-2005, *Recommended Practice for Powering and Grounding Electronic Equipment,* identifies a list of terms to be avoided because they're just not clear. Still, several of them are commonly used in the AV industry, such as the following:

- Clean ground
- Clean power
- Computer-grade ground
- Dedicated ground
- Dirty ground
- Dirty power

- Equipment grounding safety conductor
- Frame ground
- Shared circuits
- Shared ground

Don't use these terms! Electricians or other project team members might misinterpret your meaning. For example, what exactly is clean power? Because this term does not have a clear definition, your idea of clean power may be different from your co-worker's or the electrician's. Because AV integration relies so heavily on an electrician's work, avoid ambiguous terms to ensure your message gets across. And learn the electrician's power and grounding vocabulary to ensure your safety as well. Use electrician terms, such as the following:

- Panelboard
- Individual branch circuit
- Supplemental ground
- Isolated ground

These terms have clear definitions; electricians will know exactly what you mean when you use them. When in doubt on terminology, check your country's regional authority. Most countries have standardized methods and procedures, which they will publish as code for all electricians to follow. Two examples of such codes include the National Electrical Code (NEC), which is used in the United States and some other countries, and BS 7671: IET Wiring Regulations, which is used in the United Kingdom. Always check with the AHJ for the code in your area.

Codes and Regulations

AV professionals must use and reference standards and codes in their AV designs. Each local jurisdiction will normally have a code that consolidates all general and permanent legislation, organized into a code of ordinances. Building codes will be included in the municipal code, and a local jurisdiction may adopt a county's or state's building code.

Whether you're working at the local, regional, or national level, building and electrical codes will probably be adopted from one of the major code publishers. There are two major code publishers in the United States: the International Code Council (ICC), which publishes the International Building Code (IBC), the International Green Construction Code (IgCC), and others; and the National Fire Protection Agency (NFPA), which publishes the NEC and others.

It's important that you understand the relevant codes because you need to verify that your electrical infrastructure specifications and AV systems installation are compliant. You may work on a project that crosses jurisdictions, and their codes may conflict. In such cases, it is always best practice to follow the more restrictive or stringent code requirements. When in doubt, consult with the AHJ.

Electrical Distribution Systems

In all but the simplest systems, current draw, voltage, and the locations and types of receptacles required for AV equipment must be calculated, specified, and located on drawings. For a new facility or major renovation, this information will go to the electrical engineer and contractor for inclusion in their drawings and specifications. For AV integration in an existing facility, the required electrical circuits and receptacles may be coordinated through the owner, a building engineer, or an electrical contractor. In some cases, an AV firm may have a contracted electrician who can evaluate the situation and add the necessary circuits and receptacles.

In any case, you should perform simple tests on the electrical receptacles in a space to check for proper voltage and grounding prior to connecting AV equipment. In addition, you should locate overcurrent-protective devices, such as circuit breakers, for AV circuits. In larger installations, you may have to inspect the electrical system further to ensure that it meets your specifications.

Electrical contractors need to know how much power your AV system requires so they can plan accordingly. To communicate effectively, you need an intermediate understanding of power distribution.

So, where does the power for your AV system come from? At a power-generation station, the generator puts out extremely high-voltage AC, which travels to a transmission transformer for the long trip down the power lines. Because transmission at high voltage reduces the amount of current, there is less loss from resistance. This means long-distance transmission can serve a broad geographic area.

These primary transmission lines deliver power to electrical substations, which are located strategically around population areas or industrial centers. The substations have transformers that reduce the voltage before local distribution. The electricity is then distributed to a local transformer, where it is further reduced to the voltage required for your application—whether residential or commercial.

When the power from the substation's transformer reaches your local transformer, it normally has to be reduced to the voltage required for your AV systems. This reduced power can be distributed to your AV systems in two ways: *single-phase* or *three-phase,* which we will discuss next. In a single-phase system, voltage and current flow change in response to each other. In a three-phase system, there are three alternating currents that vary in phase. It's important to know which type of power you need so you can communicate with the electrician and ensure the right amount of power to get your equipment running efficiently and effectively.

Power Distribution Systems

AC power distribution systems are also referred to by the number of wires carrying the power. The most common *single-phase system* in North America is 120/240 V (Figure 10-13). The 120/240 V single-phase system uses three wires. Two-line wires carry voltage; a third is neutral. Voltage between a line conductor and neutral will be 120 V, while voltage between the two line wires will be 240 V.

Figure 10-13
Single-phase power distribution system

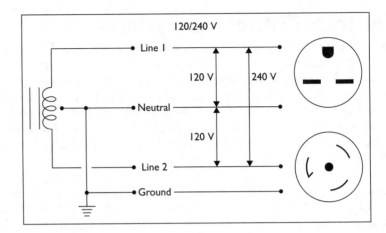

The single-phase power distribution system is used in almost all homes in North America and Europe, where the needed load is relatively small. It can also be used in small commercial buildings with lesser power demands. An additional equipment grounding conductor (EGC) is added for safety.

In commercial buildings, you'll find that power almost always comes into the building as *three-phase*. The most common three-phase systems in North America are 120/208 V and 277/480 V.

The 120/208 V three-phase system uses four wires, as shown in Figure 10-14. Three-phase wires carry electricity, while the fourth is the grounded conductor (or neutral). Voltage between a phase wire and ground will be 120 V. Voltage between any of the three

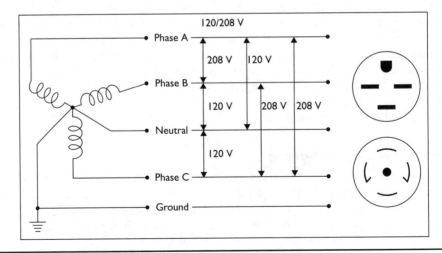

Figure 10-14   A 120/208 V three-phase system

Figure 10-15
A 277/480 V
three-phase
system

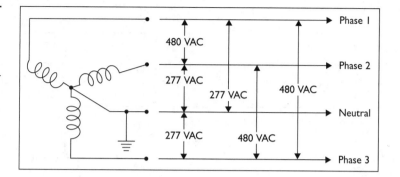

phase wires will be 208 V. An equipment grounding conductor is added for portable power distribution systems. Because of its flexible nature, this is the most popular system used in commercial, institutional, and light industrial buildings.

The 277/480 V three-phase system (Figure 10-15) is similar to the 120/208 V system. You could even say the 120/208 V system evolves from this system for AV and other receptacles.

The 277/480 V system is used in large commercial and industrial buildings. It also employs four wires and is important to be aware of because it is primarily used for room lighting, not for AV equipment. When AV systems incorporate lighting controls, you have to factor in lighting systems that use a 277 V power system.

In a perfect world, when working with three-phase systems, you want all the power for AV equipment to come from only one of the phases. Interconnected equipment powered by different electrical phases can interact with each other, causing noise.

TIP With any three-phase electrical distribution system, the electrical engineer will attempt to design a balanced load on the different phases. Keep in mind that a large, infrequently used AV system would not be placed on one phase of the building's power system. If it is, the system will be unbalanced, either when running or when idle. This can cause damage to the electrical system.

International Power Distribution Systems

Although North America, Japan, and parts of South America use 60 Hz systems, most of the rest of the world uses 50 Hz electrical-distribution systems. These systems are similar but operate at about double the voltage. The most common 50 Hz electrical-distribution systems are 230 V single-phase and 230/400 V three-phase.

A 230 V single-phase system (Figure 10-16) is similar to a 120 V single-phase system used in North America. The main difference is that the higher voltage reduces the amount of current required. This system uses three wires. The first wire carries 230 V of AC power, the second wire is the system ground, and the third wire is the EGC. This system is typically used for residential and business purposes.

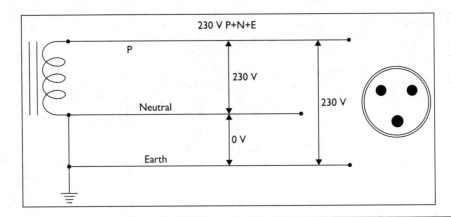

Figure 10-16   A 230 V single-phase system

A 230/400 V three-phase system (Figure 10-17) is similar to a 120/208 V three-phase system used in North America. This system uses five wires. The first three wires carry 230 V between the individual phases and neutral and carry 400 V between phases, the fourth wire is the neutral, and the fifth wire is the EGC. This system is commonly found in commercial and industrial applications that have greater power requirements, such as larger buildings, small manufacturing, and AV staging events.

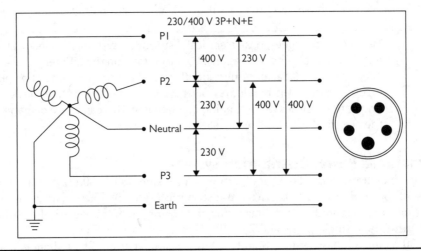

Figure 10-17   A 230/400 V three-phase system

Understanding Power Onsite

Electrical service refers to the conductors and equipment necessary for delivering energy from the electricity supply system to the wiring system of the site that it's meant to serve. Figure 10-18 shows the flow of electrical service onsite.

1. *Service drop* refers to the overhead service conductors from the last pole, other aerial support, and underground feeds outside the building, connecting to the service-entrance conductors at the building or other structure.

2. The *service entrance* is the point at which power enters the building.

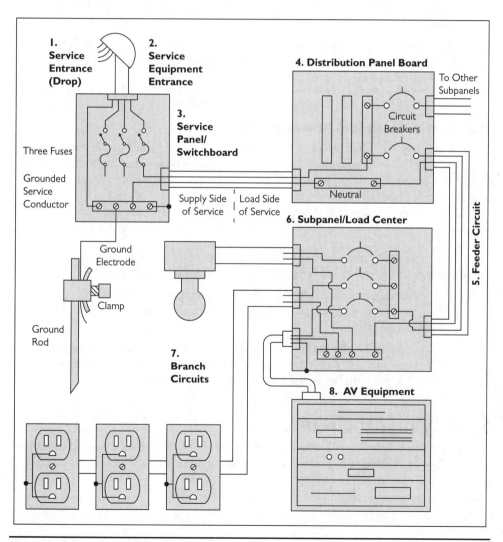

Figure 10-18   Onsite electrical service

3. The *service panel,* or *switchboard,* receives the incoming power and adds a ground conductor.

4. The *distribution panel board* distributes the power to subpanels throughout a facility.

5. The *feeders* are circuits that carry power between the service panel and the distribution panel.

6. *Subpanels* have current-limiting devices, such as circuit breakers or fuses. An individual circuit might provide power to all the lights in the room, or several electrical convenience outlets, but the total power consumed on the circuit cannot exceed the current-limiting device's rating or else the circuit breaker trips or a fuse blows.

7. From the panel, the branch circuits run power to wall outlets or directly to wired *equipment.* This powers the various amplifiers and signal-processing racks, communications equipment, and AV equipment.

The Master Technical Power Panel

A larger facility usually derives all its power from one central location: the master technical power panel. Ideally, one phase of power should be designated as the technical power supply and be fed directly by its own primary feeder and transformer, winding up at the primary power distribution center for the building.

The master technical power panel will distribute power (and the technical ground) to all other locations within a facility. Its location varies. Here are some examples:

- In a one-room studio, it may be the service-entrance panel for the entire building; there will be no feeders or subpanels, only branch circuits.

- In a small theater or studio facility, the master technical power panel is often located in or near the control room and provides all the branch circuits for local and remote locations.

- In a large complex, the master technical power panel may be in an equipment or utility room and will power feeders that, in turn, power subpanels and branch circuits. There could be several levels of subpanels in large complexes.

Specifying AV Circuits

AV designers may be responsible for calculating the number of circuits needed to support their AV systems. Projectors, screens, displays, conference room tables, lecterns, credenzas, and more may all require power.

Figure 10-19
Circuits that
power AV
equipment

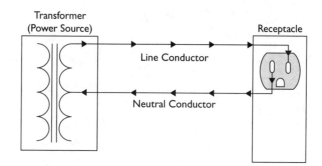

Transformer
(Power Source)

Receptacle

Line Conductor

Neutral Conductor

For starters, review your project documentation for the location of all equipment, plus other locations that require power, such as a conference table. Match the equipment to receptacle locations. Receptacles can be single, duplex, or quad, and they can be located in ceilings, walls, and floorboxes.

In circuits that carry power to AV equipment, the complete path begins with a line— or "hot" conductor—connected to one side of the local AC power transformer (the power source). The path continues through the electronic equipment, returning via the neutral conductor and back to the other terminal on the AC power transformer, ultimately returning to the power source. See Figure 10-19.

TIP In North America, the line conductor is a black, insulated wire, and the neutral is the white, insulated wire.

Branch Circuit Loads

For safety reasons, a branch circuit (Figure 10-20) can handle only a certain amount of current. In a commercial environment, a typical branch circuit is rated for 20A. If more current is drawn through the circuit, it will trip the breaker, cutting all power to the branch circuit.

Most electronics that you plug into an outlet—a coffee pot, computer, or copier— require less than 20A. However, designers must calculate the total amperage needed when the branch circuit is in typical use. In other words, can the circuit handle the coffee pot, computer, *and* copier running at the same time?

To do this, you need to know which outlets and directly wired equipment are connected to a given branch circuit. Each piece of equipment has a power-consumption rating. One may specify "120V 1.6A," while another is rated "115V 4.2A." When you add together the amperage of those devices in one system, you know the maximum current needed would be about 1.6A + 4.2A = 5.8A, which easily works for a single 20A circuit. If the needed current exceeded 20A, the circuit breaker would trip, shutting off the flow. You should plan for a decent buffer between the needed amperage and the circuit's rating. In the U.S., this buffer is defined by the NEC as 80 percent of capacity.

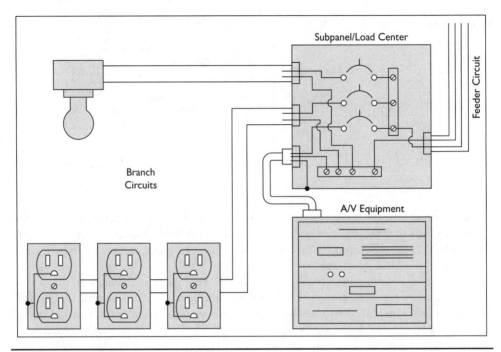

Figure 10-20 Branch circuits

 TIP Per NEC code, don't plan to use more than 80 percent of the available current in a branch circuit (in other words, 16A on a 20A circuit).

Calculating the Number of Circuits

Say you are designing a classroom for a university. The architect and electrical engineer have provided a floor plan (Figure 10-21). At this point in your design, you've already placed equipment in the room—two flat-panel monitors and two projectors for a visual system. You've got an AV rack in the back of the room and a document camera at the lectern in front.

All the AV gear requires power, so you need to ask the electrical engineer to place receptacles at these locations. Based on this drawing, you request four duplex receptacles, one by each projector and monitor, and two junction boxes, by the rack and at the lectern. Each piece of AV gear draws a certain amount of amperage. The rack requires 12A, the monitors and document cameras require 3A, and the projectors require 5A. See Figure 10-22.

You have looked up circuit information from your AHJ and determined that you will use 20A circuits, but you can use only 80 percent of that, or up to 16A of continuous load per circuit. When you add up the amperage for the devices you plan to put on an individual branch circuit, you will need to add a circuit every time you hit 16A.

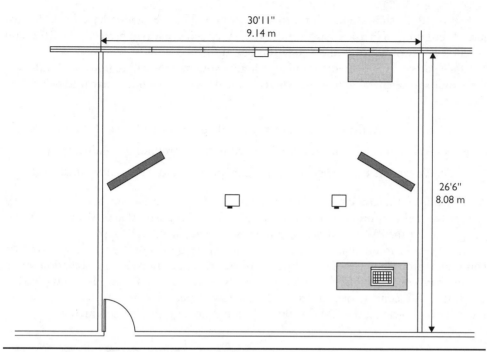

Figure 10-21 AV in a university classroom design

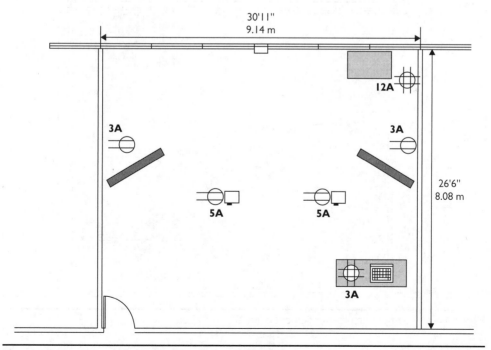

Figure 10-22 Receptacle locations in an AV installation

Figure 10-23 shows one solution for this room. The receptacles have been divided into three groups. Circuit 1 has the rack at 12A, circuit 2 has two projectors at 10A, and circuit 3 has two monitors and a junction box at 9A.

Once you've documented how many circuits your system will require, you will want to include some general notes somewhere on the drawing. The notes may read something like this:

- Circuits for AV use only. Do not share with any non-AV loads.
- All AV circuits must include auxiliary equipment grounding conductor.
- All AV circuits must originate from same phase and use the same panelboard.

At a minimum, the circuits specified for the AV system should be labeled for AV system use only. In other words, no non-AV loads should be shared with the circuits designated for the AV system or computers associated with the AV system.

Also keep in mind that the circuits for an AV system should include an auxiliary equipment grounding conductor (EGC). An electrical specification or installation might not use bare copper wire as the EGC; it may rely on the electrical metallic tubing (EMT) conduit. EMT consists of couplers and set screws. Specifying an auxiliary EGC eliminates relying solely on the EMT as the only equipment grounding conductor.

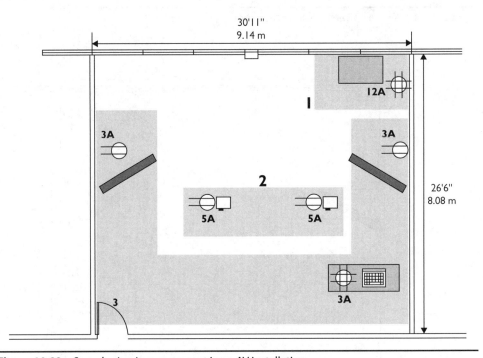

Figure 10-23   Sample circuit arrangement in an AV installation

Power Strips and Cords

When you have several devices that require power from a single location, you could use power strips (a.k.a., *relocatable power taps*). Power strips come with their own set of safety standards, such as a UL or CE mark, meaning they're listed by Underwriter Laboratories or Conformité Européenne for specific or limited usage. The UL website says, "Products that bear the UL Classification mark have been evaluated for specific properties, a limited range of hazards, or suitability for use under limited or special conditions." The CE website says, "The CE marking is the manufacturer's declaration that the product meets the requirements of the applicable EC directives."

To keep this section brief, we'll use UL as a discussion point for power strips. If you are designing within the United States, the National Electrical Code states, "Listed or labeled equipment shall be installed and used in accordance with any instructions included in the listing or labeling." Compliance with the NEC also requires compliance with how the device is listed.

UL uses the term *relocatable power taps* (RPTs) for power strips. Here are some excerpts from various UL publications regarding RPTs:

- These requirements cover cord-connected, relocatable power taps rated 250V AC or less and 20A AC or less.

- A relocatable power tap is intended only for indoor use as a temporary extension of a grounding alternating-current branch circuit for general use.

- A cord-connected relocatable power tap is not intended to be connected to another cord-connected relocatable power tap.

- Relocatable power taps are intended to be directly connected to a permanently installed branch circuit receptacle.

- Relocatable power taps are not intended to be connected (daisy chained) to other relocatable power taps or to extension cords.

- Relocatable power taps are not intended for use at construction sites and similar locations.

- Relocatable power taps are not intended to be permanently secured to building structures, tables, work benches, or similar structures, and they are not intended to be used as a substitute for fixed wiring.

NOTE You should not daisy-chain power strips, as shown in the following illustration. Power strips should be plugged directly into a branch circuit receptacle, not at the end of an extension cord. Because rack-mounted power distribution units (PDUs) fall under a different UL classification, you can plug a power strip into a PDU, but you cannot plug a power strip into another power strip. A PDU is a rack-mountable or portable electrical enclosure, connected via cord or cable to a branch circuit for distributing power to multiple electronic devices. It may contain switches, overcurrent protection, control connections, and receptacles.

And then there are power cords—a key element of getting power to an electronic device. In AV, power cord management is important. Sometimes power cords are too long, and they must be wrapped and secured neatly. Let Figure 10-24 be your guide to best practices.

You should consider neatness and accessibility when placing a cord within a rack or equipment area. The first illustration on the left shows a power cord wrapped as a coil. This is an acceptable way to tie a power cord. Folded cords, as shown in the second illustration, are also acceptable. Historically, the practice of coiling a power cable has been a topic of some debate. There are those who contend that coiling a power cord creates a large inductive loop. But there are manufacturers in the industry that have performed extensive testing and found no evidence of this effect.

The illustration on the far right is unacceptable because it would be hard to access the individual cords for service. Removing the cord for one piece of equipment would mean

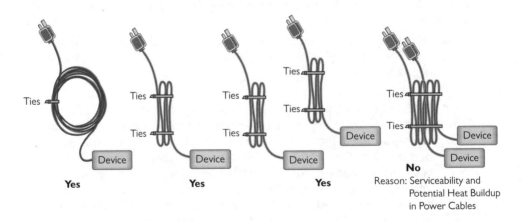

Figure 10-24   Best practices in power cord management

unbundling several cords. It also has the potential for heat buildup in the power cables. In high-current draw situations, the cords feeding the devices can become warm to the touch. Several cords wrapped tightly together can potentially create smoke or cause a fire.

For serviceability purposes, power cords that are removable from equipment can be secured with nylon ties (zip ties), whereas power cords that are permanently attached to equipment should be secured with Velcro (a.k.a., hook and loop fastener).

TIP   Longer power cords often take up more space in a rack and require extra attention. For equipment with detachable power cords, neater cable management can be achieved by replacing longer cords with shorter cords.

Grounding (Earthing)

In the context of electrical power, *ground* refers to an earth connection or something that extends an earth connection. If an electrical device is "grounded," it means the device is connected either to earth or to some conductive body that extends to the earth. The earth is used as the 0 volt reference for AC power distribution. This grounding (earthing) provides a reference point of no potential—the earth in this case—for an electrical circuit.

NOTE   In North America, the terms *ground*, *grounded*, and *grounding* are used. Outside of North America, the terms *earth*, *earthed*, and *earthing* are used. Regardless of which terms you favor, in the context of electrical power, they all refer to the same concepts.

Grounding is an important safeguard. Connecting one of a system's current-carrying conductors to earth limits the amount of voltage that can be imposed on the line. Lightning, line surges, and unintentional contact with higher voltage lines can increase the potential of the circuit, leading to a possibly fatal situation. System grounding helps reduce fires in buildings, as well as voltage stress on electrical insulation. This provides longer insulation life for motors, transformers, and other system components.

System Grounding

To protect your AV system from unexpected sources of high voltage, you need to ensure that your equipment is integrated into a system grounding scheme. System grounding will limit the voltage imposed by lightning, line surges, or unintentional contact with higher-voltage lines. It will also stabilize that voltage to earth during normal operation. System grounding is when one of the current-carrying conductors—usually the neutral—is connected to ground.

To envision what we're talking about, let's revisit the basic circuit (Figure 10-25). In this system, the receptacle is connected directly to the power source—a transformer. In reality, however, the receptacle would be connected to a panelboard. A panelboard is a component of an electricity supply system that divides electricity from a power source into individual circuits.

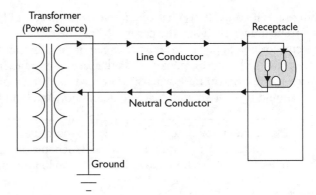

Figure 10-25
A basic circuit, with ground

Figure 10-26 shows our power and grounding system with a panelboard. It also has an overcurrent protection device called a *circuit breaker*. The circuit breaker will protect users and electrical equipment from damage due to an overload or short circuit by interrupting current flow.

The panelboard also include a *neutral bus*. A busbar is a strip of conductive material that provides a common connection point. In the case of the neutral busbar, all the neutral wires are terminated on the busbar. Figure 10-26 also shows that the neutral busbar not only is connected to the neutral return but also is connected to ground (earth). This ground connection protects people and equipment from stray electrical currents and electrical faults.

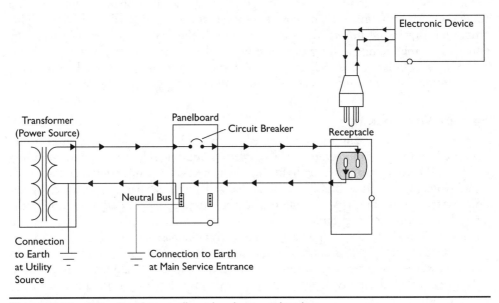

Figure 10-26   A circuit with a panelboard and a circuit breaker

TIP Keep in mind that metal panelboard housing should also be grounded.

System-Grounding Conductors

You can recognize a system-grounding scheme by its use of a neutral—or grounded—conductor. Current seeks to return to the source, and the neutral conductor is the path that current normally takes.

For safety reasons, the current-carrying neutral is also connected to a grounding electrode through the panelboard at the service entrance of a building (where electrical power comes in). The neutral wire that services the building will also be grounded at the transformer outside. In other words, in system grounding, the normal return path that current takes back to the source is on a neutral conductor attached to the ground: a grounded, neutral conductor.

Equipment Grounding

Not only should the electrical system be grounded, but the housings of electronic equipment should also be grounded. Electronic equipment with metal cases or exposed screws may become energized if they accidentally come in contact with a line conductor (an electrical fault). Equipment grounding will prevent the exposure to voltage that these cases might carry in such scenarios by opening a fuse or breaker.

The following equipment should always be grounded:

- Electrical equipment enclosures
- Panelboards, switchboards
- Junction boxes, backboxes
- Receptacles, audiovisual plates, and so on
- Raceways
- Conduit, cable trays, and so on
- Any other metallic or conductive housing that has the potential to become energized in a fault situation
- Metal housings enclosing a receptacle or power outlet, as well as panelboard enclosures

Figure 10-27 shows an example of equipment grounding. The electronic device could be a projector or other AV system.

The dotted line shows a continuous pathway to ground beginning with the metal enclosure of the electronic device, through the third prong of the electrical plug, through the electrical receptacle (socket), back to the panelboard, through the main bonding jumper, and to the neutral bus, which is connected to earth.

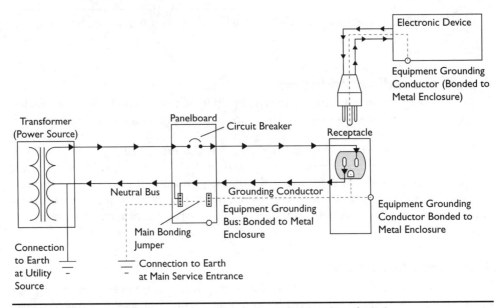

Figure 10-27 Grounding for a piece of AV equipment (the electronic device)

Equipment-Grounding Conductors

Equipment grounding is when you use a grounding conductor separate from the neutral conductor. Generally, this wire is green or green-yellow.

There are many ways to ground equipment, including bare copper or insulated wires. Equipment grounding is accomplished through an equipment grounding conductor that runs with or encloses the circuit conductors. A bare copper wire may serve as the equipment-grounding conductor, but other types may be allowable, including the following:

- Any shape of copper, aluminum, or copper-clad aluminum conductors that may be solid, stranded, insulated, covered, or bare.
- A busbar of any shape.
- Rigid metal conduit.
- Intermediate metal conduit.
- Electrical metallic tubing (EMT).
- "Listed" flexible metal conduit that meets certain code conditions. *Listed* means listed by a Nationally Recognized Testing Laboratory (NRTL) such as Underwriters Laboratory (UL).
- Cable trays as permitted.
- Surface metal raceways listed for grounding.

NOTE   Some regions may not allow EMT or conduit to serve as an equipment grounding conductor, so check your local codes and regulations.

The grounding path must not be only continuous but also reliable and of low impedance. In the case of an accidental connection between a line conductor and a grounded metallic device, this pathway must be in place to allow the current to return to the source via the equipment grounding conductor. This path must also be of low enough impedance to allow the high current required to activate the circuit's overcurrent protection device.

Ground Faults

The purpose of an EGC is to protect people. Say an integrator has installed an AV device, but the power supply becomes defective. The insulation may have melted away or some internal component came loose or failed. The result is an accidental connection, called a *ground fault*, between the line conductor and the metal enclosure of the device. This ground fault brings the metal enclosure of your AV device up to *mains voltage*.

The human body has about 1,000 ohms of resistance, depending upon where you measure the conductivity of your skin. If a human came into contact with a ground fault or energized equipment, as much as 120mA could flow through the human body—enough to cause muscle contraction, heart failure, nerve damage, or death.

In an ideal grounding system, current will flow along the line and neutral conductors. In our hypothetical situation, because of some damage or defect in the equipment, the line conductor of the electrical circuit has come into contact with the metal enclosure of the electronic device, such as a projector. The current flows from the ground fault to the EGC.

Now, when current flows from the transformer, to the panelboard, to the receptacle, and to the electronic device, the device's enclosure will carry line voltage. In other words, the electronic device's metallic enclosure will be energized to 120 or 230 V of electricity. Fortunately, the metal case is bonded to the EGC via the third prong of the device's power cord, which is plugged into a three-prong AC receptacle. Therefore, current is carried away from the device.

From there, the three-prong receptacle has an equipment-grounding screw used to attach the EGC. The EGC is run with the line and neutral conductors back to the panelboard. At the panelboard, the EGC is connected to the equipment-grounding bus, which is bonded to the neutral bus in the panelboard.

Once at the neutral bus, the current starts its return to the source. If the current draw is high enough through the low-impedance fault path, the overcurrent device (circuit breaker) will trip. This breaks the circuit, and the voltage is removed. See Figure 10-28.

PART III

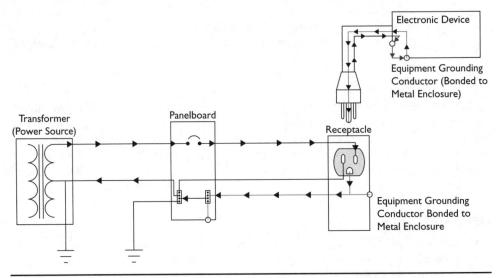

Figure 10-28   A device defect will trip the circuit breaker in a properly grounded system.

NOTE   The National Electrical Code requires that there be an "effective ground-fault current path," defined as "an intentionally constructed, permanent, low-impedance, electrically conductive path designed and intended to carry current under ground-fault conditions from the point of a ground fault on a wiring system to the electrical supply source and that facilitates the operation of the overcurrent protection device...." This permanent joining of metallic parts to form an electrically conductive path under ground-fault conditions is known as *bonding*.

A Ground Fault Case Study

Here is an AV-specific example of why you must pay close attention to the grounding in your AV system. In 2005, a pastor in Waco, Texas, was performing a baptism during a Sunday morning service. While standing waist-deep in water, he reached for a microphone so his congregation could hear him. The moment he touched the microphone, he was hit with an electric shock that killed him on the spot.

There is a possibility this tragedy could have been avoided had someone recognized the dangerous ground-fault condition in the water heater. The pool was energized, so when the pastor touched the microphone, the microphone cord's shield completed the circuit path.

The Dangers of Three-to-Two-Prong Adapters

Some AV professionals troubleshoot ground faults using a three-to-two-prong AC adapter. But have you ever considered what a three-to-two-prong adapter does? It removes the ground fault current path, which could bring the enclosure to line level.

Remember that electricity will take any and all available pathways to return to the source. When you use a three-to-two-prong adapter, you interrupt this pathway. If a person were to touch this now energized enclosure, current would flow through the person to ground.

If you have a hum problem, instead of removing the third pin or using a three-to-two-prong adapter, you should follow proper troubleshooting procedures to discover the cause of the problem.

Three-to-two prong adapters should be used only when they are secured to a grounding pin, such as a grounded faceplate screw, as pictured.

Isolated Ground

An isolated-ground system is intended to minimize interference problems, such as hum and buzz, caused by problematic *ground loops*. It also provides a more stable reference for the audiovisual circuits and can possibly reduce the noise level getting into the audiovisual system.

In an isolated-ground system (Figure 10-29), the equipment ground for the AV system power is isolated from the regular equipment ground. AV equipment racks and other AV enclosures also need to be isolated and insulated from contact with grounded objects, such as conduit, building steel, and conductive concrete floors.

Isolated ground conductors are only isolated from the normal equipment ground up to the point where the system and equipment ground conductors come together in the main panelboard. The system, equipment, and isolated ground systems all need to be bonded together at the main panelboard. This ensures that any fault current has a low-impedance pathway back to the source.

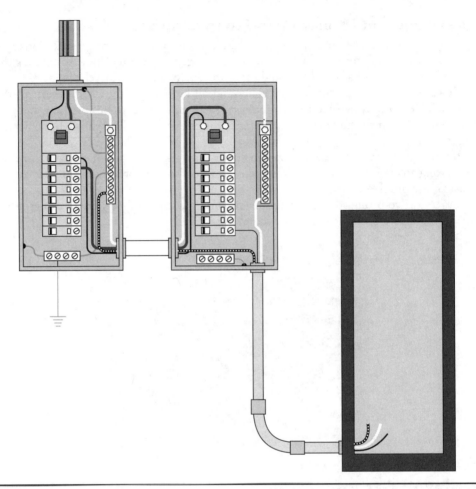

Figure 10-29 An isolated grounding scheme, indicated by the dotted wire

Some AV systems require a technical power system. A technical power system is a power system designed especially for AV systems and associated computers and utilizes an isolated ground. Such systems are useful in critical-listening environments that require a low noise floor, such as broadcast studios, postproduction facilities, performing arts centers, recording studios, and other critical listening environments.

Residual noise from interference, problematic ground loops, and more will be evident in environments with low noise floors. Assuming good design practices and properly adjusted gain structure, the normal acoustic noise floor in noncritical listening spaces will mask any system noise.

Isolated Ground Receptacles

Isolated ground systems have their own unique receptacles. Normally, as in Figure 10-30, the equipment ground pin, the flanges, the cover screw in the center of the receptacle,

Figure 10-30
Normal
receptacle

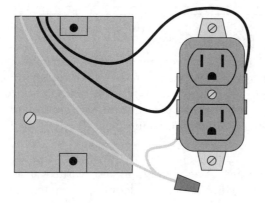

and the equipment grounding screw all have continuity among them. In other words, they're all connected electrically.

Figure 10-31 shows an isolated ground outlet. An isolated receptacle is a receptacle in which the grounding terminal is purposely insulated from the receptacle mounting. The color of such receptacles may vary, but the important identifier is the triangle symbol at the lower right of the receptacle. In an isolated ground receptacle, the equipment ground pin and the equipment grounding screw are insulated from the flanges and the cover screw.

Usually, in an isolated-grounding scheme, an insulated green wire with a yellow stripe is used as the EGC (check your local code). That isolation continues only until the bonding point at the service entrance where the neutral, equipment grounding conductor, and isolated-grounding conductor are bonded together. In Figure 10-31, there is a second green wire to the far left. This is the electrical system's normal EGC. This wire is for fault protection within the outlet's box and cover plate.

Figure 10-31
Isolated ground
receptacle

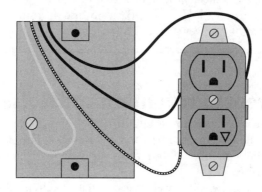

Grounding Equipment Racks

The NEC says, "Metal equipment racks and enclosures shall be grounded." So, when you create an AV design, make sure the integrator grounds them.

Powering a rack through a power distribution unit or a power strip, cord, and plug does not necessarily provide adequate grounding. However, using an auxiliary bonding conductor to connect the chassis of the PDU to the rack's bonding stud does.

Bonding ungrounded rack components, such as side panels, tops, and doors, also provides a degree of noise immunity for sensitive analog equipment. Not to mention, the high clock rates in modern digital equipment can give rise to wideband EMI radiation, which can be attenuated by the bonding of loose sheet-metal parts.

There are some practical things you can do to ensure that the racks installed in your system do not suffer from ground problems.

- There should be only one ground for the rack, and it should be via the EGC.
- The rack should not be connected to the building's metal structure.
- If a copper ground busbar is used within the equipment rack, it should be bonded to the nonpainted metal of the equipment rack using an appropriate anti-oxidizing agent.
- If a copper ground busbar is used within the rack, use it to ground the chassis of electronics that are not equipped with a ground pin on the power cord. Rack mounting a device in a rack may not adequately ground it because of the paint or finish used on the equipment or the rack.
- When racks are being used side by side and bolted together, scrape the paint off adjacent racks and use a copper jumper with a lug to connect the racks. Bolting racks together may not provide adequate continuity between racks.

Don't forget to specify the right size conductor for grounding, based on the size of the power strip's or PDU's EGC. Basically, use the same size or larger. For example, if the EGC of the power strip is 12 gauge, use a 12-gauge or larger conductor.

Interference Prevention and Noise Defense

Now that you've learned about circuit theory and power and grounding, you'll study ways to prevent interference in your AV systems. This section will help you understand basic field theory behind the causes of interference and offer strategies for combating noise.

Interference, or *noise,* is any electrical signal in a circuit that's not the desired electrical signal. The most common evidence of interference is a hum or buzz.

Hum is defined as an undesirable 50 or 60 Hz noise emanating from an audio system. It can manifest in a video system as a rolling "hum bar" on the display. *Buzz* is a hum with additional harmonic energy.

How does interference find its way into an audio or video signal? First, there has to be a source of interference and a device that's sensitive to the interference. You may hear the two referred to as *source and receiver, source and victim,* or source and receptor.

Second, there must also be a means or pathway by which the interference goes from source to receiver. This is what's known as *field theory,* or the transfer of energy from one circuit to another via an electrical or magnetic field. There is no physical contact between circuits during this energy transfer. It usually occurs either by *magnetic-field coupling* or by *electric-field coupling*.

Magnetic-Field Coupling

As current flows through a conductor, a magnetic field develops around that conductor. This magnetic field is often depicted as invisible lines of force (recall Figure 10-8), also referred to as *magnetic lines of flux*. As the current level remains constant, the lines of flux remain stationary. This explains what happens with DC, because the current is flowing in only one direction, so the field doesn't change over time.

In the case of AC, the magnetic field expands, contracts, and changes direction in response to changes in the intensity and direction of the current. With increased current flow in the conductor, the density of these magnetic lines of flux increases in direct proportion to the current flow; the lines of flux weaken as they get further from the conductor.

Current (the flow of electrons) can be made to move through a conductor when there is relative motion between conductor and magnetic field. This means that current can be made to flow either by moving a conductor through a magnetic field (thereby cutting across the magnetic lines of flux) or by making the magnetic field (the lines of flux) expand and contract around a stationary conductor.

For example, a conductor carries AC current at 60 cycles per second (60 Hz). As the current changes in intensity and direction, the surrounding magnetic field expands, contracts, and changes direction in relation to the current flow in the conductor. Now consider a second conductor placed within the changing magnetic field of the first conductor. As the magnetic field from the first conductor expands, contracts, and changes direction, the lines of flux cut across the second conductor, thereby pulling and pushing at the electrons in the second conductor.

This pulling and pushing force is voltage. Although this is a desirable effect in a transformer, it is not desirable in most other situations. In other words, the expanding, contracting, and direction-changing signal on the AC conductor—at 60 cycles per second—is transferred to the second conductor. This is called *magnetic-field coupling*.

Electric-Field Coupling

The attraction of unlike charges just described is called an *electric field*. Electric fields weaken as atoms move farther apart.

Positively or negatively charged bodies (containing either positively or negatively charged atoms) exert influence on the space surrounding them. For example, a positively charged conductor (lacking electrons) creates an electric field in the surrounding region, attracting electrons. This attraction—the electric field—creates a negative charge in a nearby conductor through what is called *electric-field coupling*. This difference in charge creates a voltage potential between the two conductors. The movement of electrons that creates this voltage potential is *current flow*. As long as there is no physical connection between the two conductors, the voltage potential will remain.

When two conductors are separated by an insulator (dielectric), along with a difference in potential between them (voltage), there's an electric field between the two conductors. The strength of the electric field increases in relation to the difference in voltage that exists between the two conductors.

With DC, the field doesn't change over time—it's static. Current is flowing in only one direction; therefore, the electric field extends out, and the lines of force are stationary. With AC, the polarity of the field changes over time, because the electric field expands and contracts. Therefore, the polarity of the electric field changes with the changes in voltage.

The capacity (ability to store a charge) of the electric field depends on the distance between the conductors, the surface area of the conductors, and the dielectric strength of the insulating material between the conductors. *Dielectric strength* refers to the maximum safe voltage of the insulating material between the conductors before the dielectric breaks down and an arc occurs, equalizing the charge between the two bodies or conductors. For example, air is the dielectric (and a good insulator) between charged storm clouds and the earth. A lightning strike is a breakdown of the dielectric—the air in this case—equalizing the charge between cloud and earth.

Although electronic components specifically designed to have high capacitance are known as *capacitors,* an electric field will exist between any two conductors with a difference in potential (voltage) between them. And as insulators are not perfect, some current will flow through the insulator (dielectric) between conductors.

 NOTE Dielectric strength is the maximum safe voltage of the insulating material between two conductors before the dielectric breaks down and an arc occurs, equalizing the charge between the two bodies or conductors.

Shielding

A shield is a metallic partition between two areas. It's used to control the propagation of electric and magnetic fields from one area to the other. Shields are used to contain electric and magnetic fields at the source or to protect a receiver from electric and magnetic fields. A shield can be the metallic chassis that houses an electronic device or the enclosure (aluminum foil or copper braid) that surrounds a wire or cable.

Shielding works bidirectionally. It prevents signals from getting out or getting in, stopping what are known as *egress* and *ingress*. The effectiveness of a shield is determined by the type of field, the material used for shielding, and the distance from the source of the interference.

AV pros can implement shielding in a variety of ways. They can provide coverage around a single insulated conductor or around individual insulated conductors in a multiconductor cable. You can also specify shields that surround multiple insulated conductors. Shields can even provide a return path for current that originates at sources of interference.

There are three basic types of cable shielding: foil, braid, and a combination of the two.

- **Aluminum foil shielding**   This employs a thin sheet of aluminum wrapped around an insulated conductor or conductors.

- **Copper-braided shielding**   This employs many tiny, interweaved wires around an insulated conductor or conductors.

- **Combination shields**   These employ both foil and braid types of shielding.

As alluded to earlier, the main criteria for specifying a shield are coverage, flexibility, and frequency range. *Coverage* is expressed in a percentage, and it indicates how much of the inner cable will be covered. *Flexibility* is a subjective measurement and correlates with a cable's flex life. And because shielding cannot protect a conductor from all sources of electromagnetic (EM) and radio frequency (RF) interference, its effectiveness is narrowed to a certain frequency range.

Shielding from Magnetic Fields

Magnetic shielding employs any magnetically permeable material to absorb and conduct magnetic lines of flux to redirect them away from an unintended victim, such as a circuit. Magnetically permeable materials include iron, nickel alloys, and steel, which vary in their ability to conduct magnetic fields. A design that puts AV cabling in steel conduit yields excellent magnetic shielding.

Non-magnetically-permeable materials include aluminum, brass, and copper, which do not have the ability to absorb or redirect a magnetic field. This means that AV cabling with aluminum-foil shielding or braided-copper shields will *not* guard against interference from magnetic fields at power line frequencies of 50 or 60 Hz.

 NOTE   Permeability is a material's ability to concentrate magnetic lines of flux. A magnetically permeable material will concentrate the magnetic lines of flux within itself, rather than let the magnetic lines of flux pass through it.

Shielding from Electric Fields

The purpose of *electric-field shielding* is to lead current to the equipment-grounding conductor and back to the source. Electric-field shielding employs electrically conductive materials to absorb and conduct electrical lines of the force and redirect them away from an unintended victim.

Foil or braided shielding does an excellent job of absorbing energy from a nearby electric field, but that energy will need somewhere to go. As discussed earlier, electricity seeks to return to the source. A pathway back to the source is provided when the shield is connected to the equipment chassis and the chassis is connected to the third prong of the power cord—the EGC. This pathway back to the source must be a low-impedance connection; otherwise, the current may take a different pathway and create interference somewhere else.

In an ideal scenario, all AV equipment would be connected to a single AC receptacle so that all shields for the interconnecting cables would be ground-referenced to that single receptacle. Often, however, this will not be the case. You may have multiple devices plugged into different receptacles, originating from different circuits, and possibly (though unfortunately) leading to different panelboards. Although all AC circuits may be referenced to the earth connection at the main service entrance, the EGCs may take different pathways. Those different pathways—even when well designed and implemented—may have slightly different impedances, which can create different potentials. When you have different potentials, current flows on the shields of the interconnecting cables.

Ground Loops

A *ground loop* is any electrically conductive continuous loop. In AV, ground loops are common but not always problematic. For example, consider two AV devices mounted together in an equipment rack and plugged into the same power strip. When the two devices are connected by a shielded cable, it creates an electrically conductive loop through the cable shield, device chassis, and third prongs (EGCs) of the power cords. Although the loop is electrically conductive, the loop area is small and of low impedance. Moreover, both devices' EGCs reference a common point in the power strip. Therefore, because the loop is of low impedance with a common reference point, there is little—if any—potential difference, and no current flows through the loop.

That said, a ground loop can manifest itself as a hum or buzz in an audio system. AV designers do not need to—nor can they—avoid all ground loops in an AV design. Instead, the design goal should be to identify areas where ground loops could be a problem and then plan accordingly.

The clearest example comes into play when designing an AV solution that spans two rooms. If the rooms use two different panelboards with different amounts of resistance between circuits, you should be able to identify potential ground-loop problems. Difference in potentials allows current to flow on the EGCs and shields of interconnecting cables. Some possible solutions might be to specify an isolation transformer or design a Cat5 or fiber-based solution.

Balanced Circuits

Signal-processing circuitry and cables are continuously exposed to noise and interference. In fact, all electrical circuits and the cabling used to connect them generate energy fields, which can interact with AV circuitry and cabling. Such interference and noise degrades the quality of an audio signal, for example. Noise introduced to a digital signal can even corrupt the data.

One way to reduce the noise in a circuit or cable is to use a *balanced electrical design*. The terms *balanced* and *unbalanced* refer to the impedance balance on two conductors and the circuitry connecting those two conductors.

A balanced circuit is a two-conductor circuit (not including a shield) in which both conductors and all the circuits connected to them have the same impedance with respect to ground. In other words, because the impedances are the same with respect to one another, they are balanced.

Figure 10-32
A balanced
circuit diagram

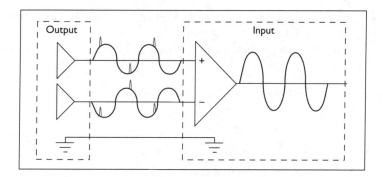

A balanced input uses a differential amplifier that responds only to the signal difference between conductors and rejects signals that appear identically—or in common—on both conductors. To help ensure that any unwanted signal or noise is induced onto both conductors as equally as possible, the two conductors are twisted around one another so that both conductors are equally exposed to the offending noise source. If the offending noise is coupled or shared equally on both conductors, it can be rejected by the differential, balanced input. We will discuss differential- and common-mode signals in more detail in the next section.

The design of balanced circuits offers a defense mechanism against noise. In Figure 10-32, the bumps on the sine waves on the output represent noise. These are called *common-mode signals* because they appear identically on both conductors. When they are combined via the differential amplifier, the input side responds only to the original differential-mode signals, which are out of phase on the two conductors. This defense mechanism removes the noise—or most of it—leaving only the intended signal. As a rule, you should use balanced components whenever you can. The cabling used with balanced circuitry requires two signal conductors. In audio, the two signal conductors are surrounded by a shield.

Differential- and Common-Mode Signals

Typically, in a balanced circuit, the audio signal will be in *differential mode* and the noise induced in a cable will be in *common mode*. In differential mode, different signals are carried on two conductors. In common mode, the same signal is carried on two conductors.

Common-Mode Rejection

The rejection of interference that is induced commonly on two conductors is known as *common-mode rejection* (CMR). The ability of a specific AV device to reject this common-mode noise is described by its *common-mode rejection ratio* (CMRR).

The CMRR is expressed in decibels, with higher numbers indicating better rejection, usually 70 to 120 dB, depending on need.

This can also be expressed mathematically. The formula for common-mode rejection is as follows:

$$(S_1 + N_1) - (-S_2 + N_2) = S_T + N_T$$

where:

- S_1 is the signal on the first conductor.
- N_1 is the noise on the first conductor.
- – indicates the difference (differential).
- S_2 is the signal on the second conductor.
- N_2 is the noise on the second conductor.
- S_T is the total signal.
- N_T is the total noise.

The CMRR equation is 20log (differential gain/common-mode gain), and it assumes an absolute value (positive value) for common-mode gain.

Although good CMRR numbers can be achieved in a laboratory, the real world is quite different. This is because the CMRR values of various electric components in a circuit are not exact values. Typical component CMRRs may vary as much as 5 percent from their stated values.

NOTE CMRR specifications should be stated in accordance with IEC standard 60268-3, which uses a 10-ohm impedance imbalance for testing.

Twisted-Pair Cables and Common-Mode Rejection

To help ensure that any unwanted signal (noise) is magnetically induced onto both conductors as equally as possible, the two conductors on a balanced cable can be twisted around one another. This purposefully and equally exposes both conductors to the offending magnetic field.

Twisting also helps to reject signals that interfere along a distance of the cable. Because of the twists, the interference will induce in one polarity for one segment of the cable, and the other polarity in the second section of the cable as a common-mode signal. This helps to reduce the level of noise generated along the length of the cable.

Transformers

One of the best defenses against common-mode noise is to specify transformers. Electronically balanced circuitry may be less expensive, but it is typically not as good at rejecting common-mode noise. An untapped transformer is inherently balanced, which leads to its excellent common-mode rejection.

Figure 10-33
A transformer

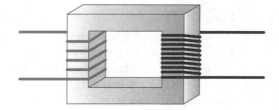

A transformer (Figure 10-33) is a passive electromagnetic device, usually consisting of at least two coils of wire (inductors) with no electrical connection between them. These coils often share an iron-based core that concentrates the magnetic lines of force in one coil, thereby inducing voltage into the other coil.

Common-mode noise will arrive on both ends of the primary side (left) of the transformer. Because it's common-mode noise, there will not be any potential difference between the ends of the primary side of the winding. Therefore, noise current will not flow through the primary side of the transformer and transfer to the secondary side.

In the real world, consider the 48 VDC phantom power supply used to power condenser microphones. Phantom power provides +48 VDC on pins 2 and 3 of an XLR connector and uses the shield as the circuit return. If, for whatever reason, phantom power is active and applied to a dynamic microphone, both ends of the coil in the dynamic microphone are presented with +48 VDC. The positive voltage is in common mode on pins 2 and 3, so no current will flow through the coil in the dynamic microphone.

Unbalanced Interface

If you do not use a balanced interface, you will need to use an unbalanced interface. In an unbalanced circuit design, the equipment outputs an unbalanced signal to a cable connected to an unbalanced input.

As with a balanced circuit, the cable may pick up noise from surrounding sources. However, with an unbalanced circuit design, there are no noise-defense mechanisms except for the shield. So if noise gets onto the signal conductor, there is no way to remove it. Moreover, if noise flows through the shield of an unbalanced circuit, it becomes part of the problem.

Cables used for unbalanced circuitry have two signal conductors. One conductor carries the signal, while the second conductor—usually the cable shield—acts as the return path. The return conductor is a low-impedance connection to the signal ground and possibly also to earth ground. The impedance of the signal circuitry is quite different than that of the return circuitry; hence, they are unbalanced.

NOTE With either a balanced or unbalanced circuit, the longer the cable run, the more it's subject to noise. Balanced circuits are less prone to suffer from noise pickup than unbalanced circuits. Unbalanced lines are limited in the distance they can cover.

The Pin 1 Problem

Another common reason for a system hum or buzz is the failure to account for the "pin 1 problem." Pin 1 is the shield connection of any device's input or output connector, regardless of the configuration or whether it's part of a balanced or unbalanced interface. On an XLR connector (pictured), for example, pin 1 is the pin to which the shield is connected. It will absorb and conduct electrical lines of the force from any nearby field and redirect them back to the source via the third prong of the power cord.

Many audio manufacturers will connect the shields of a balanced circuit to audio-signal grounds inside the equipment, which, again, is pin 1 in a three-pin XLR connector. This means that any current induced into the shield will modulate the ground where the shield is terminated. This practice of directing noisy shield currents to audio-signal ground is common and causes hum and buzz.

As the shield contact, a connector's pin 1 must have a direct connection to the device's metallic enclosure. The shield of the equipment will become an extension of the cable shield, which will keep interference away from the circuitry. This connection should occur outside the metallic enclosure, rather than inside, and will prevent the pin 1 connection from touching any circuit boards.

The best way to connect audio equipment is to use an entirely balanced, interconnected setup, where both ends of the shield are connected to chassis ground at the point of entry (see Figure 10-34). In this case, the shield of the equipment will act as an extension of the cable shield, and interference stays away from the circuitry. The bottom line is that the shield should be connected directly to the device's metallic enclosure, not to the internal electronic circuitry ground. If possible, specify an external enclosure connection, because short, internal connections may act as receiving antennas for RF interference.

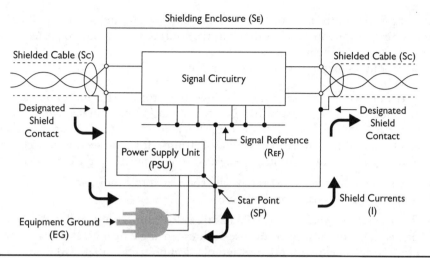

Figure 10-34 Attaching the cable shields to the equipment chassis keeps interference away from circuitry.

Specifying AV Conduit

Conduit is specified and used to protect AV cabling physically and from potential interference. To specify conduit properly, several considerations must be taken into account, such as the following:

- Compliance with local codes and regulations
- Physical protection
- Junction boxes
- Protection from potential interference
- Signal separation
- Physical distance from conduit used for electrical mains
- Avoiding damage during cable installation

Compliance with local codes and regulations includes allowable conduit fill percentages, allowable conduit bends, and junction box sizes. Restrictions on fill percentages and total allowable bends are intended to provide for heat dissipation and to prevent damaged conductors because of friction when pulling cables. Tension during the cable pulling process comes from cable weight and the friction generated between the outer cable jacket and the inner wall of the conduit.

Conduit Types

Conduit is a common means of routing cable from one location to another. Conduit permits protection from damage that might occur to exposed wires. Some conduit will offer additional protection from EMI. However, not all conduits are usable for all purposes, and it's important for you to select the right type during your design to protect your AV systems when they are being installed.

Metal conduit comes in various configurations.

- *Electrical metallic tubing* (EMT, or thinwall) is probably the most popular type of conduit. It is bendable by hand up to 1.25 in (32 mm) in diameter. If it is between 1.25 to 1.5 in (32 to 38.1 mm) in diameter, it may require a ratchet type bender, and if it is larger than 1.5 in (38.1 mm), it would require a mechanical power bender. It offers protection against stray magnetic and electric fields.

- *Flexible metal conduit* (flex) is typically connected to a movable piece of equipment and is used for short runs.

- *Intermediate metal conduit* (IMC) has threaded connections and is field bendable. Bends are accomplished by the use of threaded angle fittings. It is heavier and offers better shielding properties and physical protection than EMT.

- *Rigid metal conduit* (RMC) is also field bendable and has the same thread base as IMC, so the couplers for each type are interchangeable. Steel RMC is the best choice conduit for an electronically noisy environment because it is the heaviest conduit and offers the best physical and EMI protection.

Intermediate and rigid are interchangeable, and both can be used indoors, outdoors, underground, concealed, or exposed.

Plastic conduit offers no protection against electromagnetic interference (EMI), so it should not be used for AV cabling or any nearby AC wiring. Although plastic may be less expensive, it can also be crushed more easily than metal conduit. Plastic conduit also comes in different configurations.

- *Electrical nonmetallic tubing* (ENT) is an easily bendable PVC tube. It can be bent by hand and pushed through walls and floors.

- *Inner duct* is a fabric conduit. It is used inside other conduits, creating multiple paths in the same conduit. The interior of the inner duct tubing reduces friction when cable is pulled through it.

- *Rigid nonmetallic tubing* is stiff with a thick but lightweight wall. It is similar to plumbing tubing.

Conduit Stubs

Many jurisdictions allow properly rated cable to be run and supported freely—without conduit—in spaces such as above a drop-tiled ceiling. In this case, conduit is used to provide a pathway in a vertical and then horizontal direction beginning at a termination point, such as a wall-mounted junction box. In these cases, the conduit will run vertically from the wall-mounted box in the wall cavity, penetrating the wall cap and into the ceiling cavity, and the conduit is then bent in a horizontal direction.

With conduit stubs, the NEC requires that protection be provided at the end of the stub so that the cabling is not damaged during installation. Plastic insulation bushings will be installed at the end of the conduit stubs.

While the AV consultant or designer will specify conduit materials, sizes, junction boxes, and locations and produce a conduit riser diagram, other general specifications for the conduit infrastructure will need to be included. For audiovisual and communications cable, the specifications should be written something similar to the following:

Conduits installed for the audiovisual cabling will

- Be steel electrical metallic tubing, steel intermediate metal conduit, or steel rigid metal conduit.

- Be minimum trade size 3/4.

- Be no longer than 100 ft (30 m) or contain more than two 90-degree bends without a pull box. (Pull boxes should not be used in place of a 90-degree bend.)

- Have a bend radius of least six times the internal conduit diameter for conduits of 2 in or less.

- Have a bend radius of least ten times the internal conduit diameter for conduits larger than 2 in.

- Be reamed and free of burrs, dirt, or foreign matter (debris).

- Be fitted with insulation bushings when not terminated into a junction box.

- Have a pull string with a minimum test rating of 200 lb installed and secured.

Allowable Fill Percentages

Conduit is used to protect the cable inside and to create a pathway for the cable when it's being installed. The physical space within conduit is limited, so you must make recommendations about which cables to pull through a given conduit.

To prevent friction, conduit should not be overfilled. NEC code requires the following:

- One cable can occupy 53 percent of the conduit's inside area.

- Two cables can occupy 31 percent of the conduit's inside area.

- Three or more cables can occupy 40 percent of the conduit's inside area.

It may seem counterintuitive that only two cables should have a smaller allowable fill percentage than three or more, but this is because two conductors of the same size collectively form an oval shape. One conductor or three-plus conductors tend to form a more circular shape and rest more naturally inside the conduit.

NOTE The fill percentages here come from the NEC, so you may see similar fill percentages such as 50 percent, 30 percent, and 40 percent in other countries.

Calculating Conduit Fill

Let's say you want to run three cables in a piece of conduit. How do you know if you'll exceed that 40 percent permissible area? You can calculate conduit fill using one of the following formulas:

Conduit Capacity (One Cable)

$$D > \sqrt{\frac{d^2}{0.53}}$$

where:

- D = Inner diameter of the conduit
- d = Outer diameter of the conductor

Conduit Capacity (Two Cables)

$$D > \sqrt{\frac{d^2 + d^2}{0.31}}$$

where:

- D = Inner diameter of the conduit
- d = Outer diameter of the conductors

Conduit Capacity (Three-Plus Cables)

$$D > \sqrt{\frac{d^2 + d^2 + d^2 \ldots}{0.40}}$$

where:

- D = The inner diameter of the conduit
- d = The outer diameter of the conductors

Let's try a calculation for a single conductor or cable. What size EMT conduit is required when pulling a single RGBHV cable with an outer diameter of 0.792 in (20.12 mm), using the NEC-based, 53 percent fill as a guide?

Step 1 Substitute 0.792 for the outer cable diameter, d:

d^2 / 0.53
0.792 / 0.53

Step 2 Calculate the exponent and divide by 0.53:

0.792^2 / 0.53
0.627264 / 0.53
1.184 inches (30 mm)

Step 3 Calculate the square root to solve for the inner conduit diameter:

$D > \sqrt{1.184}$
$D > 1.09$ in (27.6 mm)

Step 4 Compare the result of 1.09 in (27.6 mm) with available conduit trade sizes:

- Trade size 1 (metric designator 27) = 1.049 in (26.6 mm)
- Trade size 1.25 (metric designator 35) = 1.38 in (35.1 mm)
- Trade size 1.5 (metric designator 41) = 1.61 in (40.9 mm)

Because 1.09 in (27.7 mm) is larger than trade size 1 but smaller than trade size 1 1/4, the latter is required.

Jam Ratio

When calculating for three conductors or cables, you will need to do some extra math. *Jamming* can occur when one cable slips in between the other two as they're being pulled so that they lay side by side in the conduit. This can occur even though you're within the 40 percent fill allowance.

Although jamming can occur in a straight run of conduit, it is more likely to take place in a bend, where the conduit may be more oval after bending.

The jam ratio formula is as follows:

$$\text{Jam} = \text{ID} / \left(\frac{OD_1 + OD_2 + OD_3}{3} \right)$$

where:

- ID = Inner diameter of the conduit
- OD = Outer diameter of each conductor

A jam ratio of 3.0 would indicate that the outer diameter of the three cables equals the inner diameter of the proposed conduit exactly. A jam ratio of anything between 2.8 to 3.2 should be avoided.

Figure 10-35
Cable jamming in conduit

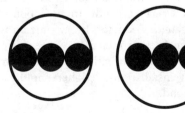

For example, take three cables, each with an outer diameter of 0.46 inches. First, calculate the proposed conduit size:

$$D > \sqrt{(0.46^2 \times 3 / 0.4)}$$
$$D > \sqrt{(0.2116 \times 3 / 0.4)}$$
$$D > \sqrt{(0.6348 / 0.4)}$$
$$D > \sqrt{(1.587)}$$
$$D > 1.259761882$$

You would need a conduit with an inner diameter larger than 1.26. A conduit with a trade size of 1.25 inches has an inner diameter of 1.38 in and would be suitable.

Because this is a three-cable scenario, you now need to check for the jam ratio. Because all three cables have the same outer diameter, the average OD is simply the OD of one of the cables: 0.46 in.

Jam ratio = 1.38 (the ID of the proposed conduit) / 0.46 (average OD of the three cables to be pulled)
1.38 / 0.46 = 3.0

In this example, if the three cables lined up in the conduit, the distance across the three cables matches the inner diameter of the conduit exactly. The next larger conduit, a trade size 1.5, should be specified. As a reminder, this is normally an issue only in a three-cable situation.

NOTE Depending on the source, you will see different numbers regarding jam ratios that should be avoided. The 2.8 to 3.2 referenced here comes from the NEC.

Conduit Bends

The NEC also limits the number of bends that installers may create in a single conduit run. The NEC says, "There shall not be more than the equivalent of four quarter bends (360 degrees total) between pull points, for example, conduit bodies and boxes." But that quote doesn't apply to AV cables.

In most cases, the AV team will be pulling much smaller gauge conductors through conduit than the 12-gauge conductors an electrician might be pulling. For example, the tension limit on a 24-gauge conductor is 4 pounds, compared to the 77-pound tension limit on a 12-gauge conductor. Every time an installer pulls through a bend, it increases friction. When friction increases, you're more likely to have damaged cable. Therefore, the 360-degree total limitation by code is not adequate for AV and communications cables. For AV installations, designers should specify a junction box after every 180 degrees worth of bend.

Chapter Review

You just learned a lot about a subject that factors relatively little in the CTS-D Exam Content Outline. You've learned about circuits, electrical power and distribution, grounding, preventing interference, specifying conduit, and more. The reason for all the detail is that electrical infrastructure is critical to the performance of AV systems and can be one of the most misunderstood areas of communication among project team members. It's not uncommon for an AV professional to use one term when trying to describe electrical infrastructure and an electrical engineer to understand something different. Think of this chapter not only as test prep but also as an important reference for professional collaboration.

Review Questions

The following questions are based on the content covered in this chapter and are intended to help reinforce the knowledge you have assimilated. These questions are not extracted from the CTS-D exam nor are they necessarily CTS-D practice exam questions. For an official CTS-D practice exam, see the accompanying CD.

1. For branch circuit loads, you should not plan to use more than _____ of the available current.

   A. 50 percent

   B. 60 percent

   C. 75 percent

   D. 80 percent

2. A power system that is designed exclusively for AV systems and associated computers and utilizes an isolated equipment ground is called a(n):

   A. Technical power system

   B. Grounded power system

   C. Balanced power system

   D. Unbalanced power system

3. The main considerations when selecting a cable shield are:

   A. Materials, permeability, and conductors

   B. Coverage, flexibility, and frequency range

   C. Impedance, flexibility, and materials

   D. Cable types, gauge, and interference

4. When installing conduit, it is important to remember that the conduit will require:

   A. Room to expand 45 percent because of latent heating

   B. Internal insulation, usually an injected polyurethane jell

   C. Adequate mounting support to withstand cable pulling

   D. A slip sleeve to ensure adequate air space for cable

PART III

5. The first step when determining conduit capacity for cable should be to determine the:

   A. Cable resistance and multiply by a factor of 5

   B. Allowable fill percentage based upon local codes and regulations

   C. Wire dimensions exclusive of insulation multiplied by 3.1459

   D. Bend radius for all cables utilized in the installation

6. An AV conduit riser diagram will show information such as:

   A. Electrical light wiring

   B. Electrical breaker boxes

   C. Junction and pull boxes

   D. Plumbing routes

Answers

1. **D.** For branch circuit loads, you should plan to use no more than 80 percent of the available current.

2. **A.** A technical power system is a power system that is designed exclusively for AV systems and associated computers.

3. **B.** The main considerations when selecting a cable shield are coverage, flexibility, and frequency range.

4. **C.** When installing conduit, it is important to remember that the conduit will require adequate mounting support to withstand cable pulling.

5. **B.** The first step when determining conduit capacity for cable should be to determine the allowable fill percentage based upon local codes and regulations.

6. **C.** An AV conduit riser diagram will show information such as junction and pull boxes.

CHAPTER 11

Elements of Acoustics

In this chapter, you will learn about

- How sound is produced
- Acoustics-related intensity and pressure
- Sound reflection, reverberation, diffusion, absorption, and transmission
- Measuring background noise and specifying maximum allowable background noise levels for a given environment and application

The first question designers consider when planning a sound system is whether such a system is even required. If a space is small, the acoustics are good, and the background noise level is low enough, there may not be a need for any system that seeks to amplify sound.

If, however, an audience can't adequately hear a presentation, performance, video-conference call, and so on, then using microphones, audio mixers, signal processors, power amplifiers, and loudspeakers to amplify a sound source electronically will probably be necessary. This way, the sound can also be distributed to a larger or more distant audience.

The second question is how much privacy a space requires, both from sound originating outside the space and from sound leaking out. Depending on the answers, infrastructure decisions will play a pivotal role in sound system design.

This chapter assumes knowledge of sound reinforcement needs assessment and specifications, which were discussed in detail in Part II, "Environment," of this guide. This chapter does not provide the level of knowledge required of an acoustician or sound engineer but will help you to make informed infrastructure decisions and design for a comfortable listening experience.

Domain Check

This chapter relates directly to the following tasks on the CTS-D Exam Content Outline:

- Domain B Task 1: Review A/E (architectural and engineering) drawings
- Domain B Task 7: Recommend acoustical criteria
- Domain C Task 1: Create draft AV design
- Domain D Task 1: Participate in project implementation communication

These tasks comprise 19.2 percent of the exam (about 24 questions). This chapter may also relate to other tasks.

Acoustic Engineering

Acoustic engineering is an important allied trade to the AV industry. Acoustics is the science and technology of sound in all its aspects. When acousticians look at a room, they consider the following properties of sound:

- **Production** How the energy is generated; in other words, the source of the sound
- **Propagation** The pathway of the energy
- **Control** How (sound) energy is generated and subsequently propagated
- **Interaction** How material responds to the sound energy imposed upon it
- **Reception** How hearers' ears and brains will respond to the stimuli placed upon them

Ideally, any application where audio quality is crucial will require an acoustical consultant's expertise during the programming phase. As an AV professional, you should be aware of your design environment's acoustic properties and be prepared to make recommendations regarding acoustic criteria.

 NOTE This chapter will cover each of the listed sound properties, but you'll find control-related information in discussions of sound transmission class (STC) and impact insulation class (IIC).

Sound Production

When you think about where sound comes from, it's probably easiest to envision vibrating objects, such as a moving loudspeaker cone or a vibrating string, producing waves in the air. However, sound is produced by any disturbance that creates changes in pressure or velocity in an elastic medium such as air. For example, air escaping from an air-conditioning outlet comes out of a vent that's much smaller than the duct. This increases the velocity of the air, resulting in a whoosh of air. The change in velocity and pressure, rather than mechanical vibration, produces the sound.

Not only is mechanical vibration not required to produce sound, you don't even really need air. Sound waves do need a physical medium in which to propagate, but that medium can be water, other liquids, or solids. The fact that sound can be carried by so many different media is part of what makes acoustics such a complex field.

In his book *Music, Physics, and Engineering* (Dover Publications, 1967), Harry F. Olson wrote, "Sound is an alteration in pressure, particle displacement, or particle velocity which is propagated in an elastic medium, or the superposition of such propagated alterations. ... Sound is produced when the air or other medium is set into motion by any means whatsoever. Sound may be produced by a vibrating body, for example, the sounding board of a piano, the body of a violin, or the diaphragm of a loudspeaker. Sound may be produced by the intermittent throttling of an air stream as, for example, the siren, the human voice, the trumpet or other lip-reed instruments, and the clarinet and other reed instruments. Sound may also be produced by the explosion of an inflammable-gas mixture or by the sudden release of a compressed gas from bursting tanks or balloons."

From these lines we learn that any disturbance that creates changes in air pressure or air-particle velocity will be processed by our ear/brain system as sound.

Sound Propagation

Sound waves have physical length, or *wavelength*. Wavelength is the distance between two corresponding points of two consecutive cycles. Knowing how a sound wave of a certain size interacts when it comes into contact with surfaces of different sizes and materials helps us to understand sound wave behavior.

You may be wondering about the effect altitude plays in relation to the speed of sound. It turns out that temperature has a much more pronounced effect on the speed of sound than atmospheric pressure.

The speed of sound depends on the temperature and molecular weight of atmospheric gas. It does not depend on pressure changes. The pressure decreases with an increase in altitude and therefore only slightly affects the speed of sound. The speed of sound in air is 1,130 ft (344 m) per second.

You can obtain the wavelength value if you divide the speed of sound by frequency, as shown in the following formula:

$$\lambda = v/f$$

where:

- λ is the wavelength measured in feet or meters.
- v is the speed of sound in feet (meters) per second.
- f is the frequency in hertz.

If the speed of sound in air is 1,130 feet per second, the wavelengths covering the entire audible spectrum, from 20 Hz to 20 kHz, range from 56.5 ft (17.2 m) long to less than 3/4 in (19 mm) long in air (in other words, 1130 / 20 = 56.5 and 1130 / 20000 = 0.0565). Considering such a vast range of wavelengths, it's important that you have a solid understanding of how waves of certain physical dimensions behave in a given space.

Although the sounds you hear every day are complex waveforms, each can be broken down into individual sine waves of all the frequencies that make up each particular sound. In Figure 11-1, a USB oscilloscope shows the complex waveforms from the left and right tracks of a music CD.

Frequency and wavelength are inversely proportional. This means that as one gets larger, the other gets smaller. The lowest frequencies have the longest wavelengths, and the highest frequencies have the shortest wavelengths.

We'll now discuss sound characteristics as they pertain to propagation, including intensity, pressure, and particle displacement.

Sound Intensity

When you talk about how "loud" a sound is, you are referring to its power. This is the amount of sound power falling on (or passing through or crossing) a unit area. Power is measured in watts, so the unit for sound power is watts per square meter (W/m^2).

However, sound is not measured using a power meter. Measuring sound power requires complex, expensive instruments capable of detecting power in watts over a specified area. Instead, sound is typically measured in terms of pressure. When you measure sound pressure, you are measuring the amplitude of sound over an area, rather than power over an area. You can measure pressure with a microphone because microphones, like the human eardrum, detect pressure.

Figure 11-1
Complex
waveforms

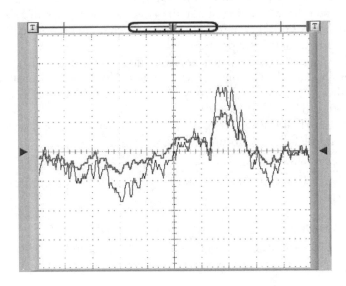

Sound Pressure

The decibel describes a base-10 logarithmic relationship of a power ratio between two numbers. It's a logarithmic scale used to describe ratios with a large range of values that can vary over several orders of magnitude.

We compare one power against another power and take the logarithmic relationship of those two powers. The result is in Bels, but Bels are a bit too large for practical use, so we multiply the result by 10 for a result in decibels (dB).

$$dB = 10log \, (P_1 \, / \, P_2)$$

That works for comparing two powers, but don't we also use decibels to compare other values such as distances and voltages? Certainly. We also use the decibel for quantifying differences in voltage and distance as they relate to power.

Voltage, distance, and sound pressure are related to power in the same way that power dissipated in an electrical circuit is proportionally related to the square of the voltage in Ohm's law. In other words, power is proportional to the square of the voltage (electrical pressure), distance, or sound pressure (see Figure 11-2).

Here we compare two voltages:

$$dB = 10log \, (V_1^2 \, / \, V_2^2)$$

The voltages are squared and compared with one another. The log of that relationship is multiplied by 10. The resulting change is expressed in decibels. The following example compares two distances:

$$dB = 10log \, (D_1^2 \, / \, D_2^2)$$

Or, we could work it in by squaring the voltages or distances or other nonpower numbers that we are comparing, but we can simplify the equation by using 20 times the log instead.

$$dB = 20log \, (V_1 \, / \, V_2)$$
$$dB = 20log \, (D_1 \, / \, D_2)$$

Figure 11-2
Power is proportional to the square of the voltage.

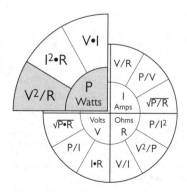

PART III

Therefore, you would use the 10log equation for comparing two powers and a 20log equation when comparing like values of anything else.

Particle Displacement

Another important part of sound measurement is *particle displacement,* measured in meters (m). Particle displacement is the distance of a particle's movement from its equilibrium position in a medium as it transmits a sound wave.

Sound Interaction

Sound energy moves out and away from the source in all directions. Unless the sound is generated in a completely free space, the energy will encounter a boundary or surface. If you are outdoors, the only likely boundaries may be the ground or nearby buildings. There are many boundaries and surfaces when you are indoors. Besides the walls, ceilings, and floors that you may be thinking of, furniture and people also affect what happens with the sound energy in the environment.

So, what happens to the sound energy produced by either a sound reinforcement system or other source of generated sound? The Law of Conservation of Energy tells us that energy can be transformed from one form to another and transferred from one body to another, but the total amount of energy remains constant.

When sound energy encounters a surface or room boundary, one or more of the following three things occurs (see Figure 11-3):

- Reflection
- Absorption
- Transmission

Before getting into the specifics of what happens to sound within a space, we'll give you a good overall view of what is occurring in that space.

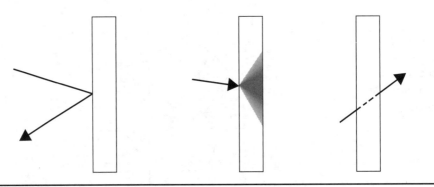

Figure 11-3   Sound interaction

The separate "sound events" that occur over time have a significant effect on the quality of sound as experienced by the listener. An acoustical consultant, understanding how a venue is to be utilized, can predict each of these events by evaluating and making recommendations regarding the venue's size, optimum shape, finishes and materials to be used, and so on.

Let's discuss each event in detail.

Reflection

Figure 11-4 shows the types of sound events that occur in a space. Of such events, you will always have *direct sound*—sound that arrives directly from the source to the listener.

If a space has boundaries (such as walls, ceilings, floors, furniture, and so on), there will also be *reflections*—sound that arrives to the listener after the direct sound as reflected energy. This sound takes an indirect path, taking more travel time before arriving at the listener.

If the sound energy is not absorbed by some material or transmitted into an adjoining space, it will be reflected back into that space. Reflections can be direct, diffuse, or somewhere in between.

Direct Reflections

Direct or specular reflections (Figure 11-5) bounce directly off a surface like light bouncing off a mirror. Like light, the incoming angle (the angle of incidence) will equal the outgoing angle (the angle of reflection).

Scattered Reflections

The second type of reflection energy is *scattered* or *diffused* (Figure 11-6). Diffusion is the scattering or random redistribution of a sound wave from a surface. It occurs when surfaces are at least as long as the sound wavelengths but not more than four times as long.

Figure 11-4
Reflection

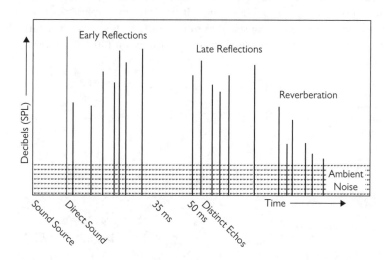

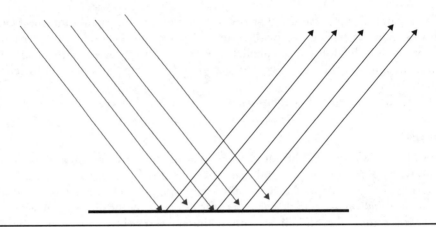

Figure 11-5 Direct reflections

When sound hits rougher surfaces, it reflects in varying directions. Whether the energy is reflected in a specular or diffused fashion depends on how "smooth" the surface is, relative to the wavelength. Either way, the energy remains in the space.

When the sound energy is diffused, it is dispersed and therefore less noticeable. Dispersed sound can have a tendency to do some self-canceling, in that as it is scattered, the hearer will receive diffused energy from all directions, causing some canceling.

This is similar to the properties exhibited by a matte-white front-projection screen. With a matte-white screen, all incident light that strikes the screen is scattered evenly in all directions. This "even scattering" or "even distribution in all directions" is easily accomplished with visible light energy because light visible to humans covers less than an octave.

Audible sound energy covers ten octaves, making diffusion or any other acoustical control over a wide frequency range difficult to implement. Again, this directly relates to wavelength. For reflecting surfaces to function as diffusers, they must be heavily textured and irregular—the dimensions of irregularities should be *nearly equal to the wavelength of sound.*

Figure 11-6
Scattered
reflections

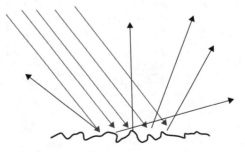

Diffusers Diffusers (pictured), as the name implies, are a good complement to sound absorption because they reduce echoes and reflections without removing sound energy entirely. Their various shapes, sizes, and materials provide a surface for sound to scatter or disperse in different directions. With diffusion, the energy is reflected back at different angles rather than the majority of the energy being reflected at a single specific angle. They are useful for breaking up dead spots from phase cancellation, but they also smooth out the peaks or the response of the room. Additionally, diffusion, like any other acoustical treatment, is effective only over a limited frequency range.

A space without diffusion can feel cavernous, so many professionals include diffusers to improve speech intelligibility and the overall experience for listeners.

 TIP Do not confuse diffusers with bass traps. Bass traps are sound absorbers for lower frequencies. They are used mainly for reducing standing waves and low frequency that build up within a space.

Flutter Echoes

One type of hard reflection is a *flutter echo*. A flutter echo is a series of reflections that continue to bounce back and forth between parallel hard surfaces, such as large walls, ceilings, windows, and floors. Flutter echoes are distracting and should be avoided.

 Take a break to check out a brief video demonstrating flutter echoes at www .infocomm.org/FlutterVideo. Note how the sound bounces back and forth off the walls of the room. Appendix C provides links to many helpful videos.

Other types of flutter echoes are "pitched-roof" flutter echoes and flutter echoes created by concave surfaces, but these concepts are beyond the scope of this guide.

Room Modes

A *mode* (or standing wave or room resonance) is the amount of energy at fixed positions within a room. Room modes significantly affect the perceived low-frequency performance in smaller rooms, such as boardrooms, conference rooms, classrooms, home theaters, music practice rooms, and small studios—really, any relatively small room.

A *standing wave* occurs when a sound wave travels between two reflecting surfaces, such as two parallel walls. At some frequency, the room's dimension equals exactly one-half a wavelength at a particular frequency, as well as multiples of that one-half wavelength. The wave reflects back on itself, producing fixed (standing) locations of high and low pressure.

For example, let's take a room that is 23 ft (7 m) deep. Dividing the speed of sound in the air of 1,130 by 46 (double the room dimension), you get 24.57 Hz. You'd get the same result if you divided 344 by 14 for the metric equivalent. Therefore, a frequency of 24.57 Hz is about 46 ft long; half of that is 23 ft.

The following are standing waves based on the example:

- **23 feet**   One-half wavelength at 25 Hz
- **46 feet**   One wavelength at 49 Hz
- **34.5 feet**   One-and-a-half wavelengths at 74 Hz
- **23 feet**   Two wavelengths at 98 Hz

In practice, the nulls (minimal pressure) can cancel well enough that they could be indiscernible from the room's acoustic noise floor.

NOTE   This chapter takes into account only axial modes (involving one pair of surfaces). There are also tangential modes (involving two pairs of surfaces) and oblique modes (involving all three room surface pairs) that are not discussed here. Critical room design would include consideration for tangential and oblique modes.

Note in Figure 11-7 that the modes would cover the full width and length of the room. It also illustrates only a slice of the modal distribution. The floor-to-ceiling dimension normally is the room's smallest dimension (RSD) and sets the frequency at which model behavior becomes dominant.

At what point do room modes dominate the low-frequency performance of the room? A simple formula is used to approximate the *Schroeder frequency*.

$$F_c = 3 \times 1130 \,/\, RSD$$

where:

- F_c is critical frequency.
- 1130 is the speed of sound in air (344 m per sec).
- *RSD* is the room's smallest dimension.

As we've already noted, the room's smallest dimension will be the distance from the floor to the ceiling. Also, F_c is not to be considered a single frequency but a transition area. Below the F_c, you would expect room modes to dominate the low-frequency performance of the space.

Figure 11-7
Fixed energy
locations in a
room

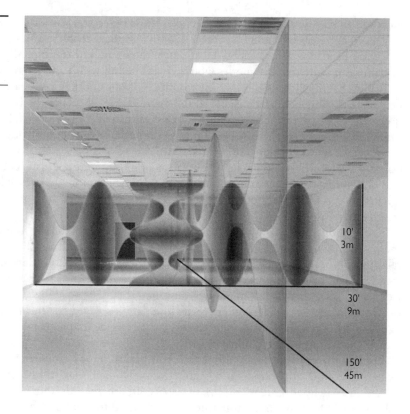

For example, take a meeting room that is 14 ft wide and 30 ft deep, with a floor-to-ceiling height of 10 ft. The distance from the floor to the ceiling is the variable used in the calculation.

$$F_c = 3 \times 1130 / 10$$
$$F_c = 339 \text{ Hz}$$

In this example, the transition area into where room modes dominate would be from around 339 Hz below.

During system equalization, placing a measurement microphone in specific locations of either high or low energy will result in an erroneous representation of the actual sound system response.

These areas of high and low energy distribution will also be revealed by the levels shown on an audio spectrum analyzer. With room modes, the energy level shown by the analyzer is completely dependent on the relationship between the microphone's position and the mode. If the microphone is placed in the location of a peak (maximum energy), the analyzer would show an excessive energy level that one might think needs to be "EQ'd out." If the microphone is placed in the location of a null, the sound energy might not show at all but would appear as part of the noise floor. And of course, there are locations for all the energy levels in between those two states. Unfortunately, there isn't a way to equalize electronically based on a room's physical characteristics.

Figure 11-7 shows fixed energy locations in the room, illustrating only a slice of modal distribution. Note that the modes would cover the full width and length of the room.

Rooms having dimensions that are multiples of one another are least desirable, a cube being the absolutely least desirable room shape. Table 11-1 lists the best room proportions suggested by various researchers. These ratios will yield reasonable low-frequency room quality, as far as the distribution of axial model frequencies is concerned.

Generally speaking, tangential modes will be −3 dB of the axial mode energy, and oblique modes will be −6 dB less than the axial mode energy. This is because tangential and oblique modes involve greater distances and involve more surfaces. The difference in levels between these types of modes will be more pronounced in a room with acoustical treatment.

Room modes will dominate the low-frequency performance of the room. Because these areas of maximum and minimum pressure (peaks and nulls) are created by the relationship between wavelength and room dimensions and are location specific, these locations will be evident and can be displayed on a spectrum analyzer. Determining the frequency below which room modes dominate helps us to know where our analyzer provides unreliable data. In other words, the data displayed by the analyzer completely depends on microphone placement at those room mode frequencies. Was it placed in an area of maximum or minimum pressure?

Because the analyzer data is unreliable, it is best to set low frequencies on an equalizer by ear. After equalizing an audio system effectively, there may still be unavoidable issues caused by the physical shape and size of a space. In other words, there is no way to "equalize a room." Different room dimensions cause sound to react in different ways.

Ultimately, the AV professional needs to know when the data seen on the analyzer is completely unreliable. Rooms with dimensions that are multiples of one another reinforce modal frequencies. This can be mitigated by spreading out the room modes—using room dimensions that are not multiples of one another. Those involved with small studio or home theater design might know these as the so-called golden room ratios.

Table 11-1		Ceiling Height	Room Width	Room Length
Room Modes		1.00	1.14	1.39
	L.W. Sepmeyer	1.00	1.28	1.54
		1.00	1.60	2.33
		1.00	1.40	1.90
	M.M. Louden	1.00	1.30	1.90
		1.00	1.50	2.50
	J.E. Volkman	1.00	1.50	2.50
	C.P. Boner	1.00	1.26	1.59

Although smaller rooms, such as conference rooms and boardrooms, are characteristically dominated by room modes, reverberation is an issue in larger rooms.

 NOTE The "sound" of a small room is impacted not only by the modal behavior at lower frequencies (around 300 Hz and below—the bottom four octaves of our hearing spectrum) but also by early reflections. Direct sound combines with the energy from early reflections (10 ms or less), and the result is severe tonality shifts. In other words, these severe tonal shifts in the sound occur when early reflected energy combines with direct energy. This doesn't require a sound system to occur and helps to explain why a small room "sounds like a small room." Small rooms sound poorly because the dimensions create this direct and early reflection problem.

Reverberation

Reverberation is the sound that persists in a room after the energy that created it is stopped. Adding audio equipment cannot compensate for a room with undesirable acoustic properties.

Reverberation is the combination of many acoustic reflections, which are dense enough that they don't sound like reflections, but rather act as a sonic decay "tail" to the sounds in a room.

True reverberation is really only a large-room phenomenon and can be a significant issue in large rooms used for speech or contemporary music styles. Examples include gymnasiums used for assembly purposes, an armory used as a reception hall, or a cathedral-style house of worship introducing contemporary-style music. Longer reverberation times are more appropriate for liturgical houses of worship, cathedrals, chamber music, and some concert halls.

You can think of a reverberant room being a sound energy storage tank. The room cannot drain off the energy being introduced into it either by absorption or by transmission.

A statistical reverberant field is reverberation that is well enough spatially diffused that it is essentially the same at all points in a room. Many of the formulas used in acoustics and sound systems assume the existence of a *statistical reverberant field,* but this does not always exist. A reverberant field doesn't exist in a small room because the sound energy is not able to develop a diffuse, uniform, random distribution.

When we talk about the reverberation time (RT_{60}) of a room, we assume the room has a statistical reverberant field.

Reverberation Time   Persistence of sound energy (reverberation) is measured in terms of time and level. It is also frequency specific. The *reverberation time* of a space (Figure 11-8) is said to be the number of seconds it takes for the sound to decay to one-thousandth of its original level, or 60 dB. Therefore, we call this RT_{60}.

The RT_{60} value will vary with frequency and environment. In general, spaces primarily intended for speech or more contemporary music require shorter RT_{60} levels than music, depending on the style. An acoustician can quantify acceptable RT_{60} times and design the venue accordingly.

Figure 11-8
Reverberation
time

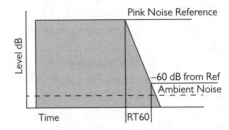

Figure 11-9 illustrates some examples of reverberation times in certain types of venues. Note how the reverberation time directly relates to the volume of a room.

Whether the reflections are either useful or distracting depends on when in time the reflection arrives to the listener after the direct sound, as well as the energy level of the reflection in comparison to the direct sound energy level. See the "Sound Reception" section in this chapter for more information about sound integration.

Absorption

Sound can also be absorbed. Absorption is about slowing down particle velocity (power) using various surfaces, such as porous absorbers. It is the friction between the air molecules and a material.

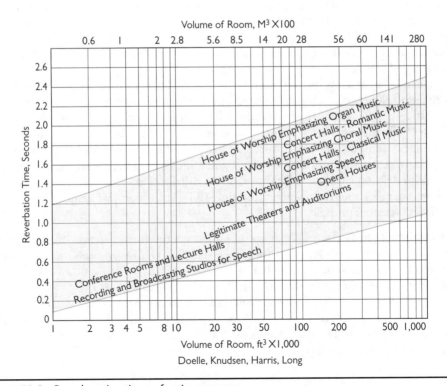

Figure 11-9   Reverberation times of various venues

The effectiveness of different types of absorbers, such as porous or resonant absorbers, is frequency (wavelength) dependent. An absorber effective for a wavelength of 6 in (152.4 mm, or approximately 2000 Hz) will be of little use for a wavelength that is more than 4 ft (1.22 m, or 250 Hz). Such effectiveness is quantified as a coefficient (sabin) over a single octave band.

The *noise reduction coefficient* (NRC) takes an average of the four middle test frequencies (250, 500, 1000, and 2000). Generally speaking, NRC values smaller than 0.20 are considered to be reflective, while values greater than 0.40 are considered to be absorptive.

While absorption reduces the amount of sound level energy within a room, absorption does not prevent sound energy from being transmitted into an adjoining room. In other words, absorption is not an acoustic barrier.

Another absorption metric gaining popularity is the *sound absorption average* (SAA). The SAA is a single-number rating that is the average, rounded off to the nearest 0.01, of the sound absorption coefficients of a material for the 12 one-third octave bands from 200 through 2500 Hz. Although the SAA replaces the NRC rating, as directed by the ASTM C423 in 2000, most product literature still uses NRC values.

While air absorption will not be a factor in a typical conference room, boardroom, or meeting room, it is a factor in larger rooms. As you get farther away from the source, the sound energy spreads out, and some of the energy is absorbed by the air as well.

The absorption coefficient of a surface is the ratio of the energy absorbed by the surface to the energy incident. It typically lies between 0 and 1, which represent nonabsorbing and totally absorbing surfaces, respectively. Values greater than 1 are often found in random incident measurements, although theoretically impossible. This usually occurs because of diffraction/edge effects. The absorption coefficient can be defined for a specific angle of incidence or random incidence as required.

Absorption coefficients are measured at 125, 250, 500, 1000, 2000, and 4000 Hz, according to ASTM C423-09a, *Standard Test Method for Sound Absorption and Sound Absorption Coefficients by the Reverberation Room Method*.

Table 11-2 shows air attenuation coefficient values for some of the frequency levels.

The amount of absorption varies with frequency (wavelength), and porous absorbers have limited effectiveness below about 250 Hz (a 4.5 ft, 1.37 m wavelength).

Porous Absorbers

As the displaced air molecules pass through a porous absorber, the friction between the molecules and the material of the absorber slows down the molecules. While there may

Table 11-2 Air Attenuation Coefficient	Frequency (Hz)	Air Attenuation Coefficient (sabins/m)	Air Attenuation Coefficient (sabins/ft)
	2000 Hz	0.009	0.003
	4000 Hz	0.025	0.008
	8000 Hz	0.080	0.025

still be some reflected sound back into the room, a much greater portion of the sound has otherwise been absorbed.

Typical porous absorbers include carpets, acoustic tiles, acoustical foams (pictured), curtains, upholstered furniture, people, and their clothing. The effectiveness of different types of absorbers, such as porous or resonant absorbers, is frequency (wavelength) dependent.

Porous absorbers are primarily effective at middle and high frequencies. Fittingly, this range is where the ear is most sensitive and where noise control is most needed in many environments.

Resonant Absorbers

Resonant absorbers are used to manage frequencies where the size or thickness of porous absorbers in those cases would be too expensive or difficult to manage. Additionally, resonant absorbers are typically placed in room boundaries or wall surfaces where porous absorbers fail to affect low-velocity sound waves. Typical resonant absorber construction consists of a gypsum panel and spacing filled with absorbent, insulating material.

NOTE   Make sure the absorber is compliant with ASTM E84, *Standard Test Method for Surface Burning Characteristics of Building Materials.* Foam material, such as craft foam, which is not fire-rated, should never be used in acoustical engineering applications.

Transmission

We know sound can be transmitted through walls and other building materials. Certain materials and construction methods can also be rated on their ability to attenuate sound passing through them.

The greater a material's mass, the higher the transmission loss. The less energy transmitted, the more energy reflected. You can predict the transmission loss of single-layer, impermeable materials using a simple formula known as the *acoustic mass law*.

$$TL = 20 * log (m * f) - 47.2$$

where:

- *TL* is the transmission loss in dB.
- *m* is the mass in kg/m^2.
- *f* is the frequency in Hz.

According to the formula, the greater a material's mass, the higher the transmission loss of any given frequency. In addition, the higher the frequency, the higher the transmission loss of any given mass of material. This explains why you can hear bass thumping outside a music venue but not the vocals.

The formula for mass law (see Figure 11-10) demonstrates a concept, but it doesn't translate directly to the real world.

As an AV professional, you won't typically be expected to perform acoustical calculations such as the total absorption of a space or the transmission loss of a partition. These are the purview of an acoustical engineer.

However, knowing the basics of how sound wave behavior can be predicted and manipulated can help you make recommendations that prevent adjacency issues and improve the performance of the AV system.

Also remember to keep these factors about mass law in mind:

- It doesn't account for acoustic effects that occur at very low frequencies (below 50 Hz) where transmission loss is more dependent on resonance effects and material stiffness than mass.

- It doesn't account for acoustic effects that decrease transmission loss at high frequencies (above 5 kHz). Transmission loss also drops at the critical frequency—the frequency at which incident sound waves graze the surface because they are parallel to it.

- Finally, the mass law cannot account for any leakage that allows sound to be transmitted through the air around the material.

Still, the mass law remains a good general guideline—denser materials provide better transmission loss, reflecting more sound than less dense materials.

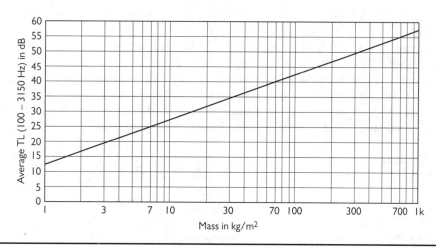

Figure 11-10   Mass law

Table 11-3	STC Range	Speech Privacy
Typical Speech Privacy Associated with STC Ratings	0–20	No privacy. Voices clearly heard between rooms.
	20–40	Some privacy. Voices will be heard.
	40–55	Adequate privacy. Only raised voices will be heard.
	55–65	Complete privacy. Only high level noise will be heard. Note that the term *complete* may not be adequate for some secure facilities.

Sound transmission class (STC) rates transmission loss at speech frequencies from 125 to 4000 Hz plotted against a standard contour as the reference. STC does not evaluate performance at frequencies below 125 Hz, where music and mechanical equipment noise levels can be high.

Table 11-3 shows typical STC ranges associated with certain expected levels of privacy, assuming background noise levels of approximately 35 dB SPL A-weighted. Note that these ranges will not provide isolation from low-frequency energy.

Also note that these ratings assume no significant flanking paths or partition openings. Slight breaches, such as gaps around conduit or plumbing or unsealed cracks at the ceiling or floor, allow sounds to come through walls that are supposed to be barriers. They are undesirable and defeat the purpose of the barrier.

 TIP Because STC doesn't account for the low frequencies produced by music and mechanical noise, it is useful only for measuring the transmission properties of a material with respect to speech.

Selecting proper building materials and construction techniques can help to keep the conference room quiet. A concrete block wall where each block is 8 in thick will yield an STC 45 rating. If there were a 92 dB SPL sound on one side of the wall, the sound could penetrate but be reduced to a level of about 47 dB SPL (barring any other means for the sound to get over, around, or through the wall).

This same block wall can become an STC 56 by applying plaster to both sides. Additional construction materials applied can further increase the STC rating.

Figure 11-11 compares the STC ratings of various wall constructions. These are using 5/8 inch (15.8 mm) gypsum and assume no penetrations or flanking paths.

The STC 36 utilizes wooden studs and absorptive material. The STC 39 and STC 44 use metal studs. Metal studs are often more effective because their flexible nature

Figure 11-11
Sound transmission coefficient ratings 36, 39, and 44

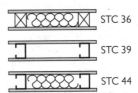

Figure 11-12
Sound transmission coefficient ratings 46 and 57

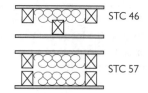

provides certain isolation from vibration. They decouple one side from another so it reduces noise transmission through the structure.

Figure 11-12 shows staggered-stud and doubled-studded wall construction, again using 5/8 in (15.8 mm) gypsum. The double-studded wall assumes a 1 in (25.4 mm) air gap.

The STC 46 uses staggering studs that also can support further mounting of shelves and hardware. Typically wood is chosen. It is difficult to stagger metal studs because of the need to use a continuous runner at the top and bottom plates. Staggered studs represent a compromise between single-stud and double-stud construction.

STC 57 implements a double-stud technique. In both cases, the studs don't touch, providing more airspace and less possibility that vibrations will resonate through the wall via the studs.

Impact insulation class (IIC) is a rating used to quantify impact sound absorption. It is an average of the attenuation in decibels that occurs at frequencies ranging from 100 to 3150 Hz. The higher the IIC rating is, the better insulation from impact noise the material provides.

The higher the IIC rating, the better the insulation from impact noise. An IIC rating of 50 is considered the minimum for flooring in residential buildings like apartment high-rises.

IIC ratings are especially important with respect to barriers between floors. Think about how the spaces above and below the AV environment will be used. How much impact noise will result from the activities in the space above yours? What about in the AV space itself? Ensure that the IIC of the floor above is sufficient to keep listeners from being distracted by impact noise. You should also make sure that the IIC of your own floor keeps the occupants of the space below from being bothered by activities in the AV space.

Table 11-4 shows IIC ratings for 6 in (152.4 mm) concrete slab with various toppings.

Table 11-4
Impact Insulation Class Ratings

Topping	IIC Rating
None	28
Vinyl flooring	35–40
Hardwood flooring	30–35
Hardwood flooring with resilient layer	45–50
Carpet and underlay	75–85

NOTE   Like STC or NRC, IIC is a one-number metric that is an average of performance across a frequency range. It doesn't tell the whole story, especially since the impact of a high-heel shoe on a tile floor produces sound at a different frequency from a boot on a wooden joist.

Sound Reception

Many things can distract from the intended message in a meeting space. The lights may emit a buzzing sound. The water cooler in the corner may turn on and off. The ventilation system may rattle as it heats or cools the room. Noise from outside the space, such as traffic or nearby construction, can intrude into the space. Each of these items adds to the overall background noise in a space.

Because excessive noise levels interfere with the message being communicated, ideally background noise–level limits will be specified by an acoustician, audiovisual consultant, or designer appropriate to the type of room and its designed purpose. In other words, the criteria and limits for background noise levels for a gymnasium will be much different from those of a conference room. The heating, ventilation, and air conditioning (HVAC) system, partitions, and any necessary acoustical treatment will be designed and applied so that the background noise–level criteria is not exceeded.

A room's acoustical properties (such as reflections and types, amount of transmission allowed) and background noise levels are significant contributors to a sound system's overall effectiveness. We'll discuss the effects of each and how they can be handled in design.

Integration Process

Within certain time frames, our ear/brain system processes direct and reflected energy as one sound event (the *integration process*). And within a certain time frame, many of these reflections can be useful, adding apparent "fullness" to the direct sound.

An important unseen effect is an increase in loudness, which occurs when the reflected sound is within what is colloquially called the *integration interval*—about 30 ms for speech and 50 ms for music, depending on the temporal structure of the sound.

Small conferencing rooms often have reflections arriving 10 ms or less after the direct sound. These short time frames often require room treatments, especially in conferencing rooms with tele- or videoconferencing capabilities. Large fan-shaped auditoriums often have late reflections arriving later than 50 ms after the direct sound.

While possibly acceptable for music (depending on musical style—more contemporary styles of music don't work well with the later reflection times), reflections arriving later than 50 ms are not acceptable in a speech application. That's because late reflections hinder speech intelligibility.

Some "early" reflections are actually useful reflections in that if they arrive close enough in time behind the direct sound, your ear/brain system actually integrates both the direct and delayed reflection and perceives only one sound. The perception of integration will depend somewhat on what you are listening to. Your brain can integrate a greater delay with music than it can with speech.

Our brain uses the comparison between direct and reflected sound to determine the direction of the sound's origin, a psychoacoustic effect called *precedence effect* and first described by Helmut Haas in his Ph.D. thesis (hence the name Haas effect). We use the direct sound—the sound arriving first at the listener—for directional cues.

This has important implications for sound system design in presentation environments.

In some situations, it may be required to have some loudspeakers on a delay line, such as underneath a balcony, for example. If you want listeners' attention to be drawn to a presentation area at the front of the room, the sound from loudspeakers at the front must reach them before the sound from loudspeakers in other parts of the room. Also, sound from the latter loudspeakers can't be allowed to drown out sound from the former. Delay and sound pressure level of loudspeakers must be set accordingly.

This integration of direct and reflected sound (see Figure 11-13) is similar to the human visual system integrating a series of still pictures resulting in apparent motion. The presentation of a moving image, either by a movie projector or by a video screen, depends on an attribute of human eyesight called *persistence of vision*. In simple terms, this means that if a succession of images are presented to us rapidly enough, we do not see them as separate images. As the presentation rate is slowed down, we become more and more aware of flicker, which can be highly objectionable.

If sound reflections arrive after these integration times listed for music and speech, we will perceive these reflections as discrete echoes, and these later reflections can diminish intelligibility.

What about reflections arriving within 10 ms of the direct sound? Again, knowing that sound travels about 1,130 feet per second or 1.13 feet per millisecond in air, you can determine the wavelength of various frequencies by using the wavelength formula (see the "Sound Propagation" section). For a frequency of 1000 Hz, the wavelength is 1.13 ft. A complete cancellation will occur at one-half that wavelength. So if a reflection takes an additional path length of 0.565 ft over the direct sound, cancellation, or a *notch* in frequency response, will occur at 1000 Hz and subsequently every multiple of 1000 Hz, creating an overall comb filter response.

You can discover the frequency of the first notch by using the following formula:

$F = 1 / 2t$

where:

- F is the frequency.
- t is the time in seconds.

Figure 11-13
Integration
of direct and
reflected sound

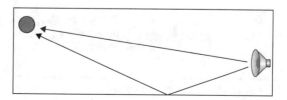

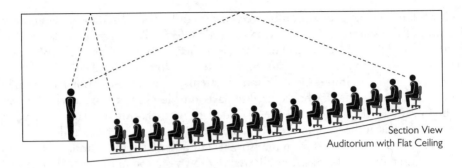

Figure 11-14 Auditorium with a flat ceiling

So, calculating for a 5 ms delay would look like this:

F = 1 / 2 (0.005) = 100 Hz

The first notch of the comb filter would be at 100 Hz and create additional notches at every multiple of 100 Hz. The first notch of a 10 ms delay would be at 50 Hz, with its subsequent multiples. These notches take out large chucks of the audible spectrum, especially in the speech region. Once you get out to about 15 ms or 33 Hz, the subsequent multiples become much denser, and the notches created by the delayed wave energy become less noticeable.

In small rooms, the additional path lengths taken by reflections are quite short when compared to larger rooms. This explains why smaller rooms devoid of acoustical treatment and with lots of hard, highly reflective surfaces, sound like they do. The listening environment in a small room is not always pleasant.

Not all reflections are bad. Figures 11-14, 11-15, and 11-16 show how an acoustician may direct reflections in an auditorium in a useful way. Bear in mind that these illustrations show only energy reflected off the ceiling. Reflections from the floor and walls should also be taken into consideration. This is where an acoustician can provide recommendations for room shapes and materials.

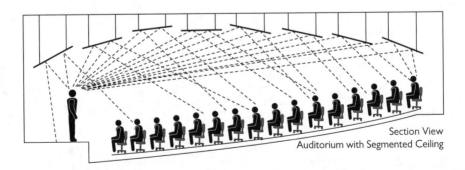

Figure 11-15 Auditorium with segmented ceiling

Figure 11-16   Auditorium with stepped flat ceiling

Noise Classes

Figure 11-17 shows a side-by-side comparison of the NC, RC, and NCB graphs. An acoustician, AV consultant, or AV designer will specify the maximum background noise limits to the architect, other consultants on the project, and the owner. These limits will inform the other parties in regard to certain decisions about construction techniques, devices, and implementation of various aspects of the building services.

The prevalent method for defining the maximum permissible background noise generated by mechanical systems in buildings has been developed by the American Society for Heating, Refrigerating, and Air-Conditioning Engineers (ASHRAE).

The method consists of comparing the octave band pressure levels of a noise with a family of curves known as *noise criteria* (NC) or *room criteria* (RC). Notice that the shape of the curves compensate for the loudness response of the ear, permitting higher levels at the low frequencies. RC curves are slightly more restrictive than the NC curves at the lowest and highest frequencies and are preferred by many mechanical system designers because the slope of the contours presumably matches more closely a well-balanced, bland-sounding spectrum.

RC ratings have suffixes that indicate the character of the sound.

- N indicates a balanced, or neutral, spectrum.
- R indicates a rumbly sound.
- H indicates a hissy sound.
- RV indicates perceptible vibration.

The *balanced noise-criterion* (NCB) curve is part of the ANSI/Acoustical Society of America (ASA) S12.2-2008 standard, *Criteria for Evaluating Room Noise*. This standard offers two methods for evaluating the sound in an occupied space. It is used before construction to specify acceptable octave-band noise levels and is used after construction to rate the noises' effect on speech communications. It can be used to identify spectral imbalance, such as noise or hiss. The curve also recommends the number of decibels of noise reduction needed to eliminate the problem.

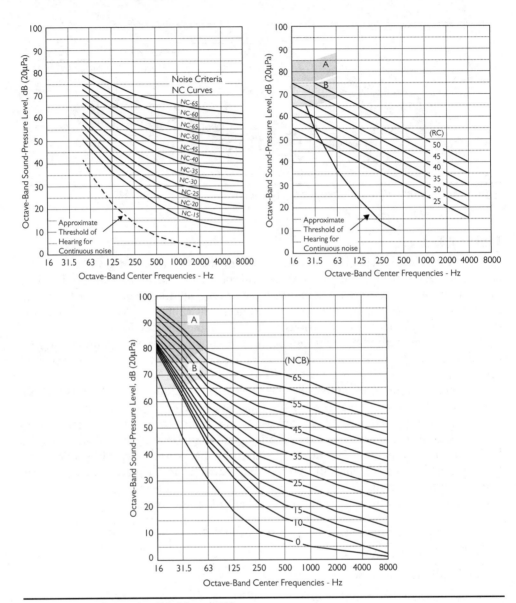

Figure 11-17 Comparing NC, RC, and NCB

Background Noise

Background noise can be a large factor in the effectiveness of an AV system. Excessive ambient noise levels result in less effective communication because of listener fatigue. Background noise can come from outside of the room and could include sounds from adjacent rooms, foot traffic from spaces above, structure-borne vibrations, and traffic on the street. Background noise can come from sources within the room as well, particularly from the HVAC system and from AV equipment such as projectors, displays, power amplifiers, and IT equipment.

Ambient noise is the background noise that originates from all sources other than the desired source. It is any sound other than the desired signal. While an electronic sound system has inherent noise in the electronic components, rooms also have noise associated with them. Unwanted background noise in a room can come from equipment fans, office machines, the HVAC system, or the actual people in the room. Noise can intrude from outside the room as well, through partitions or windows. Outside sources can include vehicular traffic, adjoining corridors, and structure-borne vibrations. See the "Reception" section later in this chapter for background noise recommendations.

Background Noise Recommendations

Table 11-5, adapted from the ANSI/ASA Standard S12.60-2010 and *Sound System Engineering, Third Edition,* provides recommendations for background noise levels for certain types of venues.

Occupancy	RC(N)	NC	Approx. dB(A)
Private residences	RC 25–30	NC 20–30	30–35
Apartments	RC 30–35	NC 30–35	35–40
Hotels and motels:			
Individual rooms or suites	RC 25–35	NC 25–35	30–40
Meeting and banquet rooms	RC 25–35	NC 25–35	30–40
Hall, corridors, lobbies	RC 35–45	NC 35–45	40–50
Service and support areas	RC 35–45	NC 35–45	40–50
Offices:			
Boardrooms	RC 25–30	NC 25–30	30–35
Business machines/computers	RC 40–45	NC 40–45	45–50
Conference rooms	RC 25–30	NC 25–30	30–35
Executive offices	RC 25–30	NC 25–30	30–35
Open plan areas	RC 35–40	NC 35–40	40–45
Private offices	RC 30–35	NC 30–35	35–40
Public circulation	RC 40–45	NC 40–45	45–50
Teleconference rooms	RC ≤ 25	NC ≤ 25	≤ 30
Church auditoriums	RC 25–35	NC 25–35	30–40
Schools:			
Classrooms	RC 25–30	NC 25–30	30–35
Large lecture halls with sound reinforcement	RC 25–30	NC 25–30	30–35
Large lecture halls without sound reinforcement	RC ≤ 25	RC ≤ 25	≤ 30
Libraries	RC 30–40	NC 30–40	35–45
Courtrooms:	RC 30–35	RC 30–35	35–40
With sound reinforcement	RC 30–40	NC 30–40	35–45
Without sound reinforcement	RC 25–35	NC 25–35	30–40

Table 11-5 Background Noise Recommendations (*Continued*)

Occupancy	RC(N)	NC	Approx. dB(A)
Multipurpose auditoriums	RC 20–25	NC 20–25	25–30
Movie theaters	RC 30–35	NC 30–35	35–40
Restaurants	RC 35–40	NC 35–40	40–45
Concert and recital halls	RC 15–20	NC 15–20	20–25
Recording studios	RC 15–20	NC 15–20	20–25
Television studios	RC 20–25	NC 20–25	25–30

Table 11-5 Background Noise Recommendations

 TIP Do not use A-weighted sound pressure levels for specification or noise analysis. dB-SPL A-weighted measurements are only rough approximations and provide no information regarding spectrum shape and frequency content.

Chapter Review

You have just reviewed the impact that a facility's acoustical properties can have on audio system design. Sound is a huge factor when you're designing in a space. There are many important considerations that you as a designer need to incorporate into your plans. Now that you know what to look out for, you'll be able to design successfully your AV systems around the space you're working in.

Review Questions

The following questions are based on the content covered in this chapter and are intended to help reinforce the knowledge you have assimilated. These questions are not extracted from the CTS-D exam nor are they necessarily CTS-D practice exam questions. For an official CTS-D practice exam, see the accompanying CD.

1. What formula is used to predict the transmission loss of single-layer, impermeable materials?

    A. Ohm's law

    B. Mass law

    C. Frequency coefficient

    D. Inverse square law

2. What is the STC range for adequate privacy?

    A. 0–20

    B. 20–40

    C. 40–55

    D. 55–65

3. If sound transmission class measures a material's ability to halt sound traveling through the air, how is transmission of sound resulting from impacts, such as footfalls on the floor above, quantified?

    A. Noise reduction coefficient (NRC)

    B. Sound transmission class (STC)

    C. Impact insulation class (IIC)

    D. Noise criteria (NC)

4. What unseen effect occurs when the reflected sound is within the integration interval—about 30 ms for speech and 50 ms or more for music?

    A. Scattering of the sound throughout the venue

    B. Echo

    C. Amplitude modulation

    D. An increase in loudness

5. Which device will reveal areas of high and low energy distribution?

    A. Peak level indicator

    B. Spectrum analyzer

    C. Oscilloscope

    D. Pink noise generator

Answers

1. **B.** Mass law allows designers to predict the transmission loss of single-layer, impermeable materials.

2. **C.** The STC range for adequate privacy is 40–55.

3. **C.** The transmission of sound resulting from impacts, such as footfalls, is quantified by impact insulation class (IIC).

4. **D.** When reflected sound is within what's known as the integration interval, you'll hear an increase in loudness.

5. **B.** A spectrum analyzer will show you areas of high and low energy distribution.

PART IV

Applied Design

CHAPTER 12

Digital Signals

In this chapter, you will learn

- How to determine signal strength based on the eye pattern of a digitally encoded signal
- How to calculate the required bandwidth in bits per second of an uncompressed digital audio or video signal
- How to differentiate between compression and encoding
- How to describe common digital video compression methods

In modern AV systems, audio and video are increasingly transported as digital signals. As an AV professional, you need to be familiar with the physical characteristics of digital signals, including how far you can transport them and what happens when the waveform collapses. You also need to be aware of digital media bandwidth requirements and the burden they can place on a shared network. Finally, you need to be conversant in common encoding and compression techniques so that you can specify AV systems with the right capabilities.

Domain Check

This chapter relates directly to the following tasks on the CTS-D Exam Content Outline:

- Domain C Task 1: Create draft AV design
- Domain C Task 2: Confirm site conditions
- Domain D Task 2: Perform system verifications

These tasks comprise 22.4 percent of the exam (about 28 questions). This chapter may also relate to other tasks.

The Analog Sunset

December 31, 2013, marked the end of the analog era. That was the day, under the Advanced Access Content System (AACS) license agreement, when AV manufacturers had to stop making devices with analog outputs. Older devices had their analog outputs disabled.

The AACS license agreement was adopted by content owners and manufacturers to protect movies and other consumer media on Blu-ray Discs and certain other sources from illegal copying. But its ramifications are felt in professional AV. Much of today's video equipment features High-Definition Multimedia Interface (HDMI) and Display-Port connectivity for transporting digital signals.

In addition, many laptop manufacturers, including AMD, Dell, Intel Corp., Lenovo, Samsung, and LG agreed to eliminate Video Graphics Array (VGA) connections in 2015. In other words, the standard analog connections that AV professionals have made for decades are slowly becoming a thing of the past. Designers still need to accommodate legacy signals, but it's more important that they embrace the digital present and future. Consider the following:

- Players manufactured after 2010 limited analog video outputs to standard-definition (SD) interlaced signals (480i, 576i, S-Video, composite).
- The end of analog computer video interfaces was announced in 2010.
- Finding a new device with an HD-15 (VGA) connection is now uncommon.
- No player manufactured after 2013 includes analog outputs.
- Intel planned to end support of VGA and low-voltage differential signaling in 2015 in its PC client processors and chipsets.

Regardless of whether a signal is analog or digital, one of the key specifications to factor into an AV design is bandwidth. Analog signals are quantified using frequency, usually in megahertz in the content of video. With digital signals, bandwidth is quantified in terms of bits per second (bps), megabits per second (Mbps), or (most commonly these days) gigabits per second (Gbps).

Here is a formulaic representation of analog (top) and digital bandwidth, for your reference:

1920 × 1080 × 60 / 2 (On/Off pixel pattern) × 3 (3rd harmonic) = 186,624,000 Hz or 186.624 MHz

versus the following:

1920 × 1080 x 60 × 3 (red, green, blue) × 8 (8-bit color) = 2,985,984,000 bps or 3 Gbps (3G) uncompressed

Digital Signals

Digital information is like a standard light switch. A common light switch has only two positions—on and off. In the world of signals, a digital signal is either on or off. These two states are numerically represented with a 1 (on) or a 0 (off).

Figure 12-1
An eye pattern

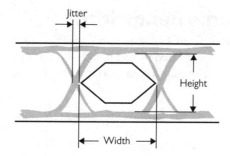

Digital formats are capable of carrying a lot more than just one signal type at a time. Some digital connections can carry video, audio, control, and Internet. Oscilloscopes visually represent signals that vary with time, with the vertical axis depicting voltage and the horizontal axis showing time.

Some oscilloscopes can take a digital signal, trace the 1s and 0s that make it up, and display important information in a visual pattern. Because of its ovular shape, this pattern is called an *eye pattern* (see Figure 12-1).

You can use an eye pattern to view many aspects of a digital signal. For example, you can view a signal's amplitude. If the amplitude of the signal is weak or if the receiver has poor sensitivity, the signal will fall within the hexagonal shape indicated in Figure 12-1. When this happens, the signal will become unstable. You may see green sparkles or other color anomalies. The audio quality may suffer as well. If the eye pattern degrades too much, you may lose your signal. When that happens, you may need to plan for repeaters along the signal path (Figure 12-2).

Figure 12-2
Repeaters help boost digital signals.

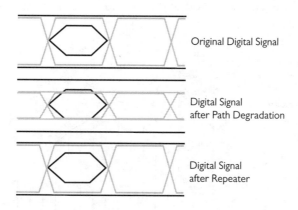

Original Digital Signal

Digital Signal after Path Degradation

Digital Signal after Repeater

Digital Audio Bandwidth

An unencoded audio signal's bandwidth requirements are in direct relationship to the signal's sampling rate (measured in hertz) and bit depth (measured in bits). See Figure 12-3. The formula for the required data throughput of a single unencoded audio stream is as follows:

Sampling Rate × Bit Depth × Number of Channels = Bit Rate (bps)

This unencoded data can be streamed over a local area network (LAN), saved to a file (for archiving or editing), or compressed with an encoder to reduce the file size even more. It should be noted that compressing a smaller file takes less processing than compressing a larger file, easing the central processing unit (CPU) load for other purposes. Note also that a 7.1 audio file will be significantly larger than a mono voice file. As always, the question is, "How good is good enough?" Is reducing bandwidth worth the quality trade-offs?

Common audio sampling rates include the following:

- **Telephone**   8 kHz
- **Audio CD**   44.1 kHz
- **DVD audio**   48 kHz
- **Blu-ray Disc**   96 or 192 kHz
- **Super Audio CD (SACD)**   2.8 MHz

 NOTE   For more in-depth information about bit depth and sampling, you can review the *CTS Certified Technology Specialist Exam Guide* (McGraw-Hill Education and InfoComm International, 2013) or *Networked AV Systems* (McGraw-Hill Education and InfoComm International, 2014).

Figure 12-3
Bit depth is like a ruler; the more granular, the more accurate the result.

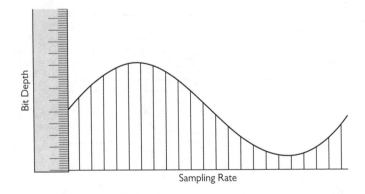

Digital Video Bandwidth

Audio and video streams are both digital representations of analog data, sound, and light. So, why does video require so much more bandwidth than audio?

It's because digitally representing video requires much more data. For video, each pixel has a bit depth—a number of possible states. The moving image has a sampling rate, represented as the number of frames per second. That total must be multiplied by the total number of pixels in the image to find the uncompressed bandwidth.

The formula for black-and-white, uncompressed digital video signal bandwidth is as follows:

$$Horizontal\ pixels \times Vertical\ pixels \times Bit\ depth \times Frames\ per\ second = Bit\ rate\ (bps)$$

The number of pixels is determined by the video format. For example, each frame of 720p digital video is 1280 pixels wide by 720 pixels high. That's 921,600 total pixels in each frame. Tables 12-1, 12-2, and 12-3 list some common video pixel resolutions for your reference.

Table 12-1
High-Definition Format

Name	Resolution
720p	1280×720
1080i/p	1920×1080
UHD (consumer 4K)	3840×2160
4K	4096×3072

Table 12-2
Common Intermediate Format (PAL)

Name	Resolution
Quarter CIF (QCIF)	176×144
CIF	352×288
4CIF	704×576
16CIF	1408×1152

Table 12-3
Standard Intermediate Format, National Television System Committee (NTSC)

Name	Resolution
Quarter SIF (QSIF)	176×140
SIF	352×240
4SIF	704×480
16SIF	1406×960

Of course, when was the last time you streamed black-and-white video? Color video is not a single signal. It's three: red, blue, and green. That means a color video stream requires even more data. The amount of bandwidth you need to stream color video depends on how that video is sampled. Here's how to calculate the bandwidth (bps) for color video, depending on the sampling method used.

4:4:4 Sampling

Color video is not a single signal. It's three: red, blue, and green. 4:4:4 sampling uses all three signals in equal proportion. A 4:4:4 color video signal requires three times the bandwidth of its black-and-white counterpart.

You may have seen the bit rate of digital video expressed as 24 or 32 bits. This is just a bit depth of 8 multiplied by the number of channels. The formula for three-channel, uncompressed digital video signal bandwidth is as follows:

Horizontal pixels × Vertical pixels × Bit depth × Frames per second × 3 = Bit rate (bps)

4:4:4:4 Sampling

Computers have a transparency layer called an *alpha channel*. This channel is the same size as the red, green, or blue signal. When you set your computer resolution, you see either 24 bit or 32 bit. 24 bit has 8 bits for quantizing red, 8 for green, and 8 for blue. Add the 8 bits for alpha channel, and you have 32 bits (and hence 4:4:4:4).

The formula for four-channel uncompressed digital video signal bandwidth is as follows:

Horizontal pixels × Vertical pixels × Bit depth × Frames per second × 4 = Bit rate (bps)

4:2:2 Sampling

Because human eyes can't detect color information as well as black-and-white detail, you can get away with limiting the color information included in the digital sample. 4:2:2 sampling includes all the luminance information, but only half the red and blue channels. The drop in quality isn't noticeable; 4:2:2 sampling is used for broadcast TV. Keep in mind, you can't use this sampling method for computer graphics because computers don't have component output.

The formula for 4:2:2 digital video signal bandwidth is as follows:

Luminance + Cr + Cb = Bit rate (bps)

where

- *Luminance = Frames per second × Bit depth × Horizontal pixels × Vertical pixels*
- *Cr (red) = Frames per second × Bit depth × 1/2 Horizontal pixels × Vertical pixels*
- *Cb (blue) = Frames per second × Bit depth × 1/2 Horizontal pixels × Vertical pixels*

4:1:1 Sampling

Digital video and some Moving Picture Experts Group (MPEG) video formats (see Chapter 17, "Streaming Design") use 4:1:1 sampling, limiting the color information even further. The full luminance signal is still present, but only one-fourth of the color information is sampled.

The formula for 4:1:1 digital video signal bandwidth is as follows:

Luminance + Cr + Cb = Bit rate (bps)

where

- *Luminance = Frames per second × Bit depth × Horizontal pixels × Vertical pixels*
- *Cr (red) = Frames per second × Bit depth × 1/4 Horizontal pixels × Vertical pixels*
- *Cb (blue) = Frames per second × Bit depth × 1/4 Horizontal pixels × Vertical pixels*

 NOTE   4:2:0 sampling is also a common choice. It is mathematically the same as 4:1:1 sampling in terms of required bandwidth, with basically the same color resolution and a different pixel pattern. Both 4:2:0 and 4:1:1 sampling suffers from blocky color patterns and poor color fidelity.

Bandwidth: Determining Total Program Size

When determining the total required bandwidth of an AV stream, it's important to remember that reducing or increasing the video or audio information changes the total data transmission rate. Yes, video requires a lot of bandwidth, but sometimes people forget the audio. Audio can require a lot more bandwidth than you might think, especially for surround-sound applications. All those channels add up. Remember also to account for overhead, namely, the addressing and control information that must accompany AV packets.

When it comes to AV program bandwidth, here is the formula:

Video bit rate + Audio bit rate + Overhead = Total required bandwidth (bps)

Once AV program bandwidth is calculated, you may find that you must choose a lower sampling rate to fit within the bandwidth limitations of your overall system. You don't necessarily have to think of choosing a lower sampling rate as sacrificing quality, though, especially when it comes to video.

Digital techniques have become far more sophisticated in recent years. Modern digital codecs can analyze image content and decide how to prioritize that detail with greater ease. With a color subsampled image, the program decoding the picture estimates the missing pixel values, uses the surrounding intact color values, and provides the link between the two. That means a 4:2:2 image can look almost as good as a 4:4:4.

Content Compression and Encoding

A single stream of uncompressed 4:1:1 video with audio and overhead can easily exceed 21 percent of the rated capacity of anything short of a gigabit LAN or optical fiber network. AV data must therefore be compressed or encoded before it can travel across an enterprise network.

Compression is the process of reducing the data size of video and audio information before sending it over a network. The information is then decompressed for playback when it reaches its destination. Compression may be "lossless" or "lossy," which is a more important distinction for AV signals than it is for, say, e-mail messages.

With lossless compression, the AV data is the same after it's been compressed and decompressed as it was originally. All the data remains intact. (In IT, lossless compression is important for maintaining the integrity of data such as financial records, text, and other non-AV information that would otherwise lose its meaning if any of it were altered.)

In AV, lossless compression schemes are important when the application demands perfect fidelity of AV data throughout its transmission—for example, in video security or command-and-control systems. Apple Lossless and Dolby TrueHD are examples of lossless audio compression; JPEG 2000 and H.264 offer lossless video compression.

Lossy compression techniques compress and discard "unneeded" data while still returning an acceptable-quality stream after decoding. The compression program examines a video or audio segment for detail that is less important or less noticeable. It then drops the data describing that detail from the stream. When the stream is re-created during decoding and playback, people are unlikely to notice the dropped information. For example, a video compression scheme might focus its work more on moving images in a stream than on static background images.

Lossy compression is common for AV applications, such as streaming media and IP telephony. Advanced Audio Coding (AAC) and MPEG-1 or MPEG-2 audio layer 3 (MP3) are examples of lossy audio compression; MPEG-2 and VC-1 offer lossy video compression. Some lossy schemes also implement lossless techniques to further decrease file sizes.

Codecs

The software or hardware that actually performs the lossless or lossy compression—as well as the decompression—is the *codec*, short for "encoder/decoder." Codecs come in an almost bewildering variety: one-way and two-way, hardware- and software-based, compressed and uncompressed, specialized videoconferencing, and so on. Deciding what type of codec to use for a design requires considering several factors, including the following:

- IT policies. The playback software that users currently have (or are allowed to have) determines the codecs their playback devices use, which in turn determines the codec you need to encode streams.
- Licensing fees associated with the codec.

- The resolution and frame rate of the source material.
- The desired resolution and frame rate of the stream.
- The bandwidth required to achieve your desired streaming quality.

When it comes to matching the bandwidth you need to a codec's capabilities, you may not be able to find technical specifications to help you. Some testing may be in order.

Digital Audio Compression: MP3

MP3 is one of the more common audio encoding formats. It was defined as part of a group of audio and video coding standards designed by the Moving Picture Experts Group. MP3 uses a lossy compression algorithm that reduces or discards the auditory details that most people can't hear, drastically reducing overall file sizes.

When capturing and encoding MP3 audio, you can choose your bit depth and sampling rate. The MPEG-1 format includes bit rates ranging from 32 to 320 kbps, with available sampling rates of 32 kHz, 44.1 kHz, and 48 kHz. MPEG-2 ranges from 8 to 160 kbps, with available sampling rates of 16 kHz, 22.05 kHz, and 24 kHz.

MP3 encoding may be accomplished using constant bit rate (CBR) or variable bit rate (VBR) methods. You can predefine CBR encoding to match your bandwidth, especially where bandwidth is limited. VBR encoding uses a lower bit rate to encode portions of the audio that have less detail, such as silence, and uses a higher bit rate to encode more complex passages. CBR encoding results in more predictable file sizes, which helps in planning for bandwidth requirements. However, VBR can result in better perceived quality.

Digital AV Compression

Compressing a data stream that contains both audio and video is considerably more complex. Because video has more information than audio, the resulting files and streams are much larger. There are many AV compression formats, but they generally fall into two categories.

The first is *intraframe compression,* which compresses and sends each frame individually (Figure 12-4). Because it sends each individual frame, intraframe compression is preferable for editing video. Motion JPEG uses intraframe compression. Not surprisingly, the resulting data files are large.

Figure 12-4
Intraframe
compression

Figure 12-5
Interframe
compression

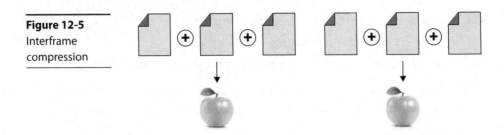

Interframe compression, on the other hand, detects how much information has changed between frames and sends a new frame only if there are significant differences (Figure 12-5). Interframe compression requires less bandwidth to stream and results in smaller files. MPEG video algorithms use interframe compression; so do most videoconferencing codecs.

NOTE You may have heard it's a bad idea for your clients to wear patterned clothes during a videoconference. It's true! An interframe codec, common in videoconferencing systems, sends a new frame every time it sees the pattern shift, resulting in a far higher bandwidth stream.

When it comes to encoding and decoding a digital signal, video frames are formed into logical groups, known as *groups of pictures* (GoPs), shown in Figure 12-6. A GoP is a set of video frames, which, when played in succession and in line with other GoPs, creates the video stream. In a GoP, there are three picture types.

- I-frames (intraframes), which are complete reference pictures. Every GoP starts with an I-frame.

Figure 12-6
A group of
pictures

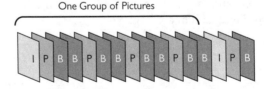

One Group of Pictures

- P-frames (predictive frames), which contain information about how the P-frame is different from the preceding I- or P-frame.

- B-frames (bidirectional frames), which contain information about how the B-frame is different from the preceding *and* following I- or P-frames.

Encoding software chooses which frames in a GoP to actually transmit in a video stream. Interframe encoding jumps from I-frame to I-frame, compressing several frames at a time.

You will learn more about compression and its role in AV systems design in Chapter 17 where we discuss streaming applications.

Chapter Review

At this point in the evolution of AV, your design is likely to transmit mostly digital signals. In that case, you need to plan your design around the proper bandwidth requirements, based on the client's needs, and understand the basics of compression and encoding.

Review Questions

The following questions are based on the content covered in this chapter and are intended to help reinforce the knowledge you have assimilated. These questions are not extracted from the CTS-D exam nor are they necessarily CTS-D practice exam questions. For an official CTS-D practice exam, see the accompanying CD.

1. Your customer wants to stream CD-quality music at 24 bits in stereo to his lobby area. How much bandwidth will this application require?

   A. 754 bps

   B. 1.5 Kbps

   C. 2.1 Mbps

   D. 1 Gbps

2. You need to stream 10 channels of 96 kHz audio. You have 25 Mbps of bandwidth available. What is the highest bit depth you can use?

   A. 24 bit

   B. 26 bit

   C. 32 bit

   D. 48 bit

3. You currently have the bandwidth capacity to stream 30 channels of 48 kHz, 24-bit audio. How many channels could you stream if you upgraded to 96 kHz, 24-bit audio?

   A. 15 channels

   B. 25 channels

   C. 30 channels

   D. 60 channels

4. What is the required bandwidth for 4:4:4, progressive digital video signal (1920 × 1080, 8 bits at 30 Hz)?

   A. 1.49 Gbps

   B. 2.60 Gbps

   C. 3.20 Gbps

   D. 460.4 Mbps

5. What is the required bandwidth for a 4:4:4 computer image (1280 × 1024, 8 bits at 80 Hz)?

   A. 2 Gbps

   B. 2.5 Gbps

   C. 3 Gbps

   D. 4 Gbps

6. What is the required bandwidth for 4:2:2 progressive digital video (1920 × 1080, 8 bits at 60 Hz)?

   A. 100 Mbps

   B. 1.99 Gbps

   C. 3.24 Gbps

   D. 1 Gbps

7. What is the required bandwidth for 4:1:1 progressive digital video signal (1920 × 1080, 8 bits at 30 Hz)?

   A. 746 Mbps

   B. 1.49 Gbps

   C. 3.30 Gbps

   D. 1.30 Gbps

8. _____ compression is common for networked AV applications, such as streaming media and IP telephony.

   A. Lossless

   B. Lossy

   C. Intraframe

   D. Apple QuickTime

Answers

1. **C.** $44,100 \times 24 \times 2 = 2.1$ Mbps

2. **B.** $96,000 \times X \times 10 = 25$ Mbps; X = 26 bit

3. **A.** $48,000 \times 24 \times 30 = 34.6$ Mbps $= 96,000 \times 24 \times X$; X = 15

4. **A.** $1920 \times 1080 \times 8 \times 30 \times 3 = 1.49$ Gbps

5. **B.** $1280 \times 1024 \times 8 \times 80 \times 3 = 2.5$ Gbps

6. **B.** *Luminance + Cr + Cb = Bit rate (bps)*; $(60 \times 8 \times 1920 \times 1080) + [60 \times 8 \times (.5 \times 1920) \times 1080] + [60 \times 8 \times (.5 \times 1920) \times 1080] = 1.99$ Gbps

7. **A.** *Luminance + Cr + Cb = Bit rate (bps)*; $(30 \times 8 \times 1920 \times 1080) + [30 \times 8 \times (.25 \times 1920) \times 1080] + [30 \times 8 \times (.25 \times 1920) \times 1080] = 746$ Mbps

8. **B.** Lossy compression is common for networked AV applications, such as streaming media and IP telephony.

CHAPTER 13

Digital Video Design

In this chapter, you will learn about

- Frame rates and resolution
- 720p, 1080i, 1080p, 4K, and other video formats
- Signal properties and uses of Serial Digital Interface, High-Definition Multimedia Interface, DisplayPort, Thunderbolt, Universal Serial Bus 3.0, and Mobile-High Definition Link
- The purpose and method of DisplayID/Extended Display Information Data communication and designing video systems that account for Extended Display Information Data issues
- Managing High-bandwidth Digital Content Protection keys in a digital video system

These days (and for the foreseeable future), video systems are digital. Because of this, AV designers need to be familiar with common digital video signal types and their applications. In many ways, these digital video signals are closer to "plug and play" than the analog signals of the past. Still, challenges exist.

When designing for interdevice communication in digital video systems, you need to consider the following:

- The properties and capabilities of your video source
- The properties and capabilities of your destination device
- How you'll get the signal from source to destination
- How you'll ensure electrical compatibility—cabling, adapter, or interface
- An Extended Display Information Data (EDID) strategy for simple and complex designs
- Digital rights management, including incorporating High-bandwidth Digital Content Protection (HDCP) keys or securing content licenses as needed

This chapter assumes knowledge of the needs analysis, video source identification and selection, and display design. These topics were covered in Part II, "Environment."

Domain Check

This chapter relates directly to the following tasks on the CTS-D Exam Content Outline:

- Domain A Task 8: Define AV needs
- Domain C Task 1: Create draft AV design
- Domain C Task 2: Confirm site conditions
- Domain D Task 2: Perform system verifications

These tasks comprise 24.8 percent of the exam (about 31 questions). This chapter may also relate to other tasks.

Digital Video Basics

Digital video devices, such as computers for driving a videowall, have processors that produce different resolutions. It is up to the AV designer to select a resolution output that looks good on the video system's displays. If an image is larger or smaller than a display's native resolution, for example, it won't look as good. If the image is a different height or width than the display, a task-specific scaler in the display may stretch or create borders around the image.

Video processors and displays have a two-way relationship. Most systems allow users to change the image resolution within the abilities of the video processor and display to optimize the image and meet the client's needs. Whenever possible, it's best to design around the native resolution of the display.

The *native resolution* is the number of rows of horizontal and vertical pixels that create the picture. For example, if a (albeit older) monitor has 1,024 pixels horizontally and 768 pixels vertically, it has a native resolution of 1024 × 768. The native resolution describes the actual resolution of the imaging device and not the resolution of the delivery signal. A higher-resolution display means more pixels, more detail, better image quality, and (most importantly) more digital information required to create the desired image.

Frame rate is the number of frames per second (fps) sent out from a video source. For instance, a 1080p high-definition video signal may have a frame rate of 60 fps. The more frames per second you display, the smoother the video will appear.

Frame rate is not the same thing as refresh rate. *Refresh rate* is the number of times per second a display will draw the image sent to it, typically measured in hertz. Displays use scaling circuitry to match the frame rate of a source. A display's refresh rate should be greater than or equal to the frame rate of the signals sent to it.

High-Definition and Ultra High-Definition Video

You know that 720p, 1080i, and 1080p are High-Definition TV (HDTV) video standards. You will likely encounter all three as you design or install various video systems, even as even higher-definition standards come to market.

- **720p** represents 720 horizontal lines, drawn onscreen using *progressive* scanning, which means the lines of each video frame are rendered in sequence. The aspect ratio for 720p video is 16:9, and its resolution is 1280 × 720. It can display up to 60 fps.

- **1080i** offers a spatial resolution of 1920 × 1080 and uses *interlaced* scanning at 30 fps. In this case, each frame of 1080i video has two sequential fields of 1920 horizontal and 1080 vertical pixels. The first field contains all the odd-numbered lines of pixels, and the second field contains all the even-numbered lines. Worldwide, most HD television channels broadcast in 1080i.

- **1080p**, sometimes referred to as Full HD, has a spatial resolution of 1920 × 1080 and uses progressive scanning up to 60 fps. It has double the resolution of both 720p and 1080i. Everything you design should be 1080p compatible to help simplify image setup and display quality. Many sources, such as Blu-ray Disc players and video game systems, output at 1080p.

Ultra high-definition video (Ultra HD or UHD) is an umbrella term used to describe video formats with a minimum resolution of 3840 × 2160 pixels in a 16:9 aspect ratio. Ultra HD formats are standard digital video formats defined and approved by the International Telecommunication Union (ITU). Two common Ultra HD formats are 4K UHDTV (2160p, or 3840 × 2160 pixels) and 8K UHDTV (4320p, or 7680 × 4320 pixels).

It's important to understand that clients who want "4K" resolution video may not understand that "4K UHDTV" and "4K" are not necessarily the same thing. The term *4K* is generally used to refer to video signals with a horizontal resolution on the order of 4,000 pixels. But to be accurate, 4K is a resolution of 4,096 pixels horizontally by 2,160 pixels vertically, or 8.8 million total pixels. This is a cinematic standard for 4K film projection (Digital Cinema Initiatives 4K or DCI 4K). What many clients may not realize is that DCI 4K carries a 17:9 aspect ratio, whereas most displays today—including those supporting 720p, 1080i, and 1080p—are built for a 16:9 aspect ratio. For years, there has been no need to accommodate various aspect ratios, but 4K has brought with it the challenge of managing two different standard resolutions.

In 2014, the ITU defined a UHD resolution that would fit a 4K-like image into the currently standard display ratio. Such an image has 7 percent fewer pixels in the horizontal aspect. On the left and right edges, 3.5 percent of the pixels are eliminated without compression or stretching so the image fits a 16:9 ratio.

Designing for 4K is a challenge, in part because creating what is truly a 4K video experience takes lots of bandwidth. Depending on how it's encoded, a 4K signal may generate between 3.5 and 20 Gbps worth of data. Today, much of what passes for 4K video requires *chroma subsampling,* which reduces color resolution by half or more (for more on sampling, review Chapter 12) to pass it through today's video infrastructure at reasonable bit rates. Either that or it must be transmitted at less than the visually smooth

60 fps that 4K systems can deliver. For example, HDMI version 1.4, which is still widely available today, can handle up to 10.2 Gbps. To transmit 4K video at 60 fps in around 9 Gbps, color information must be compressed to 4:2:0.

Depending on the application, 4:2:0 sampling may be unnoticeable to the client. However, visualization and simulation applications may require 4:4:4 sampling to maintain color fidelity. When it comes to designing a 4K system, the needs assessment is critical. Designers should ask the following:

- What is the goal for using 4K? What does the end user need to be able to see?
- What infrastructure is required to support this amount of data?
- Which type of display or projector does the end user want to use?
- Which type of receivers and processors are suitable for this system?

Consider, for example, a video device that accepts 4K. The specifications might state that it can support a UHD signal at 60 fps with 4:2:0 chroma subsampling and 30 fps with 4:4:4 chroma subsampling. Depending on the enduser's needs, those specs could factor heavily into the design.

In general, if someone tells you they want real 4K video, think to yourself "4096 × 2160 or 3840 × 2160 at 60 fps, with 4:4:4 chroma sampling and 10 bits per color or a 30-bit color depth." That will require about 22 Gbps of throughput. Then work backward to arrive at the flavor of 4K that fits their infrastructure (or the infrastructure they're willing to buy—fiber-optic cabling anyone?). It may have to run at 30 fps or use 4:2:0 subsampling or 8-bit color (8 bits per color, or a 24-bit color depth). At the end of the day, you may need to demonstrate various implementations of 4K to ensure the experience matches what they desire from a 4K application.

The Cliff Effect

When designing a video system, it's critical that AV professionals consider the length of the cables that will carry digital signals. If a digital signal is carried too far on a cable, the eye pattern will collapse, and the signal will become unreadable. This is called the *cliff effect*, as illustrated in Figure 13-1.

The edge of the cliff will vary based on the quality of the cable and the rate of the signal. Signals with a higher rate cannot run as far as signals with lower rates. For example,

Figure 13-1
The cliff effect describes how, at a certain distance, a digital video signal is unreadable.

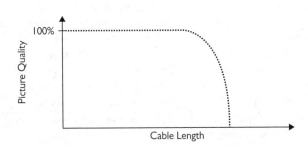

a 1080p signal might run only 66 ft (20 m), while a 720p or 1080i signal might run as far as 132 ft (40 m).

Before selecting a particular cable, check with the manufacturer to make sure it will run as far as you need it to run. Generally, if the signal needs to travel more than 30 ft, you may need to use a data-grade cable and signal extender. Examples of data-grade cables are Category 5e, 6, and 7 shielded and unshielded twisted-pair or fiber-optic cable. Allowable cable types and lengths are usually specified in a device's documentation.

When deciding on standard or high-speed cables, you need to consider all the data being sent. Some video, which might seemingly use less bandwidth than a 1080p signal, may need a high-speed cable if the video entails other data, such as for deep color or to support a high refresh rate. To be safe, you may want to specify higher-quality HDMI cables, for example, than you might immediately need for a digital video system. The cable you use to transport 1080i today may not work for 1080p, 4K, or another signal tomorrow.

You can test the stability of a signal by examining the bit error rate (BER), which is the total number of altered bits in a signal after traveling down a cable, caused by noise, interference, distortion, or synchronization errors. It's calculated by performing a BER test, which uses predetermined stress patterns consisting of a sequence of logical 1s and 0s generated by a test pattern generator.

Video Signal Types

Now that we've covered frame rates and resolutions, we'll go over signal types. When considering how digital video signals will be carried from source to sink (monitor, projector, or other type of display device), the connection format will be one of your first considerations. This includes both the signal format and the physical means of transporting that signal.

Common formats for digital display connections include the following:

- Serial Digital Interface (SDI)
- Digital Visual Interface (DVI)
- High-Definition Multimedia Interface (HDMI)
- DisplayPort
- Thunderbolt
- Universal Serial Bus (USB) 3.1 Type-C
- Mobile High-Definition Link

We'll delve further into these formats in the following sections.

NOTE DVI, HDMI, and DisplayPort are all licensed technologies and belong to different organizations. HDMI is most often used for home entertainment equipment, while DisplayPort is commonly used for computer displays. DVI was frequently used in computers but has been largely replaced by HDMI. You could potentially see any of the three on just about any piece of digital display equipment.

Serial Digital Interface

SDI is a set of video standards defined by the Society of Motion Picture and Television Engineers (SMPTE). It is an uncompressed, unencrypted, digital video signal characterized by serial, one-way communication over coaxial cable. Typical of digital signal carriers these days, it continues to go through several versions designed to accommodate higher bandwidth requirements.

SDI is commonly used for post-production, live-event, house-of-worship, and broadcast facilities. You may also find this connection used in videoconferencing applications. SDI processors typically allow for audio-channel swapping and signal control over a coaxial cable and BNC connector. Because most versions of SDI offer low latency (delay), the technology is considered excellent where lip sync is an issue.

Here are some common versions of SDI you may want to consider for your digital video design:

- SD-SDI (480i, 576i), which carries standard-definition video and audio at up to 360 Mbps using a single BNC connector
- HD-SDI (720p, 1080i), which carries high-definition video and audio at up to 1.5 Gbps using two BNC connectors
- Dual Link HD-SDI (1080p), which allows bit rates of nearly 3 Gbps over two wires
- 3G-SDI (1080p), which carries 1080p and 16 channels of embedded audio at nearly 3 Gbps on a single wire
- 6G-SDI (4K/30 fps), for UHD and 4K video at 6 Gbps
- 12G-SDI (4K/60 fps), for UHD and 4K, high-frame-rate video at 12 Gbps

The dates of SDI versions are important to consider because some are very new. For example, 3G-SDI was released in 2006; 6G-SDI and 12G-SDI came out in 2014 to support emerging 4K video applications. There is also a new 24G-SDI for handling future 8K video at up to 24 Gbps. When building a design around SDI technology, you'll have to ask yourself whether the devices you're selecting for a given project are capable of supporting newer SDI versions. And keep in mind, SDI does not have built-in support for digital rights management technology, which you will learn about later in this chapter. That could be a drawback for clients who want to employ copyrighted program material.

 NOTE   HD-SDI is better suited for connection directly to a recording device because it has a locking connector and will transport time code. HDMI has neither of these features and is better suited for connection to display devices.

Transition-Minimized Differential Signaling

Before delving further into digital video formats, let's pause to explore what might be considered a behind-the-scenes technology that supports some popular formats. Transition-minimized differential signaling (TMDS) is a technology for transmitting high-speed,

Figure 13-2
HDMI
transmission
utilizing TMDS

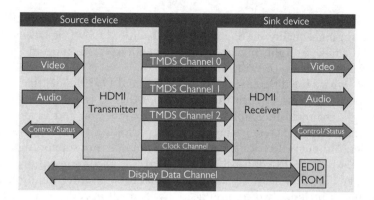

serial video data at high, native true-color resolutions. It was originally developed in 1998 by the Digital Display Working Group (DDWG) as a standardized digital video interface between a PC and a monitor. It employs differential signaling to help reduce electromagnetic interference for faster, lossless video transmission. Unlike SDI, TMDS-based formats use twisted pair, rather than coaxial cables, to help with noise reduction during transmission. The signal is balanced because of common-mode noise reduction. The opposing voltages contained in the signal create the "eye pattern" visible with an oscilloscope.

TMDS is used in both Digital Visual Interface and High-Definition Multimedia Interface technologies and helps eliminate complex analog-to-digital and digital-to-analog conversions. With all the bandwidth required for digital video transmission, the fewer the transitions, the better the signal quality and the faster it will reach its destination.

As noted earlier, Digital Visual Interface (DVI) has largely been replaced by HDMI, DisplayPort, and other formats. HDMI cables and connectors carry four differential pairs that make up the TMDS data and clock channels. These channels are used to carry video, audio, and auxiliary data. Figure 13-2 depicts the output of an HDMI source communicating with the input of an HDMI sink. The TMDS channels in the middle (0, 1, 2) are the same RGB channels you're used to seeing. The clock channel just below TMDS channels is the sync. The fifth connection on the bottom of the diagram carries Display Data Channel (DDC) information, which allows the source and display to share resolutions and other identifying information.

DVI and HDMI

Now let's drill down into two TMDS-based video formats. As DVI is largely inapplicable to professional AV applications, we'll focus mainly on HDMI. But quickly, DVI is a connection method from a source (typically a computer) to a display device. Historically, it came in analog (DVI-A), digital (DVI-D), and integrated analog/digital (DVI-I) using the same connector. Generally speaking, cable lengths for DVI connections are limited. You can move 1920 × 1200 video only about 5 meters and 1280 × 1024 video up to 15 meters.

HDMI is a point-to-point connection between video devices and has become a standard for high-quality, all-digital video and audio. HDMI signals include audio, control, and digital asset rights management information. It is a "plug-and-play" standard that is fully compatible with DVI.

So, what's the difference between HDMI and DVI besides that you're far more likely to specify the former than the latter? HDMI is DVI, with the addition of audio (up to eight channels uncompressed), a smaller connector, and support for the YUV color space. HDMI also contains functions for controlling multiple devices using a single controller. Although electrically compatible, DVI does not support digital audio or control.

HDMI meets EIA/CEA-861-B standards for uncompressed, high-speed digital interfaces and is a dominant digital video format for consumer and professional applications because it includes two communications channels in addition to TMDS. As mentioned earlier, DDC is used for configuration and status exchange between a single source and a single sink. It is the electrical channel that EDID and HDCP use for communication between a video card and a display. The DDC channel is used by an HDMI source to determine the capabilities and characteristics of the sink by reading the EDID data structure and delivering only the audio and video formats that are supported.

In addition, HDMI sinks are expected to detect what are known as InfoFrames to process audio and video data appropriately. InfoFrames are structured packets of data that carry information regarding aspects of audio and video transmission, as defined by the EIA/CEA-861B standard. Using this structure, a frame-by-frame summary is sent to the display, permitting selection of appropriate display modes automatically. InfoFrames typically include auxiliary video information, generic vendor-specific source product description, MPEG, and audio information.

An optional HDMI channel carries Consumer Electronics Control (CEC) data, which provides high-level control functions between all the various AV products in a user's environment. CEC is a single-wire, bi-directional serial bus that uses AV link protocols to perform remote-control functions for system-level automation—when all devices in an AV system support it.

Figure 13-3 offers a look inside an HDMI cable.

More About HDMI

As you see in Figure 13-4, there are 19 pins in an HMDI connector. All 19 have been in use since HDMI version 1.4. Here is a breakdown:

- Pins 1 through 9 carry the three TMDS data channels (0, 1, and 2), each with a separate shield. These three serial data channels carry component video.

- Pins 10 through 12 carry the clock and its shield. This serial data channel is typically the video pixel rate and is used by the HDMI receiver as a frequency or timing reference for data recovery on the three data channels, keeping them synchronized. Each serial data channel is a balanced pair.

- Pin 13 is for CEC information, which is sometimes disabled and used by some AV manufacturers for camera control.

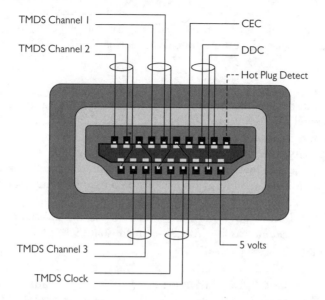

Figure 13-3
The HDMI
interface

- Pin 14 has carried the HDMI Ethernet channel (HEC) and Audio Return Channel (ARC) since version HDMI 1.4. HEC enables bi-directional IP-based applications over HDMI and accommodates for future IP networking solutions by allowing multiple devices to share an Internet connection. ARC was introduced to replace the extra cables needed to share audio between devices and allows a display to send audio data "upstream" to a receiver or surround-sound controller, eliminating the need for any separate audio connection.

- Pins 15 and 16 are for DDC and communicate EDID and newer DisplayID information, which we will discuss in the "Introduction to EDID" section. The DDC channel also transmits HDCP data for digital rights management.

- Pin 17 is the shield connection for the CEC and DDC channels.

- Pin 18 carries 5 volts of power and enables the display to provide EDID data when the display circuitry is not powered.

- Pin 19 is for "hot-plug detect," which monitors whether a display device has been turned on or off and is plugged in or unplugged. It allows the video system to identify the presence of a display automatically.

Figure 13-4
Since HDMI 1.4,
all 19 pins in the
HDMI interface
have had a
function.

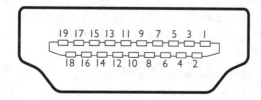

NOTE When ARC and HEC combine in one port, they are often referred to as HDMI Ethernet Audio Control (HEAC).

The most current version of HDMI—HDMI 2.0—was released in 2013. It increased per-channel throughput to 6 Gbps and raised the total bandwidth from 10.2 Gbps to 18 Gbps, just enough for 4K at 60 fps and 8-bit color. The increase in bandwidth is made possible by a new, more efficient signaling method. The interface uses the previous signaling method for traffic below 10.2 Gbps and then kicks in the new signaling above that threshold, which means it's backward compatible with HDMI 1.4 devices.

HDMI 2.0 supports 4:2:0 sampling for up to 16-bit color, 4:2:2 with 12-bit color and 4:4:4 with 8-bit color. With 4:2:0 sampling, HDMI 2.0 can send a 4K/60 8-bit signal at the same data rate as a 4K/30 8-bit signal that uses 4:4:4 sampling. HDMI 1.4a does not support 4:2:0 sampling.

NOTE HDMI 2.0a, released in 2015, adds a feature called high dynamic range (HDR) imaging, which can generate a greater range of luminance levels. Combined with 4K, HDR can deliver better contrast, light, and color in video applications, though HDR doesn't necessarily require 4K.

DisplayPort

DisplayPort is an increasingly common digital interface, developed by Video Electronics Standards Association (VESA) to replace older standards such as Digital Video Interface and Video Graphics Array and was last updated in 2014. By packetizing data in small-form "micro" packets, DisplayPort enables internal and external display connections to transmit clock signals within the data stream. This supports higher resolutions using fewer pins.

DisplayPort uses low-voltage differential signaling (LVDS), which means it is not compatible with DVI and HDMI. It also carries a 3.3 V electrical signal, rather than the 5 V signal used by HDMI and DVI. That said, DisplayPort supports a dual-mode design that can send single-link HDMI and DVI signals through an adapter, which also converts the voltage from 3.3 to 5 V.

DisplayPort 1.2 supports up to 21.6 Gbps (slightly more than HDMI 2.0 at 18 Gbps). This makes it suitable for 4K/60, 10-bit-per-color video with 4:4:4 sampling over a single cable. The newer DisplayPort 1.3 supports up to 32.4 Gbps (25.92 Gbps of uncompressed video, after accounting for overhead), which could even support 5K/60 video (5120 × 2880).

DisplayPort 1.3 also supports the same HDCP 2.2 copy protection as the latest HDMI standard. Also noteworthy is that DisplayPort 1.3 is engineered to share a port with and transmit data over USB Type-C connections.

USB 3.1 and USB Type-C

The USB 3.1 specification (also called SuperSpeed+ USB) was released and approved in 2014. Like many of the newer protocols, the personal computer and mobile device markets are the primary driving force behind adoption.

	Version	Speed	Data Rate
Table 13-1 Versions of USB	USB 1.1	Low speed/full speed	1.5 Mbps/12 Mbps
	USB 2.0	High speed	480 Mbps
	USB 3.0	SuperSpeed	5 Gbps
	USB 3.1	SuperSpeed+	10 Gbps

USB 3.1 represents a *dual-bus architecture* that is backward compatible with USB 2.0. Cables have eight primary conductors consisting of three twisted signal pairs for USB data paths and power. There are also two twisted signal pairs for the Enhanced Super-Speed data path (transmit path and receive path) and two for USB 2.0 backward compatibility.

The specification doubles the speed of USB 3.0 to 10 Gbps, though you may not achieve the full-speed capability without hardware specifically built for USB 3.1.

Table 13-1 shows four generations of USB for comparison.

USB 3.1 can utilize the new USB Type-C (USB-C) connector, which is smaller and thinner than previous generations of connectors. Manufacturers chose the same shape on both sides of the cable to support market desire for cross-platform connectors. It also has no up/down orientation, so it can be plugged in right side up and upside down interchangeably. Most significantly, the USB-C connector supports DisplayPort, HDMI, power, all USB generations, and VGA, making it a potentially significant interface for all types of AV design. Keep an eye on this product as your clients begin using devices that incorporate its capabilities.

Thunderbolt

Thunderbolt is a technology developed by Intel that transfers audio, video, power, and data over one cable—in two directions. It also permits a user to daisy-chain multiple displays and external hard drives in one link without relying on hubs. Thunderbolt 3 now also brings Thunderbolt technology to USB-C at speeds up to 40 Gbps in both directions.

Manufacturers claim Thunderbolt provides four times the data and twice the video bandwidth of any other cable, while also supplying power. This may be particularly important to consider for clients who want to use 4K video.

There are three Thunderbolt cable options (active cables include a chip to boost performance; passive cables do not).

- Passive 20 Gbps copper cables, which support 20 Gbps Thunderbolt, USB 3.1, and DisplayPort 1.2 at any length up to 2 meters

- Active 40 Gbps copper cables, which support 40 Gbps Thunderbolt and USB 3.1 at any length up to 2 meters

- Active 40 Gbps optical cables, which are under development but targeting lengths up to 60 meters

Figure 13-5
A Thunderbolt
port

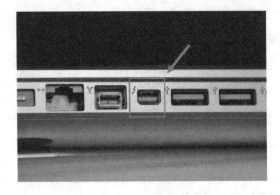

According to Intel, Thunderbolt 3 supports four lanes of PCI Express Gen 3 serial data, eight lanes of DisplayPort 1.2, and two 4K displays (4096 × 2160/60 at 10 bits per color). It is compatible with USB devices and cables, DVI, HDMI, and VGA displays via adapters, plus previous generations of Thunderbolt.

 TIP   Thunderbolt-to-Ethernet connections are possible via an adapter.

As you can see in Figure 13-5, Thunderbolt occupies the same port as Mini Display-Port, a smaller version of the DisplayPort interface often found on laptops and, recently, tablet devices. Mini DisplayPort to HDMI adapters will work with Thunderbolt-capable computers, but clients will not be able to utilize all that Thunderbolt offers without proper Thunderbolt cabling.

Mobile High-Definition Link

Mobile High-Definition Link (MHL) is a standard developed by a group of manufacturers making up the MHL Consortium. Their goal was to allow consumers to connect mobile devices and PCs to displays, monitors, and even projectors. Like other groups that have developed multifunctional, single-cable interfaces, the makers of MHL say their standard carries audio, video, data, and power charging.

The latest version, superMHL, came out in 2015 and is more like a next-generation display interface than a smartphone-connectivity solution. For one thing, superMHL features a 32-pin, full-size, symmetrical connector. It is also capable of a maximum data rate of 36 Gbps, giving it enough throughput for 7680 × 4320/120 video at 4:2:0 color sampling. See Table 13-2 for a comparison.

Both MHL 3 and superMHL support the latest HDCP 2.2 version of digital rights management and can send video to multiple displays using one cable. Another note-worthy fact about superMHL is that it uses Display Stream Compression (DSC),

Features	superMHL	MHL 3	MHL 2	MHL 1
Maximum resolution	8K/120, 4:2:0 sampling, and 36-bit color (six lanes); 4K/60 (one lane)	4K/30	1080p/60	1080p/60
Up to eight-channel audio	Yes	Yes	Yes	Yes
Blu-ray Disc audio	Yes	Yes	N/A	N/A
MHL control	Yes	Yes	Yes	Yes
Power	40W	10W	7.5W	2.5W
Content protection	HDCP 2.2	HDCP 2.2	HDCP 1.4	HDCP 1.4
Multidisplay support	Up to 32 displays	Up to 4 displays	N/A	N/A
Possible connectors	superMHL, USB Type-C, Micro-USB, HDMI, proprietary	Connector agnostic	Connector agnostic	Connector agnostic

Table 13-2 Versions of Mobile High-Definition Link

a standard developed by VESA that employs "visually lossless image compression" to improve throughout and save power. While clients may not have an immediate need for 8K resolution, superMHL's support for HDR, high frame rates, and a wide color gamut defined by ITU Recommendation BT.2020 (also supported by HDMI 2.0 and other technologies) may make it an attractive signal format for some AV designs.

Introduction to EDID

As an AV professional, the AV systems you're designing are probably expensive, sleek, and modern. But what do you do when a user wants to connect an outdated digital device to your beautiful system? Managing Extended Display Identification Data will help.

 Watch a video about EDID at www.infocomm.org/EDIDVideo. Appendix C provides links to all the helpful videos.

EDID is extremely important in today's AV world. It was originally developed for use with computer-video devices but has since made its way into the commercial AV industry.

Displays and sources need to negotiate their highest common resolutions so they can display the best image quality. EDID is a way for sources and sinks (video destinations) to communicate this information among each other, eliminating the need for people to configure a system manually. In short, EDID is how a sink describes its capabilities to a source, and vice versa.

EDID is a standard data structure defined by the Video Electronics Standard Association. In a professional AV system, an EDID handshake can be between a source and the next device in line, whether it's a display, videowall, switcher, distribution amplifier, matrix, or scaler. Without a successful handshake between source and display devices, the entire video solution could be unreliable. Therefore, creating an EDID strategy can be vital to your success as an AV designer.

During the handshake process, EDID-compliant devices swap 128-byte packets of EDID information from a table. Each of these data packets carries the following information:

- Product information, including the display manufacturer and product, serial number, and production date.
- EDID version number used for the data structure.
- Display parameters, such as whether a display accepts analog or digital inputs, its maximum horizontal and vertical size, power management capabilities, and more.
- Color characteristics, including the RGB color space conversion technique to be used.
- Timing information for audio and video sync, resolution, and more.
- Extensions, for describing extra capabilities. The most prevalent extension—CEA-861—defines the advanced capabilities of consumer devices incorporating HDMI.

Let's say the user connects a laptop to a display. The graphics card will immediately start looking for an EDID table. The EDID table contains all the possible resolutions, frame rates, and so on, that a device can support. If a device uses DVI EDID, it consists of 128 bytes. If it extends the EDID for HDMI connections, it may transmit as many as 256 bytes. Figure 13-6 shows EDID information for a specific monitor.

In a nutshell, the EDID handshake process goes like this (see Figure 13-7):

1. On startup, an EDID-enabled device will use hot-plug detection (HPD) to see whether another device is on. A source device will send a 5V signal to sink devices. This signal will discover if the sink is powered up.
2. The sink sends back a signal, alerting the source that it received the original signal.
3. The source sends a command to the sink for its EDID information.
4. The EDID information is transmitted from sink to source over the display data channel (DDC).
5. The source responds to the sink with its own EDID.
6. The source sends EDID in the sink's preferred resolution, refresh rate, and color space. The source's selection can be manually overridden.

7. If the sink's EDID contains extension blocks, the source will then request the blocks from the sink. Extension blocks can be compatible timings relevant to digital television, as well as supported audio formats, speaker allocation, and, if present, lip-sync delay.

```
--------------------------
EDID revision............ 1.3
Input signal type........ Analog 0.700,0.000 (0.7V p-p)
Sync input support....... Separate
Display type............. RGB color
Screen size.............. 470 x 300 mm (22.0 in)
Power management......... Active off/sleep
Extension blocs.......... None
--------------------------
DDC/CI................... Supported
MCCS revison............. 2.1
Display technology....... TFT
Controller............... Mstar 0x56
Firmware revision........ 4.1
Firmware flags........... 0x006345CC
Active power on time..... Not supported
Power consumption........ Not supported
Current frequency........ 65.40kHz, 60.10Hz

Color characteristics
  Default color space...... sRGB
  Display gamma............ 2.20
  Red chromaticity......... Rx 0.648 - Ry 0.335
  Green chromaticity....... Gx 0.282 - Gy 0.604
  Blue chromaticity........ Bx 0.150 - By 0.072
  White point (default).... Wx 0.313 - Wy 0.328
  Additional descriptors... None

Timing characteristics
  Horizontal scan range.... 30-83kHz
  Vertical scan range...... 56-75Hz
  Video bandwidth.......... 160MHz
  CVT standard............. Not supported
  GTF standard............. Not supported
  Additional descriptors... None
  Preferred timing......... Yes
  Native/preferred timing.. 1680x1050p at 60Hz (16:10)
    Modeline............... "1680x1050" 146.250 1680 1784 1960 2240 1050 1053 1059 1089 -hsync +vsync

Standard timings supported
    720 x  400p at  70Hz - IBM VGA
    640 x  480p at  60Hz - IBM VGA
    640 x  480p at  75Hz - VESA
    800 x  600p at  60Hz - VESA
    800 x  600p at  75Hz - VESA
   1024 x  768p at  60Hz - VESA
   1024 x  768p at  75Hz - VESA
   1280 x 1024p at  75Hz - VESA
   1152 x  864p at  75Hz - VESA STD
   1280 x 1024p at  60Hz - VESA STD

Report information
  Date generated.......... 9/10/2015
```

Figure 13-6 A monitor's EDID information

Figure 13-7
How an EDID handshake goes, if electronics could talk

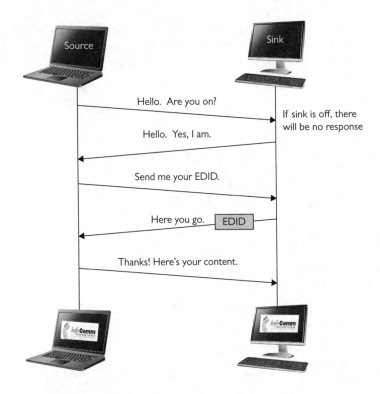

Hello. Are you on?

If sink is off, there will be no response

Hello. Yes, I am.

Send me your EDID.

Here you go. EDID

Thanks! Here's your content.

DisplayID: Next-Gen EDID

DisplayID is another VESA standard. It was developed as the next evolution of EDID and designed to be "future-proof." By structuring data in a flexible, modular way, DisplayID allows devices to identify new display resolutions, refresh rates, audio standards, and other formats as they become available. This is in contrast to the fixed header and data structures used by EDID.

DisplayID can, for example, support a single image displayed across tiled screens using multiple video processors, such as in a videowall. Each video processor handles one piece of the overall display.

Creating an EDID Strategy

Let's say you're installing a new video system for a university. Your customer has asked for a system and described it kind of like this:

> "Our professors each have their own laptops, and they like to use Power-Point slides or online videos in their lectures. We often have three or four different professors in each room per day. Because the professors do not

have a lot of preparation time before class, we need a system where they can plug in their laptops and the information shows up on the screen immediately. We just want it to work without a hassle."

Having an EDID strategy means that the projector will always be able to read the information from the professor's laptops. This makes the system easy to use, which will make your customer happy. If the same signal is sent to multiple displays, EDID will allow you to control the source signal so you get a consistent, controlled signal. The goal of an EDID strategy is to allow a display to present the signal at its native resolution without scaling. It also allows an installer to set up and configure a system based on the designer's goals.

If the system has displays of different resolutions or aspect ratios, without a proper EDID strategy, the resolution and aspect of the output will be unreliable and may vary when switching between sources.

All display devices in a video system need to have the same aspect ratio. This will prevent many EDID problems. Computers and other devices tend to have either a 16:9 or 16:10 aspect ratio, so your projectors and other display devices should reflect this. Installed display devices don't change as rapidly as personal computers and tablets do, so the unfortunate reality is that your display devices may become outdated quickly. If you have an EDID strategy, though, then the system should still work for a long time.

One way to future-proof a system is to use the most common resolution between devices as a benchmark. That way you can ensure all displays will look the same.

Even if your source and sink have an EDID strategy, sometimes non-EDID equipment such as switchers, expanders, and cables interrupt the EDID path and cause problems. Here are some strategies to make sure the system you're installing is EDID compliant.

An EDID emulator acts as a sink. It can be set to a specific aspect ratio and native resolution so that the source outputs a consistent aspect ratio and resolution. So, for example, a laptop will read the EDID information in the emulator instead of the EDID information from one of the multiple displays attached to the switcher. The laptop will output the fixed resolution set in the emulator.

You can use an EDID emulator to make sure your system is EDID compliant. Sometimes, switchers will already have these built into them. Place the emulator as close to the source as possible or in the switcher. This will give you the most accurate information about your system.

EDID Truth Tables

Whether planning or executing a design, you will benefit from containing your EDID information in one place. Creating a "truth table" will help you organize all of your EDID information. Currently there is no standard for documenting EDID information, so here is one example of an EDID truth table to help you organize and interpret this information on the job.

An EDID truth table should contain the following information for the inputs on a switcher:

- Input number on the switcher
- Type of connected source device

- Preferred resolution
- Color space support, such as RGB or component
- Audio format
- Additional notes about the source or its settings

It also should contain the following information for the outputs on a switcher:

- Output number on the switcher
- Type of connected sink device
- Device's native or support resolution
- Color space support, such as RGB or component
- Audio format
- Any additional notes about the sink device or its settings

Figure 13-8 shows how an EDID truth table might look. Note how the inputs and outputs are grouped together on this sample table.

EDID/DisplayID Truth Table

Input	Device	Resolution/s	ColorSpace	Audio	Notes	Output	Device	Resolution/s	ColorSpace	Audio	Notes
1	Laptop	720P	RGB	Stereo		1	LCD Mon 1	1080P	RGB/CCS	NA	
2	Laptop	1050P	RGB	Stereo		2	LCD Mon 2	1080P	RGB/CCS	NA	
3	Desktop	1080P	RGB	Stereo		3	LCD Mon 3	1080P	RGB/CCS	NA	
4	CATV	1080P	RGB/CCS	Stereo		4	LCD Mon 4	1080P	RGB/CCS	NA	
5	VHS Deck	NTSC-Scaler	RGB	Stereo		5	LCD Mon 5	1080P	RGB/CCS	NA	
6	BluRay	1080P	RGB/CCS	Stereo		6	LCD Mon 6	1080P	RGB/CCS	NA	
7	DocCam	1080P	RGB	NA		7	Proj 1	1920x1200	RGB/CCS	NA	
8	WallPlate 1	1080P-Scaler	RGB	Stereo		8	Proj 2	1920x1200	RGB/CCS	NA	
9	WallPlate 2	1080P-Scaler	RGB	Stereo							
10	Aux	1080P-Scaler	RGB	Stereo							

Input	Device	Resolution/s	ColorSpace	Audio	Notes	Output	Device	Resolution/s	ColorSpace	Audio	Notes
1	Laptop	720P	RGB	Stereo		1	Proj	1680 x 1050	RGB	Stereo	
2	Laptop	1680 x 1050	RGB	Stereo							
3	Desktop	1680 x 1050	RGB	Stereo							
4	WallPlate	1680 x 1050	RGB	Stereo							
5	BluRay	1080P	RGB/CCS	Stereo							
6	DocCam	1680 x 1050	RGB	NA							

Figure 13-8   An EDID truth table

Resolving EDID Issues

There a few ways to help determine whether an EDID connection is being interrupted or halted and repair the relationship. It doesn't hurt to have an EDID field toolkit for client visits if a video system is acting up and EDID might be the culprit. Such a toolkit for troubleshooting and resolving EDID issues might include software (many are free) for determining the EDID contents of devices; a video test generator to output test patterns and show native resolutions; EDID managers or emulators; HDMI or DVI line testers for quick checks of TMDS, DDC, hot-plug detection, and power in the cable; and a network-cable tester for cases of transporting signals over twisted pair.

The following are some of the common visible symptoms that there may be an EDID issue with a video system:

- There's no image on the screen (which, clearly, could indicate other issues).
- The image does not fill the screen.
- The image is fuzzy.
- The image is stretched.
- In multidisplay systems, the image quality is great on some displays but not all.

Sometimes you can look over the installation to figure out what the problem is. It could be that the source is connected to the sink over a long cable run, particularly for HDMI or DVI connections. Or maybe the source is connected to the sink over a long distance using a twisted-pair extender. Or there may be unreliable source switching. Whatever the case, if the client is blaming your design for what may be an EDID problem, try the following:

- Test the cable integrity using a signal generator.
- Confirm that the connectors (or cables) are what you specified, not low-quality, low-cost alternatives.
- Shorten cable runs to maintain integrity over a distance with solid connections and keep cable lengths within manufacturer guidelines.
- Check for possible electromagnetic interference (EMI)/radio frequency interference (RFI) and ground loops in the system; consider using shielded twisted pair if necessary.
- Use an EDID management software tool to ensure you're using the preferred resolution.
- Avoid internal switchers; use a switcher or switcher/scaler with built-in EDID.
- Determine the native resolutions of all displays in the system and select the highest common resolution among them.

EDID and Displays

Multiple displays with many resolutions will make EDID complicated. If you are responsible for designing and specifying a new video system, specify the same resolution and aspect ratio for every display in the system. If you do this, you will not have to make any compromises on preferred resolutions for the displays since they will all look the same. This will simplify your system and the amount of work you need to do.

When designing an AV system that includes only fixed sources, such as a desktop PC installed within a rack, a cable box, or a Blu-ray Disc player, you have control when it comes to how the sources will look on the displays. Choose a resolution that will be good for all of those displays, such as 1080p. If you need to make a compromise, remember to find the most common resolution between them and design around it.

If your AV system will incorporate personal devices such as a bring your own device (BYOD) system, you need to consider how the user will want their content to be displayed. Some users may prefer the display to be treated as an extended monitor, but usually users will want the display to duplicate their device's screen. In this case, they will want the native resolution of their laptop or device to appear on the display. You will therefore need to plan for your EDID to cover as many resolutions as the display can handle.

Digital Rights Management

Your customers may want to share or distribute content that they did not create, such as clips from a media library, a Blu-ray Disc video, or music from a satellite service. Unlicensed distribution of these materials can violate copyright laws.

Both you and your customers must be aware of potential licensing issues related to the content they want to use. You may need to negotiate a bulk license with a content service provider such as a cable or satellite television provider or a satellite music service. If you fail to obtain the proper licenses to stream content, you are not just risking the legal repercussions of copyright infringement. You are risking the system's ability to function at all.

Publishers and copyright owners use digital rights management (DRM) technologies to control access to and usage of digital data or hardware. DRM protocols within devices determine whether content can be allowed to enter a piece of equipment. Copy protection such as the Content Scrambling System (CSS) used in DVD players is a subset of DRM.

High-Bandwidth Digital Content Protection

When you turn on a Blu-ray Disc player, for example, it takes a moment for the device to start. This is because the AV system is verifying that everything in the system is HDCP compliant.

High-Bandwidth Digital Content Protection (HDCP) is a form of encryption developed by Intel to control digital audio and video content. If the content source requires HDCP, then all devices that want to receive that content must support HDCP.

HDCP is merely a way of authorizing playback. It can authorize the transmission of encrypted or nonencrypted content. Note that while HDCP is a way to protect content from being copied, it is not a DRM technology. Think of the process as a series of handshakes. The Blu-ray Disc player communicates to the disc asking for license information. The disc then responds that it is HDCP compliant. The two shake hands. Then the Blu-ray Disc player runs the same handshake with the display.

The past few years have seen several revisions to HDCP in part to meet demand for more session keys worldwide. Versions 1.0 to 1.4 supported DVI, HDMI, and DisplayPort. Version 2.0 added support for Unified Display Interface, TCP/IP, USB, and wireless transmission of compressed and uncompressed HD content. It is interoperable with earlier versions.

The current version of HDCP, version 2.2, added support for Intel's Wireless Display technology, Miracast, HDBaseT, MHL, and more. It entails a more advanced encryption handshake than prior versions. But there are a few other key considerations when dealing with HDCP 2.2 in an AV design.

For starters, HDCP 2.2 is *not* backward compatible. It is implemented at a hardware level, so there are no firmware solutions for upgrading devices. When it comes to 4K, native 4K sources will include HDCP 2.2; therefore, all devices between the source and sink must also be HDCP 2.2–compliant, including receivers, switches, extenders, and so on.

How HDCP Works

HDCP's authentication process determines whether both devices have been licensed to send, receive, or pass HDCP content. No content will be shared until this entire process is completed. If there is a failure at any point in the process, the whole process has to start over. The process goes like this:

1. Both source and sink calculate a shared, secret session key used for encrypting and decrypting data.

2. The source sends its key to the sink, along with a pseudorandom value generated by its cipher (or encryption algorithm).

3. The sink sends its key to the source, along with a single bit that indicates whether it's a repeater device.

4. They both generate a shared secret value that's in each device.

5. The source and sink feed the shared secret value and the pseudorandom number into their internal HDCP code cipher engine.

6. The HDCP cipher generates a secret, shared session key along with another value, which the sink sends to the source to indicate it has successfully completed its part of the authentication process.

7. The source compares the value with its own calculated value, and if the two are identical, authentication is successful.

8. The source can then start sending a stream of content, encrypted using the session key, which only the receiver can decipher.

9. If the sink is a repeater, it transmits a list of all keys connected "downstream" from it and how many levels of devices are connected to the source. This enables the source to determine whether the maximum number of allowed hops in the system has been exceeded and if the devices themselves are legitimate.

10. From then on, the sink reinitiates a handshake with source every 128 video frames or once every two seconds to verify devices are synchronized and content is accurately decrypted.

Now, even though content is streaming, the authentication process is not over. The HDCP devices must re-authenticate periodically as the content is transferred. If, during re-authentication, it is discovered that the system was hacked, the source will stop sending content.

 Watch a video about HDCP at www.infocomm.org/HDCPVideo. Appendix C provides links to all the helpful videos in this guide.

Switchers and Repeaters

All the HDCP processes explained so far have assumed that your AV system has a one-to-one relationship, with a single source for a single sink. In these systems, the keys and how they're exchanged are handled continuously between the two devices.

However, as soon as you add multiple sources and displays—and maybe a switcher to manage them—HDCP key management becomes more complicated. Some switchers maintain ongoing key exchange and encryption sessions, so the communication will not need to be restarted. These switchers can act as a source or sink to pass the protected and encrypted HDCP data to its destination. You can determine whether a switcher can manage HDCP keys by reading its specifications.

 TIP HDCP 2.2 is incompatible with legacy components, such as switchers. Under this new content protection scheme, clients wanting to utilize 4K video will need HDCP 2.2–compliant devices.

Incorporating HDCP repeaters into the AV system's design can help you manage HDCP authentication with multiple devices. When using a repeater, the HDCP authentication process occurs after the locality check and device authentication have taken place between all the devices in the system. The session key exchange has not begun yet.

1. The repeater compiles a list of IDs from all the downstream devices.

2. The repeater sends the list of IDs and number of devices to the source and sets a 200 ms timer.

3. The source reads the list and compares it to a list of revoked licenses in the media. Each new HDCP device or media has an updated list of revoked license numbers provided by Digital Content Protection LLC. If any of the downstream devices are on the revoked list, the authentication process fails.

4. The source then counts how many devices are downstream. If the number of devices is less than the maximum, the authentication process moves forward.

 NOTE The way devices such as repeaters are designed and manufactured today, each input is considered a new sink, and each output is a new source. You must have enough session keys for every device in the AV system or risk.

HDCP Troubleshooting

Once your system has been designed and installed, you need a method for verifying that the HDCP keys are being managed correctly. You know that your keys are being managed correctly if the image appears on the sink and is stable over a period of time. If the HDCP keys are not managed correctly, an image constraint token (ICT) or a digital-only token (DOT) will be displayed on your sink.

An ICT is a digital flag built into some digital video sources. It prevents unauthorized copies of content from appearing on a sink device. This encryption scheme ensures that high-definition video can be viewed only on HDCP-enabled sinks. A DOT is a digital flag that is embedded into digital sources, such as Blu-ray Discs. Its purpose is to limit the availability or quality of HD content on the component output of a media player.

There are devices on the market to help you troubleshoot HDCP problems. Some have feature sets that may include the following:

- Hot-plug/5V presence detection
- DisplayID/EDID verification
- HDCP status indication
- Indication of the number of keys accepted by the source (in other words, the maximum number of devices supported)
- Cable verification

Managing HDCP can be a challenge, but remember that if your client wants to bypass digital rights management, they shouldn't. Most countries have adopted some form of copyright law that criminalizes attempts to circumvent control access to copyrighted works. Be sure to make your clients aware of these laws when discussing their needs on a project.

PART IV

Chapter Review

Digital video is often oversimplified—either the video appears at its destination or it doesn't. Having completed this chapter, you know some of the intervening issues that come with designing digital video systems and how to manage them.

Here are some of the questions you'll work through with clients when determining their digital video needs: "What transport solutions can I employ based on the needs and budget of the client? Will I face distance limitations? Bandwidth limitations? If the client wants 4K, what implementation of 4K will satisfy their needs? Are the system's devices HDCP 2.2 compliant? Do they need to be? What should our EDID strategy be in the case of multiple displays and display formats and resolutions?" With this information and more, your digital video design will deliver what the client expects—reliably.

Review Questions

The following questions are based on the content covered in this chapter and are intended to help reinforce the knowledge you have assimilated. These questions are not extracted from the CTS-D exam nor are they necessarily CTS-D practice exam questions. For an official CTS-D practice exam, see the accompanying CD.

1. Ultra high-definition video (UHD) describes video formats with a minimum pixel resolution of:
   A. 1920 × 1080
   B. 3840 × 2160
   C. 4096 × 2160
   D. 7680 × 4160

2. To transmit 4K video at 60 fps using HDMI 1.4, color information should be sampled at a rate of:
   A. 4:4:4
   B. 4:2:2
   C. 4:2:0
   D. 4:0:0

3. A video system design to transmit 4K at 60 fps, with 4:4:4 chroma sampling and 10 bits per color, requires about _____ of throughput.
   A. 10 Gbps
   B. 16 Gbps
   C. 22 Gbps
   D. 32 Gbps

4. Both _____ use transition-minimized differential signaling to transmit high-speed serial data.

   A. DVI and HDMI

   B. HDMI and DisplayPort

   C. DVI and DisplayPort

   D. superMHL and DisplayPort

5. In a video system with multiple displays, problems with image quality in some, but not all, displays could indicate a problem with what?

   A. The video formats used

   B. The lengths of the video cables

   C. Incompatible High-Bandwidth Digital Content Protection keys

   D. Extended Display Identification Data

6. An EDID truth table should contain which of the following to describe the inputs of a switcher? (Choose all that apply.)

   A. The version of EDID used

   B. Input numbers

   C. Preferred resolution

   D. Color space support, such as RGB or a component

7. Clients who want to deploy 4K video over an integrated video system will likely need _____ devices to make it work properly.

   A. HDCP 2.2–compliant

   B. DisplayPort 1.2–compatible

   C. 8 Gbps–capable

   D. 4:2:0-sampled

8. An image constraint token onscreen indicates a problem with _____.

   A. HDMI

   B. UHDTV

   C. EDID

   D. HDCP

Answers

1. **B.** Ultra high-definition video (UHD) describes video formats with a minimum pixel resolution of 3840 × 2160.

2. **C.** To transmit 4K video at 60 fps using HDMI 1.4, color information should be sampled at a rate of 4:2:0.

3. **C.** A video system design to transmit 4K at 60 fps, with 4:4:4 chroma sampling and 10 bits per color, requires about 22 Gbps of throughput.

4. **A.** DVI and HDMI use transition-minimized differential signaling to transmit high-speed serial data.

5. **D.** In a video system with multiple displays, problems with image quality in some, but not all, displays could indicate an Extended Display Information Data (EDID) problem.

6. **B, C, D.** An EDID truth table should include information about input numbers, preferred resolutions, and color spaces.

7. **A.** Clients who want to deploy 4K video over an integrated video system will likely need HDCP 2.2–compliant devices to make it work properly.

8. **D.** An image constraint token onscreen indicates a problem with HDCP.

CHAPTER 14

Audio Design

In this chapter, you will learn about

- The difference between analog and digital audio systems
- How to compare and contrast analog and network audio transport
- How to compare and contrast different digital signal processor (DSP) architectures
- Different methods of signal metering and how to establish proper signal levels
- Comparing input and output impedances and implementing correct equalization practices
- Distinguishing between different types of audio processors and applying them to a design
- Graphic and parametric equalizers
- Applying crossover, feedback suppression, and noise-reduction filters to solve problems within an audio system

Analog technologies are so yesterday, right? No more limited dynamic range, clicks and pops from albums, flutter from tape machines, and other quality degradation. Not quite.

Humans are analog, as are microphones and loudspeakers. Communication starts with an analog voice into an analog transducer (a microphone), which converts it into an electrical signal. Eventually, that electrical signal is turned back into an analog waveform by a loudspeaker so it can be received by the ears of an analog human.

That said, what happens between the microphone element and the loudspeaker cone can be analog, digital, or both. Depending on the quality of the analog-to-digital, digital-to-analog converters, bit rates, compression rates, and so on, there can be a wide variety of what denotes "sound quality" in the digital domain.

In Chapter 6, you began to determine the parameters of a sound system design. You started by asking whether the client even needed a sound system, and then you quantified sound pressure levels, analyzed background noise, and more. If indeed you found it necessary to install a sound system, you mapped out loudspeaker locations based on coverage patterns, calculated the amount of power required at the loudspeakers, determined when to apply direct-connect or constant-voltage power amplifiers and loudspeakers, matched microphone sensitivities to the application, and explored whether the locations you chose for your loudspeakers and microphones resulted in a stable sound system.

Now it's time to consider the processors and infrastructure between microphones and loudspeakers.

Domain Check

This chapter relates directly to the following tasks on the CTS-D Exam Content Outline:

- Domain B Task 2: Coordinate architectural/interior design criteria
- Domain C Task 1: Create draft AV design
- Domain C Task 2: Confirm site conditions
- Domain D Task 2: Perform system verifications

These tasks comprise 26.4 percent of the exam (about 33 questions). This chapter may also relate to other tasks.

Analog vs. Digital Audio

When planning an audio system, a designer's first decision is to choose between analog and digital. You can have a completely analog path from microphone to mixer to processors to power amplifier to loudspeakers. This method is proven and reliable. However, it is also subject to noise and signal degradation over distance. It also requires the use of single-function components, which can be limiting when compared to digital transport methods.

If you choose to stay analog, your system will have more termination points and need a larger conduit. All those termination points will require additional labor. You'll need more space for infrastructure, and if you need to split analog signals in a point-to-multipoint configuration, you'll need to specify transformers.

Digital audio can travel over category or fiber cable. When running these cable types, you can utilize smaller conduit than you would need for analog audio. Digital audio requires less rack space but generates more heat. And if your system needs a point-to-multipoint setup, a digital system is easier to implement.

 NOTE Microphones and loudspeakers (transducers) are analog devices. You may find some "digital microphones" or "digital loudspeakers," but in truth, these are hybrids—acoustic transducers with analog-to-digital (A/D) converters (in the case of microphones) or digital-to-analog (D/A) converters (in the case of loudspeakers).

Figure 14-1 shows an example of an analog audio system. This particular schematic requires 32 pairs of cables for 64 channels of audio, for a total of 4,600 ft (1.4 km) of cabling. It also requires conduit that is 3 in (76.2 mm) in diameter. With cable and conduit costs estimated at $44,700 and a labor estimate of $1,500, the total infrastructure cost for this analog system is $46,200.

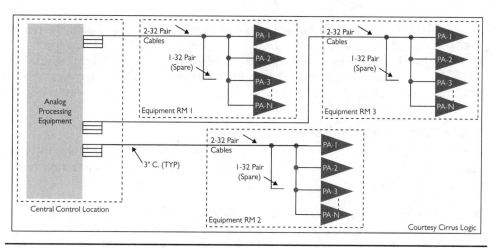

Figure 14-1   Diagram of an analog audio system

Figure 14-2 is an example of a networked, digital audio configuration. Although it may look more complex, its infrastructure is actually much simpler than the analog example. This system requires network switches and a single pair of Cat 5 copper or fiber cables. These cables carry more channels over fewer wires. Using fiber in the existing cable tray reduces the infrastructure cost to less than $3,000.

This type of infrastructure allows for more flexibility because the client can move microphones around the facility as needed, add extra loudspeakers, and locate the required DSPs in either a central location or distributed locations.

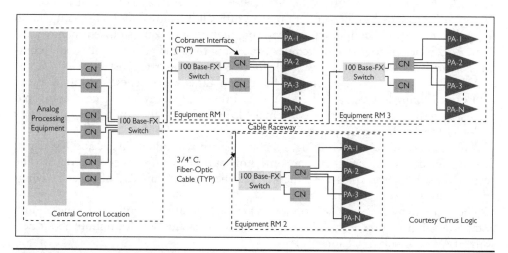

Figure 14-2   Diagram of a networked, digital audio system

PART IV

NOTE Regardless of whether an audio system is analog or digital, designers need to consider bandwidth. In the analog world, you would quantify bandwidth in terms of frequency, usually in megahertz. With digital, you would quantify bandwidth in terms of bits per second, usually in gigabits per second (Gbps).

Audio Transport Methods

Analog and digital audio use the same physical transmission media for point-to-point connections. The following are three commonly used physical interconnection types, defined by international standard IEC 60958:

- For professional audio, a Type I balanced, three-conductor, 110 ohm twisted pair with an XLR connector. This is an Audio Engineering Society/European Broadcasting Union (AES3) standard. There is another standard, AES-3id, which defines a 75 ohm BNC electrical variant of the balanced three-conductor twisted pair. Recently, more professional equipment has embraced this physical interconnection type, which uses the same cabling, patching, and infrastructure as analog or digital video that is common in the broadcast industry.

- For consumer audio, Type II unbalanced, two-conductor, 75 ohm coax with a phono connector (RCA).

- Also for consumer audio, a Type II optical fiber connection, typically plastic but occasionally glass, with an F05 connector. F05 connectors are more commonly known by their Toshiba brand name, TOSLINK.

Digital audio signals can be transmitted from one source to several endpoints over standard Ethernet networks. This point-to-multipoint transfer is sometimes referred to as *audio over Ethernet* (AoE). What's the difference between AoE and voice over IP (VoIP)? While VoIP is a speech-only application, AoE offers full-bandwidth, high-quality audio (typically at a 48-kHz sampling rate) requiring high bit rates and sufficient bandwidth. With AoE, a lack of compression reduces processing time and adds no undesirable compression artifacts, which makes it suitable for real-time audio transport.

AoE uses regular Cat 5e cabling or better and Ethernet switches. You can also use fiber-optic cabling between switches. Standard Ethernet reduces cabling costs compared to analog systems. Infrastructure costs may also be lower—the equivalent number of analog channels would require larger conduit.

AoE offers easier signal rerouting, reliability (with redundant links), and less signal degradation over distance. However, some AoE options require special interfaces. The cost of these interfaces, plus the Ethernet switches, may ultimately offset any savings realized through reduced infrastructure.

There are many different AoE options, such as CobraNet, Dante, and EtherSound. Each protocol has its own capabilities and requirements. You will learn more about networked AV protocols in Chapter 16.

DSP Architectures

More often than not, even in the middle of an otherwise analog path, you will need a central digital signal processor. It could be all-inclusive, with the mixer, signal processors, and a small power amplifier. Or it could comprise just the mixer and signal processors, or even just the signal processors.

AV professionals configure DSP devices using either the manufacturer's software interface or front-panel controls. System configurations and settings can be saved, copied, and password-protected. Specific presets can be recalled through a control system interface.

Designing around a single DSP device rather than multiple analog devices reduces the number of connections required and simplifies installation. On the other hand, too many DSPs in the signal path run the risk of introducing incompatibility among different formats. Moreover, using different sample rates and bit depths along the signal path can actually degrade audio quality.

Digital signal processors come in three basic varieties: flexible, fixed, and hybrid architecture.

- **Flexible**   *Flexible-architecture processors* are characterized by a drag-and-drop graphical user interface (GUI). In the GUI depicted in Figure 14-3, audio functions such as mixers, equalizers, filters, and crossovers can be dragged from the processing library on the left and placed almost anywhere in any order along the signal chain on the right.

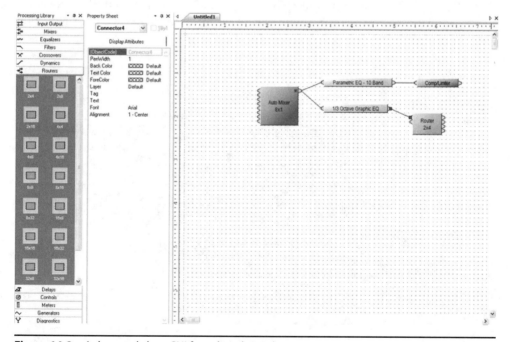

Figure 14-3   A drag-and-drop GUI for a digital signal processor

PART IV

Flexible-architecture processors give you more freedom in your design. You can manage many functions within a single box and develop complex signal paths. They are an excellent choice for systems where complexity or multiple applications may come into play, such as large-scale paging systems in airports. However, flexible-architecture processors may be more costly on a per-channel basis than fixed or hybrid systems. In addition, they require more DSP power because memory register stacks must be allocated for any eventuality and code space cannot be optimized.

- **Fixed** *Fixed-architecture processors* handle one type of function. For example, they may handle compression/limiting, equalization, or signal routing. They are often easy to set up and operate and may be good for system upgrades because you configure them much as you would their analog counterparts. However, they are functionally limited and may not be scalable.

- **Hybrid** *Fixed, multifunction (hybrid) processors* allow you to adjust multiple functions. They operate along a predictable, known pathway and are fairly cost effective, although some are limited in their routing and setup options. Generally, however, this hybrid architecture offers flexibility in signal routing, specifically with respect to which inputs connect to which outputs. It also optimizes DSP processing power because memory stacks and registers can be tightly packed.

Note in Figure 14-4 the level of control in pairing inputs and outputs while also providing for other adjustments along each path. If you look at input 1 on the left, the signal goes to an invert switch and then a mute switch, a gain control, a delay, a noise reduction

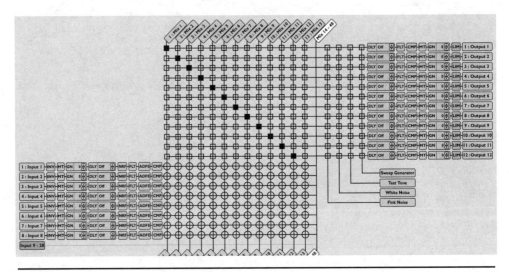

Figure 14-4   The interface for a hybrid DSP

filter, a filtering setup, a feedback eliminator, and finally a compressor. From there, you see the matrix router, which allows you to route the inputs to the different mix buses. These mix buses route to the outputs on the right. The outputs have their own set of controls, including delay, filters, compressor, muting, gain, and so on.

Signal Monitoring

Signal-level monitoring helps ensure that an audio system doesn't clip the signal or add distortion. It also helps ensure that the signal level is high enough to achieve an adequate signal-to-noise ratio without actually adding noise. Signal levels that are too low decrease the system's signal-to-noise ratio and can result in background hiss.

There are two types of meters typically used for signal monitoring. The first—and "standard"— indicator is the *volume unit (VU) meter* (Figure 14-5). The second is the *peak program meter (PPM)* (Figure 14-6).

A VU meter indicates program material levels for complex waveforms. In essence, it is a voltmeter calibrated in decibels and referenced to a specific voltage connected across a 600 ohm load. A VU meter meets stringent standards regarding scale, dynamic

Figure 14-5
A VU meter responds in a way that humans respond to loudness.

Figure 14-6
A PPM shows instantaneous peak levels and is useful for digital recording.

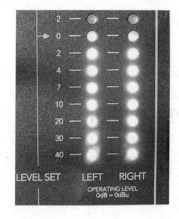

characteristics, frequency response, impedance, sensitivity, harmonic distortion, and overload. It is commonly used to monitor broadcast signals.

 TIP When using a VU meter, set the average levels to read about –6 and set the peaks to about 0.

A PPM responds much faster than a VU, showing peak levels instantaneously. It is useful for digital recording or when the level must not exceed 0 dB full scale (dBFS). Going above the full scale of a digital signal will cause clipping. You'll often find a PPM in audio mixers.

Analog vs. Digital Signal Monitoring

Although analog audio line–level signals typically operate around 0 dBu or +4 dBu, they can be as much as +18 dBu to +28 dBu before distortion (clipping) occurs. Digital signals, on the other hand, have a hard limit—0 dBFS (full scale) represents the maximum level for a digital signal. At 0 dBFS, all the bits in the digital audio signal are equal to 1.

You can use the bit depth of an audio signal to calculate its dynamic range. The formula for the dynamic range of a digital audio signal is as follows:

$$dB = 20log \ (Ns/1)$$

where:

- dB = The dynamic range of the signal
- Ns = The number of possible signal states

To find the dynamic range of a 16-bit signal, first determine the number of possible states. You'll recall that each bit has two states (0 or 1); therefore, 2^{16} yields 65,536 possible states.

- dB = 20log (65,536)
- dB = 20 (4.816479931)
- dB = 96

A 16-bit system has a dynamic range of 96 dB.

Setting Up the System

When configuring a DSP, you may need to consider many common functions. We'll go through some of these so you're clear on what they can do and how you can set them to the recommended settings.

- Input gain
- Filters (input and output)

- Equalization
- Feedback suppression
- Crossovers
- Noise reduction
- Dynamics
- Compressors
- Limiters
- Gates
- Delay
- Routing

Where to Set Gain

Regardless of whether you're working in the analog or digital domain, proper gain structure and signal monitoring are required. Although clipping an analog signal produces an undesirable and unpleasant distortion, digital clipping is annoying and harsh. Setting gain structure means making adjustments so that the system delivers the best performance and the user does not hear hiss, noise, or distortion from the loudspeakers.

Most mixers will produce +18 to +24 dBu output levels without clipping; 10 to 20 dB of headroom will support an emphatic talker or especially loud section of program material. With preamplifiers properly set and all other adjustments set at unity, the mixer's output meter should be reading about 0 (analog) or about –18 to –20 dBFS (digital) under normal operating conditions.

 TIP   Make sure to read all equipment manuals to discover what 0 really means. In an analog or apparently analog meter, does 0 mean 0 VU (+4 dBu) or 0 dBu?

There are several spots within an audio system where gain can be adjusted. Make sure to set the gain structure of each of these devices:

- Microphone preamplifiers
- Audio mixer
- Processing devices (equalizer, compressor, limiter)
- Preamplifiers in the mixer for microphone inputs
- Amplifier

You do not necessarily have to set the gain structure of all of these devices in this order. You can set unity gain in your mixer first, for example, and then set it for the microphone preamplifiers. You just need to make sure you set gain in every item. The exception? You should set the input of the power amplifiers last.

Some DSPs are equipped with microphone inputs. Like their analog counterparts, these inputs will include a microphone preamplifier. This is the most important setting in terms of getting the maximum signal-to-noise (S/N) ratio from your system. As a guide, the following input types may require as much gain as listed here:

- **Handheld vocal microphone**   35 dB minimum
- **Handheld presentation microphone**   45 dB
- **Gooseneck microphone**   45 dB
- **Boundary microphone**   55 dB
- **Any microphone farther away**   60 dB
- **Ceiling-mounted microphone**   Greater than 60 dB

When using line level inputs, an unbalanced consumer line–level input may need as much as 12 dB of gain, while a balanced professional line–level input may need little or no gain. For best results, refer to manufacturers' documentation for specifications on the amount of gain for each piece of equipment or microphone.

 NOTE   Signal-to-noise ratio is the ratio, measured in decibels, between the audio or video signal and the noise accompanying the signal.

Poor Signal-to-Noise Ratio

DSPs can help you achieve an excellent S/N ratio in your audio system. A wide S/N ratio means your audience will hear much more signal than noise, which increases intelligibility. But first, let's look at what happens when you do not have a wide S/N ratio. Figure 14-7 plots the amount of signal and noise generated by a microphone, a preamplifier, a mixer, DSP boxes, and an amplifier in an audio signal chain. The line along the bottom represents the noise. As you can see, the dynamic microphone at the beginning of this signal chain does not introduce any noise into the system, but each item afterward adds noise.

Figure 14-7
Poor signal-to-noise ratio

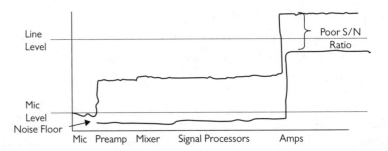

In this figure, instead of bringing the signal up to the line level (0 dBu) in the preamp, the gain was set too low, perhaps around –20 dBu. When the signal hits the amplifier, it needs to be turned up significantly to reach the desired sound pressure level (SPL) level. But do you see what also happens to the noise? It also increases significantly. In systems set like this, you will hear audible hiss from the loudspeakers.

TIP If you are trying to find the source of hiss in your audio system, check to see whether the amplifier is turned up to its maximum. This is often a dead giveaway that the hiss is a symptom of poor gain structure.

Good Signal-to-Noise Ratio

Now let's see what happens when the preamp is brought up to line level (0 dBu). As shown in Figure 14-8, you don't need to turn up the amplifier nearly as much to reach the same SPL at the listening position. This means the noise will not be amplified nearly as drastically as it was in the previous example. This gives you a wide S/N ratio, and you probably will not hear hiss in this audio system.

Figure 14-9 compares the two examples. Both systems end with the same SPL, but look at how much less you need to adjust at the amplifier when you set your gain structure at the preamplifier. This prevents too much noise or hiss from getting into your system, which makes the system intelligible and clear.

Figure 14-8
Good signal-to-noise ratio

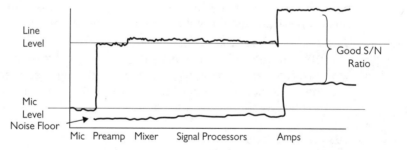

Figure 14-9
Comparing good and poor S/N ratios

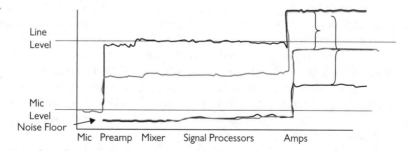

Common DSP Settings

Before we dive into DSP settings, let's go over several terms.

- *Threshold* is the level at which a desired function becomes active. Generally speaking, a lower threshold level means it will activate earlier. The recommended starting threshold for most line-level (post preamp) functions is 0 dBu.

- The *attack time* of an audio DSP determines how quickly volume will be reduced once it exceeds the threshold. If the attack time is too slow, then the sound will become distorted as the system adjusts.

- The *release time* of an audio compressor determines how quickly the volume increases when an audio signal returns below the threshold.

- *Automatic gain control* (AGC) is an electronic or logic feedback circuit that maintains a constant acoustic power (gain) output in response to input variables, such as signal strength or ambient noise level. AGC raises gain if the signal is too low or compresses the signal if it is too high. Its primary application is to capture weak signals for recording or transmission. Be careful with this DSP setting. It can create feedback if used on amplified inputs. When using AGC, start with a threshold set at 0 dB. This will help keep the gain centered at line level.

- *Ambient level control* uses a reference microphone to measure a room's noise level. It then automatically adjusts a system for noisier environments. It's a function that's useful in managing music in restaurants. The ambient level control will ensure that, no matter how loud the patrons are, the background music will remain a specified amount of dB above the ambient noise.

 TIP The reference microphone used for ambient level control may be a dedicated microphone, used only to take this SPL measurement, or it may be a designated microphone, used elsewhere in the system but designated to measure the reference signal, too.

Compressor Settings

Let's start our discussion of DSP settings with compressors. A compressor controls the dynamic range of a signal by reducing the part of the signal that exceeds the user-adjustable threshold. When the signal exceeds the threshold, the overall amplitude is reduced by a user-defined ratio, thus reducing the overall dynamic range.

Compressors represent a type of DSP that compensates for loud peaks in a signal level. All signal levels below a specified threshold will pass through the compressor unchanged, and all signals above the threshold will be compressed. In other words, compressors keep loud signals from being too loud. This reduces the variation between the highest and lowest signal levels, resulting in a compressed (smaller) dynamic range. Compressors are useful when reinforcing energetic presenters, who may occasionally raise their voice for emphasis. See Figure 14-10.

The *compressor threshold* sets the point at which the automatic volume reduction kicks in. When the input goes above the threshold, the audio compressor automatically reduces the volume to keep the signal from getting too loud.

Figure 14-10
User interface for a compressor, which keeps loud signals from being too loud

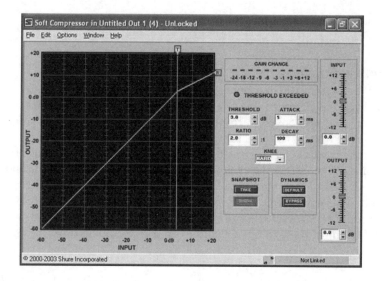

The *compressor ratio* is the amount of actual level increase above the threshold that will yield 1 dB in gain change after the compressor. For example, a 3:1 ratio would mean that for every 3 dB the gain increases above the threshold, the audience would hear only a 1 dB difference after the compressor. Likewise, if the level were to jump by 9 dB, the final level would jump only 3 dB.

You can also set the attack and release times on a compressor. Again, the attack time is how long it takes for the compressor to react after the compressor exceeds the threshold. The release time determines when the compressor lets go after the level settles below the threshold. Both of these functions are measured in milliseconds.

When setting a compressor, try starting with the following settings. You may have to make adjustments depending on the specific needs of your audio system, but these setting are a good place to start. For speech applications, such as conference rooms, boardrooms, try these settings:

- **Ratio**   3:1
- **Attack**   10 to 20 ms
- **Release**   200 to 500 ms
- **Threshold**   0

For these settings, if the initial input gain were set for a 0 dB level, it would take a 60 dB increase at the microphone to hit the +20 dB limit of input, which would result in clipping.

For music or multimedia applications, try these settings:

- **Ratio**   6:1
- **Attack**   10 to 20 ms

- **Release**   200 to 500 ms
- **Threshold**   0

Limiter Settings

Limiters are similar to compressors in that they are triggered by peaks or spikes in the signal level. See Figure 14-11. They are used to limit the impact of extreme sound pressure spikes, such as dropped microphones, phantom-powered mics that get unplugged without being muted, and equipment that's not turned on or off in the correct order. With limiters, signals exceeding the threshold level are reduced at ratios of 10:1 or greater.

Limiters protect downstream gear by preventing severe clipping and overdriving amps and speakers. Many amplifiers have built-in limiters to protect themselves.

Always set the limiter's threshold above the compressor's threshold. Otherwise, the compressor will never engage. Here are some suggested settings for your limiter. You will need to adjust these values depending on the specific needs of the audio system.

- **Ratio**   10:1 above the user-adjustable threshold.
- **Threshold**   10 dB higher than the compressor's threshold. If the compressor threshold is 0 dB, then the limiter's threshold should be 10 dB.
- **Attack time**   2 ms or more faster than the compressor's attack time.
- **Release time**   200 ms or less than the compressor's release time.

Gate Settings

Gates mute the level of all signals below an adjustable threshold. This means that the signal levels must exceed the threshold setting before they are allowed to pass. This can be

Figure 14-11
User interface for a limiter, which limits the impact of extreme sound pressure spikes

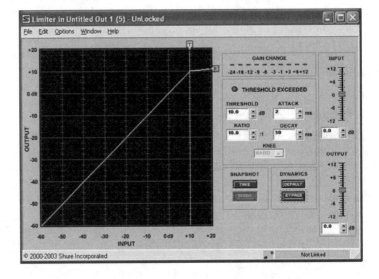

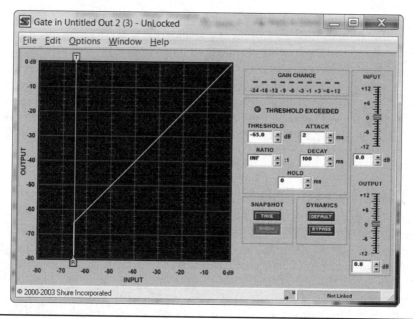

Figure 14-12 User interface for a gate, which mutes the level of signals below an adjustable threshold

used to turn off unused microphones automatically. You can control when the gate activates by setting the gate's attack and hold times. Gates are found in some automixers and are useful for noise control, such as from a noisy multimedia source. See Figure 14-12.

When setting a gate, try the following settings. As with other DSP settings, you may need to make adjustments based on need.

- **Attack**   Start with a relatively fast setting, such as 1 ms.
- **Release**   Start at 50 ms.
- **Threshold**   Your threshold setting depends on the gate's position in the audio signal chain and the number of mics used. If it's after the input gain and there is one mic, less than 0 dB is a good starting place. You may need to go lower than this if you are not getting a reliable start.

Expanders

An expander is an audio processor that comes in two forms: a downward expander or as part of what's known as a *compander*.

Downward expanders increase the dynamic range by reducing—or attenuating—the level below the adjustable threshold setting. They increase gain if the signal is low, such as a presenter with a weak voice. This reduces unwanted background noise and is especially useful in a system using multiple open microphones.

Keep in mind that expanders are primarily intended for recording and transmission. When used in an amplified environment, expanders can push a system into painfully loud feedback.

NOTE Compressors, limiters, gates, and expanders are all "dynamic filters" in that they filter audio on the basis of its dynamic range. However, some dynamics filters can also be frequency specific. For example, a compressor with a low-pass filter is good for controlling proximity effects while allowing high frequencies to pass unaffected.

Introduction to Equalization

Equalization is one of the most commonly used functions of a DSP. Equalizers, or EQs, are frequency controls that allow the user to boost (add gain) or cut (attenuate) a specific range of frequencies. The simplest equalizer comes in the form of the bass and treble tone controls found normally on your home stereo or surround receiver. The equalizer found on the input channel of a basic audio mixer may provide simple high-, mid-, and low-frequency controls.

Both the input and output signals of an audio system may be equalized. *Input equalization* is generally for tonality control—adjusting the tonal content so each input sounds similar. Output equalization is generally used for loudspeaker compensation—adjusting for "quirks" or characteristics of a loudspeaker's response.

NOTE No amount of equalization can change the acoustics of a room. Acoustic recommendations for AV spaces are covered in Chapter 11.

A *parametric equalizer* allows for the selection of a center frequency and the adjustment of the width—or Q—of the frequency range that will be affected. (The Q factor is the ratio of the height of the peak of the filter against the width of the filter at the 3 dB point; see the related Note.) This enables precise manipulation with minimal impact to the adjacent frequencies. In short, a parametric equalizer allows users to make many, large-scale adjustments to a signal with fewer filters. It offers greater flexibility than a *graphic equalizer*, which we will discuss later in this chapter.

NOTE *Wide* Q filters can be used to counteract wide peaks or dips in the frequency response. *High* Q filters, commonly used as notch filters, are used to counteract narrow bands of frequency problems. For example, they are useful for removing primary feedback from fixed microphones.

Filters are classified by their rate of attenuation on the signal. This is described in terms of decibels per octave, where an octave represents a doubling of frequency. A first-order filter attenuates at a rate of 6 dB per octave.

A second-order filter attenuates at a rate of 12 dB per octave. A third-order filter attenuates at 18 dB per octave, a fourth-order filter attenuates at 24 dB per octave, and so on. Each order has 6 dB more roll-off than the one before it.

Pass Filters

A *band-pass filter* is a low Q filter that allows the user to eliminate the highs and lows of a frequency response. While rarely seen in professional audio gear, this type of filter is useful for tone control. Many car stereos use filters like these for bass, midrange, and treble control. Telephone lines also use band-pass filters because most telephone calls do not need to pick up a lot of bass or treble signals.

A *low-pass filter* is a circuit that allows signals below a specified frequency to pass unaltered while simultaneously attenuating frequencies above the specified limit. Low-pass filters are useful for eliminating hiss in a system. If you have a source with a lot of hiss, such as a low-cost consumer-level tape deck or cheap MP3 player, you can apply a low-pass filter to eliminate the high-frequency hiss.

A *high-pass filter* is a circuit that allows signals above a specified frequency to pass unaltered while simultaneously attenuating frequencies below the specified limit. High-pass filters are useful for removing low-frequency noise from a system, such as rumble from a heating, ventilation, and air conditioning (HVAC) system or the proximity effect on a microphone.

A *shelving filter* is similar to a low- or high-pass filter, except instead of removing frequency bands, it simply tapers off and flattens out the sound again. Such filters are useful when the user may want to boost or cut certain frequency bands without eliminating any sound. A *boost shelf*, for example, will let the user boost treble or bass in a car stereo.

Crossover Filters

Crossover filters are used for bi-amplified and tri-amplified systems. By using these filters, you can send low-, mid-, and high-range frequency bands to the appropriate, separate amplifiers. Such filters are extremely useful in large-scale concert systems for reproducing live music.

A crossover separates the audio signal into different frequency groupings and routes the appropriate material to the correct loudspeaker or amplifier to ensure that the individual loudspeaker components receive program signals that are within their optimal frequency range. Crossovers are either *passive* or *active*.

Crossover filters often use high-order, roll-off filters, often in the fourth- to eighth-order range. Bass amplifiers will often take the 250 Hz or lower range, while the high-pass filter will start at 4 KHz.

The crossover point between filters is often 3 dB. (In Figure 14-13, the crossover points are represented by the large dots between the filters.) In these areas, two different loudspeakers will reproduce that particular frequency band. Because each loudspeaker has a –3 dB cut, when they each play that sound, the sound pressure in that area will be doubled, and the audience will perceive that frequency as 0 dB.

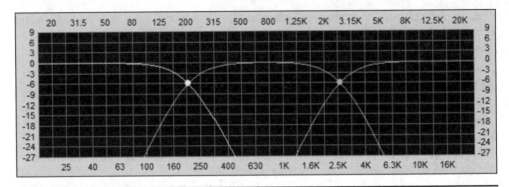

Figure 14-13 Three crossover filters

Feedback-Suppression Filters

Feedback-suppression filters are a useful option for speech-only audio systems. They are tight-notch filters that can be used to eliminate specific bands of frequencies. (A notch filter "notches out," or eliminates, a specific band of frequencies.) If you've identified a specific frequency band as a source of feedback, you can use a feedback-suppression filter to eliminate the problem.

If you have a fixed microphone in a room, such as a microphone bolted to a witness stand in a courthouse, you may find that the way the microphone interacts with reflections in the room causes feedback along specific frequencies. You can eliminate such problem areas with a feedback-suppression filter. To do so, follow these steps:

1. Turn off all microphones except for the one you're testing.
2. Before you attempt the final system equalization, turn up the gain on the microphone and note the first three frequencies that cause consistent feedback.
3. Construct three tight-notch filters at the input on those frequencies.
4. Once you've created the filters, reset them and equalize the system.

Once the system has been equalized, you are ready to set your feedback-suppression filters. Simply reengage the feedback filters you identified and see whether they improve your operational-level system. Do this for every fixed microphone in your system.

Noise-Reduction Filters

A noise-reduction filter is a popular new algorithm that samples the noise floor and removes specific spectral content. It listens for noise from things such as HVAC systems, fans, other gear near microphones (such as laptops), and electronic noise. It then reduces that particular noise from the system.

The canceller depth will depend on the amount of noise present in the room. Quiet conference rooms with little or no noise may not need a noise-reduction filter, while rooms with heavy noise, such as a training room with a large audience and loud air conditioning, may need a severe noise-reduction filter. Try these settings as a starting point:

- For eliminating computer and projector fan noise, start at 9 dB.
- For eliminating heavy room noise, start at 12 dB.

Remember that the purpose of these filters is to remove spectral content. They are not perfect, and they will affect your room response.

Delays

A *delay* is the retardation of a signal. In the context of audio processing, it is an adjustment of the time in which a signal is sent to a destination, often to compensate for the distance between loudspeakers or for the differential in processing required between multiple signals. If a delay is an unintended byproduct of signal processing, it is usually referred to as *latency*.

Delays are used in sound systems for loudspeaker alignment—either to align components within a loudspeaker enclosure or array or to align supplemental loudspeakers with the main speakers.

Within a given loudspeaker enclosure, the individual components may be physically offset, causing differences in the arrival time from those components. This issue can be corrected either physically or by using delays to provide proper alignment.

Electronic delay is often used in sound reinforcement applications. For example, consider an auditorium with an under-balcony area. The audience seated underneath the balcony may not be covered well by the main loudspeakers. In this case, supplemental loudspeakers are installed to cover the portion of the audience seated underneath the balcony.

Although the electronic audio signal arrives at both the main and under-balcony loudspeakers simultaneously, the sound coming from these two separate locations would arrive at the audience underneath the balcony at different times and sound like an echo. This is because sound travels at about 1,130 feet per second (344 meters per second) under fairly normal temperature conditions (about 71 degrees Fahrenheit), much slower than the speed of the electronic audio signal.

 NOTE At 80 degrees Fahrenheit, sound travels about 1,140 feet per second. This could impact delay settings in warmer, outdoor settings, for example.

In this example, an electronic delay would be used on the audio signal going to the under-balcony loudspeakers. The amount of delay would be set so that the sound both from the main loudspeakers and from the under-balcony loudspeakers arrive at the audience at the same time.

Delay can also be introduced to combat the *Haas effect*. The human ear has the ability to locate the origin of a sound with fairly high accuracy, based on where you hear the sound from first. Through the Haas effect—or sound precedence—you can distinguish the original source location even if there are strong echoes or reflections that may otherwise mislead you. A reflection could be 10 dB louder and you'd still correctly identify the direction of the original source.

When setting up a delay, designers can use this effect to their advantage. Rather than timing the delay of the loudspeakers to come out at the same time as the original source, add 15 ms to the delay setting (or 15 ft or 5 m). This will make the speaker generate the reinforced signal 15 ms later, which allows the listener to locate correctly the origin of the sound (the lecturer, band, and so on). Without the additional delay, the listener would perceive the source of the sound as the location of the loudspeaker, rather than the location of the original source. Just don't exceed 25 ms. Longer might be perceived as echo and compromise intelligibility.

TIP When setting electronic delay, factor in 10 ms per 10 ft (3.3 m) farther than the distance would indicate. For example, if your loudspeakers are 60.5 ft (18.4 m) from the stage, try 70.5 ms of delay instead of 60.5 ms.

Graphic Equalizers

Instead of using parametric equalizers, some audio professionals prefer to use graphic equalizers. A graphic equalizer is an equalizer with an interface that resembles a graph comparing amplitude along the vertical axis and frequency along the horizontal axis. Graphic equalizers normally come in 2/3-octave or, more often, 1/3-octave filters sets. Filters are usually set on center frequencies defined by the International Organization for Standardization (ISO). Center frequencies and bandwidth are fixed for these filters, so named because the adjustments to the sliders offer a "graphic" representation of the frequency response. Active graphic equalizers can provide boost and cut capability.

The graphic equalizer in Figure 14-14 has 31 controllable filters. This type of display gives you fine control of dozens of specific frequencies, where you can grab any control and add precise amounts of boost or cut to that particular frequency.

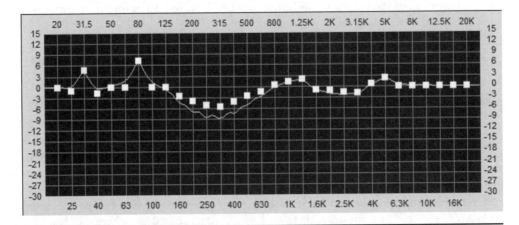

Figure 14-14   A graphic equalizer

In Figure 14-14, the line that runs near each filter control represents the combined interaction between the filters. Do you see the bumpy, rippled area around 315 Hz? That is an area with phase interference because of the way the filters around that frequency are arranged. This represents a downside of using a graphic equalizer. Parametric equalizers will avoid these phase ripples because they use fewer, smoother filters. In addition, because they use fewer filters, parametric equalizers in DSPs tend to use less processing power than a graphic equalizer.

NOTE A 1/3-octave equalizer is a graphic equalizer that provides 30 or 31 slider adjustments corresponding to specific fixed frequencies with fixed bandwidths, with the frequencies centered at every one-third of an octave. The numerous adjustment points shape the overall frequency response of the system. This makes the sound system sound more natural.

Chapter Review

Audio processing is a complex art, and doing it right takes practice. This chapter covered audio sources and destinations, analog versus digital audio, transport methods, DSP architecture types, signal monitoring, DSP functions, equalization, and filters. They're all critical to an audio design that delivers what the client wants from a sound system.

Review Questions

The following questions are based on the content covered in this chapter and are intended to help reinforce the knowledge you have assimilated. These questions are not extracted from the CTS-D exam nor are they necessarily CTS-D practice exam questions. For an official CTS-D practice exam, see the accompanying CD.

1. Stereo loudspeaker systems typically use what type of signal?

   A. Analog

   B. RGBH

   C. High gain

   D. Low gain

2. What is the advantage of converting an analog signal to digital?

   A. Digital signals have more signal headroom.

   B. Digital signals can address signal degradation, storage, and recording issues.

   C. Digital signals carry audio and video feeds that analog will not.

   D. Digital signals are more energy efficient to broadcast.

3. When creating a schematic diagram of audio signal flow for a project, what must you include in the diagram?

   A. Microphones, mixers, switchers, routers, and processors

   B. Inputs, outputs, equipment rack locations, ceiling venting

   C. Conduit runs, pull boxes, bends

   D. Construction materials, wall panels, acoustic tiles

4. Two types of meters typically used for signal monitoring are _____ and _____.

   A. VU, PPM

   B. VU, AES

   C. dBU, PPM

   D. EBU, SMPTE

5. For a handheld vocal microphone, you might want set the input gain for at least _____.

   A. 10 dB

   B. 20 dB

   C. 35 dB

   D. 60 dB

6. Which of the following is *not* a recommended compressor setting for speech applications?

   A. Ratio: 3:1

   B. Attack: 10 to 20 ms

   C. Release: 20 to 50 ms

   D. Threshold: 0

7. Eighth-order filters are useful as _____.

   A. Notch filters

   B. Crossover filters

   C. Low-pass filters

   D. Shelving filters

8. When setting a delay filter, it's useful to know that sound travels at how many feet (meters) per second at about 70 degrees Fahrenheit?

   A. 950 (390)

   B. 1,001 (305)

   C. 1,025 (312)

   D. 1,130 (344)

Answers

1. **A.** Stereo loudspeaker systems typically use analog signals.

2. **B.** An advantage of converting an analog signal to digital is that digital signals can address signal degradation, storage, and recording issues.

3. **A.** When creating a schematic diagram of audio signal flow, you should include microphones, mixers, switchers, routers, and processors.

4. **A.** Two types of meters typically used for signal monitoring are VU (volume unit) and PPM (peak program meter).

5. **C.** For a handheld vocal microphone, you might want set the input gain for at least 35 dB.

6. **C.** The recommended release setting for speech applications is actually 200 to 500 ms.

7. **B.** Eighth-order filters are useful as crossover filters.

8. **D.** Sound travels at 1,130 feet (344 meters) per second at about 70 degrees Fahrenheit.

CHAPTER 15

Control Requirements

In this chapter, you will learn about
- Modern types of control system and the devices they can control
- Control system configurations
- Control system design and performance verification

Control systems allow people to operate complex AV equipment using simple interfaces. Usually, these interfaces are located in a single convenient location within a room, such as at a lectern or on a wall near a door. Today's users also expect a control system to meet their needs regardless of the interface type.

The best control system designs fulfill users' need to collaborate as well as to control their environments in a familiar and seamless way. When all aspects of a system have been designed correctly, the AV system becomes a powerful business tool for anyone to use.

Because AV systems have become highly contextualized, control systems are the "glue" that holds systems together. They make it possible for AV professionals to create systems out of diverse components from different manufacturers.

Domain Check

This chapter relates directly to the following tasks on the CTS-D Exam Content Outline:

- Domain C Task 1: Create draft AV design
- Domain C Task 2: Confirm Site Conditions

These tasks comprise 18.4 percent of the exam (about 23 questions). This chapter may also relate to other tasks.

Types of Control Systems

What types of devices can users control today? From AV equipment to environmental/ energy components and security/access control—the number of devices that can be controlled from a central point keeps growing.

What types of control systems can users employ today? The following are just a few:

- **Traditional control system processor (i.e., relays, RS-232, input/output [I/O], and infrared [IR])**   While reliable, this type can also be expensive and require firmware updates and extensive manufacturer training for propriety control software. Examples include Crestron Pro2 Dual Bus and AMX NetLinx Integrated Controller.

- **Control built in to the system (i.e., performs actions without a secondary interface, and the same manufacturer that provides the system provides the user interface)**   While less expensive than traditional systems, this type is proprietary and less flexible. Examples include CyViz Display Controller and Cisco EX90.

- **Computer-driven control (i.e., provided and programmed by the end user)**   While highly accessible through the Web and driven by bring your own device (BYOD)/standard mobile devices, this type is dependent on operating system updates and versions and may not be scalable. One example is Opto 22.

- **Cloud-based control**   While capable of controlling large and multiple environments and providing robust backup, failure can be expensive. Examples include Jydo Controls and Surgex Axess Manager.

- **Habitual-learning systems**   While capable of learning user patterns, this type's data processing has not been perfected and may be expensive. Examples include Nest products and adaptive control systems.

Control System Components

The complete control system consists of a central processing unit (CPU), programming, external controls, connected devices, interfaces, software, control points, and the wiring. The following sections will discuss the basic subset of those components—the CPU, interfaces, and control points.

Central Processing Unit

A *central processing unit* or master control unit is the "brains" of the control system, typically consisting of a computer processor that communicates with a fixed set of devices on a local area network (LAN). The CPU is rated similarly to a computer system—based on the control protocols, control signal speed, random access and read-only memory (RAM and ROM), number and variety of bus devices, and so on. CPU capabilities determine how many keypads, push buttons, touch panels, dimmers, media players, computers, and other elements are possible within the system. Individual control systems can also be linked together to form larger, composite control systems.

A CPU can be used to control multiple zones and devices by performing a series of automatic and independent functions. The CPU requires an operating system that allows a custom or fixed program to run the processing operations. The program defines the choices, variables, calculations, and fixed functions for the processor to choose from.

Processors are a central component of a control system. Some control systems have a single master controller, while others have several. CPU-to-CPU or master-to-master systems refer to systems that enable data processing in more than one location simultaneously, for a combined effect. Small self-contained systems can be linked together to provide better reliability, redundancy, independence, and efficiency. CPU systems provide hierarchy control, with one leader (in other words, master controller) and many subcontrollers (in other words, devices). Automated systems without user interfaces use an input interface to the CPU, which in turn communicates to the input interface.

The master unit (Figure 15-1) provides an example of the range of device interfaces that may be available within a control system. In this case, the master controller provides connections supporting a wide range of devices, including legacy devices.

Control Interfaces

A *control interface* is a graphical and functional method of device control that uses programmable command sequences. For example, let's assume a user would like to turn on a light by pressing a button on a touch panel. This command is sent to the CPU, which sends the signal out across a wire/cable using the correct control point. A contact closure (in other words, the control point) activates the switch, and the light turns on.

Control interfaces can be wired or wireless. Complex wired control systems can be control rooms that operate nuclear plants and systems to control lighting and other elements of live theatrical shows. New technology merges the wired control with wireless computers that utilize graphical user interfaces, feedback displays, and push buttons.

What type of interface might your users need for their control environment? Control interfaces have different aspects that you'll need to communicate to your client so you can both decide on the best device for the space.

- The *touch-screen panels* (in other words, touch panels) are the most popular style of control (Figure 15-2). They are inexpensive, hard to lose, and easy to operate. The touch screen offers the most flexibility and style and can be wired or wireless.

Figure 15-1
The CPU master unit

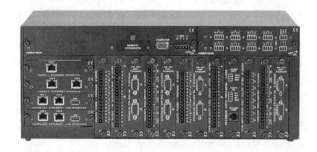

Figure 15-2
A touch-screen
control panel

- *Control panels* incorporate push buttons, knobs, and sliders. They are the predecessor of touch-screen panels and can still be found and selected for use in professional AV environments.

- *Simple wired panels* are the most common user interfaces. Simple wired interfaces are used to control devices within a typical home and can include wall switches and doorbells. In professional AV environments, they provide media player access and control.

- *Handheld remotes* and app-enhanced mobile devices may also be used in conjunction with other types of control interfaces. Handheld remotes don't typically include programmable control or graphical user interfaces (GUIs). Traditional handheld remotes are preprogrammed and have only pushbuttons, such as the remote that comes with a TV or Blu-ray Disc player. Some newer universal remotes have GUIs, while both old and new universal remotes incorporate programmable control. Many also have macro capabilities—one button turns on the TV and Blu-ray Disc player, switches the TV to Blu-ray Disc input, and so on.

AV professionals create an intuitive design to ensure the interface is easy for the user to understand and that it is installed in appropriate locations within the room, ensuring easy access within the environment (for example, out of direct sunlight that can affect visibility).

Smartphones and tablets have changed the way people interact with technology. Furthermore, these devices have changed user expectations. Users have been conditioned to expect *discoverability* and *understanding*.

Discoverability allows a user to determine which actions are possible and where or how they can perform them using a device. Understanding gives users a clear sense of how a product or device is supposed to be used. These characteristics are the key elements of *human-centered design*.

Human-Centered Interface Design

Human-centered design considers user behaviors, capabilities, and needs before technology and creativity. According to this approach, the design process begins without specifics and focuses on what the user might look for when interacting with devices. The resulting design informs the user if an action is possible, displays the action as it occurs, and notifies the user if something goes wrong.

The following are some of the characteristics of human-centered design:

- **Affordance**   Build intuitive interactions between people and their environment (for example, mail slots fit only envelopes, and balls allow for throwing or bouncing).

- **Signifiers**   Signal what actions are possible and how they should be done (for example, door knobs or handles can signal turning, pushing, or pulling).

- **Constraints**   Communicate what the design can or cannot do (for example, push versus pull on a door).

- **Mapping**   Lay out the design for clear understanding (for example, turn wheel left to turn left).

- **Feedback**   Communicate the results of an action. The feedback must be immediate, informative, and specific (for example, elevator up/down buttons).

Users could get frustrated if they can't figure out how to use the control system to make the lights dim or how to make the screen come down to project their presentations. If users can't figure out the controls, they'll be discouraged from using the interface. A human-centered interface allows the user to utilize a control system without any technical knowledge.

For example, users expect some form of feedback confirming a selection they have made in a given space. After pressing a button on a touch panel, they expect to see the drapes lowered, the projector lowered and powered on, and the button they pressed turn green. The actual devices in this scenario do not require two-way communication with the user, but users may still expect some form of positive feedback from the interface.

Consider a few of the elements when designing the user interfaces. You and your client should determine how easily the user can do the following:

- Determine what the system is for

- Figure out which device options are possible

- Identify and interpret the system state and if it is a desired state

- Figure out which buttons to press or knobs to turn in the shortest sequence possible

Control Points

A control point (Figure 15-3) is the vehicle that connects devices to the control system CPU. For example, a touch panel would be a control interface, and the control point could be RS-232 or Ethernet. When the user touches a button on the touch panel, the control point communicates the information from the CPU to the device.

The control point types range from basic (contact closure) to advanced (Internet Protocol) in complexity.

- **Contact closure**   The simplest form of remote control by opening/closing a circuit.

- **Analog voltage (in other words, voltage ramp generator)**   The analog form of data control. The voltage of a specific parameter is applied to the control point to adjust the level by a specific ratio of voltage value to the device's level.

Figure 15-3
A control point

- **Serial communication**   A one-way communication available in optical and wired formats. It most commonly uses infrared, which is a pattern of light pulses emitted from a light-emitting diode that is in turn recognized by the device's control point. Transmission requires a direct line of sight. Not all serial communication uses IR. Serial communication is also capable of bi-direction, just not in the IR form. IR is one way, unless there are two separate IR channels (IR transmitting [Tx] and IR receiving [Rx]).

- **Radio frequency (RF)**   Can be bi-directional and is mostly used by the user interface to the control system. Transmission has to be tested to prevent interference issues.

- **Network**   Works on the basis of transmitting packets of digital information (control protocols). The three forms of such transmission are as follows:

  - **Single ended**   Bi-directional between two devices.

  - **Broadcast**   A single transmitter of information and multiple receivers. All receivers "hear" the broadcast but respond only to traffic directed to itself.

  - **Multidrop**   Multiple transmitters and multiple receivers all interacting on the same wire/cable. This subtype can be complex and requires careful setup. Its formats are RS-232 and RS-422. RS-232 connects a single device back to a processor. RS-422 is a balanced connection and provides increased distance capacity via differential signaling. Differential signaling can transmit data at rates of up to 10 megabits per second or may be sent via cables up to 4921 ft (1500 m) long.

- **Internet Protocol (IP)**   Similar to network but allows for communication between the Internet, control components, applications, and so on.

- **Ethernet**   Considered a stand-alone type because of the incredible flexibility and applications it provides, although it really is a data control type (in other words, IP). It can be used to address enterprise-wide support issues and link global resources together.

   NOTE   ZigBee is a personal area network (PAN) wireless technology in the 2.4 gigahertz range that uses mesh topology to link multiple devices and can be used for sensors; lighting systems; heating, ventilation, and air conditioning (HVAC); and more.

The following sections explain the control system design and performance verification.

Control System Design

For AV control systems, the information gathered from the user during the needs analysis should be applied to every step of the design process. AV professionals must determine exactly what kinds of functionality and features the users need. Such an approach helps to avoid and solve many problems early on.

Needs Analysis

These are some general concepts to ask or listen for when interviewing the client:

- **Simplicity of operation**   Who are the users of the system? What is the user's level of technical experience?

- **Device automation**   What do they want the system to do autonomously?

- **Multiple device integration**   How many devices do they want to control?

- **Device operation from multiple locations**   Where should interfaces be located?

- **Device operation at a distance**   How do they want to control devices? Consider any pre-existing systems or future expansion issues.

- **Cost**   What is the project budget?

For each device to be controlled by AV professionals, choose an appropriate control interface by considering the following issues:

- Can the CPU accommodate all of the system's needs?

- What control interfaces are available and required for this device?

- How does the selection impact other subsystems?

CPU Configurations

Devices may need to be controlled in multiple rooms, across a college campus, or even in another part of the world. In these advanced configurations, multiple interconnected CPUs may be required. These configurations are often referred to as *centralized, client-server,* and *distributed.* Control system professionals use these terms for one or many processes.

A centralized system consists of a single CPU and many devices and is the most common configuration in the field.

Figure 15-4 shows a configuration known as *client-server.* If the control or server CPU fails, the client CPU also fails because it cannot receive instructions from the primary CPU. The client CPU can act like a pass-through. In other words, the client CPU is receiving control from the actions of the GUI connected to the control CPU. In Figure 15-4, the client has no associated control surface or GUI (touch panel, button pad, UI), so it relays only the commands from the control CPU.

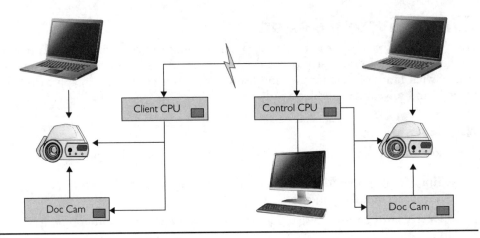

Figure 15-4 Client-server configuration

The configuration shown in Figure 15-5 is known as *distributed processing*. It has multiple independent systems linked together by a data network. If the network link fails, each system can still function independently, but the tasks between the systems are lost.

 NOTE The figures display CPU configurations, not signal flows or wiring schemes.

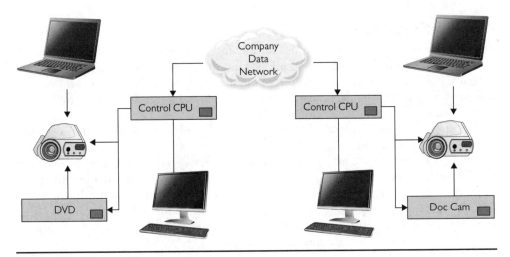

Figure 15-5 Distributed processing

Programming for Control

After they understand which devices the client needs to control, AV professionals draw or write out how these devices can be controlled with control points. This step includes transferring the list of devices and device actions to a *control functions script*.

A control functions script is an itemized list of devices to be controlled that helps to organize what needs to be done by everyone on the project, such as the client, programmers, designers, and facility engineers. It contains the required actions for each device and interconnection information, such as the control point and connector type. Some of the items on the list may not be AV related (for example, drapes, lights, and temperature sensors).

A control functions script also assists the designer in creating a control system that meets the required client needs. AV professionals discuss the control functions script and sketches with the client to receive their approval of the overall system functionality.

Establishing Control Points

In some cases, the design is complex and requires a careful selection of control points, such as in a system that consists of a large number of conference microphones, simultaneous interpretation systems, or voting systems. Regardless of the project complexity, AV professionals should refer to the approved control functions script and choose control points that most efficiently meet the design need.

Once the control points are selected, the control function script should be updated to reflect the choice. The next step in the process is to verify that the design can be implemented.

Verifying System Performance

During the system's performance verification, AV professionals ensure that devices can be controlled correctly and that the system matches up with the client's narrative. It is important to stay informed about product changes. For example, a user might not be able to control a device using a previous version of a control point three months after the implementation.

Communicate the verification results to the client, even if the system passes the verification test. Refer to ANSI/INFOCOMM 10:2013, *Audiovisual Systems Performance and Verification,* and the related guide for more information on how you can test your system's performance.

Finally, start formally designing your control systems around what you've discovered from the previous steps. This way, the problems will be taken care of and you won't have to re-design the system.

Chapter Review

In this chapter, you learned that the success of a control systems project largely depends on the choices you as an AV professional make. If your control system focuses on human behavior first and technology second, then users will be even more empowered to take advantage of all they have to offer.

PART IV

You also learned that when designing a control system, things can get pretty complex. It's especially important to establish a good rapport with clients and the users and communicate the project progress and changes on a regular basis. The next chapter will cover network design for AV systems, which you will also find useful for control system design.

Review Questions

The following questions are based on the content covered in this chapter and are intended to help reinforce the knowledge you have assimilated. These questions are not extracted from the CTS-D exam nor are they necessarily CTS-D practice exam questions. For an official CTS-D practice exam, see the accompanying CD.

1. Which of the following is a type of control system?

   A. Computer-driven

   B. Cloud-based

   C. Habitual learning

   D. All of the above

2. Which of the following control system components is used to control multiple zones and devices by performing a series of automatic and independent functions?

   A. Control interface

   B. Control point

   C. Central processing unit

   D. Control system software

3. What is the purpose of mapping in human-centered interface design?

   A. Communicate the results of an action

   B. Communicate what the design can or cannot do

   C. Lay out the design for clear understanding

   D. Signal what actions are possible and how they should be done

4. Which CPU configuration has multiple independent systems linked together by a data network?

   A. Client-server

   B. Centralized

   C. Scattered

   D. Distributed

5. What list helps to organize what needs to be done by everyone on the project?

    A. System component list

    B. Control functions script

    C. Materials list

    D. Control object list

Answers

1. **D.** Control systems can be computer-driven, cloud-based, or habitual-learning systems.

2. **C.** A central processing unit is the part of a control system used to control multiple zones and devices by performing a series of automatic and independent functions.

3. **C.** The purpose of mapping during human-centered interface design is to lay out the design so it's easier to understand.

4. **D.** A distributed CPU configuration includes multiple independent systems linked together by a data network.

5. **B.** A control functions script lists the devices to be controlled and helps organize what needs to be done by the client, programmers, designers, and facility engineers.

CHAPTER 16

Networking for AV

In this chapter, you will learn about
- Common networking components
- The layers of the Open Systems Interconnection model and the functions of each layer
- Common physical network connections and their capabilities
- The function and capabilities of Ethernet technologies
- The function and capabilities of Internet Protocol technologies
- The pros and cons of various Internet Protocol address assignment methods
- The differences between Transmission Control Protocol and Universal Datagram Protocol
- The characteristics of Audio Video Bridging/Time-Sensitive Networking, EtherSound, Cobranet, Dante, and HDBaseT protocols

You know about the audio and video technologies that form the core of the AV industry. More and more, though, those AV technologies rely on IT technologies to work. Modern AV systems use IT networks to support their systems in all kinds of ways. Technicians can monitor, control, and troubleshoot devices over the network. AV content is stored on the network. Audio and video signals can be distributed over network infrastructure in real time.

Realizing the potential of networked AV systems requires you to work closely with IT professionals. You need to be able to "talk the talk" to explain your needs and understand their concerns. In this chapter, you'll get an overview of networking technologies and gain an understanding of your networking needs so you can communicate them better to your IT counterparts.

Domain Check

This chapter relates directly to the following tasks on the CTS-D Exam Content Outline:

- Domain A Task 2: Identify skill level of end users
- Domain A Task 3: Educate the AV client
- Domain A Task 7: Research clients' business environment
- Domain A Task 8: Define AV needs (absolutes)
- Domain A Task 9: Identify scope of work
- Domain B Task 6: Coordinate IT and network security criteria
- Domain B Task 8: Coordinate life safety and security criteria
- Domain C Task 1: Create draft AV design
- Domain C Task 2: Confirm site conditions
- Domain C Task 4: Produce AV system documentation

These tasks comprise 44 percent of the exam (about 55 questions). This chapter may also relate to other tasks.

What Is a Network?

A network can consist of anything that is interconnected in a netlike manner or that is linked together to pass information. In the IT world, *network* is generally short for "computer network" or "data network."

All networks consist of two basic parts: nodes and connections. Nodes are the devices that send and receive data. In the early days of networking, a node was basically a computer. Today, a node can be a computer, a mobile device, a video server, a projector, a control panel, or some other electronic system capable of sharing data.

Connections are the means by which data travels from one node to another. They can be any signal-transmission medium: radio frequency, copper cabling, light, and so on. For our purposes, passive devices, such as patch panels, also fall into this category.

The nodes use circuit switching or packet switching to transfer data across the network. A *circuit-switched network* sends data in a continuous stream. No other devices can use the channel while the connection is active. The public switched telephone network (PSTN) is a circuit-switched network. A dedicated connection is made between two phones. Even if no one is actually talking (in other words, no data is being sent), no one else can use that channel. Circuit-switched networks provide reliable, dedicated links. But if you have a large number of devices that need to communicate with each other, circuit-switched networks are inefficient.

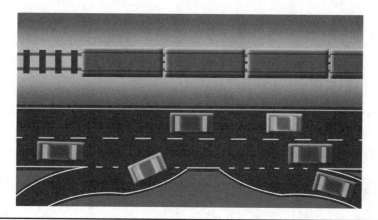

Figure 16-1 Circuit-switched networks are like a train (top); packet-switched networks resemble a highway.

By dividing data into smaller chunks, or packets, several nodes can send information on the same channel at the same time. No single device can monopolize the connection. Put another way, a circuit-switched connection is like a railroad between two cities. A train (data) can travel from one city to the other, but nothing else can use the railroad at the same time. A *packet-switched connection* is like a highway with many on- and off-ramps. Cars (packets) of various sizes can get on and off the highway at different points. See Figure 16-1 for help in visualizing the difference between circuit-switched and packet-switched networks.

Network Components

Beyond nodes and connections, network components (Figure 16-2) can be broken down into the following:

- Clients (for example, personal computers [PCs], laptops, handhelds) and servers
- Network interface cards (NICs)
- Switches (for example, an Ethernet switch), routers (for example, an Internet Protocol [IP] router), and gateways
- Wired or wireless links
- Protocols (for example, IP or Transfer Control Protocol [TCP])
- Applications (in other words, network services)

PART IV

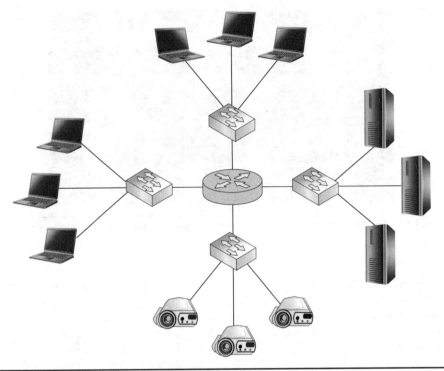

Figure 16-2   Network components: clients, servers, routers, and switches

Of these components, clients, servers, NICs, switches, routers, gateways, and links are considered hardware, while protocols and applications are considered software parts of a network. In this section, we will cover hardware components and focus on protocols later in the chapter.

Clients and Servers

Nearly all networks of significant size use servers to share resources among connected nodes. You've just learned that a server is a type of network hardware. To be more precise, a server isn't really a piece of hardware. Rather, it's a role a piece of hardware can play. If a piece of computer hardware does nothing but provide services, that computer is called a *server*. The term *server* can also refer to a program that runs on a computer along-side other programs. In a client-server network architecture, a server provides services to dependent nodes. It does resource-intensive or remotely hosted tasks that those nodes can't perform for themselves.

Servers of larger networks usually are hosted on many separate computers. Organizations may host several servers on each computer, or they can have a dedicated computer for each service. A computer whose only task is to perform a particular service is known as a *thin server*. A thin server is a server that offers only one service. Typically,

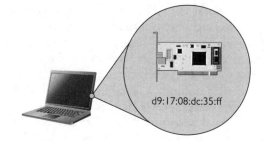

Figure 16-3
A network interface card and its sample media access control address

d9:17:08:dc:35:ff

a thin server resides on a dedicated computer configured with only the functionality required to perform the service. This increases the resources available for the server's dedicated task. It also minimizes the risk that a malicious intruder could exploit one of the operating system's unused features. It's typically a good idea to turn off any features you never use to ensure that no one else can.

Network Interface Cards

Every device that connects to the network must have a *network interface card* and associated *media access control* (MAC) address (see Figure 16-3).

A NIC is an interface that allows you to connect a device to a network. At one time, most devices had a separate card or adapter. Today, though, NICs are typically integrated into the device's main circuitry.

A MAC address is the actual hardware address, or number, of your NIC device. Every device has a globally unique MAC address that identifies its connection on the network. MAC addresses use a 48-bit number expressed as six groups of two hexadecimal numbers, separated by a hyphen or colon. The first part of the number indicates the manufacturer, and the second part of the number is a serial number for the product or circuit component.

Some devices will have more than one NIC, particularly if they need to connect to multiple networks, such as both a secure classified network and an unsecure public network. It is similar in the case of devices that are wired or wireless; both connections would require a NIC.

Let's now review the roles and differences between some common networking devices: switches, routers, gateways, and servers.

Switches, Routers, and Gateways

A *network switch* provides a physical connection between multiple devices. As each device is connected, the switch collects and stores its MAC address. This allows devices connected to the same switch to communicate directly with each other via Ethernet, using only MAC addresses to locate each other.

Unmanaged switches have no configuration options; you just plug in a device, and it connects. *Managed switches* allow the network technician to adjust port speeds, set up

PART IV

virtual local area networks (VLANs), configure quality of service, monitor traffic, and so on. Managed switches are more common than unmanaged switches in modern corporate and campus environments. Unmanaged switches are still used in some AV installations to allow for some basic network connections within their environment(s).

A *router* forwards data between devices that are not directly physically connected. They mark the border between a local area network (LAN) and a wide area network (WAN). Once traffic leaves a LAN (that is, travels beyond the switch), routers direct it until it reaches its final destination. When data arrives at a router, it examines the packet's logical address—the IP address—to determine its final destination or next stop.

A *gateway* is a router that connects a private network to outside networks. All data that travels to the Internet must pass through a gateway. Routers below the gateway will forward packets destined for any device that can't be found on the private network to the gateway. When traffic arrives from outside the private network, the gateway forwards it to the appropriate router below. Gateways also translate data from one protocol to another. See Figure 16-4 for an idea of how gateways, routers, and switches sit in a network.

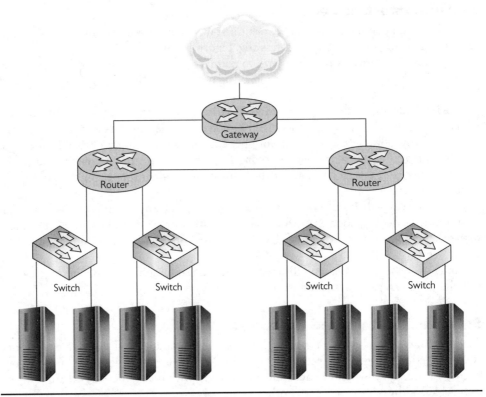

Figure 16-4   A gateway, router, and switches in a network

Figure 16-5
A common home network router combines three functionalities.

Blended Devices

Gateways, routers, and switches do not have to be physically separate devices. Much like an audio digital signal processor (DSP) that combines the separate functions of a mixer, equalizer, compressor/limiter, and so on, networking devices often include several roles in a single box. For example, routers often include the functionality of a switch. On your home network, you probably don't have a separate gateway, router, and switch. In fact, you may have only one router, which acts as both your gateway to the Internet and a switch directing traffic among the devices on your home network (see Figure 16-5).

Links

There are a lot of different physical technologies used to transport data over long distances for wide area networks: T1 lines, coaxial cable, satellite, DSL, and so on. The network connections that AV professionals have to deal with directly, though, are primarily those used within local area networks—the physical connections within a system or building. For local area network connections, the three most common physical transmission methods are as follows:

- Over copper, as voltage
- Over glass, as visible light
- Over air, as radio frequencies

Of course, it's not as simple as it sounds. Within each transmission medium, there are several options. One copper wire network cable may have very different capabilities, limitations, and internal design than another. The same is true for fiber and wireless networks. As an AV professional, you should know which medium is best for your application and why.

Twisted-Pair Cabling

As an AV professional, you are likely to encounter only the twisted-pair cabling in networking, which is available in several categories. These categories, abbreviated Cat, are Ethernet standards under the TIA/EIA-568 standard. They are also referred to as *class* cables. In most LANs, you're likely to encounter only Cat 5e and Cat 6.

Cat 5e Cabling Category 5e (Cat 5e) is the designation for 100-ohm unshielded twisted pair. It is associated with connecting hardware specified for data transmission up to 100 megabits per second (Mbps). It adds specifications for far-end crosstalk to the obsolete Cat 5 standard.

Cat 6 Cabling   The conductors in Cat 6 cables have more twists per inch. They also operate at a high speed (measured in gigabits per second), which means they have high frequencies with tiny wavelengths. All of this means that Cat 6 cables are susceptible to noise. Therefore, Cat 6 cables ought to be shielded for delivery of AV signals.

Cat 6a is an augmented form of Cat 6 cables capable of 10 gigabits per second (Gbps) data transmission. These high-frequency transmissions have to account for alien crosstalk (AXT), noise of unknown origin that can't be canceled out by active equipment like typical near and far-end crosstalk. Cat 6a cables are designed to compensate for AXT, but even so, UTP Cat 6a shouldn't be used for cable runs of more than 180.4 ft (55 m) and should be bundled loosely to limit crosstalk. STP Cat 6a cable has better protection against electromagnetic interference (EMI) and radio frequency interference (RFI) and can, therefore, be used on longer cable runs. Cat 6a is usually used to "future proof" systems more in today's commercial market.

Optical Fiber Cabling

Optical fiber is a glass medium used for transmitting modulated light from point A to point B. The makeup of optical fiber cabling (Figure 16-6) is simple.

- The core is glass medium, used to carry the light.
- Each core is surrounded by cladding, which is used to reflect the light back onto the core, keeping the signal moving down the optical fiber.
- The final layer is the coating, which protects the optical fiber from damage.

Optical fiber cabling offers high bandwidth and maintains total electrical isolation. Such characteristics allow optical fiber to maintain signal integrity in noisy environments, experiencing little signal degradation over long distances. Furthermore, optical fiber cabling is immune to EMI and RFI. Optical fiber lines are also popular for security reasons. They do not burn, withstanding aging and corrosion. Also, it is much more difficult to covertly capture data from an optical fiber line than from copper wires or radio waves. You have to physically intercept the path of the light to intercept data.

Single-Mode and Multimode Optical Fiber Cabling   There are two modes, or paths of light, behind optical fiber, known as *single-mode* and *multimode*. You should think of single-mode as a straight shot; the light path is small in diameter, which makes the signal path mostly straight, with some of the signals bouncing off the walls of the glass.

Figure 16-6
Optical fiber
cabling

Multimode is a little bit different. Some of the signal goes straight down the fiber while the rest of the signal bounces off the cladding. Because the signals are not shooting straight down the cable like they are in single-mode, the signals will take longer to reach the end of the fiber, and some light will disperse as it travels. As a result, network data can typically travel farther over single-mode than multimode.

Popular Fiber Connectors   Several types of connectors are available for optical fiber cables. Currently, the straight-tip (ST), Lucent (LC), and subscriber (SC) connectors are the most popular for the AV market.

- **ST connector**   The ST connector can be found on transmitter-receiver equipment and is similar to the Bayonet Neill-Concelman (BNC) connector. The ST connector is a bayonet connector, meaning that all you have to do is "stab and twist" to lock it into place, which keeps the optical fiber and ferrule from rotating during connection. This connector can be used on both single-mode and multimode fiber.

- **LC connector**   The LC connector is much smaller in diameter than the ST and is used for basic wiring applications. It has low loss qualities and is known as a "push, pull" connector.

- **SC connector**   The SC connector is larger in diameter than the LC. It is a "stab and click" connector, which means that when the connector is pushed in or pulled out, there is an audible click because of the attachment lock. This connector is useful for tight spaces.

Wireless Connections

Aside from wired connections, you're likely to encounter wireless connections in the field, especially with clients who want to control devices or send content wirelessly over the network.

The wireless connection known as Wi-Fi is defined by the Institute of Electrical and Electronics Engineers (IEEE) 802.11 standard and has been revised several times to keep up with the growing demands for wireless communication. The speed of a Wi-Fi connection depends on the radio frequency (RF) signal strength and the revision of 802.11 with which you connect. As signal strength weakens, the speed of the connection slows. The number of users accessing the wireless devices also affects connection speed. Wi-Fi versions a, g, and n, shown in Table 16-1, are the most commonly used in the field today.

Revision	Frequency Band	Typical Throughput	Max Throughput
802.11a	5 GHz	27 Mbps	72 Mbps
802.11b	2.4 GHz	~5 Mbps	11 Mbps
802.11g	2.4 GHz	~22 Mbps	54 Mbps
802.11n	5 GHz and/or 2.4 GHz	~144 Mbps	600 Mbps
802.11ac	5 GHz	866 Mbps to 2.5 Gbps	6.7 Gbps (theoretical)

Table 16-1   Wi-Fi Versions

Wi-Fi is extremely popular, both among users and among manufacturers. It is difficult to find laptops and desktops today that do not have wireless technology incorporated into them from the factory. Computer manufacturers assume users would rather connect wirelessly than via a network cable. This might be true for the home user. For the enterprise network, however, Wi-Fi can create more problems than it solves. Before choosing Wi-Fi as a physical connection medium, you should carefully weigh its advantages and disadvantages.

Wi-Fi Advantages   Wi-Fi is convenient, allows users great flexibility, and is less expensive than wired connections. It's also become one of customer expectations. Users expect to be able to walk into a meeting room or presentation space and launch a presentation from their laptops, tablets, or mobile phones. You could try to address this requirement by providing a connection for every device imaginable. Or, you could let users connect to the presentation system using an ad hoc Wi-Fi network. In this and many other cases, Wi-Fi just seems easier. The following are some of the reasons for the popularity of Wi-Fi:

- **It's convenient.** Wireless hotspots are everywhere. If your device is Wi-Fi capable, you can nearly always find a way to connect to the network.

- **The convenience of Wi-Fi encourages mobility and, therefore, productivity.** Workers could walk to a park, sit in a cafeteria, or ride in an airplane and still conduct business. Their work could feasibly be accomplished from anywhere.

- **It requires little infrastructure.** A wireless network is as simple as pulling an access point out of a box and plugging it into the wall. Most wireless access points are sold with a functional default installation. They're as close as a network gets to "plug and play."

- **It's scalable.** If you need to add more client nodes to a wireless network, all you have to do is add more access points.

- **It's cheap.** With copper or optical fiber networks, you have to buy the cables and connectors, pull them, install wall jacks, and incorporate switches and patch panels. With Wi-Fi, all you need is an access point.

Wi-Fi Disadvantages   Wi-Fi has a lot of potential benefits. The list of disadvantages associated with using Wi-Fi is shorter, but the disadvantages themselves are potentially catastrophic. For some applications, you simply can't use Wi-Fi. The following are the limitations of Wi-Fi:

- **Its range is limited.** Restrictions on the range of Wi-Fi devices are established by the 802.11 equipment standards and the U.S. Federal Communication Commission (FCC).

- **It's susceptible to RFI.** Interference from other wireless sources can hamper Wi-Fi performance.

- **Equipment selection and placement can be tricky.** Proper placement, antenna selection, and signal strength are key. Building construction materials impact RF propagation. Some construction materials will dampen RF signals. Others act as reflectors, enhancing signal quality.

- **It may turn out to be expensive.** Though a Wi-Fi network may seem inexpensive at first, you may find yourself purchasing additional repeaters or highly directional antennas to expand the network's range. The cost of building an extended wireless network can grow quickly.

- **It's slow.** The best Wi-Fi on the market is slower than most existing wired networks. If you need to stream live high-definition video, Wi-Fi is not a dependable option.

- **It's insecure.** Wi-Fi networks are far more susceptible to malicious attacks than wired networks because it's so easy for devices to connect. For this reason, they are often severely restricted or completely prohibited in certain business, financial, and government/military facilities.

- **The 2.4 GHz frequency is widely used in both commercial and consumer situations.** Many commonly used devices that people use every day could be utilizing this frequency.

The OSI Model

If you've studied networking, you've probably heard of the OSI model. The *Open Systems Interconnection* (OSI) model provides a mental map for the transfer of data across a network. It was created in the early days of digital networking to present a common language for the technology designers and manufacturers. The OSI model can be used to describe the functions of any networking hardware or software, regardless of equipment, vendor, or application.

As the field has matured, it has become harder to fit networking technologies into the strict categories of the OSI model. Many operate at several different layers. Still, the OSI model provides a useful shorthand for discussing networking software and devices. You'll often hear networking professionals and manufacturers talk about the layer at which a technology operates or the layer at which a problem is occurring. This section will talk you through the layers of the OSI model to help you better understand that conversation.

The OSI model is often used to describe the purpose or functionality of networking protocols, software, or devices. Knowing the OSI layer (or layers) at which a technology operates can be useful in several ways. The OSI model can do the following:

- **Tell you what a technology does and when those events occur in the data transfer process.** For instance, Application layer error checking occurs at the host and may be aware of the kinds of errors that really matter to the software application. Transport layer error checking has no awareness of the application; it just looks for any missing packets.

- **Provide a roadmap for troubleshooting data transfer errors.** The OSI model describes the signal flow of networked data. Just as you would use a signal flow diagram to troubleshoot a display system in a conference room, checking at each point in the path, you can troubleshoot a network by observing the data transfer process one layer at a time.
- **Indicate which service providers are responsible for each stage of data transfer.** Layers of the OSI model often represent a service provider handoff. For instance, an AV technology manager may be responsible for layer 1 and 2 devices and layers 5–7 software, while the network manager controls all layer 3 and layer 4 technology.

The OSI model uses a stack of layers to communicate or transmit a file from one computer to the next.

- Layers 1–3, known as the *media layers,* define hardware-oriented functions such as routing, switching, and cable specifications. These are the areas that most concern AV professionals because they're the ones that affect us directly.
- Layers 4–7, the *host layers,* define the software that implements network services. Each layer contains a broad set of protocols and standards that regulate a certain portion of the data transfer process. A data transfer on any given network likely uses several different protocols at each layer to communicate. Layer 4, the transport layer, is also important to AV professionals because it's where the transition between gear and software occurs. This layer tells the media layers which applications are sending the data. It also divides and monitors host layer data for transport.

Data is sent across a network by applications. That means when a computer sends a message, that message starts out at layer 7, the Application layer, and moves down through the OSI model until it leaves the sending device on layer 1, the physical layer.

The data travels to the receiving device on layer 1 and then moves up through the OSI model until it can be interpreted by the receiving device at layer 7, the Application layer. Let's define each of these layers, starting where the connection starts: layer 1.

OSI Model Layers

The OSI model is broken down into seven layers (see Figure 16-7).

- Layer 1 is the physical layer. The devices need to be plugged in to work. The physical layer can be copper, optical fiber, and, yes, even RF (because it requires a signal that needs to be received). The physical layer sends and receives electrons, light, or electromagnetic flux.
- Layer 2 is the interface to the physical layer; it uses frames of information to talk back and forth. The addressing scheme is MAC addresses. One MAC address talks to another MAC address. Switches use layer 2 and send and receive frames.

- Layer 3 is packet-based. Packets "ride" inside layer 2 frames. Layer 3 adds IP addressing. Routers can send, receive, and route IP addresses.

- Layer 4 works with ports. Ports are generally associated with firewalls. These ports are virtual ports and can be found at the end of an IP address such as 192.168.1.35:80. The :80 is the port number. Port 80 is generally associated with web or Hypertext Transfer Protocol (HTTP) traffic. Routers can also route ports, but for this simplistic discussion, it helps to use firewalls to set the stage.

- Layer 5 controls (starts, stops, monitors, and keeps track of) layers 4 and 3. For example, Real Time Streaming Protocol (RTSP) keeps track of the User Datagram Protocol (UDP) layer 3 traffic. It keeps track of whether the data makes it to the far end. UDP can't do that on its own; it needs a session protocol to do the work for it.

- Layer 6 opens up or transcodes between the session and the application. It is a kind of go-between. Data encryption and decryption are at this layer as well. An application can't talk data directly; it needs an interpreter, and this is it.

- Layer 7 is the application layer or the layer with which the human interacts. Using the streaming example, it is Windows Media Player. The application has the controls to manipulate the output of audio and video. It takes all the layers for a player application to retrieve the stream and play it on your desktop.

PART IV

Layer	Name	Carries	Sent to/from	Device/Function
L7	Application	Data	Application Protocols	Programs (HTTP, FTP, Email, Etc.)
L6	Presentation	Data	Data Translation Protocols	Encryption
L5	Session	Data	Session Protocols	Session
L4	Transport	Segments	Ports	Firewalls
L3	Network	IP Packets	IP Addresses	Routers
L2	Data Link	Ethernet Frames	MAC Addresses	Switches
L1	Physical	Electrons	NIC, Wire	Copper/Fiber/RF

Figure 16-7   Open Systems Interconnection layer tasks

No layer is skipped or bypassed. When troubleshooting, all layers need to be considered.

 TIP This simple mnemonic can help you remember the names of all the layers of the OSI model, from one to seven: Please Do Not Throw Sausage Pizza Away. This stands for the following:

- **P**hysical
- **D**ata Link
- **N**etwork
- **T**ransport
- **S**ession
- **P**resentation
- **A**pplication

Network Types and Topologies

When people refer to networking today, they're usually talking about a small subset of networks—packet-switched data networks. Primarily, these are ones that use Ethernet and Internet Protocol technology. Even within that narrow definition, there are different types of packet-switched networks, including the following:

- Local area networks (LANs)
- Wide area networks (WANs)
- Campus area networks (CANs)
- Metropolitan area networks (MANs)
- Personal area networks (PANs)

One of the most important characteristics of any given network is its topology. Network topology helps to determine how far data must travel to reach its destination. What path must it take? How many stops will there be along the way? Topology also bears on which network connections carry the most traffic and helps AV professionals figure out how to send AV signals over a network. Network topologies fall into two basic categories: physical topologies and logical topologies.

The *physical topology* is the "way it is wired" or how it is physically connected together. Physical topology maps the physical placement of each network device and the cable installation path. Where will the devices and cables actually be? Physical topology is constrained by the actual space the network equipment occupies.

The *logical topology* depicts electrical routing and control of data. Even though you have physically connected everything, do you really want to send all the data to all devices? Most likely not. You want to find a solution that is most efficient and moves data quickly. The logical topology is how you manage the data routes. Physical and logical topologies are like a team, and changing one player can affect what happens in the field.

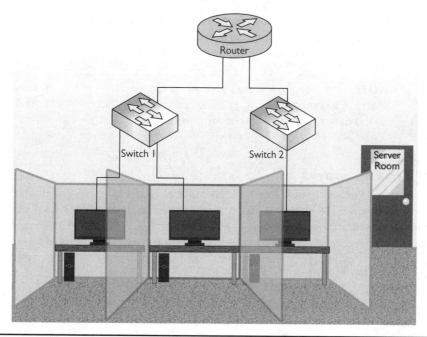

Figure 16-8 Sample logical network topology

Logical topology (Figure 16-8) maps the flow of data within a network. Which network segments and devices must data pass through to get from its source to its destination? Logical topology is not defined or constrained by physical topology. Two networks with the same physical topologies could have completely different logical topologies, and vice versa.

So, what can you learn from looking at a network's topology? Topology reveals how many devices data has to pass through before it gets to its destination—in other words, how many hops are between each device. Many real-time AV protocols have a limited number of allowable hops, usually fewer than ten. When you look at hops, you also see which devices the data has to pass through. A lot of real-time AV protocols can't travel over WANs; if the topology indicates that data has to pass through a router to get from one device to another, you know you have a problem.

Topology also shows which devices and connections have to handle the most data. This helps network engineers figure out which parts of their network need the most capacity.

Finally, topology can show where a network's weak spots are. When you look at a LAN topology, you should always look for single points of failure. A single point of failure is any one device whose failure will cause the entire system to fail. A single point of failure could be any device that a number of other devices depend on. For example, it could be a network switch that lots of other devices use to communicate, or it could be an audio digital signal processor (DSP that handles inputs and outputs from lots of other devices).

Whenever possible, you want to make single point-of-failure devices redundant, so if one fails, another device is ready and waiting to take its place. As a best practice, no more than 20 devices should be affected by any one single point of failure.

NOTE Connections, as well as devices, can be points of failure. It doesn't matter if a device is working perfectly if the cable that connects the device to the network is damaged beyond working.

Local Area Networks

Data sent across a network must be sent to an address. That address will be either physical or logical. Networks are classified according to whether nodes use physical or logical addresses to communicate.

Local area networks use physical addresses to communicate. As mentioned earlier in this chapter, the LAN's physical address is the MAC address, hard-coded into each node. LANs are usually privately owned and operated. They are fast and high capacity. Most real-time AV network protocols—for example, Audio Video Bridging/Time-Sensitive Networking, EtherSound, and CobraNet (discussed further in this chapter)—are designed for LAN speeds/capacity.

LANs require devices to be directly, physically connected (see Figure 16-9). This requirement effectively limits their geographical size. You can send an electrical signal only so far before it degrades beyond use.

Stated simply, data travels across a LAN as follows:

1. Data sent across a LAN is addressed to the MAC address of one of the devices on the LAN.

2. A switch receives the packet and examines the MAC address to which it is addressed.

3. The switch forwards the packet to the appropriate device.

Figure 16-9
Sample local area network

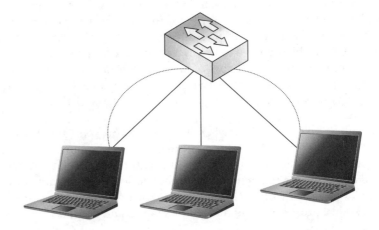

Local Area Network Topologies

Devices can be connected on a LAN in several ways.

- In a *star topology*, all nodes connect to a central point, such as a router, switch, or hub. Star networks are hierarchical. Each node has access to the other nodes through the central point. If any one node fails, information still flows. The central device is a single point of failure; if it fails, communication stops.

- Star topologies are often extended to include more than one layer of hierarchy. This is known as an *extended star topology*. If any device fails, access to the devices below is cut off, but the rest of the network continues to work. The central device remains a single point of failure; if it fails, communication stops.

- In a *mesh topology*, each node connects to every other node. Mesh topologies provide fast communication and excellent redundancy, ensuring that the failure of no one device can bring down the whole network. Providing physical connections between every device is really expensive, though. Fully meshed networks are rare.

- In a *partial mesh topology*, each node connects to several other nodes, but not all. Partial mesh topologies provide good redundancy, ensuring that several devices must fail at the same time before communications cease.

Ethernet

Ethernet is the standard for how data is sent across LANs from one connected device to another.

Ethernet has become the de facto standard for LANs. The IEEE 802.3 Ethernet standards define a data frame format, network design requirements, and physical transport requirements for Ethernet networks. When IP data is sent across a LAN, it is encapsulated inside an Ethernet frame. The Ethernet frame (Figure 16-10) is generated by the device's NIC. The frame has a header and a footer that surround the packet, which ensures that the packet will arrive intact at its destination.

The following types of Ethernet are in use today (Figure 16-11):

- 10 Mbps Ethernet
- 100 Mbps Ethernet
- 1 Gbps Ethernet
- 10 Gbps Ethernet
- 40/100 Gbps Ethernet

Each of these types of Ethernet has its own capabilities, intended applications, and physical requirements. You're only likely to encounter 10 Mbps Ethernet on legacy systems. The 100 Mbps Ethernet technologies are backward compatible with 10 Mbps, though. That means you will often see 100 Mbps referred to as 10/100 Mbps Ethernet technologies in the field. The 40/100 Gbps Ethernet is a fairly young technology and

Figure 16-10
An Ethernet frame generated by a device's network interface card

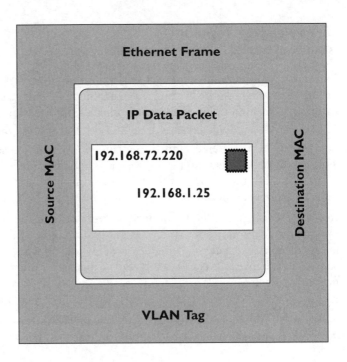

primarily intended for use as a network backbone—to connect networking devices such as routers and switches to each other, or for use by Internet service providers, rather than to connect individual client nodes to a switch. As a result, you may not work with much 40/100 Gbps Ethernet in the field.

The type of Ethernet your device sends out depends on the capability of its NIC. Not every device can handle sending and receiving data at a rate of 1 Gbps or more. Remember, the overall speed of your Ethernet connection is no faster than the slowest link in its path.

Figure 16-11
Ethernet types in use today

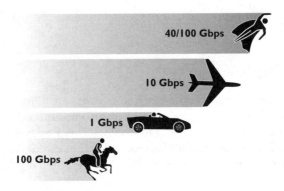

Ethernet technologies are interoperable. A frame can originate on a 100 Mbps Ethernet connection and later travel over a 1 Gbps or 10 Gbps Ethernet backbone. As a general rule, you need a faster technology to aggregate multiple slower links. If your end nodes communicate with their switches by using 100 Mbps Ethernet, the next layer of the network hierarchy may need to be 1 Gbps Ethernet, and so forth. As devices become capable of faster network speeds, even faster backbones will be required.

The IEEE released its first Ethernet standard, 802.3, in 1985. The original Ethernet standard was for 10 Mbps data transportation. "Classic Ethernet," as 10 Mbps Ethernet is sometimes called, was originally designed to operate in half-duplex because it predates switching technology. However, today you can find 10Base-T implementations that use switches to achieve full-duplex communication.

You may still see classic Ethernet in use in the field. It's sometimes used to connect end nodes such as computers and printers to switches or, in older networks, hubs. The network access equipment (for example, switches, routers, hubs, and so on) and heavily used shared resources such as servers are then connected to each other using a faster backbone.

10 Mbps Ethernet   10 Mbps Ethernet (Table 16-2) was originally designed to be transported on coaxial cable. The Ethernet standards that relied on coax cable are now considered obsolete. Like faster forms of Ethernet, classic Ethernet now runs mostly on twisted-pair Cat cable. On a campus network, optical fiber cable can also be used to span the distance between buildings.

Fast Ethernet   IEEE approved the standard for 100 Mbps Ethernet in 1995. The 100 Mbps Ethernet is also known as Fast Ethernet (see Figure 16-12). Fast Ethernet can operate in either full-duplex mode, using switches, or half-duplex, using hubs. Fast Ethernet is commonly used both to connect end nodes to switches and hubs and to connect network access equipment and servers to each other. In larger or more traffic-heavy networks, though, Fast Ethernet is not fast enough for the network backbone.

Fast Ethernet was originally designed to be backward compatible with classic Ethernet.

It uses the same frame structure and can operate over the same optical fiber and twisted-pair cables, though coaxial isn't an option. The idea was to allow networks to upgrade to Fast Ethernet without having to replace their entire cable infrastructure and all their existing devices.

However, using Cat 3 cables for Fast Ethernet is pretty limiting. Fast Ethernet over Cat 3 can operate only in half-duplex mode. Over Cat 5, Fast Ethernet can operate in half- or full-duplex. Also, when Fast Ethernet came out, existing NICs and hubs couldn't handle the faster data rates over Cat 3 cabling without the help of expensive

Ethernet Type	Physical Medium	Max Distance Between Nodes
10Base-T	Cat 3 or higher copper twisted pair	328 feet (100 m)
10Base-FL	62.5/125 micrometer (µm) multimode optical fiber, 850 nm wavelength	6,560 feet (2000 m)

Table 16-2   10 Mbps Ethernet Characteristics

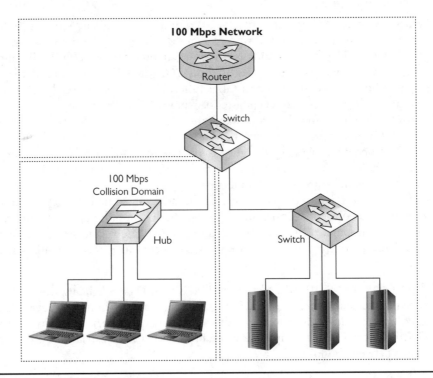

Figure 16-12 100 Mbps or Fast Ethernet

processing electronics. They could handle Fast Ethernet over higher-performing Cat 5 cables, though. Because many companies found upgrading their cables cheaper than purchasing new equipment, Fast Ethernet led to the widespread adoption of Cat 5 cable infrastructures. See Table 16-3 for further characteristics.

Ethernet Type	Physical Medium	Max Distance Between Nodes
100Base-T4	Cat 3 twisted-pair cable, using all four pairs	328 ft (100 m)
100Base-T2	Cat 3 twisted-pair cable, using two pairs	328 ft (100 m)
100Base-TX	Cat 5 twisted-pair cable or better, using two pairs	328 ft (100 m)
100Base-FX	62.5/125 μm multimode optical fiber, 1300 nm wavelength	6,560 ft (2000 m) for full-duplex; 1,352 (412 m) for half-duplex
100Base-SX	62.5/125 μm multimode optical fiber, 850 nm wavelength	1,804 ft (550 m)

Table 16-3 100 Mbps Ethernet Characteristics

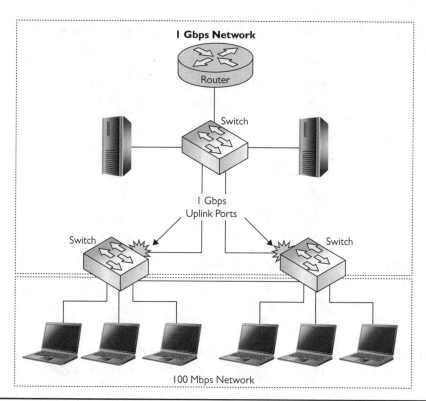

Figure 16-13 1 Gbps Ethernet

Gigabit Ethernet IEEE approved the standard for 1 Gbps Ethernet over fiber, 802.3z, in 1998. 1 Gbps Ethernet over copper, 802.3ab, followed in 1999. 1 Gbps Ethernet is also known as Gigabit Ethernet (Figure 16-13).

Some end nodes have NICs capable of Gigabit Ethernet transportation, and some don't. You'll see it used to connect end nodes to switches when required and possible, but more often, Gigabit Ethernet is deployed as a network backbone. That means it's used to connect network access equipment, such as switches and routers, and servers with Gigabit Ethernet NICs. Gigabit Ethernet is practically always implemented in full-duplex mode. Though it's technically possible to run Gigabit Ethernet in half-duplex, many network equipment manufacturers don't even make gigabit hubs—only switches.

Like Fast Ethernet, Gigabit Ethernet was designed for backward compatibility. It can run over the same multimode fiber and Cat 5 cabling as Fast Ethernet. However, unlike 10Base-T or 100Base-TX, Gigabit Ethernet over Cat 5 uses all four pairs in the cable to transmit and receive data (see Table 16-4). Gigabit Ethernet standards also allow single-mode fiber, enabling even longer distances. Gigabit Ethernet also uses four-conductor shielded cables, terminated with a DB-9 or RJ45 connector, for specific purposes, such as connecting blade servers to switches.

Ethernet Type	Physical Medium	Max Distance Between Nodes
1000Base-T	Cat 5 twisted-pair cable or better, using four pairs	328 ft (100 m)
1000Base-TX	Cat 6 twisted-pair cable, using two pairs	328 ft (100 m)
1000Base-CX	Four-conductor balanced shielded twisted pair	82 ft (25 m)
1000Base-SX	Two options: 62.5/125 μm multimode optical fiber 50/125 μm multimode optical fiber 850 nanometer (nm) wavelength	Depending on fiber type: 62.5/125 μm, up to 902 ft (275 m) 50/125 μm, up to 1804 ft (550 m)
1000Base-LX	Three options: 62.5/125 μm multimode optical fiber 50/125 μm multimode optical fibers Single mode optical fiber 1300 nm wavelength	Depending on fiber type: 62.5/125 μm, 1804 ft (550 m) 50/125 μm, 1804 ft (550 m) Single-mode, 3.1 miles (5 km)
1000Base-LX10	Single-mode optical fiber, 1300 nm wavelength	6.2 miles (10 km)

Table 16-4 1 Gbps Ethernet Characteristics

10 Gigabit Ethernet IEEE approved the standard for 10 Gbps Ethernet over fiber, 802.3ae, in 2002. The 10 Gbps Ethernet over copper, 802.3an, followed in 2006. The 10 Gigabit Ethernet operates only in full-duplex. It's primarily intended for use as a backbone to connect switches to each other. The 10 Gigabit Ethernet dramatically increased the range of Ethernet connections, enabling Internet service providers (ISPs) to use Ethernet as a WAN technology for the first time. The 10 Gigabit Ethernet can be used to do the following:

- Connect multiple switches within a LAN
- Interconnect clusters of servers
- Connect an organization directly to an ISP site
- Connect switches within an ISP network

Originally, 10 Gigabit Ethernet was designed to run on fiber over long distances. Eventually, standards for running 10 Gigabit Ethernet over copper emerged. First came short-reach, four-conductor cabling used primarily for connections within data closets—switch to switch or server to switch. Eventually, though, 10 Gigabit Ethernet also adapted the simple, ubiquitous, and inexpensive Cat cable. As in other applications, the range of 10 Gigabit Ethernet over Cat cable is significantly shorter than the range over fiber. As such, 10 Gigabit Ethernet over Cat cable isn't really intended for use as a long-range network backbone. Instead, its purpose is to provide links between server clusters in a data center—a communication pathway for supercomputers. See Table 16-5 for physical medium characteristics.

Ethernet Type	Physical Medium	Max Distance Between Nodes
10GBaseT	Cat 5e twisted-pair cable or better	328 ft (100 m) for shielded; 180 ft (55 m) for unshielded
10GBaseCX4	Four-conductor balanced shielded twisted pair	49 ft (15 m)
10GBaseS	50/125 μm multimode optical fiber, 800 nm wavelength	213 ft (65 m)

10GBaseLX4	Two options:
	  62.5/125 μm multimode optical fiber
	  9 μm single mode optical fibers
	  1310 nm wavelength
		Depends on fiber type:
		  62.5/125 μm, 984 ft (300 m)
		  Single-mode, 6.2 miles (10 km)

10GBaseLR	9 μm single mode optical fiber, 1310 nm wavelength	6.2 miles (10 km)
10GBaseER	9 μm single-mode optical fiber, 1550 nm wavelength	24.8 miles (40 km)

Table 16-5　10 Gigabit Ethernet Characteristics

40/100 Gbps Ethernet　IEEE approved a single standard for 40 Gbps and 100 Gbps Ethernet over fiber, 802.3ba, in 2010. Like 10 Gigabit Ethernet, 40/100 Gigabit Ethernet operates only in full-duplex. Again, the main purpose of the new standard is to aggregate slower connections. Recall that connections generally need to be aggregated by an even faster connection. As the use of 10 Gigabit Ethernet grows, 40/100 Gigabit Ethernet networks will be required to aggregate multiple 10 Gigabit nodes. In general, 40 Gigabit Ethernet is intended for uses in data center applications. The 100 Gigabit Ethernet is intended for aggregating 10 Gigabit Ethernet switches and providing ISP and network backbones.

As of this writing, the only available physical media for 40/100 Gbps Ethernet are fiber and four-conductor, balanced, shielded twisted pair (see Table 16-6). If history is any indication, though, Cat cabling standards won't be too far behind.

Ethernet Type	Physical Medium	Max Distance Between Nodes
40GBase-CR4	Four-conductor, balanced, shielded twisted pair	32 ft (10 meters)

40GBase-SR4	Two options:
	  OM3 multimode optical fiber
	  OM4 multimode optical fiber
		Depending on fiber type:
		  OM3, 328 ft (100 m)
		  OM4, 125 ft (410 m)

40GBase-LR4	Single-mode optical fiber	6.2 miles (10 km)
100GBBase-CR10	Four-conductor balanced shielded twisted pair	32 ft (10 meters)

100GBase-SR10	Two options:
	  OM3 multimode optical fiber
	  OM4 multimode optical fiber
		Depending on fiber type:
		  OM3, 328 ft (100 m)
		  OM4, 125 ft (410 m)

100GBase-LR4	Single-mode optical fiber	6.2 miles (10 km)
100GBase-ER4	Single-mode optical fiber	24.8 miles (40 km)

Table 16-6　40/100 Gbps Ethernet Characteristics

PART IV

Figure 16-14
Isolating LAN
devices

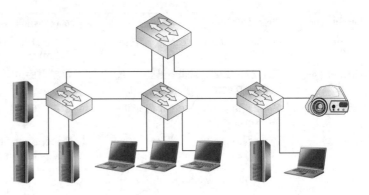

Isolating Local Area Network Devices

You don't always want all the devices on a LAN to be able to communicate directly via Ethernet. Sometimes, you want to ensure that certain devices have access only to one another and that outside devices can't easily talk to them.

This may be for security reasons. Some servers or devices host sensitive information that other devices shouldn't be able to access.

You may also want to isolate certain groups of devices to limit the traffic they receive (see Figure 16-14). All networked devices send out occasional administrative messages, called *broadcast messages,* that go to every other device on the LAN. Sometimes, you want to limit the amount of broadcast traffic a group of devices receives.

The need to limit traffic is particularly relevant to certain networked audio and video implementations. AV traffic is time sensitive. For some AV protocols, broadcast traffic from non-AV devices on the LAN is enough to cause serious quality problems. You need a way to put these devices in a cone of silence, shutting out traffic from outside the AV system.

You can simply get dedicated switches for your AV system, isolating it on its own physical LAN. This is a simple and popular solution to the problem, and sometimes it's the only feasible option.

Virtual Local Area Networks

Potentially, though, an isolated physical LAN lets existing IT infrastructure go to waste. There is a way to isolate devices on a LAN from other devices connected to the network, shutting out their broadcast traffic. You can place the devices in a *virtual local area network.* VLANs can be configured on managed switches—the MAC addresses of the devices are associated with the VLANs they belong to. When the switch forwards data from a device in a VLAN, it adds the VLAN identifier to the Ethernet frame.

VLANs aren't related to a network's physical layout. Devices in a VLAN can be connected to different switches in completely different physical locations. As long as those switches are in the same LAN (in other words, they don't have to go through a router to contact each other), the devices can be placed in a VLAN together.

Because VLANs are virtual, you can even place a device on more than one VLAN. Devices in a VLAN can send each other Ethernet traffic directly. They also receive each other's broadcast traffic. They don't receive any broadcast traffic from the other devices on the LAN.

They also can't communicate with devices outside the VLAN via Ethernet. Traffic in and out of the VLAN has to go all the way through the router.

Virtual Local Area Network Uses   Because the communication among devices on a VLAN is typically switched rather than routed, it's very efficient. Devices in separate physical locations that need to communicate mostly with each other should be on a VLAN. This makes their traffic more efficient while keeping it out of the way of other data.

Digital signage is a great VLAN application example. If you have a campuswide deployment of signs that all draw their content from a centrally located digital signage player, those devices probably belong on a VLAN. You're unlikely to need to access other systems such as file servers or mail servers from your signage player or displays. Still, if you do want to send information from a database or directory to your signs, they can still be accessed via the router.

Some AV data link protocols don't play well with others. CobraNet, for instance, is not designed to share network segments with other types of data. Placing all CobraNet devices on a single VLAN, however, isolates them on a broadcast domain. This leverages the existing physical infrastructure while putting the CobraNet traffic in virtual solitary confinement. (See "Data Link Layer Protocols" in this chapter for more information about AV data link protocols.)

Requesting Virtual Local Area Networks   If you determine that a system should be segregated on a VLAN, for either its own good or that of the network, you'll need to provide the network manager with the following information:

- What VLAN you want to create and why (for example, "I want to create an IPTV VLAN so that the network isn't flooded with streaming video traffic")
- Which devices should be included in the VLAN
- Whether any routing between the VLAN and other network locations is required or allowed

This information should all be documented as part of your system device inventory.

Wide Area Networks

A *wide area network* is a network that connects one or more LANs together (Figure 16-15). WANs use logical addresses to communicate. The form a logical address takes depends on the type of WAN. However, for the purposes of this course—and most modern WANs— the logical address is an Internet Protocol address. An IP address is assigned to a device, either manually or automatically. It may be permanently assigned, or it may change over time. It may or may not be unique.

Figure 16-15
Sample wide
area network

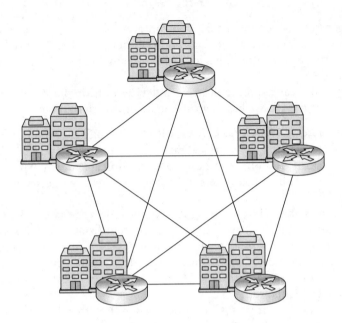

The nodes on a WAN are routers. If a LAN is connected to outside networks via a WAN, a router sits at the top of its network hierarchy. Any data that needs to travel to a device outside the LAN gets forwarded to the router. The router strips the packet of identifying LAN information, such as the MAC address of the originating device, before forwarding the packet to its intended IP address. This protects the devices on the LAN.

A WAN can be any size. It may connect two LANs within the same building. It may span the entire globe, like the world's largest WAN, the Internet. Unlike LAN connections, long-distance WAN connections are rarely privately owned. Usually, WAN connections are leased from ISPs. The speed and capacity of a WAN connection are often tied directly to how much you pay for it.

WAN communications travel farther than LAN communications. As a result, they're slower—maybe only by a fraction of a second. In live audio and video transmission, however, second fragments matter. As a result, many networked AV protocols can't travel over WANs.

Wide Area Network Topologies

WAN topologies can also be placed into a few common categories.

- **Hub and spoke** In a hub-and-spoke WAN, each LAN connects to a central location. For example, several branch offices may connect to a corporate headquarters. Like a star LAN, a hub-and-spoke WAN may have several layers of hierarchy, with several hubs connecting to several spokes.

- **Common carrier**   In a common carrier WAN, each LAN site runs a spoke to an ISP backbone.

- **Mesh**   In a fully meshed WAN, every LAN connects to every other LAN. This provides excellent redundancy.

One of the major advantages of networking is the ability to share resources. When examining a WAN topology, try to identify the best place to locate shared resources. In a hub-and-spoke topology, shared resources should be located at the hub. In a common carrier topology, the enterprise may choose to lease space at the ISP and host shared resources there, or it may choose to pay for a lot of bandwidth to and from one of its sites and locate resources there. In a mesh WAN topology, resource location is generally accomplished by building a network map, including the data throughput of all connections, and locating resources "in the middle."

Shared AV resources, such as streaming servers or multipoint control units (MCUs), will ideally be stored in the same physical location as shared IT resources. In some cases, however, you may not have access to IT server closets for security reasons.

Virtual Private Networks

Almost any large or physically dispersed organization will require some way to hold managed communication between its LANs. Services that are particularly necessary for AV applications, such as quality of service (QoS), low latency, managed routing, and multicast transmission, are impossible over the open Internet. Customers and service providers also commonly need a secure means of accessing systems remotely for monitoring, troubleshooting, and control purposes. Virtual private networks (VPNs) provide a way.

A VPN uses the Internet to create a tunnel between two or more LANs. VPNs are used to create virtual WANs and for remote monitoring, troubleshooting, and control. VPNs are typically controlled and configured by the enterprise network administrator. Each host requires the proper software, access rights, and password to log into the client network.

VPNs are often built into security devices such as firewalls. Organizations using VPNs at scale may require dedicated VPN devices. Using a VPN increases required bandwidth overhead as well, because an encryption and tunneling wrapper must be added to each packet. This additional overhead may not be significant in terms of bandwidth requirements, but it can increase the Ethernet frame size to the point where packets must be fragmented before they can be sent across the network. Packet fragmentation can be disastrous for the quality of streamed video or conferences. Always be sure your frame size is set low enough to account for VPN overhead.

There are different types of VPNs, each with their own characteristics.

Layer 2 Tunneling Protocol

Layer 2 Tunneling Protocol has the following characteristics:

- Client devices must have client software installed.

- It can transport both IP and non-IP data.

- It monitors data integrity, authenticates data origin, and protects against data "capture and replay."
- It can introduce significant latency.
- It is not commonly used in newer systems.

Internet Protocol Security

Internet Protocol Security (IPSec) has the following characteristics:

- Client devices must have client software installed.
- It is an IP-based protocol, and it provides security for any IP transport protocol (TCP, UDP, Internet Control Message Protocol [ICMP], and so on).
- It can authenticate and encrypt, or just authenticate, based on need.
- It assigns remote devices an internal address upon connection, making them effectively on the LAN.
- Remote clients have access to the same devices and resources they would on-premise.
- Client software may manage clients by requiring them to have antivirus software or a host-based firewall.
- It is commonly used for site-to-site connections.

Secure Sockets Layer

Secure Sockets Layer (SSL) has the following characteristics:

- No client software is needed—the client accesses the VPN via a web browser.
- It requires a dedicated SSL VPN server.
- It's an IP-based protocol (TCP only).
- It does not require an internal address.
- It acts as a proxy allowing only authorized users to access only approved resources; access can be configured on an individual user basis.
- It's common for mobile user–to-site connections.

Multi-protocol Label-Switching VPNs

Many of the protocols used to transport AV data over layer 2, the Data Link layer, cannot be routed over layer 3, the Network layer. This limits their scalability and prevents them from taking advantage of network layer functions such as data prioritization. Multi-protocol Label Switching (MPLS) is a "layer 2.5" technology that combines layer 2 flexibility with IP network functionality.

MPLS is a networking protocol that allows any combination of Data Link layer protocols to be transported over any type of Network layer. MPLS routes data by examining each packet's MPLS label without examining packet contents. Implementing MPLS improves interoperability and routing speed.

MPLS is frequently used to allow access to IP services over ATM networks, and vice versa. MPLS incorporates QoS class-of-service tags and network tunneling technologies. MPLS service providers therefore frequently offer MPLS-based VPNs as a service.

Many small-to-medium organizations choose to purchase VPN services directly from their MPLS ISP. There are several different options for MPLS-based VPNs, including the following:

- **Virtual Leased Lines (VLLs),** a layer 2 protocol that uses IP tunneling to create a virtual point-to-point connection

- **Virtual Private Routed Networks (VPRNs),** a layer 3 protocol that imitates private IP-based leased-line wide area networks

MPLS-based VPNs put the burden of designing and maintaining the WAN topology on the ISP. They also provide some degree of QoS. VLL and VPLS allow the user to transport a variety of data link frames over the MPLS core network, not just IP packets. MPLS VPNs require a permanent connection between customer-edge and provider-edge routers; they can't be used by mobile clients.

Network Layer Protocols

Once AV data joins other data on a routed WAN, Network layer protocols take care of logical addressing, routing, and, in some cases, prioritizing data as it moves from device to device. The rise of the Internet has made the Internet Protocol the de facto Network layer protocol for enterprise applications and networked AV systems.

Internet Protocol

IP is the postal service of the Internet that sets rules for how to package and address mail. If you don't include the right information in the address, it won't be delivered. If you don't package it correctly, it will get damaged in transit. Just like the postal service, IP assumes responsibility for making sure your data arrives at its destination, although, just like with the postal service, some messages do get "lost in transit." The IP covers several crucial functions that make WAN networking possible. IP defines the following:

- **Addressing**   Rules for how each system is identified, what the addresses look like, and who is allowed to use which addresses

- **Packaging**   What information must be included with each data packet

- **Fragmenting**   How big each packet can be and how overly large packets will be divided
- **Routing**   What path packets will take from their source to their destination

Internet Protocol Addresses

An IP address is the logical address that allows devices to locate each other anywhere in the world, no matter where they are physically. An IP address requires three distinct components.

- **Network identifier bits**   These bits identify the network. They help the IP packet find its destination LAN. The network bits are always the first digits in an IP address.
- **Host identifier bits**   These bits identify a specific node. They help the IP packet find its actual destination device. The host bits are always the last bits or least significant bits in a network address.
- **Subnet mask**   These bits tell you which bits in the IP address are the network bits and which bits are the host bits. The subnet mask also reveals the size of the network. The subnet mask is a separate address that must be included with the IP address.

IP addresses can look very different depending on which version of the Internet Protocol was used to create them. There are two versions of IP currently in use: version 4 (IPv4) and version 6 (IPv6).

IP functionality differs depending on which version is implemented, as shown in Table 16-7.

Internet Protocol Version 4 Addressing

IPv4 addressing was originally defined in 1980, in the IETF standard RFC 760. IPv4 is being slowly phased out in favor of IPv6. The fact remains that while the world will eventually need to transfer to IPv6, this hasn't happened yet and appears to be a long way from happening. IPv4 is still the most prevalent Internet addressing scheme, so you need to be familiar with its structure.

An IPv4 address consists of four, 8-bit groups, or *bytes*. Those bytes are usually expressed as decimal numbers separated by dots—dot-decimal notation. Hence, an IP address looks like this:

192.168.1.25

Remember, each of those decimal numbers actually represents 8 bits. That same address, written in binary, looks like this:

11000000 10101000 00000001 00011001

The entire range of IPv4 addresses includes every possibility from all 0s to all 1s. In dot decimal notation, that range is expressed as follows:

0.0.0.0 to 255.255.255.255

Name	Characteristics	Defined by
IPv4	• Addresses devices using four 8-bit binary octets. • A limited number of possible addresses. • Many devices may connect to a network using a single IP address via NAT. • IPSec, QoS, and multicast are handled separately from the IPv4 address. • Configured either manually or via DHCP. • Supports a 576-byte minimum packet size. • Packets may be fragmented. Example: 192.168.1.25	The IETF document RFC 791: http://tools.ietf.org/html/rfc791
IPv6	• Addresses devices using eight 16-bit binary octets. • Displayed as eight groups of four hexadecimal digits. • Includes MAC address. • Includes native support for IPSec, QoS, and multicast. • Configured automatically, without the use of DCHP. • Supports a 1,280-byte minimum unfragmented packet size. Example: FEDC:BA98:7654:3210:FEDC:BA98:7654:3210	The IETF document RFC 2460: http://www.ietf.org/rfc/rfc2460.txt

Table 16-7   Internet Protocol Functionalities by Version

In total, there are almost 4.3 billion possible IPv4 addresses. Several of these addresses are reserved for specific purposes, but that's still a lot of possible addresses. Unfortunately, 4.3 billion addresses aren't enough. Think about it—there are 7 billion people in the world. About 2.4 billion of those have Internet access. Now consider how many different Internet-connected devices you use in a day. Three? Four? More? This is why IPv4 is being phased out—it's not big enough for today's Internet.

Internet Protocol Version 4 Subnet Masks   Looking at an IPv4 address (Figure 16-16), how can you tell which bits identify the network and which bits identify the host? To interpret any IPv4 address, you need a separate 32-bit number called a *netmask,* or subnet mask.

A subnet mask is a binary number whose bits correspond to IP addresses on a network. Bits equal to 1 in a subnet mask indicate that the corresponding bits in the IP address identify the network. Bits equal to 0 in a subnet mask indicate that the corresponding bits in the IP address identify the host. IP addresses with the same network identifier bits as identified by the subnet mask are on the same subnetsubnet.

For example, subnet mask 255.255.255.0 indicates that the first three octets of any corresponding IP addresses are the network address and the last octet is the host address.

	Network ID	Host ID
IPv4 Address: 192.168.1.25 =	11000000.10101000.00000001.	00011001
IPv4 Subnet: 255.255.255.0 =	11111111.11111111.11111111.	00000000

Figure 16-16   Internet Protocol version 4 subnet mask

In its structure, an IPv4 netmask looks a lot like an IPv4 address. It consists of four bytes, expressed in dot-decimal notation. A subnet mask could be written something like this:

225.255.255.0

When you write the netmask out in binary, though, you can see the difference between an IPv4 netmask and address. A netmask never alternates 1s and 0s. The first part of the netmask will be all 1s. The second part of the netmask will be all 0s. Written in binary, the previous subnet mask would be as follows:

11111111 11111111 11111111 00000000

Used in combination with an IP address, the netmask identifies which bits in the IP address are the network identifier bits and which are the host bits. All the devices on the same network have the same network identifier bits in their IP addresses. Only the host bits will differ.

IPv4 Subnet Notation   In IPv4, there are two ways to express a subnet mask.

- You can write it out as its own full, dot decimal number.
- Or you can attach it to the end of an IP address using *Classless Inter-Domain Routing* (CIDR) notation. CIDR notation is just a slash, followed by a number. The number tells you how many of the address bits are network bits (any remaining bits are host bits).

CIDR notation is basically just a shorthand. 255.244.192.0 and /18 are two different ways of writing the same subnet mask. In binary, both are equal to 11111111 11111111 11000000 00000000.

Internet Protocol Version 6 Addressing

An IPv6 address consists of 16 bytes—that's four times as long as an IPv4 address. Because IPv6 addresses are so long, they are usually written in eight, four-character hexadecimal "words," separated by a colon. Since each hexadecimal character represents 4 bits, each word represents 16 bits. In IPv6 (see Figure 16-17), here's what the characters represent:

- The first three hexadecimal words are the network identifier bits.
- The next hexadecimal word identifies the subnet.
- The final four hexadecimal words are the host identifier bits.

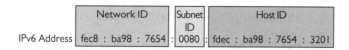

Figure 16-17   Internet Protocol version 6 address

Note that the host identifier portion of an IPv6 address is long enough to include a MAC address. IPv6 can actually use a device's MAC address as the host identifier. Some IPv6 implementations even do this automatically. Because a MAC address uniquely identifies a device, using the MAC address as the host identifier should ensure that no two devices ever have the same IPv6 address.

The IPv6 subnet mask isn't really there to tell you which bits identify the network and which bits identify the host. It's there to allow you to subdivide the network. You always have 48 bits to identify the network and 64 bits to identify the host. That means that under IPv6, there are more than 281 trillion different possible network addresses. Each network address can have more than 18 quintillion unique hosts. That's an unimaginably large number. We're not going to run out of IPv6 addresses any time soon.

IPv6 Subnet Masks   IPv6 still has netmasks, but the netmask "masks" only a certain part of the address. An IPv6 subnet mask (Figure 16-18) can be written out in eight full hexadecimal words, but the first three words of the netmask will always be all 1s, and the last four will always be all 0s. As a result, many implementations of IPv6 allow you to enter the subnet mask as a single four-character hexadecimal word. The subnet mask seen here could be written as simply c000.

You can also express an IPv6 subnet mask using CIDR notation. The CIDR suffix for an IPv6 address will almost always be between /48 and /64.

Types of IP Addresses

In both IPv4 and IPv6, certain portions of the address range are set aside for specific purposes. As a result, there are several different types of IP addresses that all look pretty much the same. Experienced network professionals can tell what types of addresses they're dealing with by looking at them. If you can recognize an IP address's type, you'll be able to distinguish which addresses can be used to identify AV devices and which cannot.

The Internet Assigned Number Authority (IANA) is in charge of giving out IP addresses or reserving them for specific purposes. IANA maintains three categories of addresses: global, local, and reserved. Most of the reserved addresses are not routed on

Figure 16-18
Internet Protocol version 6 subnet mask

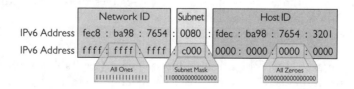

Network Address	Range	Routed?	Purpose
0.0.0.0/8	0.0.0.1 to 0.225.255.255.254	No	Used to identify an unknown IP address
10.0.0.0/8	10.0.0.0 to 10.255.255.254	No	Private network address range for large networks
127.0.0.0/8	127.0.0.0 to 127.255.255.254	No	Used as a loopback address for testing
169.254.0.0/16	169.254.0.0 to 169.254.255.254	No	Range of addresses used for automatic private IP addressing (APIPA), used in the absence of a static IP address or dynamic address assignment
172.16.0.0/12	172.16.0.0 to 172.31.255.254	No	Private network address range for medium to large networks
192.168.0.0/16	192.168.0.0 to 192.168.255.254	No	Private network address range for small to medium networks
224.0.0.0/4	224.0.0.0 to 239.255.255.254	Yes	Used for multicast communications
240.0.0.0/4	240.0.0.1 to 255.255.255.254	N/A	Reserved for experimental purposes /future use
255.255.255.255/32	255.255.255.255	No	Broadcast address used to talk to every host on a local network

Table 16-8   Reserved IPv4 Addresses

the public Internet. Table 16-8 shows the more important reserved IP addresses and their purposes.

Global Addresses   Most LANs connect to the Internet at some point. To access the Internet, you need a global IP address. That is, you need a public address that any other Internet-connected device can find. Global addresses go by many names in the networking community, including globally routable addresses, public addresses, or publicly routed addresses. IANA assigns global addresses upon request.

Any IP address that's not in one of the local or reserved address ranges can be a global address. Basically, global addresses are the "other" category. If an IP address isn't a local or reserved address, it's a global address.

Local Addresses   Not all devices need to access the Internet directly. Many devices need to communicate only with other devices on their LAN. This is particularly true for networked audio implementations. IANA reserves three IPv4 address ranges and one IPv6 address range for local networking.

The addresses in these ranges are private. Devices with private IP addresses can't access the Internet or communicate with devices on other networks directly.

There are three IPv4 private address ranges (see Table 16-9). The range you use depends on the size of your network. These ranges were defined before the development of CIDR, so the ranges correspond to the old address classes.

Network Size	Private Network	Address Range
Class A	10.0.0.0	10.0.0.1 through 10.255.255.254
Class B	172.16 to 31.0.0	172.16.0.1 through 172.31.255.254
Class C	192.168.0.0	192.168.0.1 through 192.168.255.254

Table 16-9 Internet Protocol Version 4 Private Address Ranges

If your network is so big that it would have required a Class A address under the old classful system, your IPv4 private address range will start with 10.x.x.x. If your network would have required a Class B address, your private address range will start with 172.16 to 31.x.x. Small networks use private addresses that start with 192.168.x.x.

The major advantage of private network addresses is that they are reusable. Global addresses have to be completely unique; no two organizations can use the same IP address to access the Internet. Otherwise, whenever data was sent to or from that address, there would be no way to know which network was intended. Since private addresses can't access the Internet, though, several different organizations can use the same private address range. Devices on different networks can have the same private IP address, because those devices will never try to talk to each other or to any of the same devices. As long as no devices on the same LAN have the same IP address, there's no confusion.

The obvious disadvantage of private addresses is that they can communicate only with devices on the same network. They can't be routed to the Internet. Initially, this made the networking community reluctant to use them. In 1994, the IETF introduced a new service that solved this problem: *network address translation* (NAT).

NAT is any method of altering IP address information in IP packet headers as the packet traverses a routing device. NAT is a TCP/IP service first defined in the IETF standard RFC 1631. The purpose of NAT is to resolve private IP addresses to public IP addresses, and vice versa, so that devices with private addresses can send data across the Internet. NAT is typically implemented as part of a firewall strategy. NAT operates at the Internet layer of the TCP/IP protocol stack and the Network layer of the OSI model.

NAT is typically implemented on devices at the edges of the LAN (for example, routers, web servers, or firewalls). When a device with a private IP address sends data to the public Internet, the data has to stop at one of these edge devices along the way. Before forwarding the packet, the edge device strips the private source IP address and replaces it with a global IP address. The edge device keeps track of all the data it forwards this way. Then, if any packet receives a reply from the Internet, the edge device can translate the global destination address back into the private IP address that should receive the data.

NAT has several advantages. First, it allows private IP addresses a way to access the Internet, limiting the demand for global addresses. Second, it limits the number of devices exposed to the Internet, enhancing security. Third, if you ever switch ISPs, you receive a new set of global IP addresses. Using NAT, you only have to configure the addresses of the edge devices. The private addresses don't have to change.

Broadcast Address In addition to private addresses, there are other types of addresses that can't or don't send data outside the LAN. One type of IPv4 address, when

Figure 16-19
Sample
broadcast
address

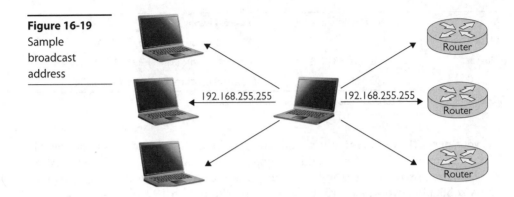

192.168.255.255

192.168.255.255

used as a destination address, will send the datagram to every device on the same network: the broadcast address (Figure 16-19).

Broadcast addresses are used as the destination IP address when one node wants to send an announcement to all network members. Broadcast messages are simplex—there's no mechanism for the other nodes to reply to the node that sent the message. An IPv4 broadcast address is any IPv4 address with all 1s in the host bits. When data is sent to that address, it goes to every device with the same network bits.

Loopback Address Both IPv4 and IPv6 have a special address type for testing devices: the loopback address. Sending data to a loopback address is like calling yourself. Data addressed to a loopback address is returned to the sending device. The loopback address is also known as the *localhost,* or simply *home.*

The loopback address is used for diagnostics and testing. It allows a technician to verify that the device he's using is receiving local network data. Essentially, it allows you to ping yourself. IPv4 and IPv6 each reserve specific addresses for loopback.

- IPv4 reserves 127.0.0.0 to 127.255.255.255 as loopback addresses. Any address in this range can be used, but most network devices automatically use 127.0.0.1 as their loopback address.
- IPv6 uses the address ::1 as the loopback address.

Subnetting

Subnetting divides a network into smaller networks (see Figure 16-20). Each smaller network is called a *subnet.* Subnets are created when the subnet mask is extended. Instead of stopping at the end of an octet, the 1s in the subnet mask spill over to the next octet.

For each bit the subnet mask is extended, the network is divided in half.

- If the subnet mask is extended one bit, you end up with two subnets.
- If the subnet mask is extended two bits, each subnet is divided again. You end up with four subnets.

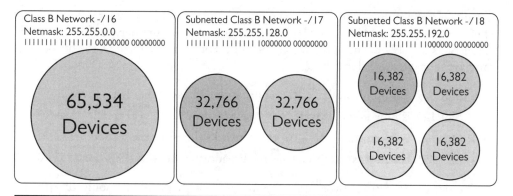

Figure 16-20   Subnetting a network

- As you divide the network, each subnet will be slightly less than half the size of the original network.

It's important for you to know about subnets because they affect how your devices communicate. For devices to communicate directly by Ethernet or belong to the same VLAN, they have to be in the same subnet.

Why do organizations subnet their networks? The main reason is to increase network efficiency. A subnet has fewer addresses than a full class network, so address resolution is faster. Fewer devices also mean less broadcast traffic—devices on a subnet receive broadcast messages only from other devices on the same subnet, not from the whole undivided network.

In certain cases, subnetting can also improve network security. For example, say you have a full class C address, with 254 possible global addresses, but only your router and your web server actually need direct Internet connections. You have 252 unused addresses lying around that someone could use to register their own device to your network. If you extend your subnet mask to /30, however, there are suddenly only two possible public addresses. Assign one to your web server and the other to your router, and there's no room for anyone else.

How Subnetting Works

A 192.168.1.x network with a subnet address of 255.255.255.0 has 256 possible unique addresses. You can think of this as 256 "slots" into which you can insert a device. The first slot, 192.168.1.0, is taken. This is the network address, and most switches won't allow you to assign it to a device. The last slot, 192.168.1.255, is taken as well. This is the broadcast address—it can't be assigned to a single device either. Any packets sent to this address go to every device on the network.

The remaining 254 slots can each contain a single device. All these devices can communicate with each other directly via Ethernet. When one of these devices sends broadcast traffic, it goes to all 254 devices.

You can subnet this network by changing the subnet mask to 255.255.255.128, or 11111111.11111111.11111111.10000000. Doing so splits the network in half at the center. Slots 0 to 127 are now in one network, and slots 128 to 255 are in the other. Now you have four unusable slots.

- **Slot 0 is still unavailable.**   It's the network address of the first network.
- **Slot 127 is now taken as well.**   It's the broadcast address of the first network.
- **Slot 128 is taken too.**   It's now the network address of the second network.
- **Slot 255 is still unavailable.**   It's the broadcast address of the second network.

The devices in each network can communicate with each other only directly via Ethernet. If the device in slot 1 wants to send a message to the device in slot 126, it can do so through the switch. If it wants to send a message to the device in slot 129, it must go through the router. Similarly, if the device in slot 1 sends a lot of broadcast traffic, only the devices in slots 1 to 126 receive it. The devices in slots 129 to 254 are in a different broadcast domain.

You can continue splitting the network into 4ths, 8ths, and so on, by extending the subnet mask. Each time you split the network, you halve the number of devices that can belong to each subnet, minus two slots for the newly created broadcast and network addresses.

IP Address Assignment

Every device that communicates across a TCP/IP network must have an IP address. Broadly speaking, there are two ways for a device to get an IP address. A device can be manually assigned a permanent address (static addressing), or it can be automatically loaned an address on an as-needed basis (dynamic addressing). Both ways play important roles in introducing AV systems to a network.

Although it requires thoughtful management, dynamic addressing requires less work in general. Instead of manually configuring an IP address for every connected device, nodes obtain addresses on their own. Because all the addressing is handled by computers, dynamic addressing avoids the risk of human error. Users won't fail to connect because someone typed an incorrect IP address.

Because it's easier to maintain, especially on larger networks, expect to see dynamic addressing used whenever possible. That said, not all devices support or should use dynamic addressing. Dynamic addresses, by nature, change. Therefore, if, for instance, you need a control system to always be able to locate a device by its IP address, you should assign that device a static address.

Assigning static addresses isn't hard. Each network operating system has its own tool for doing so. In addition, the individual device may also have a software interface that allows you to hard-code its static address. You need at least three pieces of information to manually assign an IP address: the device's MAC address, the IP address, and the subnet mask.

You might also need to know the address of the default gateway—that is, the address of the router that the device uses to access other networks. If the network uses the Domain

Name System (DNS), you also need the device's assigned domain name and DNS server. (See the section "Dynamic Name System" for more information.)

Where do you get all this information? Likely from the network manager or IT department. Whenever you add an AV system to a TCP/IP network, you'll work closely with your IT counterparts to discover and document your system's requirements. During that process, you'll let the IT department know which AV devices need IP addresses.

The IT department may give you a subnet mask and address range to use, or they may tell you specifically what address to use for each device. In either case, make sure both you and the IT department keep track of which IP addresses and MAC addresses are permanently associated with AV devices.

Static and Dynamic Addresses

Every device that communicates across a TCP/IP network must have an IP address. Broadly speaking, there are two ways for a device to get an IP address.

- The device can be manually assigned a permanent address. This is known as *static addressing*.

- The device can be automatically loaned an address on an as-needed basis. This is known as *dynamic addressing*.

Though it does require thoughtful management, dynamic addressing is less work in general. Instead of having to manually configure an IP address on every connected device, nodes obtain addresses on their own. Because all the addressing is handled by computers, dynamic addressing avoids the risk of human error. You won't fail to connect because of an incorrectly entered IP address.

Because it's easier to maintain, especially on larger networks, you can expect to see dynamic addressing used whenever possible. Not all devices support or should use dynamic addressing, though. Dynamic addresses can change. If, for instance, you need a control system to be able to locate a device by its IP address, you should assign the device a static address.

Static Addresses Assigning a static address to a device isn't hard. Each network operating system has its own tool for manually assigning addresses. The individual device may also have a software interface that allows you to hard-code its static address. You'll need at least three pieces of information to manually assign an IP address.

- The device's MAC address
- The IP address
- The subnet mask

You might also need to know the address of the default gateway—the address of the router the device uses to access other networks. If your network uses DNS, you'll also need the device's assigned domain name and DNS server.

PART IV

Manufacturer	Model #	Software Version	Firmware Version	MAC Address	IP Address	Subnet Mask	Gateway IP Address
ProjectTech	4000ZT	8.0	11.4.5	78:ab:0f:23:32:89:0c:7a	192.168.38.4	255.255.255.224	202.38.192.1

Table 16-10 Sample Static Internet Protocol Address List

Where do you get all this information? You'll need to work with the network manager or IT department. Whenever you add an AV system to a TCP/IP network, you'll work closely with your IT counterparts to discover and document the system's requirements. During that process, you'll let the IT department know what devices need static IP addresses. Be sure to specify that all the devices in the system should be on the same subnet. The IT department may give you a subnet mask and address range to use, or they may tell you specifically which address to use for each device. In either case, make sure both you and the IT department keep track of which IP addresses and MAC addresses are permanently associated.

You can document static IP address assignments using a table or spreadsheet like the one shown in Table 16-10. The AV team provides the information in the first four columns; the IT team provides the last three. You may want to include a lot more information in this spreadsheet, but these basics will help you and the IT department maintain the system and the network.

How Static Addressing Works Static addresses have to be manually entered into the device. The network manager has to document and manually keep track of which devices have static addresses and what addresses they have been assigned. If any two devices have the same addresses, most likely neither will work because of the conflict. As a result, keeping track of static addresses can be painful for network managers.

Dynamic Host Configuration Protocol

Dynamic Host Configuration Protocol (DHCP) is an IP addressing scheme that allows network administrators to automate address assignment. When a device connects to the network and the device has the "obtain IP address automatically" option activated, the DHCP service or server will take the MAC address of the device and assign an IP address to the MAC address. The pool of available IP addresses is based on the subnet size and the number of addresses that have been allocated already. Addresses are leased for a preset amount of time. After the lease time has expired, the address may be assigned to another device. The network administrator sets the amount of the lease time.

This is how an unknown device can connect to the Internet on a new network with no manual configuration. When you log onto the free Wi-Fi at a coffee shop or airport, your device is given an IP address on that network via DHCP. For DHCP to work, there must be a DHCP server on the network. One server can assign addresses to devices on multiple network segments—multiple subnets. That server keeps track of the following:

- The network's address range
- Which addresses are currently available

- Which addresses are currently in use by which devices
- The remaining lease time on each address

To use DHCP, a device must have the "obtain IP address automatically" option activated. When such a device starts up or tries to connect to the network for the first time, it will automatically request an IP address from the DHCP server. Provided the server has an address available, it will take the MAC address of the device and assign an IP address to that MAC address. Then, it will start the countdown on the address's lease time.

Dynamic Host Configuration Protocol Address Pool   The size of the available address pool depends on three factors.

- Size of the subnet the device is connecting to
- Number of addresses already in use
- Number of addresses reserved for another purpose

Once a device obtains an IP address from a DHCP server, it may or may not keep that address for a long time. The DHCP lease time is set by the network administrator. It could be three hours, three days, or thirty days—whatever the administrator thinks is appropriate. If the device renews its lease within the lease period, it gets to keep its address. If it doesn't—if it's moved to another network or is otherwise idle when its lease runs out—it will lose that address. The address goes back into the DHCP server's pool of available addresses. The next time that device connects to the network, it may or may not get the same address.

Dynamic Host Configuration Protocol Advantages   DHCP is simple to manage. If you move a device from one network or subnet to another, DHCP takes care of resetting the device's address and network settings for you. It ensures no two devices get the same address, which relieves potential conflicts. It allows more devices to connect to the network as the pool of addresses is continually updated and allocated. For example, a coffee shop may have thousands of customers using their Wi-Fi in the course of a week. Does that mean they need thousands of host addresses? Not with DHCP. With DHCP, you only need enough host addresses to cover the devices that are using the network at the same time.

The disadvantage to DHCP is that you never know what your IP address will be from connection to connection. If you need to reach a certain device by IP address, you must have a high level of confidence that the number will be there all the time, and DHCP may not give you that confidence.

How Dynamic Host Configuration Protocol Works   DHCP reserves a pool of slots to be leased for a given amount of time. The lease time is based on how many devices need addresses and how often those devices enter and leave the network. For example, at an airport, users log on and off the network at fairly quick intervals. A DHCP server's lease time there may be set to 15 minutes so that unused addresses are

PART IV

Figure 16-21
Illustrating
reserve
Dynamic Host
Configuration
Protocol

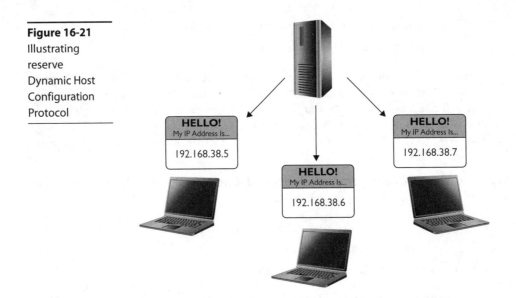

quickly surrendered back into the pool. At an office, however, the lease time may be much longer—10 or 24 hours.

Any device that requests an address from the DHCP server is assigned one from the pool. Once all the slots in the pool are occupied, no new devices can join until a lease expires. The areas above and below the DHCP pool may still be used for static addressing. Often network administrators block out several pools within a network for printers, servers, networking components, and so on.

Reserve Dynamic Host Configuration Protocol　Reserve DHCP (Figure 16-21) is a method of establishing static addresses on a DHCP server. Using reserve DHCP, a block of statically configured addresses can be set aside for devices whose IP addresses must always remain the same. The remaining addresses in the subnet will be assigned dynamically. The total pool of dynamic addresses is reduced by the number of reserved addresses.

To reserve addresses for AV devices, you need to list the MAC address of each device that requires a static address. The manually assigned static IP address and MAC address are entered into a table in the DHCP server. When the device connects to the network and reveals its MAC address, the DHCP server will see that the IP address is reserved for the device and enable it. The IP address cannot be given to any other device or MAC address.

Essentially, you're using your DHCP server to keep track of your manually configured settings. This allows you to keep all your address assignments—static and dynamic—in a single database. That way, you can avoid any risk of duplicate address allocation. If you manually configure the devices themselves instead of reserving their addresses through the DHCP server, the server doesn't know those addresses aren't available and may assign them to another device.

TIP If you have a DHCP server, it's best to use a hybrid approach rather than manually assigning an IP address to each AV device.

How Reserve Dynamic Host Configuration Protocol Works Reserved DHCP addresses are often preferred over static addresses because they are far easier to administer. A network administrator takes the device's MAC address and associates it with an IP address from within the DHCP pool on the DHCP server. This reserves the IP address and prevents it from being leased by another device. The device can then be set to obtain its address from the DHCP server. Every time it requests an address, it will be directed to the same slot. No static addressing at the individual device needs to occur.

 NOTE If the device is replaced, the MAC address needs to be reported and reconfigured on the DHCP server so that the new device can assume the old IP address.

Automatic Private Internet Protocol Addressing Sometimes, a device on a DHCP-enabled network can fail to get an address from a DHCP server. This can happen for a number of reasons.

- DHCP is not configured properly on the client.
- The DHCP server has exhausted the IP address pool.
- The DHCP server is improperly configured.
- The DHCP server has mechanically failed.
- DHCP services are bound to MAC addresses, and the client MAC address is not defined on the server.

If this happens, will the device be unable to use the network? Not necessarily. It won't be able to access other network segments or the Internet, but it may still be able to communicate with other devices on its own network segment using Automatic Private IP Addressing (APIPA).

APIPA is a form of link-local addressing defined in the IETF standard RFC 3927. APIPA automatically assigns locally routable addresses from the reserved network 169.254.0.0/16 to devices that do not have or cannot obtain an IP address. This allows devices to communicate with other devices on the same LAN. APIPA operates at the Network layer of the OSI model and the Internet layer of the TCP/IP protocol stack.

For APIPA to work, it must be enabled on the client device. If the device doesn't have an IP address and can't get one from the DHCP server, APIPA enables the device to assign itself an IPv4 address. This address must come from the reserved APIPA address range, 169.254.0.1 to 169.254.255.254. The addresses in the APIPA range are considered part of the private IP address scheme. That means they cannot be routed outside of the local network. Once a device has an APIPA address, it can communicate with other devices as long as they:

- Are on the same subnet
- Also have APIPA enabled

When a device has an IP address but can't connect to the Internet, network troubleshooters often look for link-local addresses like APIPA addresses.

Domain Name System

Devices on a network need to have unique identifiers. At the Data Link layer, devices are uniquely identified by their MAC addresses. At the Network layer, devices are uniquely identified by their IP addresses. But what if you want to find the same device over and over? Sending a message to that device's IP address won't necessarily work. The device's IP address may have changed; the lease on its old address could have run out, or the device may have been moved to another network. Even if the device has a static address, are you really going to remember that address? Committing long strings of characters to memory is easy for computers—they have hard drives for that. People need an easier way.

Naming services allow people to identify network resources by a name instead of a number. From the human perspective, names are a lot easier to understand than numeric, or alphanumeric, addresses.

DNS is the most widely used system for name-to-address resolution. If you use the Internet, you use DNS. The web addresses you type into a browser aren't actually addresses. They're DNS names. Every system that connects to the Internet must support DNS resolution.

A DNS is a hierarchical, distributed database that maps names to data such as IP addresses. A DNS server keeps track of all the equipment on the network and matches the equipment names so they can easily be located on the network or integrated into control and monitoring systems.

The goal of the DNS is to translate, or *resolve,* a name into a specific IP address. DNS relies on universal resolvability to work: Every name in a DNS must be unique so that information sent to a domain name arrives only at its intended destination.

DNS uses DNS servers to resolve names to addresses. The server contains a database of names and associated IP addresses. These servers are arranged in a hierarchy. Each server knows the names of the resources beneath them in the hierarchy and the name of the server directly above them in the hierarchy. If a server receives a request to resolve a name for a device beneath it, it can resolve that request itself. If it receives a request to resolve the name of an unfamiliar device, it will forward that request to the server above it. This is why DNS is known as a *distributed* database. No one device has to keep track of all the names and IP addresses on the Internet. That information is distributed across all the DNS servers on the network.

Internal Organizational DNS You don't need your own DNS server to resolve the names of web addresses on the Internet. You can do that through your ISP's DNS server. However, many organizations use DNS internally to manage the names and addresses of devices on their private networks. In this case, you will need your own DNS server. A DNS server is a software program. It runs on a computer. In fact, it can run on the same computer as your DHCP server. Usually, you will have a master DNS server and at least one secondary DNS server that runs a copy of the database stored on the master. This provides a backup in case the master ever fails. If an organization is really dispersed, you may want to locate a secondary DNS server at each physical site. This keeps DNS traffic off the WAN.

Using a service called dynamic DNS (DDNS), DNS can work hand in hand with DHCP. DDNS links and synchronizes the DHCP and DNS servers. Whenever a device's address changes, DDNS automatically updates the DNS server with the new address. When DHCP servers and DNS are working together, you may never need to know the IP address of a device—only its name. This makes managing the network simpler. The IP address does not need to be static. The entire addressing scheme could change without affecting the communication between devices.

A domain name has three main parts, from left to right (see Figure 16-22).

- A computer name or alias
- The domain itself
- The top-level domain (TLD)

A domain may be further divided into subdomains. This system helps prevent any two devices from being assigned the same name. Any number of computers may be called "www," as long as they belong to different domains.

A DNS is built of hierarchical text files called *resource records* (RRs). RRs can be difficult to maintain or change; doing so is usually the purview of a dedicated DNS administrator or service provider. RRs contain far more information than the domain name and associated IP address. For instance, they contain data class information that can be used as a load balancer; the DNS may round-robin web requests within a certain class. There are many different types of RRs. Service (SRV) records are particularly important. SRV records are used to identify which devices host specific services, such as Active Directory or the Session Initiation Protocol (SIP) server.

IP addresses may be dynamically assigned to domain names via DHCP. With dynamic DNS, you may never need to know the IP address of a device, only its name. Since the

Figure 16-22
Sample addressing scheme

IP address does not need to be static, this makes managing the network simpler. The entire addressing scheme could change without affecting the communication between devices.

DNS Adoption   The advantages of using DNS address assignment for a networked system seem obvious.

- Devices can be identified by easily remembered names.
- Dynamic DHCP makes control and remote monitoring systems much easier to maintain.
- DNS includes load balancing functionality.

The fact is, many AV devices still don't natively or fully support DNS address assignment. If you want to connect a device without native DNS support to a network with a DNS addressing scheme, the SRV records pointing to that device will have to be updated manually. DNS servers exist in a hierarchy, so if the device's SRV record isn't automatically published to every DNS server above it in the hierarchy, each server will have to be manually updated. If your device supports DHCP but not DNS, you're usually better off reserving a pool of DHCP addresses for your devices by MAC address than manually configuring the SRV records.

Since IPv6 is adopted alongside (and eventually replaces) IPv4, DNS should become more commonplace on AV devices. IPv6 addresses are simply too long and susceptible to errors to enter manually; IPv6 will likely force the widespread adoption of DNS.

Transport Layer Protocols

Layer 3, the Network layer, is responsible for assigning IP addresses to network devices and identifying paths from one network to another. The actual end-to-end transportation of data, however, is handled by layer 4, the Transport layer.

In the lower layers of the OSI model, each layer carries the layer above it. Physical layer technologies (layer 1) carry Ethernet frames (layer 2), which carry IP packets (layer 3). This is called *encapsulation*.

However, Transport layer protocols are not encapsulated inside IP packets. Instead, Transport layer protocols fragment IP packets into smaller chunks that fall within the maximum transmission unit (MTU) of the network connection. This process is known as *segmentation*. The transport protocol is responsible for segmenting data for transmission and reassembling it at its destination.

A transport protocol may be connection oriented or connectionless. Connection-oriented transport protocols are bi-directional. The source device waits for acknowledgment from the destination before sending data. It checks to see whether data has arrived before sending more. Connection-oriented transport includes things such as error checking and flow control to make sure data arrives as it should.

Connectionless communication is one-way. The source device sends data, which the destination device may or may not receive. Connectionless protocols are less reliable than connection-oriented protocols, but they are also faster. Many media-oriented

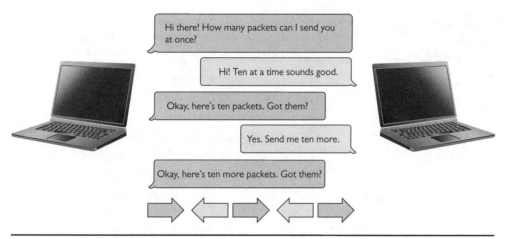

Figure 16-23   Transmission Control Protocol data transfer between two networked devices

applications, including practically all real-time protocols, use connectionless transport protocols.

In the TCP/IP protocol stack, Transmission Control Protocol is the most commonly used connection-oriented transport protocol; Universal Datagram Protocol is the most commonly used connectionless protocol. The two methods differ in speed and reliability. You must be able to identify—and in many cases decide—what kind of transport protocol your AV devices will use to send information over the network.

Transmission Control Protocol Transport

Transmission Control Protocol is a connection-oriented, reliable Transport layer protocol. TCP transport uses two-way communication to provide guaranteed delivery of information to a remote host (see Figure 16-23). It is connection-oriented, meaning it creates and verifies a connection with the remote host before sending it any data. It is reliable because it tracks each packet and ensures that it arrives intact. TCP is the most common transport protocol for sending data across the Internet.

TCP data transfer involves the following steps:

1. TCP communication starts with a "handshake" that establishes that the remote host is there and negotiates the terms of the connection; in other words, how many packets can be sent at once. The number of packets that can be sent together are referred to as a *sliding window.*

2. The origin device sends one sliding window at a time to the destination device.

3. The destination device acknowledges receipt of each sliding window, prompting the origin device to send the next one.

4. The sliding window can't move past a packet that hasn't been received and acknowledged. If any packets are damaged or lost in transmission, they will be re-sent before any new packets are sent.

Figure 16-24
Transmission
Control Protocol
stack

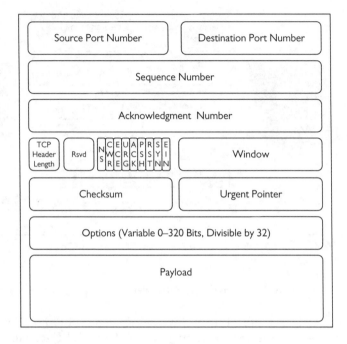

Figure 16-24 shows the TCP stack. Because TCP is reliable and connection-oriented, it's used for most Internet services, including HTTP, FTP, and Simple Mail Transfer Protocol (SMTP).

Universal Datagram Protocol Transport

TCP, the most common IP transport protocol, is reliable, but it can also be slow. UDP transport is designed to transmit information when timing is more important than missing packets.

Universal Datagram Protocol is a connectionless, unacknowledged Transport layer protocol. UDP begins sending data without attempting to verify the origin device's connection to the destination device and continues sending data packets without waiting for any acknowledgment of receipt (see Figure 16-25).

In UDP transport, it does the following:

- The origin computer does not attempt a "handshake" with the destination computer. It simply starts sending information.

- Packets are not tracked, and their delivery is not guaranteed. There is no sliding window.

UDP lacks TCP's inherent reliability. That doesn't mean all data transmitted using UDP is unreliable, though. Systems using UDP may manage reliability at a higher level of the OSI model, such as the Application layer.

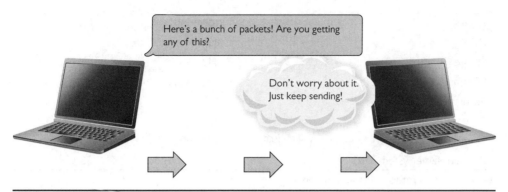

Figure 16-25 Universal Datagram Protocol communication between two devices

Figure 16-26 shows the UDP stack. UDP is used for streaming audio and video. When packets are lost in transport, UDP transport just skips over missing bits, inserting a split second of silence or a scrambled image instead of coming to a full stop and waiting for the packets to be re-sent.

UDP may also be used to exchange small pieces of information. In some cases, such as retrieving a DNS name, a TCP "handshake" takes more bits than the actual exchange of data. In such instances, it's more efficient to use the "connectionless" UDP transport.

Transmission Control Protocol vs. Universal Datagram Protocol

In TCP transport, the participants acknowledge one another, and there's a back-and-forth exchange to ensure that information is communicated clearly. With UDP transport, it is not clear how much of the message will get through to the intended recipient.

More specifically:

- TCP transport is used when the guaranteed delivery and accuracy or quality of the data being sent are most important, such as when sending control signals.

- UDP transport is used when speed and continuity are most important, such as during any real-time communications.

Figure 16-26
Universal
Datagram
Protocol stack

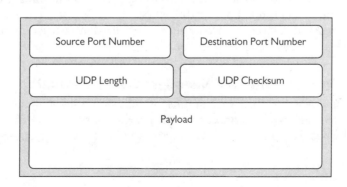

Protocol	TCP Ports	UDP Ports
HTTP	80	
Secure HTTP (HTTPS)	443	
File Transfer Protocol (FTP)	20 (data), 21 (control)	
Secure Shell (SSH)	22	22
Telnet	23	
Simple Network Management Protocol (SNMP)	161	161
Domain Name System (DNS)	53	53

Table 16-11 Protocol Port Assignments

Be aware, however, that many enterprises have policies against UDP traffic. UDP streams can be used in malicious attacks such as denial-of-service attacks, which swamp network equipment with useless requests, or Trojan horse viruses. If you want to use UDP transport for streaming media, be prepared to defend its necessity.

Ports

A port number indicates to the server what you want the data to do. Many are permanently assigned by the IANA to standardized, well-known services.

System ports, 0 to 1023, are assigned to standards-track protocols. These are also known as well-known ports. *User ports,* 1024 to 49151, are assigned by IANA upon request from an application developer. *Dynamic ports*, 49152 to 65535, cannot be assigned or reserved. Applications can use any dynamic port that is available on the local host. Table 16-11 shows TCP and UDP ports assigned to several different protocols.

Data Link Layer Protocols

As the industry advances, you will need to grow familiar with important layer 2 protocols such as Audio Video Bridging/Time-Sensitive Networking, EtherSound, Cobranet, Dante, or HDBaseT. They are all transported over standard structured cable. Most use Ethernet frames to package and transport data. As AV streaming protocols, they require a minimum data throughput of 100 Mbps.

Many AV link layer protocols require specialized infrastructure (routers, switches, and so on) specifically designed to support them.

Why Professional AV Needs Its Own Protocols

Leaving aside the massive amounts of infrastructure—billions of dollars' worth of dedicated servers and connections—that make consumer services such as YouTube and Netflix possible, professional AV really is special. Internet streaming media services can offer good-quality streams of recorded audio and video to multiple users. This AV data has been compressed and encoded before delivery to users—a time- and CPU-consuming process. Even so, users expect to have to wait for their streaming media. Many videos load for a short time before they will play, and the streaming experience is often interrupted by "buffering" while more data downloads. If there isn't enough bandwidth to deliver the full stream, the service provider may switch to a lower-quality stream or simply pause delivery for a bit.

These little inconveniences aren't permissible in many professional AV applications. Professional AV applications are often live. You're transporting audio and video that's being transduced into data in real time. Think about the difference in quality you've seen between recorded and live video feeds you see on the Internet. The live feeds are typically much lower resolution, and they often refresh only a few times per second, or even less. That level of quality isn't acceptable in a professional AV enterprise application.

When you're streaming audio and video in real time, you can't stop to buffer. If there isn't enough bandwidth to deliver all the data, the data gets lost or delayed. If the data is lost, the result is unintelligible, clipped audio and blocky video. Some amount of delay or latency may be permissible. It depends on your application. In general, the more interactive the AV application, the less latency it can tolerate. A lecture that's being streamed live to a spillover room can tolerate several seconds of latency. A live, two-way conversation cannot. A networked audio system in a stadium can't tolerate much latency either—you don't want the announcers' commentary to lag behind the action on the field.

Transporting real-time audio and video to multiple destinations on a LAN typically requires special Data Link protocols designed for that purpose. These protocols make sure that the AV data arrives in sequence, with minimal latency. They also have special network design requirements associated with them: permissible topologies, minimum Ethernet standard requirements, and so on. They may require special hardware or software. They may require AV devices to be isolated in a VLAN. Implementation can be challenging. In the end, though, these special AV protocols allow you to leverage existing IT infrastructure to transport professional-quality AV signals to hundreds of endpoints at once.

Audio Video Bridging/Time-Sensitive Networking

There are many protocols designed to deliver real-time audio or video over LANs. Most are proprietary; that is, they were developed by a private company, which owns the right to their use. They may license the technology to other manufacturers, but they will profit from any implementation of the protocol. There is at least one open, standards-based protocol for delivering real-time audio and video over Ethernet: *Audio Video Bridging* (AVB), which has recently been renamed to Time-Sensitive Networking (TSN).

AVB/TSN is a suite of standards in development by the same organization that maintains the Ethernet standards, IEEE. Right now, the complete AVB/TSN standard is still in development by an IEEE 802.1 task force. However, the AVB/TSN suite includes several standards that have already been completed and ratified. As a result, AVB/TSN is already in use in the field. The following AVB/TSN standards have already been ratified:

- **IEEE 802.1AS Timing and Synchronization in Bridged Local Area Networks** Among other functions, 802.1AS allows devices with different sampling rates to send AV media on the same system. It also ensures audio and video streams stay in sync with each other.

- **IEEE 802.1Qat Stream Reservation Protocol** This reserves a portion of network bandwidth for the AV stream. Reservation is different from traditional QoS priority. It actually closes off a portion of the network bandwidth so that only AVB traffic can use it. The percentage of the network that can be reserved is adjustable.

- **IEEE 802.1Qav Forwarding and Queuing for Time-Sensitive Streams** This guarantees that AVB traffic will arrive on time, without too much latency or too many lost packets.

Other AVB standards are still in the ratification process. This includes 802.1 BA AVB Systems, the standard that will define the defaults and profiles that manufacturers need to implement to make their LAN equipment AVB/TSN-compatible. Like Ethernet, AVB/TSN is an open standard. Any manufacturer can choose to implement and support AVB on their devices.

The aim of the complete AVB/TSN standard suite is plug-and-play networked AV. AVB/TSN-enabled devices should detect one another automatically. AVB/TSN-enabled switches should recognize AVB/TSN traffic and prioritize it appropriately. AVB/TSN networks are supposed to configure themselves, without any need for you to segregate AV equipment on a separate physical network. The catch is that every device in the system must be AVB/TSN compliant. That includes the network switches; they must be "media-aware" switches, capable of detecting and prioritizing AVB/TSN traffic. Such switches are known as AVB/TSN *bridges*.

Audio Video Bridging/Time-Sensitive Networking Topologies

AVB/TSN can use any LAN topology—bus, ring, star, mesh, and so on—but AVB/TSN data has a maximum of seven "hops." In other words, it can pass through no more than seven devices on its journey from source to destination, not counting the source and destination. Within those restrictions, latency in AVB/TSN networks is limited to 2 milliseconds.

AVB/TSN is designed to operate on a converged network—that is, alongside other data on the same LAN. It's able to do this because of its reservation and forwarding and queuing protocols. With AVB/TSN, AV data automatically occupies the top two levels of QoS on the switch. Everything else, including Voice over IP (VoIP), Internet traffic, and so on, is assigned a lower priority level. AVB/TSN allows AV traffic to travel on the same network as other traffic because it enables the AV data to cut in line at the switch and reserve up to 75 percent of network connections for itself.

TIP Not every organization will be comfortable prioritizing AV data in this manner. Even if your customers are comfortable with this, they may be unwilling to replace their LAN infrastructure with AVB/TSN-compliant devices. In that case, you're left with two options: a physically separate AVB/TSN LAN or a proprietary Data Link layer solution.

EtherSound

The first networked audio solution to make it to market was EtherSound. EtherSound was developed by Digigram and made available to the public in 2001. EtherSound is a combination of hardware, control software, and data transportation protocol technologies (see Figure 16-27 for sample topologies). EtherSound transports real-time audio and control, but it does not transport video.

The audio sources have to either be EtherSound-enabled or be connected to an EtherSound-enabled device. Digigram licenses EtherSound technology to many different audio equipment manufacturers. It uses standard networking devices, though any standard switch or hub can forward EtherSound data. EtherSound data is packaged inside Ethernet Frames. It is a Data Link layer technology and can't be routed outside the LAN.

Ethernet Requirements and Capabilities

There are two main versions of EtherSound: ES-100 and ES-Giga. As you might guess, ES-100 requires 100 Mbps Ethernet or better. ES-Giga requires Gigabit Ethernet or better. ES-100 supports up to 64 channels of bi-directional 24-bit, 48 kilohertz (kHz) audio

PART IV

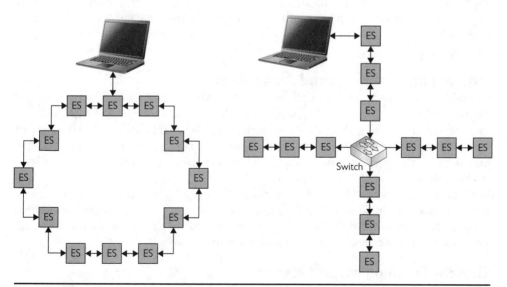

Figure 16-27 EtherSound topologies

and control. ES-Giga supports up to 256 channels of 24-bit, 48 kHz audio and control, plus 100 Mbps of standard Ethernet for non-EtherSound control signals. As usual, the maximum number of channels an EtherSound connection can support depends on the quality of the audio stream. If the audio is encoded at a lower bit depth or sampling rate, you'll be able to send more channels over a single connection.

Unlike AVB/TSN, EtherSound requires dedicated bandwidth. Typically, that means the EtherSound network should be on its own physically separate LAN. You can use existing network infrastructure, though, and place all EtherSound devices within a VLAN. In that case, you will have to reserve bandwidth for the EtherSound VLAN on all the network switches.

EtherSound Latency

You can predict the amount of latency in an EtherSound network based on its topology. There's 104 microseconds (μs) of latency native to the network because of the time it takes to buffer data into Ethernet frames. Each node the data passes through adds about 1.4 μs of latency. By counting the number of nodes between the source and destination nodes on an EtherSound network, you can calculate the amount of latency. Note that the latency will be slightly different at each daisy-chained endpoint.

CobraNet

CobraNet is a competitor to EtherSound developed by Cirrus Logic. In many ways, it's similar. CobraNet is a combination of hardware, control software, and data transportation protocol technologies. It transports real-time audio and control, but it does not transport video. The audio sources have to either be CobraNet-enabled or be connected to a CobraNet-enabled device. Cirrus Logic licenses CobraNet technology to many different audio equipment manufacturers. Like EtherSound, it uses standard networking devices—any standard switch or hub can forward CobraNet data. CobraNet data is packaged inside Ethernet Frames. It is a Data Link layer technology and can't be routed outside the LAN.

Ethernet Requirements and Capabilities

CobraNet is designed to be transported over 100 Mbps Ethernet or better. As long as the network is fully switched, CobraNet data doesn't require dedicated bandwidth. It can coexist on a LAN with other data. That said, it may still be a good idea to isolate CobraNet devices in a VLAN, shutting out broadcast traffic. You can also run CobraNet on a network that uses hubs instead of switches, but design guidelines are much stricter. In that case, a separate LAN may be required.

Over Fast Ethernet (100baseT), a single CobraNet connection supports up to 64 channels of bi-directional 20-bit, 48 kHz audio and control over a single connection. It carries fewer channels if the bit rate is higher and more if the bit rate is lower. Gigabit Ethernet and faster can, of course, support even more channels.

CobraNet Topologies and Latency

Like AVB/TSN, CobraNet can run over any Ethernet topology. Just as with AVB/TSN, the number of nodes does not affect network latency. Latency is the same at each end point.

According to Cirrus Logic, 5.33 ms of latency is introduced by the process of buffering AV data into Ethernet frames. CobraNet standards allow another 3.8 ms of latency. This could come from several different sources. Additional conversion (for example, digital to analog, sampling rate, and so on) may add another millisecond. Each switch the data passes through will also add some latency. How much depends on the overall volume of network traffic and the QoS priority of the CobraNet data. The number of hops allowed in a CobraNet network is therefore determined by the allowable latency. In general, six hops is the maximum, but more time-sensitive applications can tolerate even fewer hops.

Dante

Not all AV data transportation protocols are limited to the LAN. Dante is a proprietary Network layer audio transportation protocol developed by Audinate. AVB/TSN, EtherSound, and CobraNet all package data as payloads directly inside Ethernet frames. Dante packages audio data as a payload inside an IP packet. That means Dante traffic is fully routable—a router can send it from one LAN to another or from inside a VLAN to outside a VLAN. Like EtherSound or CobraNet, Dante transports audio and control and no video. Dante encompasses hardware, control software, and the transportation protocol itself. The audio sources have to either be Dante-enabled or be connected to a Dante-enabled device. You can turn a Windows or Apple computer into a Dante-enabled device using Audinate's proprietary software, Dante Virtual Sound Card. Any standard switch or router can forward Dante data.

Ethernet Requirements and Capabilities

Dante requires a switched Ethernet network of 100 Mbps or better, with at least a Gigabit Ethernet backbone. Dante doesn't require dedicated bandwidth. It uses the VoIP DiffServ category to prioritize audio and control data over other data. Therefore, it can coexist on a LAN with other data. Over Fast Ethernet, a single Dante connection can carry 48 channels of bi-directional 24-bit, 48 kHz audio. Over Gigabit Ethernet, a single Dante connection can carry 512 channels of bi-directional 24-bit, 48 kHz audio. As always, the actual limit on the number of channels depends on the quality of the audio stream. High-quality equals fewer channels, and vice versa.

Dante Topologies and Latency

Like AVB/TSN and CobraNet, Dante can run over any Ethernet topology. The latency of the Dante network is set by the system administrator and managed by the Dante control software. You set the latency based on the size of the network. For live sound, Audinate recommends setting a latency of no more than 1 ms. If the Dante packet arrives at its destination device before the set latency period is up, the device will actually delay it a little. This ensures that all Dante nodes remain in sync.

However, unlike AVB/TSN and CobraNet, Dante devices don't need to have the same latency at each node. Using the Dante control software, you can configure some network paths to allow more latency (for example, the path to a recording device), thereby freeing up more bandwidth for time-critical network paths (for example, the paths to your loudspeakers). Be forewarned: This flexibility has a price. Lower latency requires more bandwidth. Lowering your latency will limit the number of possible channels. Dante networks have a maximum of 10 hops.

Q-Sys

Q-Sys is a proprietary networked audio transportation protocol developed by QSC. Like Dante, Q-Sys is a Network layer audio transportation protocol. It too packages audio data inside IP packets, meaning it can be routed from one LAN to another. Like Ether-Sound, CobraNet, and Dante, Q-Sys transports audio and control signals and no video. Q-Sys encompasses hardware, control software, and the transportation protocol itself. A Q-Sys network requires several proprietary QSC audio products to work, including a Q-Sys Core central processor and server, I/O frames that convert analog audio to and from Q-Sys packets, and network design software. Any standard switch or router can forward Q-Sys data.

Ethernet Requirements and Capabilities

Q-Sys requires end-to-end Gigabit Ethernet or better. Q-Sys doesn't require dedicated bandwidth or physically separate networks, but like Dante and AVB/TSN, they do require QoS. Q-Sys requires that its clock data be in the network's highest QoS class and its audio streams be in the high-middle "assured forwarding" class. Q-Sys control data and management data can be in the "best effort" class. Depending on the Q-Sys Core used, a single Q-Sys connection may carry up to 512 channels of bidirectional audio.

Q-Sys Topologies and Latency

Q-Sys employs centralized processing—the Q-Sys Core performs the audio processing for the network. As a result, Q-Sys networks typically employ a star or extended star logical topology, with the Core at the center of the network (see Figure 16-28). As in a Dante network, the amount of latency in a Q-Sys network is configurable, from 2.5 ms up to 4.5 ms in a larger network. Q-Sys networks have a maximum of seven hops.

HDBaseT

HDBaseT is an alternative approach to networked AV. Unlike AVB/TSN, EtherSound, CobraNet, Dante, and Q-Sys, it is not carried in Ethernet frames or IP packets. It cannot pass through conventional network switches and routers. IT and HDBaseT networks use the same Cat 5e or better cables and RJ-45 connectors, but that's where the similarities end. An HDBaseT network is a dedicated network, built with special components. It doesn't interface with the IT network except as a system source. It bears mentioning here as an alternative to Ethernet-based AV networks.

HDBaseT was developed by the HDBaseT Alliance, a group of manufacturers. It was originally intended for use in the consumer market but has made inroads into the professional AV market as well, particularly in digital signage and surveillance cameras. All devices in the HDBaseT signal chain must be capable of transmitting and/or receiving HDBaseT.

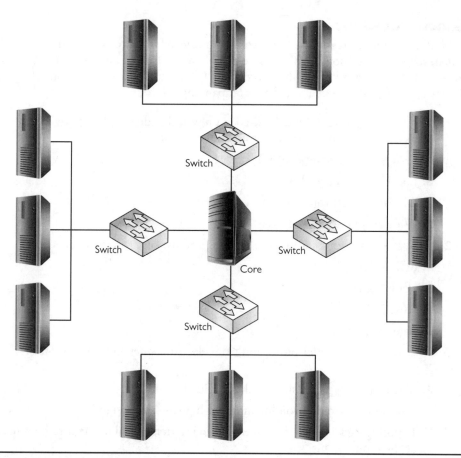

Figure 16-28 Q-Sys topology

HDBaseT Capabilities

HDBaseT carries uncompressed 2K/4K video, as well as audio and control signals. It is also capable of carrying up to 100 watts of power—you might not even need to plug HDBaseT displays and other end nodes into the wall. HDBaseT can also carry 100 Mbps Ethernet. This capability allows HDBaseT devices to access content on connected computers.

Chapter Review

Before you can send any signals across a network, especially AV signals, you have to understand how data travels through the network. In this chapter, you learned about network components, types, and topologies, as well as how different protocols play out in the design and operation of AV/IT networks. You're now ready to take on streaming design, which is the focus of Chapter 17.

Review Questions

The following questions are based on the content covered in this chapter and are intended to help reinforce the knowledge you have assimilated. These questions are not extracted from the CTS-D exam nor are they necessarily CTS-D practice exam questions. For an official CTS-D practice exam, see the accompanying CD.

1. A _____ uses unique, hard-coded physical addresses, known as media access control (MAC) addresses, to send data between nodes.

   A. Personal area network (PAN)

   B. Local area network (LAN)

   C. Global area network (GAN)

   D. Wide area network (WAN)

2. What standard best identifies the purpose and use of a wireless connection?

   A. SCP X.25

   B. IEEE 802.11

   C. RFC 761

   D. Signaling system 7

3. Twisted-pair cables offer protection from electromagnetic interference by _____.

   A. Shielding each pair inside a foil or braided shield

   B. Physically separating conductors from higher-voltage signals

   C. Exposing each wire to the same outside interference, allowing it to be canceled at the input circuit

   D. Comparing the signal that arrives at the destination device against a checksum

4. An organization needs its own DNS server if it _____.

   A. Needs to statically associate certain names and IP addresses

   B. Uses DNS internally to manage the names and addresses of devices on the private network

   C. Has more than one LAN

   D. Needs to access the Internet

5. Reserve DHCP allows you to _____.

   A. Limit the use of a pool of addresses to a particular VLAN or subnet

   B. Establish a pool of additional addresses in case the primary pool of addresses runs out

   C. Assign static IP addresses to devices using a DHCP server

   D. Set an unlimited lease time for all devices using a DHCP server

6. TCP transport should be used instead of UDP transport when _____.

   A. Speed and continuity of transmission are more important than guaranteed delivery or accuracy of data

   B. Data accessibility is more important than security of the data transmission

   C. Security of the data transmission is more important than data accessibility

   D. Guaranteed delivery and quality of the data is more important than the speed or continuity of the transmission

7. The term *Fast Ethernet* refers to _____.

   A. 10 Mbps Ethernet

   B. 100 Mbps Ethernet

   C. 1 Gbps Ethernet

   D. 10 Gbps Ethernet

8. The speed of Ethernet your device can send and receive depends on the _____.

   A. Type of WAN physical medium the organization uses to access the Internet

   B. Capability of its network interface card (NIC)

   C. Type of cable used to connect the device to the network

   D. Speed of the switch to which it is directly attached

9. To transport audio using AVB/TSN, you must have at least _____ Ethernet.

   A. 10 Mbps

   B. 100 Mbps

   C. 1 Gbps

   D. 10 Gbps

Answers

1. **B.** A local area network uses unique, hard-coded physical addresses, known as media access control (MAC) addresses, to send data between nodes.

2. **B.** The IEEE 802.11 standard defines many aspects of wireless connectivity.

3. **C.** Twisted-pair cables offer protection from electromagnetic interference by exposing each wire to the same outside interference, allowing it to be canceled at the input circuit.

4. **B.** An organization needs its own DNS server if it uses DNS internally to manage the names and addresses of devices on the private network.

5. C. Reserve DHCP allows you to assign static IP addresses to devices using a DHCP server.

6. D. TCP transport should be used instead of UDP transport when guaranteed delivery and quality of the data is more important than the speed or continuity of the transmission.

7. B. The term *Fast Ethernet* refers to 100 Mbps Ethernet.

8. B. The speed of Ethernet your device can send and receive depends on the capability of its network interface card (NIC).

9. B. To transport audio using AVB/TSN, you must have at least 100 Mbps Ethernet.

CHAPTER 17

Streaming Design

In this chapter, you will learn about

- Conducting a needs analysis for streaming AV systems
- Conducting a network analysis for streaming AV systems
- Designing an AV streaming system that takes into account bandwidth, latency, and other requirements
- Quality of service (QoS) and its effect on streaming AV systems
- The network protocols used for streaming
- The difference between unicast and multicast and the basics of implementing multicast distribution on an enterprise network

The network environment is as important to a streaming application as a physical environment is to a traditional AV system. When it comes to designing for a streaming AV system, you need to analyze the network as carefully as you would a physical room by exploring its potential, discovering its limitations, and recommending changes to improve system performance.

Streaming media comprises Internet Protocol television (IPTV), live video and audio streaming, and video on demand. It is also the foundation for other networked AV systems, such as digital signage and conferencing.

To design a successful streaming application, you must think carefully about the client's needs and how they impact service targets. For example, how much bandwidth will your AV streams require? How much latency and packet loss can users tolerate? Some answers depend on the network itself; others depend on how content is encoded to travel over that network. As you begin to discover the number and quality of streams your client needs, you may set off some bandwidth alarm bells. Video and audio streams require significantly more bandwidth than other AV signals, such as control. If you understand the concepts underlying the compression, encoding, and distribution of digital media, you're on your way to designing a variety of streaming solutions.

Streaming Needs Analysis

When conducting a needs analysis for a streaming solution, you need to discover not only what the client wants, but also what the current networking environment can deliver. Typical questions related to traditional audiovisual applications—regarding room size, viewer positioning, and so on—may be impossible to answer because the client may not know with any certainty where end users will be when they access streaming content. Instead of asking about the room where an AV system would reside, you need to delve into issues relating to streaming quality, bandwidth, latency, and delivery requirements. You need to think in terms of tasks, audience, end point devices, and content. And you need to explore these issues in the context of an enterprise network, not a particular venue.

Ultimately, what you learn in the needs analysis will help inform the service-level agreement (SLA) for your streaming AV system—and possibly other, more encompassing SLAs. Not to mention, as you're collecting information about the client's need, you should always ask yourself, "How is this going to impact network design?" because, eventually, you may have an IT department to answer to.

Streaming Tasks

In the design of any AV system (networked or non-networked), form follows function. The needs analysis begins with discovering the purpose of the system. Assume you've already established your client needs to stream AV. Why? What tasks will streaming AV be used for?

Decisions regarding bandwidth allocation, latency targets, and port and protocol requirements should be driven by a business case that is established in the needs analysis. How do the tasks that the prospective streaming system will perform contribute to the organization's profitability, productivity, or competitiveness? If you can make a valid business case for why your streaming system requires a high class of service, opening User

Datagram Protocol (UDP) ports, or 30 Mbps of reserved bandwidth, you should get it. But you need to understand the following:

- "The picture will look bad if we don't reserve the bandwidth" is not a business case.

- "The picture will look bad if we don't reserve the bandwidth, and if the picture looks bad, the intelligence analysts won't be able to identify the bunker locations" is an excellent business case.

If there's no business case for high-priority, low-latency, high-resolution streaming video, for example, then the user doesn't need it, and it probably shouldn't be approved. In that case, be prepared to relinquish synchronous HD streaming video if the client doesn't really require it. Just be sure you document the lower expectations as your system's service target.

Streaming Task Questions

What tasks will the streaming system be used for? This is the most basic question of a needs analysis. Answering it in detail should reveal the following:

- The importance of the system to the organization's mission

- The scope of use in terms of number and variety of users

- The frequency of use

If the task is a high priority, the streamed content will require priority delivery on the network, which will affect the bandwidth allocated and the class of service assigned to it. The nature of the task will also impact latency requirements. As you delve further into the tasks that the streaming system must support, you may ask questions such as, "Do users need to respond or react immediately to the streamed content?" If so, latency requirements should be very low—such as 30 milliseconds.

Furthermore, find out the answer to this question: "Will any delay in content delivery undermine its usefulness?" This question is also aimed at determining how much latency is acceptable in the system, outside of immediate-response situations. And the answers will help address follow-on questions: "Can we use TCP transport, or is UDP necessary?" and "How should the data be prioritized in a QoS architecture?"

Audience

The user is the star of the streaming needs analysis (or any needs analysis, for that matter). In fact, *who* the audience is specifically may be a major factor in a business case for a high-resolution, low-latency streaming system. We're talking about the organization's hierarchy here. If the main users are fairly high in the hierarchy—management, executives—they may demand a high-quality system to match their status.

If, on the other hand, the system will be used broadly throughout the organization, you may need to consider the bandwidth implications of such widespread use. Would a multicast work? (We will cover multicasting in detail later in this chapter.) Should different groups of users be assigned different service classes? You'll understand better when you identify the audience.

Where the audience is located, however, may be your primary challenge in offering a streaming system that meets the client's need. It's actually a far more complex issue when it comes to streaming applications than traditional audiovisual systems. Asking about location should reveal whether all users (the audience) are on the same local area network (LAN) or wide area network (WAN) and whether some users will access streaming content over the open Internet. How does that impact design? There are various reasons, including the following:

- Bandwidth over a WAN is limited.
- QoS and multicast are impossible over the open Internet.
- LAN-only solutions have a far greater array of data link and quality options.

End Points

Related to audience are the end points people will use to access streaming content. Your client may need to stream data to a handful of overflow rooms, hundreds of desktop PCs, or thousands of smartphones. The number and type of end points have a direct impact on service requirements.

How many different end points does the client need to stream to? With unicast transmissions, the bandwidth cost will rise with each additional user. If the user needs to stream to a large or unknown number of users within the enterprise network, you need to consider using multicast transmission or reflecting servers to reduce bandwidth. What *kind* of end points will people be using? Different end points support different resolutions, for example. If end points will be especially heterogeneous, you may want to implement a variable bit-rate intelligent streaming solution. If most users will be using mobile devices, content must be optimized for delivery over Wi-Fi or 3G/4G cellular networks.

Content Sources

The type of content the client will stream has a direct impact on the network, which in turn affects the streaming system design. Like other parts of the needs analysis, the content will factor in its bandwidth usage, latency targets, and class of service. The following are some basic questions to ask:

- Do you need to stream audio, video, or both? Video requires far more bandwidth than audio. Codec options will also differ based on type of media.
- How will content be generated? Video content generated by a computer graphics card may require more bandwidth than content captured by a camera. You'll also have different codec options for different sources.

- Will streaming images be full-motion or static? Still images, or relatively static images, require a lower frame rate than full-motion video.

- Will the client be streaming copyrighted material or material that's protected by digital rights management (DRM)?

You will also need to consider how and where content will enter the network. This is often referred to as the place where content is *ingested* (or uploaded) and can be a computer, a server, a storage system, or a purpose-built network streaming "engine." You should determine how many ingestion points there will be and ensure each has the bandwidth required for expedient uploading. In addition, how many concurrent streams, or "channels," must be uploaded? The answer should help establish how many video servers will be needed.

Moreover, can you exercise any control over the format, bandwidth, and so on of the content that will be ingested for streaming? If your clients are ingesting several different formats, they may need a transcoder, which automatically translates streams into formats that are compatible with the desired end points or are bandwidth-friendly toward certain connections.

And when it comes to the streaming content itself, you may want to make recommendations on frame rates, resolutions, and other streaming media characteristics based on the network design you anticipate. For video, how much motion fidelity do users need to accomplish their tasks? Lower acceptable fidelity will allow you to use a lower frame rate. Higher fidelity will result in increased latency or higher bandwidth.

What level of image quality or resolution is required for the task? Again, the focus is on *requirement*, not the desire. Use the answer to these questions to help establish a business case: At what point will limiting the video resolution detract from the system's ability to increase the client's productivity, profitability, or competitiveness? How low can the video resolution be before the image is no longer usable?

Using Copyrighted Content

Your clients may want to stream content that they didn't create, such as clips from a media library or music from a satellite service. Unfortunately, such digital distribution can violate copyright laws.

Make sure clients are aware of the potential licensing issues related to the content they want to stream. You may need to negotiate a bulk license with a content service provider, such as a cable or satellite television provider or a satellite music service.

If you fail to obtain the proper licenses to stream content, you aren't just risking legal repercussions; you're risking the system's ability to function at all. Publishers and copyright owners use DRM technology to control access to and usage of digital data or hardware. DRM protocols within devices determine what content is even allowed to enter a piece of equipment. Copy protection such as the Content Scrambling System (CSS), used in DVD players, is a subset of DRM. Actual legal enforcement of DRM policies varies by country.

High-bandwidth Digital Content Protection (HDCP) is a form of DRM developed by Intel to control digital audio and video content as it travels across Digital Video

Interface (DVI) or High-Definition Multimedia Interface (HDMI) connections. It prevents the transmission or interception of nonencrypted HD content.

HDCP support is essential for the playback of protected high-definition (HD) content. Without the proper HDCP license, material will not play.

It can be difficult—though possible—to stream to multiple DVI or HDMI outputs. All the equipment used to distribute the content must be licensed. When in doubt, always ask whether a device is HDCP-compliant.

 NOTE IPTV and streaming are similar, given that both utilize most of the same technology, so for the purposes of this book, the two will be handled as one topic. IPTV is a system that delivers television services over a packet-switched network, such as a LAN or the Internet. Streaming is traditionally the transfer of audio and video files that are played at the same time they're temporarily downloaded to a user's computer or other device.

Streaming Needs Analysis Questions

Use the following questions to gather information from clients about streaming applications. Consider how the users' needs with respect to each item could impact the system's design, cost, or network.

Tasks

- What tasks will the system be used to perform?
- Do users need to respond or react immediately to the streamed content?
- Will any delay in content delivery undermine the usefulness of the content?

Audience

- Who is the intended audience?
- Where is the intended audience (onsite, within the LAN; offsite, within the company WAN; offsite, outside the company WAN; and so on)?
- What are the audience access control requirements?

End Points

- How many different end points (devices) do you need to stream to?
- What kind of end points will your end users be using to view content (desktops, mobile devices, large displays, and so on)?

Content

- What kind of content do you need to stream (for example, full-motion video and audio, full-motion video only, audio only, still images only, still images and audio, and so on)?

- How will content be generated?
- Will you be streaming Voice over IP (VoIP)?
- How will content be ingested into the network?
- For motion video, how much motion fidelity is required?
- What level of quality and/or image resolution do you require (standard definition, high definition, best possible, adequate, and so on)?
- How many concurrent upload streams, or "channels," do you require?
- How many concurrent download streams, or "channels," do you require?
- What are the accessibility requirements, if any?

Storage

- Will content be available on demand?
- How long will content need to be stored?
- How quickly does content need to be propagated from storage?
- What are the backup or redundancy requirements?

Streaming Design and the Network Environment

You've talked to users to find out what they need from a streaming media solution, so now it's time to visit the client's IT department. The network environment is as important to a streaming application as the physical environment is to a traditional AV system. You need to analyze the network as carefully as you would a physical room by exploring its potential, discovering its limitations, and recommending changes to improve system performance. Let's get started.

Topology

In the needs analysis stage, you determined whether streaming users would be accessing content inside or outside a LAN. Remember that a LAN in this case is a single, openly routable location. Until you've had to traverse a firewall, you're still on a LAN.

If your streaming system will remain within a single LAN, you're lucky. The system's routing will be considerably less complex, multicasting will be far easier to implement, and bandwidth availability is unlikely to be a problem. If you're streaming content over a WAN, however, you have several additional factors to consider, including the following:

- The physical location of streaming servers
- Bandwidth availability on every network segment
- The possible need for hybrid unicast/multicast implementation
- The addressing scheme of the organization

The addressing scheme will determine what information you need to gather about your ports and protocols (see Chapter 9). It will also impact how access control and system control will be managed. Can the system identify authorized users via the Domain Name System (DNS)? Do you need to reserve a set of Internet Protocol (IP) addresses for the streaming servers on the Dynamic Host Configuration Protocol (DHCP) server?

Bandwidth: Matching Content to the Network

Bandwidth availability represents the single largest constraint on most networked AV systems. It will drive your choice of transmission method and codec for streaming applications. We will cover these considerations later in this chapter.

Remember that the network is only as fast as its slowest link. The rated capacity of the network should be based on the bottlenecks—the lowest-bandwidth throughput link that data will have to traverse. Whatever the rated capacity of the network is, you can't use all of it. That would be like mounting a display with bolts that can hold exactly the display's weight; the first time someone bumps into the screen, it will tear right off the wall. How much of the network can you use?

Realistically, only 70 percent of rated network capacity is available. The remaining 30 percent should be reserved to accommodate peak data usage times and avoid packet collision. Some industry experts recommend reserving as much as 50 percent of the network for this purpose. Ask the network manager what network capacity is available for each client.

In a converged network, of the 70 percent considered "available," only a portion should be used for streaming media—about 30 percent of the available 70 percent. Otherwise, you won't have enough bandwidth left for other network applications.

Depending on the importance of the streaming application, you may want to reserve this bandwidth with Resource Reservation Protocol (RSVP). RSVP is a Transport layer protocol used to reserve network resources for specific applications. The reservation is initiated by the host receiving the data and must be renewed periodically. RSVP is used in combination with differentiated service (DiffServ). At the least, DiffServ QoS will be required for WAN streaming. We will discuss DiffServ later in this chapter.

Your goal, then, is to design a streaming application that consumes no more than 30 percent of the available network capacity. You may also need to implement some form of bandwidth throttling to prevent the streaming application from overwhelming the network during peak usage, setting the limit at that 30 percent mark. Traffic shaping will introduce latency into the stream, causing it to buffer but preserving its quality. Traffic policing drops packets over the limit, which reduces video quality but avoids additional latency. What's more important to your client: timeliness or quality?

 NOTE Based on estimates that only 70 percent of rated network capacity is considered available and only 30 percent of the available capacity is available for streaming, consider 21 percent of a network's rated capacity available for streaming. See Figure 17-1.

Figure 17-1
The bandwidth available for streaming may be a small part of a network's capacity.

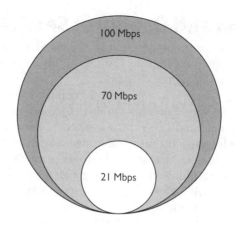

100 Mbps

70 Mbps

21 Mbps

Image Quality vs. Available Bandwidth

Working with the client and the client's IT group, you must determine whether the amount of bandwidth allocated for streaming will be driven by current network availability or the end user's quality expectations. It may be anathema to AV professionals, who pride themselves on high-quality experiences, but the client may be willing to sacrifice quality in favor of network efficiency. In that case, it's your job to ensure that the client knows what he's giving up and that the SLA reflects an acceptable balance between efficiency and quality.

In general, streaming bandwidth will be driven by network availability when the client is extremely cost-conscious or the streaming service is being added to an existing network that's difficult to change. Streaming bandwidth will be driven by the user's need for quality when high image resolution and frame rate are required to perform the tasks for which the streaming service will be used or when the tasks for which the streaming service will be used are mission critical. The need for quality also seems to get a boost when your client audience is from the C-level suite.

What can you do when you discover that streaming requirements exceed available network resources? If quality takes precedence, either add bandwidth, optimize existing bandwidth, assign streaming a high QoS class, or reserve bandwidth using RSVP. We will cover QoS and RSVP in more depth later in this chapter.

If availability takes precedence, you may need to reduce image resolution, frame rate, or bit rate; cut the number of channels by implementing multicast streaming or cache servers; or implement intelligent streaming.

TIP When discussing bandwidth capacity with a network administrator, make sure you're on the same page. Ask yourself, "Is the admin telling you how much bandwidth the whole network is rated for?" If so, you can use only 21 percent of that for streaming. Is the admin telling you the average bandwidth availability? If so, you can use 30 percent of that for streaming. Is the admin telling you the availability during peak usage? If so, it will help you determine QoS requirements.

PART IV

Streaming and Quality of Service

Quality of service is a term used to refer to any method of managing data traffic to provide the best possible user experience. Typically, QoS refers to some combination of bandwidth allocation and data prioritization.

Many different network components have built-in QoS features. For example, video-conferencing codes sometimes have built-in QoS features that allow various devices on a call to negotiate the bandwidth requirements. Network managers may also use software to set QoS rules for particular users or domain names. AV designers need to be more concerned with QoS policies that are configured directly into network switches and routers.

The bandwidth required for streaming video makes QoS a virtual requirement for streaming across a WAN. If you're adding a streaming application to an existing network, you need to find out the following:

- **Whether QoS has been implemented across the entire WAN**   To provide any benefit, QoS must be implemented on every segment of the network across which the stream will travel.

- **What differentiated-service classes have already been defined for network-based QoS (NQoS)**   Every organization prioritizes data differently. You may think that AV data should always be assigned a high service class because it requires so much bandwidth and so little latency. However, a financial institution may value the timely delivery of stock quotes above streaming video. Where will the streaming application fit within the enterprise's overall data priorities?

- **Whether RSVP can be implemented to reserve bandwidth for the streaming application**   RSVP must be implemented on every network segment to function, which is a labor-intensive process. Start by finding out whether RSVP is currently implemented on the network—whether or not you should use it is a separate question. Does the importance of the streaming application really merit reserving 21 percent of the network for its traffic at all times?

- **What policy-based QoS rules are already in place, if any?**   Assigning QoS policies to particular user groups can be helpful for networked AV applications. You may want to place streaming traffic to and from the content ingest points in a higher class of service than on the rest of the network, for instance. If remote users are accessing the system via IPSec, you may have to use policy-based QoS. The ports, protocols, and applications of IPSec traffic are hidden from the router.

- **Whether traffic shaping can be used to manage bandwidth**   Again, traffic shaping policies will have to be implemented on every router on the network. However, if your client doesn't mind the additional latency, traffic shaping can be an effective way to prevent the network from being overwhelmed by streaming traffic. Of course, if traffic policing has been implemented, you need to know this too. Find out where bandwidth thresholds have or will be set for streaming traffic and set expectations for dropped or delayed packets accordingly.

Understanding DiffServ

The underlying strategy of network-based QoS is to prioritize time-sensitive traffic over other traffic. One way to accomplish this is to assign each type of traffic on the network to a particular QoS DiffServ class. Each class is handled differently by network switches and routers. Some classes are designed to preserve data without losing any packets (low loss), some classes are designed to transport data as quickly as possible (low latency), and some prioritize data arriving in the exact order in which it was sent (low jitter). The lowest-priority class is "best effort." Data in this class will arrive when and how it arrives, with no guarantees of integrity or timeliness.

Each application your client will use is assigned a DiffServ class on the network routers and switches. When traffic enters the network, these devices automatically detect which application it comes from and tags it with a DiffServ class. The DiffServ class then defines how the network devices prioritize the traffic. Here are some AV-related DiffServ classes you'll want to consider for your designs:

- **Signaling service class**   This class is for traffic that controls applications or user end points. For example, signals that set up and terminate a connection between conference call end points would belong in this class.

- **Telephony class**   This class is intended for VoIP traffic. It can be used for any traffic that transmits at a constant rate and requires low latency.

- **Real-time interactive class**   This class is for interactive applications that transmit at a variable rate and require low jitter and loss and low delay. Examples include interactive gaming and some types of videoconferencing.

- **Multimedia conferencing service class**   This class is for conferencing solutions that can dynamically reduce their transmission rates if they detect congestion. If a conferencing class can't detect and adapt to network congestion, the real-time interactive class should be used instead.

- **Broadcast video service class**   This class is for inelastic, noninteractive media; that is, media streams that can't change their transmission rate based on network congestion. This class is used for live-event AV streaming as well as broadcast video.

- **Multimedia streaming service class**   This class is for noninteractive streaming media that can detect network congestion or packet loss and respond by reducing its transmission rate. This class is used for video-on-demand services.

Latency

If your application will include live streaming, the amount of latency inherent to the network can be nearly as big a concern as bandwidth availability. What latency is present, and what causes it?

Find out whether your client has an internal speed-test server. If it does, work with the network manager to determine the inherent latency of the network. You can use a WAN speed test to verify network upload and download bit rates, as well as latency inherent between IP addresses.

If your client does not have an internal speed test server, free WAN speed test tools are available from many sites, including www.speedtest.net, www.speakeasy.net, and www.dslreports.com.

Varying degrees of latency are acceptable, depending on your client's needs. Here are some examples:

- **Videoconferencing** 200 milliseconds
- **High-fidelity audio** 50 microseconds
- **Streaming desktop video** 1 second

Eliminating latency entirely from streaming applications is impossible. The trick is to document in your SLA how much latency your client can tolerate for the application. Keep in mind, if your client has a transportation security requirement, more latency will be introduced into the network. Encryption and decryption take time.

Network Policies and Restrictions

Remember, what the network is *capable* of doing and what the network is *permitted* to do are two separate issues. You must determine not only whether bandwidth optimization and latency mitigation strategies, such as differentiated service, policy-based QoS, multicasting, and UDP transport, are possible but whether they are permitted. Many of these strategies are extremely labor-intensive to implement, and some, such as multicast and UDP transport, may represent significant security risks. For a review of UDP, see Chapter 16.

You should also always investigate what software and hardware the enterprise already has. You can bet that staying within an organization's existing device families will ease the process of getting approval to connect devices to the network. For example, the software that users currently have (or are allowed to have) will determine what codecs are available on the end-user playback device, which in turn determines the encoder your system should use.

Cheat Sheet: Streaming Network Analysis Questions

Use the following questions to gather information from your client's IT department about supporting streaming media applications. Consider how network policies with respect to each item could affect the streaming system's design, cost, and network impact. Some of the technical issues in these questions are covered in greater depth later in this chapter.

Topology

- Will content be streamed within a LAN, within a WAN, or over the open Internet?
- If content will be streamed over a WAN, what is the network topology?
- What is the addressing scheme (DNS, DHCP, static)?

Bandwidth Availability

- What is the network's total available end-to-end upload bandwidth?
- What is the network's total available end-to-end download bandwidth?
- What is the network's typical available worst-case upload bandwidth?
- What is the network's typical available worst-case download bandwidth?
- If content will be streamed to the Internet, what upload and download bandwidth is provided by the Internet service provider (ISP)?
- If traffic will be streamed over a WAN, has QoS been implemented? If so, what queue level will AV traffic occupy?
- If traffic will be streamed over a WAN, has traffic shaping been implemented?
- If traffic will be streamed within a LAN, has Independent Group Management Protocol been implemented? If so, what version?
- Is a hybrid solution required to preserve bandwidth? If so, is protocol-independent multicast available to transport?
- Do you need to relay multicast streams across domains?

Latency

- How much latency is inherent to the network?
- Will there be transport-level security requirements?

Network Policies

- Are multicast and UDP transport permitted?
- Are there restrictions on protocols allowed on the network?
- Are there restrictions on what software may be installed on the hosts?
- How is access control currently managed on the network?
- What video player software is currently installed on the hosts? What codecs does it include?

Designing the Streaming System

Most live video with low latency requirements will be delivered via UDP transport. That's because if a stream is time sensitive, it's generally preferable to drop a few packets than wait for the source to confirm delivery and have to resend dropped packets.

Multicast transmissions are always delivered via UDP. UDP packets include little data, however, because they're designed to deliver data as efficiently as possible.

Real-time Transport Protocol (RTP) is a Transport layer protocol commonly used with UDP to provide a better AV streaming experience. (RTP also works with Transmission Control Protocol [TCP], but the latter is more concerned with reliability than speed of transmission.) In addition to a data payload, RTP packets include other information, such as sequence and timing. RTP helps prevent jitter and detects when video packets arrive out of sequence. It also supports one-to-many (multicast) video delivery.

RTP is often deployed in conjunction with the Real-time Transport Control Protocol (RTCP), a Session layer protocol for monitoring quality of service for AV streams. RTCP periodically reports on packet loss, latency, and other delivery statistics so that a streaming application can improve its performance, perhaps by lowering the bit rate of the stream or using a different codec. RTCP does not carry any multimedia data or provide any encryption or authorization methods. In most cases, RTP data is sent over an even-numbered UDP port, while RTCP is sent over the next higher odd-numbered port.

Other Streaming Protocols

When setting up a streaming system, in addition to transport protocols, you should also consider streaming protocols. Streaming-specific protocols serve different functions and are based largely on the types of end points clients will use to view content.

Real Time Streaming Protocol (RTSP) comes in handy if all end points are desktop computer clients. This is because RTSP supports RTCP, while *MPEG transport stream* (MPEG-TS), for example, does not. RTSP is a control protocol that communicates with a streaming server to allow users to play, pause, or otherwise control a stream. For its part, RTCP sends back user data, allowing the streaming device to dynamically adjust the stream to improve performance.

If any of the end points are set-top boxes or similar devices (maybe a streaming box behind a screen in a restaurant), you'll probably use MPEG-TS. The frequency of some displays used with set-top-style boxes can sometimes cause a perceived lag between audio and video. MPEG delivery prevents this from happening by combining audio and video into a single stream. MPEG-TS is defined as part of MPEG-2, but it is the transport stream used to deliver MPEG-4 audio and video as well.

Session Description Protocol (SDP) is a standardized method of describing media streamed over the Internet. The information carried by SDP generally includes session name, purpose, timing, information about the media being transported (though not the media itself), and contact information for session attendees. In short, SDP is used to kick off a streaming session—ensuring all invited devices are in contact and understand what's coming next. The information contained in SDP can also be used by other protocols, such as RTP and RTSP, to initiate and maintain a streaming session.

High-Quality Streaming Video

As you probably know, the Motion Picture Engineering Group defines the compression formats commonly used for streaming high-quality video: MPEG-1, MPEG-2, and MPEG-4. There used to be an MPEG-3 format, but it's no longer used and shouldn't be confused with the MP3 audio compression format.

All three major MPEG standards stream over UDP. Today, MPEG-2 and MPEG-4 are the most prominent for networked AV systems, though MPEG-1 is also ubiquitous—MP3 audio is part of the MPEG-1 standard. For our purposes, we'll explore further the flavors of MPEG you're most likely to use for a streaming design.

MPEG-2

MPEG-2, also known as H.222/H.262, is the most common digital AV compression format. It's an international standard, defined in ISO/IEC 3818. MPEG-2 is used to encode AV data for everything from DVD players and digital cable to satellite TV and more. Notably, MPEG-2 allows text and other data, such as program guides for TV viewers, to be added to the video stream.

There are various ways to achieve different quality levels and file sizes using MPEG-2. In general, however, MPEG-2 streams are too large to travel on the public Internet. MPEG-2 streams have a minimum total bit rate of 300 Kbps. Depending on the frame rate and aspect ratio of the video, as well as the bit rate of the accompanying audio, the total bit rate of an MPEG-2 stream can exceed 10 Mbps.

MPEG-4

MPEG-4 is designed to be a flexible, scalable compression format. It is defined in the standard ISO/IEC 14496. Unlike MPEG-2, MPEG-4 compresses audio, video, and other data as separate streams. For applications where audio detail is important, such as videoconferencing, this is a major advantage. MPEG-4 is capable of lower data rates and smaller file sizes than MPEG-2, while also supporting high-quality transmission. It's commonly used for streaming video, especially over the Internet.

The MPEG-4 standard is still developing. It is broken down into parts, which solution providers implement or not, depending on their products. It's safe to say there are a few complete implementations of MPEG-4 on the market, but it isn't always clear what parts of MPEG-4 an MPEG-4 solution includes. Therefore, it's important to understand the major components of MPEG-4.

MPEG-4 Levels and Profiles

Within the MPEG-4 specification are levels and profiles. These let manufacturers concentrate on applications without getting bogged down in every aspect of the format. Profiles are quality groupings within a compression scheme. Levels are specific image sizes and frame rates of a profile. This breakdown allows manufacturers to use only the part of the MPEG-4 standard they need while still being in compliance. Any two devices implementing the same MPEG-4 profiles and levels should be able to interoperate.

MPEG-4 Part 10 is the most commonly implemented part of the MPEG-4 standard for recording, streaming, or compressing high-definition audio and video. It is also known as H.264 Advanced Video Coding (AVC). AVC can transport the same quality (resolution, frame rate, bit depth, and so on) as MPEG-2 at far lower bit rates—typically half as low as MPEG-2.

AVC profiles include but are not limited to the following:

- Baseline profile (BP), used for videoconferencing and mobile applications
- Main profile (MP), used for standard-definition digital television
- Extended profile (XP), used for streaming video with high compression capability
- High profile (HiP), used for high-definition broadcast and recording, such as digital television and Blu-ray Disc recording

AVC also includes intraframe compression profiles for files that might need to be edited—High 10 Intra Profile (Hi10P), High 4:2:2 Intra Profile (Hi422P), and High 4:4:4 Intra Profile (Hi444P).

MPEG-H and H.265

MPEG-H is the latest group of standards under development. It includes H.265, also known as High Efficiency Video Coding (HEVC), which is the successor to H.264. With H.265, AV designers can double the data compression ratio of a stream compared to H.264/MPEG-4 AVC without sacrificing video quality. On the flip side, they can offer much better video quality at the same bit rate. H.265 is said to be able to support 8K ultra high-resolution video at up to 8192×4320.

Because networked AV applications can have voracious bandwidth appetites, H.265 is a significant advance. The most recent version of HEVC/H.265 was approved as an ITU-T standard in 2015. Companies are slowing introducing H.265 products, but the industry is still just on the cusp of H.265 adoption.

Unicast and Multicast

As someone who's probably watched a little TV in your time, you know what broadcasting means. To broadcast is to transmit data to anyone who can receive it at the same time. This doesn't happen much in networking. When it comes to streaming, we talk in terms of unicast or multicast.

Unicast streaming establishes one-to-one connections between the streaming server that sends the AV data and client devices that receive it. Each client has a direct relationship with the server. The client sends a request to the server, and the server sends the client a stream in response. Because the server is sending out a separate stream to each client, each additional client consumes more of the available bandwidth. Streaming media to three clients at 100 Kbps actually uses 300 Kbps of bandwidth. Unicast streams may use either UDP or TCP transport, although with TCP transport, you can assume there will always be some *measure buffering,* or client devices waiting for parts of the stream to arrive before playing it.

An encoder can typically produce only five or six unicast streams, depending on the streaming device's available resources. If your client needs more than a handful of unicast streams, you'll need a streaming or caching server to replicate and manage them.

That said, unicast is easier to implement than multicast, and it's cheaper for small applications. Consider using unicast for point-to-point streaming, and even point-to-point plus recording. If you're unicasting to thousands of users, however, you'll have to invest in streaming devices that sit at the network's edge for handling the extra streams, which can be expensive.

Multicast streaming is a one-to-many transmission model. One server sends out a single stream that multiple clients can access. Multicast streams require UDP transport. They can be sent only over LANs or private networks, not over the open Internet. So-called Class D IP addresses are set aside for multicast transmissions (see Table 11-1). In multicast streaming, the following happens:

1. A server sends the stream to a designated Class D IP address, called the *host address*.

2. Clients subscribe to the host address.

3. Routers send the stream to all clients subscribing to the host address.

Subscribing to an active multicast host address is like tuning into a radio station: All the users receive the same transmission, and none of them can control the playback. There is no direct connection between the server and the clients. Because the server is sending only one stream, the transmission should theoretically take up the same amount of bandwidth no matter how many clients subscribe. Sounds efficient, right?

However, not all networks are capable of passing multicast streams. For multicast to work, every router in the network must be configured to understand multicast protocols and Class D addressing. If the router doesn't recognize the Class D IP address as a multicast host address, the clients will have no way to access the stream. As a result, multicasting can be very labor-intensive to implement. Only small portions of the Internet are multicast-enabled, so it's usually not possible to multicast over the open Internet. If you want the client's IT department to allow multicast, you'd better make a good case. Figure 17-2 illustrates the main differences between unicast and multicast streaming.

Unicast vs. Multicast

How do you choose whether to stream using unicast or multicast? The decision should be based on your streaming needs and network capabilities. In many cases, you won't have the option to use multicast streaming, particularly if the network you're working with isn't multicast-enabled. Managed switches must be capable of multicasting. Independent Group Management Protocol (IGMP) should be implemented on the router, and if you want to send multicast streams over a wide area network, you have to set up a protocol-independent multicast (PIM) relay, which forwards only the unicast streams that are in use. (We'll cover IGMP, PIM, and more later in this chapter.) All the routers in the network have to support this functionality.

If the network isn't ready for multicasting, use unicast streaming. Moreover, as long as the projected number of clients and the bit rate of the streams won't exceed the network's bandwidth capacity, stick with unicast because it's much easier to implement. And if you're implementing video on demand, you want to use unicast so users can control playback.

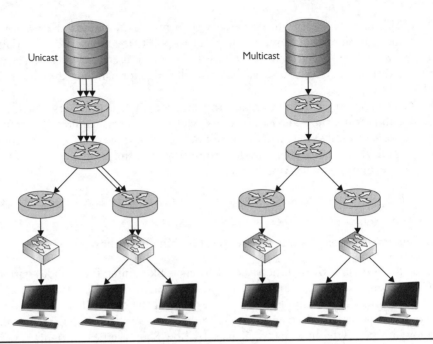

Figure 17-2   Differences between unicast and multicast

On the other hand, when you need to stream to a large number of client devices on an enterprise network, multicast can help limit your bandwidth usage. For example, streaming a live lecture to all the student desktops on a campus might benefit from multicasting. Multicasting is typically used for IPTV systems, with each channel sent to multiple hosts.

Compromise between unicast and multicast is possible. For example, using a caching or reflecting server, you can convert a multicast stream to a unicast stream to pass it over a network segment that cannot accept multicast transmissions. This hybrid approach is the most common approach for WAN implementations.

You Decide: Unicast or Multicast?

Q: You want your server to be able to send out the same stream at multiple bit rates so that each client can receive the highest-quality stream of which it is capable. Should you use unicast or multicast?

A: To take advantage of multiple bit rate encoding and intelligent streaming, you must use unicast transmission. Multicast transmission sends out a single stream at a single bit rate. Unicast servers send out a different stream for each client and may vary the bit rate according to information in the client handshake.

Q: You're designing a streaming application for a high school that will allow video announcements to be streamed live to 100 classrooms at 300 Kbps every morning. Should you use unicast or multicast?

A: It depends on the size of the LAN. If the school has 1 Gbps Ethernet, you should probably use unicast because it's easier to manage. If it has 100 Mbps Ethernet, however, use multicast.

Q: You want to be able to retrieve a detailed record of which clients have accessed the stream. Should you use unicast or multicast?

A: If you want to be able to retrieve a detailed client list, use unicast. Unicast clients have a direct connection to the server, while multicast transmissions are connectionless. No connection, no record.

Implementing Multicast

To review, if you need to send a large number of streams or you need to stream to many users over a LAN, you'll probably use multicast. It is a great preserver of bandwidth, but it takes an enormous amount of configuration to implement. For starters, every router on the network must be configured to understand what are called *group-management protocol requests*. These requests allow a host to inform its neighboring routers that it wants to start or stop receiving multicast transmissions. Without group-management protocols, which differ depending on the Internet Protocol version a network uses, multicast traffic is broadcast to every client device on a network segment, impeding other network traffic and overtaxing devices.

Internet Group Management Protocol (IGMP) is the IPv4 group-management protocol. It's gone through a few revisions. IGMPv1 allowed individual clients to subscribe to a multicast channel. IGMPv2 and IGMPv3 added the ability to unsubscribe from a multicast channel. IGMP is a communications protocol used by hosts and their adjacent routers to allow hosts to inform the router of their desire to receive, continue receiving, or stop receiving a multicast.

Multicast Listener Discovery (MLD) is the IPv6 group-management protocol. IPv6 natively supports multicasting, which means any IPv6 router will support MLD. MLDv1 performs roughly the same functions as IGMPv2, and MLDv2 supports roughly the same functions as IGMPv3.

IGMPv3 and MLDv2 also support source-specific multicast (SSM). SSM allows clients to specify the sources from which they will accept multicast content. This has the dual benefit of reducing demands on the network while also improving network security. Any device that has the host address can try to send traffic to the multicast group, but only content from a specified source will be forwarded to the group. This is in contrast to any-source multicast (ASM), which sends all multicast traffic sent to the host address to all subscribed clients.

Protocol-Independent Multicast

With the amount of configuration required to implement multicast streaming, many IT managers are hesitant to implement it beyond a single LAN. Multicast routing beyond the LAN is made possible by protocol-independent multicast (PIM).

PIM allows multicast routing over LANs, WANs, or even, theoretically, the open Internet. Rather than routing information on their own, PIM protocols use the routing information supplied by whatever routing protocol the network is already using, which is why it's protocol independent. PIM is generally divided into two categories: dense mode and sparse mode.

Dense mode sends multicast traffic to every router of the network and then prunes any routers that aren't actually using the stream. By default, dense mode re-floods the network every three minutes. PIM-DM is easier to implement than sparse mode but scales poorly. It's suitable only for applications where the majority of users will join each multicast group.

Sparse mode sends multicast traffic only to those routers that explicitly request it. This is the fastest and most scalable multicast implementation for WANs. We'll examine it further.

PIM Sparse Mode

PIM sparse mode (PIM-SM) sends multicast feeds only to routers that specifically request the feed using a PIM join message. The multicast source sends its stream to an adjacent router. That router must be configured to send the multicast traffic onward to a specialized multicast router called a *rendezvous point* (RP). There can be only one RP per multicast group, although there can be several multicast groups per RP.

Here's how it works:

1. The destination host sends a join message toward the multicast source or toward the rendezvous point.

2. The join message is forwarded until it reaches a router receiving a copy of the multicast stream—all the way back to the source if necessary.

3. The router sends a copy of the stream back to the host.

4. When the host is ready to leave the multicast stream, it sends a prune message to its adjacent router.

5. The router receiving the prune message checks to see whether it still needs to send the multicast stream to any other hosts. If it doesn't, it sends its own prune message on to the next router.

Packets are sent only to the network segments that need them. If only certain users will access the multicast stream or if many multicast streams will be broadcast at once, sparse mode is the most efficient use of network resources. IPTV, for example, is typically implemented using PIM-SM.

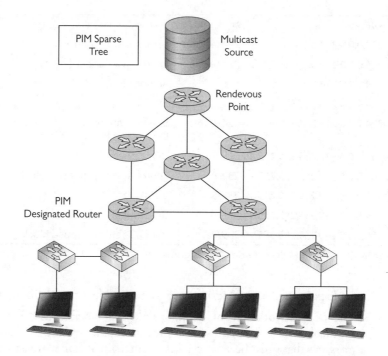

Figure 17-3
Setting up
a multicast
network using
PIM sparse mode

However, PIM-SM also requires the most configuration (see Figure 17-3). All routers on the network must be aware of the multicast rendezvous points. Routers should also be configured with access lists so that only designated users will have access to the multicast group. RPs themselves must be configured with a traffic threshold. Once the threshold is exceeded, join messages will bypass the RP and go directly to the source. This threshold is usually set to zero automatically, which means the RP will direct all join requests to the source by default. It can also be lifted entirely. The decision depends on how much multicast traffic each network segment can bear.

NOTE PIM "sparse-dense" mode is not a type of PIM but rather a router setting on Cisco routers that allows the interface to act in both PIM sparse mode and PIM dense mode simultaneously (on different multicast groups) to support a network with both modes used for different multicast groups and applications.

Multicast Addressing

You can't use just any IP address as a multicast host address. The Internet Assigned Numbers Authority (IANA), the same organization responsible for assigning port numbers, has divided the Class D IP address range into a series of address blocks allocated to different types of multicast messaging. See Table 17-1.

Address Range	Mask	Description
224.0.0.0-224.0.0.255	224.0.0/24	Local network control block
224.0.1.0-224.0.1.255	224.0.1/24	Internetwork control block
224.0.2.0-224.0.255.255	n/a	Ad hoc block
224.1.0.0-224.1.255.255	n/a	Unassigned
224.2.0.0-224.2.255.255	224.2/16	Session Announcement Protocol (SAP)/Session Description Protocol (SDP) block
224.3.0.0-231.255.255.255	n/a	Unassigned
232.0.0.0-232.255.255.255	232/8	Source-specific multicast block
233.0.0.0-233.255.255.255	233/8	GLOP block
234.0.0.0-238.255.255.255	n/a	Unassigned
239.0.0.0-239.255.255.255	239/8	Administratively scoped block

Table 17-1 IANA Multicast Address Assignments

Each block in the Class D address assignment table serves a different function.

- The local network control block, or link-local block, is used for network protocols that will remain within the same subnet. Control or announcement messages that must be sent to all the routers in a subnet are addressed to destinations in this range.

- The internetwork control block is used to send multicast control messages beyond the local network segment. For example, in PIM sparse mode, rendezvous point information may be communicated across broadcast domains using an address in this range.

- Ad hoc addresses are assigned by IANA to multicast control protocols that don't fit clearly into the first two blocks. However, much of the ad hoc block was assigned prior to the existence of usage guidelines, so many addresses in this range are simply reserved for commercial uses.

- The SDP/SAP block is reserved for applications that send session announcements.

- The source-specific multicast block provides multicast host addresses for SSM applications.

- The GLOP block (see the following note) provides multicast host addresses for commercial content providers.

- Some address ranges remain unassigned for experimental or future uses.

- The administratively scoped block is reserved for private multicast domains. These addresses will never be assigned by IANA to any specific multicast technology or content provider. You're free to use these as multicast host addresses within the enterprise network, but they can't be used to send multicast content over the Internet.

Any multicast host address used by a private enterprise (other than a commercial content provider, such as an ISP or television network) will come from either the SMM or the administratively scoped block.

> **NOTE** GLOP is not an acronym. It turns out the original authors of this request for comment (RFC) needed to refer to this mechanism by something other than, "that address allocation method where you put your autonomous system in the middle two octets." Lacking anything better to call it, one of the authors simply began to refer to this as "GLOP" addressing, and the name stuck.

Streaming Reflectors

A streaming video reflector (sometimes called a *relay*) subscribes to a video stream and re-transmits it to another address. This re-transmission can be any combination of multicast or unicast inputs and outputs. In the case of forwarding multicast across a VPN, a pair of reflectors can be used. In such a situation, a streaming source outputs a multicast stream. The reflector service subscribes to the stream and de-encapsulates layers 3 and 4 (IP and UDP headers). It then re-encapsulates the data with new TCP and IP headers and forwards the packet. The receiving end receives the unicast stream and performs the reverse process, forwarding a multicast stream.

When implementing multicast reflecting, you need to consider the following:

- **Administration** The reflector is typically configured by the same administrator who is responsible for the streaming service. Beyond the initial configuration at installation, no network configuration is required to change the reflector service. For occasional use, such as company announcements, a reflector at the source site can be configured and left active with the receive-side reflectors for the duration of the event.

- **Bandwidth** Because the reflected streams are individually configured, there is no risk of inadvertently forwarding multicast streams. The receive-side reflector requests the stream based on local administration. While the receive-side reflector service is enabled, the bandwidth is used even if no one is subscribed to the multicast stream. There is a small packet overhead increase with the conversion from UDP to TCP.

- **Scalability** A single reflector at the source location can reflect to multiple receive-site reflectors, but the bandwidth is unicast, so each receive-side reflector gets a separate stream.

- **Configuration** A separate PIM rendezvous point will need to be configured at the receiving site. Multicast addresses do not need to map between the sites. Each site can have its own addressing scheme. For IPTV applications, a separate channel guide will have to be implemented if the multicast addresses do not map between the sites.

Chapter Review

Streaming is an increasingly important component of AV systems design. Once you've performed the requisite analyses for a streaming system, you need to be able to identify the impact of bandwidth restrictions and network policies and the impact of inherent network latency on the streaming application. You should also calculate the required bandwidth for uncompressed digital AV streams and factor in the appropriate transport and distribution protocols for the client's streaming needs.

Always keep in mind that streaming AV consumes network resources—perhaps more resources than a network manager anticipated. Document everything, from the needs analysis to network restrictions to the technical specifications of your proposed solution. If you can make the case that your streaming system meets the customer's needs and you've created a design that respects the requirements of the larger enterprise network, you will be successful.

Review Questions

The following questions are based on the content covered in this chapter and are intended to help reinforce the knowledge you have assimilated. These questions are not extracted from the CTS-D exam nor are they necessarily CTS-D practice exam questions. For an official CTS-D practice exam, see the accompanying CD.

1. If your streaming AV system does not support High-bandwidth Digital Content Protection (HDCP), it's likely the system _____.
   A. Won't be able to play high-definition video content
   B. Won't be able to play standard-definition video content
   C. Won't be able to play live video streams
   D. Won't be able to play protected audio streams

2. In a converged network, where 70 percent of the bandwidth capacity is available and 30 percent of the available capacity is available for streaming, what percentage of the network's rated capacity is available for streaming?
   A. 21 percent
   B. 30 percent
   C. 50 percent
   D. 70 percent

3. What might be considered acceptable latency for streaming desktop video?
   A. 50 microseconds
   B. 30 milliseconds
   C. 200 milliseconds
   D. 1 second

4. Which of the following protocols might you use in a streaming AV system? (Select all that apply.)

    A. User Datagram Protocol

    B. Real-time Transport Protocol

    C. Real-time Transport Control Protocol

    D. MPEG

5. Which of the following statements apply to unicast streaming?

    A. It consumes more bandwidth the more people who need to view the stream.

    B. It uses group-management protocols to control streaming channels.

    C. It requires special routers called *rendezvous points*.

    D. It uses special IP addresses assigned by the Internet Assigned Numbers Authority.

6. If your multicast streaming AV system runs on an IPv6-based network, the group-management protocol to use is called _____.

    A. Internet Group Management Protocol

    B. Multicast Listener Discovery

    C. Source-Specific Multicast

    D. Protocol Independent Multicast

Answers

1. **A.** If your streaming AV system does not support High-bandwidth Digital Content Protection (HDCP), it's likely the system won't be able to play high-definition video content.

2. **A.** In a converged network, where 70 percent of the bandwidth capacity is available and 30 percent of the available capacity is available for streaming, 21 percent of the network's rated capacity is available for streaming.

3. **D.** In general, streaming desktop video can tolerate one second of latency.

4. **A, B, C.** When designing a streaming AV system, you might use User Datagram, Real-time Transport, and Real-time Transport Control Protocols.

5. **A.** Unicast consumes more bandwidth the more people who need to view the stream. The three other statements apply to multicast.

6. **B.** If your multicast streaming AV system runs on an IPv6-based network, the group-management protocol to use is called Multicast Listener Discovery.

CHAPTER 18

Security for Networked AV Applications

In this chapter, you will learn about

- Documenting security objectives
- Evaluating a client's security posture
- Creating a risk register for an AV/IT network
- Implementing a risk response for common security risks

Consider how and why you protect your home, whether you use an alarm system or simply lock your doors. You secure your home for the same reason your customers protect their IT networks—to protect the valuables inside. As AV systems migrate to enterprise data networks, user organizations expect them to maintain a security posture in alignment with their overall information security goals. AV designers must understand their clients' security requirements and take them into account when designing a system.

Every client's security needs are unique and evolve over time. Like the all-important needs assessment that designers conduct before creating an AV system, there is a process they should follow to ensure they discover clients' security needs and design a system that meets them.

Domain Check

This chapter relates directly to the following task on the CTS-D Exam Content Outline:

- Domain B Task 6: Coordinate IT and network security criteria

This task comprises 4 percent of the exam (about five questions). This chapter may also relate to other tasks.

Security Objectives

As AV systems migrate to enterprise data networks, clients expect those AV systems to be in alignment with their information security goals. In many cases, those goals may be more than just best practices; they may be required for regulatory compliance. Healthcare facilities in the United States must protect data in compliance with the Health Insurance Portability and Accountability Act. Financial institutions in the United States must comply with the Sarbanes-Oxley Act, among others. Industrial companies and others around the world may seek to comply with ISO-27000, a security framework that is now required for all ISO-9000 series-certified companies. To the extent that an AV system interfaces with IT systems or handles data that falls under various compliance frameworks, design and integration choices that put them out of compliance may impede installation.

Even when regulatory compliance isn't a central concern, most clients have a similar set of security objectives.

- **Confidentiality**   Ensuring that people who shouldn't have access to information don't.
- **Integrity**   Ensuring that people who are permitted to access information can trust that the information has not been changed or altered.
- **Availability**   Ensuring that access to information is unimpeded. This extends to any type of information, including multimedia, video sources, and more.

Think of these objectives as the CIA triad. No security system is perfect, and each organization weighs these objectives differently. Some companies can trade off tighter security measures for easier access to files. Others can tolerate downtime if it means keeping their data secure. Typically, as you communicate with clients, you may find that two of the three legs of the CIA triad are most important.

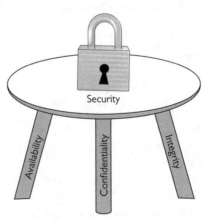

Any technology that is connected to an enterprise network could potentially impact one or more of these security objectives. As an AV designer, you are not likely to specify or configure firewalls, intrusion detection devices, or other network security technologies. Your job is to be aware of a client's security requirements, communicate that information to the AV team, and, where possible, address and mitigate security risk in your AV design.

Perhaps the most important aspect of discovering security objectives and requirements, regardless of how extensive they may be, is documenting them. During any security needs analysis, designers should document everything they can about security and risk. When planning a project, allocate more time than you think necessary to document security requirements, issues, and strategies. You'll be glad you did.

Identifying Security Requirements

A recurring issue in the AV industry—and an impediment to getting paid—is that security requirements are often discovered during installation or commissioning. There is nothing worse than performing your final systems verification, expecting final sign-off, and finding there's a security requirement you didn't know about, rendering the project unacceptable. Therefore, it's critical to identify security requirements and set expectations up front, before the client signs off on the initial design (see Figure 18-1). This will give you time to communicate the requirements and, if necessary, submit change orders to ensure equipment is specified that can support those requirements. You may also need to budget cost and time to complete International Organization for Standardization (ISO) surveys and risk mitigation plans.

If possible, move the identification of security requirements into the needs analysis phase of the AV design. This may not always be possible; a company may not want to expose its security profile or requirements to just anyone who bids. But you can at least begin to understand what compliance frameworks the client operates under and which legs of the CIA triad are priorities.

At a minimum, designers should identify security requirements and address them in the design prior to sign-off. This is usually the last time in the process when it is reasonably easy to make changes without impacting schedules or equipment costs.

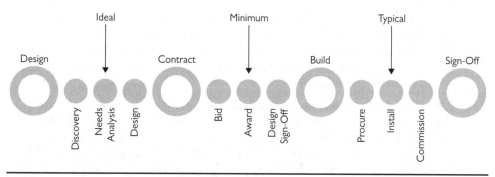

Figure 18-1 Ideally, you should identify security requirements upfront. Typically, AV pros wait too late.

Security requirements and the steps needed to meet them should be appended to the statement of work and listed as system sign-off criteria. This is to protect both the client and the AV designer/integrator.

Determining a Security Posture

AV systems help facilitate communication, but they can also create vulnerabilities in your client's system. The client's *security posture* may limit what equipment can be in an AV installation. For example, some customers may forbid the use of wireless microphones because their signals can be intercepted. Other customers may not allow you to use a projector with nonvolatile memory (NVM) for fear that images could be retrieved from the projector if it were stolen.

With respect to networked AV systems, you have to consider whether the AV system provides a way to access the rest of the network or any other information the customer wants to protect. Can you guarantee that a hacker can't use the digital signage outside the boardroom to access the chief executive officer's (CEO's) schedule or use the videoconferencing system to spy on confidential meetings? You need to understand the elements of a security posture that are relevant to your AV design.

A security posture describes what an organization is trying to protect and how vigorously it needs to protect it. When it comes to AV systems, the security posture should be set by the client. AV designers don't create security postures; they make their systems compliant with an existing posture.

Security postures will likely be unique to each job because each customer will have different requirements. You might hear security postures described as lax, realistic, or paranoid. Security postures are often influenced by external oversight, such as an industry or regulatory authority that sets security standards, or internal operations, such as a company security policy.

There are several steps to determining a security posture.

- **Learn the client's mission.** The AV system you're designing should help achieve an organization's mission. Knowing the vision or goals of the organization will help you see the value of the AV system from the client's perspective and prioritize which aspects the client needs to secure.

- **Learn the concept of operations.** The concept of operations describes how the client fulfills its mission. How does the organization function? How will the AV system help the organization function better? Examine its current security processes and procedures. Can any of them be applied to the AV system? Will any of them have to change?

- **Assess the data's importance.** Specifically, this concerns data traveling through the AV system. Where does the information in your AV system fit into the organization's mission and concept of operations? Is the AV system essential to operations, or does it simply carry casual information among departments? Is there an existing system that carries similar information that can be used for reference?

- **Learn the client's risk profile.** This may involve signing a nondisclosure agreement. A risk profile is how tolerant a customer is of risk. How worried is the customer about security breaches? A customer's risk profile may vary for different content. What type of intrusions does the customer worry about most? For instance, a university may not care much if an outsider hacks into its streaming video server and watches all the recorded lectures. It may be concerned, however, about protecting the content servers that store footage from its medical research facility. The organization's security policies will be a reflection of its risk profile.

- **Identify stakeholders.** This especially includes those with the power to approve and negotiate. The project stakeholders are the best sources of information about security posture. Document the role of each stakeholder so that various members of the project team know whom they can contact to learn different information about security posture. Negotiation is an integral part of the security and risk management process. Within your stakeholders, you will need to identify who has approval authority or negotiation power.

- **Identify governance structure.** You need to know at least the sections that apply to your AV system, which will probably need to exist within the customer's IT framework. Because of the complexity of IT systems, mature organizations create control objectives that govern how to run the system. They may adhere to a standardized IT governance structure, such as Information Technology Infrastructure Library (ITIL) or Control Objectives for Information and Related Technology (COBIT). Even if the client doesn't use a specific standardized governance structure, its IT policies should cover similar categories, including the following:

  - How do the systems and processes help the organization meet its mission?

  - What are the usage policies, and which best practices does your customer follow?

  - Who are your user groups, and will any of them use the system remotely?

  - What are the audit guidelines and processes?

  - How does the system compare to industry best practices for similar systems?

  - How does your customer measure the success of a system?

- **Identify project constraints.** Constraints include budget, time for completion, and policies that affect the eventual installation. The client's security policies may impose certain constraints on the project. For example, there may be a policy against using Wi-Fi. In that case, you may only select devices without Wi-Fi or with the capability to disable Wi-Fi. Constraints will likely impose financial burdens on the project. A cost-benefit analysis of those burdens may result in the revision of policies or requirements. For instance, the client might agree that, given the cost of running new cable, a few encrypted Wi-Fi devices are OK after all.

TIP You've landed two projects with the same client. One is a videoconferencing system for the international board of directors. The other is a video-streaming system for HR training. To learn the risk profile for the videoconferencing system, research security measures taken on other systems used by the board of directors. For the video-streaming system, research how the client protects other HR educational materials.

Stakeholder Input

Information security always supports business goals, and not every department in an organization has the same business goals. The amount of time, effort, and cost spent on security depends on those goals. There is no one-size-fits-all, "secure enough" system. Designers need to come to agreement with various parties on what security requirements are important.

Verify that you have input from all relevant stakeholders. Typically, an AV designer/integrator needs to address three areas of security, so it is important to speak to stakeholders with experience in each area.

- **Operational** These are the stakeholders who own data. They determine what needs to be protected and how vigorously. The other two areas support operational security.
- **Network** These are the IT stakeholders who specify and administrate network policies. There are generally two types of IT network stakeholders: those responsible for the ports and protocols, firewalls, and routers in a network; and those responsible for access control (see "The Triple-A of Access Control").
- **Physical** These are traditional security stakeholders, responsible for physical access to gear, spaces, and more. They can help you create policies on how to secure gear and cabinets to prevent theft.

Here is an example of an AV-specific operational security concern that may not involve network security: Say your client just finished renovating their office building. They have a beautiful conference room on their lobby level with three glass walls. If the CEO displays the company's three-year financial plan on the conference room videowall, anyone in the lobby could read it. These are the types of security concerns an AV designer must be aware of.

The Triple-A of Access Control

When specifying IT security for AV applications, you need to consider access control, which can be described by three *A*s:

- **Authentication** The person using the system is who they say they are. This is proven with certificates, passwords, and tokens.

- **Authorization** The person using the system is allowed to use it and take specific actions. This is managed through permissions in the system and directories or authorized users.

- **Accounting** Those who manage authentication and authorization also have an accurate record of what happens with the system and over the network in general. This accounting supports a concept called *nonrepudiation,* which includes producing records proving who was using a networked system and what they did while they had access.

Without all three *As*, nonrepudiation can't work.

Assessing Risk

Put yourself in this position: You are considering for your design an AV device that supports a bunch of standard network protocols, including Telnet, Secure Shell (SSH), HTTP Secure (HTTPS), Hypertext Transfer Protocol (HTTP), and File Transfer Protocol (FTP). It has a default password of "password" and only one user account named "admin," which can't be changed. Here are some potential vulnerabilities:

- HTTP, Telnet, and FTP are clear-text protocols, meaning anyone with access and a simple network analyzer can see exactly what's going across the wire, including usernames and passwords.

- The default password could be found easily on Google.

- The default username can't be changed.

- The client can't set up multiple accounts for nonrepudiation.

- The client can't set up accounts with different user permissions.

Now you're in a meeting with representatives of the client. You bring up the possible vulnerabilities of your proposed AV device and engage the client in the question of "Big deal or not a big deal?" What you're doing is helping identify risk or possible threats to the AV system.

A threat usually requires a vulnerability and someone or something that might want to exploit that vulnerability. In most cases, if there's a vulnerability, you should assume someone will want to exploit it. Depending on the value of what the client must protect or the ease by which a vulnerability might be exploited, you may determine that a threat is larger or smaller and requires commensurate protective measures.

AV designers should attend risk-response meetings with a list of potential vulnerabilities. This is not necessarily a list of bugs and exploits but rather a list of services and functions handled by AV devices that may need a security policy. Depending on the security posture and any required procedures within the organization, this may be a general list of functions or a list of specific gear.

Risk Registers

Once you're aware of the threats and risks to an AV system, you should create a *risk register*. A risk register is a methodology for prioritizing the threats that you can mitigate. It usually takes the form of a comprehensive table or spreadsheet and helps you assign value to risks depending on two factors: probability (how likely something bad will happen) and impact (how bad things will be if it does).

Risk registers are used across all forms of business, not just security. There are many methodologies and templates for assigning risk, and the process can be simple or complex, depending on the details and the client's security posture. A risk register might include information such as a description of the risk, the type of risk, the likelihood it will occur, the severity of its effects, a current status of the risk, and any internal stakeholders responsible for managing the risk. In general, if your client already has a risk management process or template, use theirs.

A risk register also includes an entry for countermeasures—basically how the risk might be handled. Typically, there are four ways to handle a risk.

- **Avoid it.** Limit or avert the risky activity.
- **Accept it.** Because the probability or impact is low enough, the client is willing to take the risk.
- **Transfer it.** The client can purchase insurance or maintenance plans or adopt cloud-based technology services.
- **Mitigate it.** Make changes to design, configuration, or operational procedures to lower the probability or impact of a risk to the point where it's acceptable.

Designers should consult with clients about their options and assign a response to each risk in the risk register.

Mitigation Planning

The most common risk response is mitigation, one of the final steps in a security strategy (see Figure 18-2). A mitigation plan includes the action proposed to mitigate a risk, a contingency (what to do if something bad happens even after you've mitigated the risk), the name of someone responsible for the mitigation plan, and a due date.

The responsible party and due date will usually come from the client, not the designer/integrator. For example, let's assume you have a projector that can be controlled only via Telnet. The vulnerability is that Telnet usernames and passwords are sent via clear text and can therefore be discovered and the system accessed. The potential impact is fairly low because the worst thing a hacker could do is turn off a projector. But the probability it will happen is fairly high because of how easy it is to find out the password and break in.

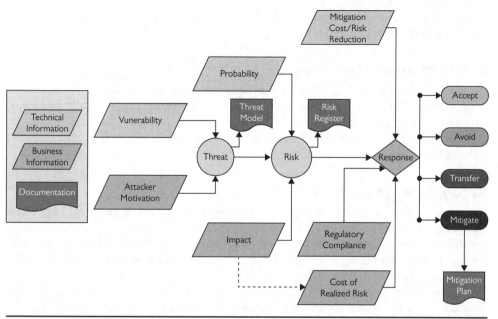

Figure 18-2 Planning for AV system security involves many steps.

A mitigation plan for this system may be to create an AV-specific virtual LAN (VLAN) for just the projector and the devices that need to talk to it, such as a control system. Then create an access-control list on the router to that VLAN that blocks all Telnet traffic. That way, only a computer or device that is physically connected to that VLAN can see the network traffic and Telnet into the vulnerable projector. Typically, the job of creating the VLAN would be assigned to the client's network team, with a due date before the installation date.

In general, you may find that segregating AV applications onto separate VLANs is a good mitigation strategy for a variety of situations. In most cases, this is a design-level consideration, rather than a configuration task, so address it early.

The following are some other risk-mitigation strategies.

Change Default Passwords

Default passwords should never be left in a system. This is a huge security risk that is easy to fix. Before integration, change all default passwords to a job-specific password. You can use some standard combination of numbers and job name. For example, 246*Info-Comm could be your job password. This gives you a measure of security and makes it easy for project team members to access the system.

After systems verification and commissioning, when you turn over systems documentation to the client, give them a list of devices with usernames, job passwords, and instructions for changing the passwords. That way, they can implement password security that meets their own company policy.

Create Multiple User Roles

If a piece of AV equipment is going to be accessed over the network for day-to-day use—as opposed to just configuration—create separate accounts for users and administrators with only the permissions required to perform their job functions. It's bad practice to allow anyone who might need to use or schedule an AV system to have configuration rights, too.

Accounts for Every User

The most secure password management strategy is to set an account for every user and then assign individual roles based on their access requirements. The challenge is scalability. What if you have 100 projectors that require two admins and eight users each? And what if the eight users are different based on where each projector is used? And what if somebody quits?

This is where directory servers come in handy. Directory servers are a centralized system used to keep, change, and store passwords. Most clients usually have a directory server for enforcing company password policies on laptops or other computing devices. You can integrate AV systems with an existing directory server for authentication and authorization.

Authentication is the username and password that proves the person requesting access to a system is who they say they are. Authorization takes that identity and matches it to a group membership. By being a member of the group, the person inherits the group's permissions. Say a member group is called *projector admins*. If someone wants to administer a projector, the projector authenticates that person and then checks to see whether the person is a member of the projector admin group. If so, the projector grants access.

The following are among the advantages of using a centralized directory:

- It greatly lowers the amount of administration required. You can administer policies for 100 projectors in one place.

- It is much more likely that password policy will be adhered to because users have to change only one password for every device.

- Because you may be able to leverage directory servers that are already in place for IT purposes, you can hand off password policy to the organization.

Keep in mind, however, the ability to use a centralized directory is not universally supported by all AV products.

Disable Unnecessary Services

AV devices tend to be "Swiss army knives," with many different functions and connection capabilities, which may or may not be used on a given job. Best practice is to disable services such as Telnet, FTP, or HTTP when they are not being used for a particular installation. This gives a potential attacker fewer doors to try to break into.

Enable Encryption and Auditing

Use encryption where possible. This prevents people from reading passwords and potentially compromising data. Use HTTPS instead of HTTP, SSH instead of Telnet, and so on. Then, disable the nonencrypted version.

Plus, any systems that have an audit function, which tracks access and security failures, should be enabled. This offers a record of who logged in when, any failed login attempts, and more. Such an audit report not only can help catch and punish bad guys, but it can also help the client figure out how they got into a system to further mitigate risk down the road.

Chapter Review

AV designers aren't necessarily in the business of securing their clients' systems. But it is their job to understand and document clients' security requirements, recognize threats and vulnerabilities, help assess risk, and offer plans for mitigating or otherwise address risk as part of their designs.

In this chapter, you learned how to identify a client's security objectives, requirements, and posture. You also learned how to use a risk register not only to describe the possible threats to a client's information systems but also to plan for ways of addressing those threats. If you come away with nothing else from this chapter, remember always to document everything about a client's security requirements and how they might be impacted by your AV design. You never want to learn too late that you've created an insecure AV system.

PART IV

Review Questions

The following questions are based on the content covered in this chapter and are intended to help reinforce the knowledge you have assimilated. These questions are not extracted from the CTS-D exam nor are they necessarily CTS-D practice exam questions. For an official CTS-D practice exam, see the accompanying CD.

1. A client's security objectives can often be described with respect to the CIA triad. CIA stands for:

    A. Central Intelligence Agency

    B. Confidentiality, integrity, availability

    C. Confidentiality, information, access

    D. Communication, infrastructure, authorization

2. Which of the following is not a step in assessing a client's security posture?

    A. Assessing how important the client's data is

    B. Testing the client's network for vulnerabilities

    C. Identifying stakeholders

    D. Understanding project constraints

3. When you've identified a security risk, you can avoid it, accept it, transfer it, or
_____.

    A. Eliminate it

    B. Change it

    C. Mitigate it

    D. Reconfigure it

4. Which is an important consideration for AV designers concerning a client's wireless network?

    A. QoS could be minimized.

    B. Integration of POS equipment into the system.

    C. Data security/encryption issues.

    D. Variable bandwidth dynamics issues.

5. Which of the following is a mitigation strategy for addressing security risks introduced by AV systems?

    A. Building a firewall

    B. Setting all passwords to "password"

    C. Hiring a security expert

    D. Putting AV systems on a VLAN

Answers

1. **B.** A client's security objectives can often be described with respect to confidentiality, integrity, and availability.

2. **B.** When assessing a client's security posture, it's important to assess the importance of the client's data, identify stakeholders, and understand project constraints. Testing the network for vulnerabilities is not a designer's job.

3. **C.** When you've identified a security risk, you can avoid it, accept it, transfer it, or mitigate it.

4. **C.** With respect to a client's wireless network, AV designers need to consider data security and encryption issues.

5. **D.** To mitigate security issues introduced by AV systems, consider putting those systems on a virtual LAN (VLAN).

CHAPTER 19

Conducting Project Implementation Activities

In this chapter, you will learn about

- The audiovisual performance verification process, including for discrete audio and video systems
- Troubleshooting methods
- The verification standard for system closeout
- Closeout documentation
- Customer training
- Obtaining customer sign-off

As the AV industry establishes standards and best practices on and off the job site, owners, consultants, and integrators will need to conform to the standards and follow the guidelines for the proper design, fabrication, installation, and integration of AV systems. In this chapter, you will learn about the system performance verification standard and resources provided by several organizations. You will also learn how to troubleshoot common problems.

For starters, you should familiarize yourself with various AV-related standards. This is an excellent time to verify that the system that was installed is compliant with all relevant standards. You will also need some specific test and measurement tools for calibration and verification of both audio and video.

Your knowledge of the basic principles and theories involved in electronics, audio, video, and networking technologies will be well utilized during the final stretch of AV system integration. Once you have studied the theory and conducted verification of the system on the job site, you will be able to set up and verify new AV systems with confidence.

Domain Check

This chapter relates directly to the following tasks on the CTS-D Exam Content Outline:

- Domain D Task 1: Participate in project implementation communication
- Domain D Task 2: Perform system verifications
- Domain D Task 3: Conduct system close out activities

These tasks comprise 9.6 percent of the exam (about 12 questions). This chapter may also relate to other tasks.

Performance Verification Standard

The ANSI/INFOCOMM 10:2013 standard, *Audiovisual Systems Performance Verification*, can help determine whether an AV system has met your client's objectives and is performing to design expectations.

Benefits of using this standard include the following:

- Streamlining verification tests and reporting
- Providing a verifiable outcome
- Creating a common language between all parties
- Aligning outcome and performance expectations at an early stage in the project
- Creating reporting that completes the project documentation
- Reducing project risk through early identification of problems, thereby reducing the likelihood of remedial work

This standard should be used in conjunction with ANSI/INFOCOMM 2M-2010, *Standard Guide for Audiovisual Systems Design and Coordination Processes*, as well as other relevant performance standards. The 2M standard provides a framework and supporting processes for determining elements of an audiovisual system that need to be verified, the timing of that verification within the project delivery cycle, a process for determining verification metrics, and reporting procedures. The standard includes 160 reference verification items.

As shown in Figure 19-1, verification of conformance to the 2M standard must include the delivery of the Audiovisual Systems Design and Coordination Processes Checklist.

The 2M standard serves to verify the following:

- **Documentation of applicability** An outline that indicates which sections of the standard are applicable to the project according to contractual agreements, as well as any services not applicable (indicated as N/A)

Standard Guide for Audiovisual Systems Design and Coordination Processes Checklist

Project Title ______________________ Description ______________________

Location ______________________ Architect ______________________

Designer ______________________ Date ______________________

Integrator ______________________ Client ______________________

Activity Codes: Meeting – M Coordination – C Task – T Deliverable – D Other – O NA – Not Applicable

Note: There may be more than one activity code on each line

Date	Activity Code	Responsible Party	Accepted By	
I. Project Planning and Coordination Meetings				
_____	_____	_____	_____	1. Schedule and agreement for meetings

Figure 19-1 Title block of Audiovisual Systems Design and Coordination Processes Checklist

- **Consideration** Written verification that the service providers have read and understand this standard and agree to be referred to as the Responsible Party for the applicable sections
- **Completion** Written verification that the service providers have completed the approved services, indicated by the party authorized to sign as Accepted By

The verification can be as simple as checking off boxes when you complete a task. By documenting your work along the way, you are setting yourself up for success when you hand over the system to the client.

The Audiovisual Systems Design and Coordination Processes Checklist includes three check boxes for each item for the project team to address.

- **The Activity Code** This identifies the type of item, such as deliverable (D), coordination (C), task (T), meeting (M), other (O), or not applicable (NA).
- **The Responsible Party** This is the designer, contractor, or integrator who is delegated and contracted to perform the activity. This may be more than one party and should be identified as such.
- **Accepted By** The client, designer, contractor, or integrator who is authorized and contracted to verify that the activity has been performed. This may be more than one party and should be identified as such.

Figure 19-2 provides an example of how a checklist line item could be filled out. The task is "schedule and agreement for meetings." This is an activity code M, C, and D, which stands for "meeting, coordination, and deliverable." The integrator has been contracted to perform the activity, and the consultant is authorized to verify that the activity has been performed.

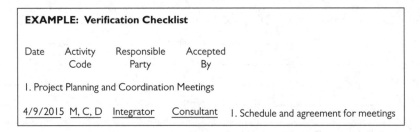

Figure 19-2 A sample checklist line item filled out in accordance with the *Standard Guide for Audiovisual Systems Design and Coordination Processes*

System Verification Process

The performance verification process involves many phases, starting with pre-integration and all the way through final acceptance by the client, as shown in Figure 19-3. The actual testing of system performance starts with turning on the system for the first time and ends with handing off the remotes and documentation to your client. Therefore, it starts in the middle of a typical AV project, after planning, fabricating, and installing the equipment at the job site.

The verification process in each of the phases is as follows:

- **Pre-integration verification** Refers to items that take place prior to systems integration. These items will generally verify existing conditions, such as the presence of device enclosures, or items such as backing/blocking/framing that require coordination among the trades for AV system installation.

- **Systems integration verification** Refers to items that take place while the audiovisual systems are being integrated or built, including off-site and onsite work. These items will generally verify proper operation or configuration so that the system can function (for example, equipment mounted level, phantom power, termination stress, AV rack thermal gradient performance).

- **Post-integration verification** Refers to items that take place after the audiovisual systems integration has been completed. These items will generally verify system performance against verification metrics as defined in the project documentation (for example, projected image contrast ratio, audio and video recording, control system automated functions).

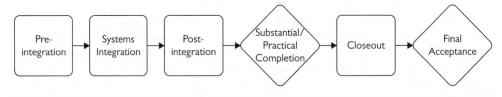

Figure 19-3 Performance verification phases and milestones

- **Substantial/practical completion verification** Indicates conditional acceptance of the project has been issued by the owner or owner's representative, acknowledging that the project or a designated portion is substantially/practically complete and ready for use by the owner; however, some requirements and/or deliverables defined in the project documentation may not be complete. This milestone occurs at the end of the post-integration verification phase.

- **Closeout verification** Refers to items involved with closing out the project. These items will generally be related to documenting the As-Built/As-Is status of the systems and transfer of system software, among other items such as control system test reporting, As-Built drawings complete, and warranties.

- **Final acceptance verification** Indicates that acceptance of the project has been issued by the owner or owner's representative, acknowledging that the project is 100 percent complete; all required deliverables, services, verification lists, testing, performance metrics, and sign-offs have been received; and all requirements defined in the project documentation have been satisfied and completed that occur at the completion of the closeout verification phase. No further project activity will take place after this milestone is verified.

Certain verification items may need verification at multiple times during a project. The reference verification items provided in the ANSI/INFOCOMM 10:2013 standard, *Audiovisual Systems Performance Verification,* define the verification phases at which those items should be tested. Where additional items are added on a project-specific basis, they will also be allocated a verification phase.

Regional Regulations

You need to know how codes, regulations, and safety procedures apply to your job site. To do that, you need to identify in the location of your project the authority having jurisdiction (AHJ) or the regional regulatory authorities, as they are known in some areas of the world. These organizations typically monitor compliance with codes and laws. Standards and best practices are typically established by organizations consisting of representation from various sectors of the industry.

Codes and laws are mandated methods, practices, and collections of standards that are enforceable by law. You can be legally punished for not following them. Generally, an inspector will be present to verify that the work is being done according to code. Each jurisdiction may have its own set of regulations.

If you encounter conflicting codes, follow the most restrictive code for the region in which they are working. In other words, if you find the interpretations of applicable codes and standards are in conflict, follow the requirements of the more stringent code or standard.

Standards are documents that provide requirements, specifications, guidelines, or characteristics that can be used consistently to ensure that materials, products, processes, and services are fit for their purpose. They are often prepared by a standards organization or group and published with an established procedure.

Best practices are the best choice of the available methods for accomplishing a specific task in an industry. Best practices are recognized as the proper way to do a certain task. They can be a generally accepted industry practice or unique to a specific company.

Resources for Regional Codes

As noted earlier, codes, regulations, and safety procedures vary by location. You will need to check these for the area of your project. Several organizations provide resources to locate regional or industry-specific codes.

The National Electrical Code (NEC) is an electrical wiring code for the United States, and there are similar organizations in countries around the world. The NEC provides comprehensive information including the following resources:

- The *NEC Codebook* provides the detailed and comprehensive descriptions of electric standards. The codebook is usually used as a reference by individuals interested in the details affecting an electrical system installation.

- The *NEC Handbook* provides the complete electrical code, along with extensive additional commentary. The commentary includes drawings, additional articles, wiring diagrams, tables with supplementary data, and photographs to provide a better understanding of the NEC's requirements.

There are many different codes and standards that apply to various regions in the world. Every country has its own resources for standards. If you need to access standards by your region or industry, you can begin by searching the following two websites:

- The International Organization for Standards (http://iso.org) publishes standards to ensure that products and services are safe, reliable, and of good quality. For business, they are strategic tools that reduce costs by minimizing waste and errors and increasing productivity. The ISO has technical committees working on standards for a large number of industries.

- NSSN (http://nssn.org), administered by the American National Standards Institute (ANSI), is a search engine that provides users with standards-related information from a wide range of developers, including organizations accredited by ANSI, other U.S. private-sector standards bodies, government agencies, and international organizations.

Verification Tools

You're not necessarily an installer, but during pre-installation preparations, your team should have developed a verification checklist; revisit it to make sure you or someone on the team has the tools for calibration and verification of audio and video signals listed in Table 19-1, including general items such as crimpers and tape. In addition, you may want to use software-based signal analyzers for some of the components in your design. Note that Table 11-1 does not provide an exhaustive list; you may have more tools that are specific to certain work on various projects.

General and Network	Audio	Video
Verification list	Impedance meter	HDMI signal generator
Continuity tester	Tone and signal generators	HDMI signal analyzer
Multimeter	Signal analyzer	
Copper and fiber-optic cable certification testers	SPL meter	
Network cable testers	Real-time analyzer (RTA), dual-channel FFT analyzer, and measurement microphone	

Table 19-1 Test and Measurement Tools for AV System Verification

Audio System Verification

The audio system can be one of the most challenging aspects of an AV system design. It can be challenging to ensure a system provides an undistorted, high-quality signal with adequate levels to all specified destinations.

An audio system requires final adjustment after all the components have been installed for it to produce the desired or specified volume and quality. It is part of your job to set the audio gain and system equalization (EQ) and to adjust the various digital signal processing (DSP) components for the system to sound as good as it possibly can.

You will need to verify the performance of many components in an audio system and at many points along the signal path. You will want to use the ANSI/INFOCOMM 10:2013, *Audiovisual Systems Performance Verification* standard. The list of verification items found in that standard will make it easier for you to document the status of the AV system and to keep track of what you and your team have already inspected.

Audio-Testing Tools

You will need to use different test instruments to measure and verify various aspects of the audio signal along its path from microphone or other audio source to the loudspeakers. Audio-testing tools range from handheld devices to computer software programs; some are available for single-function testing and others for testing multiple functions.

Piezo Tweeter

A tweeter is a special type of loudspeaker, usually horn- or domed-shaped, that produces audio frequencies in the range of 2,000 Hz to 20,000 Hz (which is considered to be the upper limit of human hearing). Special tweeters can deliver high frequencies up to 100 kHz.

A piezo tweeter contains a piezoelectric crystal coupled to a mechanical diaphragm. An audio signal is applied to the crystal, which responds by flexing in proportion to the voltage applied across the crystal's surfaces, thus converting electrical energy into mechanical.

PART IV

The conversion of electrical pulses to mechanical vibrations and of returned mechanical vibrations back into electrical energy (transduction) is the basis for ultrasonic testing. The active element is the heart of the transducer as it converts the electrical energy to acoustic energy, and vice versa.

Audio Signal Generators

An audio signal generator is a piece of test equipment that produces calibrated electronic signals intended for the testing or alignment of electronic circuits or systems.

As shown in Figure 19-4, audio signal generators generate sine, square, or other waves at specific frequencies or combinations of frequencies. Many signal generators also generate pink noise, a quasi random noise source characterized by a flat amplitude response per octave band of frequency, and white noise, a sound that has the same energy level at all frequencies. In addition to showing frequency sweeps, these devices can also be used to test for polarity.

Sine waves are used as good, steady references for setting signal levels and to reveal distortion added by the equipment being evaluated. Common sine wave frequencies used include the following:

- **1 kHz** Used for setting levels and setting system gain using the unity gain method
- **400 Hz** Used in conjunction with a piezo tweeter to listen for clipping, as well as setting system gain using the optimization method

With the right software or app installed, a quality audio interface, and a properly calibrated signal, you can also use your computer, tablet, or smartphone as a signal generator. A tone generator creates a stable, constant signal that can be measured by a signal analyzer set to, for example, a 1 kHz signal at 0 dBu. This establishes the baseline measurement for setting gain.

Figure 19-4
A signal
generator

Sound Pressure Level Meters

Sound pressure level (SPL) is a measurement of all the acoustic energy present in an environment. It is typically expressed in decibels (dB SPL). Sound pressure refers to the pressure deviation from the ambient atmospheric pressure caused by the vibration of air particles. Sound pressure level refers to that variation of level above and below ambient atmospheric pressure and is referenced to 20 µPa or 0.0000204 dynes/cm^2, the threshold of human hearing. Sound pressure levels are expressed in decibels to correlate with the human perception of changes in loudness.

An SPL meter gives a single number measurement of the sound pressure at the measurement location. The meter consists of a calibrated microphone and the necessary circuitry to detect and display the sound level. Its function is simple; it converts the sound pressure levels in the air into corresponding electrical signals. These signals are measured and processed through internal filters, and the results are displayed in decibels, as shown in Figure 19-5.

When selecting an SPL meter, you want to use one that can take accurate readings. Sound pressure level meters are classified based on the allowable tolerances of the measurement. Devices that are not classified do not conform to a standard, so they are not reliable for measurement and testing purposes.

- **Class 0**   A lab reference standard. It has the strictest tolerances and is used when extreme precision is needed.

- **Class 1**   For precision measurement. It is useful for taking flat, engineering-grade accuracy measurements instead of wide-range or field measurements.

Figure 19-5
Meters for measuring sound pressure level

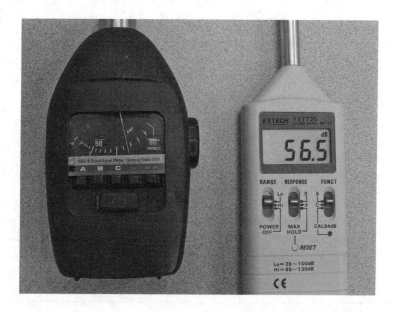

- **Class 2** For general-purpose use. It has the widest tolerances with respect to level linearity and frequency response. Class 2 meters are required only to have A-frequency weighting. Other weightings are optional. For many audio purposes, a Class 2 meter is acceptable.

- **Class 3** Intended for noise surveys. It is a simple sound level meter meant to determine whether a noise problem exists. If a problem does exist, further diagnosis will require a higher class meter.

Always reference the project specifications for the SPL meter settings necessary for proper verification. If the verification requirements do not specify settings for the SPL meter, you can use SPL meter weighting guidelines to select one.

You can apply weighting to the SPL meter measurement to correlate the meter's reading to how people perceive loudness. Figure 19-6 shows how loud different frequencies must be for the human ear to perceive them as equally loud as another. The dotted curve represents the threshold of human hearing, which is what the human ear perceives using a 1 kHz reference. The x-axis of the graph shows actual frequency, and the y-axis shows actual decibels SPL. A 40 Hz tone must be about 50 dB SPL louder before the human ear can perceive it equally as loud as 1 kHz. A 200 Hz tone, however, would have to be only 15 dB SPL louder to be perceived equally as loud as the 1 Hz tone. It is an absolute value, using 0 dB SPL as a reference.

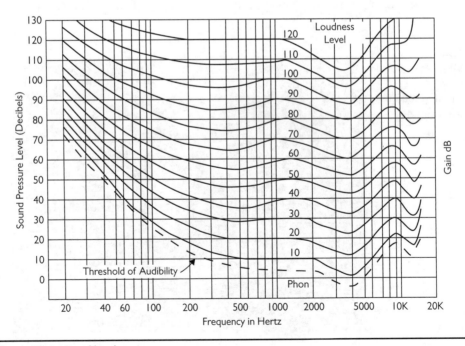

Figure 19-6 Equal loudness curve

The weighting curve represents standard filter contours designed to make test instruments approximate the response of the human ear. Therefore, the different weighting curves are meant to represent what the ear hears at various intensity levels. These measurements are a relative value and depend on where or what you are referencing for your measurement. The SPL meter will typically have three weighting settings: A, C, and Z (for zero).

- **A weighting**   Setting commonly used for environmental, hearing conservation, and noise ordinance enforcement. It closely reflects the response of the human ear to noise and its relative insensitivity to lower frequencies at lower listening levels.

- **C weighting**   More uniform response over the entire frequency range.

- **Z weighting**   No filtering. This is referred to as flat or Z (zero) weighting. A meter may be equipped with settings for A, C, and Flat or settings for A, C, and Z. Flat and Z would be unweighted settings.

You can see the differences in SPL weighting by examining the weighting curves. The line marked A in Figure 19-7 represents the A-weighted filter setting on an SPL meter. You can see that A weighting discriminates against low-frequency energy. The A weighting curve is almost the inverse of the equal loudness curve at a low listening level. The human ear perceives low-frequency energy as a lower decibels SPL than it actually is. The energy is still there; you are just not as sensitive to it at these listening levels. The A weighting reflects that perception.

Figure 19-7
SPL weighting curves

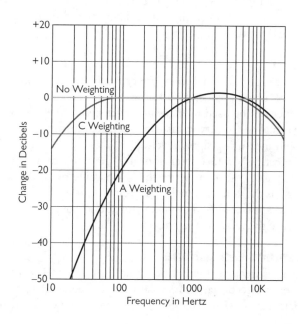

A weighting is useful in situations with low listening levels, including most speech applications. It lowers the decibels SPL reading of low-frequency sounds to reflect how a human being perceives those sounds. As the listening level increases to 85–140 dB SPL, the human ear response "flattens out." You may then choose a C-weighted filter (indicated by the line marked C in Figure 19-7), whose curve is far less steep.

For example, because they reflect the response of the human ear at low listening levels, A-weighted measurements are frequently used to quantify ambient background noise. While there are better metrics for quantifying background noise levels and their effects on the listener, an SPL measurement provides a simple one-number rating.

The ANSI/ASA S12.60 standard shows that maximum one-hour SPL levels, including those from building services such as heating, ventilating, and air conditioning (HVAC), should not exceed 35 db SPL A-wtd (weighted) for spaces not exceeding 20,000 square feet (566 square meters) in classrooms and other learning spaces.

Given the maximum background noise level of 35 db SPL A-wtd from the standard and that a space should have a minimum 25 dB signal-to-noise (S/N) ratio acoustically, a goal of speech level is at least 60 db SPL A-wtd. However, a sound reinforcement system for speech may more typically operate in the range of 70 to 75 dB SPL.

In addition to choosing a weighting for your SPL meter, you will need to select a response time. A fast response is used for capturing transient, momentary levels. A slow response will capture consistent noise levels. This is useful for averaging rapid fluctuations in sound pressure levels and more closely mimics the way your ears react.

A system may need to be compliant with a specific standard. Internationally, sound level meter performance falls under two different standards: International Electrotechnical Commission (IEC) and ANSI. The IEC standard relates to frontal incidence correction, while the ANSI standard relates to random incidence correction. In other words, does the microphone have to be oriented directly on an axis with the noise source or can it be off the axis up to a certain point? These two different standards relate to response rather than weighting.

Multimeter

Since electronic audio signal levels are typically measured in decibels or decibels to volt, both of which are referenced to a known voltage, an alternating current (AC) voltmeter or multimeter can be used to measure or set signal levels. You can also use a multimeter for testing signal continuity, measuring voltage, measuring DC voltage to test equipment batteries, and measuring signal levels.

When selecting a multimeter, look for the true "root mean square" (RMS) feature, which will enable you to measure the RMS value of an AC voltage. RMS, rather than peak voltage, is the conventional measurement most often used to compare voltage readings in audio applications. The meter must also have wide enough bandwidth to accurately measure the reference signal.

Measurement Microphone

A test and measurement microphone is used to accurately capture system performance. It should be omnidirectional, have a flat on-axis frequency response, and have a preferred-capsule diameter of 1/2 in (6.35mm). The microphone should also give consistent results.

Oscilloscope

An oscilloscope is a test device that enables measurement and evaluation of electronic signals by displaying a waveform. In audio system verification, an oscilloscope may be used to identify clipped sine waves when using the optimization method for setting system gain.

Now that you have a foundation in the properties of audio-testing equipment, you can apply this theory to testing and evaluating the audio signal pathway and listening environment.

Video System Verification

Ensuring appropriate signal levels across all video equipment, adjusting video cameras and displays, and checking audio/video synchronization are all part of the video verification process. As you close out a project, you should test and verify several items using the Video System Performance Verification Items and the Audio/Video System Performance Verification Items from the ANSI/INFOCOMM 10:2013, *Audiovisual Systems Performance* Verification standard.

Verifying the Video Signal Path

When verifying a video system, you first should check the wiring and cabling of the video equipment. Once all connections have been completed, verify that the wiring methods and cable pathways are correct. This is typically a visual inspection process because you will compare the technical drawings, such as a signal flow drawing, against what you discover in the rack and elsewhere.

As with audio system wiring, during the inspection process, you need to look for the following:

- Correctly terminated connectors. Look for defects such as bent pins or frayed shields.
- Correctly connected cables. They should be attached to terminals as indicated on your system drawings.
- Cabling in the pathways that are properly organized in the walls and in the ceiling. Also, check for proper bend radius at all junction and pull boxes.

As you work through this process, record any errors or discrepancies for immediate repair. Permanent changes that occurred during installation should be documented and submitted to the designer for updating.

Signal Extenders

When distributing signals, cables attenuate the signal over distance. The longer the cable, the more the signal will be attenuated. In some cases, you may elect to use a balun to convert between a balanced signal and an unbalanced signal. A balun is a device named from the combination of *bal*anced and *un*balanced signals. Baluns generally use transformers and are passive devices, and signal distance limitations must be observed.

Digital signals are already balanced and don't generally use baluns. Many of the early HDMI "baluns" (two-cable systems) were just powered extenders (think "balbal" versus "balun"). Many had a distance limitation of less than 110 ft, depending on resolution. Later versions were single-cable extenders that tried to "multitask" wires for multiple signals. They were vulnerable to electromagnetic interference and had a somewhat short lifespan.

If your customers need to use category cable for transporting signals over long distances, a balun can be a great tool. There are also active devices that contain circuitry to boost and reclock the signals. Active devices require power and are sold in pairs, one for transmission and one for reception. This pair of devices takes AV formats and converts them into a format that can be transferred over longer distances. They are also more affordable alternatives to long HDMI cables since they send data over category or fiber-optic cables; the cost of copper cabling is reduced, and there is smaller conduit.

 TIP Active extenders reclock the signal and output a duplicate of the original signal. Passive extenders change the physical medium but do not reclock the signal.

In a simple way, HDMI extenders take the signal in and repeat it back out.

Regardless of application, active transmitter and receiver devices must be the same type because they are designed to work in pairs only. Also, keep in mind that signals between older transmitters and receivers cannot go through a network switch or router. (Digital video extenders now send signals through network systems and switches by using digital video extenders that convert the signals to packetized data.)

There are several common issues to be aware of when including HDMI in your design.

- Most HDMI connectors will pass through a 7/8" (23 mm) hole. Be sure to check that the connector you are using can pass through the conduit and enclosures you are using. In addition, check the bend radius of the conduit to ensure that it can support the length (not just the width) of the HDMI connector.

- HDMI can also be sent over Cat 5e, Cat 6, Cat 7, or fiber. Often, there should be an extender at both ends of the cable for this transmission, though HDMI now can also go directly from interface to switch, and vice versa.

- HDMI-compliant switchers must be powered because a switcher fully decodes, retimes, and resets the signal.

Signal EQ with Drivers

Signals lose voltage level over distance, so your integrator may need to boost the signal to "drive" it to the far end. After this boost, the voltage at the receiving end would be at the "proper" level. This would be 0.7 volts for RGB analog, for instance.

When verifying performance, check to see that the driver is installed on the front end by the source. It pre-amplifies and pre-EQs the signal so it arrives at the destination at the proper level across the frequency band. Notice that the driver does not affect the noise level in the system. (When located near the far end, the driver amplifies noise.)

Higher frequencies will exhibit greater loss over distance. To compensate for high-end loss, you will need to make peaking, EQ, or slope adjustments as well. The peaking over-amplifies the high end, so by the time the signal reaches the far end, it will have reduced to the proper level. You don't necessarily lose noise over distance because you are probably picking up new noise along the way.

When boosting or repeating digital signals, make sure the repeater is at the far end. The process is entirely different, however. In the case of digital signals, you input the signal and reclock or reshape it. In other words, you create a new sharp signal. It is not possible to do this with analog signals.

Verifying Video Sources

After installation, the AV team will need to fine-tune camera adjustments and complete projector calibration. Light sources play a big part in how the eye perceives color images. When flat or low-contrast lighting is used, images can look washed out and dull. Proper lighting will create images that have vivid contrast ratios and are interesting to watch.

Color temperature can also become a factor when verifying display images with true and accurate color. The color temperature of the light produced is a concern in some critical viewing environments. The color temperature of the light sources used to light the environment should be consistent. Light from the sun is around 5600 Kelvin, which casts a bluer light. Interior lighting is around 3200 Kelvin, which casts a yellowish light. Combining different light sources in a space can cause images to look unnatural. For example, a person in a poorly lit room might appear blue on one side of their face, while the other might appear yellow.

Camera Adjustments

Video cameras are common in meeting rooms and training centers. Clients tend to use cameras for videoconferences and to record events in their facilities. Similar to other AV devices, cameras should be set up for the environment in which they operate. Often, cameras are connected and powered on, and that is the extent of the setup. The designer or integrator should make some standard adjustments to a camera's image if the image produced with default settings is of poor quality.

Focus

The focus adjustment allows the camera to deliver a sharp, clearly visible image of the subject. To set the focus, follow these steps:

1. Have a subject stand in the general location where the camera would normally be recording.

2. Zoom the camera lens tightly to the subject and adjust the main focus until the subject image appears sharp and crisp. A focus chart can make the process easier; the contrasting black-and-white sections allow for very accurate focusing.

3. Zoom back out to frame the shot for best coverage.

This process will prevent recorded images from appearing hazy, blurry, or out of focus.

Back-Focus

Lenses must stay in focus as the lens is zoomed from wide-angle shots to narrow fields of view. Adjusting the back-focus on the lens will keep zoomed-out images focused. To adjust back-focus, follow these steps:

1. Locate the back-focus setting on the camera lens. If your camera has this setting, it will likely be a manual, hardware-dependent adjustment near the focus setting.

2. At the target area, zoom into the same chart you used to set the focus, and focus as before.

3. Zoom all the way out and adjust the back-focus until the shot is again in focus.

Repeat this process until the lens stays in focus throughout its range. If possible, lock the setting in place.

Iris Settings

On a video camera, the iris controls how much light comes through the lens. Most AV systems require some iris adjustments on the lens to allow the camera to adjust for lighting changes. This prevents captured images from appearing too dark or too bright. This adjustment is generally found on the body of the camera.

The automatic iris adjustment takes in the light through the lens and creates a voltage, which in turn controls the iris's opening. The opening in the iris controls the amount of light that can pass through the lens. Auto iris settings are calculated within a camera in a few ways, such as taking an average of the amount of light on the entire screen or only the center of the image. AV professionals therefore need to deliver the appropriate amount of light so the subject on the screen has the proper light level.

Generally speaking, there are two important areas of lighting that will affect the auto iris: foreground (or subject lighting) and background (or wall lighting). Once the person on the screen is properly lit, you can adjust the background lighting to open or close the auto iris. For example, if your background is dark, then the person in the image will be brighter because the iris will be open more. Conversely, if the background is bright, the person will appear dark because the iris is closed more. By adjusting the lighting balance between foreground and background, you can achieve good image quality with an automatic iris camera.

Backlight Adjustment

Sometimes, the contrast between the camera object and the background image is so great that it adversely affects the auto-iris settings. For example, if the camera's subject is standing in front of windows at noon, the intense light from outside will cause the iris to close, making the person in the image appear dark. Backlight adds a 3D effect and separates the person on camera from the wall behind them.

The backlight adjustment adjusts, or *trims,* the auto-iris setting. This backlight setting adjusts the auto iris a step more or less bright as compared to the default auto-iris setting. It is used in cases where there is not enough range on background light settings. The auto-iris setting should be performed first, and the backlight adjustment should be used after, if needed.

 TIP When adjusting the exposure on a video camera to produce a better picture of a backlit subject, use the manual iris setting to a lower f-stop number or switch on the "backlight compensation" function when available.

Automatic Gain Control

In darker rooms, faithful reproduction of recorded images will be harder to produce. To compensate for the lower levels of light, gain can be increased in the camera. Adding gain in these situations can improve images but will also magnify any noise in the camera image. This noise can be a problem if you are sending the camera images to a videoconferencing codec. Try the automatic setting first. If the resulting image is still poor, adjust the camera gain.

Shutter Adjustments

An electronic shutter controls the amount of light that a camera must process. If your room has windows that will bring in substantial light during portions of the day, it might be a good idea to turn the automatic shutter on. This will reduce the possibility that facial features will become washed out. In situations where there is fast movement, the shutter may make the image become too stuttered or jerky. Try increasing the shutter speed slightly on the camera.

White Balancing

Many cameras used in the AV industry offer an automatic white balance circuit as a standard feature. This circuit looks for bright or white objects and self-adjusts to then reproduce proper colors. This is the reason that color balancing is performed using a flat white object such as a piece of white cardstock (white is an equal mix of all colors). If the automatic feature is off, a manual white balancing is required. Most professional video cameras have a white balance button.

Follow these steps to manually white balance a video camera:

1. Place a large piece of white paper in the object location.

2. Zoom into the white paper.

3. Press the white balance button. This will set the color reference level for optimum color reproduction for a given lighting condition.

Some cameras have preset color balance settings that may be selected. Selecting one of these presets will lock the white color temperature of the camera. Be cautious with these presets. Use this setting only if the light settings in the meeting room environment rarely change.

Framing the Image

After the camera has been correctly set up to capture the image accurately, an AV professional needs to frame the subject. The method for doing so depends on the type of camera system used. If the camera is on a pan-tilt-zoom system, then the technician needs to make sure that any presets point and focus the camera in the proper points in the room. If the camera is in a fixed location, however, the technician will need to point, zoom, and focus the camera.

One method of framing is to pretend that the camera shot is split into three equal-sized, horizontal rows. The subject's eyes should line up near the top of the second row. If the shot is not framed this way, a large amount of the wall may be shown. Or, the person's head may be cut off at the top of the screen. The bottom of the image should end between the shoulders and elbows.

Display Setup

Display setup requires general knowledge of signal generators and the purposes of common test patterns. A knowledgeable technician can make the necessary adjustments based on the viewing environment. Technicians are working with multiple types of displays. All these display types require different procedures for correct setup. The job is only partially complete if the technician connects the displays, turns them on, and walks away.

Before turning over a project, a designer may need to verify the setup. Going back to the project documentation, identify the parameters of the display device, which could be a projector or a flat-panel display. Then determine the input signal types that will be used on the display. The signal will probably be HDMI, although Digital Video Interface (DVI) and Red Green Blue Horizontal Sync Vertical Sync (RGBHV) are still occasionally used in existing systems.

Determine the aspect ratio of the image. Two common ratios are 16:9 and 4:3. This information may be in the owner's manual, or you can calculate it by dividing the width by the height of the displayed image. Be cautious because it is possible to display an image that was designed for a 4:3 display on a 16:9 display. The resulting image could be stretched. It is also possible to display an image that was designed for a 16:9 display on a 4:3 display. The resulting image may have letterboxing (16:9 image on a 4:3 display) above and below the image or pillaring (4:3 image on a 16:9 display) on the left and right of the screen. This just means that the image may not fill the entire screen.

Once you've identified the display's viewing parameters, make sure that the source signal fills the screen correctly. You can use two patterns for this step: the *crosshatch* and *geometry* patterns. The crosshatch pattern is used to determine the maximum viewable screen size, ensuring that the image fits the screen.

Using a crosshatch pattern (Figure 19-8), adjust the horizontal and vertical controls until the outer lines of the pattern are exactly at the edge of the screen or display. You can use electronic controls on a direct view display. If you are adjusting a projector, you can

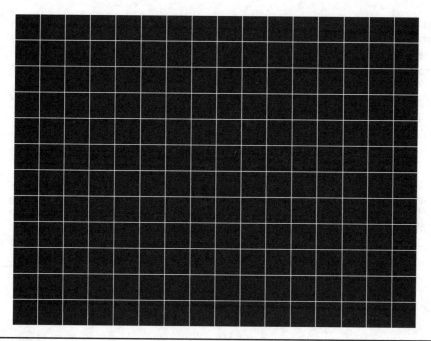

Figure 19-8   Crosshatch pattern

physically position the projector or use lens shift. The crosshatch pattern verifies that the image fills the screen and is centered. You can also use it to check linearity.

A geometry pattern (Figure 19-9) is used to indicate the correct aspect ratio. The image contains a large circle or several circles. Using the geometry pattern that matches

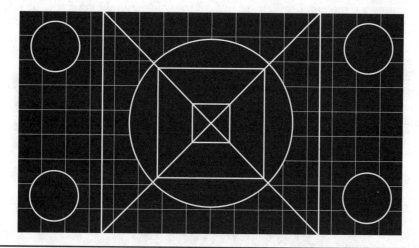

Figure 19-9   16:9 geometry pattern

the aspect ratio of the video source (not the display), examine the display. If the circles appear to be an oval, then either the display is set to the wrong aspect ratio or the display may be stretching or compressing the pattern. There are two common versions of this pattern: 4:3 and 16:9. The one depicted is the 16:9 version.

Set the Chroma Level

Color bars are test patterns that allow technicians to make specific adjustments to the color of displays. They are used to set a display's chroma level and hue shift. RGB sources do not typically have hue and saturation controls. Component and composite sources may or may not have saturation and hue controls.

In general, adjust for black and white (brightness/contrast) before adjusting for colors. A commonly used test pattern is the Society of Motion Picture and Television Engineers (SMPTE) high-definition (HD) version. Alternatively, you may come across the Association of Radio Industries and Businesses (ARIB) version. This is an HD-specific color bar variant.

 Watch a video about using color bar test patterns at www.infocomm.org /ColorBarVideo. Appendix C provides a link to this and other videos.

Set Contrast

The pattern shown in Figure 19-10 is used to set contrast. The white rectangle in the center is "white," or the brightest item on the screen. The two very black rectangles beside it are "blacker than black," and the black background that surrounds the white and blacker rectangles are "black." The goal is to strike a balance between all the shades in the image. Make adjustments until all the bars are clearly distinct and visible. Ensure the white bars look white and the black bars look black. They should also appear in even, gradual steps.

If the black sections of the image are too dark, increase the brightness control. If the image sections are too bright, increase the contrast. It may take several adjustments to balance the image and ensure that all variations of white and gray can be clearly seen.

Figure 19-10
Test pattern to
set contrast

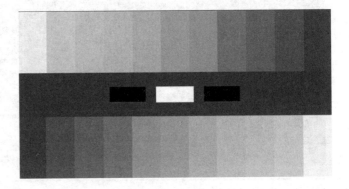

Here is the process for adjusting brightness and contrast:

1. Display a grayscale test pattern.

2. Adjust the contrast level down and then increase the level while watching the white rectangle in the center of the screen. Adjust up until the white does not get any whiter.

3. Adjust brightness until you cannot see any difference between "black" and "blacker than black."

4. Repeat the adjustments until both settings are achieved.

Once complete, the gray strips should gradually increase/decrease in value in a linear fashion. Repeat these steps until all bars appear in even, gradual steps.

Projector Verification

When setting up projectors, you will also need to align the image on the screen. You should complete this task after you have verified that the projector is in its proper position in the room. The professional way to align a display is with test pattern generator images. These can come from a computer or a dedicated pattern generator.

Because projected images are often the centerpiece of AV systems, the image contrast ratio is one of the most important criteria for performance. The ANSI/INFOCOMM 3M-2011 standard, *Projected Image System Contrast Ratio,* was developed to ensure high-quality image projection.

The 3M standard applies to front- and rear-projection systems; it looks at the contrast ratio performance of the entire system, including the projector, screen, and ambient light. It defines four minimum contrast ratios based on the tasks performed within a space. These four contrast ratios are as follows:

- 7:1 for passive viewing
- 15:1 for basic decision making
- 50:1 for analytical decision making
- 80:1 for full-motion video (home theater)

The following sections describe how the standard defines these contrast ratios.

Passive Viewing

The viewer is able to recognize what the images are on a screen and can separate the text or the main image from the background under typical lighting for the viewing environment. The content does not require assimilation and retention of detail, but the general intent is understood. There is passive engagement with the content (for example, non-critical or informal viewing of video or data).

Basic Decision Making

The viewer can make basic decisions from the display image. The decisions are not dependent on critical details within the image, but there is assimilation and retention of information. The viewer is actively engaged with the content (for example, information displays, presentations containing detailed images, classrooms, boardrooms, multipurpose rooms, and product illustrations).

Analytical Decision Making

The viewer can make critical decisions by the ability to analyze details within the displayed image. The viewer is analytical and fully engaged with these details of the content (for example, medical imaging, architectural/engineering drawings, forensic evidence, and photographic image inspection).

Full-Motion Video

The viewer is able to discern key elements present in the full-motion video, including details provided by the cinematographer or videographer necessary to support the story line and intent (for example, home theater, business screening room, and broadcast post-production).

The standard includes a set of simple measurements to verify that the system conforms to the desired contrast ratio of the viewing task. First, you must identify five measurement locations, as shown in Figure 19-11. The five locations are recorded on a viewing area plan.

- **Viewing location 1**   Viewing location closest to the screen and farthest to the left in the plan view. (In other words, this is the viewing location closest to the screen, situated laterally to the left of the vertical center line axis of the screen.)

- **Viewing location 2**   Viewing location closest to the screen and farthest to the right in the plan view. (In other words, this is the viewing location closest to the screen, situated laterally to the right of the vertical center line axis of the screen.)

- **Viewing location 3**   Viewing location at the central point of viewing locations 1, 2, 4, and 5. In the case where this central viewing location is obstructed (such as by a conference table), the measurement location will be the first available viewing location on the screen center line behind the obstruction.

- **Viewing location 4**   Viewing location farthest from the screen and farthest to the left in the plan view. (In other words, this is the viewing location farthest from the screen situated laterally to the left of the vertical center line axis of the screen.)

Figure 19-11
The contrast ratio should be measured from five locations within the viewing area.

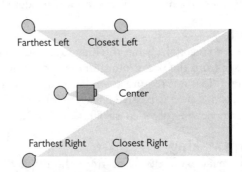

- **Viewing location 5**   Viewing location farthest from the screen and farthest to the right in the plan view. (In other words, this is the viewing location farthest from the screen situated laterally to the right of the vertical center line axis of the screen.)

After you have identified the viewing locations, measure the contrast ratio of the system using a 16-zone black-and-white checkerboard (intraframe) pattern. You will also need a luminance meter or spot photometer with up-to-date calibration.

Here is the procedure for verifying the projected image contrast ratio:

1. Display a 16-zone black-and-white checkerboard test pattern on the projection screen under conditions that represent the actual viewing environment.

2. From the first measurement position identified on the viewing area plan (viewing location 1), measure and record the luminance values at the center of each of the eight white rectangles.

3. From the same measurement position, measure and record the luminance values at the center of each of the eight black rectangles.

4. Calculate the average of the eight white measurements and the average of the eight black measurements.

5. Divide the resulting average white value by the average black value to obtain the contrast ratio at that measurement position. *Contrast Ratio = Luminance average max / Luminance average min.*

6. Repeat the contrast measurement procedure at each of the five measurement positions identified on the viewing area plan.

7. Record the resulting contrast ratios for each of the measurement positions on the viewing area plan.

If the contrast ratio meets or exceeds the minimum laid out in the ANSI/INFO-COMM 3M-2011 standard, *Projected Image System Contrast Ratio,* at all five viewing locations, then the system conforms to the standard. If the contrast ratio of one but no more than four measurement (viewing) locations falls below the required ratio for the identified viewing category by no more than 10 percent, the system partially conforms. If the contrast ratio at any one of the measured locations falls below the identified viewing category by more than 10 percent, then the system fails to conform to the ANSI/INFOCOMM 3M-2011 standard, *Projected Image System Contrast Ratio.*

 Watch a video about measuring contrast ratio at www.infocomm.org/ContrastVideo. Appendix C provides a link to this and other videos.

Audio/Video Sync

In many AV systems, the audio and video signals may take significantly different paths to get from the source to the point at which the user will experience them, such as in a seat within a local venue, at a remote location, or following distribution of a recording.

The audio and video signals may also undergo very different amounts of processing, each with their own inherent delays.

In systems where associated video and audio signals may be transported or processed separately and are then subsequently combined for transmission or display, one of those signals could be delayed more than the other, creating synchronization errors sometimes known as lip-sync errors. These errors are typically corrected by applying delay to the least delayed signal so that it aligns with the most delayed signal. For a good user experience, the signals should arrive in synchronization at the point at which the user will experience them, regardless of whether that point is local or remote.

A "blip-and-flash" test is a common method for measuring the synchronization of audio and video signals. A test signal consisting of one full frame of white video, accompanied by an audio tone of the same time length, is required. An alternative signal may be an image changing from full-frame white to full-frame black at regular intervals, with each change accompanied by a brief "click" or tone burst. This can be generated by a laptop running a slideshow.

The signal at the point of reception can then be analyzed using a dual-channel digital storage oscilloscope to record the timings at which the audio and video signals are received.

If a metric is not being measured, then a subjective reception test using the same test signal can be used, in addition to replaying video material that depicts a person such as a newsreader speaking. The subjective effect of any delay can then be assessed for a pass-fail assessment.

Tests should be undertaken at the inputs of recording devices, at the inputs to transmission devices such as videoconferencing codecs and broadcast circuits, and locally within the presentation space at both near-screen and farthest-viewer positions.

Here is a procedure for measuring the time alignment of signals. This is assuming that the AV system has been installed and all recording devices, presentation equipment, and link equipment/circuits are operational.

1. Set up a blip-and-flash source.

2. Measure delay (synchronization error) between audio and video at the nearest and farthest viewer positions within the room.

3. Measure delay at inputs to all recording devices.

4. Measure delay at inputs to all transmission devices, such as VC codecs, and broadcast circuits.

5. Note if the measured delay is within the specifications as stated in the project documentation or within +15/−45ms (audio/video) in the absence of other information.

Alternative subjective tests may be undertaken using source video with no synchronization error where a person is seen speaking. Validate subjective synchronization delay at the locations listed earlier.

Correcting Audio/Video Sync Errors

In a perfect audiovisual system, the users will perceive the audio and video signals at the same time. For example, if the video is of a person who is speaking, the audio of their voice should match the movements of the person's lips. However, you may encounter problems that disrupt this synchronization.

Downstream video processing can cause delay. Some displays have built-in video processors, which, when used in conjunction with audio processors, scalers, and other processors, will cause lag in the signal.

Unfortunately, there is no clear way to predict how much, if any, delay will occur in the AV system. The amount of delay introduced depends on the digital signal processors within the system, and the specific amount varies by manufacturer. In most cases, you will probably be able to depend on the HDMI lip sync feature, which will automatically compensate for delays in the video signal. In these cases, EDID can be used as a tool for correcting the sync issues. HDMI uses EDID to communicate delay information to upstream devices. It will measure the amount of milliseconds of delay introduced and send that to the sink for automatic correction. This is often sufficient for systems with a single display, but when you start working with larger systems that involve multiple displays and rooms, EDID becomes less reliable. After all, if EDID detects eight different displays with eight different delay values, how does it know which display to optimize?

In these cases, the integrator can manually introduce delay into an audio distribution system. Delay is a function typically found within digital signal processor boxes or switchers or as a stand-alone, dedicated box.

Delay allows you to extract the audio at the beginning of the signal chain and send it right to the infrastructure. If you are responsible for selecting the digital signal processors for your system, you should consider including a DSP that corrects for delay. That way, if you do encounter this problem, you can fix it by using a "blip-and-flash" test reel and adjusting the delay until the signals are back in sync.

Conducting System Closeout

After verifying that the system is working properly, you must demonstrate to the client or the client's representative that it meets the performance specifications of the AV design. To obtain customer sign-off, you will need to complete several tasks as part of the system closeout process.

Handing over documentation to your client is an essential part of system closeout. If troubleshooting or requested changes remain undocumented or incomplete, the project remains open and could require additional staff hours to resolve. This could possibly delay payments and project conclusion. On some projects, your work may involve training the client's staff on how to operate the systems.

Adhering to the standard ANSI/INFOCOMM 10:2013, *Audiovisual Systems Performance Verification,* can help you smoothly close out your project. This standard requires you to meet with project stakeholders to determine what verification tests will be performed on the system and what metrics will be used to assess system performance. It includes guidance as to when in the process each step should be performed.

The standard requires the AV team to turn in verification testing reports for each phase of construction.

When you use this standard to manage system verification, you are also forming a shared understanding with your client and other stakeholders of what constitutes a complete, fully functional system. Your performance and outcome expectations are explicitly stated and aligned early in the project. This reduces risk by identifying potential problems or disagreements early, thereby reducing the need for remedial work. The standard also helps both you and your client verify the project outcome by mandating documentation of each stage of construction and testing as it is completed. Both you and the client know when the system is done.

Closeout Documentation

The importance of documentation at every stage of an AV project can scarcely be overstated. From the first meetings through installation and verification, documenting every change is crucial for several reasons, including future maintenance of the system. Closeout documentation includes all the information gathered during the project as well as drawings of record, operational documentation, and a punch list (see later in this chapter).

Table 19-2 is Section 9.6, "System and Record Documentation Reference Items," of the ANSI/INFOCOMM 10:2013 standard, *Audiovisual Systems Performance Verification*. You can use this table as a checklist to ensure your client receives the relevant documentation.

A critical factor in ensuring that documentation deliverables are up to date is determining who is responsible for each document. You must understand both your specific role and the tasks involved in your team's closeout documentation. Knowing who is responsible for which items will enable you to gather successfully all the relevant documentation for closeout.

Drawings of Record

After a project has been completed and verified, the AV team should hand over comprehensive documentation, including the drawings of record to the project manager. Drawings and documents of record reflect changes made onsite to the original AV design. The original plans often cannot take into account product changes that may require changes on the job site. By carefully keeping track of changes to wiring, changes in model numbers of devices, audio and video signal modifications, and other system design elements, these drawings of record become valuable references during service calls and routine maintenance in the future.

Document every single change, even if it is just a connection point changing. Note the changes on the system plans. This step is vital not only in communicating system changes to all parties currently involved in the project but also to those who will work on changes to the system in the future.

Operational Documentation

Operational documentation should be included with a contract at the end of a project. Even if user documentation is not specified in a contract, training or job reference

Item Number	Item Name	Pre-integration	Systems Integration	Post-integration	Closeout
DOC-100	Final Inventory of AV Equipment	X	X	X	
DOC-101	Approval of Samples	X			
DOC-102	Delivered Product Against Samples		X		
DOC-103	Wireless Frequency Licensing		X		
DOC-104	Consultant's Testing			X	
DOC-105	General Contractor's Testing			X	
DOC-106	Integrator's Testing			X	
DOC-107	Manufacturer's Testing			X	
DOC-108	Owner's Testing			X	
DOC-109	Third-Party Testing			X	
DOC-110	Substantial/Practical Completion			X	
DOC-111	As-Built Drawings Complete				X
DOC-112	Audio System Test Reporting				X
DOC-113	Control System Test Reporting				X
DOC-114	Final Commissioning Report and System Turnover				X
DOC-115	Required Closeout Documentation				X
DOC-116	Software Licensing				X
DOC-117	User Manuals				X
DOC-118	Video System Test Reporting				X
DOC-119	Warranties				X
DOC-120	Final Acceptance				X

Table 19-2 System and Record Documentation Reference Verification Items

manuals should be prepared for the customer. System documentation may include the following:

- System-specific operating instructions and manufacturer equipment manuals
- System design and block drawings
- Control system configuration, settings, and Internet Protocol (IP) addresses

- DSP software files
- Network device inventory information
- Drawings of record
- Spreadsheet listing all equipment provided and serial numbers
- Description of recommended service needs and schedules of maintenance
- Warranty information (both manufacturer and AV system as a whole)
- Support telephone numbers

Other deliverables should include remote-control devices, adapters, cables, spare parts, and discs (CDs or DVDs) with software programs and user documentation.

Best Practice for Equipment Manuals and Software Documentation

- Arrange equipment manuals in alphabetical order and group by function. For example, all display device manuals would be placed in one group.
- Leave a copy of the equipment operation documents with the equipment rack, the project manager, or the client's end user.
- Create backups of all computer files associated with the equipment, especially if the files contain records of the system settings.

Punch List

You may need to answer questions about the AV system and address issues as they are discovered. Therefore, a "punch list" is useful. It contains the corrections or changes that need to be made to conform to the scope of the project. Here are some of the items a punch list may contain:

- Minor changes such as correction of illegible labels on equipment inputs
- Physical changes such as moving a wall-mounted connector to a higher location
- Functional changes such as adjusting a monitor
- Technical changes such as rewiring a rack that was not properly dressed

Even if your client does not require this document, the use of a punch list has become standard practice in the construction industry. In fact, it could be the document that protects you and your company from any future misunderstandings. When all the work on the punch list cannot be completed immediately, make plans for follow-up and arrange to meet with the project manager to review the changes the next day.

Troubleshooting

There are going to be times when your AV system will not work correctly. When this happens, you may need to help troubleshoot the systems to find where the issues are coming from. Troubleshooting is a process for investigating, determining, and settling problems. The most important process in troubleshooting problems is to be systematic and logical.

The following are some basic troubleshooting best practices:

- Change only one thing at a time.

- Test after each change.

- Use signal generators to provide a known reference to measure against. Use signal analyzers to obtain quantifiable information.

- Document your procedures and findings.

A maintenance log is essential for fixed AV systems. It should include every item examined and repaired and the service performed. Maintenance logs are easy to update, especially right after service has been performed. They may include the date and time the system was checked, who checked it, and the status of the system. They may also include problems that were discovered and what measures were taken to fix them. You should make it standard practice to record corrective measures that were taken to restore system performance or recommended actions and whether they were acted upon. From time to time, equipment may need to be updated. For example, in a boardroom, a streaming device may replace a Blu-ray Disc player. The date this took place should be documented, as well as how the signal was rerouted.

Regularly check the system by running test signals to ensure they are up to specifications. Despite rigorous preventive care, from time to time a piece of equipment will need repair. This, too, should be entered on a maintenance log. By documenting exactly what needs repair and how much it might cost, your client will know when a device needs to be repaired or replaced and perhaps save money in the long run. Inspect connectors and wiring. Also make sure the area is clean.

Customer Training

After you have completed all the procedures, work with the client to schedule a training session for the typical users of the system. There may be several levels of training required for different groups of users. Each training session should be catered to the needs and interests of the audience. Different training groups might include the following:

- Technical staff who will be responsible for operations in the future and require in-depth training on all systems.

- Power users to nontechnical users who take full advantage of a system's functionality. They may hold frequent videoconferences or multimedia presentations.

- Casual users who make limited use of the system's functionality.

You may also want to conduct in-depth "train the trainer" sessions with individuals from within the owner organization so that training can continue in the future.

First study the system. If you are training people on the system's operations, you should be completely familiar with them yourself. Lack of familiarity or uncertainty on the part of the trainer can result in similar uncertainty in the trainees. More operational mistakes are likely if the trainer is uncertain or ineffective.

The client briefing should be informal. It is preferable to demonstrate operations by working with the newly installed system in front of the end users. Sometimes this will be done with the designer as part of the commissioning process. You, your project manager, or a sales team member may also brief the client.

Not all users require the complete and detailed operating procedures. Knowing the appropriate end users for extended training is most important.

It is also necessary to provide some level of documentation to customers describing how to operate a system. Detailed operating instructions for every piece of the AV system are only one portion of the total package.

End-user training should at least include the following:

- How to turn the system on and off
- How to switch between the various program sources
- How to turn on and mute microphones
- How to adjust the volume levels of audio sources
- How to use the control system interface
- How to adjust internal HVAC and lighting presets/settings

When creating this documentation, also keep in mind that presenters using the system may only have time to glance at instructions. They will only need bullet-point instructions.

You may at times need to connect your customer with the manufacturer for additional training or support during closeout. The technology manager in charge often requires more extensive training than you may be able to provide. Remember your steps for escalating questions or concerns to address this type of briefing.

Client Sign-Off

To obtain client sign-off, you should review the overall project. Before beginning this review process, you need to have completed the following tasks:

- You have completed a step-by-step approach to testing all the parts of the AV system.
- You have identified any problems or issues associated with the system and setup of equipment and have addressed them prior to turning over the system to the customer.
- You have provided a means for your company to demonstrate to the customer that the system meets both design and performance specifications and standards.

Either at or following the training, ask the consultant or client to sign closeout documentation as specified. Having everything at the training provides an opportunity for sign-off with all parties present.

Chapter Review

When an AV project has been competed—when your design has become a reality—a designer's job is not over. Because your most important task is ensuring the client gets exactly what he expected, it's critical to oversee a comprehensive process of systems verification. This includes everything from determining whether the systems were properly installed to whether they are performing as expected. An AV designer's knowledge of basic AV and familiarity with certain testing and verification equipment will come in handy.

And once it's been determined that the system is performing properly, it is important to deliver all documentation to the client, train users on the system as necessary, and obtain final signoff. Then, and only then, is your AV design complete.

Review Questions

The following questions are based on the content covered in this chapter and are intended to help reinforce the knowledge you have assimilated. These questions are not extracted from the CTS-D exam nor are they necessarily CTS-D practice exam questions. For an official CTS-D practice exam, see the accompanying CD.

1. What are the benefits of using the ANSI/InfoComm 10:2013 standard, *Audiovisual Systems Performance Verification*? (Select all that apply.)

   A. Reducing project risk

   B. Aligning outcome and performance expectations

   C. Providing a verifiable outcome

   D. Creating reporting that completes the project documentation

2. Which of the following are features of an audio signal generator? (Select all that apply.)

   A. Generates sine wave and other signals used for setting system levels

   B. Usually has both 1 kHz and 400 Hz signal outputs

   C. With a properly calibrated signal can determine signal bit rate

   D. Can be helpful in measuring distortion

3. According to the ANSI/INFOCOMM 3M-2011 standard, *Projected Image System Contrast Ratio,* what is the minimum contrast ratio of basic decision-making tasks?

   A. 7:1

   B. 15:1

   C. 50:1

   D. 80:1

4. Which of the following are associated with sound pressure levels? (Select all that apply.)

   A. Is typically measured in decibels (dB SPL)

   B. Is the ultimate method for quantifying background noise levels

   C. Eliminates distortion in speech reinforcement

   D. Can most accurately be measured with a Class 0 precision SPL meter

5. What type of video is best used to verify audio/video synchronization?

   A. Landscapes with orchestra music

   B. News anchors speaking

   C. Team sports

   D. A blip-and-flash test reel

6. Contrast ratio should be measured from _____ locations within the viewing area.

   A. All

   B. Two

   C. Four

   D. Five

7. After a project has been completed and verified, the AV team should hand over comprehensive documentation, including _____.

   A. Drawings of record

   B. Copies of relevant standards

   C. Test patterns

   D. A business card

8. To "train the trainer" is to _____.

   A. Learn the AV system so you can train the client

   B. Train individuals at the client location who can train other users

   C. Train the client on aspects of the user interface

   D. Host classes at the designer's office

9. Comprehensive training of end users and support staff is essential to customer satisfaction and also _____.

   A. Is not expensive or time-consuming because the manufacturer pays for it

   B. Reduces service calls as well as improper use and equipment damage

   C. Reduces AV contractor costs because it is a tax-deductible expense

   D. Enables the AV contractor to continue to keep paid personnel at the site

10. Where would the person in charge of verifying system performance locate performance criteria?

   A. Call the installers of the system.

   B. Typically, there isn't any documentation; using personal experience is best.

   C. Project specification documentation.

   D. Owner's manuals.

Answers

1. **A, B, C, D.** Using the ANSI/INFOCOMM 10:2013 standard, *Audiovisual Systems Performance Verification,* will help reduce project risk, align outcome and performance expectations, provide a verifiable outcome, and create reporting that completes project documentation.

2. **A, B, D.** An audio signal generator will generate a sine wave and other signals used for setting system levels. It usually has both 1 kHz and 400 kHz signal outputs and can be helpful in measuring distortion.

3. **B.** 15:1 is the minimum contrast ratio for projected images used in basic decision-making tasks.

4. **A, D.** Sound pressure levels are typically measured in decibels and can most accurately be measured with a Class 0 precision SPL meter.

5. **D.** A blip-and-flash test will reveal video latency.

6. **D.** Contrast ratio should be measured from five locations within the viewing area.

7. **A.** After a project has been completed and verified, the AV team should hand over comprehensive documentation, including drawings of record.

8. **B.** To "train the trainer" is to train individuals at the client who can train other users in the future.

9. **B.** Comprehensive training of end users and support staff is essential to customer satisfaction and also reduces service calls, as well as improper use and equipment damage.

10. **C.** The person in charge of verifying system performance should be able to locate performance criteria in the project specification documentation.

PART V

Appendixes

Math Formulas Used in AV Design

How long has it been since you solved a word problem or used a math formula? Many CTS-D exam candidates have not done math in a formal setting in years. You may be familiar with the skills and tools in this appendix, but then again, you may need a refresher.

Most AV math formulas use only the four common operators: add, subtract, multiply, and divide. However, some formulas require a solid foundation in the order of operations. The order of operations helps you correctly solve formulas by prioritizing which part of the formula to solve first. It is a way to rank the order in which you work your way through a formula. This appendix will review and test your knowledge of applying the order of operations.

This is the order of operations:

1. Any numbers within a pair of parentheses or brackets

2. Any exponents, indices, or orders

3. Any multiplication or division

4. Any addition or subtraction

If there are multiple operations with the same priority, then proceed from left to right: parentheses, exponents, multiplication, division, addition, subtraction. The order of operations can be remembered by using one of these acronyms: PEMDAS, BEMDAS, BIDMAS, or BODMAS.

Steps to Solving Word Problems

All math formulas summarize relationships between concepts. Word problems are designed to test how well an individual can apply that relationship to a new situation.

By following a simple strategy, you can turn a complicated word problem into a few straightforward steps. This section provides a structured approach to solving problems. Within this structure, you will find many strategies for solving different types of problems. This strategy is based on *How to Solve It: A New Aspect of Mathematical Method* by George Polya.

Step 1: Understand the Problem

As typical within the AV industry (and in general), the first step is to understand the problem you're trying to solve. Here are the tasks to complete for this step:

1. Read the entire math problem.

2. Identify your **goal** or unknown. What information are you trying to determine?

3. Identify what you have been **given**. What data, numbers, or other information in the problem can help you determine the answer?

4. Predict the answer if you can. What range of values would make sense as an answer?

Example: Calculate the current in a circuit where the voltage is 2 V and the resistance is 8 ohms.

First, identify your goal. What are you trying to solve for? When you see the word *calculate,* generally the word that follows is your goal. Other words that identify the goal include *determine, find,* and *solve for.* Your **goal** in this problem is to calculate current.

An easy way to identify your **given information** is to find the numbers in the problem. In this example, the numbers are 2 and 8. Look for context clues or units to identify what those numbers represent. *The voltage is* identifies 2 as a voltage. The *ohms* after the 8 identifies 8 as the resistance.

Sometimes it is unclear what each number represents. In that case, drawing a diagram can help you make sense of what the problem is trying to say. You may want to make a chart of your given and unknown information for quick reference. For more complex problems, tables of given information can be extremely helpful.

Givens and Goal	Values
Current	?
Voltage	2 V
Resistance	8 ohms

Step 2: Create a Plan

The second step in this process is to translate the words in the problem into numbers you can enter into a formula. Begin with the following:

1. Assign appropriate values to the **goal** and **given information**.

2. Determine a formula that describes the relationships between your variables.

If there is a single formula that has all your variables in it, move on to the next step.

In some cases, you may be unable to identify a formula that will determine your **goal** based on your **given information**. If you're stuck, consider the following strategies:

- Use an intermediate formula to solve for the information you are missing.
- Use an outside reference, such as a chart or graph, to find information not listed in the problem.
- Use a strategy that has worked to solve similar projects in the past.
- Diagram the scenario described in the word problem. Use the diagram to keep track of the relationships between values. For instance, as listeners move **farther away** from a sound source, you know to expect a **loss** of sound pressure.

Example: Calculate the current in a circuit where the voltage is 2 V and the resistance is 8 ohms.

Again, start by assigning variables to your given and unknown information. Note that some items are represented by different variables in different contexts. If you are having trouble determining which variables to use, consider drawing a diagram and labeling it with your given information, like this:

Givens and Goal	Values	Variables
Current	?	I
Voltage	2 V	V
Resistance	8 ohms	R

Once you have assigned variables, think about the relationship between the information. There should be a formula that describes the relationship. For complex problems, you may need to use several formulas.

You may know formulas from memory. If you don't, look them up (we've provided several useful formulas at the end of this appendix). It is helpful to think about a time when you solved for the value previously or a similar problem you may have solved in the past. Try to think of a problem that used the same givens and unknowns.

For example, you might not remember how to solve for current using voltage and resistance. But if you remember how to solve for voltage using current and resistance, you can solve this problem. Voltage is equal to current multiplied by resistance.

Step 3: Execute Your Plan

The third step is to put your plan in action, as follows:

1. Write the formulas.
2. Substitute the **given information** for the variables.
3. Perform the calculation.
4. Assign units to your final answer.

Example: Calculate the current in a circuit where the voltage is 2 V and the resistance is 8 ohms.

Once you have determined the appropriate formula, write it down and then replace the placeholders with the numbers for this problem. People who skip this step are prone to making mistakes.

Formula: $V = I * R$
Substitution: $2 = I * 8$

To solve this equation, you need to get the I by itself. The 8 is currently being multiplied. To move it to the other side of the equation, perform the opposite mathematical function. In this case, that function is division.

$2 / 8 = (I * 8) / 8$
$2 / 8 = I$
$0.25 = I$

You need to assign units to your answer before it is final. Because I represents current, you would assign 0.25 the unit for current, which is amps (A).

$I = 0.25$ A

Step 4: Check Your Answer

Your final step is to make sure the numbers you've calculated still make sense when translated back into words. Compare your answer to the scenario described in the problem. Is the result reasonable? Is it within the range you originally predicted?

For example, suppose you are calculating the voltage present in a boardroom loudspeaker circuit. A result of 95 V is probably a reasonable answer. A result of 50,000 V indicates that you made a mistake in your calculations.

If you have an incorrect answer and use it to solve other parts of a process, it will result in cascading problems.

Example: Calculate the current in a circuit where the voltage is 2 V and the resistance is 8 ohms.

In this example, is "less than 1 A" a reasonable answer? Understanding the problem is essential here. A D battery has a voltage of 1.5 V. When a D battery is attached to a circuit, there is not much current. So, the small number of 0.25 amps is a reasonable answer.

Rounding

Many of the results listed have been rounded to the nearest tenth. When solving multistep problems, you may be tempted to round at each step. The earlier or more often you round in a multistep problem, the less accurate your result will be. Round only your final result.

AV Math Formulas

This section presents some common math formulas that may be useful for AV design professionals.

Estimated Projector Throw

The formula for estimating projector throw distance is as follows:

*Distance = Screen width * Throw ratio*

where:

- *Distance* is the distance from the front of the lens to the closest point on the screen.
- *Screen width* is the width of the projected image.
- *Throw ratio* is the ratio of throw distance to image width.

Projector Lumens Output

The formula for estimating projector brightness is as follows:

$$\text{Brightness} = \frac{\left(\dfrac{L*C*A}{Sg}\right)}{Dr}$$

where:

- L is the ambient light at the screen location (lux or footcandles).
- C is the desired contrast ratio.*
- A is the area of the screen (in square meters or square feet).
- S_g is the gain of the screen. Assume a screen gain of 1 unless otherwise noted.
- D_r is the projector derating value. Assume a derating value of 0.75 unless otherwise noted.

* The desired contrast ratio depends on the use case in the ANSI/INFOCOMM 3M-2011 standard, *Projected Image System Contrast Ratio*. The following are the four contrast ratios in the standard:

- 7:1 for passive viewing
- 15:1 for basic decision making
- 50:1 for analytical decision making
- 80:1 for full-motion video (home theater)

Image Height to Farthest Viewer Distance Ratio

The formula for determining image height based on viewing task is as follows:

$$I_H/I_D = D_T/V_T$$

where:

- I_H is the image height.
- I_D is the distance from the farthest viewer to the image.
- V_T is the viewing task ratio (distance).
- D_T is the viewing task ratio (height). This will always be 1.

For the viewing task ratio, which is based on levels of detail, use a factor of 8 when viewers will observe content (general viewing), use 6 when viewers will inspect content with clues (reading with clues), and use 4 when the viewers will inspect content without clues (inspection).

Decibel Formula for Distance

The formula for decibel changes in sound pressure level over distance is as follows:

$$dB = 20 * log (D_1 / D_2)$$

where:

- dB is the change in decibels.
- D_1 is the original or reference distance.
- D_2 is the new or measured distance.

The result of this calculation will be either positive or negative. If it is positive, the result is an increase, or gain. If it is negative, the result is a decrease, or loss.

Decibel Formula for Voltage

The formula for determining decibel changes for voltage is as follows:

$$dB = 20 * log (V_1 / V_R)$$

where:

- dB is the change in decibels.
- V_1 is the new or measured voltage.
- D_2 is the original or reference voltage.

The result of this calculation will be either positive or negative. If it is positive, the result is an increase, or *gain*. If it is negative, the result is a decrease, or *loss*.

Decibel Formula for Power

The formula for calculating decibel changes for power is as follows:

$$dB = 10 * log (P_1 / P_r)$$

where:

- *dB* is the change in decibels.
- P_1 is the new or measured power measurement.
- P_r is the original or reference power measurement.

The result of this calculation will be either positive or negative. If it is positive, the result is an increase, or *gain*. If it is negative, the result is a decrease, or *loss*.

Current Formula (Ohm's Law)

The formula for calculating current using Ohm's law is as follows:

$$I = V / R$$

where:

- *I* is the current.
- *V* is the voltage.
- *R* is the resistance.

Power Formula

The formula to solve for power is as follows:

$$P = I * V$$

where:

- *P* is the power.
- *I* is the current.
- *V* is the voltage.

Series Circuit Impedance Formula

The formula for calculating the total impedance of a series loudspeaker circuit is as follows:

$$Z_T = Z_1 + Z_2 + Z_3 \ldots + Z_N$$

where:

- Z_T is the total impedance of the loudspeaker circuit.
- Z_x is the impedance of each loudspeaker.

Parallel Circuit Impedance Formula: Loudspeakers with the Same Impedance

The formula to find the circuit impedance for loudspeakers wired in parallel with the same impedance is as follows:

$$(Z_T) = Z_1 / N$$

where:

- Z_T is the total impedance of the loudspeaker system.
- Z_1 is the impedance of each loudspeaker.
- N is the number of loudspeakers in the circuit.

Parallel Circuit Impedance Formula: Loudspeakers with Different Impedances

The formula to find the circuit impedance for loudspeakers wired in parallel with differing impedance is as follows:

$$Z_T = \frac{1}{\frac{1}{Z_1} + \frac{1}{Z_2} + \frac{1}{Z_3} \cdots + \frac{1}{Z_N}}$$

where:

- Z_T is the total impedance of the loudspeaker circuit.
- Z_x is the impedance of each individual loudspeaker.

Series/Parallel Circuit Impedance Formulas

Two formulas are used to calculate the expected total impedance of a series/parallel circuit.

First, the series circuit impedance formula is used to calculate the impedance of each branch, as follows:

$$Z_T = Z_1 + Z_2 + Z_3 \ldots + Z_N$$

where:

- Z_x is the impedance of each loudspeaker.
- Z_T is the total impedance of the branch.

Then, the parallel circuit impedance formula is used to calculate the total impedance of the series/parallel circuit, as follows:

$$Z_T = \frac{1}{\frac{1}{Z_1} + \frac{1}{Z_2} + \frac{1}{Z_3} \cdots + \frac{1}{Z_N}}$$

where:

- Z_x is the total impedance of each branch.
- Z_T is the total impedance of the loudspeaker circuit.

Needed Acoustic Gain

The formula for calculating needed acoustic gain—how loud speakers need to be for listeners to hear the intended audio—is as follows:

$$NAG = 20log\ (D_0/EAD)$$

where:

- D_0 is the distance from the source to the listener.
- EAD is the equivalent acoustic distance, or the farthest distance one can go from the source without needing sound amplification or reinforcement to maintain intelligibility.

Potential Acoustic Gain

The formula for calculating potential acoustic gain (gain before feedback) is as follows:

$$PAG = 20log\ [(D_0 * D_1)/(D_2 * D_S)]$$

where:

- D_0 is the distance between the talker and the farthest listener.
- D_1 is the distance between the closest loudspeaker to the microphone and the microphone.
- D_2 is the distance between the loudspeaker closest to the farthest listener and the farthest listener.
- D_S is the distance between the sound source (talker) and the microphone.

Audio System Stability (PAG/NAG)

The formula for checking audio system stability by determining that needed acoustic gain (NAG) is less than potential acoustic gain (PAG) is as follows:

$$20log\ (D_0/EAD) < 20log\ [(D_0 * D_1)/(D_2 * D_S)] - 10log(NOM) - FSM$$

where:

- *NOM* is the number of open microphones.
- *FSM* is the feedback stability margin.
- *EAD* is the equivalent acoustic distance.
- D_0 is the distance between the talker and the farthest listener.
- D_1 is the distance between the closest loudspeaker to the microphone and the microphone.
- D_2 is the distance between the loudspeaker closest to the farthest listener and the farthest listener.
- D_S is the distance between the sound source (talker) and the microphone.

Conduit Capacity

The formula for calculating conduit capacity is as follows:

$$ID = \sqrt{\frac{OD^2 + OD^2 + OD^2 \ldots}{FP}}$$

where:

- *OD* is the outer diameter of the cables.
- *ID* is the inner diameter of the conduit.
- *FP* is the permissible fill percentage of the conduit based on the number of cables.

Permissible fill percentage is determined by the authority having jurisdiction (AHJ). For example, the National Electrical Code (NEC) requirements are as follows:

- One cable: 53 percent
- Two cables: 31 percent
- Three or more cables: 40 percent

Jam Ratio

The formula for calculating jam ratio is as follows:

$$Jam = ID / \left(\frac{OD_1 + OD_2 + OD_3}{3} \right)$$

where:

- *OD* is the outer diameter of the cables.
- *ID* is the inner diameter of the conduit.

Jam ratio is applicable only to conduits with exactly three cables.

Heat Load Formula

The formula for calculating heat load is as follows:

$$Total\ BTU = W_E * 3.4$$

where:

- W_E is the total wattage of all equipment used in the room.
- 3.4 is the conversion factor, where 1 watt of power generates 3.4 BTU of heat per hour.

This formula does not account for the heat load generated by amplifiers.

Power Amplifier Heat Load

The formula for calculating the heat load of a power amplifier is as follows:

$$Total\ BTU = W_E * 3.4 * (1 - E_D)$$

where:

- W is the wattage of the amplifier.
- E_D is the efficiency of the device.

Power Amplifier Wattage (Constant Voltage)

The formula for calculating required amplifier wattage is as follows:

$$W_t = W * N * 1.5$$

where:

- W_t is required wattage.
- W is watt tap used at the individual loudspeaker.
- N is total number of loudspeakers.
- 1.5 is 50 percent of the amplifier headroom.

Wattage at the Loudspeaker

The formula for the electrical power (EPR) required at a loudspeaker is as follows:

$$EPR = 10^{\left(\dfrac{L_p + H - L_s + 20\log\left(\frac{D_2}{Dr}\right)}{10} \right)} * W_{ref}$$

where:

- L_p is SPL required at distance D_2.
- H is required headroom.
- L_s is loudspeaker sensitivity at 3.28 ft (1 m).
- D_2 is distance from loudspeaker to listener.
- D_r is distance reference value.
- W_{ref} is the wattage reference value. Assume a wattage reference value of 1 unless otherwise noted.

Simplified Room Mode Calculation

A simplified formula for discovering frequencies where room modes will be present is as follows:

$$3 * (velocity\ of\ sound)\ /\ RSD = Hz$$

where:

- The *velocity of sound* = 1,130 feet per second (343 meters per second) at 72 degrees F
- *RSD* = The room's smallest dimension
- *Hz* = Frequency

Loudspeaker Coverage Pattern (Ceiling Mounted)

The formula for calculating the diameter (twice the radius) of the circle that represents the coverage area of a loudspeaker is as follows:

$$D = 2 * (H - h) * tan\ (C\angle\ /\ 2)$$

where:

- D is the diameter of the coverage area.
- H is the ceiling height.
- h is the height of the listeners' ears.
- $C\angle$ is the loudspeaker's angle of coverage in degrees.

Loudspeaker Spacing (Ceiling Mounted)

The formula for calculating the space between ceiling-mounted speakers depends on how much overlap of each speaker's coverage pattern is desired. Here are formulas for three typical coverage patterns, based on overlap:

- Edge-to-edge (no overlap): $D = 2 * r$
- Minimal overlap: $D = r * \sqrt{2}$
- Center-to-center (maximum overlap): $D = r$

In all cases:

- *D* is the distance between loudspeakers.
- *r* is the radius of the loudspeakers' coverage circles.

Digital Video Bandwidth

The formula for calculating digital signal bandwidth for uncompressed, color (RGB) video is as follows:

bit rate (bits per second) = horizontal pixels × vertical pixels × bit depth × frames per second

Analog Video Signal Bandwidth

The formula for calculating analog video signal bandwidth is as follows:

$$HF = \frac{H_{pix} * V_{pix} * f_v}{2} * 3$$

where:

- *HF* is the highest frequency in hertz.
- H_{pix} is the total number of horizontal pixels.
- V_{pix} is the total number of vertical pixels.
- f_v is the refresh rate.

Minimum Video System Bandwidth

The formula for calculating minimum video system bandwidth is as follows:

*SF = HF * 2*

where:

- *SF* is the system frequency in hertz.
- *HF* is the highest frequency in hertz of the computer signal.

InfoComm Standards

The American National Standards Institute (ANSI) is the official U.S. representative to the International Organization for Standardization (ISO). The InfoComm International Certified Technology Specialist–Installation (CTS-D) exam, for which you are studying, is ANSI-accredited under the ISO and the ISO/IEC 17024:2012 standard, *Conformity Assessment–General Requirements for Bodies Operating Certification Schemes of Persons.*

In addition, InfoComm is an ANSI-accredited Standards Developer (ASD), creating voluntary standards for the commercial audiovisual industry. Accreditation by ANSI signifies that the processes used by standards development organizations (SDOs) to develop ANSI standards meet ANSI's requirements for openness, balance, consensus, right to appeal, and due process. InfoComm also develops non-ANSI standards for use within the AV industry.

InfoComm standards provide guidance for AV system performance. This includes system performance standards, management standards, documentation standards, and verification standards. The standards take into account technology, physiology, architecture, and other variables in determining the best way to design, implement, and manage the performance of all types of AV systems. You can keep up with news about current standards and those in development by visiting InfoComm's website (www.infocomm .org/standards).

Do not be surprised if you see references to some of these standards on the CTS-D exam. It is important for CTS-D professionals to be able to understand and apply relevant standards. As a CTS-D certified AV professional, you should consider standards when designing AV system projects.

This appendix provides a brief synopsis of the existing InfoComm standards. Members can download all the InfoComm standards from the InfoComm website for free.

ANSI/INFOCOMM 1M-2009, *Audio Coverage Uniformity in Enclosed Listener Areas*

One of the fundamental goals of sound system performance for both speech reinforcement and program audio is delivering consistent coverage in the listening area. A well-executed audio system design is one that allows all listeners to hear the system at approximately the same sound pressure level throughout the desired frequency spectrum range, no matter where positioned in the designated listening area. This standard provides a procedure to measure this spatial coverage, as well as criteria for use in the design and commissioning of audio systems.

ANSI/INFOCOMM 2M-2010, *Standard Guide for Audiovisual Design and Coordination Processes*

A successful professional audiovisual system installation depends on the clear definition and coordination of processes, resources, and responsibilities of the design and installation project teams. A properly documented audiovisual system provides the information necessary to understand and implement the system goals and project requirements in a logical and efficient manner. The documentation should complement and coordinate related architectural, engineering, and construction documentation. This standard outlines a consistent set of the standard tasks, responsibilities, and deliverables required for professional audiovisual systems design and construction.

ANSI/INFOCOMM 3M-2011, *Projected Image System Contrast Ratio*

This standard provides metrics for measurement and requirements for minimum contrast ratios for rear- and front-projection audiovisual projected image systems.

It also applies to both permanent and temporary installations and defines the projected image system's contrast ratio and its measurement. It defines four contrast ratios based on content viewing requirements: passive viewing, basic decision making, analytical decision making, and full-motion video. The system contrast ratio refers to the image as it is presented to viewers in a space with ambient light. Metrics to measure and validate the defined contrast ratios are also provided.

The standard puts the needs of the viewer ahead of all other considerations. Its requirements move beyond individual performance factors of a projector and a screen because the contrast ratio they can deliver is ultimately affected by the light in the space.

This standard provides important metrics for evaluating, planning, and designing projected image system installations, setting minimum contrast ratios, and measuring the contrast ratio provided by the system.

ANSI/INFOCOMM 4:2012, *Audiovisual Systems Energy Management*

This standard defines and prescribes processes and requirements for ongoing power-consumption management of the audiovisual system. The standard identifies requirements for the control and continuous monitoring of electrical power for audiovisual systems, whereby power is conserved whenever possible and components operate at the lowest power-consuming state possible without compromise to the system's performance for the needs of the user. Audiovisual systems in conformance with the standard will meet the defined requirements for automation, measurement, analysis, and training.

An audiovisual system designed to minimize power consumption includes power monitoring and automated control of components in an effort to use the least amount of electrical power possible when the AV system is in operation, when it is in standby modes, and when the system is not being used.

Energy conservation can be managed through ongoing active monitoring and reporting of power consumption. Design of the technical architecture of the AV systems and components, implementation based on design documentation, and thorough testing procedures of installed systems are critical to the success of an energy management program.

ANSI/INFOCOMM 10:2013, *Audiovisual Systems Performance Verification*

This standard provides a framework and supporting processes for determining elements of an audiovisual system that need to be verified, determining the timing of that verification within the project delivery cycle, determining verification metrics, and creating reporting procedures. The standard includes 160 reference verification items. Consultants, integrators, manufacturers, technology support staff, owners, third-party commissioning agents, and architects who have verification processes in place can integrate existing processes into the framework this standard provides, adding customized verification items to those already defined in the standard.

CEA/CEDIA/INFOCOMM J-STD-710, *Audio, Video and Control Architectural Drawing Symbols Standard*

This document provides a standardized set of architectural floor plan and reflected ceiling plan symbols for audio, video, and control systems, with associated technologies such as environmental control and communication networks. It also includes descriptions and guidelines for the use of these symbols.

INFOCOMM F501.01:2015, *Cable Labeling for Audiovisual Systems*

This standard defines requirements for audiovisual system cable labeling for a variety of venues. The standard provides requirements for easy identification of all power and signal paths in a completed audiovisual system to aid in operation, support, maintenance, and troubleshooting.

Video References

InfoComm has produced several short videos that can help you prepare for the CTS-D exam. Most of these videos are referenced throughout this guide and are less than 15 minutes long. They are presented here in the order in which they're introduced in the preceding chapters. Others offer additional insight but are not specifically referenced in the guide.

Videos in This Guide

Title	Link	Length
Applying for the CTS-D Exam	www.infocomm.org/CertVideo	7:44
Ohm's Law and the Power Formula	www.infocomm.org/OhmsVideo	4:15
Planning an AV Design	www.infocomm.org/PlanningVideo	4:46
The Design Phase	www.infocomm.org/DesignPhaseVideo	7:14
Scaled Drawings	www.infocomm.org/ScaleVideo	6:57
Components of an AV Design Package	www.infocomm.org/PackageVideo	1:40
AV Design Package Tour	www.infocomm.org/DesignTourVideo	12:41
Writing a Program Report	www.infocomm.org/ProgramReportVideo	5:12
Ergonomics Part 1	www.infocomm.org/Ergo1Video	11:57
Ergonomics Part 2	www.infocomm.org/Ergo2Video	11:39
Determining Viewing Area	www.infocomm.org/ViewingVideo	16:48
Determining Image Specifications	www.infocomm.org/ImageSpecVideo	15:56
Equal Loudness Contours	www.infocomm.org/LoudnessVideo	5:08
Flutter Echoes	www.infocomm.org/FlutterVideo	0:18
How EDID Works	www.infocomm.org/EDIDVideo	0:59
How HDCP Works	www.infocomm.org/HDCPVideo	1:55
Measuring Contrast Ratio	www.infocomm.org/ContrastVideo	2:17
Color Bar Test Pattern Tutorial	www.infocomm.org/ColorBarVideo	2:45

Additional Videos

Title	Link	Length
Multiple Choice Breakdown	www.infocomm.org/QuestionsVideo	10:26
Study Better	www.infocomm.org/StudyVideo	5:04
Frequency Response	www.infocomm.org/FrequencyVideo	4:14
Loudness of an Audio System	www.infocomm.org/AudioLoudnessVideo	3:20
SPL and Weighting Curves	www.infocomm.org/SPLVideo	6:11
Logarithms	www.infocomm.org/LogarithmsVideo	4:30
Loudspeaker Impedance	www.infocomm.org/ImpedanceVideo	3:57

About the CD-ROM

The CD-ROM included with this book comes with Total Tester practice exam software with a complete practice exam and a PDF copy of the book. The software can be installed on any Windows XP/Vista/7/8 computer and must be installed to access the Total Tester practice exams.

System Requirements

The software requires Windows XP or higher; the current or prior major release of Chrome, Firefox, Internet Explorer, or Safari; and 30MB of hard disk space for full installation.

Installing and Running Total Tester

From the main screen you may install the Total Tester by clicking the Software Installers button and then selecting the Total Tester CTS-D Certified Technology Specialist-Design Practice Exams button. This will begin the installation process and place an icon on your desktop and in your Start menu. To run Total Tester, navigate to Start | (All) Programs | Total Seminars or double-click the icon on your desktop.

To uninstall the Total Tester software, go to Start | Settings | Control Panel | Add/ Remove Programs (XP) or Programs And Features (Vista /7/8), and then select the CTS-D Certified Technology Specialist-Design Total Tester program. Select Remove and Windows will completely uninstall the software.

Total Tester

Total Tester provides you with a simulation of the CTS-D Certified Technology Specialist-Design exam. The practice exam can be taken in either Practice or Final mode. Practice mode provides an assistance window with references to the exam tasks, listed as objectives, and domains, an explanation of the correct answer, and the option to check your answer as you take the test.

Both Practice and Final modes provide an overall grade and a grade broken down by certification objective. To take a test, launch the program and select CTS-D Certified Technology Specialist-Design from the Installed Question Packs list on the left. You can then select Practice Exam or Exam Simulation.

Free PDF Copy of the Book

The contents of this book are provided in PDF format on the CD. This file is viewable on your computer and many portable devices.

To view the file on your computer, Adobe's Acrobat Reader is required.

 NOTE For more information on Adobe Reader and to check for the most recent version of the software, visit Adobe's website at www.adobe.com and search for the free Adobe Reader or look for Adobe Reader on the product page.

To view the electronic book on a portable device, copy the PDF file to your computer from the CD, and then copy the file to your portable device using a USB or other connection. Adobe offers a mobile version of Adobe Reader, the Adobe Reader mobile app, which currently supports iOS and Android. The Adobe website also has a list of recommended applications.

Video Links

The CD also includes a Video References file excerpted from the book. The file includes links to a library of design-related videos provided by InfoComm. These are the same links provided in the book, but they have been provided separately for quick access.

Technical Support

For questions regarding the Total Tester software or operation of the CD-ROM, visit www.totalsem.com or e-mail support@totalsem.com.

For questions regarding the PDF copy of the book, e-mail techsolutions@mhedu.com or visit http://mhp.softwareassist.com.

For questions regarding book content, please e-mail customer.service@mheducation .com. For customers outside the United States, e-mail international.cs@mheducation.com.

1/3 octave equalizer   A graphic equalizer that provides 30 or 31 slider adjustments corresponding to specific fixed frequencies with fixed bandwidths, with the frequencies centered at every one-third of an octave. The numerous adjustment points shape the overall frequency response of the system. This makes the sound system sound more natural.

4K ecosystem   Video cameras, media players, servers, displays, distribution, and networking technologies used for recording and delivering video at 3840×2160- or 4096×2160-pixel resolution.

8K   A video resolution format. It offers a 7680×4320-pixel resolution, which is 16 times the resolution of full HD.

9-pin connector   The most common type of RS-232 connection that is used within a control system.

acceptable viewing area   The viewing range for a screen suggested as a 45-degree line extending outward from the left-side edge and right-side edge of a displayed image.

access point   A network device that handles a wireless network connection.

acoustic echo canceller   Used in a conferencing system. The canceller will attempt to compensate for environmental echoes that are created by the far-site sound bouncing around the walls and furniture and returned to the microphones.

acoustics   Explains and quantifies the interaction of cyclical mechanical compression and rarefaction of a medium, typically air, occurring within a commonly accepted frequency range of 20 Hz to 20 KHz (the audible spectrum) and the physical environment in which those waves occur.

acuity   An eye's ability to discern fine details. There are several different kinds of acuity, including resolution acuity, which is the ability to detect that there are two stimuli, rather than one, in a visual field, and recognition acuity, which is the ability to identify correctly a visual target, such as differentiating between a *G* and a *C*.

AES   Audio Engineering Society.

allied trade   A business that collaborates with AV professionals to complete a project.

alternating current (AC)   An electric current that reverses its direction periodically.

ambient light   Lighting throughout an area that produces general illumination.

ambient noise Sound that is extraneous to the intended, desired, or intentional background noise.

amplifier An electronic device for increasing the strength of electrical signals.

amplitude The strength of an electronic signal as measured by the height of its waveform.

amperage The amount of electric current flow within a circuit. Amperage is measurement in amps and expressed using the symbols I or A.

analog A method of transmitting information by a continuous but varying signal.

analog-to-digital/digital-to-analog (AD/DA) converters Used to convert signals from analog to digital or from digital to analog.

angularly reflective screen A screen that reflects light back to the viewer at a complementary angle.

ANSI American National Standards Institute.

aperture An opening in a lens regulating the amount of light passing through the lens to the imager.

arrayed loudspeaker system A loudspeaker arrangement that delivers sound from a single point in space. It is also known as a *high-pressure system*.

artifact A small disturbance that affects the quality of a signal.

aspect ratio The ratio of image width to image height.

attack time A setting within an audio digital signal processor that determines how quickly the volume will be reduced once the volume exceeds the threshold. If the attack time is too slow, then the sound will become distorted as the system adjusts.

attenuate To reduce the amplitude (strength) of a signal or current.

Audio Coverage Uniformity measurement locations (ACUML) The test points within a venue that have been determined to carry out the measurements for the Audio Coverage Uniformity test.

Audio Coverage Uniformity Plan (ACUP) A stand-alone document that identifies the Audio Coverage Uniformity measurement locations for a particular venue, using the InfoComm indication symbol.

audio processor An electronic device used to manipulate audio signals.

Audio Return Channel (ARC) Introduced to the HDMI standard with version 1.4. ARC allows a display to send audio data upstream to a receiver or surround-sound controller, eliminating the need for a separate audio connection.

audio signal An electrical representation of sound.

audio transduction   The process of converting acoustical energy into electrical energy or electrical energy back into acoustical energy.

Audio Video Bridging (AVB)   A standards-based audiovisual Data Link layer protocol defined under IEEE 802.1-AVB. It uses standard Ethernet cabling but requires AVB-enabled switches and network components. AVB does not require separate network infrastructure or dedicated bandwidth; AVB components automatically prioritize data. AVB was recently renamed Time-Sensitive Networking to reflect the standard's applicability to communication among different types of devices, such as network sensors. See *Time-Sensitive Networking*.

audiovisual infrastructure   The physical building components that make up the pathways, supports, and architectural elements required for audiovisual technical equipment installations.

audiovisual rack   A housing unit that protects and organizes electronic equipment. The inside of a typical AV industry rack is 19 in (482.6 mm) wide. Many of the technical specifications for a rack, including size and equipment height, are determined by standards that have been established by numerous standard-setting organizations. The outside width of the rack varies from 21 to 25 in (530 to 630 mm).

authority having jurisdiction (AHJ)   An organization, office, or individual responsible for enforcing the requirements of a code or standard or for approving equipment, materials, installation, or procedure. In some areas of the world, the authority having jurisdiction is known as a *regional regulatory authority*.

automatic gain control (AGC)   An electronic or logic feedback circuit that maintains a constant acoustic power (gain) output in response to input variables such as signal strength or ambient noise level.

Automatic Private IP Addressing (APIPA)   A form of link-local addressing defined in the IETF standard RFC 3927. APIPA automatically assigns locally routable addresses from the reserved network 169.254.0.0/16 to devices that do not have or cannot obtain an IP address. This allows devices to communicate with other devices on the same LAN. APIPA operates at the Network layer of the OSI model and the Internet layer of the TCP/IP protocol stack.

balanced circuit   A two-conductor circuit in which both conductors and all circuits connected to them have the same impedance with respect to ground.

balun   Short for BALanced-to-UNbalanced, a transformer used to connect a balanced circuit to an unbalanced circuit. For example, a transformer used to connect a 300-ohm antenna cable (balanced) to a 75-ohm antenna cable (unbalanced).

band   A grouping or range of frequencies.

bandwidth (BW)   1. A range of frequencies. 2. A measure of the amount of data or signal that can pass through a system during a given time interval. 3. The range of frequencies used or allowed.

bandwidth (networking)　Bandwidth is the available or consumed data communication resources of a communication path, expressed in terms of bits per second. It is also called *throughput* or *bit rate*.

bandwidth limiting　The result of encoding a higher-quality signal into a lower-quality form, such as RGB converted into S-Video.

baseband　A video signal that has not been modulated.

benchmarking　The process of examining methods, techniques, and principles from peer organizations and facilities, which can be used as a basis for designing a new or renovated facility.

bend radius　The radial measure of a curve in a cable, conductor, or interconnect that defines the physical limit beyond which further bending has a measurable and/or harmful effect on the signal being transported.

bidirectional polar pattern　The shape of the region where some microphones will be most sensitive to sound from the front and rear, while rejecting sound from the top, bottom, and sides.

bill of materials (BOM)　A complete equipment list of components that must be procured in order to build the system as designed. The BOM also lists the costs associated with each aspect of designing and implementing the system.

bit　Shortened form of binary digit, symbolized by 1s and 0s. A bit is the smallest unit of digital information.

bit depth　The number of bits used to describe a sampled voltage level.

bit error rate (BER)　The total amount of error bits present in a signal after being sent across a cable. It is calculated by performing a BER test.

bit rate　The measurement of the quantity of information over time in a digital signal stream. The higher the bit rate, the better the signal quality will be. Bit rate is quantified in bits per second (bit/s or bps).

block diagram　An illustration of the signal path through a given system from sources to destinations.

Bluetooth　A wireless technology for low-cost, short-range radio links between mobile phones, computers, personal digital assistants (PDAs), and other consumer devices. It uses a short-range wireless connection wireless personal area network (WPAN), which allows devices with transceiver chips to talk to each other.

BNC connector　A professional type of video connector featuring a two-pin lock. The BNC is the most common and most professional coaxial cable connector because of its reliability and ruggedness. They are used to transport many different types of signals such as radio, frequency, component video, time code, sync, and power.

bonding   Joining conductive material by a low impedance connection, thus ensuring that they are of the same electrical potential.

boundary microphone   A microphone design where the diaphragm is placed close to a sonic "boundary" such as a wall, ceiling, or other flat surface. This prevents the acoustic reflections from the surface from mixing with the direct feed and causing phase distortions. This microphone is commonly used in conference and telepresence systems.

branch circuit   The circuit conductors between the final overcurrent device protecting the circuit and the outlets.

breaker box   See *panelboard*.

broadcast domain   A set of devices that can send Data Link layer frames to each other directly, without passing through a Network layer device. Broadcast traffic sent by one device in the broadcast domain is received by every other device in the domain.

building information modeling (BIM)   A data repository for building design, construction, and maintenance information, used by multiple trades on a single project.

bus   A wiring system that delivers power and data to various devices.

busbar   An electrically conductive block or bar of metal, typically copper or aluminum, that serves as a common connection for two or more circuits.

buzz   A mixture of higher-order harmonics of the 50 or 60 Hz noise (hum) originating from the AC power system and audible in the sound system.

byte (B)   An 8-bit word. The abbreviation for byte is B.

cable   An assembly of more than one conductor (wire).

cable tray   An assembly of units made of metal or other noncombustible material to provide rigid continuous support for cables.

candela   The luminous intensity of a source that emits monochromatic radiation of frequency 540×1012 Hz and has a radiant intensity in that direction of $1/683$ watt per steradian. The candela has replaced the candlepower standard.

capacitance   The ability of a nonconductive material to develop an electrical charge that can distort an electrical signal.

capacitive reactance (XC)   Opposition a capacitor offers to alternating current flow. The capacitive reactance decreases with increasing frequency or, for a given frequency, the capacitive reactance decreases with increasing capacitance. The symbol for capacitive reactance is XC.

capacitor   A passive electrical component in which plates of conductive material are separated by a dielectric. For a given capacitance value, expressed in farads, a capacitor will have a greater opposition to AC current flow at lower frequencies than at higher frequencies.

cardioid polar pattern   A heart-shaped region where some microphones will be most sensitive to sound predominately from the front of the microphone diaphragm and reject sound coming from the sides and rear.

carrier   Modulated frequency that carries video or audio signal.

Category 5 (Cat 5)   The designation for 100-ohm unshielded twisted-pair (UTP) cables and associated connecting hardware whose characteristics are specified for data transmission up to 100 Mb/s (part of the EIA/TIA 568A standard).

Category 5e (Cat 5e)   An enhanced version of the Cat 5 cable standard that adds specifications for far-end crosstalk (part of the EIA/TIA 568A standard).

Category 6 (Cat 6)   A cable standard for Gigabit Ethernet and other interconnections that is backward-compatible with Category 5, Cat 5e, and Cat 3 cable (part of the EIA/TIA 568A standard). Cat 6 features more stringent specifications for crosstalk and system noise.

center tap   A connection point located halfway along the winding of a transformer or inductor.

central cluster   A single source configuration of loudspeakers. In a central cluster, the sound is coming from one point in the room. The central cluster is normally located directly above (on the proscenium), and slightly in front of, the primary microphone location.

central processing unit (CPU)   The portion of a computer system that reads and executes commands.

charged-coupled device (CCD)   A semiconductor light-sensitive device, commonly used in video and digital cameras, that converts optical images into electronic signals.

chassis   Also called a *cabinet* or *frame,* an enclosure that houses electronic equipment and is frequently electrically conductive (metal). The metal enclosure acts as a shield and is connected to the equipment grounding conductor of the AC power cable, if so equipped, to provide protection against electric shock.

chassis ground   A 0 V (zero volt) connection point of any electrically conductive chassis or enclosure surrounding an electronic device. This connection point may or may not be extended to the earth ground.

chroma   The saturation, or intensity, of a specific color. It is one of the three attributes that define a color; the other two are hue and grayscale.

chrominance   The color portion of a composite or S-Video signal.

cliff effect   The sudden loss of digital signal reception. When a digital signal is carried too far on a cable, the eye pattern will collapse, and the signal will become unreadable.

clipping   The deformation of an audio signal when a device's peak amplitude level is exceeded.

clock adjustment   Also called *timing signals,* used to fine-tune the computer image. This function adjusts the clock frequencies that eliminate the vertical banding (lines) in the image.

coaxial (coax) cable   A cable consisting of a center conductor surrounded by insulating material, concentric outer conductor, and optional protective covering, all of circular cross section.

CobraNet   CobraNet is a proprietary digital audio Data Link layer protocol designed by Cirrus Logic. It uses standard Fast Ethernet cabling, switches, and other components. CobraNet signals are nonroutable.

codec   An acronym for *coder/decoder*. An electronic device that converts analog signals, such as video and audio signals, into digital form and compresses them to conserve bandwidth on a transmission path.

collision domain   A set of devices on a local area network (LAN) whose packets may collide with one another if they send data at the same time.

color difference signal   A signal that conveys color information such as hue and saturation in a composite format. Two such signals are needed. These color difference signals are R-Y and B-Y, sometimes referred to as Pr and Pb or Cr and Cb.

color rendering index (CRI)   The effect a light source has on the perceived color of objects relative to an incandescent source of the same correlated color temperature, which has a CRI of 100.

color temperature   The quantification of the color of "white" light, as rated on a numerical scale. Low color temperature light (~2000K) has a warm (red-ish) look, while light with a high color temperature (~6000K) has a colder (blue-ish) appearance.

combiner   In a process called *multiplexing,* puts signals together onto one cable, constituting a broadband signal.

common mode   1. Voltage fed in phase to both inputs of a differential amplifier. 2. The signal voltage that appears equally and, in phase, from each current carrying conductor to ground.

common-mode rejection ratio (CMRR)   The ratio of the differential voltage gain to the common-mode voltage gain; expressed in decibels.

compander   An audio processing device that combines compression and expansion.

component video   Color video in which the brightness (luminance) and color hue and saturation (chrominance) are handled independently. The red, green, and blue signals—or more commonly, the Y, R-Y, and B-Y signals—are encoded onto three wires. Because these signals are independent, processing such as chroma keying is facilitated.

composite video signal   The electrical signal that represents complete color picture information and all synchronization signals, including blanking and the deflection synchronization signals to which the color synchronization signal is added in the appropriate time relationship.

compression   1. An increase in density and pressure in air molecules. 2. A process that reduces data size.

compressor   A device that controls the overall amplitude of a signal by reducing the part of the signal that exceeds an adjustable level (threshold) set by the user. When the signal exceeds the threshold level, the overall amplitude is reduced by a ratio, also usually adjustable by the user.

compressor ratio   The compression ratio of an audio compressor determines how much the volume reduces depending on how far above the threshold the signal is.

compressor threshold   The compressor threshold sets the point at which the automatic volume reduction kicks in. When the input goes above the threshold, an audio compressor automatically reduces the volume to keep the signal from getting too loud.

condenser microphone   Also called a *capacitor microphone,* a microphone that transduces sound into electricity using electrostatic principles.

conductor   In electronics, a material that easily conducts an electric current because some electrons in the material are free to move.

conduit   Can mean any pathway, but in the AV and electrical industry it is a circular tube that houses cable.

cone   The most commonly used component in a loudspeaker system and found in all ranges of drivers.

constant voltage   25 V, 70 V, 100 V; a method of distributing power to loudspeakers over a large area with less loss than a typical connection would provide. This can also be called a *high impedance system.*

Consumer Electronic Control (CEC)   A single-wire, bidirectional serial bus that uses AV link protocols to perform remote-control functions. It is an optional feature of the HDMI specification that allows for system-level automation when all devices in an AV system support it.

contact closure   A contact closure is the simplest form of remote-control communication. It is a switch. This type of control point operates a device by opening or closing an electrical current or voltage loop. It has the most basic protocol language: "on" (closed circuit) or "off" (open circuit).

content delivery network (CDN)   A distributed network of caching servers that can provide hosted unicast distribution of media for an organization. They are most often utilized by organizations whose content is in high demand.

contrast   Absolute difference in luminance between the peak white and black levels, where white and black luminance is displayed simultaneously.

contrast ratio   Describes the dynamic video range of a display device as a numeric relationship between the brightest color (typically white) and the darkest color (typically black) that the system is capable of producing. Two methods are used to specify contrast ratio; the full on/full off method describes the dynamic contrast ratio, and the ANSI measures the static contrast ratio.

control system   A subsystem that simplifies the operation of an AV system.

correlated color temperature (CCT)   The color appearance of a light source as measured on the Kelvin scale.

coverage pattern   The predictable pattern of sound energy that every loudspeaker emits. The coverage pattern is based on the frequency of the sounds and the physical size of the loudspeaker.

critical distance (Dc)   The point where the sound pressure level of the direct reverberant sound field are equal.

critical path schedule   Reveals the interdependence of activities and assesses resource and time requirements and trade-offs. It also determines the project's completion date and provides the capability to evaluate activity performance.

crossover   Separates the audio signal into different frequency groupings and routes the appropriate material to the loudspeaker or amplifier to ensure that the individual loudspeaker components receive program signals that are within their optimal frequency range.

crosstalk   Any phenomenon by which a signal transmitted on one circuit or channel of a transmission system creates an undesired effect in another circuit or channel.

current   The amount of electrical charge that is flowing in a circuit, measured in amperes.

curvature of field   A blurry appearance around the edge of an otherwise in-focus object (or the reverse) when the velocity of light going through the lens is different at the edges than at the center of the surface. Curvature of field is due to the lens design.

Dante   A proprietary digital audio Network layer protocol designed by Audinate. Dante sends audio information as Internet Protocol (IP) packets. It is fully routable over IP networks using standard Ethernet switches, routers, and other components. Dante traffic requires no separate infrastructure; it can coexist with other data traffic. Dante controller software manages data prioritization and audio routes.

dB SPL   A measure of sound pressure level represented in dynes per centimeter squared. Its reference, 0 dB SPL, equals 0.0002 dynes/cm². dB SPL is used as a measure of acoustical sound pressure levels and is a 20-log function.

decibel (dB)   A base-10 logarithmic relationship of a power ratio between two numbers. This is used for quantifying differences in voltage, distance, and sound pressure as they relate to power.

delay   An audio signal-processing device or circuit used to retard the speed of transmission on one or more audio signals or frequencies.

demodulator   An electronic device that removes information from a modulated signal.

depth of field   The area in front of a camera lens that is in focus from the closest item to the camera to the item farthest away.

detail drawing   A detail drawing enlarges small items to show how they must be installed. They depict items too small to see at the project's typical drawing scale.

dielectric constant   Describes the ability of a material between two conductors to store an electrical charge. Dielectric strength is determined by the material's type and thickness and is the amount of voltage that insulation can stand before it breaks down.

differential mode   1. Voltage fed out of phase to both inputs of a differential amplifier. 2. Signals measurable between or among active circuit conductors feeding the load but not between the equipment grounding conductor or associated signal reference structure and the active circuit conductors.

differentiated service (DiffServ)   A network quality-of-service strategy wherein data from specific applications or protocols are assigned a class of service. Flows assigned a high priority are given preferential treatment at the router, but delivery is not guaranteed.

diffusion   The scattering or random redistribution of a sound wave from a surface. Diffusion occurs when surfaces are at least as long as the sound wavelengths but not more than four times as long.

digital media player   Digital media players are devices that allow users to play back or stream audio and video content from digital media servers, the Internet, or computer hard drives.

digital-only token (DOT)   A digital flag that is embedded onto digital sources, such as Blu-ray Discs. Its purpose is to limit the availability or quality of HD content on the component output of a media player.

digital signage   Digital signage is customized content shown on strategically located displays intended to attract specific types of viewers. It is sometimes referred to as dynamic signage to differentiate it from large-format static signs. Digital signage is displayed on LCD and LED panels, kiosks, and projection screens. These displays are placed in public spaces, museums, stadiums, corporate and educational buildings, retail stores, hotels, restaurants, and other locations.

digital signage media player   A hardware device or computer server used to store and forward or play back digital signage content on display screens. Some commercial digital signage displays have integrated media players on a chip. Digital signage players are often located in close proximity to the display screen but may also be located remotely. Network-ready media players enable the control and management of content remotely.

digital signage template   Customizable layouts used for standardizing content across all displays on the network. They enable multiple messages or content from multiple sources to be displayed on a screen by presenting the information in zones.

digital signal processor (DSP)   Combines processor functions such as mixers, limiters, and equalizers, typically into a single device.

digital-to-analog converter   An electronic device that converts digital signals into analog form.

direct couple   A loudspeaker system in which the amplifier is connected directly to the voice coil wires of the loudspeaker.

direct current (DC)   Electricity that maintains a steady flow and does not reverse direction, unlike alternating current (AC). It is usually produced by batteries, AC-to-DC transformers, and power supplies.

direct sound   Also known as *near-field,* sound that is not colored by room reflections.

direct view display   Houses the light-producing elements and screen in one piece of equipment.

directivity   The specific coverage pattern that designers must consider when determining the placement of loudspeakers required to provide full coverage for all the listeners within a space.

dispersion   An effect that can be seen when a white light beam passes through a triangular prism. The different wavelengths of light refract at different angles, dispersing the light into its individual components.

Display Data Channel (DDC)   The electrical channel that EDID and HDCP use for communication between a video card and a display. It is a collection of protocols maintained as a standard by the Video Electronics Standards Association (VESA).

DisplayID   A standard developed by VESA outlining how video display data is structured to describe its performance and capabilities when communicating with other devices. By structuring data in a flexible, modular way, DisplayID enables devices to identify new display resolutions, refresh rates, audio standards, and other formats as they become available. For example, the standard can support a single image segmented across tiled displays using multiple video processors.

DisplayPort   A digital display interface developed by the Video Electronics Standards Association (VESA) to replace VGA and DVI and used to connect a video source to a display device. It can also carry audio, USB, and other data.

distributed sound system   A sound system using multiple loudspeakers separated by distance. It typically operates in a lower sound pressure level than a high-pressure system. The loudspeakers are most often suspended over the heads of the listeners.

distribution amplifier (DA)   An active device used to split one input into multiple outputs, while keeping each output isolated and the signal level constant.

diversity receiver   A diversity receiver is an RF receiver that uses a pair of antennas to receive a transmitted RF signal. Diversity receivers constantly calculate phase differences between signals to dynamically shift between the two antennas and avoid cancellation.

DLP   Digital Light Processing by Texas Instruments. A projection system that has technology based on the digital micromirror device (DMD). It uses thousands of microscopic mirrors on a chip focused through an optical system to display images on the screen.

Domain Name System (DNS)   A hierarchical, distributed database that maps names to data such as IP addresses. A DNS server keeps track of all the equipment on the network and matches the equipment names so they can easily be located on the network or integrated into control and monitoring systems. See *reserve DHCP*.

dome   A type of loudspeaker driver construction. Fabric or woven materials are used to create a dome-shaped diaphragm, and the coil is attached to the edge of the diaphragm.

driver   In audio, an individual loudspeaker unit.

dual channel   In a measurement scenario, indicates that two inputs are used for measuring something under test. The two channels used are a test reference signal and a measured signal.

DVD   Digital Video Disc or Digital Versatile Disc. This is an optical storage medium for data or video.

DVI   Digital Visual Interface. This is a connection method from a source (typically a computer) and a display device that can allow for direct digital transfer of data. The connection is limited to a distance of 5 meters (16 feet) for resolutions up to 1920×1200. Lower resolutions such as 1280×1024 can reach up to 15 meters (49 feet). DVI has largely been replaced by HDMI, DisplayPort, and other formats.

Dynamic Host Configuration Protocol (DHCP)   An IP addressing scheme that allows network administrators to automate address assignment.

dynamic microphone   A pressure-sensitive microphone of moving-coil design that transduces sound into electricity using electromagnetic principles.

dynamic range   The difference between the loudest and quietest levels of an audio signal.

early reflected sound   Sound created by sound waves that are reflected (bounced) off surfaces between the source and the listener. The sound waves arrive at the listener's ear closely on the heels of the direct sound wave.

echo   A reflected version of sound energy acoustically, or a duplicated version of a signal electronically, that arrives to the listener with sufficient delay and separation from the original signal to allow the delayed signal to be perceived distinctly and later in time from the original signal.

echo cancellation   A means of eliminating echo from an audio signal path.

electret microphone   A type of condenser microphone. It has prepolarized material, called *electret,* which is applied to the microphone's diaphragm or backplate.

electrical service   The conductors and equipment for delivering energy from the electricity supply system to the wiring system of the site served.

electromagnetic interference (EMI)   Disruption of operation of a circuit (noise) due to the effects of interference from electric and/or magnetic fields.

elevation drawing   A two-dimensional view of a single surface. It is commonly used for creating a true picture of what a surface will look like.

emissive technology   Any display device that emits light to create an image.

encoded   A signal that has been compressed into another form to reduce size or complexity, as in a composite video signal.

energy management plan   A document that details a systematic approach to implementing the most effective power consumption methods and procedures to achieve and maintain optimum energy usage.

equalizer   Electronic equipment that adjusts or corrects the frequency characteristics of a signal.

equipment grounding   The connection to ground (earth), or to a conductive body that extends that ground connection, of all normally noncurrent-carrying conductive materials enclosing electrical conductors or equipment or forming part of such equipment. The purpose is to limit any voltage potential between the equipment and earth.

equipment grounding conductor (EGC)   The conductive path installed to connect normally noncurrent-carrying metal parts of equipment together and to the system's grounded conductor, to the grounding electrode conductor, or to both.

equipment rack   A centralized housing unit that protects and organizes electronic equipment.

equivalent acoustic distance (EAD)   The farthest distance one can go from the source without the need for sound amplification or reinforcement to maintain good speech intelligibility. It is a design parameter dependent on the level of the presenter and the noise level in the room.

ergonomics   Also known as human factors or human factors engineering. This is the scientific study of the way people interact with a system. It focuses on effectiveness, efficiency, reducing errors, increasing productivity, improving safety, reducing fatigue and stress, increasing comfort, increasing user acceptance, increasing job satisfaction, and improving quality of life.

Ethernet   A set of network cabling and network access protocol standards administered by the 802.3 subcommittee of the IEEE. Ethernet signals are transmitted serially, one bit at a time, over the shared signal channel to every attached station.

EtherSound   A proprietary digital audio Data Link layer protocol designed by Digigram. It uses standard 100 Mbps or 1 Gbps Ethernet cabling, switches, and other components. EtherSound signals are nonroutable.

expander   An audio processor that comes in two types: a downward expander and as a part of a compander.

extended display identification data (EDID)   A data structure within a sink that is used to describe the sink's capabilities to a source. These capabilities include native resolution, color space information, and audio type (mono or stereo).

external configuration   Refers to the ability of one device to configure other devices and subsystems.

far field   The sound field distant enough from the sound source so the SPL decreases by 6 dB for each doubling of the distance from the source.

farthest viewer   The viewer positioned at the farthest distance from the screen as defined by the viewing area.

feedback   1. In audio, unwanted noise caused by the loop of an audio system's output back to its input. 2. In a control system, data supplied to give an indication of status, such as on or off.

feedback stability margin (FSM)   Extra margin that represents additional gain that a sound system may need. It is the possibility of feedback due to the nonlinearity across the frequency band of a sound system.

fiber optic   A technology that uses glass or plastic threads or wires to transmit information.

field   In video, one-half of a video frame containing every other line of information. Each standard video frame contains two interlaced fields.

filter   Removes or passes certain frequencies from a signal.

firewall   Any technology, hardware, or software that protects a network by preventing intrusion by unauthorized users and/or regulating traffic permitted to enter or exit the network. A firewall controls what traffic may pass through a router connecting one network to another. Firewalls control access across any network boundaries, including between an enterprise network and the Internet or between local area networks (LANs) within an enterprise.

firmware   A type of software that has been permanently stored in a piece of hardware.

fixture   A fixture is a lamp housing that is mounted or fixed in place.

flex life   The number of times a cable can be bent before it breaks. A wire with more strands or twists per inch will have a greater flex life than one with a lower number of strands or fewer twists per inch.

focal length (FL)   1. The distance, in millimeters, between the center of a lens and the point where the image comes into focus. 2. The value given to a lens, stated in inches or millimeters. The shorter the focal length, the wider the angle of the image will be.

footcandle (fc)   An English unit of measure expressing the intensity of light illuminating an object. A footcandle equals the illumination from one candle falling on a surface of 1 square foot at a distance of 1 foot.

footlambert (fl)   The footlambert (fl) is a U.S. customary unit of measurement for luminance. It is equal to 1/pi candela per square foot.

frame rate   The number of frames sent from a display source per second.

frequency   The number of complete cycles in a specified period of time. It is formerly expressed as cycles per second (cps), now specified as hertz (Hz).

frequency domain   A signal viewed as amplitude versus frequency is in the frequency domain. This allows you to view the amount of energy present at different frequencies.

frequency response   The amplitude response versus frequency for a given device.

Fresnel lens   A flat glass or acrylic lens in which the curvature of a normal lens surface has been collapsed in such a way that concentric circles are impressed on the lens surface. A Fresnel lens is often used for the condenser lens in overhead projectors, in rear-screen projection systems, and in studio spotlights.

front-screen projection   A system that employs a light-reflecting screen for use when the image will be projected from a source in front of the screen.

full-duplex communication   A form of bidirectional data transmission in which multiple messages may travel on the same medium simultaneously.

full HD   An HDTV high-definition video mode characterized by 1080 horizontal lines of vertical resolution and progressive scanning. It is commonly notated as 1080p.

fundamental frequency   Known as *pure tone,* the lowest frequency in a harmonic series.

gain   1. Electronic signal amplification. 2. The ability of a projection screen to concentrate light.

gain control   A gain control is an electronic adjustment through which the operator can increase or decrease the amplitude of a defined signal element.

gain-sharing automatic mixers   A gain-sharing automatic mixer is an audio mixer that automatically turns up microphone channels that are in use and turns down microphone channels that are not being used.

gate   An audio processor that allows signals to pass only above a certain setting or threshold.

gated automatic mixer   An audio mixer that turns microphone channels either "on" or "off" automatically.

gateway   The highest router in the hierarchy of routers. It connects a local network to an outside network, and all traffic must travel through it. A gateway will pass traffic to the routers below, and the routers below look to the gateway to find names (DNS addresses) that are not found on the local network.

gauge   A thickness or diameter of a wire.

genlock   To lock the synchronization signals of multiple devices to a single source.

graphic equalizer   Equalizer with an interface that has a graph comparing amplitude on the vertical with frequency on the horizontal.

graphical user interface (GUI)   Often pronounced "gooey"; provides a visual representation of the system features and functions.

graphics adapter   Commonly referred to as a *video card,* outputs computer signals.

grayscale   The brightness and darkness of a color. It is sometimes called *value.* It is one of the three attributes of color; the other two are hue and chroma.

grayscale test pattern   Displays the broadest range of intensities between black and white on the screen.

ground   1. The earth. 2. In the context of an electrical circuit, the earth or some conductive body that extends the ground (earth) connection. 3. In the context of electronics, the 0 V (zero volt) circuit reference point. This electronic circuit reference point may or may not have a connection to earth.

ground fault   1. An unintentional, electrically conducting connection between an ungrounded conductor of an electrical circuit and a normally noncurrent-carrying conductor, metallic enclosure, metallic raceway, metallic equipment, or earth. 2. The electrical connection between any ungrounded conductor of the electrical system and any noncurrent-carrying metal object.

ground loop   An electrically conductive loop that has two or more ground reference connections. The loop can be detrimental when the reference connections are at different potentials, which causes current flow within the loop.

ground plane   A continuous conductive area. The fundamental property of a ground plane is that every point on its surface is at the same potential (low impedance) at all frequencies of concern.

ground potential   A point of no potential in a circuit.

ground reference   The 0 V (zero volt) reference point for a circuit.

grounded conductor   A system or circuit conductor that is intentionally grounded.

ground-fault circuit interrupter (GFCI)   A safety device that deenergizes a circuit (or a portion of that circuit) within an established period of time when a current to ground exceeds the values established for a Class A device. Class A GFCIs trip when the current to ground is 6 mA or higher; they do not trip when the current to ground is less than 4 mA.

ground-fault current path   An electrically conductive path from the point of a ground fault on a wiring system through normally noncurrent-carrying conductors, equipment, or earth to the electrical supply source.

grounding   Connecting to ground or to a conductive body that extends the ground connection. The connected connection is referred to as *grounded*.

grounding conductor   A conductor used to connect equipment or the grounded circuit of a wiring system to a grounding electrode or electrodes.

grounding electrode   A conducting object through which a direct connection to earth is established.

grounding electrode conductor   The conductor used to connect the system grounded conductor or the equipment to a grounding electrode or to a point on the grounding electrode system.

group management protocol (GMP)   Allows a host to inform its neighboring routers of its desire to start or stop receiving multicast transmissions. Without a GMP, multicast traffic is broadcast to every client device on the network segment, impeding other network traffic and overtaxing device CPUs.

group of pictures (GoP)   A set of successive frames that are required to display a complete series in a digital AV signal. It includes the visible picture, timing/sync information, and compression frames.

half duplex   A form of data transmission in which only one network node at a time sends data.

harmonic distortion   A multiple of a fundamental frequency that does not exist in the original signal.

harmonics   Higher-frequency sound waves that blend with the fundamental frequency.

HD-15 connector   An HD-15 connector, sometimes called a VGA connector, is a video connector that is typically associated with the output of a computer graphics card. It has three rows of five pins, which carry analog red, green, blue, and sync signals along with display data channel information.

HDCP key   A long number that a program uses to verify authenticity and encode /decode content. HDCP processes use multiple types of keys. These keys are strongly protected by Digital Content Protection, LLC.

HDCP receiver   A device that can receive and decode the HDCP signals. A television is an example of a receiver.

HDCP repeater   A device that can receive HDCP signals and transmit them to another device, such as a switcher or distribution amplifier.

HDCP sink   A device that receives and decodes the HDCP signals.

HDCP source   A device that sends HDCP-encoded signals and content.

HDCP transmitter   A device that can send HDCP-encoded signals and content. A Blu-ray Disc player is an example of an HDCP transmitter.

HDMI Ethernet Audio Control (HEAC)   In HDMI, the combining of HEC (HDMI Ethernet Channel) and ARC (Audio Return Channel) into one port or cable. See *HDMI Ethernet Channel (HEC)* and *Audio Return Channel (ARC)*.

HDMI Ethernet Channel (HEC)   Consolidates video, audio, and data streams into a single HDMI cable. A dedicated data channel enables high-speed, bi-directional networking to support future IP solutions and allow multiple devices to share an Internet connection.

HDTV   High-definition television.

headend   The equipment located at the start of a cable distribution system where the signals are processed and combined prior to distribution.

headroom   The difference in dB SPL between peak- and average-level performance of an audio system.

heat load   Heat load is the heat that is generated and released by a piece of electronic equipment. It is measured in British thermal units.

heat sink   A device that absorbs and dissipates heat produced by an electrical component.

hemispheric polar pattern   The dome shape of the region that some microphones will be most sensitive to sound. This pattern is used for boundary microphones.

hertz (Hz)   Cycles per second of an electrical signal.

High-Bandwidth Digital Content Protection (HDCP)   A form of encryption developed by Intel to control digital audio and video content as it travels across Digital Video Interface (DVI) or High Definition Multimedia Interface (HDMI) connections. It prevents transmission or interception of nonencrypted HD content.

High Definition Multimedia Interface (HDMI)   A point-to-point connection between video devices for all-digital video and audio. HDMI signals include audio, control, and digital asset rights management information. It is fully compatible with DVI.

high-pass filter   A circuit that allows signals above a specified frequency to pass unaltered while simultaneously attenuating frequencies below the specified limit.

hiss   Broadband higher-frequency noise typically associated with poor audio system gain structure.

horn   A loudspeaker that reproduces mid to high frequencies.

hot plug   A low-level signal sent by a source that indicates whether a sink or display is connected.

hue   The attribute of a color that represents a red, a purple, a green, and so on. It is one of the three attributes that define color; the other two are grayscale and chroma.

hum   Undesirable 50 to 60 Hz noise emanating from a sound system or evidenced by a rolling hum bar on a display.

IEEE   The Institute of Electrical and Electronics Engineers.

illuminance   Light falling on a surface, measured in lux (lx) or footcandle (ft-c or fc) [1 lux = 0.09 fc]. It is not visible to human eye other than in the form of reflected luminance.

image constraint token (ICT)   A digital flag built into some digital video sources. It prevents unauthorized copies of content from appearing on a sink device. This encryption scheme ensures that high-definition video can be viewed only on HDCP-enabled sinks.

image resolution   Image resolution is the total number of pixels of the display. It is normally expressed as a ratio of horizontal pixels to vertical pixels.

imager   A light-sensitive electronic chip behind a video camera's lens made up of thousands of sensors, called *pixels,* which convert the light input into an electrical output. In normal operation, an imager will output a frame of captured video at the frame rate of the video standard.

impedance (Z)   The total opposition to current flow in an AC circuit. Like a DC circuit, it contains resistance, but it also includes forces that oppose changes in the current (inductive reactance) and voltage (capacitive reactance). Impedance takes into account all three of these factors. It is measured in ohms, and its symbol is Z.

impedance matching   Having an impedance value on an input that an output is expecting. It does not necessarily mean having comparable impedances on an input and an output.

impedance meter   Used to measure true impedance of an electrical circuit.

inductance (L)   The property of a conductor that opposes any change in current, represented by the symbol L and measured in henries (H).

induction   The influence exerted on a conductor by the movement of a magnetic field.

inductive reactance (X_L)   Opposition to the current flow offered by the inductance of a circuit. It is dependent on frequency and inductance. Its symbol is X_L.

InfoFrames   Structured packets of data that carry information regarding aspects of audio and video transmission, as defined by the EIA/CEA-861B standard. Using this structure, a frame-by-frame summary is sent to the display, permitting selection of appropriate display modes automatically. InfoFrames typically include auxiliary video information, generic vendor-specific source product description, MPEG, and audio information.

infrared (IR)   A range of light frequencies used to send information. IR transmission requires line-of-sight between transmitter and receiver. Infrared signals may be either wired or wireless.

input   A connection point that receives information from another piece of equipment.

I/O port   Typically used for input binary signals to a control system to indicate the state of a connected device, such as active or inactive, on or off, or connected or not connected.

insulation   Also known as the *dielectric,* material applied to a conductor that is used to isolate the flow of electric current between conductors and to provide protection to the conductor.

Integrated Services Digital Network (ISDN)   A communications standard for transmitting voice, video, and data over digital phone lines or the traditional telephone network. Common applications of ISDN include telecommuting, Internet access, video conferencing, and data networking.

intelligibility   A sound system's ability to produce an accurate reproduction of sound allowing listeners to identify words and sentence structure.

Internet Corporation for Assigned Names and Numbers (ICANN)   A nonprofit organization chartered to oversee several Internet-related tasks. ICANN manages Domain Name System (DNS) policy, including the top-level domain space for the Internet.

Internet Group Management Protocol (IGMP)   The IPv4 group management protocol. IGMPv1 allowed individual clients to subscribe to a multicast channel. IGMPv2 and IGMPv3 added the ability to unsubscribe from a multicast channel.

interlaced scanning   The scanning process that combines odd and even fields of video to produce a full frame of video signal.

internal configuration   Refers to the setup and customization of a management or control device.

Internet Protocol (IP)   A TCP/IP protocol defined in the IETF standard RFC 791. IP defines rules for addressing, packaging, fragmenting, and routing data sent across an IP network. IP falls under the Internet layer of the TCP/IP protocol stack and the Network layer of the OSI model.

Internet Protocol Television (IPTV)   A system that delivers television services over a packet-switched network such as a LAN or the Internet.

inverse square law   The law of physics stating that some physical quantity or strength is inversely proportional to the square of the distance from the source of that physical quantity.

IP   See *Internet Protocol (IP)*.

IR   See *infrared (IR)*.

isolated ground (IG)   An equipment grounding method permitted by the NEC for reducing electrical noise (electromagnetic interference) on the grounding circuit. The isolation between IG receptacles and circuits and the normal equipment grounding is maintained up to the point of the service entrance (or a separately derived system) where the grounded (neutral) conductor, equipment grounding, and isolated equipment grounding conductor are bonded together and to earth ground.

isolated grounding circuit   A circuit that allows an equipment enclosure to be isolated from the raceway containing circuits, supplying only that equipment by one or more listed nonmetallic raceway fittings. The equipment is grounded via an insulated grounding conductor.

isolated receptacle   A receptacle in which the grounding terminal is purposely insulated from the receptacle mounting means. Isolated receptacles are identified by a triangle engraved on the face and are available in standard colors. The receptacle (and so the equipment plugged into the receptacle) is grounded via an insulated grounding conductor.

jacket   Outside covering used to protect cable wires and their shielding.

junction box   A metal or plastic enclosure for enclosing the junction of electrical wires and cables. A junction box can be used as a termination point with a custom connector plate or interface plate. A junction box can also be installed and used as a pull box for longer cable runs.

keystone error   The trapezoidal distortion of a square-cornered image because of the optical effect of the projection device being located in an improper position with respect to the screen.

lamp   The bulb or source of light output.

latency   Response time of the network. It is expressed as the amount of time in milliseconds between a data packet's transmission from the source application and its presentation to the destination application.

lavalier   A small microphone designed to be worn either around the neck or clipped to apparel.

Law of Conservation of Energy   States that the total energy cannot be created or destroyed. Energy can be transformed from one form to another and transferred from one body to another, but the total amount of energy remains constant.

least favored viewer (LFV)   The farthest usable seat from the image. The LFV depends on the viewing angle toward the screen, image size, and content being displayed.

lenticular   A screen surface characterized by silvered or aluminized embossing, designed to reflect maximum light over wide horizontal and narrow vertical angles.

lighting fixture   An installed lighting instrument.

limiter   An audio signal processor that functions like a compressor except that signals exceeding the threshold level are reduced at ratios of 10:1 or greater.

limiter ratio   Defines how much the limiter will compress signals that exceed its threshold. The limiter compresses only the portion of the signal that exceeds its threshold, after the signal has already passed through the compressor.

limiter threshold   Defines which portions of the signal the limiter will affect. All decibel levels below or equal to the threshold will pass through the limiter unchanged. All signals above the threshold will be compressed.

line driver   Used for gain and peaking to compensate for signal attenuation created by cable resistance for longer cable runs.

line level   The strength of an audio signal. Line levels perform signal routing and processing between audio components, such as loudspeakers.

liquid crystal display (LCD)   A video display that uses liquid crystals to produce an image. These devices do not emit light directly.

liquid crystal on silicon (LCoS)   A reflective, fixed-resolution LCD imaging technology. LCoS panels resemble LCD panels in size and function. A liquid crystal layer is applied inside an LCoS panel to a reflective complementary metal-oxide semiconductor (CMOS) mirror substrate. The LCoS chip has a fixed matrix of pixels, each backed by a mirrored surface.

listed   Equipment, materials, or services included in a list published by a Nationally Recognized Testing Laboratory (NRTL), such as Underwriters Laboratories (UL), that is acceptable to the authority having jurisdiction (AHJ).

load center   An electrical industry term used to identify a lighting and appliance panelboard designed for use in residential and light-commercial applications.

local area network (LAN)   A computer network limited to the immediate area, usually the same building or floor of a building. A LAN connects devices within a small geographical area, such as a building or campus.

local monitor   A device used to monitor the output of a signal from a system or other device in the local vicinity.

logarithm   The exponent of base-10 that equals the value of a number.

logic network diagram   A tool that helps sequence and ultimately schedule the project's activities and milestones. It helps determine whether all the activities necessary to complete the program are present.

looping scheme   Features electronics with the ability of passing on the video signal to another device. Looping distributes a video signal to multiple devices (usually displays) simultaneously.

lossless compression   A process that retains the original quality of a file after it has been compressed and decompressed.

lossy compression   A form of compression that gives an approximation of the original data by eliminating redundant or unnecessary information.

loudspeaker   A transducer that converts electrical energy into acoustical energy. A loudspeaker is basically a driver within an enclosure.

loudspeaker circuit   A group of wired loudspeakers. Each loudspeaker in the circuit will have an impedance value.

low-pass filter   A circuit that allows signals below a specified frequency to pass unaltered while simultaneously attenuating frequencies above the specified limit.

low voltage   An ambiguous term. It may mean less than 70 V AC to an AV contractor, while an electrician may use the same term to describe circuits less than 600 V AC. The term may also be determined by the authority having jurisdiction (AHJ).

lumen   A measure of the light quantity emitted from a constant light source across 1 square meter.

Luminaire   A complete lighting instrument comprised of a light source, globe, reflector, and housing.

luminance (Y)   Also called *luma,* part of a bandwidth-limited video signal combining synchronization information and brightness information. Its symbol is Y.

lux   A contraction of the words *luminance* and *flux.* 10.7 lux is equal to 1 footcandle.

MAC address   The actual hardware address, or number, of an NIC device. Each device has a globally unique Media Access Control (MAC) address to identify its connection on the network.

matrix decoder   A decoder that produces red, green, and blue from Y, R-Y, and B-Y.

matrix switcher   An electronic device with multiple inputs and outputs. The matrix allows any input to be connected to any one, several, or all the outputs.

matte-white screen   A screen that evenly disperses light 180 degrees uniformly, both horizontally and vertically, creating a wide viewing cone and wide viewing angle.

maximum transmission unit (MTU)   The size in bytes of the largest frame that can pass over a Data Link layer connection. Any header information must be included within the MTU.

mechanical switcher   A switch that mechanically connects cables or circuits. It functions like a wall switch, meaning there is a mechanical connection or disconnection between two conductors.

meshed topology   Where every local area network (LAN) connects to every other LAN.

mic level   A very low line-level signal. It creates only a few millivolts of electrical energy.

microphone sensitivity   A specification that indicates the electrical output of a microphone when it is subjected to a known sound pressure level.

middleware   Software that provides services to applications that aren't available from the operating system. In a streaming system, for example, middleware software may perform transcoding, compression, or remote access authentication functions, enabling users to access content from diverse endpoints.

midrange   A loudspeaker that reproduces midrange frequencies, typically 300 Hz to 8,000 Hz.

milestone   A significant or key event in the project, usually the completion of a major deliverable or the occurrence of an important event. It can often be associated with payment milestones, and client approvals.

millwork   Items that are custom cut for the project, such as moldings or trim.

mixer   A device for blending multiple audio sources.

mix-minus system   A type of speech reinforcement system that allows both meeting presenters and participants to be heard. Each loudspeaker is given a separate subsystem, which mixes the microphone signals, minus the closest microphone.

Mobile High-Definition Link (MHL)   Originally a standard audio/video interface for connecting mobile electronics to high-definition televisions and audio receivers. The latest version, superMHL, is capable of 36 Gbps and up to 8K resolution, making it a possible option for more general AV applications.

modular connector A connector used with four, six, or eight pins. Common modular connectors are RJ-11 and RJ-45 (8P8C).

modulator A device that converts composite or S-Video signals, along with corresponding audio signals, into modulated signals on a carrier channel.

Multicast Listener Discovery (MLD) The IPv6 group management protocol. Multicast is natively supported by IPv6; any IPv6 router will support MLD. MLDv1 performs roughly the same functions as IGMPv2, and MLDv2 supports roughly the same functions as IGMPv3.

multicast streaming A one-to-many transmission, meaning one server sends out a single stream that can then be accessed by multiple clients. Class D IP addresses are set aside for multicast transmissions.

multimeter A multipurpose test instrument with a number of different ranges for measuring current, voltage, and resistance.

multiplexing The process used by the combiner to put together a number of modulated signals.

multipoint Also called *continuous presence*, videoconferencing that links many sites to a common gateway service, allowing all sites to see, hear, and interact at the same time. Multipoint requires a bridge or bridging service.

Multi-Protocol Label Switching (MPLS) A networking protocol that allows any combination of Data Link layer protocols to be transported over any type of Network layer. MPLS routes data by examining each packet's MPLS label without examining packet contents. Implementing MPLS improves interoperability and routing speed.

native resolution The number of rows of horizontal and vertical pixels that create the picture. The native resolution describes the actual resolution of the imaging device and not the resolution of the delivery signal.

near-field The sound field close to the sound source that has not been colored by room reflections. This is also known as *direct sound*.

needed acoustic gain (NAG) The gain the sound system requires to achieve an equivalent acoustic level at the farthest listener equal to what the nearest listener would hear without sound reinforcement.

needs analysis A needs analysis, also referred to as the *programming phase*, consists of identifying the activities that the end users need to perform and then developing the functional descriptions of the systems that support those needs.

Network Address Translation (NAT) Any method of altering IP address information in IP packet headers as the packet traverses a routing device. NAT is typically implemented as part of a firewall strategy. The most common form of NAT is Port Address Translation (PAT).

network bridge   Connects two different types of networks. It translates one network protocol to another protocol. An example of a bridge is a computer modem. A cable modem converts, or *bridges,* the Ethernet protocol to a cable TV protocol.

network interface card (NIC)   An interface that allows you to connect a device to a network. Many NICs are now integrated into the device's main circuitry.

network segment   A network segment is any single section of a network that is physically separated from the rest of the network by a networking device such as a switch, router, or hub. A segment may contain one or more hosts.

network switch   Connects multiple devices together so they can communicate with the other devices that are also connected to the switch. As each device is connected, the switch collects and stores the MAC address of the device that it communicates with. When one device wants to communicate with a second device, the switch looks up the destination device's location in its memory and then sends the information to its destination.

network topology   The physical connection that aids in the communication between devices in an area network.

neutral conductor   See *grounded conductor.*

nit   The metric unit for screen or surface brightness.

noise   Any electrical signal present in a circuit other than the desired signal.

noise criterion (NC) rating   Developed to establish satisfactory conditions for speech intelligibility and general living environments. Measurements are taken at eight center octave frequencies from 63 to 8,000 Hz and plotted against a standardized curve.

noise-masking system   Introduces background noise to hinder communication and increase privacy. These are also sometimes called *sound-masking* or *speech-privacy* systems.

noisy ground   An electrical connection to a ground point that produces or injects spurious voltages into the computer system through the connection to ground (IEEE Std. 142-1991).

nominal impedance   The low point in the usable frequency area in a loudspeaker.

notch filter   A filter that notches out, or eliminates, a specific band of frequencies.

number of open microphones (NOM)   Takes into account the increased possibility of feedback by adding additional live microphones in a space. Each time the number of open microphones is doubled, you lose 3 dB of gain before feedback.

Nyquist-Shannon Sampling Theorem   States that an analog signal can be reconstructed if it is encoded using a sampling rate that is greater than twice the highest frequency sampled. For example, since the range of human hearing extends to 20 kHz, the sampling rate for digital audio should be greater than 40 kHz.

octave   A band, or group, of frequencies. The relationship of the frequencies is such that the lowest frequency is half the highest. 200 Hz to 400 Hz is an octave; 4,000 Hz to 8,000 Hz is an octave; and so on.

Ohm's law   A law that defines the relationship between current, voltage, and resistance in an electrical circuit as proportional to applied voltage and inversely proportional to resistance. The formula is $I=V/R,$ where I is the current (in amps), V is the voltage (in volts), and R is the resistance (in ohms).

omnidirectional   Describes the shape of the area for microphones that have equal sensitivity to sound from nearly all directions.

on-axis   The center point of a screen, perpendicular to the viewing area for a displayed image. This is considered to be the best location for viewing.

organic light-emitting display (OLED)   Consists of layers of organic compounds that emit light when an electric current flows through it. There are separate organic layers for red, green, and blue.

oscilloscope   A test device that allows measurement of electronic signals by displaying the waveform on a CRT.

OSI model   Open Systems Interconnection model. This is a reference model developed by ISO in 1984, as a conceptual framework of standards for communication in the network across different equipment and applications by different vendors. Network communication protocols fall into seven categories, or layers.

overcurrent   Any current in excess of the rated current of equipment or the ampacity of a conductor. It may result from overload, a short circuit, or a ground fault.

overcurrent protection device   A safety device designed to open a circuit if the current reaches a value that causes excessive or dangerous temperatures in conductors or conductor insulation. Examples are circuit breakers and fuses.

packet filtering   A technique that uses rules to determine whether a data packet will be allowed to pass through a firewall. Rules are configured by the network administrator and implemented based on the protocol header of each packet.

panelboard   A single panel or group of panel units designed for assembly in the form of a single panel, including buses and automatic overcurrent devices. A panelboard may be equipped with switches for the control of light, heat, or power circuits. It is designed to be placed in a cabinet or cutout box placed in or against a wall, partition, or other support, and accessible only from the front.

parallel circuit   A circuit in which the voltage is the same across each load, but the current divides and takes all the available paths and returns to the source.

parametric equalizer   Allows discrete selection of a center frequency and adjustment of the width of the frequency range that will be affected. This can allow for precise manipulation with minimal impact of adjacent frequencies.

peak The highest level of signal strength, determined by the height of the signal's waveform.

peaking An adjustment method that allows compensation for high-frequency loss in cables.

peaking control Electronic adjustments within a video component that can be used to compensate for system losses, particularly in cable capacitance.

permissible area The maximum amount of space that cables should occupy inside the conduit.

phantom power A DC power source available in various voltages.

phase A particular value of time for any periodic function. For a point on a sine wave, it is a measure of that point's distance from the most recent positive-going zero crossing of the waveform. It is measured in degrees; 0 to 360 degrees is a complete cycle.

phono The European name for an RCA connector.

phosphor The substance that glows when struck by an electron beam, providing the image in a CRT. The higher the quality of the phosphor, the brighter and more vivid the image.

pink noise A sound that has equal energy (constant power) in each 1/3-octave band.

pink noise generator (PNG) Intended to provide an unintelligible noise source that represents an equal amount of energy per octave through a sound system. It is commonly used to evaluate and align a sound system in an environment.

pixel A combination of two words, *picture* and *element*. The smallest element used to build a digital image.

plan view A plan view is a drawing of a space from the "top view," taken directly from above. Examples include a floor plan and site plan.

plane of screen Identification of image position on a plan or drawing relative to other plotted locations. It is a notional line, whether in plan view or elevation, that aligns with the front surface of the screen (that is, image position) used as a datum to define viewers' relative positions.

plasma display panel (PDP) A direct-view display consisting of an array of cells, known as *pixels,* which are composed of three subpixels, corresponding to the colors red, green, and blue. Gas in the plasma state is used to react with phosphors in each subpixel to produce colored light (red, green, or blue) from a phosphor in each subpixel.

playback system A playback system is a music reinforcement system that has a wide frequency response bandwidth and is capable of high sound pressure levels. A playback system does not include microphones; it simply plays prerecorded material.

plenum space   The plenum space is also called *environmental air space.* It is an area connected to air ducts that forms part of the air distribution system.

point source   A sound system that has a central location for the loudspeakers, mounted high above, intended to cover a large area. This type of sound system is typically used in a performance venue or a large house of worship.

point-to-point   Conferencing where two sites are directly linked.

polar pattern   Also known as *pickup pattern,* the shape of the area that a microphone will be most sensitive to sound.

polar plot   A polar plot is a graphical representation of the relationship between a device's directionality and its output.

port   In a TCP/IP network, a 16-bit number included in the TCP or UDP Transport layer header. The port number typically indicates the Application layer protocol that generated a data packet. A port may also be called by its associated service (e.g., port 80 may be called HTTP, or port 23 may be called telnet).

Port Address Translation (PAT)   A method of Network Address Translation (NAT) whereby devices with private, unregistered IP addresses can access the Internet through a device with a registered IP address. Unregistered clients send datagrams to a NAT server with a globally routable address (typically a firewall). The NAT server forwards the data to its destination and relays responses to the original client.

post tension type construction   A type of structure that uses metal cables embedded within the concrete slab to support the structure. The cables act as a suspension support system that allows for wider spacing of columns within a building.

potential acoustic gain (PAG)   The potential gain that can be delivered by the sound system without ringing and before feedback occurs. It is based upon the number of open microphones and the distances between sources (like a presenter) and microphones, microphones and loudspeakers, and listeners and loudspeakers.

power   Energy expended in one form manifesting itself into another form: motion, heat, or light. This is power, or the rate at which work is done. It is represented by the letter P and is measured in watts (W).

power amplifier   Boosts the audio signal enough to move the loudspeakers.

power conditioners   Enhance the quality of power going to equipment by regulating voltage, eliminating noise or correcting other issues.

power distribution unit (PDU)   A rack-mountable or portable electrical enclosure that is connected by a cord or cable to a branch circuit for distribution of power to multiple electronic devices. A PDU may contain switches, overcurrent protection, control connections, and receptacles.

power sequencing   The act of powering on and off equipment that often requires warm-up or cool-down time. Sequencing also helps prevent tripping circuit breakers by limiting the excessive surge of electricity when devices are first turned on.

preamplifier   Boosts the electronic signal captured by the microphone before it is sent to other equipment.

primary optic   The lens that focuses the image onto the screen.

program report   A document that describes the client's specific needs, system purpose and functionality, and the designer's best estimate of probable cost, in a nontechnical format for review and approval by the owner. This is also known as the AV narrative, or discovery phase report, return brief, or concept design report.

progressive scanning   Scanning that traces the image's scan lines sequentially, such as with an analog computer monitor.

Protocol Independent Multicast (PIM)   Allows multicast routing over LANs, WANs, or even, theoretically, the open Internet. Rather than routing information on their own, PIM protocols use the routing information supplied by whatever routing protocol the network is already using; that's why it's protocol independent.

pulling tension   The maximum amount of tension that can be applied to a cable or conductor before it is damaged.

pure tone   See *fundamental frequency*.

Q factor   The ratio of the height of the peak of the filter against the width of the filter at the 3 dB point.

quality of service (QoS)   Any method of managing data traffic to preserve system usefulness and provide the best possible user experience. Typically, QoS refers to some combination of bandwidth allocation and data prioritization.

quiet ground   A point on a ground system that does not inject spurious voltages into the computer system. There are no standards to measure how quiet a quiet ground is.

raceway   An enclosed channel of metal or nonmetallic materials designed for holding wires, cables, or busbars, with additional functions.

rack   See *equipment rack*.

rack elevation diagram   A rack elevation diagram is a pictorial representation of the front of a rack and the location of each piece of equipment within that rack, typically labeling the number of RUs used for each piece of gear.

rack unit (RU)   A unit of measure of the vertical space in a rack. One RU equals 1.75 inches (44.5 mm).

radio frequency (RF)   The portion of the electromagnetic spectrum that is suitable for radio communications. Generally, this is considered to be from 10 kHz up to

300 MHz. This range extends to 300 GHz if the microwave portion of the spectrum is included.

radio frequency interference (RFI)   Radiated electromagnetic energy that interferes with or disturbs an electrical circuit.

rarefaction   A decrease of density and pressure in air molecules.

ratio   A mathematical expression that represents the relationship between the quantities of numbers of the same kind. A ratio is typically written as X:Y or X/Y.

RCA connector   Also known as a *phono* connector, a connector most often used with line-level audio signals.

reactance (X)   Opposition to alternating current resulting from capacitance and inductance in the circuit.

rear-screen projection   A system in which the image is projected toward the audience through a translucent screen material, for viewing from the opposite side.

reference level   In the context of decibel measurements, the reference level is the established starting point represented by 0 dB. The reference level varies according to linear unit and application.

reference point   The point of no potential used as the 0 V (zero volt) reference for a circuit.

reflected ceiling plan   Used to illustrate elements in the ceiling with respect to the floor. It should be interpreted as though the floor is a mirrored surface, reflecting the features within the ceiling.

reflecting server   Takes in a unicast stream and broadcasts out a multicast stream. It is often used for live data streams.

reflection   Light or sound energy that has been redirected by a surface.

reflective technology   Any display device that reflects light to create an image.

refraction   The bending or changing of the direction of a light ray when passing through a material, such as water or glass. How much light refracts, meaning how great the angle of refraction, is called the *refractive index*.

refresh rate   The number of times per second a display, such as a monitor, television, or projector, will draw the image sent to it.

release time   The release time of an audio compressor determines how quickly the volume increases when an audio signal returns below the threshold.

relocatable power tap   A cord-connected product rated 250 V AC or less and 20 A or less with multiple receptacles. This tap is intended only for indoor use and plugged directly into a branch circuit. It is not intended to be connected to another relocatable power tap.

reserve DHCP   A hybrid approach to IP addressing. Using reserve DHCP, a block of statically configured addresses can be set aside for devices whose IP addresses must always remain the same. The remaining addresses in the subnet will be assigned dynamically. The total pool of dynamic addresses is reduced by the number of reserved addresses.

resistance   The property of a material to impede the flow of electrical current, expressed in ohms.

resistor   A passive electrical component that produces equal impedance to current flow. Current passes through a resistor in direct proportion to voltage, independent of frequency, as outlined in Ohm's law.

resolution   1. The amount of detail in an image. 2. The number of picture elements (pixels) in a display.

reverberant sound   Sound waves that bounce off multiple surfaces before reaching the listener but arrive at the listeners' ears quite a bit later than early reflected sound.

reverberation   Numerous, persistent reflections of sound energy.

RF   See *radio frequency (RF)*.

RF control   RF control is generally employed as a user interface to the control system. Some manufacturers' devices provide control links into their components using RF transmission, as this affords the ability to control devices when line of sight is not possible.

RF system   A closed-circuit system with the composite video and audio signals modulated at a certain frequency, called a *channel*. RF systems require a display device (such as a television) with a tuner set to a selected channel to display the information modulated onto that frequency.

RGBHV signal   A high-bandwidth video signal with separate conductors for the red signal, green signal, blue signal, horizontal sync, and vertical sync.

RGBS signal   A four-component signal composed of a red signal, a green signal, a blue signal, and a composite sync signal.

RGsB signal   A three-component signal composed of a red signal, a green signal with composite sync added to the green channel, and a blue signal. It is often called *sync on green*.

rigid metal conduit   Rigid metal conduit, called *rigid,* is the heaviest conduit and offers the best physical and EMI protection.

rigid nonmetallic tubing   Rigid nonmetallic tubing is very stiff with a thick wall but lightweight. It is similar to plumbing tubing. Because it is not flexible, it is available in preformed pieces at various angles.

ring   A network topology that connects terminals, computers, or nodes in a continuous loop.

room criteria (RC) rating   With measurements taken at eight center-octave frequencies from 31.5 to 8,000 Hz, the average of the measurements taken from 500, 1,000, and 2,000 Hz. This includes additional steps to rate the background noise as (N) for neutral, (R) for rumbly, or (H) for hissy.

room mode   Also called a *standing wave*; occurs between parallel surfaces of an enclosure (could be a room, a loudspeaker cabinet, and so on) where the dimension between those parallel surfaces equals one-half wavelength (and the harmonics thereof). The wave is thus reflected on itself out of polarity, creating location-specific areas of maximum and minimum pressure.

router   A device that works on the OSI layer above the Network and Transport layers. A router knows the IP address of sent packets, and it can send them to specific locations on the network. The IT manager can use a router to change how the network works and allows for redundancy in the network.

RS-232   The interface between data terminal equipment and data circuit-terminating equipment employing serial binary data interchange. It supports a single-ended mode of operation with one driver and one receiver. It supports a maximum cable length of 50 feet (15 m) with a data rate of 20 kbps.

RS-422   Provides the electrical characteristics of balanced voltage digital interface circuits. It is a balanced signal with one driver and 10 receivers with multidrop capability. The maximum cable length for RS-422 is 4,000 feet (1,220 m) with a data rate of 10 Mbps.

RS-485   RS-485 supports a differential mode of operation with 32 drivers and 32 receivers and multidrop capability. The maximum cable length for RS-485 is 4,000 feet (1,220 m) with a data rate of 10 Mbps.

RsGsBs   Red, green, and blue signals with composite sync added to each color channel. This requires three cables to carry the entire signal. It is often referred to as *RGB sync on all three*.

RT$_{60}$ The time taken for the energy in an initially steady reverberant sound field to decay by 60 dB after the source of the sound ceases.

RU   See *rack unit (RU)*.

sampling rate   The number of samples taken per unit of time (typically seconds) when converting a continuous (analog) signal to a discrete signal (typically a digital signal).

scale   One number being equivalent to another number in a ratio, for example, 1/4 inch = one foot.

scaler   A feature in a display device that changes the size of an image without changing its shape. Scaling may be required when the image size does not fit the display device.

scan rate   The frequency of occurrence of a display drawing one line of information.

scattering   When light hits a textured surface, the incoming light waves get reflected in multiple angles because the surface is uneven.

scene   A recallable preset of lighting levels for one or more zones.

scope statement   A written agreement between the client, the project sponsor, the key stakeholders, and the project team that defines the boundaries of the project.

screen gain   Describes the distribution of light reflected off a projection screen. The amount of gain is compared to a matte-white screen, which reradiates light and distributes it with perfect uniformity.

SDTV   Standard-definition television.

section drawing   A section drawing is a view of the interior of a building in the vertical plane. Section drawings show a bisected wall, which allows you to view what is behind it.

sensitivity specification   A way to determine a device's ability to convert one form of energy into another form of energy. It is used to define the device's efficiency in converting from one form to another.

serial digital interface (SDI)   An uncompressed, unencrypted, standardized digital video signal.

series circuit   When all the current supplied by the source will flow through the entire circuit. The electrons leaving the source of power go through each component of the circuit and return to the source. While all the current flows through all the circuit, the voltage is divided between the three resistors (loads) as well as the wire that connects them.

series/parallel loudspeaker circuit   When groups of loudspeakers called *branches* are wired together in series. Typically, loudspeakers in the same branch have the same impedance. Each branch is connected to the positive and negative lines of the amplifier in parallel.

server   A powerful computer, typically with large amounts of storage and more memory, computing capacity, and redundancy than a desktop computer.

service level agreement (SLA)   Used to document agreements between an IT service provider and a customer. It describes the services to be provided; documents service-level targets; and specifies the roles and responsibilities of the service provider(s) and the customer(s).

shear   The tendency of a mount to tear or cut off from the structure.

shield   A metallic partition placed between two regions of space. A shield is used to control the propagation of electric and magnetic fields from one of the regions to the other. It contains electric and magnetic fields at the source or to protect the receiver from electric and magnetic fields. A shield can be the chassis (metallic box) that houses an electronic device or the metallic enclosure (aluminum foil or copper braid) that surrounds a wire or cable.

shotgun microphone   A long, cylindrical, highly sensitive, unidirectional microphone used to pick up sound from a great distance.

sightline   The unobstructed view between a person and the object he needs to see. A sightline study determines the most appropriate seating layout for a clear field of view, including the lowest visible point on the display wall, nearest viewers' line of sight, farthest viewers' line of sight, distortion of image from off-axis seat locations, and other ergonomic factors for a preferred field of vision and viewing comfort tolerances.

signal flow   The traceable path of signals through a system.

signal generator   A test equipment instrument that produces calibrated electronic signals intended for the testing or alignment of electronic circuits or systems.

signal ground   1. A 0 V (zero volt) point of no potential that serves as the circuit reference. 2. A low-impedance path for the current to return to the source.

single-phase power   Alternating current electrical power supplied by two current-carrying conductors. This type of power is used for residential and some light-commercial applications.

single-point ground (SPG)   In the context of IEEE Std. 1100, refers to implementation of an isolated equipment grounding configuration for the purposes of minimizing problems caused by circulating current in ground loops.

signal-to-noise (S/N) ratio   The ratio, measured in decibels, between the audio or video signal, and the noise accompanying the signal. The higher this ratio, the better the quality of the sound or picture.

Simple Network Management Protocol (SNMP)   A set of Internet Engineering Task Force (IETF) standards for network management, including an Application layer protocol, a database schema, and a set of data objects. SNMP exposes management data in the form of variables on the managed systems, which describe the system configuration. These variables can then be queried, and sometimes set, by managing applications.

socket   In a TCP/IP network, the combined port number, Transport Layer protocol identifier, and IP addresses of communicating end systems. A socket uniquely identifies a session of a given transport protocol.

sound pressure level (SPL)   In the context of Standard 1M, all sound pressure levels are expressed in unweighted decibels.

sound reinforcement system   The combination of microphones, audio mixers, signal processors, power amplifiers, and loudspeakers that are used to electronically amplify and distribute sound.

source-specific multicast (SSM)   In streaming, allows clients to specify the sources from which they will accept content. This has the dual benefit of reducing demands on the network while also improving network security. Any device that has the host address can try to send traffic to the multicast group, but only content from the specified source will be forwarded to the group.

specification   A written, precise description of the design criteria for a piece of work. Specifications define the level of qualitative and/or quantitative parameters to be met and the criteria for their acceptance. All specifications must be formulated in terms that are specific, measurable, and verifiable and unambiguous.

specular reflection   A mirrorlike reflection of energy, in which most of the energy is reflected back in a single direction.

speech privacy system   A sound system that adds background noise to an environment to cover up human speech and prevent privacy issues.

speech-reinforcement system   An audio system that reinforces or amplifies a presenter's voice to be heard over a larger audience.

splitter   An electronic device that divides a signal into different pieces to route to different devices.

spot photometer   A type of meter used to measure luminance.

standing wave   Occurs between parallel surfaces of an enclosure (could be a room, a loudspeaker cabinet, and so on) where the dimension between those parallel surfaces equals one-half wavelength (and the harmonics thereof). The wave is thus reflected on itself out of polarity, creating location-specific areas of maximum and minimum pressure.

star topology   A network topology where all network devices are connected to a central network device, usually a hub or a switch.

static IP address   A manually assigned permanent IP address.

stereophonic   Commonly shortened to *stereo,* describes when input from all microphones is split into at least two channels before driving the signal through the loudspeakers.

streaming video/streaming audio   Sequence of moving images or sounds sent in a continuous, compressed stream over the Internet and displayed by the viewer as they arrive. With streaming video or audio, a web user does not need to wait to download a large file before seeing the video or hearing the sound.

subnet   A logical group of hosts within a local area network (LAN). A LAN may consist of a single subnet, or it may be divided into several subnets. Additional subnets may be created by modifying the subnet mask on the network devices and hosts.

subnet mask   A binary number whose bits correspond to IP addresses on a network. Bits equal to 1 in a subnet mask indicate that the corresponding bits in the IP address identify the network. Bits equal to 0 in a subnet mask indicate that the corresponding bits in the IP address identify the host. IP addresses with the same network identifier bits as identified by the subnet mask are on the same subnet.

subwoofer   A loudspeaker that reproduces lower frequencies, typically 20 Hz to 200 Hz.

supercardioid polar pattern   The exaggerated heart shape of the area that a highly directional microphone is most sensitive to sound.

surface-mount microphone   Also called a *boundary microphone,* a microphone placed on a table to pick up sound. This type of microphone is often used in boardrooms and other environments where a number of talkers must be picked up and the microphone needs to remain unobtrusive.

surround-sound system   A stereo playback system that uses from two to five channels for realistic sound production, producing an experience where the sound appears to surround listeners. This is best achieved using surround-encoded material, a receiver, and surround loudspeakers.

S-Video   A video signal, also known as Y/C. Y is the luminance, and C is the chrominance. Y and C are transmitted on separate conductors.

switcher   A peripheral or sometimes integrated device used to select one of a group of signals.

sync   Synchronization. The timing information that keeps images displaying properly.

system   In the AV industry, a compilation of multiple individual AV components and subsystems interconnected to achieve a communication goal.

system black   The lowest level of luminance a system is capable of producing for its task operating conditions. The system includes projector, screen, the light the projector produces, and ambient light.

system grounding   The intentional grounding of one of the current-carrying conductors in a manner that will limit the voltage imposed by lightning, line surges, or unintentional contact with higher-voltage lines, and that will stabilize that voltage to earth during normal operation.

tap   A connection to a transformer winding that allows you to select a different power level from the transformer.

task lighting   Lighting directed to a specific surface or area that provides illumination for visual tasks.

tensile strength   The maximum force that a material can withstand before deforming or stretching.

three-phase power   Alternating current electrical power supplied by three current-carrying conductors, each offset by 120 degrees from one another. A fourth conductor, a neutral, is used as the return conductor. This type of power is used for commercial and industrial applications.

threshold   The level at which the desired function becomes active. Generally speaking, a lower threshold level means it will activate earlier. Recommended starting threshold for most line-level (post-preamp) functions is 0 dBu.

throw distance   The distance from a projector to a focusing surface or the screen.

Thunderbolt   Interface technology developed by Intel that transfers audio, video, power, and data over one cable in two directions. Thunderbolt versions 1 and 2 use the same connector as Mini DisplayPort (MDP), while Thunderbolt 3 uses USB Type-C.

time code   A method of numbering video frames according to the Society of Motion Picture and Television Engineers (SMPTE) standards. The code is the eight-digit address representing the hour, minute, second, and frame recorded on the videotape's control track.

time domain   A view of a signal as amplitude versus time, which allows you to see the amount of acoustical energy present over a period of time.

Time-Sensitive Networking (TSN)   In 2012, the IEEE working group overseeing the Audio Video Bridging standard was renamed Time-Sensitive Networking to reflect the standard's applicability to communication among different types of devices, such as network sensors. See *Audio Video Bridging (AVB)*.

transduction   The process by which one type of energy changes to another.

transformer   A passive electromagnetic device commonly consisting of at least two coils of wire (inductors) with no physical connection between them. Most often, these coils share an iron-based alloy core. This common core aids in concentrating the magnetic lines of force created by the current flow in one coil (primary), thereby inducing a voltage into the other coil (secondary).

transient disturbance   A momentary variation in power, such as a surge, spike, sag, blackout, or noise.

transition-minimized differential signaling (TMDS)   A technology for transmitting graphics to a display at high speeds. It supports high resolutions, such as 9.2 megapixel (3840×2400) displays, and native 16 million true-color resolutions.

transmission   Passing of sound energy through partitions or structure-borne vibrations.

Transmission Control Protocol (TCP)   A connection-oriented, reliable Transport layer protocol. TCP transport uses two-way communication to provide guaranteed delivery of information to a remote host. It is connection-oriented, meaning it creates and verifies a connection with the remote host before sending it any data. It is reliable because it tracks each packet and ensures that it arrives intact. TCP is the most common transport protocol for sending data across the Internet.

transmission loss   Attenuation that occurs when sound goes through a barrier or partition, expressed in decibels, and is affected by the barrier or partition's mass, stiffness, and damping.

transmissive technology   Any display device that creates images by allowing or preventing light to pass.

tweeter   A loudspeaker that is designed to reproduce frequencies above 3000 Hz.

twisted-pair   Any number of wires that are paired together and twisted around each other. The wires can be shielded or unshielded.

Ultra HD   A term used to describe video formats with a minimum resolution of 3840×2160 pixels in a 16×9 aspect ratio.

unbalanced circuit   A two-conductor circuit in which one conductor carries the signal and the other conductor carries the return. The return conductor is usually the cable shield and is a low-impedance connection, as it is connected to the signal ground and possibly also to the earth ground. The impedance of the signal circuitry is quite different from the return circuitry, which is why the impedances of the two conductors are quite different—the impedances are unbalanced with respect to one another.

unicast streaming   Unicast streaming is a one-to-one connection between the streaming server sending out the AV data and client devices listening to the stream. Each client has a direct relationship with the server. The client sends a request to the server, and the server sends the client a stream in response. Since the server is sending out a separate stream for each client, each additional client takes up more bandwidth. Streaming media to three clients at 100 Kbps actually uses 300 Kbps of bandwidth. IP Unicast streams may use either UDP or TCP transport, although with TCP transport, there will always be some buffering.

unity gain   Derived from the number 1, refers to no change in gain.

Universal Serial Bus (USB)   An industry standard for connecting, communicating, and supplying power between computers and electronic devices. Version 3.1 of USB is capable of 10 Gbps—enough to transmit 4K video. USB 3.1 can utilize a USB Type-C (USB-C) connector, which supports DisplayPort, HDMI, power, all USB generations, and VGA.

unshielded twisted-pair (UTP) cable   Typically used for data transfer, UTP cable contains multiple two-conductor pairs twisted at regular intervals, employing no external shielding.

vectorscope   A vectorscope is a specialized oscilloscope used in video systems to measure chrominance accuracy and levels.

vertical scan rate   The vertical scan rate describes the number of complete fields a device draws in a second. This may also be called the *frame rate, vertical sync rate,* or *refresh rate.* The vertical scan rate is measured in hertz (Hz) or cycles per second.

video wall   A video wall features several monitors, video screens, display cubes, video projectors, or TV sets that are set up on top of each other or side by side to form a single, large contiguous display.

viewing angle   Determines how far off-axis (screen centerline) a viewer can sit and still see a good-quality image. This is no greater than 45 degrees off the projection axis.

viewing area plan   A plan-view drawing of the viewing environment that identifies five viewing locations as defined in the requirements section of the ANSI/INFOCOMM 3M-2011 Standard.

viewing cone   The best viewing area for the audience. The term *cone* is used because there is width, height, and depth to the best viewing area, and this area emanates from the center of the screen.

virtual local area network (VLAN)   Connects separate LANs to form a logical group. For instance, the LANs at each branch of a large company could be combined into one company-wide VLAN.

virtual private network (VPN)   Uses the Internet to create a tunnel between two or more local area networks (LANs). VPNs are used to create virtual wide area networks (WANs) and for remote monitoring, troubleshooting, and control. VPNs are typically controlled and configured by the enterprise network administrator. Each host requires the proper software, access rights, and password to log into the client network.

visual field   The point of space that can be seen when a person's head and eyes are absolutely still. It is measured in angular magnitude, or degrees. The visual field of a single eye is termed *monocular vision,* and the visual field where the perceived image from both eyes overlap is called *binocular vision.*

Voice over Internet Protocol (VoIP)   Allows the digital transmission of phone calls and multimedia over the Internet and other networks. VoIP is relayed over smartphones and other Internet devices and requires equipment such as VoIP routers, phone adapters, telephone sets, and more.

volt (V)   The basic international unit of potential difference or electromotive force.

voltage   The electrical potential to create current flow in a circuit.

watt   The measurement of the amount of power consumed by a system. It is represented in math by the symbols P or w.

waveform monitor   A specialized oscilloscope used to display and analyze the video signals sync, luminance, and chroma levels.

wavelength   The distance between two corresponding points of two consecutive cycles measured in meters.

wayfinding   The use of visual guides or signage in strategic locations to help travelers more easily navigate to a destination.

webcasting   Allows the broadcast of digital media such as audio or video over the Internet, which audience members can stream live or access on demand. Essential equipment for webcasting includes computers, streaming servers, production software, recording gear, appliances, and more.

white noise   A sound that has the same energy level at all frequencies.

wide area network (WAN)   A data communications system that uses telecommunication circuits to link local area networks (LANs) that are distributed over large geographic distances. A wide area network (WAN) covers a large geographical area, such as a state or country. The Internet, which covers the entire world, is one large WAN.

wire   A single conductive element intended to carry a voltage or electronic signals.

wireless local area network (WLAN)   A network that shares information by radio frequency (RF).

woofer   A loudspeaker that has low frequencies, typically 20 Hz to 200 Hz.

work breakdown structure (WBS)   A deliverable-oriented grouping of project elements that will ultimately organize and define the total scope of the project. Each descending level represents an increasingly detailed definition of a project component.

XLR connector   A popular type of audio connector featuring three leads: two for the signal and one for overall system grounding. This is a secure connector often found on high-quality audio and video equipment. It is sometimes called a *cannon connector*.

Y/C   A video signal, also known as *S-Video*. Y is the luminance, and C is the chrominance. Y and C are transmitted on separate synchronized conductors.

zone   In the context of lighting, a zone is a grouping of luminaires (lighting fixtures) that are controlled together. In the context of digital signage, a zone is an area where separate content may be placed. A different playlist must be created for each zone.

INDEX

Numbers

A